Churches and the Holocaust
Unholy Teaching, Good Samaritans, and Reconciliation

Churches and the Holocaust
Unholy Teaching, Good Samaritans, and Reconciliation

Mordecai Paldiel

Sages, give heed to your words lest . . . the disciples who come after you drink [the evil waters]. . . . and the Name of Heaven be profaned.
Mishnah, Ethics of the Fathers 1:11

"Thy priests will be clothed with righteousness and Thy saints will shout for joy" (Psalms 132:9). "Thy priests," these are the Righteous of the Nations, who are God's priests in this world.
Midrash, Tanna de-Vei Eliyahu Zuta 20:33–34

KTAV Publishing House, Inc.

Library of Congress Cataloging-in-Publication Data

Paldiel, Mordecai.
  Churches and the Holocaust : unholy teaching, good samaritans, and rec-
onciliation / Mordecai Paldiel.
      p. cm.
  Includes bibliographical references and index.
  ISBN 0-88125-908-X
  1. Righteous Gentiles in the Holocaust. 2. World War, 1939–1945--
Jews--Rescue. 3. Holocaust, Jewish (1939–1945)--Foreign public
opinion. 4. Holocaust (Christian theology). 5. Judaism--Relations--
Catholic Church. 6. Catholic Church--Relations--Judaism. 7. John Paul
II, Pope, 1920–2005--Relations with Jews. 8. Jews--History--1945–
9. Clergy--Europe--Political activity. I. Title.
D804.65.P353 2005
940.53'183508827--dc22   2005028487

Published by
Ktav Publishing House, Inc.
930 Newark Avenue
Jersey City, New Jersey 07306
www.ktav.com
orders@ktav.com
Fax 201-963-0102

CONTENTS

INTRODUCTION

In 1953, Yad Vashem was created by the Israeli parliament (Knesset) as the country's national memorial of the Holocaust. The legislature stipulated that the new institution was also established for the sake of the "Righteous Among the Nations who had risked their lives to save Jews." Nine years later, in 1962, in the wake of the Eichmann trial, Yad Vashem decided to set up a public commission, chaired by a Supreme Court judge, to set criteria for the attribution of the title of "Righteous Among the Nations." This term is not new but has its roots in rabbinic Judaism of the first century, which used it to designate non-Jews who followed certain moral prescriptions—sometimes referred to as the Seven Noachide Laws—that would entitle them a place in paradise. The honorific was reinterpreted and applied to non-Jews who had risked their lives to save Jews from the Nazis during the Holocaust. To date, over 21,000 men and women have been awarded the "Righteous" title. The principal criteria followed by the commission include risk to the life and liberty of the actors of the rescue operation, personal and direct involvement in the rescue act, no material or other reward and compensation exacted by the rescuer as a condition of his/her help, that the rescuer was not allied to an organization that committed physical harm to Jews or other people, and finally, that verification of the rescue story was grounded on eyewitness accounts, principally of the beneficiary party, and/or reliable documentary material.

Since the program's inception, historians have narrated the deeds of these Gentile rescuers of Jews, while sociologists and psychologists have probed the mystery of their motivations.[1] The religious obligation to extend help to those in distress was found to be a salient motivation. In the present study, we shall delve into the world of the Christian clerics who have been declared "Righteous" by Yad Vashem, and whose number, at the date of this book's publication, is close to 600. Other than the religious obligation to assist others in need, as in the example of the Good Samaritan, which undoubtedly motivated many clerics to act, the question before us is how this applied to Jews on the run, in light of the church's generally negative teaching about Jews and Judaism. A concomitant question is whether there was an attempt to exploit the misery and helplessness of Jewish fugitives seeking the aid of Christian clerics in order to induce them, subtly or openly, to accept the Christian faith.

As we shall further see, the record shows that in the majority of cases the driving motivation was simply to assist people in dire destitution without any openly manifested ulterior consideration. Some clerics may have held to the Christian belief that the Jews were being punished for the "crime" of having rejected Jesus, the person who remains the nexus of every Christian's belief, but they nonetheless still saw it as their religious duty to try to save them. This went hand in hand with an admiration for the resilience of Jewish existence and a religious-mythical view of the Jews as still a Chosen People, whose existence was preordained and whose presence was required for the unfolding of the final messianic drama.

For a better appreciation of these motivational elements, one must delve a bit into the special place Jews and Judaism occupy in the thinking of Christianity. One must, moreover, constantly keep in mind that the relationship of Christianity to Judaism has no parallels to the church's relation to any other of the world's major religions. Christianity is the only religion that venerates a person who was born a Jew, and who absorbed the religion of Judaism and later taught it to his followers in his own special way, but, for reasons to be further explained, has remained outside the religious pantheon of the Jewish people and religion. This has confounded Christian thinking down the ages to the point of repeated explosions of violence against Jews. In the face of a still vibrant Judaism, which by its very existence seemed to question the essentials of Christian belief, the response of a triumphant church was a combination of continuous attempts to delegitimize the contending faith, including laws and regulations that reduced the Jews to the status of a pariah people and, paradoxically, a mystification at the continued virile condition of Jewish existence.

The reasons for this ambivalence all go back to the very foundations of the Christian religion; to the fact that Jesus of Nazareth was born Jewish, and remained committed to Judaism to the end—his tragic death. This is no mere speculation, but is authenticated and enshrined in Christian scripture, the New Testament. Christians have for ages been mystified by the fact that Jesus, who proclaimed himself as the long-awaited Jewish Messiah, and several centuries after his appearance was officially elevated to the rank of a divine figure by his later non-Jewish followers, was not accepted by his own people, and remained excluded from Jewish religious lore. This led to the creation of an unsolvable problem in the minds of Christian theologians: what to do with the Jews, especially after Christianity became the triumphant religion in the Roman world. The problem gave birth to a deep animosity toward Judaism in nascent Christianity, which saw itself as the true inheritor of the biblical mantle, the true Israel, with tragic consequence for the Jewish people, while at the same time the church continued to feel threatened by the continued vibrancy of the Jewish faith and people. Only in the aftermath of the Holocaust, a monstrous murderous action carried out by baptized, if not believing, Christians, has the church been led to rethink and reevaluate the "teaching of contempt," a phrase coined by the French Jewish historian Jules Isaac. Major positive changes were initiated by Pope John Paul II who placed Judaism on a par with Christianity and went further than any preceding pontiff in holding the Jews in high esteem—a shift followed by his successor, Benedict XVI, as evidenced by his visit to a restored synagogue in Cologne, Germany, very soon after the start of his pontificate. Be that as it may, Christians still continue to view Jews in mythical terms, often referring to their continued existence and refusal to accept Jesus as the Messiah as a divine "mystery," to be resolved, if not immediately, then at least in the final messianic era.

Bearing all this in mind, this book will deal with both aspects of clerical aid to Jews during the Holocaust; first, with how the Christian tradition shaped the minds of religious leaders with regard to Jews and the position adopted by ecclesiastical officials when faced with Nazi antisemitism; second, with the Good Samaritans—stories of help extended to Jews by clerics of the three major denominations: Catholicism, Protestantism, and Eastern Orthodoxy. It goes without saying that clerics could with greater ease be of greater help than lay people, thanks to their access to large institutions and facilities, built to absorb and feed people in need of assistance. In addition, clerics maintained contacts with each other in many and far and distant places, and thus found it easier to obtain alternative hiding places, as well as to acquire forged credentials when the situation so required. We shall begin by briefly examining how the Jewish refusal to acknowledge Jesus is portrayed in the New Testament and further explained by the church fathers. For this purpose, the ongoing and legitimate debate on whether this or that passage in the gospels represents the true, original, and authentic thoughts and expressions of Jesus or is an addition introduced by later redactors is only of secondary importance. For what shaped the minds of the clergy over the centuries was their belief in the truth and sanctity of every word and statement in the New Testament.

Before starting, a personal note is in order. I am a Jew, the scion of a Hasidic family, deeply dedicated to the Jewish faith and tradition, while at the same time holding in deep esteem other people's religious beliefs and devotions. What I state in the following pages is therefore, of course, my personal interpretation, and not in any way intended to impinge on the religious sensibilities of other people. What follows is one Jew's attempt to make sense of how the origins of Christianity and the perception of the Jews have molded the minds of Christian believers through the centuries and may have affected both laymen and clerics when faced with the challenge to assist Jews, doomed to destruction by a regime whose followers, if not always believing Christians, at least had been born and baptized into the Christian faith.

Chapter 1
ANTECEDENTS

*Do not boast over the branches. . . . Remember it is not you that
support the root, but the [Jewish] root that supports you.*
Paul of Tarsus

*[The synagogue is] a haunt of infidels, a home of the impious, a
hiding place of madmen, under the damnation of God himself.*
Bishop Ambrose of Milan

Jesus and Paul

Christian theologians often ask how Jewish Jesus really was. If Jewish, did
he remain so, not only at the beginning, but also to the end of his ministry?[1]
Born in Nazareth, several years before the turn of the millennium, he was
named Yeshua, which means "God will help" (the name "Jesus" is the Greek
transcription *Iesous*), a not uncommon name among Jews of those days.[2] Like
all Jewish boys, he was circumcised eight days after his birth. His "parents,"
according to the custom of pious Jews, went to Jerusalem for purification and
offered a sacrifice, and repeated these visits every year at the feast of Passover,
at times taking Jesus with them.[3] Before the start of his ministry, at approximately the age of thirty, Jesus was a humble Jewish artisan, eking out a living
in his hometown, Nazareth. The whole span of his ministry was probably as
little as one year or perhaps as much as three years. As a Galilean Jew, Jesus
did most of his preaching near the shores of the Sea of Galilee, in the years
27–29 C.E. He had brothers and sisters.[4] His language was Aramaic, closely
related to Hebrew and spoken by the common folk.[5] All this we are told by
the New Testament.

Much as some Christian theologians interpreted the teachings of Jesus as an
end to the Law (the faulty Greek translation of "Torah"), Jesus stands out as
very much a religious Jew if we are to follow the account in the New
Testament, although he reserved to himself the right to reinterpret and suggest
changes. He is described as working among Jews and only among them. In the
words of the apostle Paul, Jesus was foremost "a servant to the circumcised."[6]

1

Some of his followers addressed him as "rabbi," a term especially popular for designating teachers and interpreters of the Torah.[7] "As was his custom," he attended Sabbath services, and most of his preaching took place in synagogues, and he went on pilgrimages to the Temple in Jerusalem to celebrate the great religious festivals, such as Tabernacles (Sukkot) and Passover.[8] The gospels report that while in Jerusalem, in the closing phase of his ministry, he directed his disciples to the place where they were to celebrate the Passover dinner, most probably the traditional Seder.[9] His interpretation of biblical verses took place in the traditional Jewish setting, allowing people to speak and interpret biblical passages, sometimes in spirited debates with others. He also preached in the Temple, a Jew among Jews.[10]

As for his teachings, the nineteenth-century biblical scholar Ernest Renan was among many Christian scholars who thought that Jesus preached the abrogation of the Torah laws and its prescriptions; that he was "a destroyer of Judaism. . . . In other words, Jesus was no longer Jewish. . . . The Law would be abolished, and he would be the one to abolish it."[11] However, this extreme view is not what the New Testament wants us to believe. On the contrary, in the Sermon on the Mount, Jesus is reported as saying: "Think not that I have come to abolish the law and the prophets. . . . I have come not to abolish but to fulfill them. For truly, I say to you, till heaven and earth pass away, not an iota, not a dot, will pass from the law."[12] There has been some debate about the hidden meaning of "to fulfill them." According to one interpretation, in the original Greek version of the New Testament, the term *plerosai* means, "to fill, to cram full, to fecundate," as against *katalusai*, "to dissolve, destroy, overthrow. In other words, Jesus is saying, "I have not come to overthrow but to fill, to give fullness." Indeed, true to his word, he on several occasions urged his listeners to abide by the Torah's prescriptions. Thus, after healing a person from leprosy, Jesus told the man, "Go, show yourself to the priest, and offer for your cleansing what Moses commanded."[13]

As an observant Jew, Jesus most likely recited the daily obligatory creedal statement known as the Shema. Thus, when questioned as to "which commandment is the first of all? Jesus immediately responded, "The first is, Hear [Shema], O Israel, the Lord our God, the Lord is one. You shall love the Lord your God with all your heart, and with all your soul, and with all your mind. This is the great and first commandment. And a second is like it, 'You shall love your neighbor as yourself.' On these two commandments depend all the law and the prophets.' " Or, for instance, when breaking bread, he made a blessing, as still practiced today by observant Jews.[14] On the essential daily prayer to God, there are close parallels between the formula used by Jesus, known as the Lord's Prayer, and the one retained today in the Jewish Kaddish sanctification. In the former: "Our Father, who art in heaven, hallowed be thy name. Thy kingdom come. Thy will be done, on earth as it is in heaven."[15] In the Kaddish, recited three times daily: "Exalted and hallowed be God's great name. In this world of his creation. May his will be fulfilled. And his sovereignty revealed. . . . Speedily and soon."[16]

While not challenging the ritual aspects of the Jewish religion, Jesus seems to have placed a greater emphasis on the ethical comport of the religion. As noted by Flusser, when it came to the question of the plucking of heads of grain on the Sabbath, otherwise forbidden, Jesus justified it on the argument that "the Sabbath was made for man, and not man for the Sabbath." Here, too, parallels may be found in rabbinic thought, as in the following saying: "The Sabbath has been handed over to you, not you to the Sabbath."[17] On many other significant religious issues, Jesus even took a more extreme stand than what Judaism, as interpreted by the rabbis, allowed. For example, on the question of divorce, Jesus deviated from the more lenient Mosaic regulations by prohibiting what was permitted. Then come some more rigorous ethical demands. Repeatedly opening with "You have heard it was said . . . But I say to you," Jesus prohibited murderous thoughts (as against murder *per se*), adulterous thoughts (as opposed to the act of adultery), all oaths (rather than only false oaths), retaliation (as opposed to the biblical demand for punishment equal to the crime), and even advocated self-mutilation to avoid sinning ("If your hand or your foot causes you to sin, cut it off and throw it away").[18] This, then, cannot be construed as an abrogation of the Mosaic code but rather an ethical deepening and extension of the Torah prescriptions, perhaps the ultimate moral perfection demanded of believers, one which rabbinical Judaism in the long run did not advocate because of its lack of realistic application in daily life. The gist of his ethical teaching he summed up in what is known as the Golden Rule: "So whatever you wish that men would do to you, do so to them; for this is the Law and the prophets." Here too, parallels can be found in Jewish teachings, in fact with Jesus' great predecessor Hillel, whose ethical dictum was: "What is distasteful to yourself, do not do to your neighbor; that is the whole Torah, the rest is but a commentary thereof," and "Judge not your neighbor lest you find yourself in his place."[19] Thus, it seems that both Jesus and Hillel before him saw the Golden Rule as summarizing the ultimate meaning of the Mosiac code, and the biblical saying "You shall love your neighbor as yourself"—but not at the price of abandoning Torah prescriptions—as applying also to strangers.[20] This teaching comes out clearly in the story of the Good Samaritan, a sect in conflict with Judaism, who assisted a hapless and wounded Jew who had been attacked by bandits while on his way from Jerusalem to Jericho. "Go and do likewise" Jesus told his interlocutor, who had asked him for the secret of obtaining eternal life.[21]

"Repent, for the kingdom of heaven is at hand," Jesus repeated to all who were ready to hear and follow him, because this was a time when many people expected the Messiah's advent, although no one knew when exactly the messianic age would begin, but Jesus was convinced it was close at hand, very close. "There are some standing here who will not taste death before they see the kingdom of God."[22] Jesus was certain that he was the long-awaited Messiah. Therefore, when passing through his hometown Nazareth, and upon reading from Isaiah the prophetic messianic passage "He has sent me to proclaim release to the captives," Jesus proclaimed: "Today this scripture has been fulfilled in your hearing." In fact, the term "Christ," used by Christians, is a translation of the Hebrew Messiah, or "anointed one." It is no surprise that Matthew and Luke placed Jesus' birth in Bethlehem, the city of David, the forefather of the prophetically predicted Messiah.[23] In Jewish tradition, the Messiah was to be a liberator of his people, mostly in the political sense, which was to be followed with the start of a new era characterized by peace and justice. As Jesus addressed crowds from place to place, many of the listeners—not just his select dozen disciples—began to believe that he was the long-awaited Messiah, and they acclaimed him as such. Had it not been so, the Roman governor Pilate, who ordered Jesus' crucifixion, would not have mockingly insisted that the sign above the cross read "King of the Jews."[24]

Upon entering Jerusalem, the city where, according to the biblical prophets, the Messiah was to make his triumphal appearance, the crowd greeted him with shouts of "Blessed is the King who comes in the name of the Lord" and "Hosanna to the Son of David!"[25] Jesus' followers, like the other Jews of the period, had in common the expectation that the Messiah would deliver them from Roman rule. A new Messiah meant a new rebellion, although in fairness it must be pointed out that Jesus was no supporter of a revolt against Rome. "Render to Caesar the things that are Caesar's, and to God the things that are God's," he counseled his listeners.[26] Notwithstanding this demurral, the Roman governor's main concern, at the trial of Jesus, was the messianic agitation caused by his appearance. Pilate presented Jesus to the assembled crowd with the words "Behold your King!", an allusion to the messianic king who, much to the satisfaction of the Romans, had not fulfilled the hopes of his followers.[27] Here it should be underlined that even those who believed him to be the Messiah perceived him in human terms, and not as a divine figure second only to God, as later professed by the nascent church.

In the Gospel of John, Jesus's fellow Jews are, in general, portrayed as being against Jesus and constantly eager to do him harm, even to the point of killing him. John dispenses with even a modicum of polite exchanges between Jesus and his detractors, and has Jesus accusing his own people, "You are of your father the devil. . . . He was a murderer from the beginning, and has nothing to do with the truth, because there is no truth in him . . . for he is a liar and the father of lies," evidently referring to Satan, the Devil.[28] It is questionable whether Jesus actually pronounced these highly charged words in the way presented by John, written many years afterwards, but for the purpose of our study, what matters is that these inflammatory words were considered authentic by believing Christians. At the same time, the same John who singled out the Jews as Jesus' bitter opponents has him say to a Samaritan woman that "salvation is from the Jews."[29]

However, contrary to the impression created in John's gospel, the record of the other three gospels makes it clear that Jesus was actually popular with the crowds that came to listen to him. In Capernaum, they "could not get near him because of the crowd," and so forth throughout the Synoptic Gospels. Another example are the thousands who stayed on for long hours to listen to him and then had to be fed, when it is told the Jesus performed the miracle of the fish and loaves of bread. In fact, everywhere he went, crowds followed him. Only in his native Nazareth was he not well received, and they even wished to harm him.[30] In Jerusalem, Jesus taught in the Temple, where he drew large crowds (witness the cries of "Hosanna to the son of David"), and was received by some as a prophet. His popularity with the crowd, indeed, at first prevented the priestly authorities from arresting him, "for all the people hung upon his words . . . [and the high priests] feared the people." As noted by Jules Isaac, a favorable reception of Jesus was the rule, a hostile reception the exception.[31] Even later, on the way to his crucifixion, "there followed a great multitude of the people, and of women who bewailed and lamented him." Some offered Jesus wine mixed with myrrh to help numb the agonizing death he faced. After witnessing the crucifixion of Jesus, "all the multitudes . . . returned home beating their breasts." When he was removed from the cross, it was not the Romans but two Jews, Joseph of Arimathea and Nicodemus, both leading members of the city council of Jerusalem, and the latter one of the richest patricians in the city, who looked after the burial arrangements, with Nicodemus arranging for Jesus' body to be anointed with a mixture of myrrh and aloes. [32]

As for the Pharisees, who in the New Testament are generally depicted in disparaging terms, they play no role in the gospel accounts of the arrest and trial of Jesus, and are mysteriously absent as antagonists in the Passion narratives, where the priests appear as the main culprits. Indeed, a leading Pharisee scholar, Gamaliel, is recorded as counseling not to impose punitive measures against the apostles.[33] The reason for this is simple: the Pharisees, and Jews in general, regarded the handing over of a Jew to a foreign power as a repulsive and criminal act. In Jewish religious lore, informers and betrayers are listed among those who sins are "unforgivable" and whose punishment lasts forever.[34]

5

When Jesus decided to move his sphere of preaching from the Galilee to Jerusalem, it is clear from a reading of the text that his words and actions in Jerusalem, including his prediction of the Temple's destruction, precipitated the catastrophe. The Sadducean priesthood, despised by most people, had its sole support in the Temple. The ominous forecast of the Temple's imminent destruction, pronounced by Jesus literally on the Temple grounds, coupled with his series of clashes with the Temple hierarchy and the violent expulsion of the moneychangers, represented a clear threat to the priestly caste, and they decided to move against him. Also to be taken into consideration was the fear of Caiaphas, the chief priest, that the Jesus movement would trigger violent Roman intervention. The leader of another messianic movement, Theudas, had recently been captured and executed by the Romans.[35]

Moving to Jesus' arrest, one must keep in mind that since the disciples are all recorded to have fled from the scene, one must follow with caution the narrative in the New Testament of what actually took place in the garden of Gethsemane. According to John 18:3, the Temple guard arrived, accompanied by a Roman cohort and a disciple of Jesus named Judas Iscariot. Here one must wonder why it was necessary for Judas to point out and identify Jesus, who frequently visited and taught in the Temple compound, in the sight of everyone, much of it in direct confrontation with the Temple priesthood. At any rate, at this point all eleven disciples abandoned their master during this most critical phase of his ministry.[36] As earlier noted, the high priests did not dare arrest Jesus in public because "they feared the people," and "lest there be a tumult among the people," "for all the people hung on words." At the same time, the chief priest could not allow Jesus to go on with his preaching, which he felt threatened the high position of the priestly caste, for "if we let him go on thus, every one will believe in him."[37] Not a word here on the supposed hostility of the Jewish crowd.

What else do we know about the Jewish role in the trial itself, which later formed the basis of the terrible charge of deicide against the Jewish people as a whole? As stated, not one of the apostles was able to witness it, because they deserted their master at the moment of his arrest. The only exception was Peter, who followed from a safe distance and made his way into the courtyard of the high priest, but when questioned, he denied knowing Jesus and stood aside.[38] How, then, is one to assess with certainty what actually took place at the pretrial hearing before the priestly hierarchy? Under Roman rule the Jewish religious high court, known as the Sanhedrin, had lost the right to pass capital punishment, so the high priest had no other choice than to defer the matter to the Roman governor, who happened to be staying in Jerusalem. But was it an official assembly of the Sanhedrin that condemned Jesus to death? John knew nothing about it. In Luke, a verdict by that body is not even mentioned. In addition, since the arrest of Jesus took place in the dead of night and his arraignment was at daybreak, we know nothing of how the people at large felt about this incident.[39] Nowhere is it reported that the masses of people, in a city overflowing with tens of thousands of pilgrims for the Passover festival, had any part in the intrigue woven against Jesus, but as the four evangelists testify, the priestly leadership acted unbeknownst to the people, despite them, and in fear of them.[40]

As for the later Christian accusation that the Jewish people, *in toto*, rejected Jesus and participated in his death, the following facts should be underlined. In the Galilee, Jesus visited no more than a handful of towns, in a region where, according to the historian Josephus, there were more than 200 important Jewish communities and fifteen fortified towns. Furthermore, in the time of Jesus, the dispersion of the Jewish people had been an accomplished fact for centuries, with the Jews of Palestine forming a minority. In all likelihood, the majority of the Jewish people inside and outside of Palestine did not know Jesus. As for the real size of the crowd stirred up by the chief priests in front of the Roman governor's palace out of the several millions who according to Josephus made the pilgrimage to Jerusalem during the Passover festival, how many, one may legitimately ask, would have been able to squeeze themselves into the narrow enclave of the governor's inner yard and then scream, as recounted by Matthew: "His blood be on us and on our children"? A few hundred, at the most—at any rate, a very small percentage of the human mass at Jerusalem at the time, and even more infinitesimal in relation to the mass of the Jewish people in the world of antiquity.[41]

We now come to the Roman governor, Pontius Pilate, the dictatorial ruler of the country on behalf of the Roman Empire, in whose hands now lay the fate of Jesus. What do we know of him, other than his lukewarm presentation in the New Testament as somewhat innocent, passive, and naive in the confrontation with Jesus? If the words of Flavius Josephus, the principal Jewish historian of the period (and considered a credible recorder of events) are to be taken into account, Pilate was anything but a forgiving person. The same with the apostle Luke, who in 13:1 relates how Pilate ordered a massacre of Galileans which took place during Jesus' ministry. Pilate was eventually ordered to return to Rome to explain his behavior, which he did not do, but according to the church historian Eusebius elected to commit suicide. Another credible historian, Philo, described Pilate as "a man of an inflexible, stubborn, and cruel disposition," and listed his seven mortal sins: "his venality, his violence, his thievery, his assaults, his abusive behavior, his frequent executions of untried prisoners, and his endless savage ferocity." He was a man "full of briberies . . . robberies . . . outrages . . . wanton injuries . . . [and] executions without trial."[42] It stands to reason from this cruel narrative that in the hands of Pontius Pilate the life of a man, even more so a Jew suspected of messianic agitation, could not have weighed very heavily. One uncontested fact emerges clearly: Jesus was scourged, then crucified at the command of the Roman procurator. Having scourged Jesus, he delivered him to be crucified. We shall, of course, never know what really transpired in the mind of this man, whom his masters in Rome, not known for their benign treatment of conquered and rebellious peoples, recalled to Rome because of his unspeakably cruel governance of the Jews.[43]

After Pilate's sentencing, not the Jews, but the Roman soldiers had their turn at degrading Jesus. They dressed him in a purple cloak, plaited a crown of thorns, and set it on his head. They also placed a reed in his right hand. They then genuflected, prostrating themselves before him as before an oriental despot, and saluted him: "Hail! King of the Jews!" Then they spat on him, wrenched away his reed scepter, and struck him on the head with it. As to the reaction of the Jewish crowd outside the governor's place, according to the New Testament, on the way to the execution, Jesus was accompanied by "a great multitude of people and of women who bewailed and lamented him."[44] Also worth mentioning is that crucifixion was a Roman form of punishment for criminals and political agitators. In conclusion, on the orders of Pilate, Jesus was flogged and crucified by Roman soldiers. These are the facts.

It stands to reason that for the rising Christian church, slowly spreading throughout the Roman Empire, the tradition of the crucial Roman role in the crucifixion of Jesus, already hailed as a divine figure, was an embarrassment, to put it mildly, and the church handled it by subtly shifting the blame on the Jews. This proved a comfortable solution, for by the time of the final redaction of the gospels, the great Jewish revolt against Rome had ended in a crushing defeat, and the Jews had lost much favor with the Romans; note the Arch of Titus in the Roman Forum, and the minting of special coins with the inscription *Judea Capta*—"Captive Judea." For ages thereafter, Christians blamed the Jews, all Jews at the time and throughout the following centuries, for the death of Jesus. Christian theologians never stopped to ask themselves why all Jews should be blamed for the role of a few Jews in the death of another Jew, a person viewed at the time in strictly human terms? Were Jews, moreover, to be held responsible because three hundred years after the crucifixion, at the Council of Nicea, a non-Jewish religious movement declared this person to be a divine figure, co-equal with God? It took the Roman Catholic Church almost two millennia after this event to admit in 1965, at the Second Vatican Ecumenical Council, that "what happened in His passion cannot be blamed upon all the Jews then living, without distinction, nor upon the Jews of today."[45] Many Christians, however, still hold the Jews to blame for the crime of deicide— the death of a godly figure.

As for the disciples of Jesus, after their master's disappearance, they continued to hope and preach the message of his reappearance, but they also continued to uphold the precepts of the Torah, the most zealous being James, "the brother of the Lord," and the recognized leader of the Christian community in Jerusalem. They visited the Temple at the hour of prayer, and their preaching there attracted new converts. When they were faced with arrest and punishment by the city council, which was dominated by the priesthood, the rabbinic sage Gamaliel (a leading Pharisee) came to their defense and effected their release. James and the elders also counseled the newly converted apostle Paul to "live in observance of the law."[46] However, as we shall soon see, this apostle had a totally different understanding what Jesus signified to the new church.

* * *

One tends to speculate what form the sect calling themselves Christians ("Messianists") would have taken had Saul-Paul not appeared on the scene. The man who undoubtedly had the greatest influence in shaping the theology of Christianity as we still know it today was born as Saul, in Tarsus, a city in Asia Minor (modern Turkey), but is better known by his Greek name, Paul. In contrast to his fellow disciples, Saul had not known Jesus personally. He claimed to have studied in Jerusalem under the guidance of the benign Pharisee Gamaliel, although judging from his later thinking it is most likely that Hellenist influence may have predominated over his Judaic studies. However, quite paradoxically, the greatest advocate of Christianity began by allying himself with the priestly caste and taking a direct role in persecuting the followers of the recently crucified Jesus. After urging that Stephen, one of the newly converted followers, be stoned to death, Paul, in the words of Acts, "was ravaging the church, and entering house after house, he dragged off men and women and committed them to prison." Not content with persecuting the Christian community in Jerusalem, he wished to extend "his raging fury" against Christians in foreign cities, and for that purpose, "breathing threats and murder against the disciples of the Lord," he asked to be sent to Damascus, so that "any belonging to the Way, men or women," should be bound to Jerusalem for punishment. However, on the way there, he suddenly saw Jesus in a vision, who implored him, "Saul, Saul why do you persecute me?" From that moment, he became an adept disciple, and very much so. In fact, Christianity cannot be properly understood without him.[47]

Paul's basic and fundamental premise, as evidenced from his many Letters to the faithful, is that all men are shackled under the power of sin. Moreover, since sin so permeates the very nature of man, making him unable to extricate

himself from its grip, this must be wrought outside of him; in fact, by a supernatural power, who is none other than Jesus Christ, a divine figure, who having become man, then as a mortal experienced death, had by this act atoned for
all the sins of mankind, and released them from the bondage of sin. This was
quite a novel idea, and had no parallel in Jewish thought.[48] Paul's second premise was that the Law (in other words, the Torah) awakens and makes known to
man his predisposition to sin and evil deeds—again, an idea which went counter to every teaching in Judaism, of whatever tendency. Is then the Torah to
blame for making us conscious of our sinful nature? Paradoxically not! "Yet, if
it had not been for the law, I should not have known sin. I should not have
known what it is to covet if the law had not said, 'You shall not covet.'" So the
Law, while fundamentally "holy . . . and just and good," works at cross-pur-
poses, since sinful man, who is by nature "carnal, sold under sin," by the introduction of the Torah's prohibition suddenly becomes cognizant of his sinful
nature, and this state of affair he finds unbearable. Sharpening his critique of
the Torah, Paul claimed that "the sting of death is sin, and the power of sin is
the Law." This revolutionary idea was so far removed from what Jews of all
factions held to be the true nature of the Torah that it is hard to understand how
Paul could later still claim for himself the title of Pharisee![49]

The solution to man's sorry state, which began with Adam's trespass (later
known as the Original Sin), is by acknowledging Jesus as a divine figure who
assumed a human form and upon his death took upon himself the sins of all
who believed in him. This is to Paul the true significance of Jesus' coming.
Through faith in Jesus, Paul argued, every person, whether Jew or Gentile,
finds release from sin, apart from and without obedience to the Torah. While
the Law is not to be cancelled, it has in fact lost its sacerdotal importance, and
is of no further religious value, since "a man is not justified by works of the
law but through faith in Jesus Christ." The Torah, in fact, has with the coming
of Jesus become irrelevant, a meaningless conformity to obsolete religious
regulations. For whereas the Law is a "curse" and "kills," faith in Christ
"gives life." Little, if anything, is said of Jesus's ethical teachings.[50]

What about Paul's brethren, the Jews, who opposed this novel interpretation of the Torah and the figure of a divine Jesus? Paul sadly concluded that
while "they have a zeal for God . . . it is not enlightened." Israel is said to have
"stumbled." At the same time, Israel's history remained the locus of divine
revelation, and the irreplaceable witness of salvation history; this, in spite of
their "blindness" and obnoxious stance. The election simply preserves them in
present darkness for a future redemption, not for their own sake, but "for the
sake of their forefathers"; this, until the ingathering of the gentiles into the
new faith. "A hardening has come upon part of Israel," and "to this day whenever Moses is read a veil lies over their minds."[51]

Yet, despite his derogation of the status of Judaism, Paul did not quite slam the door in its face. In Romans, chapters 9–11, while sharply critical of Judaism, Paul allowed himself to deviate from his other and more common supersessionist claims by retaining for the Jews a dignified role in the divine economy. In these two chapters Paul argued that the Jewish "root" as well as its "branches" remained "holy." As for the new Gentile converts, Paul viewed them as merely "wild olive shoots" which were grafted in the place of some of the broken-off unbelieving Jewish shoots, so that the Gentiles may share in "the richness of the olive tree." Paul consequently cautioned the Gentile Christians, "Do not boast over the branches. . . . Remember it is not you that support the root, but the [Jewish!] root that supports you," since the Gentiles were cut off from a "wild olive tree," and grafted "contrary to nature, into a cultivated olive tree." This was a novel complimentary gesture by Paul to his people, and in these passages we have the most generous approach to the Jews and Judaism in the New Testament; it may well have preserved them from extinction (though not persecution) at the hands of Christians for many centuries to come. A full reading of these passages, however, discloses that the message for the Jews as a whole remained unmistakably problematic. As pointed out by Rosemary Ruether, Paul, perhaps unwittingly, laid the foundations for the idea developed by Augustine that not until the Jews are converted will Christ return and the salvation of the world, of church and synagogue, be complete. For, as Paul underlined, "if the casting away of them is the reconciling of the world, what shall the receiving of them be, but life from the dead?" Thus, the Jews are to be preserved, and Romans 9–11, therefore, had a profound impact upon a later triumphalist Christianity in not destroying the Jews, but preserving them for centuries to come, although in a low and demeaning status, and ever hoping that they would eventually convert and thereby allow Christianity to enter into the final salvific stage for mankind.[52]

In summary, while scholars still dispute Paul's real position on the Torah's precepts, which he himself presumably practiced to the full, there is no parallel in any Jewish literature to some of his extreme statements in that regard. It is surprising that Paul, a man who undoubtedly had the mind of a genius, could so completely misrepresent the true nature of Judaism. A basic principle of Judaism is that man can gain God's favor by his own conduct. But if this so, then the role of Jesus as a fully or near-divine sin-forgiving figure is superfluous. At this early stage of Christianity, it already seems that compromise was hard to come by. Quite aside from the question of whether the Jewish followers of Jesus, at this early stage, saw in his death a divine sacrifice to atone for the sins of mankind, it was because of Paul that this belief was finally adopted by the nascent church. With Paul, Jesus is transformed into an a-historical figure, a visitant from outer space with a purely spiritual mission devoid of political content. The Jews, who refused to see it this way, had, in the eyes of Paul and the rising church, completely missed the point, and were to suffer the consequences of their "blindness" and stubborn objection to the new faith. Paul probably did not wish it so, but the result of his teaching was to make the Jews the adversary.[53]

The Nascent Church

One cannot be unmoved by the some of the lofty thoughts expressed in the New Testament, such as the Sermon on the Mount and the Parable of the Good Samaritan, and Paul's laudation of pristine love.[54] At the same time, the New Testament is also a text filled with a critique and harsh words against Judaism; from a Jewish perspective, it seems that Paul and later the church fathers had completely misread the true nature of Jewish faith. Be that as it may, as the texts of the New Testament were being put down in writing, edited and redacted, Jews underwent one of the most tragic epochs in their history, as the two revolts against Rome in 66–70 and 132–35 C.E. left the country in ruins, the Jewish people divested of its holy Temple, and the holy city of Jerusalem declared off-limits to Jews, with its name changed to Aelia Capitolina, in honor of a Roman emperor. The New Testament was also written at a time when the conflict between the followers of Jesus and their opponents within what was now rabbinic Judaism had reached a boiling point. The New Testament is in some respects a polemical work, of the truth of the new religion against the backdrop of a still vibrant Judaism, in whose bosom the new religion was born. While it is not bereft of statements calling into question the Pharisaic-rabbinic self-appreciation of Judaism, the editors of the New Testament could not dispense with the Hebrew Bible, now renamed the Old Testament, since they found it necessary to find biblical legitimization of their claim to at least Jesus' messiahship, if not his divine stature. Here lie the roots of the incredible hostility manifested by the church fathers toward the Jews, who by denying the Christian claim of a close link with the Hebrew Bible were questioning the legitimacy of the new-born religion. One senses an almost tragic inevitability in the animosity of the church toward its parent religion; a fuming bitterness lasting to modern times, with tragic consequences for the Jewish people.[55]

The New Testament, however, did contain antidotes to the anti-Jewish animus. Since Jesus was presented as a kindly and beneficent figure who healed the sick and spoke up for the downtrodden, a Christian who wished to emulate him could take an example from the master's love and thus be swayed to a charitable stance, even toward the Jews. But this proved a difficult task for many Christians, especially theologians. For the paradox remained that all

12

Christians drew inspiration from the New Testament, a religious text that contained not a few unfriendly statements about Judaism, and there is sufficient anti-Jewish material in its pages, when taken out of context, to feed the fires of prejudice and religious passion.[56]

The new religion, now fully Gentile after the original Jewish component dwindled and disappeared from the scene, had also to contend with counterarguments from pagan thinkers in the Roman world, such as Celsus, who pointed to the anomaly of a Christianity at odds with its own roots, asking how the Gospel could base its validity on its being the fulfillment of Jewish prophecy, yet be repudiated by the holders of title to that prophecy.[57] Taking Celsus' challenge very seriously, an early church theologian named Marcion proposed a radical solution. His position was that there was, indeed, a tension that had to be resolved. If Christianity was truly "new," and if it had truly abandoned the Torah, it had to relinquish the "old" book and the God who enacted it. That God, he claimed, was humankind's enemy, the Creator of this evil world, whereas Jesus had appeared suddenly as the revelation of "newness," as well as of a new, previously unknown God. The Hebrew Bible was, consequently, to be shoved aside and replaced with the New Testament; here, too, not all of it, only a few newly edited books and some of Paul's letters. The church fathers braced themselves against this new challenge—especially Tertullian, who defended the God of the Old Testament, arguing that this God did not act unfairly. Proof? The punishment of the Jews, by having their Temple destroyed. To Marcion's rejoinder that if the Torah was to be abandoned, how could one take seriously the God who enacted this inferior law in the first place, Tertullian replied that the Law was not due to any inferiority on God's part but to the inferiority of the people with whom God was working at that time, since the Law was meant to restrain the "gluttonous" appetite of the idolatry-prone Jews. While Marcion's solution of two Gods and a new Bible was repudiated, and his dualism rejected, a Marcionist radical strain was retained, threatening to resurface and gain dominance, as it did with the German Christian movement in Nazi Germany. Marcionism also left a strong imprint in the form of an ongoing hostility and contempt toward the Jews.[58]

Led by the Nicean formula, in 325 C.E., where the church finally regulated the question of the divine-human nature of Jesus ("begotten from the Father, . . . from the substance of the Father, God from God, light from light, true God from true God, . . . of one substance with the Father, . . . who for the sake of us men and for the purpose of our salvation came down and became incarnate, becoming man"),[59] Christianity conquered the souls of the weakened Roman Empire, and extended its reach among the tribes and lands of the new kingdoms in Europe. This stupendous victory, however, did not pacify the wrath of the church leaders against the Jews. It became imperatively necessary for the edification of the faithful that the Jewish people as a whole be proven fundamentally evil, unworthy, laden with crimes, opprobrium and maledictions. Thus began the elaboration of a theology which became wedded to Christian thinking up to the modern period; of the Jews as both a criminal and a witness people; wretched witnesses "of their own iniquity and of our truth" (Augustine); marked by God with a sign, as was Cain, which both preserved them and singled them out for the loathing of the Christian world.[60]

These anti-Jewish fulminations were not simply peripheral and accidental, but woven into the core of the Christian message, right up to the Holocaust. The church was utterly convinced that it was the legitimate successor of Israel.[61] At the same time, the church could not bring itself to outlaw Judaism, as it did with pagan religions and with its own heretical movements. So paradoxically, while pagan temples were destroyed or confiscated, Judaism remained the only non-compliant religion allowed to subsist, although in a pariah status. Perhaps assuming a neutral position vis-à-vis Judaism, such as a parallel faith-community with "equal rights to exist," would have undone Christianity at its core, and perhaps not. However, the danger persisted that if Judaism was not declared reprobate for rejecting Jesus as its Messiah, then perhaps the Messiah had not come and Christian faith was founded on delusion, even as Judaism claimed. The solution to this dilemma was to allow Jews to subsist, but to make them detestable and contemptible in the eyes of Christians.[62]

Almost all of the church fathers took turns at bashing the Jews in texts known as *Adversos Judaeos*. Names such as Cyprian, Gregory of Nyssa, Tertullian, Ignatius, Aphrahat, John Chrysostom, Ephrem, Eusebius, Jerome, Justin Martyr, Origen, John Damascene, Irenaeus, Eusebius, Lactantius, Ambrose, and Augustine—theological pillars of the Christian pantheon—are all associated with this campaign of defamation. It was virtually impossible for a Christian writer or preacher to teach from the scriptures without alluding to the anti-Judaic theses. The following are only a few examples. Judaism, Ignatius claimed, was nothing "but funeral monuments and tombstones of the dead," a mass of frivolities and absurdities except as a preliminary to the Gospels. Jerome sneered at the "old wives' tales" of the Jews. "Many of them are so disgusting that I blush to mention them," and the prayer of Jews is as pleasant to God as a donkey's braying. Cyprian reminded the Jews not to forget that they had been replaced by the Gentiles. Ephrem termed the Jews: "Thou shameless one and harlot!" John Damascene claimed that the Sabbath was given to the Jews because of their "grossness and sensuality" and "absolute propensity for material things." Hippolytus discussed at length the "fornication of Israel." To Augustine, the Jews were the murderous elder brother now forced to wander the earth as a reprobate among the nations.

Eusebius concluded that Jewish reprobation was permanent and irrevocable. "They would be dispersed among the Gentiles throughout the whole world with never a hope of any cessation of evil or breathing space from troubles." Ambrose mocked the Jews for their state of "confusion." The list of the basest accusations is unending. There is little attempt in the patristic tradition to maintain the Pauline idea of a Jewish remnant in the church as the stem into which the Gentiles were "ingrafted." The relationship became primarily one of substitution, with the "reprobate, unbelieving" Jews cast off.[63]

The derogation of Israel went hand in hand with an appropriation and reinterpretation of the Hebrew Bible, on the charge that the Jews had failed to properly understand their own scriptures. As stated by the second-century Justin: "Your scriptures, or rather not yours but ours, for you, though you read them, do not catch the spirit that is in them." For, as the church now claimed, if the Gentiles are the true Israel, the Jews must have all the time been sailing under false colors. The Gentile church was seen as already implicit in the Old Testament (itself a derogatory term), and was prefigured and foretold in the ancient heroes and prophets. Eusebius held that the patriarchs were not Jews but, like the Christians, part of a universal race, when virtue reigned without the Torah, but through the universal law of conscience inscribed on the heart. The church was, therefore, the restoration of the original covenant, represented by the patriarchs before the Mosaic period. The Torah laws were explained as a way to limit the uncontrollable appetites of the Jews, such as the dietary laws, given to the Jews to restrain their gluttonous ways. According to Eusebius, everything that Moses forbade the Jews had previously existed among them without restraint: idolatry, polytheism, lying, incest, and murder; indeed, all the crimes forbidden in the Law. To Justin, "circumcision was given you as a sign, that you may be separated from other nations, and from us, and that you alone may suffer . . . and that your land may be desolate, and your cities burnt with fire. These things have happened to you in fairness and justice."[64] The Jews, who over the centuries had carefully written and preserved their sacred texts, were now told that they had misread and misunderstood their own writings, and had to be corrected by a rival religion that had not existed at the time that these scriptures were put in writing. How ironic and tragic!

This ongoing vilification unavoidably led to the next step—the demonization of the Jews. One finds it hard to perceive the Jew, as encountered in the pages of some of the church fathers, as a human being. He is described as the embodiment of all that is unredeemed, perverse, stubborn, evil, and demonic in this world. The noted bishop of Antioch, John Chrysostom, outdid the other church fathers in this respect. In eight sermons, which he delivered in 387 in Antioch, he accused the Jews of the most outrageous sins and crimes, such as sacrificing their sons and daughters to devils. As for the synagogues, they were merely dens of debauchery; "no better than to visit a brothel, a robber's den, or any other indecent place . . . a resort of demons, or a citadel of the Devil. . . . What is more, the synagogue is not only a whorehouse and a theater; it is also a den of thieves and a haunt of wild animals. . . . The demons inhabit the very souls of the Jews, as well as the places where they gather." Alluding to the charge of deicide, Chrysostom rhetorically asked: "If someone had killed your son, could you stand the sight of him or the sound of his greeting? Wouldn't you try to get away from him as if he were an evil demon; as if he were the Devil himself? The Jews killed the Son of your Master . . . Will you so dishonor Him as to respect and cultivate His murderers, the men who crucified Him?"[65] From here, it was but a short step to incitement to murder, although Chrysostom did not have to spell it out, and in fact the church fathers, while strongly condemning the Jews, stood back from Chrysostom's vitriolic hatred. It is to be noted that the same Chrysostom composed some very uplifting hymns in praise of God, and is considered a saint in the Greek Orthodox church.

The gradual disenfranchisement of the Jews came after they had finally been granted full Roman citizenship under the pre-Christian Roman emperor Caracalla, and were now made to suffer from a steady reduction of their civil rights. The practice of forcing the Jewish community to listen to Christian conversion sermons began in the fifth century.[66] The first recorded example of compulsory baptism took place in 558, in Uzes (near Nîmes), France, to be followed by other instances elsewhere. As for Jewish houses of prayer, the first recorded burning of a synagogue took place at the behest of Innocentius, bishop of Dertona in northern Italy, who died in 355. It is related that "the Christians together with their bishop destroyed the synagogue, and erected a church on the site." Similarly in Antioch, a clergyman prevented the rebuilding of a synagogue destroyed by rioters in 423. The burning of a synagogue in the frontier town of Callinicum, in 388, in Asia Minor, nearly caused a rift between the highest levels of the secular and ecclesiastical powers—between the emperor Theodosius and one of the most lauded bishops of Christianity, Ambrose (who personally baptized Augustine). When the emperor ordered the local bishop to provide funds to restore the synagogue, Ambrose in a letter to the emperor declared that he would be happy to himself take a hand in the burning of a synagogue, adding that for a bishop to rebuild a synagogue would be tantamount to apostasy, since the synagogue was "a haunt of infidels, a home of the impious, a hiding place of madmen, under the damnation of God himself." Theodosius modified this order to a simpler restoration of the sacred articles stolen from the synagogue, while the actual rebuilding was to be financed by the state. But this too was unacceptable to Ambrose, who insisted that there were to be no reparations and no punishment whatsoever of the culprits. When the emperor refused to give in, Ambrose seized the occasion of the emperor's presence at the Divine Liturgy in the cathedral of Milan to confront him. Coming down from the altar to face him, the bishop declared that he would not continue with the Eucharist until the emperor obeyed. The emperor bowed to this threat of excommunication, and the rioters at Callinicum went unpunished and not even admonished.[67] In contrast to Ambrose, Pope Gregory the Great (509–604) ordered the bishop of Caglieri to restore a synagogue, on the logic that Jews were not allowed to build new ones. He also forbade forced conversions of Jews by religious enthusiasts, and favored conversion only as the outcome of sincere conviction. At the same time, he cautioned that the Jews were not to be allowed too much freedom, and in his biblical commentary, in line with his *Adversos Judaeos* predecessors, he portrayed the typical Jews as a demonic unbeliever whose trail of perfidy and apostasy led unavoidably to the killing of Christ.[68]

The official church position on the Jews guaranteed their existence, but as a pariah people—testifying both to the present election of the church and to the need for them to be on the scene to witness its final triumph. The concept of a "witness people" received its clearest and most influential expression in the writings of Augustine, one of Christianity's foremost theologians. He wrote that the Jews were dispersed over the world to bear witness through their Scriptures, as proof "that we have not fabricated the prophecies about Christ." It followed that although "the Jews do not believe in our Scriptures, their own Scriptures are fulfilled in them, while they read them with blind eyes. . . . The Jews are our attendant slaves, who carry, as it were, our satchels, and bear the manuscripts while we study them." Therefore, "do not slay them," but "scatter them by our might. . . . They are our supporters in their books, our enemies in their hearts, our witnesses in their scrolls." The Augustinian witness-people formula, which prevailed in Christendom up until the modern period, allowed the Jews to survive but never to thrive, since their misery was to serve as proof of the truth of Christianity. Like Cain, they were to carry a sign signifying their damnation, but they were not to be killed.[69]

Through the Ages

Over the centuries, the teaching of contempt of the Jews as a reprobate people knew no pause, and continued to be taught and preached in mainland Christendom, in Catholic as well as Protestant churches. Leading theologians continued to castigate the Jews even though the Jews, who desired nothing but to keep out of the fray, offered no prompting or provocation. The principal Catholic theologian of the medieval period, Thomas Aquinas, wrote that it was permissible "to hold the Jews in perpetual servitude because of their crime . . . with the sole proviso that they do not deprive them of all that is necessary to sustain life. . . . We must bear ourselves honestly, even to those who are outcasts, lest the name of Christ be blasphemed." In the sixteenth century, the Protestant Reformer John Calvin stated that the Jews "cut themselves off from all hope of salvation. . . . the whole race is utterly cut off from the kingdom of God." The French Catholic theologian Jacques Bossuet allowed the Jews to continue to exist, but denounced them as "stamped by their reprobation, visibly blighted by their unfaithfulness to the promises made to their fathers, banished from the Promised Land, having no land to cultivate even, slaves everywhere they are, without honor, without freedom, without form as a people." This negative theology, what Ruether terms Christianity's "left hand," did not abate even in modern times, when the church no longer held undisputed sway over the minds of people. The French theologian Jacques Maritain, who spoke up against antisemitism, remarked that the Jews must pay "forever" for their "error" of rejecting Jesus. Edith Stein, a Jewish convert to Catholicism, also held fast to this idea. Upon her deportation to Auschwitz (for to the Nazis what mattered was not her belief but her Jewish racial ancestry), she reportedly stated that she offered her life to God "for the atonement of the unbelief of the Jewish people." These ideas still held sway even in the post-Holocaust era. For example, the Jewish theologian Richard Rubenstein related his shock, on meeting with the Protestant Pastor Heinrich Grüber (who had helped Jews avoid capture by the Nazis and was honored as a "Righteous Among the Nations" by Yad Vashem), to hear Grüber explain that Hitler had been a rod of God's anger against the Jews. Rubenstein marveled that an anti-Nazi of the stature of Grüber, who had suffered incarceration in a Nazi concentration camp for his help to Jews, remained bound to a teaching that justified, from a theological viewpoint, the suffering of the Jews.[70]

The theological conviction that Jews merited suffering did not mean that uncontrolled physical violence against Jews was permitted. On the contrary, Christian theologians continued to warn against excessive harm to Jews. Thus, in 1146, Bernard of Clairvaux wrote: "The Jews are not to be persecuted, killed, or even put to flight"; and "whosoever touches a Jew to take his life is like one who harms Jesus himself." The reason given is the oft-repeated statement that "the Jews are for us the living words of Scripture, for they remind us always of what our Lord suffered. They are dispersed all over the world so that by expiating their crime they may be everywhere the living witnesses of our redemption." As for the popes, while continuing to castigate Jewish "unbelief" and "culpability," they warned against physical violence, while at the same time, in the style of Gregory the Great, they continued to castigate the Jews as "preachers of Antichrist," in whom the devil dwells.[71]

Undoubtedly, the most serious of charges, one still believed by many Christians, is that of deicide—the murder of a divine figure in the form of Jesus Christ. Officially, the church position is that Jesus's death was preordained and had to happen. Anselm of Canterbury, in the eleventh century, stated bluntly that a ransom was due God because of Adam's disobedience and fall, and this "satisfaction" for the Original Sin was paid in full by God himself, by sacrificing his Son, thereby substituting for man's sins. Yet the Jews had to be blamed for his death, although in truth, the official Catholic position, spelled out in the sixteenth century at the Council of Trent, blamed the death of Jesus on all sinners, not merely the Jews. The council affirmed that "this guilt seems the more enormous in us than in the Jews, since according to the testimony of the same Apostle [Paul]: 'If they had known it, they would never have crucified the Lord of glory' (1 Cor. 2:8), while we, on the contrary, professing to know him, yet denying Him by our actions, seem in some sort to lay violent hands on Him." In spite of this, however, Christian theologians continued to attribute the death of Jesus solely to the Jews; not merely the Jews of Jesus' time, but all Jews, past and present, who, it was asserted, bear the "curse" of this deed. Among the church fathers, Gregory of Nyssa branded the Jews "murderers of the Lord," and he was not the only one. In the medieval period, Pope Innocent III likened the Jews to the biblical Cain, who committed the first recorded murder. This, Innocent III cautioned, did not mean open season on the Jews, "yet as wanderers ought they to remain upon the earth, until their countenance be filled with shame and they seek the name of Jesus Christ the Lord." The Catholic theologian Jacques Bossuet charged the Jews with committing "the greatest of all crimes: an unprecedented crime, that is, deicide, which also occasioned a vengeance the like of which the world had never seen." This accusation reverberated in the minds of philosophers down to the modern age. Such as Sören Kierkegaard, who wrote of the effect of this rather explosive charge on the tender minds of children: "The child would have decided that when he grew up he would slay all those ungodly men who had dealt thus with the loving One." Finally, Pope Paul VI, the successor of John XXIII (who tried to make amends to the Jewish people), restated the charge of the Jews, who "just at the right moment, not only did not recognize Him but fought Him, abused Him, and finally killed him."[72]

Martin Luther, the great Protestant reformer, stands out as one of the most vicious Jew-baiters of the late medieval period. Surprisingly, in 1523, soon after his break with the Catholic Church, he penned a brochure with the title *In That Jesus Christ Was Born a Jew*, where he appeared as a stout defender of Jews. He even averred that Jews had been right to resist Catholic efforts to convert them. "If I had been a Jew," he stated, "I should rather have turned into a pig than become a Christian." Two decades later, disappointed that the

Jews had not flocked to his church, he penned another brochure, this time with the enflamed title, *On the Jews and Their Lies*, a book littered with the filthiest insults, in the style of John Chrysostom, with frenzied summonses to the worst violence. He castigated the Jews as "venomous beasts, vipers, disgusting scum, cancers, devils incarnate . . . pig excrement," and urged that "their private houses must be destroyed and devastated; they could be lodged in stables," and called for the burning of their synagogues, "and whatever escapes the fire must be covered with sand and mud." He warned his followers: "Know, my dear Christians, and do not doubt that next to the devil you have no enemy more cruel, more venomous and virulent, than a true Jew." Finally, as a last resort, "we will be compelled to expel them like mad dogs." This from a thinker who wrote the spiritually elevating hymn *A Mighty Fortress!* His rage against the Jews knew no bounds. He urged German rulers to act "like a good physician who, when gangrene has set in, proceeds without mercy to cut, saw, and burn flesh, veins, bone and marrow."[73] Sadly, another German, four centuries later, did exactly that.

In 1215, Pope Innocent III, presiding over the Fourth Lateran Council, decreed the obligatory wearing of a special identifying dress for all Jews, including a conical hat and a "Jew badge" (usually a yellow circle, symbolic of the Jew as betrayer of Christ for "gold"). Other canonical rules included that synagogues be low and miserable buildings. In Spain, in 1492, the Grand Inquisitor Torquemada, persuaded the Ferdinand and Isabella, the king and queen, to expel all Jews who were not baptized, so that the Inquisition could settle down to hunting out the secret Judaizers—that is, those forced to convert but suspected of secretly still practicing Judaism.[74] In July 1555, at a time when Italy was emerging from the Dark Ages and flourishing into the Renaissance, all of Rome's Jews were rounded up and brought to a district besides the Tiber River that would thenceforth serve as a ghetto until 1870. While imprisoned there, Jews were forced by order of the popes to attend conversionist sermons in the few synagogues left to them. Pope Paul IV (1555–59) went further by forbidding Jews to possess any religious book except the Bible, and placed the Talmud on the Index of Forbidden Books. In July 1555, he issued the bull (an official papal edict or announcement) *Cum Nimis Absurdum*, which stated that in papal lands Jews were to own no real estate, attend no Christian university, and hire no Christian servants; they were required to wear distinctive clothing and badges, and were not to be addressed as "sir" by Christians. As Europe emerged from the medieval period into the modern age, the Jews still found themselves reduced to political servitude, social ignominy, and in many places locked behind ghetto walls; to economic ruin, vulnerability to violence from below, and arbitrary exploitation and expulsion from above. At various times, the Jews of England, France, Spain,

Portugal, and much of Germany had been expelled, or forced to practice their religion in hiding.[75] The crux of the Christian ambivalence toward Jews and Judaism remained a mixture of contempt, denunciations, and vilifications, but also of a secret admiration at the resiliency of the Jewish people and religion, and the hope that they would eventually admit their "error" and embrace the church. As stated in the 1930s by the German bishop Michael von Faulhaber: "After the death of Christ, Israel was dismissed from the service of Revelation . . . and from that time forth Ahasuerus wanders, forever restless, over the face of the earth . . . and one day, at the end of time, for them too the hour of grace will strike (Rom. 11:26)."[76]

Karl Barth best exemplified this ambivalent attitude. A founding member of the Confessing Church in Germany, which took a stand against the Nazi encroachment of the churches, he also spoke out against the persecution of Jews and declared that antisemitism was anti-Christian, and "irreconcilable with the Christian point of view." In 1933, Barth wrote that the blood of the Jewish people was "in his veins, the blood of the son of God . . . Jesus Christ was a Jew. . . . How can we, each time we think about this, not be obliged to think above all of the Jews?" Responding to *Kristallnacht*, the torching of all the synagogues in Nazi Germany, in November 1938, Barth (from his base in Switzerland) stated: "He who is on principle an enemy of the Jews . . . is to be recognized as on principle an enemy of Jesus Christ." Yet in the first volume of *Church Dogmatics*, written in the same year (CD I:2), he stigmatized the Jews as "a hard and stiff-necked people, because it is a people which resists its God. It is characterized as the people which in its own Messiah finally rejected and crucified the savior of the world and therefore denied the revelation of God." That whereas the Christian symbolized man with his face turned toward God's grace, the Jew symbolized the same man with his face turned away from God's grace. In the second volume of *Church Dogmatics* (CD II:2), written in 1942, at the height of the Holocaust, Barth painted the Jews as representing "the divine judgment," while at the same time same time emphasizing that Israel's election was permanent and inescapable despite its refusal to accept the Christian gospel. Having stated this, he quickly drew back, asserting that because Israel hears but does not believe ("refuses to hear properly and perfectly"), it places itself in a difficult position; that of the man who resists his election. At the same time, despite Israel's disbelief, "even its loud no in response to divine election" cannot release Israel from the role it is to play in salvation history. It cannot evade its "appointed service," which is to represent the judgment of God in the same way the church represents God's mercy. In this role, Israel is a vessel of dishonor, as it gives "wretched testimony" of its lack of faith. In his further writings on this subject, in 1950, Barth referred to the Christian God as "continually to be rejected by Israel," and the Jews are therefore judged severely. While admitting that unfortunately all Christians suffer from the disease of antisemitism (was Barth also alluding to himself?) because of jealousy of Israel's chosen status, the Jews represented the "mirror" in which are reflected "who and what we all are, and how bad we all are"— that of sinful humanity; of displaying "the primal revolt, the unbelief, the disobedience in which we are all engaged." Antisemitism, according to Barth, is nothing else but "annoyance" with Jews because they force non-Jews to recognize the pitiful nature of the human condition; hence, antisemites "desire that the mirror should be removed." But this will do no good to the Christian. For "what is the good of turning the mirror to the wall, or even smashing it? That will not alter the fact that we are still what we saw ourselves to be in the mirror." The Jews cannot, therefore, disappear from the stage of Christian history, for they serve as a "witness" of man's fundamental condition of sinfulness, as they themselves "are no more than the shadow of a nation, the reluctant witnesses of the Son of God and Son of Man . . . whom they rejected, yet who has not ceased to call them." These words of the staunch anti-Nazi Barth reveal the dialectical tension present in the traditional Christian obsession with Judaism, combining a deep aversion with a profoundly irrational attraction.[77]

Some view the Holocaust as the final and logical stage which began with the patristic anti-Jewish campaign, and was nourished by the centuries-long teaching of contempt. The Nazis shattered the Christian ambivalence and double-edged relation vis-à-vis the Jews, and took the Jewish Question to its ultimate Final Solution. As pointed out by John Carroll, because the hatred of Jews had been made holy, it became lethal. The anti-Jewish teaching, disseminated from generation to generation by hundreds and thousands of voices, often the most eloquent, often also the most grossly insulting, created in the minds of Christendom a picture of Judaism and Jews which engendered repulsion and hate. To which one may add the words of Richard Rubenstein: "The more one studies the classical utterances of Christianity on Jews and Judaism . . . the more one is prompted to ask whether there is something in the Christian philosophy of history, when pushed to a metaphysical extreme, that ends in the justification of, if not the incitement to, the extermination of Jews." However, as further pointed out by Rosemary Ruether, while in the Christian drama the Jews would eventually embrace Jesus, and mankind would enter into the final stage of divine salvation, to the antisemitic as well as anti-Christian Hitler, there was no room for the Jews in the Final Judgment, and the generations-long teaching of contempt was brought to its ultimate murderous culmination in the Nazi gas chambers.[78]

In the following chapters we shall narrate, country by European country, the personal involvement of Christian clerics in the rescue of Jews during the Holocaust, as culled from the record of those honored by Yad Vashem as

"Righteous Among the Nations." These accounts will be preceded with brief outlines of Jewish life and the Christian teaching on the Jews in each of these countries. We shall simultaneously attempt, as far as the record on hand allows, to identify the possible motivations of the clerical rescuers. Whatever the reasons, the fact that hundreds of members of the clergy were prepared to risk their lives and personal freedom to save Jews from destruction remains an encouraging sign and a hopeful indication that a new dawn may yet be at hand.

Chapter 2
GERMANY

The Church of Christ has never lost sight of the thought that the "chosen people," who nailed the redeemer of the world to the cross, must bear the curse for its action through a long history of suffering. . . . The conversion of Israel, that is to be the end of the people's period of suffering.
Dietrich Bonhoeffer (April/May 1933)

This people which can neither live nor die because it is under a curse which forbids it to do either. . . .We see a highly gifted people which produces idea after idea for the benefit of the world, but whatever it takes up becomes poisoned. . . . We cannot change the fact that until the end of its days the Jewish people must go its way under the burden which Jesus' decree has laid upon it: "Behold, your house is left unto you desolate."
Martin Niemöller (1935)

I spiritually oppose the deportation [of Jews] with all its consequences, because it goes against the chief rule of Christianity— "You should love your neighbor as you love yourself," and I consider the Jews also my neighbor who have immortally created souls after the image and likeness of God. . . . I state with steadfast conviction that the National Socialist ideology is incompatible with the teaching and commands of the Catholic church.
Bernhard Lichtenberg (1941)

Jews, Antisemitism and the Final Solution

Jews in Germany's history go back to Roman times, as merchants in Roman military and trading outposts along the Rhine River, such as Cologne. In the Middle Ages, Jewish religious life flourished in various parts of the country and at the same time weathered the terrible religious persecutions unleashed by the Crusaders starting in 1096, and followed by the Black Death

24

scare in the fourteenth century, which led to the decimation of many Jewish communities along the Rhine. By the time of the Reformation in the sixteenth century, the Jews' life swerved between intermittent expulsion and readmittance in most German cities, with many moving eastward, where they found a safe haven in nearby Poland. With the unification of Germany in a single state, in 1871, in the form of the German Empire (also known as the Second Reich), Jews obtained full civil rights. By then Jews had already made important contributions in all spheres of German public life. During the Weimar Republic, following World War I, Jewish cultural assimilation reached its apogee in the theater, music, philosophy, and science. With Hitler's assumption of power in January 1933, the Jewish population of Germany numbered 522,000 (566,00, according to Nazi racial definitions), representing 0.9 percent of the population, with 377,000 (or 66.8 percent) in Berlin alone. Most Jews had by then been fully acculturated into German life, and the rate of conversion to Christianity and intermarriages numbered in the thousands. This ongoing peaceful acculturation was to take a sudden and terrible turn for the worse.[1]

"Antisemitism" is relatively a modern term, coined in 1879 by Wilhelm Marr, a German journalist, who penned a pamphlet entitled *Der Sieg des Judentums über das Germanentum* ("Jewry's Victory Over Germanism") in which he claimed that the Jews had gained control over the country's life, thanks to their special gifts, endurance, and resilience, and had thus become a power to contend with. This was not meant as a compliment, but as a warning that the Jews were preventing Germany from attaining world supremacy. Marr also had no kind words for Christianity, which he characterized, as he did all religions, as a disease of the human spirit, and hence a source of corruption.[2] While before World War I, antisemites were unable to marshal more than a fraction of the German electorate, anti-Jewish sentiments were popular among many segments of the population. For instance, the celebrated historian Heinrich Treitschke coined the slogan, much in favor later by the Nazis, that "the Jews are our misfortune." On the religious front, Rev. Adolf Stöcker, a Lutheran clergyman who served as imperial court chaplain and was the founder of the Christian Social Workers Party, railed against the Jews from the perspective of the traditional Christian anti-Jewish bias, and the religious historian Paul Bötticher, better known as Lagarde, viewed the Jews as a mortal enemy of Christianity, which, according to him, was perverted already at its birth by the "legalistic" thinking of Paul of Tarsus. He foresaw a mortal contest between Jews and Aryans, and called for taking the most drastic measures against the Jews, even physical liquidation. Other less-known figures continued to beat the drum of Jew-hatred; some with a theological twist, such as Karl Eugen Dühring, who rejected the Old Testament as too Jewish, whereas

Jesus was to be retained based on the preposterous theory that he had no Jewish blood, but was clearly an Aryan, having been fathered by a Roman soldier of Germanic origin. While Jesus could be retained, this did not apply to the church in its present form, since Dühring claimed it was nothing but a Jewish front meant to enslave the world. Houston Stewart Chamberlain, a British national who made Germany his home and whose writings had a great impact on many readers in Germany and elsewhere, also took up the notion of Jesus' Aryan origin. "The probability that Christ was no Jew, but he had not a drop of genuinely Jewish blood in him, is so great that it is almost equivalent to certainty," he asserted, adding that Jesus' teaching was not the perfecting of the Jewish religion, but its negation, a reaction against Jewish "formalism and hard-headed rationalism." For him as for Marr, the two races that stood facing each other were the Jews and the Germans, and struggle between them was unavoidable. Max Bewer, another exponent of the Aryanized Jesus idea, in his *The German Christ* (1907), explained that the Incarnation was nothing but the overcoming of the Aryan blood in Jesus over his Semitic blood. "God in him had triumphed, German blood over Jewish blood." While Bewer, Duehring, and Chamberlain retained Jesus as an Aryan superheroic figure, they felt that Christianity was incompatible with the German spirit, since the teaching of humility, altruism, brotherly love, and otherworldliness led to what they asserted was a paralysis of the spontaneous power of one's true nature, and was therefore a false spiritualization, besides being an unjust mortification of the flesh. These antisemitic currents gained strength after Germany's defeat in World War I, and the Nazis, who then appeared on the scene, represented but a small part of a powerful reactionary and racist current that flooded the traumatized country.[3]

Another idea current in Germany in the pre-Holocaust period, as well as in other countries, was that of racism: the doctrine that one group of people is morally or mentally superior to others, and that its superiority arises out of inherited biological differences, as reflected in a higher physical, intellectual, moral, and cultural life. The idea of racism was wedded to the idea that the higher races, such as the white race or the Germanic peoples (often referred as Nordic or Aryan), had a moral right to dominate the other, inferior races, so as to preserve civilized life, and for this purpose they were even permitted, if necessary, to enslave the lower races. Racists warned against intermarriage between races, or as they derisively termed it, "mongrelization," which they claimed led to the lowering and degeneration of cultural life, since it was opposed to "nature." Houston Stewart Chamberlain, mentioned earlier, was the most extreme protagonist of racist antisemitism. He spelled out his ideas in his *Foundations of the Nineteenth Century*, which appeared in 1899 and earned wide circulation. He was one of the greatest popularizers of the idea of the superiority of the Germans and their destiny to rule. He also predicted a life-and-death struggle between two conflicting philosophies of life, represented on the one hand by the Jewish "race" and on the other by the "Germanic-Aryan race," the outcome of which would settle the future course of civilization—degeneration or continued creativity. Chamberlain's prophetic call for a struggle against the Jews made a deep impact on Hitler, who visited the aged philosopher in Bayreuth to pay his respects, and Chamberlain is one of the few authors to whom Hitler referred in *Mein Kampf* by name; he also mentioned him during the war years in the so-called *Table Talk.* Thus, by the time Hitler appeared on the scene, the process of the demonization of the Jews, coupled with the glorification of the Germans and the idea of an apocalyptic contest between both, had already entered the mainstream among wide circles, including the country's intellectual elite.[4]

As for Hitler, historians differ as to whether he possessed a clear and fully systematically thought out ideology. One cannot, however, dispute that insofar as the Jewish issue was concerned, Hitler was consumed with a mythical obsession of unmitigated hatred. Hitler's *Weltanschauung* (a term much in use by him, and signifying a world-encompassing philosophy of life) was a mixture of racism, antisemitism, and Social Darwinism that he saw as having an internal logic of its own—and this all-embracing ideology resembled in some respects a secularized form of a religious mold. Repeating ideas current with racists and Social Darwinists, Hitler believed in the eternal struggle for the survival of the fittest and in the blood purity of separate races, the latter expressed with religious zeal, such as that "cross-breeding constitutes a sin against the will of the Eternal creator," and that the most sacred task was the preservation of the Aryan-Germanic pure blood "given us by God." He summarized this thinking in a single divine commandment: "Thou shalt preserve the species." These ideas were repeated over and over again in his speeches, conversations, and writings, and he never deviated from them to any significant extent.[5]

The most passionate component of Hitler's thinking was his hatred of the Jews, who in his mind were a world power lurking behind the scenes to blot out Aryan supremacy in order to better control the lives of everyone on the planet. To achieve this aim, he claimed, the Jews employed an ideological arsenal that included such ideas as egalitarianism, democracy, pacifism, internationalism, and, yes, even Christianity—all this to weaken the healthy fiber of those they wished to subdue and control. He also blamed the Jews for spreading diseases of every kind, including syphilis and prostitution, all of which are liberally mentioned in his *Mein Kampf.* The Jew was no less than the enemy of life itself. In a 1931 speech, Hitler predicted that the contest between Jew and Aryan was "the great question that will be decided, one way or the other." He warned that in the event that the Jews gained mastery over the world, that will constitute "the funeral wreath of humanity"; even more portentous, the end of human life on this planet, which afterwards "will move through the ether without men as it did millions of years ago." Hitler's hatred of the Jews made up the most constant factor of all his beliefs, a "negative religion" in one historian's estimate. Hitler writes of his adoption of antisemitism in terms that suggest a conversion experience. "In fighting against the Jew, I am fighting for the work of the Lord," he stated in *Mein Kampf.* It was the dominant aggressive drive, possibly the only one of his ideological convictions that was not open to opportunistic manipulation. It remained one of the strongest beliefs, the most durable object of his intense hatred, right from the beginning until his suicide in 1945, cursing them in his *Political Testament,* before shooting himself.[6]

In addition to the antisemitic content, Nazi history created a cosmic drama that included the coming of a providentially appointed messianic figure, the Fuehrer, who was to lead his beleaguered *Herrenvolk* ("master race") out of the wilderness of defeat and disintegration. Indeed, Hans Kerrl, the minister of church affairs, minced no words when he affirmed that "National Socialism is itself a religion."[7] Obsessed as he was with a false missionary zeal, Hitler often spoke of himself in religious terms. Indeed, the extent of Hitler's references in his writings, speeches, proclamations, and *Table Talk* to God, the Almighty, the Great Creator, Providence, Christianity, and the like is indeed enormous. Such as his words in a May 1933 speech, where he invoked God to help him to achieve his goals: "Lord, you see we have changed our ways. . . . The German people is again strong in its will. . . . Lord, we shall not give you peace! Bless our fight for our freedom." Earlier, in *Mein Kampf,* he wrote that he was determined "that God's will is also, in fact, done and that God's work is not desecrated." Perhaps this is not surprising for a person who grew up in an intensely Catholic milieu. As a boy, he attended the school of a Benedictine monastery, and as he stated in *Mein Kampf,* he was intoxicated with the solemn magnificence of church festivals, actually singing in the church choir and serving as an altar boy. No wonder that he once considered entering the priesthood—"the highest ideal worth striving for," he wrote, was to become the abbot of a monastery—"as was only natural," he stated, in *Mein Kampf.*[8] Yet, by the time he took over the leadership of Germany, he had nothing but contempt for Christianity.

Hitler was, of course, careful to keep his anti-Christian views to himself, and in public put on the appearance of a faithful supporter of the churches. Thus in a face-to-face meeting with Bishop Wilhelm Berning and Monsignor Steinmann, on April 26, 1933, Hitler stated that he had been reproached with being an enemy of Christianity and this reproach had hurt him deeply.

However, in private conversations to his stalwarts, Hitler spoke a different language. "National Socialism is a form of conversion to a new faith," he told them." In 1933, he stated: "Neither of the two faiths has any future. At least, for Germans. [Italian] Fascism may make its peace with the church. I may, too. Why not? But that will not prevent me from banishing Christianity from Germany root and branch." According to Rauschning, Hitler told him in 1933: "A German church, a German Christianity, is a distortion. One is either a German or a Christian. You cannot be both. . . . I shall give them [the priests] a few years' reprieve. Why should we quarrel? They will swallow anything in order to keep their material advantages. Matters will never come to a head. They will recognize a firm will, and we need only show them once or twice who is master. They will know which way the wind blows." Hitler clung to the belief that the Christianization of the ancient Germans was superficial and incomplete, and definitely a mistake of historical proportions. "The heaviest blow that ever struck humanity was the coming of Christianity," Hitler told his dinner guests on July 11, 1941. . . . The time will come when I'll settle my accounts with them [the clergy], and I'll go straight to the point. . . . In less than ten years from now things will have quite another look." To a close aide, Hitler predicted "the end of the Christian church—and the opening of our own temples and shrines. . . . The Ten Commandments have lost their validity. . . . Providence has ordained that I should be the greatest liberator of humanity. I am freeing man from the restraint of a . . . degrading self-mortification of a chimera called conscience and morality." In his self-stylized messianic image, Hitler saw himself as a deliverer entrusted with a mission. "In fighting against the Jew," he stated in *Mein Kampf,* "I am fighting for the work of the Lord."[9] Even clerics in the church were misled into enthusiastic pronouncements. In 1934, the Evangelical Church thanked God for giving Germany a "pious and trusty overlord," with one Lutheran minister declaring Hitler's advent in 1933 "a divine gift and miracle," and another bishop adding: "He has been sent to us by God." At times Hitler was ready to accept Jesus as an Aryan, whereas he stigmatized Paul as the Jew who "used Christ's teachings to mobilize the underworld and to organize a pre-Bolshevism." At other times he lauded Christianity as "this wonderful thing," even though he contended that it had been "murdered" by the Jews of the ancient world. He even vaguely identified with Jesus. As early as 1922, he said: "I would be no Christian . . . if, like our Lord 2,000 years ago, I were not to wage a battle against those who today plunder and exploit this nation."[10]

The process of depersonalization of the Jews had been largely accomplished in the minds of most Germans long before Hitler entered the scene. As pointed out by John Weiss, even the most powerful speaker cannot convert those who are not already prepared to believe. While, as pointed out by

Yehuda Bauer, most people who voted Nazi were not prepared for anything approaching the Final Solution as it finally evolved and took form, at the same time antisemitism was the most virulent of all the components of the Nazi program. It was the one that was most loudly proclaimed, most insistently pursued, most sincerely believed in. It was an ideological obsession. The Nazi demand for a radical solution of the "Jewish Question" in order to "save" all of human society led the historian Saul Friedlaender to coin the term "redemptive antisemitism" for Nazi hatred of the Jews; that is, the redemption of Germany and other peoples would come about with the physical removal of the Jews. To the Nazis, the Jewish Question was a global, universal, even cosmic problem of the greatest magnitude. On its "solution" depended the future of mankind, and certainly that of Germany. This is what makes Nazi antisemitism unique. Since the Jew was the epitome of everything hated by the Nazis, he was the total enemy, and therefore his elimination had to be total as well, in contrast to the policy on other peoples whose survival was allowed as enslaved subjects.[11]

The first months of Nazi power, in early 1933, saw a surge of physical attacks on the country's 522,000 Jews, many of whom were subjected to public humiliation with the police standing by. This went hand in hand with laws aimed at excluding Jews from influential positions, cultural life, journalism, and academic institutions. On April 7, 1933, all professors of law who were Jews were driven from their universities in humiliating circumstances, and all Jewish judges were suspended. Cities and towns vied with each other in displaying posters: "Jews not wanted here." While all this was happening, the country's civic and religious leaders kept their silence. Some 300,000 Jews left in the following years, and well into the first two years of World War II. In September 1935, the Nuremberg Laws were promulgated, which annulled the citizenship of the country's Jews, and forbade marriage and sexual relations between Jews and non-Jews, as racially defined. The new law defined a Jew as a person with at least three Jewish grandparents. A person with two Jewish grandparents and two "Aryan" ones was considered a mongrel, or *Mischling,* First Grade. A person with only one Jewish grandparent was a *Mischling* Second Grade. The *Mischlinge* constituted a separate race, not fully Jewish and not fully Aryan. In some cases, they could marry among themselves, but rarely with full Aryan-blooded spouses. The *Mischlinge,* of whom there were more than a hundred thousand (the exact figure is not known), found themselves removed from certain sectors of the country's economic life, but to a lesser degree than full-Jews. In October 1938, passports held by Jews were marked with a large *J*; the same for personal identity cards. A year earlier, Jews had been required to add Jewish identifying middle names on their ID cards: Israel for men and Sarah for women. In 1938, Jews were ordered concentrated in special "Jewish" houses, and were forced to sell their holdings in real estate, as well as other large enterprises, at prices a fraction of their real value—a process euphemistically termed Aryanization. Jews were eventually prohibited from leaving their homes after dark, and certain sections of the cities were placed out of bounds for them. With the start of the war on September 1, 1939, further restrictive decrees followed one another in quick succession, such as the requirement to hand over jewelry, radios, cameras, electrical appliances, and other valuables. In September 1941, all Jews aged six and above were ordered to wear the Jewish Star. Jews "fit for work," meaning practically everyone, were assigned to the most menial and difficult tasks. A year before the start of the war, on the evening of November 9–10, 1938, several hundred Jewish synagogues, as well as thousands of Jewish small-scale enterprises and homes, were either torched or vandalized throughout Germany (which now included Austria and the Sudeten region of former Czechoslovakia), in a government-orchestrated orgy of horror that came to be known as *Kristallnacht,* or "Night of Broken Glass." Close to a hundred Jews were murdered and 35,000 Jews were carted off to concentration camps (at this stage, most were released upon the presentation of transit visas to other countries). This was followed with a restriction on movement by Jews in public places, and the closing of all Jewish journals and Jewish organizations. Here too, non-Jewish civic and religious leaders kept their silence, only voicing concern at the economic losses of these destructive acts. No public protest was heard, save from one or several lone pastors. About 164,000 Jews (of the 215,000 counted in September 1939) were still living in the expanded Reich on October 1, 1941, when a ban was declared on further emigration. Large-scale deportation of Jews to conquered Poland and the Baltic countries began in October 1941. Those who had earlier left for neighboring countries fell victim to the Nazis when their host countries came under German occupation. The remaining Jews faced the final murderous brunt of the regime.

With the German invasion of the Soviet Union on June 22, 1941, the Nazi regime turned to murder as a government policy, in the form of the mass extermination of Jews in the newly conquered territories, carried out by special killing units known as *Einsatzgruppen.* German Jews deported to Riga and Minsk were liquidated upon arrival. The years 1942 and 1943 saw the continuing deportation of tens of thousands of Jews, who were sent to the killing facility of Auschwitz. The more privileged were initially deported to the "model" camp of Theresienstadt, established to fool the deportees and international agencies, such as the Red Cross, into believing that the camps were nothing worse than detention centers. After one Red Cross team had left the scene, those made to pose for them were immediately dispatched to the gas chambers in Auschwitz. In sum, a total of 137,000 Jews were deported from

Germany, of whom only 9,000 survived the inferno of the Holocaust. An estimated 20,000 Jews survived inside Germany—15,000 of them in the open, protected by their marriages to non-Jewish spouses. By the time of Germany's surrender on May 8, 1945, an estimated 3,000 to 5,000 Jews had survived in hiding. In neighboring German-speaking Austria, annexed to Germany in March 1938, the Jewish population there was 185,000–170,000 in Vienna alone. A pattern of civil and economic disenfranchisement on the model of Nazi Germany followed in quick succession. Up to the start of the war, some 126,000 Jews managed to emigrate. The rest were deported to concentration camps in Poland, where most perished. At the end of the war, only 1,000 Jews were to be found in Vienna; most were partners in mixed marriages, but some 200 had survived by living underground. A total of 65,000 Austrian Jews perished at the hands of the Nazis, with only 1,700 surviving the horrors of the camps and death marches.[12]

Responses by the Churches

Ian Kershaw, the British historian of the Nazi phenomenon, wrote that the Final Solution "would not have been possible . . . without the silence of the church hierarchies, who failed to articulate what opposition there was to Nazi racial politics." This is not surprising, given that even staunch anti-Nazis among the clergy held tightly to the traditional Christian delegitimization of Jews and Judaism, as we shall later demonstrate in the cases of Martin Niemöller and Dietrich Bonhoeffer. The response of the clergy to the official antisemitic policy of the regime was of great importance, since the churches were practically the only non-Nazified bodies in Germany and retained enormous influence that could have fostered public opinion counter to Nazi propaganda and policy. For any cleric with eyes to see and ears to hear, there could be no doubt that the Nazi teaching stood diametrically opposed to the basic tenets of Christianity, especially to the Christian commandment to love one's fellow man of whatever race; especially the weak and the downtrodden. Racism, the central tenet of the Nazi *Weltanschauung,* stood in irreconcilable conflict with the basic Christian teaching of the equality of all men before God. In light of this, instead of being in the forefront to combat Nazi teachings, the response was at best too little and too late, with some clergy even espousing Nazi ideas. [13]

Turning first to the Protestant churches, they counted about 45 million registered members, who belonged to one of the twenty-eight regional (*Land*) churches, of which the largest was the Old Prussian Union, with 18 million members. In 1932, church members who openly supported Hitler founded the German Christians' Faith Movement (better known as the German Christians), and supported the introduction of racist ideas within the church, including the exclusion of the thousands of baptized Jews from any involvement in church teaching, liturgy, and preaching. By 1933, some 3,000 pastors belonged to the German Christians, and their number kept growing. In opposition to the German Christians, Niemöller and Bonhoeffer created the Confessing Church, which upheld traditional Christian teachings and rejected racial distinctions among believers. Be that as it may, even the Confessing Church found it difficult to stand up in defense of Jews—that is of people who chose to remain faithful to their tradition. Some in the Confessing Church even continued to make anti-Jewish statements, and disclaimed any interference in the Nazi regime's radicalization of anti-Jewish measures. In 1936, Karl Barth, one of the founders of the Confessing Church, accused it of living under the spell of Nazi ideology, so that "whoever did not believe in Hitler's mission was ostracized, even in the ranks of the Confessing Church." Many clerics, too many indeed, agreed with the Nazis that the Jews constituted an alien body within the German nation and were responsible for much of the malaise in public life, and thus merited whatever suffering befell them.[14]

As for the German Christians—created in 1932, they stated that race and nation were God-given attributes, and that God commanded their preservation. In 1934, a German Christian group in Dortmund proposed that all Hebrew-sounding hymns and liturgical passages with names and expressions such as "God Sabaoth," "Hosanna," "Abraham's seed," "Jehovah," "Jacob's salvation," and "Zion" be stricken from the worship service. On November 13, 1933, the German Christians staged a mass demonstration in Nazi Party style in the Sports Palace in Berlin. Speaker Dr. Reinhold Krause demanded the elimination of the Old Testament with its Jewish "commercial morality" and unedifying stories of "cattle-dealers and pimps," and the rejection of the theology of "Rabbi Paul." One German Christian cleric defended the New Testament by terming it the most anti-Jewish book in the whole world. Heinz Eisenhuth, professor of systematic theology at the University of Jena, in July 1939, after terming the Old Testament the expression of a racially foreign soul, urged that it be stricken, including the prophetic literature, and that the New Testament be purged of all texts except the four gospels, Paul being considered a Jewish theologian. It is as though one were witnessing a Marcionite renaissance. Other pastors took up the notion of the supposedly Aryan origin of Jesus, since they claimed it was unthinkable to accept him as Jewish, for in that case one would have to ask why "a beautiful flower should not grow on a muck-heap." Dr. Kuehlewein, bishop of Baden, in 1936, repeated words voiced by Bonhoeffer and Niemöller, that "when the Jews crucified Jesus, they crucified themselves, their revelation, and their history. Thus the curse came upon them. Since then the curse has worked itself out from one generation to another. This people has, therefore, become a fearful and divinely ordained scourge for all nations, leading to hatred and persecution." The Lutheran publicist Wilhelm Stapel tried to temper the impression created by these harsh words by stating that a Jew who had become a Christian through baptism was to be regarded as "our Christian brother but not our German brother . . . as man an alien, as Christian a brother. . . . The one will move through the world as a German, the other as a Jew . . . a reality that baptism in no wise alters." "Which of us is not able to suppress a shudder at the sight of him?" one cleric exclaimed at the sight of a Jewish-born Christian pastor ministering in church.[15]

Most Protestant clerics, and especially Lutherans, expressed unmitigated exuberance at Hitler's accession to power, in January 1933, as in the following proclamation. "A powerful national movement [i.e., the Nazis] has seized and exalted our German Volk. . . . To this turning point in history, we speak a grateful Yes, God has granted this to us." The lauding of Hitler continued side by side with the bashing of Jews. Consider, for instance, Hugo Pick, a church superintendent in Thuringia, in 1938: "The Fuehrer of our Volk has now been called to lead an international fight against world Jewry."[16] Later, when Hitler launched World War II, the churches again congratulated him on the conquest of Poland, rejoicing that "an ancient German land [*sic*] will be returned to the motherland." Upon the conquest of Yugoslavia and Greece, in April 1941, the churches again gave thanks to the Fuehrer, as well as upon the attack on the Soviet Union, in June 1941. "You, our Fuehrer, you conquered the Bolshevik threat in our country, and now you are calling our people, and the peoples of all European nations, to a crusade against the enemy of every Western Christian regime and culture." These words of praise of the Nazi leadership went hand in hand with the continued denunciation of the Jews. At the same time that the Nazi leadership was waging a war of extermination against the Jewish people, in December 1941, church leaders of Saxony, Nassau-Hesse, Mecklenburg, Schleswig-Holstein, Anhalt, Thuringia, and Lubeck, announced that "the severest measures" were to be taken against the Jews, since they, rather than Germany, were responsible for the war. At the University of Jena, the New Testament scholar Walter Grundmann, in 1942, argued that "the elimination of Jewish influence on German life is the urgent and fundamental question of the present German religious situation." Earlier, in 1938, following *Kristallnacht*, Martin Sassse, bishop of Thuringia, took pleasure in the coincidence that the date of the synagogue burnings (November 10) was the birthday of Martin Luther, who had also thundered against the Jews. "Only ignorance of the true facts," Sasse wrote, "can induce Christians to tolerate Jews. Only absolute misapprehension as to Luther's aims and ideas can permit Christians to take the part of and intercede for Jews."[17]

As for the Confessing Church, its main concern was not the welfare of the Jews, but opposition to the Aryan Clause; that is, to the introduction of divisions inside the church based on the racial composition of its members, particularly affecting tens of thousands of baptized Jews, since this was a violation of a fundamental Christian tenet. Hermann Sasse, a Bavarian Lutheran theologian, put it quite bluntly, stating that the effect of the introduction of the racial laws into the church would be to outlaw Jesus Christ, the Son of David after the flesh, from the preaching ministry. As late as February 1942, a Confessing Church memorandum stated: "If we exclude Christian non-Aryans, we shall be compelled to banish all of the apostles and Jesus Christ himself on account of their belonging to the Jewish race." At the same time, Martin Niemöller, in November 1933, urged clergy of Jewish descent to "exercise restraint so as not to offend. It would be unsatisfactory for a pastor of non-Aryan descent to hold office in the church administration or an especially prominent position in home missions." The reference was to the thirty-seven pastors of Jewish descent, of whom twenty-nine still held office—an infinitesimal figure in relation to the nearly 18,000 Protestant pastors in Germany. Exact figures are hard to come by, and one estimate puts the number of evangelical non-Aryans at 300,000, and perhaps slightly more, of whom 50,000 were born full Jews (by the Nazi definition); 210,000 were classified as *Mischlinge* First Grade (half-Jews); 80,000 as quarter-Jews. To this must be added the many tens of thousands of converts and *Mischlinge* in Austria, after its annexation to Germany in March 1938. The *Paulusbund* (Association of Paul), an alliance of baptized Jews in the Protestant churches, had by 1936 some 80,000 members. It existed for only six months, and was ordered disbanded by the Gestapo in 1937. A parallel Catholic organization, the *St. Raphael Verein* (headed by Bishop Berning of Osnabrück), helped Catholic-baptized Jews to emigrate.[18]

The debate on the fate of baptized Jews continued to torment the churches, with many conferences and religious conclaves debating what to do with these people who had, of their free will, and without pressure, joined the Christian community, and now found themselves ostracized. A Baden church statement underlined that "the church expects, of course, that these foreign brothers and sisters in the faith [will] seriously attempt to discard those qualities inherited from their fathers that are foreign to what is German, to integrate themselves into our *Volkstum* [national heritage], and to exercise restraint in public life, so as not to hinder the practice of brotherly love or disturb the present community of life and faith."[19] Yet even those who opposed the Aryan paragraph, as applied to converts, were not free of antisemitic sentiments. Walter Künneth, a young university lecturer on the topic of "The Church and the Jewish

Question in Germany," believed that state measures to restrict Jews were necessary "to protect the German people," as long as it was done in compliance
with "Christian ethics," whatever that may have meant to Künneth. Wilhelm
Haffmann, a Confessing Church cleric in Schleswig-Holstein, wrote
(1936–37) that "we of the church must say, based upon almost two thousand
years' experience with the Jews: the state is right. It is attempting to protect
the German people." Another Confessing Church pastor, Gerhard Schmidt, in
a 1937 essay, defended Martin Luther's anti-Jewish tirade, since in Schmidt's
opinion, Luther "does not reject the Old Testament because of the Jews, but
rather the other way around: because of the Old Testament, he rejects the
Jews." Schmidt, strangely, accused the Nazis of wishing to destroy the Jews
in order to do away with the Old Testament.[20]

Other clerics took a more favorable stand vis-à-vis baptized Jews, and
favored continued evangelization, but for reasons which demonstrated a total
lack of any appreciation and respect for Judaism and Jews. Pastor Gerhard
Jasper, who reportedly later assisted persecuted baptized Jews, was in favor of
continued evangelization among Jews so as to arouse them to "holy jealousy"
by treating them as equals in the church. He urged his fellow believers to overcome their dislike of Jews, their "shudder" at the Jews in the words of one
clergyman. Another Protestant cleric, Dannenbaum, wrote in 1935 that the
Jews, after being purified in the furnace of suffering, "and who knows through
what bloody torments of antisemitism they will yet be harassed," would then
be ripe for conversion. "In crucifying Jesus, they came under the curse of the
divine judgment, an abomination to all peoples. When they accept Jesus, there
will be an endless time of grace, a source of blessing for the whole world!"
Unhappily, for Dannenbaum, for daring to suggest that the Jewish people were
redeemable, he was scornfully criticized in the foremost Nazi newspaper, the
Völkischer Beobachter.

As sadly noted by H.D. Leuner, "nothing paralyzed the church's fight for
the oppressed from the beginning as much as the distinction made between
baptized and unbaptized Jews. . . . The unbaptized Jew, i.e., the Jew as such,
was to be left to the devil." Only very late, when the Jewish Question had been
"solved" by deportation and extermination, did a synod of the Confessing
Church, in October 1943, strike a different note, declaring that "the life of all
men belongs to God alone. It is sacred to him, and that applies also to the life
of Israel."[21] By then, most of the remaining German Jews had already been
dispatched to their death.

Some in the Confessing Church went so far as to equate the Nazi phenomenon with nothing less than pre-Christian Judaism. Adolf Schlatter, for
instance, a Tübingen theologian, and a noted Hebraist and New Testament
scholar, viewed Judaism as an ally of the Nazi state in the struggle against

Christianity. "Today . . . he [the Jew] can only rejoice when the celebration of the reascending sun supplants Christmas, and when it is impressed upon young people that their sole confession from now on is that they are Germans because the name 'Christ' has become meaningless for them." Schlatter equated Judaism with the "Nordic racism" of Nazism and the Nazi understanding of community as an "association" formed by "the compulsion of the blood." Other Confessing Church pastors followed suit, and in a total reversal of positions accused the Jews of being in league with the Nazis to undermine Christianity. Heinrich Fausel, one of the most thoroughgoing and resolute of the Confessing Church pastors, wrote in 1934 that to accept the racist definition as a guideline for admittance, the church would repeat the Jewish error of restricting or destroying the divine freedom by means of an earthly ruling. This viewpoint was repeated in the Confessing Church's Bethel Statement, of 1933: that a church which would block entry to the church because of racial considerations would itself become a legalistic Jewish Christian church.[22]

Paul Althaus, Otto Dibelius, and Gerhard Kittel were three prominent Protestant theologians who fell prey to the Nazi seduction and its anti-Jewish stance. In 1933, Althaus exultantly praised Hitler's assumption of power. "We as believing Christians thank the Lord God that He has in our need presented us with the Fuehrer as pious and faithful overlord, and that in the National Socialist political system he will provide us with good government, a government with discipline and honor. We therefore acknowledge before God our responsibility in our profession and calling to assist the work of the Fuehrer," a person whose coming Althaus lauded as a "gift and miracle from God." By late 1938, Althaus's enthusiasm for Hitler had waned. As for Otto Dibelius, in the years preceding the Nazi takeover he wrote: "There is no doubt whatever that in all the murky happenings of the last fifteen years, the Jewish element has played a leading role." In a 1928 Easter message to the pastors in his district, he stated, "I have always considered myself an antisemite. It cannot be denied that Judaism plays a leading role in all the corruptive phenomena of modern civilization." In 1933, he recommended closing Germany's eastern border against immigration by eastern Jews as a protective measure and appealed to the German "steadfastness . . . that will not succumb to an alien race." Finally, Gerhard Kittel, a distinguished New Testament scholar and a leading authority on ancient Judaism, was an enthusiastic member of the Nazi Party and a supporter of the German Christian movement. In 1937, Kittel told an audience in Cambridge that Hitler carried a New Testament in his vest pocket and read from it daily! Earlier, in 1933, he wrote in *Die Judenfrage* ("The Jewish Question") of his great reverence for and sympathy only for Orthodox Jews, coupled with an antipathy toward secularized and emancipated Jews. Intermixing with other peoples, he stated, was the gravest sin even in ancient Israel, since the struggle for the purity of Israel was a thread running through the whole of the Old Testament from the time of Moses right down to the post-exilic period. While the religiously practicing Jew should be afforded honorable guest-status in the country, marriages between Jews and Gentiles should be forbidden. Jews, Kittel stated, should have the courage "to accept the divinely prescribed role of a restless and homeless alien wandering over the earth, waiting patiently for the Promised Day of the Lord." As for the convert, he can never become a German but remains a Jew after his baptism, although a Christian. " 'My Christian brother' but never 'my German brother.' " Kittel also accused the Jews of trying to make much out of other races by pushing Jewish blood onto them, "until a power rose up against them, which once again brought an end to their push, raised up a new set of laws, and for the last time directed Jews back behind the gates: National Socialist Germany and its Fuehrer, Adolf Hitler! . . . [who] has taught the German people anew to listen to its genuine instinct and to feel good about it. In no way is this barbarity or cruelty unreasonable toward the Jews." Interestingly, in 1914, many years before the advent of Hitler, the younger Kittel had published *Jesus und die Rabbiner* ("Jesus and the Rabbis"), in which he pointed out the great similarity between rabbinical teachings in the Talmud and Jesus' teachings in the New Testament. In 1926, he again reiterated that every ethical teaching attributed to Jesus can find its counterpart in the Jewish tradition. Then, as happened to others, toward the late 1930s, he fell under the hypnotic spell of Hitler and Nazism.[23]

Especially distressing are the positions taken on the Jewish issue by the two staunchest anti-Nazi Protestant clerics, Dietrich Bonhoeffer and Martin Niemöller. Bonhoeffer's anti-Nazi credentials are unquestionable. In a letter to Bishop George Bell, of Chichester, England, in March 14, 1934, Bonhoeffer wrote: "The question at stake in the German church is no longer an internal issue but is the question of existence of Christianity in Europe. . . . Church and Christianity as such are at stake." Later that same year, to Bishop Ammundsen of Denmark, he emphasized that a decision must be made between Nazism and Christianity. During the war years, asked for whom he prayed, Bonhoeffer responded: "Truth to tell, I pray for the defeat of my country, for this is the only possibility of atoning for all the suffering which my country has inflicted during the war." However, his position vis-à-vis Judaism showed him to be tainted with the traditional anti-Jewish virus, which he shared with other anti-Nazi clerics. In a article written in mid-April, printed and published in June 1933, over four months after Hitler's accession to power, "The Church and the Jewish Question," Bonhoeffer, in the words of the church historian Klaus Scholder, wrote "one of the most illuminating and most significant works produced during these years—politically as well as theologically." He never retracted (at least publicly) the following harsh words written against the Jews: "The Church of Christ has never lost sight of the thought that the 'chosen people,' who nailed the Redeemer of the world to the cross, must bear the curse for its action through a long history of suffering. . . . When the time comes that this people humbles itself and penitently departs from the sins of its father to which it has clung with fearful stubbornness to this day, and calls down upon itself the blood of the Crucified One for reconciliation . . . then He will gather this people from all nations and bring it back to Canaan. . . . The conversion of Israel, that is to be the end of the people's period of suffering." As to whether the church should intervene to oppose state measures (at the time, already the Nazi state) against the Jews, Bonhoeffer's position was surprising, when compared with his otherwise anti-Nazi stance. For he urged that the church stay aloof from any involvement on behalf of the Jews. This, he explained, was due to the church's traditional acceptance of secular rule as the lesser of two evils. Therefore "the action of the state remains free from the church's intervention." Is this rule also to be applied with regard to the state's actions against the Jews? Certainly! "Thus even today, on the Jewish Question, it cannot address the state directly and demand of it some definite action of a different nature." There are only two exceptions to this rule, when intervention is a religious obligation. The first case is when the state fails in its duty to preserve law and order; a situation that Bonhoeffer defines as "too little order." Second, when the state enforces "too much law and order," which prevails when it acts for "the forced exclusion of baptized Jews from our Christian congregations." In that situation, and only then, is the church obligated "to throw themselves into the spokes"—not in defense of Jews in general, but only of baptized Jews. These sentences, written directly under the impact of the initial Nazi anti-Jewish laws, make it clear that in the spring of 1933 Bonhoeffer still allowed the Nazi regime freedom of action to regulate the Jewish issue by special discriminatory legislation. Bonhoeffer slightly modified this hands-off approach toward the state by adding that the church had an unconditional obligation to the victims of any ordering of society, even if they did not belong to the Christian community. But here again he backtracked by drawing a clear distinction between plain Jews and baptized Jews; the latter were to be protected by the church. In the words of Stephen Haynes, "Bonhoeffer communicates a profound anti-Judaism. . . . He utilizes rhetoric whose anti-Jewish implications appear to elude him. . . . His opposition to the Aryanizing of the church did not compel him to repudiate, or even acknowledge, his own deep seated anti-Judaism." As furthermore noted by Alan Davies, "Bonhoeffer's Jewish stance makes it somewhat easier to understand the nonchalance with which the majority of German Christians initially accepted Nazi rule." In the words of Eva Fleischner, there is no evidence that

Bonhoeffer "ever repudiated the notion of a divine curse hanging over the Jewish people." James Kelley, another student of Bonhoeffer's theology, notes that the latter's adherence to a "theological antisemitism" unwittingly gave respectability to those favoring a more radical and Nazi-style solution of the Jewish Question, and stilled the voices of others, who did not feel prepared to risk themselves on behalf of the Jews. "If the synagogues burn today, the churches will be on fire tomorrow," was his terse comment when learning of the atrocities of *Kristallnacht*. Not a word about whether Christians should take action and protest the burning of hundreds of synagogues.[24] Imprisoned in 1943 because of his anti-Nazi views, and held in jail, Bonhoeffer was executed on April 9, 1945.

Martin Niemöller was a decorated World War I submarine commander, and then a Protestant minister who served a Berlin-Dahlem congregation. In 1933, together with Bonhoeffer, he formed the Pastors Emergency League, the forerunner of the Confessing Church. He at first welcomed the Nazi revolution, and preached with swastikas decorating the altar, but was quickly disenchanted with the new regime, and spoke out against it. Arrested in 1937, he remained in prison until the end of the war, on Hitler's order. In a 1935 sermon, he saw fit to take on the Jews—with a theological vengeance! "The gospel lessons of this Sunday throw a light upon the dark and sinister history of this people which can neither live nor die because it is under a curse which forbids it to do either. We speak of the 'eternal Jew' and conjure up the picture of a restless wanderer who has no home and who cannot find peace. We see a highly gifted people which produces idea after idea for the benefit of the world, but whatever it takes up becomes poisoned, and all that it ever reaps is contempt and hatred because ever and anon the world notices the deception and avenges itself in its own way. I say 'in its own way,' for we know full well that there is no charter which would empower us to supplement God's curse with our hatred. Even Cain receives God's mark, that no one may kill him; and Jesus' command 'Love your enemies!' leaves no room for exceptions. But we cannot change the fact that until the end of its days the Jewish people must go its way under the burden which Jesus' decree has laid upon it: 'Behold, your house is left unto you desolate.' . . . What is the reason for this punishment which has lasted for thousands of years? Dear brethren, the reason is easily given: the Jews brought the Christ of God to the cross. . . . [The Jewish people] bears a curse because it rejected him and resisted him to the death when it became clear that Jesus of Nazareth would not cease calling to repentance and faith, despite their insistence that they were free, strong and proud men and belonged to a pure-blooded, race-conscious nation. . . . The choice has been made. . . . Now it bears the curse. Because it rejected the forgiveness it drags about the frightful burden of the unforgiving blood guilt of its fathers.

The blood of all the righteous men who were ever murdered because they testified to the holy will of God against tyrannical human will has come upon its head, as well as the blood of Jesus and the blood of all his messengers." As for the converted Jews, in 1933 he sided with Bonhoeffer that they enjoyed full-fledged rights—"whether we like it or not," he significantly added. Repeating an antisemitic canard, Niemöller explained: "As a people that has had much to bear under the influence of the Jewish people," he went on to ask that clergy of Jewish descent "exercise restraint so as not to offend. It would be unsatisfactory for a pastor of non-Aryan descent to hold office in the church administration or an especially prominent position in home missions." At his trial in February 1938 for his anti-Nazi views, he reiterated his viewpoint that the Jews were alien and uncongenial to him. It had, he added, to be accepted that God had seen fit to reveal Himself in a Jew, Jesus of Nazareth. "This painful and grievous stumbling-block has to be accepted for the sake of the Gospel."

Soon after the war, in January 1946, Niemöller expressed deep remorse, not for his Nazi-period antisemitic stance, but for not protesting the actions taken against the Jews. "I am guilty . . . I kept silent! I only began to speak up when the church was affected. I feel that I am guilty!" Five years later, in 1950, he repeated this mea culpa: "We openly declare that through indifference and silence we became before the God of Mercy accomplices to the vile deeds committed by the people of our nation against the Jews. . . . I regard myself as guilty as any SS man. We let God wait ten years." Again, in 1970: "There was not one single voice to be heard affirming in public that murder is murder." Asked whether he still felt ill at ease in the presence of Jews, Niemoeller avoided a direct answer. "As a Christian, I must conduct myself not according to my sympathies or antipathies, but must see in each human being, even if he is unsympathetic to me, the fellow human being for whom Jesus Christ hung on His cross as much as for me." In light of the above, one should treat with some reservation Niemöller's much-touted postwar statement (spoken in 1945): "First they came for the Communists, and I didn't speak up, because I wasn't a Communist. Then they came for the Jews, and I didn't speak up, because I wasn't a Jew. Then they came for the Catholics, and I didn't speak up, because I was a Protestant. Then they came for me, and by that time there was no one left to speak up for me." The statement is not entirely correct. Insofar as the Jews are concerned, he did speak up—against them![25]

Bishop Theophil Wurm, head of the Lutheran church, also gave his blessings to the anti-Jewish measures by the Nazi state, though with some reservations. He took pride in the contribution of the Evangelical clergy in keeping itself "so free from specific Jewish characteristics and that has made such proof of its readiness to champion the cause of Volk and Fatherland," including the right of the state "to combat the Jews as a dangerous element in the population." At the same time, in a letter to Nazi Justice Minister Franz Guertner, while praising the state's actions against the Jewish population, he cautioned against overstepping the necessary bounds, for "sooner or later, transgressions against the commands of God must have their revenge." He then mellowed this warning by fawning allegiance to the Nazi state. "In no way do I dispute the right of the state to resist Judaism as a dangerous element. Since my youth, I have held the judgment of men such as Heinrich von Treitschke and Adolf Stoecker [both self-declared antisemites] on the corruptive effect of Jewry in the religious, moral, literary, economic, and political spheres to be correct, and, as director of the city mission in Stuttgart thirty years ago, I led a public and not unsuccessful struggle against the Jewish intrusion into the welfare system." (Wurm later "bitterly regretted" these last words.) In his memoirs, he admitted that "a spell was laid upon us, and it was as if our mouths were kept shut by an invisible power." In December 1941, he turned down a request by Pastor Hermann Diem that Württembrug pastors be allowed to read a statement condemning the persecution of the Jews. Somewhat later, in a letter to Dr. Drill, of the Interior Ministry, Wurm wrote that while supporting the exclusion of the Jews, he was opposed to their extermination. "One is depressed by how the struggle against other races and peoples is being conducted, [especially] the systematic murder of Jews and Poles in the occupied territories. Even those who years ago considered Jewry's dominance in the most diverse areas of public life to be severely detrimental, at a time when almost the entire press was philosemitic, cannot accept that one people is justified in exterminating another people with measures that affect every individual, regardless of personal culpability." The continuing German military reverses in 1943 led Wurm to further distance himself from his previous staunch antisemitism, and on July 16, 1943, he took the highly unusual step of writing directly to Hitler: "In the name of God and for the sake of the German people [we call upon] the responsible leadership of the Reich [to] check the persecution and annihilation to which many men and women under German domination are being subjected, and without judicial trial. Now that the non-Aryans [in other words, Jews] who have been the victims of the German onslaught have been very largely eliminated, it is to be feared, in the light what has already happened in certain individual cases, that the so-called 'privileged' non-Aryans [Jews married to non-Jewish spouses] who have so far been spared are in renewed danger of being subjected to the same treatment." Not receiving a response, Wurm wrote to the head of Hitler's chancellery, Hans-Heinrich Lammers, in December 1943, adding: "I must declare, not from any kind of philosemitic tendencies, but simply out of religious and ethical feeling, that we Christians perceive this policy of extermination conducted against Jewry to be a grievous injustice and an ominous one for the German people." This time, he received a stiff and threatening response from Lammers, in a March 1944 letter, demanding that Wurm limit himself strictly to the ecclesiastical sphere, and cease to pronounce upon questions of general politics, if he wished to avoid possible consequences to himself. Frightened into submission, Wurm kept silent.[26]

* * *

There were a few lone voices that dared to speak up amidst the general cacophony of anti-Jewish statements—but just a handful. Their number is so small, hardly a dozen, as to blot out any influence that their words of protest may have carried. But they deserve mention, if for no other reason than to acknowledge their good deed. Such as some members of the Protestant Provisional Church Administration, who in a May 1936 memorandum to Hitler, decried the concepts of blood and race as eternal values, and protested the incitement of hatred against the Jews. "If, in the framework of National Socialist ideology, an antisemitism is forced upon the Christian that obliges him to hate the Jews, then the Christian commandment to love one's neighbor stands in opposition to this." This rather innocuous statement provoked a vehement reaction from the Nazis. Several of those involved were arrested, and Friedrich Weissler, a Jewish lawyer who worked with the Confessing Church, was hauled off to Sachsenhausen camp and murdered. In the village of Oberlenningen, Wuertemburg region, Pastor Julius von Jan reacted to the *Kristallnacht* pogrom in very strong terms, in his sermon on November 16, 1938. Paraphrasing the Hebrew prophet Jeremiah (22:29), he despairingly asked, "Where in Germany is the prophet sent to the king's house to utter the word of the Lord? Where is the man who, in the name of God and of justice, will cry like Jeremiah, 'Maintain righteousness, rescue those deprived of their rights out of the hands of the transgressor. Do not oppress the stranger, the orphan, and the widow. Do no one violence, shed not the innocent blood'? God has sent us such men. They are today either in a concentration camp or reduced to silence. . . . Our bishops have not recognized it as their duty to stand shoulder to shoulder with those who have spoken the Lord's Word. . . . Wild passions have been released, God's commandments disregarded, Houses of God which were sacred to others razed to the ground without punishment, men who have served our German people loyally, and have conscientiously fulfilled their duty, have been thrown into concentration camps, merely because they happened to be of another race. A dreadful seed of hatred has been sown. A frightful harvest will grow out of it, unless God in Grace allows our people to show sincere repentance. . . . Thou, O earth, earth, earth, hear the word of the Lord. Amen." A few days later a mob of about twenty Nazi Party members raided the vicarage. Von Jan was forcefully removed from his Bible class and hauled on top of the roof of a shed, where he was publicly whipped, and then taken to prison. The police did not intervene. But he survived, as a soldier on the front line, and returned in 1945 to his former parish.

In the Dahlem section of Berlin, Pastor Helmut Gollwitzer also denounced the pogrom from the pulpit, without mentioning the Jews by name, but everyone knew who was meant.[27] In 1943, during the war years, church members in Munich (their signatures omitted, with the exception of Pastor Hermann Diem from Würtemburg), on Easter 1943, presented Bishop Hans Meiser with the following petition: "As Christians we can no longer tolerate the church in Germany keeping silent about the persecution of the Jews. . . . [In the parable of the Good Samaritan, Jesus] ruled out each and every limitation of neighborly love that makes it apply merely in the case of those holding the same faith or belonging to the same race or people. Every non-Aryan, whether he be Jew or Christian, has today in Germany 'fallen among murderers,' and we are asked whether we are going to encounter him as Priest and Levite or as Samaritan. The recognition that there is a 'Jewish Problem' cannot absolve us from such a decision. . . . God has fastened upon this particular people as the instrument of His Revelation. The church must, therefore, as the first Apostles did after Golgotha!—testify unwearingly to all Jews. . . . This witness the church can accomplish convincingly for Israel only if she simultaneously espouses the cause of the Jew who has 'fallen among murderers.' . . . The church has to bear witness to the redemptive significance of Israel, and to withstand to the utmost every attempt to solve the Jewish Question according to a self-manufactured political gospel involving the annihilation of Jewry. . . . [The church] must testify that along with Israel she and her Lord Jesus Christ Himself are being attacked." Meiser took no action, other than passing the petition to Bishop Wurm.[28] Pastor Hermann Hesse, in Barmen/ Eberfeld, contested the church's stand on the Jewish issue in a sermon in June 1943: "As Christians we can no longer tolerate the silence of the church in Germany over the persecution of the Jews. The Jewish Question is an evangelical, not a political issue. The church, over against the state, has to testify to the saving (*heilsgeschichtlich*) significance of Israel, and promote resistance to any effort to liquidate Jewry. . . . The church . . . is inextricably bound up with Jewry. . . . She has . . . to testify that when Israel is assailed, she and her Lord Jesus Christ Himself are also attacked." By order of Himmler, Hesse was removed to Dachau camp. His son Helmut, also a minister, who presided with his father in the church service, was also deported to Dachau, where he died from privations.[29] There were also some, but only a handful, who spoke up courageously only on behalf of the baptized Jews. Such as Katharina Staritz, a

Confessing Church vicar in Breslau, who in September 1941 protested the requirement for baptized Jews, among them members of her congregation, to wear the yellow star. Word reached the Gestapo, which confiscated the remaining copies of her letter. Soon thereafter, a direct attack against her appeared in the SS journal *Das Schwarze Korps*. Arrested on March 4, 1942, she soon found herself in Ravensbrück camp. As a final indignity, the Breslau Consistory suspended her salary. Released on May 18, 1943 on probation, she remained under surveillance and had to report twice weekly to the Gestapo until the end of the war.[30]

* * *

Like their Protestant colleagues, Catholic prelates also failed to take a strong stand against Nazi antisemitism, and some even betrayed signs of a racist attitude. An additional troubling factor for the Catholic establishment was the Concordat reached between the Vatican and the Hitler regime on July 8, 1933, which precluded any open Catholic opposition to Hitler. Before that, membership in the Nazi Party had been ruled impermissible for Catholics by not a few bishops (in Bavaria, Freiburg, Mainz, and Rottenburg), since as they then explained, Nazism "is not only a political party, it also represents a total world outlook. As such it involves an attitude toward religion and it poses demands in the area of religion." Bishop Konrad von Preysing of Eichstaett (later Berlin) stood out as one of the most consistent opponents of Nazism (and the strongest critic of Papal Nuncio Cesare Orsenigo's lack of opposition to Nazi transgressions). In 1931, at Fulda, the bishops reiterated the prohibition against joining the Nazi Party, "which pretends to be no more than a political party with justified national goals, but which in fact stands in clearest conflict with fundamental truths of Christianity and with the organization of the Catholic church of Christ's founding." The bishops, nevertheless, left it to the determination of the clergy whether to permit formal membership in the party but without participating in its ideology and propaganda. In March 1933, after Hitler's assumption of power, the Catholic bishops changed course and withdrew their prohibition against joining the Nazi Party. Then, after the Concordat with the Vatican, Catholic opposition to the Nazis came to a virtual halt. Some Catholic theologians even tried hard to find similarities between Nazism and Christianity. Professor Joseph Lortz, a church historian, declared that both were opposed to Bolshevism, liberalism, relativism, atheism, and public immorality. Michael Schmaus, professor of dogmatic theology at Münster, felt that Catholicism and Nazism could and should march hand in hand, and that both shared a "just concern for maintaining the purity of the blood, the basis for the spiritual structure of the people." The Catholic journal

Reich und Kirche praised "the success of that great work of German renewal to which the Fuehrer has summoned us… It will point the way toward the kind of fruitful cooperation that is outlined in the *Reichskonkordat*." The Catholic Church in Germany had given up its fight against Nazism at this early stage of Hitler's accession to power. Henceforth, only timid voices were to be heard from that quarter.[31]

As for the Catholic position on the Jews, it too could rely on a solid tradition of Jew baiting, from a theological perspective which continued well into the modern period. In the nineteenth century, Professor August Rohling, a Catholic priest in Münster, was responsible for many antisemitic pamphlets published in the region. His most famous work, *Talmud-Jew,* which appeared in 1871, and earned wide publicity, portrayed Jews as masters of finance, captains of industry, organizers of terrorist groups, and members of another race. In the 1920s, Bishop Keppler described the Jews as a perverted people that constitutes "a thorn in the side of Christian peoples, reduces them to servitude with the golden chains of millions and with pens saturated with poison, contaminates the public wells of education and morality by throwing into them sickening and purulent substances." His words fell on listening ears. A certain Brother Kaller, in 1927, wrote that "modern Jewry undermines everything that is Christian and any religion and morality. . . . That is the Jewish danger against which we defend ourselves and which we must overcome by and all permissible means." While German Catholicism, before the Concordat, saw itself as opposed to the growing Nazi movement, antisemitism was not one of the primary bones of contention. On the contrary, many Catholic publicists— like the Franciscan father, Erhard Schlund—agreed with the Nazis on the importance of fighting the Jews' "hegemony in finance, the destructive influence of the Jews in religion, morality, literature and art, and political and social life." Not surprisingly, in a face-to-face meeting with Bishop Berning and Monsignor Steinmann, on April 26, 1933, Hitler touched upon the Jewish Question and stressed the fundamental agreement between Nazism and Catholicism, reminding the prelates that the church always had regarded the Jews as parasites and had banished them into the ghetto. He innocently stated that he was merely doing what the Catholic Church had espoused and done for 1,500 years. The reaction of the two church dignitaries to these words is not known. As late as March 1941, Archbishop Konrad Gröber, in a pastoral letter abounding in anti-Jewish utterances, blamed the Jews for the death of Christ and added that the "self-imposed curse of the Jews, 'His blood be upon us and upon our children,' had come terribly true until the present time, until today."[32]

While the highly revered Cardinal Michael von Faulhaber, in Munich, spoke in defense of the Old Testament in his 1933 Advent sermon, he went out of his way to make clear that he did not have in mind the Jews of his own day. We must distinguish, he told the faithful, between the people of Israel before the death of Christ, who were vehicles of divine revelation, and the Jews after the death of Christ, who have become restless wanderers over the earth. But even the Jewish people of ancient times could not justly claim credit for the wisdom of the Old Testament. So unique were these laws that one was bound to say: "People of Israel, this did not grow in your own garden of your own planting. This condemnation of usurious land-grabbing, this war against the oppression of the farmer by debt, this prohibition of usury, is not the product of your spirit." In Faulhaber's estimation, "the greatest miracle of the Bible is that true religion could hold its own and maintain itself against the voice of Semitic blood." At any rate, since the crucifixion, Israel had been dismissed from God's service, "the Daughter of Zion was given the bill of divorcement, and Ahasuerus [the legendary wandering Jew] has restlessly wandered the earth ever since." The embarrassing fact that Jesus had been a Jew was handled in a pastoral letter of 1939 by Archbishop Gröber, who conceded that Jesus could not be made into an Aryan, but the Son of God had been fundamentally different from the Jews of his time—so much so that they had hated him and demanded his crucifixion, and "their murderous hatred has continued in later centuries." This Catholic free-for-all open season against the Jews went a bit too far for a Bavarian priest named Alois Wurm, editor of the monthly journal *Seele,* who on April 5, 1933, addressed a complaint to Faulhaber "that in this period when the most extreme hatred is being fomented against Jewish citizens, surely more than ninety-nine percent of whom are innocent, not a single Catholic paper, as far as I can see, had the courage to proclaim the teaching of the Catholic catechism that one may not hate and persecute any human being, least of all for his race. To very many people that appears to be a Catholic failure."[33]

In addition, the world-renowned Catholic theologian Karl Adam, in Tübingen, argued not only that Nazism and Catholicism were not in conflict one with the other but that they belonged together as nature and grace. Furthermore, in Adolf Hitler, Germany at last had found a true people's chancellor. Adam adopted the vocabulary of Nazism, arguing that German blood was and remained "the substantial carrier of our Christian reality," tying together Catholics and others within the German people. He defended the preservation of the German people's pure blood as a justified act of self-defense, for blood was the physiological basis of all thinking and feeling, and "the myth of the German, his culture and his history are decisively shaped by blood." The repulsion of the Jewish mentality in the press, literature, science, and art presently undertaken by the state was a necessary measure, although Adam cautioned that "the Christian conscience must insist that these legal ordinances be implemented in a spirit of justice and love"—whatever that meant. As for Hitler, "Now he stands before us, he whom the voices of our poets and sages have summoned, the liberator of the German genius. He has removed the blindfolds from our eyes and . . . has enabled us to see and love again the one essential thing: our unity of blood, our German self, the *homo Germanus.*" This praise of Hitler was seconded by the Jesuit monthly *Stimmen der Zeit,* which wrote that the swastika had proven its creative potential, "the person of Hitler has become the symbol of the faith of the German nation in its existence and future." "The Fuehrer of the Third Reich," declared the *Handbuch* of Archbishop Konrad Gröber, "has freed the German man from his external humiliation and from the inner weakness caused by Marxism and has returned him to the ancestral Germanic values of honor, loyalty, and courage." From all these Hallelujahs, the simple man in the street had no problem in deducing that the Fuehrer, praised by church and state alike, was indeed a blessing for Germany, and his policies, including his radical antisemitism, were evidently not to be questioned and challenged.[34]

On the question of the status of baptized Jews in the Catholic Church, Cardinal Adolf Bertram, in a letter to his episcopate on September 17, 1941, suggested that priests advise Jewish Catholics to attend the early Mass whenever possible, so as to avoid "substantial difficulties" of having to mingle with Aryan Catholics, including officials and members of the Nazi Party. He ended by repeating Paul's injunction that in principle there is neither Jew nor Greek among those who believe in Christ, for all are one in Jesus Christ (Romans 10:12; Galatians 3:28). Paul, the Jew, could of course never have imagined that had he lived in the Germany of Cardinal Bertram, he would have been requested not to attend Mass alongside other Christians of a different ethnic-racial background. Some help to converted Jews was made available when, in 1938, Bishop Konrad von Preysing and other Catholic prelates (including Wilhelm Berning) created an agency to assist persecuted Jewish-Christians, the Relief Agency of the Berlin Chancery (*Hilfswerk beim Bischoeflichen Ordinariat Berlin*). It served primarily to meet the spiritual and material needs of baptized Jews, including financial subsidies, food, and arrangements for emigration. Unable to prevent the deportation of Catholic Jews to the death camps, the Catholic Church limited its demand to asking that non-Aryan or half-Aryan priests and nuns volunteer to accompany the deportees in order to hold services for them and provide religious instruction for the children on their way to their death. In November 1943, Bertram wrote to the Ministry of Interior and to Gestapo headquarters about the conditions under which baptized Jews were living in camps, where a large number of the sufferers had already succumbed, with a lack of proper pastoral care. The episcopate, he mentioned, would gladly designate priests for divine services and the administration of the sacraments in the camps. Not a word on the justice of the deportations themselves. Bertram's next and final letter, in January 1944, asked that the *Mischlinge* not be treated in the same manner as Jews. The *Mischlinge*, he stated, were Germans and Christians, and had always been rejected by the Jews.[35]

As is well known, Bishop Clemens August von Galen dared to openly confront the Nazis on an important moral issue, the euthanasia program. In his sermons he preached obedience to the state without reservation, while at the same time denouncing Gestapo seizures of ecclesiastical institutions. Then, in his sermon of August 3, 1941, he unreservedly condemned the "mercy" killing of mentally infirm people by government agencies, based on the "Thou shalt not murder" of the Ten Commandments. Once humans were treated like machines or animals that were no longer useful, he warned, there was no way of being sure where the killing would stop. Even invalids, cripples, and wounded soldiers could no longer feel sure of their lives. "Woe unto the German people, when innocents not only could be killed, but their slayers remain unpunished." When news of the bishop's words reached the Nazi higher echelons, several officials proposed that Galen be hanged, but Goebbels, fearing "that the population of Muenster could be regarded as lost during the war if anything were done against the bishop, and in that fear one safely could include the whole of Westphalia," counseled patience. This calmer advice prevailed, for Hitler, though furious at Galen, was forced to defer his desired vengeance, and the euthanasia program was officially halted. Would a similar declaration by the brave bishop on the Jewish issue also have made a dent in the Nazi plan of the Final Solution? One cannot be certain. Guenther Lewy thinks it would have been worth trying. For "here was an example of the strength, power, and influence of public opinion in Hitler's state ruled by brute force, and that at a time when the Fuehrer stood at the zenith of his military successes. Had German public opinion shown a similar response against other crimes of the Nazi regime committed on an even greater scale, such as the extermination of the Jews of Europe, the results might well have been similarly telling… That German public opinion and the church were a force to be reckoned with in principle and could have played a role in the Jewish disaster as well—that is the lesson to be derived from the fate of Hitler's euthanasia program." Other than the euthanasia issue, and his fight against Nazi raids on Catholic institutions, Galen continued to support the Nazi regime. In a September 14, 1941, sermon, he offered thanks to God for the invasion of the Soviet Union, to thwart a "Judeo-Bolshevik conspiracy [which] was attempting to start fires all over Europe." That same month, Galen received a letter from an anonymous source. The writer, who introduced himself as a World War I veteran, asked if Bishop von Galen was aware that Jews in conquered

Poland were dying of hunger in ghettos, and that the fate of thousands of other Jews remained uncertain. He then asked: "Will you stand up and be our helper?" Galen, in line with other high-placed Catholic dignitaries, chose to remain silent. By December 1941, the majority of Muenster's 135 Jews were being deported. Others followed in next months, including women and elderly Jews. Of the 271 Jews deported from Muenster, only 24 survived. Throughout this tragic event, Bishop von Galen did not speak up.[36]

The silence of the German bishops in the face of Nazi atrocities led Konrad Adenauer, a Catholic and president of the West German republic, to state after the war: "I believe that if all the bishops had together made public statements from the pulpits on a particular day, they could have prevented a great deal. That did not happen and there is no excuse for it. It would have been no bad thing if the bishops had all been put in prison or in concentration camps as a result. Quite the contrary— but none of that happened, and therefore it is best to keep quiet."[37]

As in the case of Protestant clerics, there were a few Catholic clergy who dared to speak out, too few to make a dent. A certain Brother Albrecht Kopschina, of the Assumption parish in Hoppenwalde, in 1937, told seminarians that when Jesus exhorted his disciples to "Go into all the world and teach all people," he did not say "with proof of Aryan ancestry." Another monk, Brother Johannes Seidel, vicar of the Holy Cross Church in Frankfurt-an-der Oder, was denounced in 1938 for mentioning in positive terms the "chosen state of the Jewish *Volk*." Questioned by the Gestapo, he stated that the Jews were "chosen by God to carry divine revelation and to preserve the belief in one God." To avoid punishment, he then made a sharp distinction between the Jews before and after Christ. Brother Kurt Willig, pastor of St. Konrad Church, in Berlin-Schoenberg, remarked in 1941, "Jesus was a Jew and a member of the chosen people. . . . Jews are the chosen *Volk*. No one can change that." He received a stern warning not to repeat such words. Earlier, in February 1936, Father George Althaus was sentenced to six months imprisonment for his prayer of intercession at church services that included a special prayer "for the poor persecuted people of the Jews." Others suffered punishment for speaking up against the mistreatment of baptized Jews. In the words of H.D. Leuner, "There is no doubt that innumerable pastors were detained, maltreated, and deliberately murdered in concentration camps, but most of them underwent their martyrdom in loyalty to their religious convictions rather than as the outcome of intercession for Jewish victims."[38]

Bernhard Lichtenberg stands out as the exception to the rule; as the single most well known Catholic cleric who openly disagreed not only with the persecution of baptized Jews, but of Jews in general, and was martyred for this. During the Nazi period, he served as rector, then provost, in St. Hedwig's

Cathedral, Berlin, with the title of monsignor, awarded him by the pope in 1926. In March 1933, when the Nazis declared an official boycott of shops and businesses owned by Jews to take place on April 1, Lichtenberg provided Oscar Wasserman, the Jewish director of the Deutsch Bank in Berlin, with a recommendation to see Cardinal Adolf Bertram to request church intervention in the boycott—which Bertram declined. In July 1935, Lichtenberg had a Vatican-published article read from the pulpit, attacking Nazi leader Alfred Rosenberg's thesis of Nazism as a substitute for Christianity. The head of the SS, Reinhard Heydrich, asked Kerrl, minister of church affairs, to bring charges against Lichtenberg, but fortunately for Lichtenberg nothing came of it. When he received news of the horrible conditions in Esterwegen, a little-known concentration camp, including the forcing of Jewish prisoners to pick up manure and clean toilet refuse with their hands, Lichtenberg delivered in person (not by mail) a letter of protest to the Prussian Ministry of Interior and asked to speak directly with Goering. This was not allowed. Instead, a lower official met with Lichtenberg to receive the prelate's protest. Theodor Eicke, SS inspector of the concentration camp, took this report as a personal affront on his "camps" and requested preventive detention against Lichtenberg. Again, nothing came of it. Immediately following the November 1938 *Kristallnacht* pogrom, Lichtenberg publicly stated: "We know what happened yesterday. We do not know what tomorrow holds. However, we have experienced what happened today. Outside, the synagogue burns. That is also a house of God." During the evening Mass in St. Hedwig's Cathedral, Lichtenberg began to pray publicly for both Jews and Jewish Christians as well as imprisoned priests; this on a daily basis, until his arrest in 1941. In November 1940, Lichtenberg took up Catholic theologian and priest Karl Adam on his espousal of the Nazi state. Adam had recently lectured on the "positive" aspects of Nazism, and argued that the highest obligation of Catholics in Germany was loyalty to the Third Reich. To this, Lichtenberg reacted strongly. Acknowledging the right of the state to govern and act as a servant of God for the good of its citizens, he rhetorically asked: "And how is it in the cases in which the secular authority is not 'God's helper for your own good'?" The obvious answer was that "one must obey God more than humans." On November 23, 1940, Adam responded to Lichtenberg's critique in language that revealed more clearly than before his support of the Nazi state. Stating that God's will "is to be fulfilled on earth," he added, "the highest earthly worth remains for me—and for those who do not want to be unfaithful to their German blood—the unity of the German *Volk* in the new Reich. The people of Germany stood today a racially bound community (*Volksgemeinschaft*) of which ancient cultures had no knowledge." To this Lichtenberg responded, on November 30, 1940, that the idea of the

Volksgemeinschaft was unchristian, and "the Holy Spirit goes wherever it wishes, irrespective of whatever *Volk*."

On October 23, 1941, the Gestapo finally acted against Lichtenberg, several months after two visitors to St. Hedwig's Cathedral, on August 29, 1941, overheard Lichtenberg openly pray for the "poor persecuted Jews." Upset by this prayer, they immediately left the cathedral and shared their experience with a friend, whose father, an official in the SS, denounced Lichtenberg. Already long since on the Gestapo's black list, Lichtenberg was charged with "hostile activity against the state." Searching his home, the Gestapo found a declaration that Lichtenberg had written and planned to read from the pulpit the upcoming Sunday, in which he denounced a recently published Nazi anti-semitic pamphlet, that Goebbels' Propaganda Office had distributed throughout the country in an effort to stir up hatred against the Jews. In his prepared sermon, Lichtenberg wrote: "An anonymous smear against the Jews is being distributed to Berlin houses. This pamphlet states that every German who supports Jews with an ostensibly false sentimentality, be it only through friendly obligingness, practices treason against his *Volk*. Let us not be misled by this unchristian way of thinking but follow the strict command of Jesus Christ: 'You shall love your neighbor as you love yourself.'" At his interrogation, Lichtenberg declared that since the Nazi world outlook (*Weltanschauung*), as described in Hitler's *Mein Kampf*, stood in conflict with Christianity, he must reject it "as a Catholic priest . . . and also reject it *de facto*." As a Catholic priest he could not say "yes and Amen to every decree and measure that comes from the government." As examples of his disagreement, he cited "deliberate killing of life allegedly unworthy of life, [and] persecution of the Jews." With regard to Jews, he added, "I spiritually oppose the deportation with all its consequences, because it goes against the chief rule of Christianity, 'You should love your neighbor as you love yourself,' and I consider the Jews also my neighbors who have immortally created souls after the image and likeness of God." Lichtenberg admitted to praying regularly for "the severely harassed non-Christians, for the Jews, for prisoners in the concentration camps, particularly for the imprisoned priests and religious. . . for those with lack of faith . . . for those who despair and attempt suicide, for the millions of nameless and stateless refugees, for the fighters, wounded and dying soldiers on both sides, for the bombed-out cities in allied and enemy lands . . . for the Fatherland, and leaders of the *Volk*." In answer to questions relating to his critical notations in his copy of *Mein Kampf,* Lichtenberg stated: "Hitler is not an infallible prophet. . . . I do not consider Hitler as a prophet sent by God. . . . I state with steadfast conviction that the National Socialist ideology is incompatible with the teaching and commands of the Catholic Church." Placed on trial, on March 21, 1942, he was found guilty of a treacherous attack on state and party, and sentenced to a two-year imprisonment.

Bishop Konrad von Preysing wrote to the pope, informing him of Lichtenberg's arrest for praying for the "arrested Jews." Pius XII, while praising Lichtenberg's steadfastness, declined to intercede. Preysing succeeded in obtaining a concession from the Gestapo that if Lichtenberg remained silent and accepted a self-imposed prohibition on preaching during the war period, they would restore his freedom upon the termination of his two-year prison term. Lichtenberg, however, refused to assent to this, stating, "What better can happen to a person than to die for his holy Catholic faith? Today, I am ready, in facto this, to die for it!" He had only one request, to allow him to accompany the deported Jewish Christians and Jews to the Litzmannstadt/Lodz ghetto in order to serve as a pastoral minister to the people there. Preysing failed to dissuade Lichtenberg from this request, and his fate was doomed. On October 22, 1943, upon the end of his term in Berlin's Tegel prison, Gestapo officials took Lichtenberg to the work camp at Wuhlheide. There he was forced into a garbage room by a SS man along with a kapo prisoner, beaten, and left alone in the room for two days. On November 3, he was moved to Hof, a town that served as a collecting point for prisoners awaiting transportation to Dachau camp. As his health deteriorated, Lichtenberg was moved to a nearby state hospital, where he died on November 5, 1943. In the words of Guenther Lewy, "Lichtenberg's protest remained a solitary act of witness. His bishops remained silent in the face of the burning temples and the first round-up of the Jews." Yad Vashem honored him with the "Righteous" title.[39]

Clergy Rescuers of Jews

We will now move on to the relatively few German clerics honored by Yad Vashem for their rescue of Jews, and we start with a well-known name, Dean (*Probst*) Heinrich Grüber. His interest was first confined to baptized Jews, but with the increasing anti-Jewish measures, he turned his attention also to helping ordinary Jews. Surprisingly, like many other World War I veterans frustrated at Germany's loss in the First World War, Grüber joined the ultra-right Stahlhelm, a paramilitary organization dedicated to the overthrow of the Weimar republic and the restoration of monarchy. In early 1933, while serving as the director of a church school, he even fell under the spell of the Nazis and joined the party. Whatever his motivations, his flirtation with Nazism was short-lived, and he soon joined the Pastors Emergency League, established in September 1933 by Martin Niemöller in protest against attempts to discriminate against baptized Jews in the churches. As a result, Grüber lost his job at the church school, but was then appointed pastor in a Berlin suburb. In 1937, the unofficial leadership of the Confessing Church (the successor of the

Pastors Emergency League) commissioned Grüber to create a central relief agency for Protestants of Jewish descent. This was the origin of the famous Grüber Bureau, which opened in Berlin barely three weeks after the November 1938 *Kristallnacht* pogrom, with offices in other parts of the country. It soon became one of the most significant rescue and relief centers for racially persecuted people in prewar Nazi Germany. The Grüber office helped in many ways and was aided by other pastors, such as Confessing Church pastor Eitel-Friedrich von Rabenau, who headed a school for victims of racial discrimination. Among the branch offices, in Breslau it was headed by the earlier-mentioned Katharina Staritz; in Heidelberg by Pastor Hermann Maas, and it had offices in Thuringia, Cologne, and Leipzig. Close cooperation was maintained with Catholic and Quaker welfare organizations. Grüber also explored emigration outlets to Ethiopia, Australia, New Zealand, the Philippines, and Brazil. In the meantime, the Gestapo tolerated Gruber's activity, since it fell in line with the Nazis' own forced emigration policy at the time. While the bureau's original purpose was to help baptized Jews, it gradually extended its help to non-baptized Jews. Rabbi Leo Baeck and other leaders of the government-controlled Jewish Association worked hand in hand with Grüber to ease the plight of fellow Jews. When Grüber protested against the forced expulsion of the Jewish population in Stettin, Pomerania province, to Lublin, in occupied Poland, he was summoned to the Gestapo and warned not to interfere again in such matters. Still, in February 1940, Grüber tried again to intervene on behalf of deported Jews from Stettin. As a result, he was summoned to the Gestapo headquarters and warned that this would be the last time before retribution. When he received alarming reports on the desperate plight of German Jewish deportees to the Gurs camp in southern France, Grüber decided to examine the situation at first hand. He was preparing for the trip when, on December 19, 1940, he was summarily arrested, and held in Sachsenhausen and Dachau concentration camps for two and a half years, where he was subjected to severe physical and mental torture. Released on June 23, 1943, he was broken in body (he could not, for instance, go down the stairs without assistance), though not in spirit. The bureau itself had been dissolved in the wake of his arrest, and most of its staff, consisting largely of baptized Jews, had been deported to the death camps in the East.

In 1961, Grüber traveled to Israel to testify for the prosecution at the trial of SS chief Adolf Eichmann. Speaking of his impressions of the man, whom he had met on several occasions, he related his response to a question shot at him by Eichmann: "Why do you care about the Jews at all? No one is going to thank you for your efforts." To which Grüber responded to Eichmann, who had once visited Palestine, "You know the road from Jerusalem to Jericho? . . . Once on that road there lay a Jew who had fallen among thieves. Then a man passed by, who was not a Jew, and helped him. The Lord, whom alone I obey, tells me, 'Go thou and do likewise,' and that is my answer.'" It was the well-known parable of the Good Samaritan. Eichmann was unmoved. Recalling that dark period during the Eichmann trial, Grüber noted: "What always depressed me in those days above all was that people who otherwise thought it their duty to act so courageously were conspicuously lacking in what we call the courage of one's convictions (*Zivilcourage*)."[40] While in prison, Grüber's assistant, Rev. Werner Sylten, continued the bureau's operation for a few months. His classification as a *Mischling* (half-Jew) in accordance with the racial laws (his father was a converted Jew) made his position highly precarious. Before joining Grüber's office, he was viciously attacked in the Nazi daily *Voelkische Beobachter*, on September 20, 1935, on the charge of "daring to teach German girls salvation by the Jewish God Jahweh," which led to his dismissal from his teaching job. In 1941, he was arrested and sent to Dachau camp. While there, he was confined to the Disabled Barracks due to his ill health, and was treated contemptuously by the SS doctor, who referred to him as the "Jewish pastor." The cruelties and privations of the concentration camp undermined his health and he died on August 26, 1942, and was sent to the camp's crematorium. Sylten's patriotic credentials, including service in the German army during World War I, in which he was decorated, and in the right-wing *Freikorps* militia after that war, did not save him from death at the hands of his captors, who treated him more brutally because of his part-Jewish descent.[41]

Pastor Hermann Maas was Grüber's colleague in Heidelberg. He was unique in many ways, but especially in his great fondness for the Jewish people—a sentiment highly irregular in the charged anti-Jewish atmosphere of most Protestant pastors, even those opposed to the Nazis. Maas remembered his grandmother once telling him when they encountered a Jew while he was a small child: "You must always show respect to Jews; they are the children of God." "This saying," Maas underlined, "accompanied me throughout my life." In 1903, three years after his ordination, while in Basle, he visited the Sixth Zionist Congress, headed by the movement's founder, Theodor Herzl, who made a deep impression on him. "From that day on, I subscribed as a reader of the [Zionist] journal *Die Welt*. I considered myself a Zionist. I paid the shekel, and these sixty years [actually fifty-nine years] I have been a Zionist. On a visit to Palestine in 1933, he was moved at the sight of the new Jewish settlements. When he decided to return to Germany that July, his Jewish friends pleaded with him: "You belong with us; now stay here." Maas responded: "Indeed, I belong to you, and will always belong to you in truth. Now I have to start the struggle against the regime for and on behalf of the Jews." Returning to Heidelberg, "I posted a mezuzah on the door of my home, so that Jews knocking on my door would know that 'we are permitted to come here always and at any time.' . . . Thus I acted since 1933, and openly—in full view of the Gestapo." He also contributed articles to the German Zionist paper, the *Jüdische Rundschau*, translated poems of the celebrated Hebrew poet Nachman Bialik, participated in the Passover celebration (Seder), and attended the Jewish High Holy Day services in the Heidelberg synagogue, where a seat was always reserved for him. This led to his being exposed to a concerted campaign of vilification and threats by local Nazis, who demanded that the "pastor of the Jews" be excluded from the pulpit. Joining Niemoeller's Pastors Emergency League, he worked to extend help to baptized Jews, and also assisted Jews in Heidelberg to leave the country in whatever way possible. "Once I took out forty families in one train." Attending Christian ecumenical meetings outside Germany, "I had to struggle on behalf of the Jews. . . . On that occasion, I declared: Christians who from this moment confess in the guilt of the Jews, and who wish to avoid further guilt, must come out openly and in public. At first, they accepted this with great difficulty, for they hesitated to take the responsibility upon themselves. They felt that I was inserting something strange in the Oecumene." Forced by the Nazis to relinquish his clerical post, in 1943, he underwent harassment by the authorities. As Maas recalls, "The eyes of the Gestapo were always open, and constantly trailing me, and I was always in great danger. . . . When they often asked me: 'Why are you helping people to leave the country?' I would answer: 'I want to save them from death, from danger, from imprisonment, or from concentration camp.' I then added: "Here's another reason (of course, this was my personal invention). It is my fervent wish for these people to be outside the country; for these people will proclaim to the entire world that in Germany there are still people who are not hostile to them and who help them. This could be of benefit to Germany. It is important that something of another Germany should shine its light.' Quite surprisingly, they liked this, and they said, 'Fine; please go on with your work.'" After Grüber's arrest, Maas feared that he was also on the list, but for reasons unexplained, he was not apprehended. "Thus I had the opportunity to distribute food ration cards to people and help them in various ways, and my mezuzah was still affixed on my door. People knew they could expect help." This tranquil situation, however, was bound to change. Finally, in 1944, he was arrested and moved to a labor camp in occupied France. "So, I said, 'I am sixty-seven years old.' It does not matter; you are still able to work." Maas stayed at an undisclosed place in France, until the approach of the Allies. He then, with others, wandered toward the German border, where he saw the liberation on March 29, 1945, in the town of Karfreitag.

The postwar period saw Maas strengthening his ties to the Jewish people. In letters to friends, he expressed deep sorrow at what his people had done to the Jews. "We can do so little! We can only cover our heads in shame, and with a broken spirit fall on our knees and lament the murdered people of Israel. I tell you this in a state of deep distress, and I beg for forgiveness." In another letter: "My only guilt is that I am still alive. I should have shouted much louder, I should have protected and saved more people, so that in the end they [the Nazis] would have also murdered me. . . . I can only repay it by loving even more those who were put into my heart by our merciful God, who has chosen Israel as His people to suffer so immensely, but whom he never allows nor will allow to perish." In a letter to Rachel Auerbach of Yad Vashem, in 1963, he gave voice to his great love of the Jewish people: "Please, do not refer to me as 'a friend of the Jews'; I only want to be 'a Jewish brother.' " Earlier, in 1960, he wrote, "We love the Jewish people not *in spite of* their being Jews, but *because* they are Jews. . . . When we come to Israel, we come home—yes, a real home. Thus, we are bound to each other, and thus we wish to remain." In 1968, he again wrote of his abiding love for the Jewish people "Truly, the mystery of Israel has accompanied me each day, forever to this day. One cannot apprehend Israel religiously enough. . . . The life of a Jewish heart passes through numerous shades and hues; through hatred and coldness, but also through warmth and sparkling streams of shining silver." There was no other German clergyman who matched Hermann Maas's deep and intimate attachment to the Jewish people. A tree in his name adorns the main thoroughfare in the Avenue of the Righteous at Yad Vashem.[42]

We have earlier noted the somewhat ambivalent and mostly negative attitude of Confessing Church pastors toward Judaism and the Jews. Yet there were not a few such pastors who were active in sheltering both baptized as well as plain Jews. One of the most fascinating stories in this context is that of the Krakauers, husband and wife. Two years after the war's end, in 1947, Max Krakauer published *Lichter im Dunkel* ("Lights Amid Darkness"), relating the rescue of himself and his wife Ines by several dozen pastors of the Confessing Church—starting in Berlin, and continuing in the Pomerania and Stuttgart regions. Before the Nazi period, Krakauer was a successful businessman in the film industry. On January 29, 1943, friends warned the Krakauers that the Gestapo had called at their flat in order to deport them. After brief stays with several German friends, they were sent to Pastor Friedrich von Rabenau of the Confessing Church, who referred them to other pastors, in various locations; such as Pastor Johannes Strecker, of the Wusterhause vicarage, in Pomerania province, where they were cordially welcomed and after a time brought to Bad Polzin, where they found asylum in the house of Mrs. Dr. Goldmund, a theologian of the Confessing Church who had just been divorced by her husband, a fervent Nazi. They were then moved to different locations and for a time the couple had to separate, because no shelter for both could be arranged. As the situation in Pomerania became unsafe, the Krakauers returned to Berlin, where they rotated among several hiding places. They were eventually dispatched to Stuttgart, a center of Confessing Church activity. After a nightmarish journey of several days, they were received by a certain Pastor Mueller, who passed them off as a homeless couple from bombed-out Berlin. From Stuttgart, they were moved to Koengen, and sheltered by two pastors, Stoeffler and Goelz (whom we will meet again later). They then passed through several the hands of rural deans, including Pastors Rapp in Owen and Zeller in Waiblingen, Dilger in Cannstaff (an invalid with one leg), Otto Mörieke in Korntal, Brecht in Calw, Haar in Stuttgart-Sillenbuch, Elisabeth Goes, whose husband, Pastor Albrecht Goes, was away with the army, and Dilger; finally with Zeller in Waiblingen, where they met liberating American troops on April 23, 1945. More than sixty men and women had been instrumental in saving their lives, in forty-three different places, and staying at local vicarages for periods of only three to four weeks each, so as not to arouse suspicion. The Krakauers were Jewish by religion. They experienced only one incident of being refused asylum for declining to convert to Christianity. Nobody else dropped even the slightest hint that this was expected.[43] We now move to a further account of some of the pastors who aided the Krakauers and were honored with the "Righteous" title.

Otto Mörike was a member of the clandestine *Brüderrat* (Fraternal Council) of the Confessing Church in Württemberg, which, in response to an appeal by its Berlin office, provided refuge and help to Jews on the run, especially during the latter phase of World War II. Mörike had a history of brushes with the Gestapo because of his outspoken anti-Nazi views. In November 1943, he and wife Gertrud took the Krakauers into their home in the village of Flacht, where he served as a parish minister. To dispel suspicion, Mörike appeared with the Jewish couple in public and let it be known that they were "Aryan" acquaintances and fugitives from air-raid bombings in Berlin, a sight quite familiar in those days. Though the Krakauers could stay in Flacht no longer than four weeks, since this would have entailed registration with the police, Mörike took upon himself the overall responsibility for organizing the Krakauers' further sheltering with trustworthy Protestant ministers in the region.[44] One of them was Alfred Dilger, parish minister in Cannstatt, who had lost a leg in World War I. On October 11, 1943, he and wife Luise welcomed the Krakauers (under their assumed name of Ackerman) into their household for a five-week stay. "Naturally, our children and relatives were not aware of the secret," Dilger noted in his diary, "other than Luis, who knew how to keep the matter strictly confidential." Dilger's church superiors, however, did not look kindly at this sheltering of a Jewish couple. Pastor Karl Hartenstein, from Stuttgart, on a visit to Dilger, told him he knew very well the true identity of his guests, "and that I should be fully aware not to expect any assistance from the church elders, for the pastor's Lutheran house is state property." Dilger responded that "in admitting persecuted Jews I am placing myself under the protection of an authority higher than that of the church. I had not considered it necessary to seek permission for this undertaking." After the Krakauers' departure, the Dilgers sheltered a baptized Jewish woman. [45]

Eugen Stöffler and wife Johanna, in Koengen, Wuerttemburg province, also sheltered the fleeing Krakauers. As related by the Stöfflers' daughter, Ruth, her parents were fully aware of the danger for their six children and themselves. "However, they didn't hesitate to offer 'at least some drops of help' in the midst of the unspeakable suffering of the Jewish people." Ruth Stöffler remembers other Jews who stopped by at her house, such as a certain Mrs. Braun from Berlin, or a woman from Duisburg, or Mrs. Vogel, whose husband, Rudi Vogel, had once been mayor of Munich. "We, the children, knew that among our guests there were 'special guests', but our maid didn't know this." Max Krakauer described Eugen Stöffler as "a man whose spiritual nature never failed him, not even at the prospect of being sent to a concentration camp for hiding Jews, and we had not been the first Jewish guests in his house. No matter how serious a particular case was, he understood how to minimize it, at least in our presence, although deep down he might have been troubled occasionally. . . . Already the pastor's oldest son had lost his life in this murderous war. Yet this personal loss was borne with the deepest of Christian faith, the same faith that saw in our arrival a call by God. . . . We were allowed to stay in this house on three occasions, once even without advance notice. Because the transportation system started to break down more frequently, it became impossible to announce our arrival in advance. In spite of this, we were welcomed as if we had been expected impatiently for some time. During our three stays in Koengen, we were introduced to a good many people. . . . Most important was being introduced in Koengen to a large number of pastors who belonged to the '*Sozietät*' and who took an active interest in our predicament. . . . My wife was able to help out in the house, and I worked in the yard and at the typewriter. Work, after all, relaxed us most. . . . We had stayed there for three weeks, and if we hoped to avoid arousing any suspicion we had to move on." From there, Max Krakauer moved to the house of Pastor Goelz, in Wankheim, while his wife was taken to a different location. [46]

Richard Goelz had initiated a movement to reform church music while serving as a parish minister in Wankheim, Württemberg province. In autumn

1943, he and his wife, Hildegard, hosted Max Krakauer for four weeks. While there, Krakauer helped out in the harvesting. Dr. Hermann Pineas, a Jewish physician from Berlin, was another fugitive who found refuge in Goelz's house. After Pineas' departure, Goelz was arrested and interrogated by the Gestapo. He was sent to Welzheim, a forced-labor camp northeast of Stuttgart, where he was incarcerated for eight months. The experience there completely altered the man, and after his release, on April 18, 1945, he showed signs of mental stress, which was exacerbated by the death of his son Gottfried in a submarine accident in the last year of the war. Disappointed by the failure of his endeavor for a radical reform of the Protestant prayer book within the Protestant establishment, he converted to the Russian Orthodox Church and in 1958 left for the United States.[47]

Following is the story of how many members of the Confessing Church helped a baptized Jewish woman named Beate Steckan. In a postwar account entitled *Night on Germany,* she writes of the dedicated care she received from these pastors. Such as Pastor von Rabenau, from the Apostle Paul Church in Schoeneberg, "who came to see me many times to give me consolation in my faith." When Mrs. Steckan was informed of her deportation, in November 1941, she had just come home from communion. "No doubt, I had hoped that as the widow of an Aryan killed in World War I—a name carved on a wall of the municipality of Schoeneberg—I might be spared. Back from church, I opened the door and there was the letter that was to decide my destiny, asking me to come the next morning to the Jewish community office, which had been charged by the Gestapo with preparations for the deportation of Jews and baptized Jews alike." She informed Pastor Rabenau, and he immediately showed up to comfort her. Reporting to the Jewish community as "Sarah" (every racially born Jewish woman was required by the Nazi government to carry the middle name "Sarah"; for men "Israel"), she was informed that her deportation had been postponed for the sake of her late husband, a decorated soldier. In February 1942, her pension and other retirement payments were cancelled. "From one moment to another, I became a poor person. In my despair I called Pastor von Rabenau. He said: 'Frau Steckhan, you have not yet learned what it means to be a member of a Christian congregation. All of us will stand behind you.' And then all of them came to help," including Pastors Burckhardt and Jannasch, "who was especially caring for non-Aryan Christians, and his entire congregation stood behind him," and in whose charge baptized Jews were allowed to sit (with their obligatory yellow star) next to their fellow Aryan believers, instead of being segregated, as prevailed in other churches. "A circle of clergymen, among them the late Superintendent Rott, read the Bible with us once a week in a private flat. Above all, they instructed us in case we were deported, how to be able to help other Christians. We were to get instructions by the Confessing Church to hold services and other church activities, if there were no clergymen to be found." Rabenau insisted on accompanying her on her 25-minute walk home; "he didn't listen to my protests that I was marked as a Jew by the yellow star." She then was forced to do menial forced labor. In August 1942, Steckan received a second deportation summons. "I asked Pastor Jannasch to give me the last blessings and the Holy Communion." This took place as the Gestapo came to take her away, and Jannasch in his religious robe stood behind her. "I asked them to give me sufficient time to take communion," which the Gestapo obliged. In her words, impressed by the communion, and by the large oil painting of her husband in uniform with the Iron Cross medal, the Gestapo officers had a change of heart. "You are no Jewish woman," they exclaimed. "You belong to us. Your husband was an Aryan and an officer; you are a Christian yourself—we can't take you with us," and they left. However, fearing a sudden return visit by the Gestapo, Steckan was advised by friends not to rely on miracles but immediately go into hiding. A friendly pastor procured for her a faked identity card under the name of Edith Juckeling. She then moved from one home to another, from one parsonage to the next; first in the Berlin vicinity; then in distant places, such as the parsonage of Pastor Richard Goelz, at Wankheim, who welcomed her with the words: "Next Sunday we must sing a Te Deum, as we are honored with the presence of the House of Israel." Goelz also arranged alternative hiding places for her, including the Eugen Stoeffler household, in Koengen, both already mentioned in the story of the Krakauers. Her peripatetic movements took her to pastors' homes in distant Munich. The final year of the war found her on the estate of a duchess in Prenzlau. As a baptized Jewish woman who took her new religion seriously, she found many pastors ready, willing, and volunteering to help her. Very few baptized Jews were that lucky.[48]

In Berlin, we have the story of Harald Poelchau, who since 1932 had been the chaplain in the Tegel prison. In that capacity, he was required to be present at an ever-increasing number of executions of political opponents of the Nazi regime, including those involved in the attempted assassination of Hitler on July 20, 1944. Unknown to the Gestapo, since 1941 Poelchau himself had belonged to the circle of anti-Nazi resisters gathered round Count von Moltke, known as the *Kreisauer Kreis*, and had attended their meetings. With the start of the deportation of Jews, Poelchau was often solicited to provide shelter and other forms of assistance to Jews on the run. In one dramatic incident, in early 1945, he and his wife Dorothee admitted Rita and Ralph Neumann, who suddenly appeared in Poelchau's apartment at midnight, just as the pastor and his wife were preparing to go to bed after a prolonged and excruciating stay in the air-raid shelter. The Jewish brother and sister had been arrested and interrogated, and had managed to flee their captors during an air-raid alarm. They ran for two and a half hours until they stood at the doorway of Poelchau's home, pale, worn out, and out of breath. Ralph Neumann knew the place because of errands he had performed for the pastor and his wife while he still in hiding with his previous benefactors, the Wendlands. Poelchau and his wife admitted them without hesitation, fed them, invited a doctor to treat Ralph's wounds, and accommodated the two in their small apartment—at great personal risk— until the end of the war. In another act of mercy, Pastor Poelchau helped another fleeing Jew, Konrad Latte, on several occasions, by arranging places for him to stay under an assumed name.[49]

Before arriving at Poelchau's doorstep, Ralph Neuman was helped by Ruth Wendland. She was the daughter of Protestant Pastor Walter Wendland, and was affiliated with the Confessing Church. In August 1943, Ruth Wendland and her mother, Agnes, admitted into their home seventeen-year-old Ralph Neumann and his sister Rita, who were leading an illegal existence in Berlin. Ralph slept at night in a small room in the house and left early in the morning, as though going out to work. In February 1945, Neumann was arrested on the street by a military patrol. Under torture by the Gestapo, he divulged the names of his helpers. Ruth Wendland's mother was arrested and jailed. When she fell ill, Ruth offered to substitute for her sick mother and was jailed in her stead. Fortunately, the end of the war was near, and Ruth managed to come out relatively unharmed. Her mother, Agnes, however, had contracted typhoid and passed away in August 1946, at the age of fifty-five. After the war, Ruth Wendland continued her career in the church, and in August 1964, she was ordained as the first woman pastor of the Altstadt community in Muelheim, in the Ruhr region, a post that she held for close to thirteen years, until her death in 1977.[50] In Berlin as well, in 1944, Pastor Guenther Brandt helped the Jewish lawyer Dr. Hans Gumpel, who was living with his wife incognito in Potsdam, by issuing them a stamped confirmation that they were refugees from Stettin. This facilitated their passage through various official controls. An earlier beneficiary of Brandt's help was the half-Jewish daughter of Susanne Vogel (herself of Jewish descent and married to a non-Jew), who was taken into the Brandt house as a household maid, while at the same time attending her confirmation ceremony in the church. In still another instance, in 1944, the Brandts accommodated in their home for a few weeks a Jewish widow by the name of Gertrud Leopold.[51]

Still in Berlin, we have the story of Erik Myrgren, a minister of the Swedish Protestant church. In December 1944, he was passing through Berlin after having left Stettin, now a frontline city. The church there was in ruins, and he was on his way home to Sweden, where he hoped to celebrate Christmas with his family. Passing through Berlin, he was met by the Swedish vicar Erik

Perwe, who had to go to Sweden for consultations and asked him to stay on for two weeks in his stead. Perwe, according to author Leonard Gross, was "the brains and guts of the most organized effort in all Berlin to save its remaining Jews." He arrived in Berlin in September 1942 with his wife Maria, after the preceding minister, Birger Forell, was expelled by the Nazis. Perwe considered it God's calling, as he noted in his diary: "God calls, I must obey." The Swedish church was in the Wilmersdorf section. With the help of his staff (including Sister Wide Ohmann, a trained nurse), the church gave refuge to itinerant Jews (twenty at a time on occasions). Perwe also provided false baptismal certificates and maintained contacts in the Gestapo, some of whom were ready to "sell" their Jews in return for payment. "So, it happened," Myrgren continues, "that for the first time, I met Jews that Reverend Perwe was hiding in the cellar of the [Swedish] church," Myrgren noted. "I had no objections. I would still be able to go home for Christmas, if nothing happened." But something did happen: the worst thing possible! Perwe's plane crashed, and all the passengers were lost at sea. When news of this tragedy spread, Perwe's Jewish benefactors turned to Myrgren for help. "At night, his special friends came, the *U-Boote* [submariners], Jews whom he had hidden and promised further help; people to whom he had been the difference between life and death. I can still hear their cries of sorrow. Trembling old people, youngsters with despair in their eyes, hunted for years, and now—so they believed—they were deprived of their last hope. The only person who to a certain extent knew of Perwe's many activities was Erik Wesslen [also from Sweden]. . . . He bribed guards and policemen to let arrested Jews disappear . . . Jews for coffee, liquor, chocolate, money, and jewels. Slowly, slowly, I myself became part of the machinery which Perwe and his famous predecessor, the vicar Birger Forell, had built up so carefully, the purpose of which was to save lives and to help persecuted and bereaved people. My own work was humble compared to that of the others, but it lasted six intensive months. . . . Together with the others in the church, Wesslen, Vide Ohmann, . . . I did what had to be done. People needed help—that was all. Help with food and clothing, a place to hide, a transport to a secure place, some money, maybe medical care, or just some words of comfort and hope. . . . Many Jews came to us and stayed either a few days or two to three weeks, and were then placed elsewhere, the moment we found a safe hiding place. Some examples. Herbert Friedemann once had an important job. Now he was fifty but looked like seventy, was extremely thin and frightened. He was living like a shadow, afraid he would be caught and transported away. Perwe had promised to take him to Sweden. When that hope was swept away, he was in despair. 'Is there a place for me here in the church?' he kept asking. I knew that Friedemann lived in a relatively secure place, so I answered: 'We have already far too many here in the church. Be patient, maybe we will find something.' '*Aber lieber Herr Pfarrer, ich kann nicht mehr. Bitte, bitte, lassen Sie mich bleiben!*' (But dear Mr. Pastor, I cannot take it any longer. Please, please, let me stay here). In order to calm him down, I promised to deal with the matter and asked him to return after a week. 'After a week I may have a solution.' [The following day he returned, and I said to him] 'Dear Friedemann, I know that you phoned yourself. Forgive me. I have obviously not understood how difficult it is for you.' Then I was interrupted. I was scared to see him falling down on his knees creeping against me crying: 'Let me stay! Let me stay! I ask you!' It was so painful so I had to look away. I was so ashamed. But within me came a burning hatred against that system which so deeply humiliated a people and crushed its dignity so that an old man found it necessary to beg a young man for his life at his feet. It was terrible. But it was good for me. It strengthened my inner readiness. It was there before. Now it received maturity and strength. What had I to fear? Death was always close. The bombs were falling day and night. To take an additional risk meant so little. But to some people it was a matter of surviving. Friedemann could stay some days in the church where a few other Jews took care of him. . . . The stream of people passing through the church became more and more strong. Sometimes thirty, forty, fifty, spent the night there at the same time filling every little corner." Responding to his elevation to the "Righteous" title, in a 1987 letter to Yad Vashem, Reverend Myrgren downplayed his role in the rescue of Jews: "I feel very humble, and surely I'm not worthy being honored with such a prominent distinction. Whatever I did during my time in Berlin I had no idea there was something extraordinary about it. On the contrary I always had a feeling [of] not doing enough. Still I tried to act as much as I could in the way my pious parents taught me: bring help to your fellowman, whoever he is, whatever he needs."[52]

Moving out of the Berlin area to Kassel, we note the rescue of Rahel Schild, who in 1918 had married a non-Jewish dental surgeon, Dr. Ernst Plueer, after the two met in a German military hospital during World War I. Their son, Wolfgang, born in 1921, and considered a half-Jew by the Nazis, lived under certain restrictions and in January 1945 was deported to a labor camp in the Ruhr area. In the meantime his father, Ernst Plueer, in Kassel, was summoned by the Gestapo and given the alternative to either divorce his Jewish-born wife or be denied his dental practice. Upon his refusal, he was summoned, at the age of sixty-five, to report for physical labor. At this point, Rahel realized that she stood in danger of arrest. To free her husband from the obligation of strenuous physical labor, she concocted a suicide note without his knowledge and took care that it fell into the hands of the Gestapo. Then, following the advice of a family friend, she approached Pastor Walther Disselnkoetter in the nearby village of Zueschen. An active member of the Confessing Church, Pastor Disselnkoetter was on the Gestapo watch list, and agents had occasionally searched his home. He wrote of his meeting with the forlorn Rahel in a 1994 letter to Yad Vashem: "At noontime of January 28 [1945], a worried-looking woman stood in front of the door of our presbytery in Zueschen, and told my wife [Anna] she was Mrs. Schmidt, from Allenstein, who had fled from the Russians, and her belongings and papers were stolen. She wanted to find shelter among friends in Kassel, but the houses there were fully destroyed and its inhabitants killed. So she was looking for a temporary place. 'Frau Schmidt' appeared very worried and disoriented. My wife did not believe the 'refugee story,' but she nevertheless took Mrs. Plueer in without further ado. When I returned home that same evening, she told me that she had taken a woman into the house who appeared to her to be a fleeing Jewish woman or . . . from a camp or labor firm. We concluded that 'Frau Schmidt' probably was a fleeing Jewish woman, and decided not to question her further but admit her in the house." The next day, the pastor's wife registered her under the assumed name Schmidt at the local municipality, and received in return food coupons and a temporary identity card. The pastor added: "For us the situation was very dangerous, for in case of detection we faced the death penalty, or at least to be taken away to a concentration camp. We had four children, aged four to thirteen years, and I was considered 'politically unreliable' for being a pastor in the Confessing Church." With the liberation of Zueschen in April 1945, Mrs. Plueer informed the American authorities of her true identity, and they took care to notify her husband, with whom she had lost contact. Reverend Disselnkoetter then penned a letter to Dr. Plueer, in Kassel, informing him of his wife's survival, and her weak medical condition, and urging him to come as soon as possible to fetch her.[53]

Or consider the story of Wilhelm Mensching. While working as a missionary in Africa, he was arrested by the British at the start of World War I, and taken with his wife and two children to India, where he came under the influence of Mahatma Gandhi. Returning to Germany after the war, he served as pastor in the village of Petzen, near Bueckeburg. He was by then a convinced pacifist, and sympathetic to the Quaker movement. The Nazis confiscated his pamphlets on this subject, and he avoided arrest only through the intercession of the local mayor, a Nazi himself. Mensching's son Ernst died in the war as a soldier, in 1944. A year earlier, Mensching helped out Ruth Caecilie Lilienthal. Born to a Jewish father and a non-Jewish mother, she belonged to the Jewish community and was thus listed by the Nazis as fully-Jewish (*Geltungsjuedin*) instead of *Mischlinge* Grade 1 because she had elected not to be Jewish. Beginning December 1942, she went underground in Berlin. From there she moved, in October 1943, to Bueckeburg/Schaumburg Lippe, where she was sheltered by a family she knew from Berlin. When she could no longer stay there, and did not know where to turn next, she contacted Reverend Mensching's daughter, Hanni Mensching, with whom she had earlier corresponded through their membership in the Quaker movement, and Hanni, in turn, asked her father to help out. "This is how I landed in mid-October 1943 in the pastor's house in Petzen, and remained there hidden until approximately the end of March 1944," Ruth wrote. During that period, she contacted a serious illness in her feet, which forced her to stay in bed. "Pastor Mensching arranged for me to be admitted to a hospital in Bueckeburg—naturally under a false name, as Rose Schwendinger. There I remained for about five weeks." With the help of electrical treatment, she slowly regained the use of her legs. Then, in early 1944, she found employment, under her borrowed name, with a pharmaceutical firm in Bueckburg, which made it possible for her to leave the reverend's home and rent a room for herself. "I remember with great appreciation Pastor Mensching and his family, who hosted me with much kindness during my illness."[54]

We conclude with the story of Julius Seebass, a pastor in the village of Bornecke. In April 1945, he answered a knock on his door, and was shocked at the sight facing him. There stood Rudolf Klepfisz and Adolf Weissmark, who had escaped from Langestein-Zwieberge, an affiliate of Buchenwald concentration camp. The two totally exhausted Jewish prisoners were quickly admitted inside. Then the pastor, together with his wife Hertha and their two daughters, Ricarda and Renata, began to care for the two escapees, including washing their typhus-stricken bodies. As a result, twenty-year-old Ricarda became infected and succumbed to this deadly disease. The two Jewish escapees recovered and lived on.[55]

Turning to Catholic rescuers, the record is even sparser than for Protestants. Let us note the few so far uncovered. In 1929, Josef Arkenau joined the Dominican Order as a novice, and when ordained assumed the name Aurelius. Interestingly, like many other clerics, at first Arkenau welcomed the Nazi assumption of power. However, after witnessing many acts of Nazi terrorism after he arrived in Berlin in April 1934, where he had been sent to do pastoral work, he had a change of heart. In 1940, he was assigned to the Dominican chapel in Leipzig-Wahren, where he remained until the end of the war. Soon thereafter, he became involved in helping people persecuted by the regime. At first, those helped were converted Jews, such as members of the *Paulusbund* in Breslau, who were hidden until a way was found to get them out of the country, legally or not. Later, deserters from the army, underground socialists, and various opponents of the Nazi regime, as well as Jews in general were also aided. Kaethe Sackarndt was one of his Jewish beneficiaries. After the death of her non-Jewish husband, she was confined to a Jewish-inhabited home, with her son, Joachim Label. Her friend Johanna Langraf arranged several temporary hiding places for her. Finally, running out of options, Johanna was referred to Father Arkenau. At first, he provided Mrs. Sackarndt with food rations, which Johanna received for Kaethe once per month. Then, Arkenau referred Johanna to a priest in Berlin, who gave her a new identity card for Kaethe. With this document, Kaethe found a place to live in Halle. As to her later conversion, Kaethe Sarckarndt underlined, in a 1998 statement, that "never did Father Aurelius ever suggest that I convert or even hint at it. On the contrary; he urged me to give it careful and lengthy consideration. My conversion was the result of a two-sided conviction held by me and my friend, who unfortunately died during the period of the air- raid bombings. Our common conviction was based on the belief that we were treading a road that many of our forefathers had already trodden during the past two thousand years." In a letter to Yad Vashem, Father Arkenau wrote, "When once, in 1941, at a railway station at night, I saw how the Nazis treated the Jews, far worse than we ever treated our animals on my father's farm, I knew that I had the duty to help and save as many Jews as possible. Because of this duty, I had no problem, as a priest, about what I had to do for this human duty—to fake, falsify, bribe, lie, and smuggle. Whom should I have asked for permission for this? My bishop, our abbot, or the pope? It was not the time to discuss such theological questions. It was the time to act and to do the right thing, and that was to help the victims of Nazi persecution."[56]

Turning to another story: Father Heinrich Middendorf, in 1919, joined the missionary order of the Priests of the Heart of Jesus (*Herz-Jesu-Priester*), taking upon himself the three lifelong vows of poverty, chastity, and obedience. In 1938 he was appointed rector of the Stegen monastery in Breisgau, about 20 kilometers from Freiburg, a post he held until 1946. The Stegen monastery was located in a secluded setting, situated in a remote valley at the foot of the picturesque Schwarzwald mountain range. There, Father Middendorf admitted Lotte Paepcke, the Jewish wife of a non-Jewish husband, during the later war years, and her 1935-born son, Peter. Living in Leipzig in a "privileged" mixed marriage, the Paepcke family at first felt safe from deportation. However, as the prospects of the Third Reich dimmed, Jewish partners in mixed marriages were increasingly targeted. In 1943, Mrs. Paepcke was assigned to forced labor, clearing rubble of bombed-out houses. Sensing that something even worse was in store for her, the following year she fled to Freiburg. There, in the autumn of 1944, with the help of friends, she made contact with Father Middendorf. He sent a small truck for her, in which mother and son were hidden among sacks of potatoes. Once in Stegen, Middendorf placed Lotte Paepcke in a monk's cell, where she stayed out of sight. Her son was placed among a group of orphans evacuated from northern Germany because of the air bombardments. He served as an acolyte, assisting the cleric with the religious service, with no one paying attention to the fact that he was not a Catholic. This situation lasted until the liberation in April 1945. Apart from the Paepcke family, Father Middendorf sheltered in Stegen several other fugitives from Nazi racial persecution, including Irmgard Giessler, the Jewish wife of a Catholic journalist, and Eva and Dieter Bacheimer, the children of a Christian mother and a converted Jewish father.[57]

We have, furthermore, the story of Joseph Hoeffner, a parish priest in Kiel, who together with his sister Helene Hesseler sheltered the seven-year-old Esther Sara Meyerowitz from Berlin, under the name of Christa Koch, as well as Edith Nowak and her non-Jewish husband. In the 1960s Hoeffner was a bishop of Munster; then archbishop in Cologne. In 1969, he was consecrated a cardinal.[58] Finally, August Ruf and Eugen Weiler; respectively priests in Singen and Wiechs, both aided Katherina Sara Lasker-Meyer, in April 1942, to illegally cross the German-Swiss border in the Bodensee region. As a result the two were arrested; Weiler was incarcerated in Dachau, which he luckily survived. As for Ruf, he faced a worse fate. Imprisoned in Ludwigsburg, he was released in April 1944, as he was on the point of dying. He passed away five days later.[59]

Chapter 3
FRANCE

Pétain is France, and France today is Pétain.
Cardinal Pierre Gerlier (November 1940)

*Jews are men, Jewesses are women. . . . All is not permitted
against them. . . . They are part of the human race. They are our
brothers like so many others. A Christian cannot forget it.*
Archbishop Jules-Géraud Saliège (August 1942)

*These people [Jews] have come to seek help and protection
among the Protestants of this region. I am their pastor; in other
words, their shepherd. It is not the role of a shepherd to betray
the sheep placed under his protection.*
Pastor André Trocmé (August 1942)

Historical Background and Nazi Period

Jews began arriving in France in Roman times, and later settled in various
parts of the Frankish kingdom that replaced the Roman Empire in the region
originally known as Gaul. Already as early as the sixth century there were
attempts to compel Jews to accept Christianity, and in 576 Bishop Avitus of
Clermont-Ferrand offered the Jews of his town (who numbered over 500) the
choice of either baptism or expulsion. In spite of these local encumbrances,
which rose and ebbed with time, the number of Jews in France increased in
the following centuries. Under Charlemagne, in the ninth century, Jews were
not harmed, and some even obtained high positions in the king's court. Later,
in 845–46, when church councils sought to legislate hostile canons, King
Charles the Bald (840–77) refused to ratify these canons. In the coming centuries Jewish religious learning prospered. The most famous figure of this era
was the biblical and talmudic commentator Rashi, in Troyes. The period of the
Crusades (11th–12th cent.) saw the Jews undergoing intense persecutions,
including loss of life, interspersed with expulsions from various cities, only to
be readmitted later, and expelled again. Jews also underwent forced conver-

sions in Rouen and Metz, and in 1171, thirty-one Jews were burned at the stake in Blois on the false charge of ritual murder of a Christian child. French kings continued to hamper the Jews with restrictive measures, including the public burning of the Talmud in Paris in 1240, based on a bull issued by Pope Gregory IX. After a series of massacres and burnings at the stake, Jews were banished from France in 1306; some were readmitted, then finally banished in 1322. Jewish communities continued to exist only in the newly incorporated provinces of Alsace and Lorraine, and in the Bordeaux region, where "New Christians"—Jews who had been forced to convert in Spain and Portugal—were allowed to settle as Christians (though secretly practicing their erstwhile Judaism). In the eighteenth century, some Jews were also allowed to settle in Paris, but under restrictive conditions. The 40,000 Jews in France on the eve of the French Revolution were granted full civic rights in 1791. In 1806, Napoleon tried to regulate Jewish religious life by reinstituting the Sanhedrin as the highest religious court, but this attempt faltered with the fall of Napoleon. The late nineteenth century saw the appearance of antisemitic papers, and in 1883, the daily *La Croix*, published by the Catholic Assumptionists, accused Jews and Freemasons of having orchestrated the French Revolution. In 1886, Edouard Drumont published *La France Juive,* which became a bestseller. In its pages he accused the Jews of running the country to their own advantage. Drumont's popularity led him, in 1892, to publish an antisemitic daily, *La Libre Parole,* filled with anti-Jewish diatribes. From there it was but a small step to the trumped-up trial of Alfred Dreyfus, a Jewish army officer, charged with having spied for Germany. The trial and public humiliation of Dreyfus were accompanied by cries of "Death to the Jews" shouted by antisemitic crowds. After World War I, France absorbed many Jews, seeking shelter from persecution in other countries, who hoped to bask in the freedom offered by its secular and liberal laws. On the eve of World War II, Paris counted 180,000 Jews, and there were more than 300,000 Jews in the country. They were soon to face a new and more dangerous threat for which they were not prepared.[1]

Following the swift and stunning German defeat of the French army in the short campaign of June 1940, the country was divided into two zones. About two-thirds, including Paris and the whole Atlantic coast, was under direct German occupation, and a third, consisting of Lyon and the southeast up to and including the Mediterranean coast, was under a semi-puppet government with headquarters in Vichy, headed by a famed World War I hero, Marshal Philippe Pétain. The Vichy government saw no way to preserve a semblance of French sovereignty over a limited portion of the beloved homeland other than by aligning itself with a victorious Nazi Germany. Pétain was hailed, not as a collaborator like Quisling in conquered Norway, but as the man of the hour who, as when he made his heroic stand at the battle of Verdun in the previous war, would be able to restore national pride and withstand the demands of the German overlords. One of the first items on the new agenda was a change in the status of the Jews; in other words, the revocation of the rights enjoyed by the Jews since the French Revolution.

The Vichy government did not wait for the Germans to exert pressure on them on this issue. Acting on its own, on October 3, 1940, it decreed the first Jewish Statute (*Statut des Juifs*), which identified as Jewish anyone with only two Jewish grandparents if the person was married to a Jew. Such people, and other Jews, were automatically excluded from public service, the armed forces, and the liberal professions; such as teaching, journalism, the cinema, theater, and radio. The following day, an additional law authorized the prefects who administered the provinces to intern or assign to supervised residences any non-naturalized Jews (who numbered close to half of the 325,000 Jews in the country), as they saw fit. This was followed, on October 17, with a government statement accusing the Jews of "abusing our hospitality" and "contributing not a little to our defeat." It further castigated the Jews for their "decomposition", and the "evil effect of their activity." Having said that, the government assured the Jewish population that it did not want to harm them, only to prevent them from causing "anarchy" in society. "This is not a matter of mass vengeance," it stated to calm Jewish fears, "but of indispensable security." But worse was yet to come.[2]

On June 2, 1941, a second Jewish Statute, replacing the earlier one, defined a Jew as anyone with three Jewish grandparents, regardless of the person's current religious affiliation, as well as anyone with two Jewish grandparents who was married to a Jewish spouse. If not married to a Jewish spouse, such a person had to produce a baptismal certificate from before June 25, 1940, the date of France's defeat. Additional professions added to the prohibited list included court jury, banking, advertising, real estate, loans, higher education (only 3 percent of the total students in some disciplines), and a host of other jobs. A month later, all Jewish-owned industrial and commercial businesses were placed under government-appointed administrators, as were houses owned by Jews and their furniture contents. These decrees were applicable in both the Vichy "free" zone and the German-occupied zone. As noted by a clandestine journal: "At this hour, Jews find it almost entirely impossible to find any gainful employment." In Paris, the Vichy-appointed police chief, in a decree posted in December 1941, prohibited Jews from spending the night outside their homes, and non-Jews from taking them in, "under pain of the gravest penalties." In fact, Jews had been reduced to second-class or even lower-grade citizens, with a stroke of the pen. Under the new law, a census of all Jews living in the Vichy zone was made mandatory.

When asked whether a priest of Jewish origin, considered Jewish by the new law, was required to register, the Toulouse regional head of the newly founded General Commissariat for Jewish Questions responded on August 2, 1941: "If Pontius Pilate had ordered a census of Jews, Jesus Christ himself would have obeyed. The humblest of his representatives on earth must therefore also submit themselves to the requirements of the law." This government agency (hereinafter referred to by its French initials CGQJ), created in March 1941, and mandated to propose additional discriminatory steps against Jews, was first headed by Xavier Vallat, a self-declared antisemite of the old French vintage (not the Nazi-racist brand), who was later replaced by the more strident antisemitic Louis Darquier de Pellepoix. Vallat justified the new anti-Jewish measures as a return to the prerevolutionary status of Jews, which he stated was based on the religious notion of the Jews as "a cursed race, condemned never to have a homeland due to the collective sin of deicide."[3] In addition, all Jewish organizations were placed under a government-supervised Jewish umbrella organization known as the Union Général des Israélites de France (UGIF). In accordance with these draconian measures voluntarily imposed by the French government, thousands of Jews were interned in French internment camps, again without German prodding, and 3,000 died due to lack of proper nourishment and medical facilities, and exposure to the elements. Thus the first Jewish victims in France died on French soil. In the words of Susan Zuccotti, "they died because of French, not German, persecution."[4] The internment camps were supervised by the Vichy government and guarded by French gendarmes. The better-known ones in the Vichy zone were Gurs, Rivesaltes, Récébédou, Noë, Vernet, Argèles, Agde, Les Milles, and Vénissieux; in the Occupied Zone: Drancy and Beaune-la-Rolande.

Fearing negative repercussions from the Vatican because of the racist underpinnings of the Jewish Statutes, Pétain, on August 7, 1941, asked the French ambassador there, Léon Bérard, to inquire whether the Holy See had any reservations with regard to these anti-Jewish measures. Bérard's exhaustive report, on September 2, 1941, stilled Pétain's fears. He pointed out that the anti-Jewish program was of little concern to the Vatican except for the law's racist definition of who was a Jew. Bérard assured Pétain that he had consulted an authoritative person in the Vatican, but without naming him, who pointed out that whereas the principle of the unity of mankind was to be upheld, there were "ethnic particularities" within this large assembly of peoples which had to be taken into consideration, and which justified certain limitations and restrictions. Such restrictions, the Vatican official explained, had already been justified by the great medieval Catholic theologian Thomas Aquinas, who had recommended that Jews be barred from government posts and be limited in the exercise of their professions. Not to miss out on anything, Bérard also reported his interlocutor's observation that regulations for the wearing of special dress, should it come to that, were also not new to the church. According to the unnamed high Vatican source, it was imperative that Jews have no authority over Christians, and therefore "it is legitimate to deny them [the Jews] access to public office; also legitimate to admit them only in a fixed proportion to the universities and the liberal professions." However, Bérard continued, the church could not accept that a Jew duly converted to Catholicism should still be considered a Jew, as the statute provided. This was the sole point on which the law of June 12, 1941 was in opposition to an important church principle. All in all, Bérard was assured that insofar as the anti-Jewish measures were concerned, there would be no opposition from the Holy See. "As an authorized source at the Vatican told me, they don't intend to get into a fight over the Jewish Statute" as long as the sacrament of marriage is not questioned. At the same time, the Vatican urged that these measures be applied with due consideration "for justice and charity." Pétain felt greatly relieved by Bérard's report, to the point that when the papal nuncio, Monsignor Valério Valeri, complained to him about the racist content of the Jewish Statute, Pétain jestingly replied that Valeri was perhaps not up-to-date with the policy of his superiors in the Vatican.[5] Vichy could continue to oppress its Jews, with the silence, if not the blessings, of the Holy See.

* * *

The Catholic hierarchy in France shared the Vatican's position, or so it would seem from its silence at the promulgation of the anti-Jewish measures. In addition, many clerics saw Pétain as the man who would bring France back to its Christian principles; a sort of savior, promising order, hierarchy, discipline, and respect for religious and traditional values. Adulation for the aged marshal (eighty-four in 1942) was voiced by all the princes of the Catholic Church in France. The church's primate, Cardinal Pierre Gerlier, led the chorus of praises for Pétain and the so-called National Revolution proclaimed by Vichy ("family, homeland, and work"). "Pétain is France, and France is today Pétain," Gerlier told a large crowd who welcomed Pétain on his visit to Lyon on November 19, 1940. Gerlier added: "France needed a chief who would lead her to her eternal destiny. God has allowed for you to be here." Praises for Pétain were also voiced by Cardinal Emmanuel Suhard in Paris, Monsignor Delay in Marseilles, and Monsignor Gabriel Piguet, bishop of Clermont-Ferrand. On July 24, 1941, cardinals and archbishops in the occupied zone gathered in Paris, and issued a statement declaring their "veneration" for Pétain, and calling on all Frenchmen to collaborate with the puppet regime: "We call upon our faithful to place themselves next to him in the work of restoration which he has undertaken on the three principles of family, work, and homeland." Similar paeans of loyalty were voiced by the bishops of Poitiers, Reims, Amiens, Nantes, Nancy, La Rochelle, and other cities. Some prelates, like Abbé Valery, went so far in their enthusiasm for Pétain as to compare him with the resurrected Christ.[6]

Going a step further, some church leaders saluted the Vichy regime for its repressive measures against the Jews. The bishop of Grenoble, in his Easter sermon of 1941, lauded Pétain for moving against that "harmful power, the aliens, of which the Jews are a particularly outstanding specimen." True enough, Cardinal Gerlier cautioned against a too strict application of the anti-Jewish measures, but he had no objection to the principle behind the Jewish Statute. According to Vallat, Gerlier told him: "Your law is not unjust . . . but it lacks justice and charity in its enforcement." He was, on the other hand, "extremely understanding from the economic and final viewpoints. The Jewish problem exists, he [Gerlier] told me; it is indeed inescapable, and I approve [the anti-Jewish measures] within the framework of justice and freedom." Even the venerable Monsignor Saliège, bishop of Toulouse, who in the summer of 1942, as we shall later see, was the first to break the silence and condemn French participation in the deportation of Jews, stated a year earlier, according to Vallat, that "Vallat's position from the viewpoint of Catholic doctrine is incontestable" (according to another version, "irreproachable"). No wonder that after the war, Xavier Vallat stated in his defense that had the Catholic hierarchy protested any aspect of the anti-Jewish laws, he would either have modified the laws or resigned from office.[7] From the ecclesiastical standpoint, anti-Jewish measures were apparently not only permissible but also desirable—but, in line with classical church tradition, only up to a certain point.

Pastor Marc Boegner, head of the French Protestant churches, was the first high cleric to voice a protest against the anti-Jewish laws—as early as the spring and summer of 1941. However, he did so not in public but in private letters to the Vichy government and to Cardinal Gerlier. Since he did not want to distance himself completely from Vichy, Boegner's protest was somewhat restrained. He signaled that he, too, like the high Vichy officials, differentiated between French Jews and immigrant Jews. "I underline French, for . . . I have indicated clearly our belief that the immigration of great numbers of non-French Jews and massive and unjustified naturalization do pose a problem for the state." In the same vein, in his letter to Pétain of June 27, 1941, he stated that he had "always felt that there was for France, as for all nations, a Jewish problem," but he protested the way Vichy was adopting the German model to deal with this "problem," which was "neither Christian nor human." He repeated his request for a differentiation between immigrant and naturalized

Jews. As noted by Michael Marrus, Boegner, like other clerics who in private entertained friendly relations with Jews, accepted the idea of the state's right to pass legislation to solve the "Jewish problem," and upheld some form of discrimination, at least against part of the Jewish community—the foreign Jews.[8] A bit later, a conclave of lower-ranking Protestant clerics took a more forceful stand when, in September 1941, a group of fifteen pastors met in Pomeyrol and adopted a resolution that included a "solemn protest against any statute rejecting the Jews." The pastors, however, also repeated the canard "that the state finds itself faced with a problem which it has to solve" but warned "against any law placing Jews outside the human community." In summary, there were at this early stage no public outcries by either the Catholic or the Protestant religious establishment against the notion of measures against the Jewish population, as long as they were within certain limits.[9]

Among Catholics, as with Protestants, stirrings were felt mostly within the lower clergy. In June 1941, four Catholic professors of theology (Fathers Joseph Chaine, Louis Richard, Joseph Bonsirven, and Henri de Lubac) met in Lyon and issued a document condemning the racial laws. A similar lone voice was voiced by Father Riquet, who asked the assembled cardinals and archbishops in Paris, in July 1941, to condemn the racial laws as "a scandal for the Christian conscience" because they were meant to suppress another religion. His request was denied. That same year, Cardinal Gerlier lectured a visiting Jewish delegation on the "sins" of the prewar government of Premier Léon Blum (who happened to be Jewish) and the need for "expiation."

Despite such efforts, the voices of protest among the rank and file of the Catholic Church could not be stilled. These crystallized, toward the end of 1941, in the publication of a clandestine journal, *Témoignage Chrétien* ("Christian Witness"), in Lyon, edited by Father Pierre Chaillet, and distributed over the following years to thousands of Catholic and Protestant clerics throughout the country. The first issue, which appeared in November 1941, carried the motto: "France, take care lest you lose your soul" (*France, prends garde de ne perdre ton ame*), and was written by Father Gaston Fessard, a Jesuit priest, who had denounced the anti-Jewish laws as early as December 1940. He now reminded readers of the statement of Pope Pius XI in 1938 that "spiritually we are Semites," and he protested against the internment of Jews in French camps as well as the antisemitic campaign and vilification of Jews in the press. In subsequent issues, the paper declared antisemitism incompatible with Christian doctrine. *Témoignage Chrétien* minced no words in its condemnation of the anti-Jewish laws and urged its readers to declare their "disgust and indignation that one could practice such a human hunt on our soil . . . . If need be, we must have the courage to prevent the delivery to the Gestapo of the victims of these arbitrary measures. Saving an innocent person is not a rebellious act, but obedience to the unwritten laws of justice and charity." *Témoignage* also quoted the Catholic theologian Jacques Maritain, who warned against the antisemitic virus "which is in most of us, in a more or less latent or active condition" and held that this "spiritual disease" was nothing more than a revolt against Christianity. Furthermore, when assaulting Jews, antisemites are actually "spitting" on Christ, for they cannot forgive the Jews for having introduced to the world a message that stands opposed to tyranny and material gain. As for the Jewish refusal to accept Christ, which continued to trouble Maritain, he was sure that this "tension" would eventually resolved through a reconciliation between the synagogue and the church. Most of the articles in *Témoignage* were written by Jesuit priests, and in collaboration with the Protestant pastor Roland de Pury, of Lyon, up to his arrest in 1943. Some members of the Catholic hierarchy suspected that non-Catholic circles were behind these harsh anti-ecclesiastical statements, and Monsignor Delay, the bishop of Marseilles, publicly reprimanded the journal's severe criticism.[10] As it turned out, the widely read *Témoignage Chrétien* had a great impact in shaping the minds of many clerics to a more active stand against the antisemitic measures of the Vichy regime.

Among Protestants, we have already noted Boegner's guarded protest of the government's anti-Jewish measures. Boegner assumed wrongly that Vichy was acting under pressure from the Germans. When he met Prime Minister Darlan, Boegner was reassured that the anti-Jewish measures were mainly directed against the foreign and non-naturalized Jews. Not yet fully satisfied, Boegner asked to see Pétain and met with him on January 18, 1942. According to Boegner, who at the time was still sympathetic to *le Maréchal*, Pétain said that the anti-Jewish laws caused him much suffering, but that he was powerless to prevent abuses in their application. Pétain also said that he was surprised at the relative indifference of the churches to what was happening on the Jewish issue. After the war, Pastors Elie Brée and Laurent Olivès admitted that Protestants had not been totally free of antisemitic sentiments, and had professed too much loyalty to Pétain, the victor of Verdun. At the same time, there was a strong pacifist current in the Protestant camp, mainly among a group known as the Social Christians. Insofar as the Jews were concerned, these clerics continued to debate their guilt for the crucifixion. Pastor F. J. Leenhardt, who lectured at the theological faculty in Geneva, held to the traditional deicide charge: "Israel has rejected Christ. . . . Jews are for us believers who, while knowing the true God, pushed aside his Son. . . . They have been, since then, broken, dispersed, repulsed by others, and, religiously speaking, rejected by God." To help the Jews put an end to their constant wandering and suffering at the hands of their host nations, Jacques Maritain urged a greater evangelization of the Christian message among them, while simultaneously rejecting all forms of antisemitism. How these two aims were to coalesce was not explained.[11]

* * *

In May 1942, the Germans decreed that all Jews over the age of six in the occupied zone were required to wear the yellow star. Here Vichy put its foot down and refused to extend the decree to the Vichy zone, for fear of shocking public opinion, and the Germans did not insist, even after they overran the Vichy zone in November 1942. On the other hand, Vichy ordered all vital documents held by Jews (identity card, work permit, and ration card) to be stamped *Juif* or *Juive* by December 11, 1942, an act already enforced in the occupied zone over a year earlier. To Monsignor Carmine Rocco, representing the papal nuncio Valeri, Pierre Laval (restored as prime minister in April 1942, replacing Admiral Darlan) sarcastically remarked that the star decree should not be a surprise to the Vatican, since it was the popes who had first introduced the yellow hat to mark out Jews from other people.[12] The star imposition was followed, in July 1942, with the start of the mass deportation of Jews to concentration camps in occupied Poland. Per agreement between SS chief Reynhard Heydrich and French police head René Bousquet, the arrest of Jews in both zones was to be carried out by French police and gendarmes, who were also to guard them while they were temporarily held in the Drancy internment camp before being handed over to the Germans. On the morning of July 16, 1942, some 9,000 French police and gendarmes launched a city-wide dragnet of Jews in Paris, arresting close to 13,000, who were first held in the Vélodrome d'Hiver sports stadium, in stifling heat and lack of hygienic conditions, before being moved to Drancy. In the "free" zone, Vichy agreed to hand over only foreign Jews to the Germans, but this included the aged, the sick, as well as children over the age of two belonging to those arrested, even if born in France and naturalized. Some exemptions were granted—women about to give birth or with children under two, and Jews married to non-Jews. More Jews continued to be arrested in the coming months and years, and eventually French-naturalized Jews were included whenever a quota had to be filled. Deportation levels dipped somewhat in 1943, but rose again in 1944, and continued unabated. By the time of France's liberation, a total of over 75,000 Jews were turned over to the Germans for destruction in the death camps, a figure that certainly would have risen had the Allies not liberated France in August 1944. Of these, only 2,800 survived. To this death toll must be added the 3,000 who died in French internment camps, and about 1,000 executed in France, for a total death toll of approximately 77,000—or 24 percent of the French Jewish community. The fact that the French police seized far more Jews than the Germans remains a stain on France's name and national reputation.[13]

The start of mass deportations in the summer of 1942 sparked the first public protests by church dignitaries. Monsignor Jules-Géraud Saliège, in Toulouse, led the way. When he received news of the brutal way the deportations were carried out in his diocese, the aged and partially paralyzed archbishop penned a pastoral letter, which he ordered read in his diocese on July 30,1942, and in which he condemned the deportation of Jews in no uncertain terms. He chose his words carefully: "That children, women, fathers, and mothers should be treated like animals, that family members should be separated and sent off to an unknown destination, it has been reserved for our time to witness this sad spectacle. . . . Jews are men. Jewesses are women. Foreigners are men and women. All is not permitted against them, against these men, these women, these fathers and mothers. They are part of the human race. They are our brothers like so many others. A Christian cannot forget it." Saliège tempered these words by exempting the French government from this crime. "France, beloved homeland . . . I have no doubt that you are not responsible for these horrors." One had to take care not to precipitate an open breach with Vichy.

Most of the priests in Saliège's diocese obeyed their archbishop and read the letter from the pulpit. Reprinted in resistance pamphlets distributed widely in France, it had an electrifying effect on public opinion and encouraged clerics to actively participate in rescue efforts. Three months later, Saliège wrote in the religious journal *Sémaine Religieuse*: "The death of our Savior is not to be imputed to the sons of men. Israel's infidelity is no more to blame than the infidelity of modern nations." Much earlier, in 1933, he had written: "I cannot forget that Jesus' stem flourished in Israel, and produced its fruit. The Virgin, Christ, and the first disciples were of the Jewish race. How can you think that I do not feel tied to Israel like the bough which the trunk has borne."[14] In addition, Saliège provided the Jewish activist Georges Garel with a letter of introduction that opened the doors of many Catholic relief organizations and religious institutions.

Not daring to move personally against Saliège, Vichy solicited an article from a pro-regime theologian who, quoting Pope Benedict XIV and Thomas Aquinas, tried to prove that antisemitism was in line with traditional Christian doctrine. Prime Minister Laval refrained from moving against the aged and semi-paralyzed bishop. On June 9, 1944, the Germans came to arrest Saliège, but taking note of his weak physical state, the Gestapo left. Instead they arrested the bishop of Montauban, Jean-Marie Théas, who, like Saliège, had issued a pastoral letter to be read from the pulpits in his diocese in which he blasted in no uncertain terms the antisemitic measures of the Vichy regime. Théas had declared "the indignant protest of the Christian conscience, and I proclaim that all men, Aryan or non-Aryan, are brothers, for they are created by God." Going further than Saliège, Théas stigmatized Vichy's antisemitic laws. "The present antisemitic measures are a contemptible attack on human dignity, a violation of the most sacred rights of the individual and the family." Théas had also allowed the Jewish activist Ninon Hait to work out of his office preparing false documents for Jews in hiding. In addition, he arranged for a Jewish-born Catholic prelate, Abbé Alexandre Glasberg, sought by the Gestapo for his role in helping fleeing Jews, to be sheltered in his diocese, under an assumed name. Arrested, Théas was moved to Compiegne, where he remained imprisoned until August 29, 1944—that is, France's liberation.[15]

Several others bishops in the Vichy zone followed suit, although in less condemnatory terms. In Marseilles, Monsignor Delay denounced the indiscriminate arrest of men, women, and children who are being sent "possibly to their death." But he weakened, if not nullified, the effect of his message by giving vent to antisemitic notions: "We do not ignore the fact that the Jewish Question poses difficult national and international problems. We are well aware that our country has the right to take all appropriate steps to defend itself against those who, especially in recent years, have done her so much harm and to punish those who abuse the hospitality that has so liberally been extended to them." But this justification, in his words, did not allow "the mass arrest, simply because they are Jews and strangers, men, women, and children, who committed no personal infraction." Cardinal Gerlier waited a full month after Saliège before himself issuing a public protest, on September 6, 1942, condemning the deportation of Jews for no fault of their own. At the same time, he intimated his approbation of some of the anti-Jewish measures, for "there is a problem for the French authorities to resolve." Of those who publicly protested, only Saliège and Théas felt no need to allude to a "Jewish problem." All in all, fewer than half of the bishops in the Vichy zone made public statements from the pulpit, and not one in the occupied zone. In Paris, Cardinal Suhard confined himself to a private letter to Pétain in which he spoke up in defense of the "inviolable rights of the human person," and urged restraint in the measures taken, especially against mothers and children.[16]

Having issued these appeals, Catholic dignitaries felt it necessary to take a step backwards by reconfirming their allegiance to the Vichy regime. Saliège wrote that he objected to "the indecent use that certain people have made of his letter," and continued by renewing "his complete loyalty to the *Maréchal*." Cardinals Suhard and Gerlier made similar pronouncements of loyalty, to be followed by the archbishops of Rheims and Besançon, and the bishops of Châlons, Verdun, Mans, Chartres, Soissons, Beauvais, Nancy, Saint-Dié, Langres, Troyes, and Vannes. To signal their appeasement of the regime,

Suhard and Gerlier, the two princes of the Catholic church in both zones, appeared together with Laval and Pétain at a military review in Vichy on October 29, 1942. When the deportations resumed the following year, the French bishops did not renew their protests, with the exception of Suhard, who wrote to Pétain asking him to moderate the conditions of the arrested Jews, and told a satisfied Pétain that "everyone knows that the French government cannot be held entirely responsible for the steps taken." Suhard's concern was limited to asking only that these measures "would at least" not be done "with excessive severity and inhumanity." In other words, the deportations could continue, but without excessive brutality. On September 20, 1942, Monsignor Jean-Joseph Moussaron, of Albi, also had a protesting letter read from the pulpit, expressing "the consternation which the deportation of Jews has caused among us," especially in that "women were separated from their husbands, children from their parents. Religion and humanity cannot but protest against this violation and disregard of the sacred rights of the human person and family and of the divine law of charity." Moussaron then mellowed his statement by acquitting the Vichy regime of any responsibility. "Let no one see in our words a diminution of loyalty toward the government which we have not ceased to praise. The government is not to be blamed. Far from having taking the initiative in these measures, so counter to French tradition and the Christian spirit, it had to submit to them as a consequence of the defeat."[17]

Spurred by their religious elders, many members of the clergy lent a hand in the rescue of Jews. Perhaps for the first time, there was a crossing of denominational lines as Catholic priests and Protestant pastors worked hand-in-hand in a combined effort to help Jews avoid arrest and deportation. On the Catholic side, Archbishop Saliège, following his pastoral letter of July 1942, offered the facilities of his religious institutions to Jews in need. Meeting in his office with Georges Garel, of the Jewish children's welfare organization, known by its acronym OSE, Saliège handed him a personal letter of introduction that opened of the doors of many religious institutions to Garel and his aide, Andrée Salomon, in their effort to find sheltering places for Jewish children. Garel and Salomon placed their first twenty-four children with the *Oeuvre de Sainte-Germaine*, a Catholic philanthropic organization in Saliège's diocese. While Saliège's coadjutor, Monsignor Louis de Courrèges d'Ustou, was also of immense help to Garel, it is Saliège whom Garel remembered with great affection. "From my first contact with him," he wrote, "I knew I was in the presence of a superior man. That man, I can and I must say, had the stuff of a saint." Garel added that in every department and diocese he was able to find religious or lay institutions willing to help hide children. Similarly, in Nice, the Jewish activist Moussa Abadi was helped immensely by Bishop Paul Rémond, while in Montauban, Archbishop Théas, in the words of Jewish activists Edouard and

Shatta Simon, "opened for us, as for others, the Collège de Sorreze, that of St. Antoine de Padoue near Brive, and other religious secondary establishments, where we were able to place a very large number of young people."[18] Also meriting mention is the *Amitié Chretiénne* association, created in Lyon in May 1941, representing both the Catholic and Protestant churches, and headed by Father Pierre Chaillet and Abbé Alexandre Glasberg. Its program called for assisting refugees of all sorts, but especially fleeing Jews. *Amitié* produced thousands of identity and ration cards, with funds coming mainly from the American Jewish Joint Distribution Committee. Amitié was at first tolerated by Vichy, but as its activities took on a more clandestine aspect, it moved its offices to Grenoble and then went underground. In January 1943, Chaillet was arrested by the Germans, but as he was using an assumed name, they failed to identify him, and he was released.[19]

On the Protestant front, the earlier pro-Pétain spell shared by Boegner and the vast majority of other clerics had dissipated by the summer of 1942. On September 6, 1942, Boegner brought more than sixty-seven pastors together in a conclave in Mas Soubeyran (Gard) and called upon them to save Jews. Addressing the gathering, Boegner urged the assembled clerics to keep faith "until death," and remain Good Samaritans toward the suffering Jews. According to Pastor Idebert Exbrayat, Boegner stated that with the roundup of Jews by the French police, the Vichy government was now a tool in the hands of the Germans, and therefore it was morally right to deny the government the right to arrest Jews. In some individual cases, he was instrumental in arranging hiding places for fleeing Jews. Earlier, in a letter to Pétain on June 27, 1942, Boegner still spoke of "the Jewish problem," but objected to baptized Jews having to wear the yellow star ("to wear ostensibly before men the title of Jew while they themselves are proud to wear before God the title of Christian"). Two months later, with the deportations in full swing, Boegner minced no words in his second letter to Pétain, on August 20, 1942, where he expressed the Protestant churches' "immense sadness at the decisions taken by the French government with regard to the foreign Jews (whether baptized or not). No Frenchman could remain indifferent to what has been happening since August 2nd in the sheltering [*sic*] and internment camps," where men and women are delivered to the Germans, "many of whom know in advance the fate which awaits them. . . . Christian churches, whatever their confessional diversities, would be unfaithful to their main teachings if they did not raise their painful protests in the face of the violation of such teachings." Boegner ended his message with a plea to Pétain to take steps to keep France from "inflict[ing] upon herself a moral defeat of incalculable weight."

This was followed by a tête-à-tête confrontation between Boegner and Prime Minister Pierre Laval on September 9, 1942. The meeting ended badly.

As reported by Boegner, it went as follows. *Boegner:* "Will you hunt down people?" *Laval:* "We will seek them wherever they're hiding." *Boegner:* "Do you agree that we save the children?" *Laval:* "Children must remain with their parents." *Boegner:* "But don't you know that they will be separated?" *Laval:* "No." *Boegner:* "I tell you that yes." *Laval:* "What do you want to do with the children?" *Boegner:* "French families will adopt them." *Laval:* "I don't want this; not one must remain in France!" Boegner tried to persuade Laval that the Jews were not being deported for field labor, as officially proclaimed, but to be killed. "I talked to him about massacres, and he responded about gardening!" Before leaving, Boegner told Laval: "I am forced to impress upon you the gravity of the situation. The churches cannot remain silent in the face of such facts." Laval shot back: "The churches? They have behaved quite differently! I told this to the representative of the nunciature who came to see me. Besides, let them do what they wish; I will continue doing what I have to." With this the conversation came to an end. After this encounter, Boegner was even more determined to urge his followers to offer help to Jews, but the Protestant community did not need much persuasion to act, and its share in the rescue effort was appreciably larger than its representation in the general and mostly-Catholic population. Protestants make up about a third of all French clerics honored by Yad Vashem.[20]

The relatively greater participation of Protestant clerics was largely due to two principal reasons: their own history as a persecuted minority, which made them more sensitive to the persecution of other ethnic-religious groups,[21] and their acceptance of a Christian fundamental belief in the special role of the Jewish people in the overall divine providence, and the religious obligation to come to their aid when circumstances required it. Many Jews found shelter in two heavily Protestant enclaves, Le Chambon-sur-Lignon and the Cevennes. The pastors there had no problem in mobilizing their parishioners for this purpose, although many of them had never met a Jew or even knew that they existed. In the words of Pastor G. Gillier: "Jews, for us, were rather a myth. They were a biblical people. However, in all of the Cevennes, we did not know them. In any case, I never saw one. . . . The Jewish Question was not merely a biblical question, but a reality. From that point on, action could begin." In addition, the CIMADE movement, a Protestant relief organization founded in 1939, and headed by Madeleine Barot and Pastor Jean Delpech, to help people evacuated from the war zones of Alsace-Lorraine, quickly turned its attention to helping Jews imprisoned in French detention camps with food and medicine, and then facilitating their escapes to safe havens inside the country or across the border in Spain or Switzerland. For this purpose, the CIMADE opened four sheltering centers in the south, in Chambon-sur-Lignon, Marseilles, Vabre, and Pomeyrol, where most of the residents were

Jews liberated from French internment camps. The Quakers, too, participated in the rescue of Jews. Helga Holbek, a Quaker associate, was active in spiriting children out of Gurs camp and either placing them in private homes or arranging their surreptitious crossing into Switzerland. In the Lyon area, Gilbert Lesage, another Quaker, played a pivotal role in the rescue of children during the Venissieux incident, an incident we shall describe later.[22]

As for the mostly Protestant community of Le Chambon-sur-Lignon, in the mountainous region of Haute Loire, starting in the summer of 1942 many Jews began to pour into the region, arriving there from many directions—Lyon in the north and Marseilles in the south. In Marseilles, the Jewish activist Joseph Bass (known as Monsieur André), who had set up his own rescue network, directed many Jews to Le Chambon. Some continued on to the Swiss border with the help of couriers like Mireille Philip, the wife of a minister in the London-based Free French government of De Gaulle. No exact figures exist on the number of Jews who sought refuge in the Le Chambon area, although estimates run into several thousands. In some hamlets, Jews could be found in almost every house. Twenty-three church ministers served the Plateau Vivarais, where Le Chambon is located, including twelve Protestant parishes, and counting among them Darbyists, Catholics, and Swiss ministers. The Darbyists, a dissident Protestant sect founded by John Nelson Darby in the early nineteenth century in Ireland, held to no established clergy, and very little respect for the secular authorities. In July 1941, when Le Chambon received an order to sound the bells of the chapel on August 1 in honor of the Vichy-created French Legion, the Darbyist woman guardian of the chapel, known as Amélie, decided that this was not to be obeyed, since "the bells are meant not for the *Maréchal*, but only for God!"[23]

There were seven institutional houses in Le Chambon that sheltered Jews and other fleeing refugees. Utilizing coded messages when passing Jews from one to another, the Protestant pastors would say, for instance, "I'm sending you three Old Testaments." The leading spirit of the rescue enterprise was undoubtedly Pastor Andre Trocmé, also known for his staunch pacifism, which led him to oppose armed resistance in the region, a stand over which he was challenged by other Protestant pastors. His closest collaborator was Pastor Edouard Théis, who founded the Collège Cévenol secondary school, which in 1942 counted 300 students, many of them fleeing Jews. Many relief organizations operated in the Le Chambon area, including the Protestant CIMADE, the Red Cross, the American-based Quakers and Fellowship of Reconciliation, and the Swiss Children's Aid, as well as Jewish organizations, such as OSE. Funding came from various Protestant organizations. Local residents who kept Jews in their homes refused to register them in their town halls, as required by Vichy laws. The spirit of the Protestants in the region is best captured by the words of Magda Trocmé (the wife of Pastor Trocmé): "It was not decided from one day to the next what we would have to do. . . . A person doesn't sit down and say I'm going to do this and this and that. We had no time to think. . . . Sometimes people ask me, 'How did you make a decision?' There was no decision to make. The issue was: 'Do you think we're all brothers or not? Do you think it is unjust to turn in the Jews or not? Then let us try to help!' "[24]

Another Protestant enclave deeply involved in the rescue of Jews was located in the mountainous Cévennes region, to the south of Le Chambon, and lying astride the two regional departments of Lozère and Gard. According to one estimate, between 800 and 1,000 Jews found refuge in this mountainous redoubt, an area of about 2,000 square kilometers, and counting some 40,000 inhabitants. Villages such as Saint-Germain-de-Calberte, Vébron, and Vialas were termed by one observer as "rescue villages." Before the war, many residents had left the region to seek better economic advantages elsewhere, as a result of which there were many empty homes waiting to be leased to whatever new arrivals happened to wander in—resistance fighters, as well as fleeing Jews. People started arriving in September 1942, and were assisted by local pastors to find places to stay, while simultaneously lending a hand in agricultural work. Among the rescuing pastors were Raoul Lhermet in Saint-André-de Valborgne, Elie Brée, in Caveirac, Roland Polex and Edmond Peloux, in St.-Jean-du-Gard, Robert Joseph in Clarensac, Franck Robert in Meyrueis, André Gall in Florac, Laurent Olivès and François Chazel in Vébron et Rousses. One typical story is that of Majer Landau, originally from Germany, who, fleeing arrest in October 1942, arrived in Saint-Germain-de-Calberte. He was standing in the middle of the village, uncertain what to do, when he was approached by Paul Tinel, an officer in the Salvation Army, who in straightforward language addressed him, "My brother, you are in need of assistance!" When Majer told him he was a Jew, armed with forged identity documents, and with a wife and daughter waiting in Montpellier, Tinel told him: "You are coming to my place, and we will arrange a separate place for your wife and daughter," and so it was. Later, in the spring of 1943, when some gendarmes came to look for foreign Jews, Majer's daughter Sylvie was picked up by Pastor Gaston Martin and his wife, in St. German de Calberte. Over dinner, the Martins asked the eleven-year-old Sylvie about her religion, to which she responded that she had none, adding: "I know that I am Jewish . . . [but] I don't know what that means." The pastor responded that out of respect for her as a person, even though she was not a practicing Jew, he would no longer intone a Christian prayer over dinner. Somewhat later, Sylvie was taken by Tinel and placed in a Salvation Army home in Grenoble.[25]

At times Jewish children sheltered in religious institutions faced the problem of dealing with subtle conversion efforts by their caretakers. This was especially so in Catholic institutions, where children could not avoid being exposed to religious artifacts, such as crucifixes and depiction of saints, with no similar opportunity for a counter-balanced exposure to Jewish religious symbols. Abuses, often unintentional, were unavoidable on the part of the nuns and monks who showered the children with warmth and sometimes also with religious messages. In the case of the previously mentioned Sylvie Landau, Tinel had originally arranged for her to stay in the Salvation Army Home in Grenoble. Later, due to the fear of a Gestapo raid, she was sent to the Notre-Dame-de Sion convent in the city and told to tell the Mother Superior her true identity and her desperate situation. It is well to remember that this order was founded by baptized Jews, for the purpose of missionizing among Jews, and many of its nuns were converts. In Sylvie's words: "The Mother Superior then took me on her knees; she kissed me; she was very kind and advised me on what one should say and not say. The problem was that I was of the age where all girls already had their first communion. I could participate in the catechism . . . but not communion." Everyone was told that the communion was being postponed until the return of her father from a German prison. "I owe these people a tremendous debt of gratitude; there was never any conversion attempt whatsoever." However, one day, the institute chaplain asked her whether she wished to convert. Sylvie declined, and was not bothered again. On August 15, 1944, Grenoble was liberated, and Sylvia left the convent.[26]

Things did not go so smoothly for Rosa Liwarek, who had to regularly listen to accounts of the guilt of the Jews. Sheltered in a village in the Brittany region, she was urged to convert by the local priest. In her words, "the priest knew I was Jewish. While I was being baptized he said that he was pleased to do so; the Jews had killed Christ but I would be forgiven." Similarly for Denise Baumann, in the same place, who recalled a priest coming every Thursday to show the Jewish children films on the death of Jesus. "He told us at the same time that it was the Jews who had killed him and that our parents had been deported because they had not believed in him. If we concerted, we would be saved."[27]

One should note in this context that such outright abuses were the exception, and the Catholic hierarchy was mostly opposed even to subtle attempts, and went so far as to revoke conversions improperly implemented by overzealous nuns. An especially touching case is that of Saul Friedländer, who entered a Catholic boarding school with a letter from his father consenting to baptism. At the end of the war, he had decided to become a priest. Then, in January 1946, a Jesuit priest told him about Auschwitz and spoke disapprovingly about antisemitism. The sympathetic approach of the Jesuit priest had a profound impact on Saul, especially the way the priest tempered his words about the Jews with much emotion and respect. "He did not press me to choose one path or the other—and perhaps he would have preferred to see me remain Catholic—but his sense of justice (or was it a profound charity?) led him to recognize my right to judge for myself, by helping me to renew the contact with my past." Saul Friedländer decided to return to the Jewish fold.[28]

In one celebrated rescue operation, Catholics, Protestants, and Jews acted in concert to save over a hundred Jewish children from deportation. This took place at the Vénissieux camp, outside Lyon, where about 1,200 foreign-born Jews were arrested on August 26, 1942, and were waiting to board a deportation train arriving the next morning from the south with its load of imprisoned Jews. At first, Vichy announced that children unaccompanied by their parents could be released. Acting on this loophole, Father Alexandre Glasberg (Catholic), Madeleine Barot (Protestant-CIMADE), Gilbert Lesage (Quaker, and also representing a Vichy agency for supervising foreign workers), and Georges Garel (Jewish) were allowed inside the camp that evening as a screening commission to pick out the unaccompanied children under age sixteen and have them freed. In the early hours of August 29, a total of 110 children were ready to leave. Glasberg was, at this critical moment, in the camp's office, waiting for the commandant to return, when a message was received from the regional prefect, Angeli, canceling the previous authorization to let unaccompanied children go free. Glasberg quickly stuffed the message in his cassock. The commandment, on his return, never found out about the message from his superior and authorized the children's departure. The children were immediately taken by bus to a former convent in Lyon that was being used by the Jewish Scouts organization (EIF) and then were quickly dispersed to various locations: some in Chambon-sur-Lignon; others, with the help of the Catholic activist Germaine Ribière, in Catholic institutions, such as the Oeuvre Sainte-Germaine in Toulouse, headed by Sister Louise Thèbe; still others, with the assistance of the Jewish activist Renée Neher, to other safe locations.

Of special interest is Cardinal Gerlier's peculiar behavior during this incident. Father Roger Braun reported attending a meeting in Gerlier's office on September 2, 1942, with the participation of Abbé Glasberg, Father Chaillet, Abbé Alphonse Lagarde, and Jean-Marie Soutou. Suddenly the phone rang; it was Prefect Angeli on the line, furious at having been outwitted and determined to have the children returned. He told Gerlier that at 6:00 p.m. that evening a car would be added to a train bringing Jewish deportees from Camp des Milles, outside Marseilles, on the way to Drancy camp; this added car was to be filled with the escaped Vénissieux children. Angeli insisted that they had to be put on the train. Gerlier was heard responding: "*Monsieur le Prefet*, the families have charged me with the guardianship of their children. You are not going to force a father to deliver his children to the police." It was a long conversation. "What upset me," said Braun afterwards, was that Monsignor Gerlier continuously placed his hands on the receiver to tell a joke, and this was really not the right moment." Finally, Gerlier was heard to say: "Well, *Monsieur le Prefet*, if you wish to come to the archdiocese, then come to the archdiocese! But you will not have the children"; and he hung up. He then said to the assembled clerics: "Get lost, all of you. I can no longer be seen with you; the prefect is on his way here to ask me to turn over the children, and I don't especially want to know where they are. Try to manage. *Au revoir*." Before leaving, he asked the three to disclose the whereabouts of the children who were still in the Lyon region, promising to keep it secret. Glasberg and Chaillet were dumbfounded, hesitant to refuse a request from the head of the Catholic Church. According to Glasberg, Soutou was about to turn over the addresses when Glasberg stopped him. "I was ready to kill him," Glasberg related in a postwar statement. Soutou calmed him, stating that he was giving the cardinal false addresses, since according to Soutou, "I have no confidence whatsoever in Gerlier" (or did he perhaps mean that he did not trust the promise made by Angeli, who according to Gerlier had told him over the phone that he was prepared to agree not to deport the children as long as they were turned over?). According to another account, Father Chaillet also declined the cardinal's request, and was told by him to go into seclusion for his own safety. Chaillet hid in the psychiatric hospital in Privas. Later, sought by the Gestapo, he moved to Saint-Julien-de-Ratz under an assumed name. As for Prefect Angeli, he was furious at having been outwitted, but decided not to tackle the highest authority of the Catholic Church, and finally gave up his quest for the children's return. The 110 children were thus saved from the clutches of the Germans and their Vichy collaborators.[29]

The Jewish survival rate in France was relatively high in comparison to the figures for other West European countries. About 75 percent of the original 325,000 Jewish population in France on the eve of the German invasion saw it through the Holocaust. Of these, approximately 5,000 were able to leave the country legally before exit travel was banned in November 1942 and an estimated 50,000 escaped to Spain or Switzerland; 20,000–30,000, mostly children, were placed by Jewish rescue organizations with non-Jewish families; about 30,000 Jews were able to live openly in Paris because the Germans did not round them up; and well over 100,000 Jews, perhaps as many as 150,000, survived in some form of hiding or by blending into the population as a whole. Favoring Jewish survival were geographical and political considerations, such as the Vichy regime's concern to protect the 190,000 naturalized Jews at the expense of the foreign Jews. Moreover, the Italians, in the seven departments they administered, placed severe obstacles on the deportation of the close to 50,000 Jews in their region. In several instances, they forced the French police to release Jews already arrested in Annecy and Grenoble. The widespread activities of clandestine Jewish rescue organizations also contributed to the large number of Jews saved, as well as the favorable public opinion regarding Jewish victims of persecution and—of great importance—the involvement of many members of the Christian clergy of all denominations in the rescue of Jews. At the same time, Jews constantly had to be on the alert to avoid arrest and not fall victim to the Germans, the French police, and the Milice, a Vichy government–sanctioned militia that right up to the end pursued Jews in hiding even more relentlessly than the Germans and physically assaulted their res-cuers.[30]

Help by Catholic Clergy

Turning to individual clerics who helped Jews on the run, for lack of space we can only note a few of the stories of these Good Samaritans—stories with a special interest and significance. We begin with Father Théomir Devaux, in Paris, who served as a parish priest at the St. Sulpice Church, and also head-ed the Fathers of Our Lady of Zion monastery. Passing the word around trust-ed confidantes, Jewish children were brought to him (sometimes thirty-five in one day) and then dispersed to sheltering homes or institutions in the Paris region. He facilitated the rescue of hundreds of children (some claim as many as 400 or more), in collaboration with Sister Francia of the Sisters of Zion convent, and in coordination with various Jewish organizations (UGIF, OSE, Rue Amelot, and WIZO). The children were armed with forged papers, some of which he produced himself. In this, he was assisted by Father Emile Planckaert, and also worked closely with Sister Josephine (Denise Paulin) of the Notre Dames de Sion in Grenoble. One person saved in this manner was Fanny Baruch, whom Devaux placed in the Institution de la Croix in Antony, where other Jewish girls were also hidden. In some instances, children were hidden in his own home for a night or two before proceeding on their journey for safekeeping. He reportedly refused to take advantage of the situation by seducing the children away from their religion, and after the war he was active in returning them to their parents or to Jewish organizations. In his journal, *Les Cahiers Sioniens*, which was suppressed during the occupation and resumed publication after the war, he wrote in praise of Jews and Judaism.[31]

The story of Lucien Louis Bunel, better known under his religious name as Père Jacques, ended in tragedy. A member of the Carmelite order, he headed the St. Thérèse Petit-Collège, a private Carmelite boarding school in Avon, near Fontainebleau, for children of middle-class and aristocratic families. At first, like most other Frenchmen, he supported the Pétain regime, and he kept a portrait of the *Maréchal* in the main study hall. But this quickly turned to disappointment. His first act of defiance against the antisemitic laws took the form of hiring a Jew, Emil Weil, a local botanist, prohibited from teaching under the Vichy antisemitic laws, to teach mathematics to his pupils, and another Jew, Maurice Bas (known as Maurice Lefèvre), as a domestic servant. He followed this up by admitting three Jewish boys to the school under assumed names: Jean Bonnet (Hans-Helmut Michel, originally from Nazi Germany), Maurice Sabatier (Maurice Schlosser), and Jacques Dupré (Jacques Halpern). Before arriving there, Hans-Helmut's parents had first contacted the Sisters of the Order of Zion in Paris, and were referred by Mother Superior Louisa to Father Devaux, who sent Hans, under the name Jean Bonnet, to Father Jacques. Tipped off by an informer, on January 15, 1944 the Gestapo raided the premises and arrested the three boys, as well as Father Jacques. As a lesson and warning, the school's pupils were ordered to line up in the courtyard and watch as their beloved principal taken away by the Gestapo. Before that, the Gestapo questioned the pupils: "Three Jewish students were arrested in this school. Are there any Jews among you?" "No. We did not know they were Jewish." "You did know it." "These are our comrades, like the others." "You are not comrades to Negroes; you are not comrades to Jews." Father Jacques's parting words, "*Au revoir les Enfants*," was the title of a 1980s film by one of his students, turned filmmaker. He also managed to say: "See you soon; continue without me." The assembled children shouted back: "*Au revoir, Mon Père*." That same day, the Germans closed the school. Emil Weil, his mother and sister, were also arrested in their Fontainebleau home, and taken away. Maurice Bas, the Jewish servant, who was housed in a room across the street from the school, was able to flee in time. Interrogated by the Gestapo, Father Jacques was asked why he had disobeyed the laws of the Germans. To which he reportedly answered: "I don't know these laws. I only know one law, that of the Gospels and of charity. You may shoot me if you so wish. I have no fear of dying. On the contrary—it would be for me the greatest joy… Instead of killing fathers of families, and making their wives widows and their children orphans, take me and shoot me." Gestapo agent Korf later remarked: "This is a man. What a man! He only has one flaw. He is not a Nazi." Father Jacques was moved to several camps, and eventually landed in Mauthausen concentration camp. Transferred to a hard-labor assignment in Gusen camp, he was liberated by advancing U.S. troops on April 25, 1945, but by then his body had been terribly weakened by the deprivations of camp life. Taken to a nearby hospital, in Linz, he died on June 2, 1945, while murmuring: "Avon, Avon." His body was returned to Avon for burial, in a ceremony attended by Chief Rabbi Jacob Kaplan. Before his arrest, he is reported to have said to a friend: "It is quite possible that serious things will soon happen to me. If I am shot, take comfort in the fact that I have achieved my goal: to give my life for all those who suffer." The three Jewish boys, together with Emil Weil and his family, all disappeared in the Holocaust.[32]

Moving south of Paris, in Oullins, a suburb of Lyon, Father Auguste Mayrand, headed a Dominican monastery and boys' school, where he saved dozens of Jewish children and many adults by offering them shelter in his school. The Gannatolskies, husband and wife, left their eight-year-old son Charles with Mayrand from 1942 until 1944, under a borrowed identity. To mask the child's identity, Father Mayrand taught him how to feign saying the prayers by moving his lips, and how to properly cross himself. As Charles recalled, he was told to repeat to himself, "My name is Gannat; I am Catholic; I don't know where my parents are (and this was true), I will never admit that I am Jewish." In the summer of 1944, Mayrand moved Charles to his native village of Channaleille, near Le Puy (Haute-Loire). After a long stay under Mayrand's fatherly care, Charles asked to be baptized, Mayrand vigorously turned him down on various pretexts, repeatedly stressing his Jewishness, and even forbade him to join the church choir. After the war, Father Mayrand disclosed to Charles and his sister Viviane that he had sheltered forty-four Jewish children, as well as six adults under the guise of gardeners of the monastery's park.[33]

Roger Braun was a Jesuit priest who served as a chaplain in French internment camps in southern France, side by side with representatives of Protestant and Jewish rescue organizations. In this capacity, he obtained forged documents and ration cards and distributed them to those in need, and he also participated in the smuggling of Jewish children across the borders to Switzerland and Spain. After the German occupation of southern France, in November 1942, he hid all rabbinical seminarians in Limoges in a section of the church used by the choir. When Rabbi Avraham Deutsch was imprisoned in Limoges, Braun visited him and brought him his prayer shawl (tallith) and phylacteries. While a young student in Strasbourg, Braun once explained, he was shocked by the representation on the façade of the main cathedral of the burning of the city's 2,000 Jews in 1349, after they refused to embrace Christianity. He was overcome with an awesome feeling of the need of forgiveness and reconciliation between the two faiths, a belief that continued to inspire him in the postwar period. He once stated, "For myself, I gained much spiritually from contacts with Jews. I acquired a greater respect for God, a greater love as well, and a much greater respect for the Law (Torah)." Before dying from a terminal illness, he specifically asked that the Kaddish, the Jewish prayer for the dead, be pronounced during the burial ceremony—and Chief Rabbi René-Samuel Sirat obligingly performed the request of the dying man. [34]

In September 1943, Werner Epstein, fleeing from Nice, was referred to Father Jean Adrien of the Marist order, who was the head of the Sainte-Marie institution, in Saint-Chamond, Lyon region. Epstein wanted to teach languages and drawing in a Catholic seminary in Charace, near Gap (Hautes Alpes), and asked Adrien to intercede on his behalf. After hearing an account of Epstein's peripatetic wandering, Adrien told him that he would decide the following morning. Next day, Epstein returned, his heart beating with uncertainty, and was told that he had been accepted. Adrien assigned the relieved Epstein to teach fourth and fifth graders in one place, and third graders in another location, in return for food and lodging. In addition, he would be allowed to earn something by giving private lessons. Adrien then instructed Epstein on the practices of the Catholic religion. "He made me learn the 'Our Father' and 'Hail Mary' prayers. He advised me that on Sundays, I should leave my dwelling, and perhaps pass by the church. Thus people would believe that I had attended Mass. 'During the prayers and blessings, remain standing in a dignified position. I don't want you to make the sign of the cross, but move slightly your hand in front of your chest, so that the students and others, accustomed to the sign of the cross, would think that you also did it as a good Catholic.' " Epstein worked as a teacher from November 1943 until April 1944, when, during the Easter vacation, he fell ill while visiting his wife in Gap, and he stayed there until the liberation of the area in August 1944.[35]

Moving south to Castres (Aveyron), in the Tarn region, Father Pierre-Marie Puech, who headed the *Le Petit Seminaire* boarding school, hired Marcel Bernfeld (under the pseudonym of Bernede), in 1943, as an English teacher in the school, and provided for his accommodation. Bernfeld related that among the pupils, many were Jews under assumed names. Henri Englander (aged fifteen), another Jewish youth admitted as a student, wrote that Puech "thanks to his constant, unending (even daily) and patient support, coupled with a spirit of respect toward my religious belief, he gave me the moral support to stand off the stress of the occupation and avoid a mental or spiritual collapse. . . . His behavior was that of a *tzaddik*]righteous person]." Abbé P. Mathieu, a former resident of the school, recalled some of the suspicions and complaints raised some of the students did not comply with certain religious regulations, suspecting foul play about their identity. For the peace of mind of all the students, the Jewish children were urged to attend the obligatory religious instruction. However, their silence and unresponsiveness during these sessions raised new questions. To solve the situation, in the words of Abbé Mathieu, "Abbé Mantoy received them in his office and told them: I will ask you such-and-such a question, and you will answer this way." Thus, the secret of the boys' true identity was reinforced until the end of the occupation. In a letter to Yad Vashem, Father Puech, who after the war was elevated to bishop

of Carcassonne, wrote, "I was always happy and proud to have avoided a tragic and unjustified fate to youth and adults, whose only fault was to belong to
a race despised by the Nazis. I acted with discretion, with no expectation of
any reward, but conscious of having simply done my duty. . . . A new link has
since united me with a people that I love and that has suffered so much."[36]

In some instances, Catholic clerics sheltered Jews, not in religious institutions, but in their own homes. One celebrated incident in Lille led to a long-
lasting friendship between rescuer and rescued. Before the war, Father
Raymond Vancourt, born in 1902, for a time taught theology at the Greek
Melkite seminary in the St. Anne Church in Jerusalem, and in 1932 he earned
a doctorate degree in Eastern Orthodox theology. In Lille since 1934, he lectured at the Jeanne d'Arc school at Lille University. In addition to his spe-
cialization in Oriental Christian thought, he was also adept in the philosophies
of Hegel and Kant.[37] With the coming of the war, he was assigned as chaplain
at the St. Camille clinic, and soon thereafter he met Irene Kahn. Born in
Mannheim, Germany, in 1921, Irene moved to Lille in 1934, where she lived
with relatives and worked translating orders and bills for the Peugeot auto
company, and supplemented her income by tutoring children in English and
German. Fleeing the Germans again in the spring of 1942, she was taken at
night by a friend, Louise Siauve, to an undisclosed location. As Louise and
Irene entered the dimly lit hall of a building, they faced a tall man in priestly
garb, and standing near him, a young woman. It was Father Raymond
Vancourt and his niece and housekeeper, Raymonde Lombard. "I was very
exhausted from tension," Irene recalled; she fell ill, and was bedridden for a
few days. "It was like a nervous breakdown, and the cardiologist who was
called, suggested that I get up and find some interest to keep my mind and
body going." After a while, Vancourt surprised her by asking her to help him
translate some German text into French—whole chapters, indeed, as he was
working on a translation of Nicolai Harmann's *Grundzuge einer Metaphysik
der Erkenntnis* ("Fundamentals of the Metaphysics of Knowledge"). Irene
Kahn gladly obliged, and the book appeared, in French translation, in 1947,
under the title *Principes d'une Métaphysique de la Connaissance*. It included
a special acknowledgment to Irene Kahn, "who during her years of seclusion
forced on her by the antisemitic persecutions, helped us in this translation,
thanks to her knowledge of German." While in Vancourt's home, where she
also did household chores, Irene stayed indoors all the time. "I never opened
the door to anyone ringing the bell; I never went to a window while the curtains were drawn open. . . . At night I often lay in bed hearing the sound of
boots coming nearer, stopping—my heart would stop, and they would stomp
the sidewalk again, and my heart would race ahead of my breath, while I was
lying in a cold sweat. . . . However, a few times the bell would ring, Mr.

L'Abbé would go to the door: it was sometimes German soldiers, and polite-
ly he would direct them away from the house, towering over them, determined, sure of himself and probably praying with every fiber of his being . . .
but he would never let me know." People who visited were told she was a
friend of Raymonde, the priest's nephew. Vancourt's house also served as
shelter for two teenage Jewish girls before they were taken to a convent for
safekeeping. At a later period, Vancourt also admitted Irene's Ehrlich family
relatives. The abbé's house now became crowded; additional beds and cots
were brought in. The Ehrlich children of fifteen and eleven years had to be
kept busy and quiet; they were forbidden to step outside in spite of the balmy
spring weather in 1944. As the liberation neared, the Germans launched
house-to-house searches, and Vancourt's charges were moved to a nearby
monastery.

One day, touched by her rescuer's religious serenity, Irene asked Father
Vancourt to convert her. She was surprised by his response: "His usually calm
face turned to pain; I saw him upset for the first time. Then he took both my
hands into his, and in a firm voice looking down at me, he said, 'Irene, I love
you as a human being, and my respect for you as a Jew is deep and sincere;
that's what you are. Don't ever ask me to do that. Even if you asked me on
bent knees, I would not do it and that's that.' " Similarly, the Ehrlich daughter, Eliane, who after the war married a rabbi (Jacques Ouaknim); she stated
that Vancourt never took advantage of the situation to steer his Jewish charges
away from their religion. "He insisted that we feel at home, that my father don
his phylacteries [for the morning prayer] as customary, and to celebrate the
Sabbath and the holiday." At the ceremony in Yad Vashem, in his honor, in
1975, Father Vancourt had this to say. "It was indeed a great honor for us to
be chosen by Providence to share, even in a very humble way, the immense
ordeals known by Jewish people during the last world war. As a man and as a
priest, it has always been my understanding that one aspect of my duty was to
help reduce the suffering of those who came across my way, to restore to them
as much as possible a measure of self-confidence and joy. Thus, when circumstances brought Irene into the flow of our lives, Mlle. Lombard and mine,
a German Jewish woman who needed shelter, and later on, her uncle's family, and yet a whole host of Jewish children destined to the crematorium
ovens—we could not and we did not have the slightest shade of hesitation. We
did, quite naturally, what any other person would have done in our situation,
and we felt honored that God would want to use us as His humble servants and
help our fellow men in their sufferings. . . . Once again, from that time on, it
is us who owe you our gratitude. . . . I repeat in all sincerity and from the depth
of my heart—the honor we are receiving from you today, and by which we are
touched, only reflects in our view the very great honor imparted to us when

we were called upon to restore a measure of security and happiness to brethren crushed by tragedy."[38]

Clerics living close to the Spanish and Swiss borders could be of great help in facilitating the flight of Jews to safer havens. The Swiss border offered a greater attraction for several reasons: its geographical proximity to central France, which made it more accessible, and particularly the greater easiness afforded by communities who lay astride the border—by comparison with the Spanish border with its formidable and uninhabitable Pyrenees Mountains. Father René De Naurois, for one, guided a family of German Jewish refugees across the Alps to safety in Switzerland. After the German invasion of southern France, in November 1942, he fled to Spain. De Naurois related that before the war, while in Germany, he learned of the existence of the Dachau and Oranienburg concentration camps, and in Berlin met people who had been there, who showed him the scars received in these camps. This experience had a strong impact on him during the war years. "That is why, for me, my attitude did not change from 1933 until 1945." When he asked permission to flee to England to join a combat unit, Monsignor Saliège turned him down. "Your obligation is to stay here," so as to help people in need. In August 1942, while heading a Catholic women's summer camp near Argentieres (Haute Savoie), he learned of a Jewish family in distress. He guided the family on a six-hour trek over the Alps (at one point, at 2,000 to 2,200 meters altitude) until their safe arrival in Switzerland. Not content with this, he thundered against Vichy's antisemitic measures from the pulpit during Sunday masses. "I exploded, literally speaking. . . . Christ was Jewish, Joseph was Jewish, Maria was Jewish, Abraham, etc. . . . Moses. . . . Vichy police grumbled during the sermon." In December 1942, he crossed into Spain, and joined De Gaulle's Free French Army as a military chaplain.[39]

Also near the Franco-Swiss border, in the town of Annecy, Father Camille Folliet, a chaplain for the Catholic youth movement, on many occasions escorted fleeing Jews on the dangerous border-crossing trek, and was assisted by other Catholic clerics in the region, such as Fathers Marius Jolivet and Jean-Joseph Rosay. When an attempt to smuggle the Schiffmanns and their two daughters across the border failed, Folliet took them to his parents' home, and attended to all their needs until an alternative hiding place was found for them. Jenny Schiffmann remembered her errands on behalf of Folliet, carrying bread and food ration cards for members of the resistance. "He never asked us to change our religion," she added. Abbé Simon Gallay, in Evian-les-Bains, whom we shall meet again later, and who termed Folliet "a childhood friend," told of Folliet's concern for Jews in flight. "He would call me from Annecy, 'Go to the train station to pick up two parcels'" [Jews who had to be taken across the border]. Folliet obtained many false documents from Jeanne

Brousse, who worked as a secretary at the Annecy prefecture. Father Abel Jacquet, in Juvigny, recalled the 1942 Christmas eve when Folliet showed up late, missing the evening Mass. "He arrived at 11:00 p.m., broken-hearted and tired. He had traveled with a Jewish family that had been arrested at the St. Cergues station and taken to the gendarme station in Machilly. 'I gave the gendarmes a little sermon,' he smilingly related, recalling to them the significance of Christmas. Why take away these people who did no wrong and whose only fault was in being born Jewish? . . . We are on the eve of Christmas. The whole world is about to celebrate the holiday of hope and peace, promised to men of good will. Imagine what would have happened on the first Christmas if they had hunted Jews all the way to Bethlehem! The Savior would not have been born in a cave but in a prison, behind bars and barbed wires.'" After the midnight Mass, Folliet jumped on a bike and headed to Machilly to look after his imprisoned wards. He managed to have them freed and led to the frontier. During Mass, the following morning, Folliet's face was radiant, happy to have succeeded in saving a group of Jews. In June 1943, the Italians, who controlled the area, arrested him for clandestine activity and sentenced him to ten years imprisonment, but he was released in March 1944. With the liberation of France, he joined the French army as a chaplain, and tragically died of wounds sustained in battle in April 1945.[40]

In the spa and resort town of Evian-les-Bains, located on Lake Leman, separating France and Switzerland, several clerics helped fleeing Jews cross into Switzerland, either by land or by boat. Abbé Simon Gallay helped many Jews, including the author's family. As related by the author's father, Shlomo Wajsfeld, in September 1943, after the Germans took over the Italian zone, the family fled from the village of Varces, south of Grenoble, and headed north toward the Swiss border, where they had previously been told by a Jewish activist to look up a certain priest in Evian-les Bains; a man who would certainly assist them to cross over into Switzerland. Perhaps in the hope that the unknown priest would be more responsive to the pleas of a woman, Mrs. Hinde Wajsfeld went ahead to investigate and appraise the man's responsiveness, leaving the children behind with her husband. Arriving in front of the indicated church, she knocked on the door and was led into a room. "A little while later, a man appeared. He was handsome, tall, with blond hair and blue eyes, and another priest, a bit older. I was led into a beautiful room and they asked me what I needed. I began to weep and told them my whole story; that I was temporarily here with three children: Rachel, Mordecai, and Leah, and the others were with Papa behind in Varces village. They asked me to immediately bring the others. I was then taken with the children to a nursing home, where the nuns gave us something to drink and a room with mattresses on the floor for us to rest. The priest, 'Mr. le Bain,' told us to wait until the time was ripe to smuggle us over. He would then tell me when to bring the rest of the family." Mrs. Wajsfeld immediately informed her husband to join her with the other three children, including two ten-month-old twins, and Hinde's mother. "A couple of days later, [the priest] came over and said: 'Now it's time.' I was crying and wanted to give 'Mr. le Bain' my wedding ring for his good deed, but he said to me, 'My dear lady, keep the ring, jut remember me.' I remember him to this day. His lovely and friendly face." The priest told them to head for Thonon-les-Bains, and from there by bus to a certain village, where a *passeur* would be waiting for them near the local bistro. When the right person appeared, he led the family through fields to a crossing point. After being apprehended by Swiss border guards, the family was taken to a camp in Geneva, and allowed to stay in the country, although under restricted conditions. It turned out that the 'Mr. le Bain' was none other than Father Simon Gallay, who was fondly called 'Plebeian," from the Latin *plebs*, 'people;' that is, 'man of the people'—apparently a title sometimes given a rural pastor.[41]

As for the other priest who welcomed the fleeing Jewish family, it was Abbé Albert Simond. In a letter to Paldiel, in 1984, Gallay wrote: "Yes, it is I who took care of you at Evian and arranged your passage to Switzerland. I helped many Jews cross into Switzerland, but I was not alone in doing it." He mentioned several other clerics, such as Albert Simond, Camille Folliet, and Jean Rosay." According to Sister Aline (Josephine Tremblet), who knew Simond and Gallay well, she especially praised Gallay for organizing passages into Switzerland. "He exhausted himself on account of this, and often worked away at night to arrange a passage—to the point of falling asleep the next morning in church." Abbé Pierre Mopty, the parish priest of Evian, seconded Gallay in the common rescue efforts. Interestingly, Abbé Mopty had a canoe that he often used to row people across the lake. He once ferried three Jews across Lake Leman, but was arrested by French customs officers, and later released through the intercession of Cardinal Gerlier. Not forgetting the three Jews, after his release, Mopty sought them out in Rivesaltes camp, and somehow miraculously managed to have them released to him, and later again took them across the lake in his boat—this time successfully. It was learned after the war that when Gallay and Simond were informed that the Milice planned to torch the local Jewish synagogue, they hurried and fetched the Torah scrolls in time, and concealed them in their church. After the war, the sacred scrolls were returned to the Jewish community.

Ruth Lambert was also involved in the rescue of Jewish children in French internment camps. One evening, in Rivesaltes camp, there was a knock on the door of a room where she was conferring with Abbé Albert Gross (a chaplain for Caritas-Suisse) and the Jewish activist Andrée Salomon. "A young priest with a black umbrella and a big smile entered: " '*Bonjour*, I am Abbé Mopty.

I am here to save Jews.' . . . We were stunned. Abbé Gross got up: '*Bonjour,* I am from Lausanne.' 'And I am from Evian,' Mopty replied." He then explained that a priest in Lyon had asked him to take three people across into Switzerland, who were being sought by the Gestapo because they were Jews. He had come quite simply "to get them out of here." In the words of Lambert, "It was then that we were able to appreciate his determination to go to the full extent of his loving-kindness in order to help these three people; first, in a taxi, then to hide them behind the altar of a church in Perpignan; to go to the prefecture and use his charm to solicit the aid of a high official (who was with the resistance); finally, to lead these three people to Evian. Arriving with his three companions at the Evian harbor. Mopty boarded a suitable canoe, and all four left for Ouchy, on the Swiss side, where Abbé Gross was waiting for them. Mopty returned alone to Evian that same evening, and returned the canoe to its mooring place. It belonged to the police chief! No one had noticed." "He often told me," Ruth Lambert recalled, that "wanting what God wants is the only profession which gives me relaxation."[42]

An unusually extraordinary story in this context is that of the clerics who ran the *Ecole St. François* ("Juvenat") Catholic seminary, in Ville-la-Grand, a building that literally straddled the Franco-Swiss border, and thereby presented an unusual advantage for people wishing to cross at this point. The seminary's garden ended on one side at a wall that formed the border at this point. It so happened that after the German border guards had passed within feet of the school on their regular patrol rounds, they were out of sight for a few minutes. During this precious and short interval, it was safe to place a ladder on the wall and quickly cross over to the Swiss side.

The decision to get involved in this giant rescue operation was taken by Father Pierre Frontin, the seminary's head. It worked as follows. Father Raymond Boccard, in charge of the school's garden, had a room under the roof that dominated the wall forming the border. "From there, one sees very far," Boccard related; "thus, I was able to easily observe the arrival of patrols. At a favorable moment, when the German border guards, who scrupulously followed all the curves of the wall bordering the frontier, could no longer see what was happening in our area, I gave the signal from my window by raising my cap. The fugitives had two minutes and thirty seconds time to make the crossing. One therefore had to hurry."

David Bar-Stav (formerly, Wagner) related that when he and his wife arrived at the seminary, in September 1942, they were warmly greeted by Father Louis Favre. "He had the look of a saint. His eyes were full of goodness. He said to me: 'Oh, my son, how lucky for you to be already here.' One had the feeling that this was a man ready to sacrifice himself to save other people." Favre led David to an upper floor of the building, where he showed him the garden, and beyond it the barbed wire and the spot where he was to make the crossing. David and his wife crossed exactly at noon, as told, and ran for 200 meters before being apprehended by the Swiss border guards. Luckily for both, they were not sent back to France after the guards had verified by phone David's claim that he had assured himself of employment with a French electric company, which had an affiliate in the Geneva region.

The seminary's clerics estimate to have saved 2,000 people (perhaps an exaggerated figure), the majority of whom were Jewish. Not surprisingly, an operation on so large a scale could not go unnoticed for too long, and eventually, the Germans got around to what was happening there. In February 1944, Father Favre was arrested, and he was executed on July 16, 1944. The seminary was ordered closed, and the clerics and students expelled, to be replaced by German customs officials. This situation lasted for only one month, for in August of that year the whole area was liberated by advancing Allied troops.[43]

Turning to Catholic nuns, Sister Clotilde Régereau's story is especially touching. On the night of July 19, 1942, Mr. Muller and his two sons, Henri (born 1930) and Jean-Isaac (born 1931), knocked on the door of the Maison de *Soeurs de la Charité*, on Rue du Bac, Paris. They told the surprised nun at the door of their escape from the great roundup of July 16; they had wandered aimlessly for four days, and on the metro (subway) a nun had referred them to this convent, where they now, at the end of their wits, hoped to be admitted. The nun was a bit hesitant, and called the Mother Superior, Sister Régereau, to determine what to do. Upon listening to the father's tale, she immediately decided to take the boys to the *St. Vincent de Paul* hospice, in Hay de Rose, where they remained for over a year; then to an orphanage in Neuilly-sur-Seine. She also fetched an additional brother and sister (Michel and Annette) from the Rue Lamarck children's center, which at the time was still administered by the Jewish community. Posing as a visitor, and disregarding rules, Sister Régereau simply walked out with them and placed the two in safe locations. By saving the four Muller children, Sister Régereau made it possible for their father to seek a safe place for himself. Unfortunately, the children's mother was deported to Auschwitz.[44]

West of Paris, in Flers (Orne), in the Normandy region, Sister Marie-Louise Pannelay was the Mother Superior of a *St. Vincent de Paul* institution serving women who came to Flers from the surrounding towns and villages to work and needed a place to stay; it also provided accommodations to a handful of local elderly women. The three Roth daughters (Renée, born 1931; Denise, 1933; and Liliane, 1934) stayed there from August 1942 to September 1944. After the war, Renée Roth documented the story of her survival in a children's book, *Touch Wood*. In her testimony to Yad Vashem, she described how

Mother Superior Pannelay saw to it that these three Jewish girls learned the catechism and the rudiments of the Catholic religion. "We attended the local parochial schools, the *Pensionnat Notre Dame*, where the teachers, a group of lay nuns, taught us and 'knew' of our situation. We attended Mass and Vespers on Sundays and learned the prayers and hymns. We didn't take communion or go to confession, since we were not baptized—a prerequisite for these sacraments." Renée's mother visited her daughters only once during their two-year stay there. "It was Mother Superior who was mostly responsible for establishing a safe 'network' for us. She presented [to others] the *petites Roth*, as we were called, as three little city girls whose parents wanted them safe from bombings and severe food shortage in Paris. At no time did we feel coerced into conversion." However, in March 1944, when German troops were seen entering Flers, Sister Pannelay decided to quickly baptize the girls. Renée noted that her mother had previously urged Pannelay to do whatever she deemed necessary to ensure the girls' safety. "We could then take communion and go to confession; that is, be totally 'invisible' and not arouse any suspicion. And a predated baptismal certificate would protect us in case of a surprise raid by the German authorities. We were therefore baptized in March 1944. As for the motivation guiding the nuns' actions, I am sure it was out of their genuine belief to 'help' anyone in need. As mentioned above, they believed in 'charity' in the religious sense." The three sisters also underlined the special attention they received from two of the Sisters, Anne-Marie Le Cahérec and Madeleine Malolepszy, who was of Polish origin. Malolepszy was the cook "and the one who was closest to us. We could run to her with special questions and problems, and she used to sneak in some extra food to the three of us whenever possible."[45]

In the hilly region of Corrèze, Sister Marie-Gonzague Bredoux was the Mother Superior of the *Abbaye Saint-Etienne* convent in Aubazine, which had been converted into a home for elderly people. Together with the home's chief administrator, Sister Marie-Thérèse Berger, they admitted twelve Jewish girls who had been referred to them, including a certain Kraindel Dornfest and her daughter Betty, in September 1942. While there, Mrs. Dornfest helped out in the convent's kitchen, but as an observant religious person, she was exempt from work on the Sabbath and Jewish festivals. Her daughter, Betty, helped out by sewing dresses for the twelve Jewish girls in hiding. When Betty asked the Mother Superior for candles, which her mother wished to light for the Sabbath, Sister Bredoux immediately fetched them from inside the chapel. When the convent ran out of candles, Bredoux supplied them with oil and cotton so that they could continue to observe this religious requirement. With the approach of the Passover holiday, Dornfest and her daughter needed special food for the eight-day holiday period. Luckily, for them, a former Jewish scout instructor brought two kilograms of matzos (unleavened bread) for the two women. In Betty's words: "The Mother Superior asked me the significance of this holiday, and its accompanying customs. I explained to her everything linked to this holiday: the requirement of special utensils and the matzos. I added that we would limit ourselves to eating solely matzos for eight days. To my great surprise, several days before the holiday the Mother Superior called me and led me to a room no one had entered before and showed me a stove, new utensils, a sack of potatoes—everything that she had prepared for Passover. Thus, for eight days we observed the holiday. Afterwards, the Mother Superior called me from time to time to ask me about Judaism. She never tried to convert us." Liberation, in September 1944, took place close to the Rosh Hashanah holiday. Here too, Mother Bredoux was of assistance, by instructing the two women how to reach the synagogue in nearby Brive, and she supplied them with hard-to-find potatoes, and a letter to a French family to provide housing for the two women during the two-day holiday. The Dornfests stayed in the convent until the spring of 1945.[46]

In Rulhe, Aveyron region, Sister Antoinette Masserey ran an old-age hospice where she sheltered two dozen Jews, mostly teenage girls and several adults, and was sensitive to the religious needs of her wards, such as exempting them from work on Saturdays. During the stay in the hospice, they performed various chores, such as kitchen duty, laundry, feeding the animals, tending the bean garden, and chopping firewood. Ever sensitive to the religious needs of her wards, Sister Masserey arranged a clean white tablecloth for the Friday evening meal. In the words of one of her wards, "She allowed us to hold courses on the Bible and Jewish subjects; we danced the Zionist-inspired hora; she often participated in our sessions and conversations. Briefly, she did the impossible to facilitate for our young ones to maintain a Jewish link and spirit." For Passover, knowing that it was forbidden to eat bread, Sister Masserey made available sufficient quantities of potatoes and eggs. For the Rosh Hashanah (Jewish New Year) holiday, she exchanged food with the farmers in return for chocolate, honey, and fruit. "All this to help us celebrate and have a good year, as prescribed by the Jewish religion." At the close of the Yom Kippur fast day, she arranged for a light soup to be ready to break the fast. Sister Jeanne-Françoise Zufferey was one of Masserey's principal aides. She slept in the same large dormitory hall as the teenage Jewish girls, separated by only a curtain, and was assigned to the care of these youths and their integration in the home's population in such a way that the others would not suspect the girls Jewish origin (they were presented as refugees from the Alsace region). While other nuns and not a few residents suspected otherwise, they kept their silence—in the spirit of passive assistance.[47]

Much farther to the south, in Perpignan, not far from the Spanish border, when the Germans extended their hold over the whole of France, in November 1942, the Florentine family sought alternative safe havens, and a friendly neighbor took Collete Florentine and her parents (Isaac and Corinne) to a Catholic school in St. Flour, in the Cantal region, for possible shelter. But the woman school supervisor turned them down. Before they departed, she suddenly told them that a nun was leaving in about ten minutes to go to another religious institution, and there might be room for the fleeing Jewish family in that place. This stranger nun made an on-the-spot affirmative decision. "It was like a thunderbolt," Collete Florentine recalled her family's reaction. Collete had herself baptized before leaving for the small religious school, in Allanche, which was headed by two nuns: Mother Superior Jeanne Dessaigne (Sr. Marie Angèle) and Philomène Rolland (Sr. Marie Etienne), where Collete passed the winter of 1942–43. In July 1943, her mother, Corinne, fleeing the Germans in Perpignan, was also admitted to this school, in the guise of a person recuperating from an illness, and she stayed there for a full year. Also admitted was Collete's cousin, Jacqueline Eskinazi, who appeared there under the name of Esteve. Similar to Colette, Jacqueline decided to go through baptism so as not to stand out among the other residents of the Catholic institution. "I learned the catechism, and attended services in church. I also went through confirmation, during which I dressed in a beautiful white robe. This was so completely new and also so 'attractive' that I gave myself completely." After the war, the two nuns accepted the girls' renewed Judaism "with full understanding." In one of her letters to Colette, Sister Marie-Etienne reiterated her happiness at having had the opportunity to save her from the ravages of the Holocaust, and then asked forgiveness for not having had the means to keep Colette's room sufficiently warm during her stay there. She then added her hope that "we Christians do not forget that we have our roots in the Jewish people." Finally, "what else can I say to you, other than what you already know by heart, that I love you all, and that I embrace you with all my heart."[48]

Monsignor De Courrèges d'Ustou, who served as coadjutor to Cardinal Saliège, placed some forty children, released from French internment camps, in the Sainte-Germaine boarding school in Vendine, 30 kilometers from Toulouse, which was headed by Sister Louise Thèbe. She, in turn, appealed to Sister Denise Bergon, who managed a children's summer camp, *Notre Dame de Massip*. By Christmas 1942, the first five children arrived in Massip, and the number eventually rose. With the increased danger of German roundups in the Toulouse region, eventually eighty-two Jews, mostly children (including some of the Vénissieux camp escapees), found a safe haven there for various lengths of time. Other than Sister Bergon and the home's director, Sister Marguerite Roques, and the school's chaplain, and two more Sisters, the other eleven nuns were not told the truth about the Jewish children's true origin. To explain the broken French spoken by these children, some of who were from Germany, the other children were told that the new arrivals came from the distant region of Lorraine, which had been annexed to Germany, and whose residents spoke an accented French. It is reported that Bishop Saliège told Bergon that he was sure she would not take advantage to proselytize among the children, and added: "You will have to lie; lie then whenever necessary; I give you all my absolutions in advance." During communion, the Jewish children remained sitting, and Sister Bergon explained to the surprised others that the parents of these sitting children did not practice any religion. Some of the boys were later placed with local families.

Denise Markx, one of the children sheltered in Massip, was fifteen years of age in 1944. Taken with her sister to Capdenac by Sister Bergon, the arrangement was for Denise to stay intermittently in Catholic boarding schools in Massip and nearby Figeac. "In Massip as in Figeac, we were made to participate in the religious services and catechetical lessons for understandable reasons, so as not to arouse suspicion." Sister Roques served as home director, and she also gave lessons in mathematics. In Massip, Sister Bergon often took Denise out for walks. "This is how I learned that she had hidden beneath a slab in her office papers and money which my parents had left in her care, that there was an underground passage beneath the chapel which was set aside for hiding adult Jews; that she had prepared an escape plan to the mountains by forming groups of elders who would take care of the younger ones." In September 1943,when the French Milice, tipped off by informers, came to arrest Michel Frejer and his brother, both managed to flee the place in the nick of time. By sheer luck, and the devotion of the Sisters, all the children in the Massip boarding school saw it through safely and returned to their families. Sisters Bergon, Roques, and Thèbe were responsible for the rescue of over eighty Jewish lives.[49]

In Cimiez, Nice region, Mother Superior Henriette Gret (Sr. Anne-Marie) headed the Clarisses Sainte-Claire convent, where many Jewish children were sheltered whose parents had entrusted them to the nuns. One of these children, Glika Rappaport (born in 1936), was hidden with her eleven-year-old brother Raphael, beginning late in 1943, in a small shack at the edge of the convent garden. Another sheltered child, Lisette Lévy (born in 1929), was found wandering the streets of Nice after her parents had been picked up and deported. She was spotted by a certain Sister Emmanuelle, who took her to the Clarisses convent. Far from attempting to convert them, Sister Anne-Marie and her nuns encouraged the Jewish girls to maintain their faith and not forget their Jewish identity. Close to Passover, they tried, although unsuccessfully, to obtain matzos (unleavened bread) for the hidden girls. On one occasion, a Franciscan priest came to give lessons in French, and made use of the occasion to also teach some Hebrew to a Jewish man hidden there. The children did participate in Mass, but this was done only to dispel any suspicions of their real origin. Jewish children streamed through the convent during the war, some in transit and some for longer periods. Sisters Anne-Marie, Emmanuelle and Rose also regularly met with the children's parents, who were in hiding elsewhere, to update them on their children's well-being. When danger of arrest by the Gestapo threatened, the nuns removed the girls to another institution housing deaf-and-dumb children. Informed of the three nuns' elevation to the "Righteous" title, the 1991 head of the St. Claire convent, Sister Marie-Pascal, wrote to Yad Vashem that her predecessors had only carried out the command of "You shall love the Lord your God with all your heart . . . and your neighbor as yourself." She then added another biblical verse, from the Book of Psalms, chapter 126:5–6, "He that goes forth weeping, bearing the seed for sowing, shall come home with shouts of joy, bringing his sheaves with him." To which she added: "This is our life as pilgrims here below, but afterwards, we shall all be united to sing: 'Render thanks to the Lord, for He is good, for His love is forever.' "[50]

Mention should also be made of the German-born Sister Cläre Barwitzky, who worked in a lay home for children in the southeastern mountainous region of Chamonix, where thirty Jewish children were sheltered. She had arrived in France in 1932, and was assigned by Father Remillieux, in Lyon, to work on behalf of French-German reconciliation (Compagnons de St. François). During the war years, she moved to St. Etienne, trying to keep her German identity a secret, and was active with other religious in placing Jewish children with non-Jewish families. Then, in 1943, with the increasing danger of arrest of these children, some of them were removed and sent to a remote summer camp near Chamonix at the foot of Mt. Blanc, and Sister Bartwitzky volunteered to care for them there. Hanna Szmidt and Fella Szmidt, who were assigned as teachers in the summer camp, relate the music lessons given by Sister Barwitzky to the children. "She was always ready to give everything, even her overcoat. . . . Every morning Cläre prayed together with the children the *Shema Yisrael* [Hear, O Israel] in French. On Fridays, Cläre cared for the Christian children, so as to allow us to celebrate the Sabbath with the Jewish children."

With the onset of the winter season in late 1943, the municipality of Chamonix agreed to Barwitzky's plea to move the children to one of the closed winter hotels. "Then began for us an unforgettable year; a year full of goodness, of relating to others, of trust, love, joy, and sisterly cooperation. I cannot recall in my life another time equal to this. . . . The children especially loved the discussions on the position of the Holy Scriptures. Juliette [Guy] and Marinette [Vidal]—two non-Jewish women active in the rescue of children]—gave everyone as a gift a complete Bible, the Old and New Testament. The children were free to select the text they wished to discuss. Mostly, they preferred the Book of Proverbs." Luckily for everyone, the children's location was never raided. In her farewell letter to the children in December 1944, Sister Barwitzky had words of counsel for her former wards: "Exert yourself, as I did with my weak strength, to protect and respect the dignity of every person, even at the risk of one's own life. . . . The house in St. Etienne, where I worked for many years, and through which I saved the lives of Jewish children, carried the name of 'Peace and Joy.' This title was the motto of my life. I beg of you, exert yourself in the cause of peace! Oppose injustice wherever you come across it. Be a protagonist for life, whenever it is in danger. Consider your life as a mission for peace and happiness. Your life would then not be a waste. The peace and joy that you grant others will flow back to you. I thank my God, that he has shown me the way of peace and forgiveness."[51]

Our final story of nuns helping Jews takes place in Paris. It concerns Maria Skobtsova, of the Russian Orthodox Church. Born in 1891 as Yelizaveta Pilenko in Riga, Latvia, then part of the Russian Empire, she composed poetry, such as *Scythian Shards* and *Ruth*, both of which were well received in literary circles. When the Russian Revolution broke out in March 1917, Elizabeth was a member of the socialist SR Party, which she believed would help reawaken Old Mother Russia, and bring about a religious revival. Angry at the Bolshevik leader Leon Trotsky for forcefully breaking up the SR convention, she planned to assassinate him, but was dissuaded by her party colleagues. Instead she went to Anapa, on the Black Sea coast, to organize the revolutionary cause there, and was elected the town's mayor. With the capture of the town by the White forces of General Denikin, she was arrested and put on trial. Her defense swayed the president of the court, Danilo Skobtsov, to dismiss all charges. The two eventually married. With the advance of the Red Army, the Skobtsovs fled via Tiflis and Istanbul to Yugoslavia, and then to Paris, where they arrived in 1923. In the meantime she bore Danilo a daughter and a son named Yuri. In 1932, upon the premature death of her four-year-old daughter from meningitis, she decided to become a nun in the Russian Orthodox Church. Taking her vows, she chose the name Maria, and decided not to withdraw from the world, but to dedicate herself to the cause of the needy, especially the distraught Russian emigrants in France, for whom she opened a dormitory in Saxe, near Paris, including a free kitchen. In 1935, her church purchased a building in Rue de Lourmel, Paris, which became the base of her charitable work. She was seconded by Father Dimitri Klepinin, also a Russian emigrant, who was ordained in the Russian Orthodox Church in Paris in 1937, but before that was already married to Tamara, a YMCA worker in Paris, who bore him a daughter, Helen.

With the German occupation of France, Maria Skobtsova decided to direct her aid to Jews, first by making the free kitchen available to them; then by providing temporary shelter at her center for those in need. A hidden mill inside the convent turned out false identifications. Lourmel soon became known as a "Jewish church," as many Jews flocked there for assistance. An entire Jewish family was hidden in Klepinin's private room, another in Yuri's room. She provided a false certificate to the sister of the historian Leon Poliakov, and equally for the wife of the future historian Georges Wellers. In July 1942, when the yellow star edict was promulgated by the Germans, she countered with her celebrated poem "Israel," which read:

Two triangles, a star,
The shield of King David, our forefather.
This is election, not offense.
The great path and not an evil one.
Once more is a term fulfilled.
Once more roars the trumpet of the end
And the fate of a great people.
Once more is by the prophet proclaimed,
Thou art persecuted again, O Israel.
But what can human ill will mean to thee,
Thee, who have heard the thunder from Sinai?

During the great roundup of Parisian Jews at the Winter Sports Stadium in July 1942, she succeeded in penetrating the closely guarded stadium and saving two Jewish children (hidden in trash bins). Toward the end of 1942, she was warned by friends that the Gestapo was on her trail. However, she rejected all pleas to cease helping Jews; she could no longer change course, she stated, since an invisible hand was dictating her work. On February 8, 1943, she was arrested by the Gestapo, together with her son Yuri and Father Klepinin. She readily admitted to helping Jews, to the issuing of false baptismal certificates and to transferring funds to Jews in hiding. Gestapo agent Hoffmann lectured Maria's mother: "You educated your daughter very stupidly. She only helps Jews." The old woman replied: "That is not true. She is a Christian who helps those in need. She would even help you, if you were in trouble." Hoffmann replied, "You will never see your daughter again." Then came the turn of Klepinin. *Hoffmann:* "If we release you, will you give an undertaking never again to aid Jews?" *Klepinin:* "I can say no such thing. I am a Christian, and must act as I must." At this, Hoffmann struck Klepinin across his face and screamed: "Jew-lover! How dare you talk of helping those pigs as a Christian duty!" Recovering his balance, Klepinin raised the cross from his cassock and facing Hoffmann quietly said: "Do you know this Jew?" Another blow from Hoffmann landed Klepinin on the floor. Deported to Ravensbrück camp, Maria Skobtsova succumbed on March 31, 1945, days before the camp's liberation. In her prewar writings, the following statement is found: "At the Last Judgment, I will not be asked whether I satisfactorily practiced asceticism, nor how many bows I made before the divine altar. I will be asked whether I fed the hungry, clothed the naked, visited the sick, and the prisoner in his jail. That is all that will be asked." Her son Yuri, also arrested, died earlier, in February 1944, in Dora camp; on the following day, Father Klepinin, in the same camp, succumbed to pneumonia. On October 12, 1945, a memorial service was held in a Parisian synagogue in Skobtsova's memory, with the cantor and congregation in tears.[52]

More Special Catholic Rescue Stories

Some stories of rescues by Catholic clergy do not fit any particular category, but stand in a class by themselves. Such as Father Jean Fleury, in Poitiers, who provided spiritual care to his gypsy co-religionists incarcerated in a nearby camp on Route de Limoges (and was therefore dubbed "Father of the Gypsies"). Attached to this camp was one reserved for Jews. Father Fleury availed himself of this opportunity, and his association with the underground, to help remove Jewish children from the camp and, with the help of others, arm them with forged credentials and find them safe havens in southern France. Rivkah-Régine Breidick, who worked with the local rabbi, Elie Bloch, met Father Fleury in 1942. After the arrest of Rabbi Bloch in February 1943, Régine took over the responsibility of looking after the children who had been turned over to private foster families. "I frequently consulted Father Fleury, at the College Saint-Joseph in Poitiers, where he lived. He himself used to visit sick Jews." In September 1943, facing arrest, Régine turned to Fleury, who arranged her transfer elsewhere. She eventually reached Grenoble, where she stayed out the war. After the liberation, she learned the names of some of the people helped by Fleury, such as Dr. Wolfsohn (a Jewish Communist), Mr. Kraviec, Roger Copferman, and Richard Kamelgarn." She stated, "Father Fleury helped and saved within the measure of his possibility, be it a Jew, Gypsy, or Communist, while placing his own life in danger. He did it for love of fellow-men." Similarly for Régine's brother, Jacques Breidick, who was living in relative peace with his sister in the village of La Milliere par Romagne, when one evening at the end of September 1943, a certain Hélène Marzellier came to see them. "She had been sent by Father Fleury and told us that the Germans were preparing to deport all the Jews to concentration camps. She took us to a Christian school, where we spent the night, and the next morning we left on foot for another village fifteen kilometers away.

There, we went to some peasants whose address we had been given by Hélène Marzellier. Two weeks later, a closed truck came to take us to a monastery in Poitiers. There Father Fleury received us. He gave us forged documents and a train ticket to southern France, via the convent of *Notre Dame de Sion*, in Lyon." Some estimate the number of Jews helped by Father Fleury and his associates to run to more than a hundred souls.[53]

In 1942, when Nicole Bloch (of the Jewish Scouts, known as the "Sixth," in the Toulouse region) was told of a certain sympathetic Abbé Albert Gau in Carcassonne, who was much involved in Catholic youth activities, then "without referring to my superiors, I decided to risk meeting him. He welcomed me enthusiastically, beyond any expectation. He hid s young men and girls for us in different religious homes, such as: Sisters in Pezens, Sisters in Narbonne, Dominicans in Fangeaux, *Mission de Restauration Paysanne*, and so on, or with families. . . . Besides, he obtained food for us in appreciable quantities." Renée Baras, a social worker during the war, near Carcassonne, remembered receiving from Gau numerous Jewish children and adults for hiding. She stated that Abbé Gau continued his work "in spite of the objections of the church," a statement which she did not elaborate. Abbé Gau reportedly utilized the baptismal forms and seals at the diocese for his rescue work. In a special chapter titled: "Protection of Jews," in a book on the Catholic youth movement, Gau wrote that when asked by Nicole Bloch to help her in the rescue of Jews, "I could not say no to her." In his upstairs office, Nicole Bloch and her associate, Anny Latour, fabricated false credentials with the use of certain chemicals. As for the false baptismal certificates handed out to Jews, Gau agreed to this on the sole condition that they would not, as a consequence, be required to be baptized. Gau was eventually trailed by the French police, and on one occasion, as the police were questioning him, his Jewish associates were working on false documents in one of the back rooms of his home. On another occasion, when the police wished to inspect a certain room, Gau replied angrily: "This room is reserved for the diocese. You have no right to enter it without the bishop's permission. I've had enough of this," he shouted, and turning his back he walked away from the door. One policeman was heard saying: "Let's get the hell out of here; it's over." Later, with the arrival of the Germans on scene, the Gestapo decided to arrest Gau, and he went into hiding from March 1943 until the country's liberation. In hindsight, Abbé Gau writes: "From a distance, I am convinced that I was never more fully a priest than during that period when I was a recluse from society." At a ceremony in his honor at Yad Vashem in 1987, he expanded on the special role of the Jewish people, and called for Jews and Christians to practice a "union within differences." He continued, "Jews and Christians, let us remain the children of the same covenant. Let us not forget that the commandment of 'You shall love your neighbor as yourself" is to be found in the Law of Moses." Steering from his prepared speech, he turned to the assembled audience and stated: "I turn to you, people of God, and I dare say: 'You have nothing to offer our pagan world but your fidelity to the word of God, and the long, never-ending history of your martyrdom. A people that some claim to be domineering but which is, at the same time so fragile and strong as to be able to survive all other peoples; a people always persecuted, for it proves an annoyance to moribund peoples and empty souls; a people which lives in the horror of its spilled blood, of the blood which for twenty centuries has flowed from its own children—continue your jolting role; do not fail us, for without you, we would lose direction. People of Jesus, I love you. . . . We love you."[54]

In Nice, on the Mediterranean coast, Bishop Monsignor Paul Rémond was known for his initial support of Vichy; like other bishops, he hailed Pétain and urged his flock to pay obedience to him, and also encouraged people to join the newly formed Vichy Legion, on whose request he celebrated an open-air Mass in May 1941. Then, by mid-1943, he underwent a transformation. This may have came about through the prodding of a Syrian-born Jew named Moussa Abadi—a professional theatrical expert, born in Damascus, who had fled from Paris to Nice. Abadi related how, in the summer of 1943, he learned from an Italian army chaplain of the horrors perpetrated on Jews in distant Ukraine by the Germans, including mass executions. Fearing that the Jews in Nice might soon meet a similar fate, Abadi asked to see Bishop Rémond. As later related by Abadi, he addressed the bishop in the following terms. "Monsignor, I am a Jew, I come from afar, and hail from one of the oldest ghettos in the world. I have come to ask you to take risks. Try to live according to your Gospels like I am going to try living according to my Bible. You can throw me out, you can chase me away, but without you I will not be able to save the children."   Taken back by this somewhat discourteous approach, Rémond pulled himself up and in a trembling voice said: "What you're asking me is a very grave matter. In other words, you expect the occupation of Nice by the Germans, and you must imagine that the Nazis could storm in right here, arrest me, arrest my secretary, Abbé Rostand, deport them, interrogate them!" "Precisely that," Abadi shot back." "In that case, I ask you to let me reflect on this, but I am going to ask you one question before leaving—will your future activity include the use of arms?" "No." With these words the two parted. When Abadi returned to see Rémond, as agreed, the bishop began by giving various explanations and excuses, which to Abadi sounded like a cop-out. Abadi then related that he thought to himself: "The game is up; he is going to give me his blessings, wish me good luck, and end with this." But he heard Rémond say: "I have considered it, and well, we are going to try to do something together." Abadi then said that doing things together would mean doing it in one of the rooms of the bishop's residence. For what purpose, the bishop asked. To fabricate false papers, Abadi replied. Rémond agreed to this, even for the making of false baptismal certificates. Both also agreed for a new name for Moussa Abadi. It was to be Monsieur Marcel.

With the help of Rémond's aide, Abbé Rostand, a list of Catholic institutions was drawn up who would be approached for assistance in the rescue of children. To open the doors of Catholic institutions, Abadi needed a cover, so Rémond appointed him a general inspector of the diocesan educational institutions, and gave him an appropriate letter of introduction. Monsignor Rémond also signed a statement, certifying that Abadi's close aide, Yvette Rosenstock, under her new name of Sylvie Delattre, was a social worker commissioned by the diocese to care for the diocesan children, adding: "I insist that Mrs. Delattre be given full satisfaction."

With the German takeover of the Italian zone in Nice on September 8, 1943, Abadi went immediately into action, placing children in Catholic institutions, under forged names. By virtue of these initiatives, and the help of Monsignor Rémond, Abadi's rescue network was able to save over 500 threatened Jewish children, many of them placed in dormitories of Catholic institutions. Abadi recalled that one day, as he was working on his new credentials in Rémond's residence, the bishop came down the stairs and into Abadi's room. "I have come to give you a hand," and he began to write out ration cards. Abadi turned to Rémond and said: "Monsignor, this is madness what you're doing! Your handwriting is known in the whole diocese; this is going to lead to your arrest, torture, and perhaps be shot." Rémond replied: "Well, in that case, you will ascend into heaven with me, and you will not be in such bad company." And he continued working on the documents.

Monsignor Rémond also, on his own initiative, arranged sheltering places for individual Jews, adults and children. Such as for René Schwod, whom he placed in a Catholic-run sanatorium in Thorenc. He also provided the writer Joseph Joffo and his brother with certificates of baptism under new names, and subsequently intervened to have both released from prison. Eight-year-old Greta Herensztat remembered being brought by her mother to Rémond in his study and left there. In Greta's words, Rémond looked at her and spoke in a muffled voice: "You are [from] now Ginette Henry. You were born in Orange and your parents are dead. You are going to stay in a convent until we locate your godparents. Then you will go to live with them as soon as possible. Do you understand? You cannot tell where you were born, and you cannot talk about your parents. Now repeat your name and your birthplace to me." Greta/Ginette was then taken to the cloister of the Clarisses Sisters in Cimiez, where she and other Jewish children were sheltered. Thus, an unabashed Pétain supporter had, by the turn of events, staked his safety and reputation in an active effort to save Jewish children in a city where the infamous Nazi Jew-hunter Alois Brunner was on a furious rampage to catch as many Jews as possible and deliver them to the death camps.[55] Of the 15,000 Jews in Nice, only 2,200 were eventually caught by the Germans, in spite of the increasing rewards promised by the Gestapo: from 100 to 1,000 francs per individual, to as much as 5,000 francs for an important person. At the time, the average monthly salary was 3,000 francs.

We conclude with Father Marie-Benoît (hereinafter referred to as Benoît), whose story has no equal in the annals of help to Jews by clergy during the Holocaust. Born in 1895 as Pierre Péteul to a family of flour millers in northern France, he was admitted to the Capuchin order as a novice in 1913. Then came World War I, in which he participated as a stretcher-bearer, was wounded, and decorated. After the war, he continued his theological studies, including the Gregorian College in Rome; then taught theology in Rome. When Italy entered the war against France in June 1940, Benoît left and moved to the Capuchin monastery in Marseilles, which soon became a beehive of clandestine activities on behalf of fleeing Jews. It may have begun with the visit of a young woman, Fernande Leboucher, in mid-1942, who came to seek his help to free her Jewish husband, Ludwik Nadelman, from the Rivesaltes detention camp, near Marseilles. He promised to help. His motivation, as reported by Leboucher was as he stated: "The law under which Ludwik is imprisoned is an immoral one, and one is not allowed to ignore such laws but should actively resist them. There is no doubt in my mind that this is such a law, and such a time."[56]

Together with Leboucher, Benoît devised a plan to help Jewish internees flee to the Italian zone of occupation in Nice. From his Capuchin center, Benoît turned out false identity documents and organized the flight of Jews across the Swiss and Spanish borders. He worked in tandem with other prelates, Catholic and Protestant, as well as Jewish clandestine operatives, such as Joseph Bass (codenamed Monsieur André), whom he termed "my very dear friend." The bishop of Marseilles had authorized Benoît to visit the internment camps in the region, including the Camp des Milles and Hotel Bompart inside Marseilles, where women were interned, and this enabled him to transmit reports on conditions there. His activities could not for long go unnoticed by the police, "but I had devoted friends among the police who aided me to prevent danger." Despite this, caution was the order of the day, especially as many people flocked to Benoît's center at 51 Rue Croix de Regnier.

After the arrival of the Germans in Marseilles in November 1942, Benoît turned his eyes toward the Italian zone of occupation, centered in nearby Nice, where tens of thousands of Jews had flocked. It was common knowledge that the Italian authorities, still allied to Nazi Germany, refused to be partners in the anti-Jewish excesses practiced by their ally, and they allowed the Jews in their midst to live almost undisturbed. Taking advantage of this situation, Benoît gradually began to spirit Jews to Nice and Cannes, in collaboration with the Jewish organizations there. In Nice, Benoît met the Jewish banker Angelo Donati, who doubled as an intermediate between the Jewish organizations and the Italian authorities. One day, Donati introduced him to Guido Lospinoso, Mussolini's special emissary in the Italian zone to deal with Jewish matters, ostensibly in cooperation with the SS command in France. After meeting Benoît, Lospinoso decided to act contrary to his mandate; that is, instead of helping to arrest Jews, he would now protect them from arrest by the Vichy authorities. Relating, in 1948, Lospinoso's conversion in favor of protecting Jews, Benoît reported that the Italian official at first "wished to know if the God of the Jews is the same as the one for the Christians, and why I, a Catholic, was involved with them. I did not find it difficult to enlighten him and to justify myself, and he then declared that he only wished to be benevolent toward the Jews." This situation lasted until the end of the Italian occupation in France in September 1943.

In the meantime, in late June 1943, his superiors called Benoît back to Rome. At this point, the Italians, battered by their losses in the war, were thinking of withdrawing their troops from France, and it was feared that the Germans would soon occupy the Italian zone, trapping the estimated 45,000 Jews there. Arriving in Rome, Benoît asked for and was granted an audience with the pope. Meeting Pius XII on July 16, 1943, Benoît began by describing the situation of Jews in France, including the deportations carried out by the Vichy regime. According to Benoît, Pius XII reflected for a moment, then said: "One would not have believed this on the part of France."[57] Then Benoît turned to the other matters on his agenda. Specifically, he asked the pontiff for the Vatican's support on four matters: to obtain news for the families of French Jews deported to Germany; to obtain guarantees of humane treatment for Jews imprisoned in French detention camps; to intervene with Spain to aid in the repatriation of Jews in France claiming Spanish ancestry; and finally, and this interested Benoit the most, to apply pressure on the Italian government to facilitate the transfer of thousands Jews from the former Italian zone in France into Italy proper before the expected German takeover of that area. As recorded by Benoît, the Holy See failed to commit itself and respond favorably to any of these requests, advancing various excuses.

On July 25, 1943, when Mussolini was overthrown and replaced by Marshal Badoglio, Benoît felt it wiser to ask for the Jews in the Nice region to be moved, not to Italy proper (where Benoît feared a German takeover), but instead directly to North African sites. The original plan was accordingly redrafted and together with Donati, Benoît elaborated a plan for transferring many of the Jews in the Nice region, aboard ships, to recently liberated North African camps. For this purpose, Benoît met in Rome with D'Arcy Osborne and Myron Taylor, the British and American representatives at the Vatican, to work out the details of this gigantic rescue operation. The new Italian government, for its part, was prepared to provide four ships to undertake three voyages from Nice to North Africa with 2,500 people on board for each crossing, thus allowing some 30,000 Jews to escape. Both Taylor and Osborne supported the plan, though Osborne less enthusiastically. The Italian had begun to requisition eighty trucks to bring the Jews to seaside harbors, and the American-based Jewish Joint representative in France had promised to underwrite the operation. However, tragically, the plan was scuttled by the premature announcement of the surrender of Italy to the Allies on September 8, 1943, and the immediate takeover of the Italian zone in France by the Germans, who, headed by the notorious SS chief Alois Brunner, began a massive manhunt for Jews in Nice and surrounding areas. As sadly recalled by Benoît, "Thus were condemned innumerable Jews, the salvation of whom had been our dearest wish." With the Germans in full control of Nice, and on the lookout for Benoît, he had no choice but to remain in Rome, and his activities there are further described in the chapter on Italy.[58]

Help by Protestant Clergy

As indicated earlier, the Protestant share in the rescue of Jews was proportionally higher than that of Catholic clergy; they made up a third of all French clerics honored as "Righteous" by Yad Vashem but represented only 2 percent in the general population. Following are a few select stories. Pastor Albert Delord served his parish in Carmax (Tarn) and ran a summer camp where forty-six Jewish children were placed among the overall 200 children—collected by Delord and his wife from the surrounding area after the deportation of their parents. Let us listen to Delord's description of his involvement in the rescue of Jews. "We lived in total ignorance of the fate of the Jews in Europe, and we only learned of this accidentally during the great roundups in the southern zone. We were at the time busy with a summer camp containing 100 children, when some parents told us to immediately return their two daughters to them. They told me that they were Jewish and were about to be arrested. This news was so upsetting to me that at first I did not believe it. . . . A few days later, I learned that these people had indeed been deported. I was in a state of shock, having discovered with one blow the situation of the Jews in Europe. I then went to the only French Jews I knew and told them to spread the message to their co-religionists that I was placing myself at their disposal. Within the next 48 hours, dozens of Jewish families came to see me. I was overwhelmed to discover their distress, and felt completely incapable of helping them. I started by opening my house to them and looked up contacts able to help them. . . . I called a meeting of some parishioners on whom I could count and shared my concerns with them. Their commitment was total from the first day; each according to his capacity and situation pledged to take part in our activities: struggle, information, false papers, social work. We had the unbelievable luck to be able to carry out our work for three years without a single arrest! . . . It was for me a great joy to discover the Jewish community. During all these years, I sheltered Jews of all tendencies and became very close to them. A little problem in the midst of all this drama was the question of baptism. Many Jews asked us to be baptized in order to escape danger—so they believed. While I was ready to make a false document, I categorically refused such a ceremony, and this cost me much lack of understanding. By contrast, I made many friends, who have remained so to this day. . . . When I now look back on this period, I have the feeling of simply having been a gatherer of good dispositions. Thanks to God, we were able to perform our simple task to its full completion."[59]

The Vivarais heights are situated in the southeastern corner of the Haute-Loire department, and count some twenty villages and hamlets, with Chambon-sur-Lignon and Mazet-St.Voy the main centers, and had a population of slightly above 6,000 souls, mostly Protestants, descendents of the Huguenots. When hunt for Jews began, thousands flocked to this region and were welcomed with open arms and sheltered almost everywhere in this Protestant enclave. In Le Chambon, various Protestant organizations sheltered Jews in hostels which had earlier hosted people in need; such as the Coteau Fleuri, Les Grillons, Tante Soly, Les Roches, La Guespy, Faidoli, and Les Heures Claires—by CIMADE, Red Cross, the American Quakers, and the pacifist Fellowship of Reconciliation. In Tante Soly, for instance, 80 percent of the residents were Jews, according to its wartime owners, Solange and Emile Seches. The mostly Protestant people of this area practiced a down-to-earth Christianity, rooted in the Hebrew Bible and the New Testament. As repeatedly stated by them, an important biblical injunction in their belief was "You shall love the Lord with all your heart and love your neighbor as yourself." One Chambonnais gave the following explanation: "How can you call us 'good'? We were doing what had to be done. Who else could help them? And what has all this to do with goodness? Things had to be done, that's all, and we happened to be there to do them. You must understand that it was the most natural thing in the world to help these people." Simple and yet profound words.[60]

While many religious figures participated in this vast rescue operation, Pastor André Trocmé was undoubtedly the leading spirit. Born in 1901 in northern France to an old French Huguenot family on his father's side, and a German family on his mother's side, he witnessed the horrors of the First World War, which probably moved him toward a militant pacifism, abhorring all forms of violence, even so-called justified military actions. In 1926, he met and married the Italian-born Magda Grilli while in New York studying at the Union Theological Seminary and tutoring David and Winthrop Rockefeller. Returning to France, he filled several clerical posts, and in 1934, when he was accepted as pastor in Chambon-sur-Lignon (a post he held until 1948), he promised not to overtly propagate his pacifistic views. In his first sermon there, he nevertheless stated: "No government can force us to kill; one has to find a way to resist Nazism without killing people." This was to be found, as he then wrote, by following the peaceful teachings in the Gospels, such as the passage "Love thy neighbor as thyself," the Sermon on the Mount, and the Parable of the Good Samaritan; "one should obey God rather than men," and the biblical texts on the cities of refuge (Numbers 35, Deuteronomy 4 and 19). His daughter Nelly described him as a "spiritual and intellectual volcano"; others noticed his "turbulent stream," and "holy anger" at the sight of evil. Interestingly, in spite of his strong pacifism and his abhorrence of war, in the 1930s he once considered assassinating Hitler. In his private unpublished memoirs he wrote of the mental conflict he underwent when he realized the danger presented by Hitler. "Having known the First World War, I struggled against an inner sensation within myself. . . . However, should I not take advantage of my knowledge of German to slip into Hitler's entourage and assassinate him before it was too late, before he threw the world in a wide catastrophe?" What stopped him was his determination not to deviate from his religious beliefs on nonviolence, as well as his widening pastoral obligations in Le Chambon.[61]

On June 22, 1940, the day France surrendered, Trocmé preached a sermon that was to guide his action during the occupation years. "The duty of Christians is to respond to the violence that will be brought to bear on their consciences with the weapons of the spirit. . . . We will resist whenever our adversaries demand of us compliance contrary to the orders of the Gospels. We will do so without fear, as well as without pride and without hate." Reacting to the mass arrest of Jews in Paris, on July 16, 1942, Trocmé stated from the pulpit, "This is a humiliation for Europe and for us French. . . . The Christian Church must get down on its knees and ask forgiveness of God for its impotence. . . . I can no longer keep silent. I do not say this with a spirit of hate but of sadness and humiliation for the people of our country." Earlier, with the news of the internment of thousands of Jews in French camps, Trocmé convened a church session at which he proposed visiting one of the internment camps as a goodwill ambassador to distribute food. Arriving in

Marseilles, he met Burns Chalmers of the American Quakers, who told him of the difficulties incurred in finding families willing to shelter people released from these camps. Turning to Trocmé, Chalmers asked: "Do you wish to be such a community?" Trocmé recalled thinking, "The unexpected challenge was there, in front of me." He asked Chalmers, "But these children, one has to shelter them, to nourish and teach them. Who will do it?" Burns: "Find the homes and the instructors. The Quakers and the Fellowship of Reconciliation will support you financially." Returning to Le Chambon, he asked his cousin, Daniel Trocmé, to open one such home. It was to be Les Grillons. Additional homes followed, and the rest is history. Le Chambon-sur-Lignon had been converted into a city of refuge, as commanded by laws of Moses.

The young Jewish activist Denise Siekierski, who worked with Joseph Bass out of Marseilles, guided many Jews into the Chambon area. "I had a room in Chambon, where we hid hundreds of Jews," she recalled. Soon, people of all backgrounds, languages, and religions were seen circulating freely in Le Chambon, "believers and nonbelievers, Christians and Jews." Jewish teachers, who had lost their jobs as a result of the regime's racial laws, were hired in the private school opened in 1938 by Trocmé's trusted companion, Pastor Edouard Théis.

Such as Daniel Isaac, who recalled that he arrived in Chambon in July 1941 with his wife and children at the request of André Trocmé to teach philosophy at the Collège Cévénol, after his dismissal by the Vichy regime. He eventually made his escape from France to join the Free French Army being organized in Africa. His wife, children, and in-laws remained in hiding. As for his father, the famed historian Jules Isaac, and his mother, they came to Le Chambon in 1942 in search of safety. It was there that Jules Isaac began to interest himself in the origins of antisemitism within Christianity, which he believed was at the origin of the current antisemitism holding sway in Nazified Europe. In 1943, he began putting these thoughts in writing in *Jesus and Israel*. André Trocmé recalled how impressed he was by Jules Isaac in the many conversations between the two, especially when, in 1943, Isaac showed him the manuscript of his book, and in Trocmé's words "he beseeched me, together with him, to exonerate the Jews from the crime of deicide, for which they had been accused for nineteen centuries. Of course, I did not have to be convinced." In 1943, Jules Isaac and his wife, together with their families left the Chambon area for a different place, where they were betrayed, and with the exception of Jules Isaac, were deported to die in a concentration camp.

The historian Eli Ben Gal was another recipient of help from the Le Chambon community. "It was one of the best times of my life," he stated. "I spent the time fishing for frogs, hunting snakes, chasing butterflies, and I shall never forget it." The Bible-believing people there considered the Jews to be the People of God. As stated by Marie Brottes, a Le Chambon rescuer, in the film by Pierre Sauvage, *The Weapons of the Spirit*, "What? God has sent His people and we would not receive them?"[62] To the author Anny Latour, Trocmé revealed after the war that he had forbidden any form of proselytizing. "To the Jews who asked me to baptize them as a way of escaping antisemitic laws, I always replied, 'I cannot offer baptism unless it is asked for in complete honesty, and for religious conviction. There are other ways of saving you.' During the occupation, not one Jewish child received improper Christian upbringing: to not respect the consciences of children who had been entrusted to us by parents who had disappeared; this would have been an abuse. What gave us such a right?" [63]

When asked by the regional prefect to welcome Vichy Youth Minister Georges Lamirand, who would be arriving on an official visit on August 15, 1942, Trocmé gave him a polite but cool reception—no flags in the windows, and no one cheering him from the sidewalks. When Lamirand left the local Protestant chapel, after delivering a brief pro-Vichy message, a group of students from the Collège Cévénol presented him with a petition, believed to have been drafted by Trocmé, which read. "Mr. Minister. We have learned of the terrible scenes that took place in Paris three weeks ago, when the French police on orders of the occupying power arrested in their homes all the Jewish families in Paris for their deportation. Fathers were torn from their families and deported to Germany; children were torn from their mothers, who shared the fate as their fathers. . . . We wish to let you know that we have among us a number of Jews. However, we make no distinction between Jews and non-Jews. This is contrary to the teaching of the Gospels. If our comrades were to receive an order to be deported or even to register, for the sole reason that they belong to another religion, they will disobey such orders, and for us, we will do our best to hide them among us." Stupefied and at a loss for words, Lamirand's face turned red with rage. Standing next to him was the regional prefect, Robert Bach, who angrily turned to Trocmé: "Mr. Pastor, you have gone too far! We know you're behind this speech of theirs! On this day of national harmony, you sow dissention." Trocmé shot back: "There can be no question of national harmony when our brothers are threatened with deportation." To this, Bach reportedly angrily retorted: "It is true that I've already received orders, and I will carry them out. The Jews, who are strangers in this region, are not your brothers. They do not belong to your church or your homeland. . . . The Fuehrer, as an intelligent man . . . has ordered to concentrate the Jews of Europe in Poland. There they will have their own lands and houses; they will lead a life that is suitable for them and will cease to corrupt the West. In a few days, my men will come to register the Jews in Chambon." Unflinchingly, Trocmé replied: "We ignore what is a Jew. We only know what are human beings." Bach, losing his patience, warned: "Mr. Trocmé, you would do better to be prudent. Seven of your citizens write to me on a regular basis about your subversive activities. Up to now, I have taken no account of their letters, but I am keeping track. If you're not prudent, it is you whom I will be forced to deport. You've been warned. Goodbye!"

Two weeks later, on August 25, 1942, the regional police chief came to see Trocmé, and without mincing words straightforwardly asked him to turn over the list of Jews in the region. Trocmé, no less defiant as before, responded: "I know nothing of these people. But even if I possessed such a list, I would not furnish it to you. These people came to seek aid and refuge among the Protestants in this region. I am their pastor, in other words, their shepherd. It is not the role of a shepherd to turn over the sheep placed in his care." The police chief warned Trocmé that if he persisted in this refusal, he would be arrested, and left. Soon thereafter, several police vans appeared on the scene, and asked the Chambon inhabitants to show them where the Jews were staying. At the end of the day, only one Jew (of the hundreds, if not thousands, in the region, at this time) was apprehended, a refugee from Austria, who was released when it turned out that he was only a half-Jew. The gendarmes remained in town for three weeks, staging sudden inspection raids on homes and isolated hamlets, then left empty-handed.

After his confrontation with Lamirand and Bach, Trocmé feared immediate arrest, but nothing happened until some six months later, when, on February 13, 1943, Trocmé and two of his principal assistants, Pastor Edouard Théis and Roger Darcissac (the town's educational head), were arrested and interned in camp St. Paul-D'Eyjeaux, near Limoges. During their five-week imprisonment, Pastor Boegner interceded with the Vichy authorities for their release. Finally, as a condition of their liberation, Trocmé and his companions were asked to sign a statement committing themselves not to criticize Pétain or disobey Vichy orders. Trocmé and Théis refused. A day later, the three were released. It was reported that the other prisoners in the camp were deported, and apparently there were no survivors. On June 29, 1943, the Gestapo entered the fray, raiding the Maison des Roches, which was administered by Daniel Trocmé, and where twenty-three refugee students were housed, including some Jews. The students were taken away, with the exception of one who was very ill, and another student who, it was reported, had saved a convalescing German soldier from drowning in the Lignon River and was let go. As for Daniel Trocmé, he was imprisoned and eventually deported to Majdanek camp, where he perished on April 4, 1944. After this Gestapo raid, Trocmé and Théis were urged to go underground, and they stayed in hiding until the spring of 1944. Historians differ on the number of Jews who benefited from the aid of the Protestants of the Plateau, but most agree it runs to at least several thousand. One Le Chambon rescuer, honored by Yad Vashem, reportedly was told by a gendarme, "Be careful, Madame, you're being watched." To which, she replied, "But not by you! I am guarded by God above," and she pointed upward.[64]

In the Cevennes, another large Protestant community, in the mountainous region to the south of Le Chambon (astride both the Lozère and Gard departments), many pastors were involved in welcoming fleeing Jews in their midst. In one such story, in July 1942, Fanny Hadari, her parents Helene and Elias Gutwirth, and brother Azriel, arrived in Mende, and were helped by local inhabitants with shelter here and there. In the spring of 1944, in light of the increasing dangers, Fanny's mother, Helene, went to see Pastor Joseph Bourdon, who taught at a Protestant seminary. He referred her to Pastor André Gall in nearby Florac, while the family's two children were sent to Pastor François Chazel in Vébron village. In Vébron, Pastor Chazel procured new credentials for the other family members under the name of Delrue. "Whenever I needed advice," Fanny Hadari wrote, "I always went to Chazel's home. He was always patient with me, loaned me books, and discussed philosophy and religion with me." Chazel's wife, Liliane gave more details on the help to fleeing Jews. "About fifty Jewish refugees came to our villages. The problems were many and daily: false credentials, ration cards, lodgings, work for certain people, subsidies for those lacking it. One had to encourage, at the same time, those welcomed and those who welcomed them." She went on to list the people helped by her and her pastor husband: Mrs. Benzoname, with her little son Michel and a little nephew; the Goldzahl family, Walter Poli, his wife, and their little Willi, originally from Germany (who later were able to flee to Switzerland); the Kahn-Steinitz family; Dr. Joseph Mandl, the Gutwirths with their son and daughter, originally from Belgium; Maxime Cohen, who later fell captive to the German, was tortured and executed; Hermann and Anny Flack and their son Thomas (from Austria); the Zygels (from Poland), who arrived with five children; the eldest, Henri, worked as a tailor in the presbytery, but left to join the Maquis when he learned of the Normandy invasion in June 1944 and fell in combat two months later; finally, Mr. Stampa, from Poland, whose wife died in a hospital, and who one day decided to join an acquaintance in the Alps region without leaving a forwarding address. "The little that Pastor François Chazel was able to do during this great turmoil," his wife explained in 1977, "was thanks to the One who said: 'You shall love the Lord your God with all you soul, with all your strength and with all your thoughts, and your neighbor as yourself.'. . . Great was our joy and our gratitude to see coming out alive of this turmoil almost all those whose lives was entrusted to us. *Glory to God alone*." In this context, one may also mention some more pastors, such as Franck Robert in Meyrueis (Lozere), who located farming families willing to shelter Jews, and provided them with false credentials, while temporarily sheltering them in his home; Robert Joseph in Clarensac, who assisted Elisabeth Zerner and her husband; Roland Pollex in St. Jean du Gard, who helped the Lazarsfeld family; Laurent Olivès in Ardailles, who assisted Renata Villain and her baby son Alain; finally, Gaston Martin in St. Germain de Calberte, who together with Paul Tinel (of the Salvation Army) shared in the rescue of Sylvie Schaub and her father.[65]

Pastor Elie Brée, in Caveirac (Gard), who assisted the earlier-mentioned Elisabeth Zerner and her two children, explained in 1993 how he had become involved in rescue work. One day, a woman who had escaped from an internment camp in nearby Beaucaire knocked on his door and asked for help to reach distant Switzerland; Brée found a sheltering home for her. Then on another day, a nearby camp commander confided to Brée that he had been ordered to hand over the "non-Aryan" prisoners, in other words Jews. Brée asked whether he knew which agency was authorized to issue Aryan certificates. The commander did not know. So Brée suggested that perhaps this could be done by the Protestant chaplaincy (Brée being the camp chaplain). "I did all the certificates. We knew they were worth nothing, but this gave them time to breathe. It worked for a time, while we tried to 'put away' those most in danger"; that is to hide them." At a conference in 1996, Brée explained what had led him into this sort of illegal work. "There was clearly an adversary. [One was confronted by] the famous choice: Where lie the good and the bad?—one stood before a wall; one had to react, and thus there were two choices; [for a while] I feel crushed, and wait for this to pass; then, suddenly, no! One cannot allow it. Now one must act. At this moment, one must find a way to act. This was the moment when I told my wife: 'You know, one cannot remain like this.' "[66]

Still in the Cevennes, we note the story of Pastor Marc Donadille in Saint-Privat-de-Vallongue (Lozère), who hid Marianne Ahlfeld and her children in an old house in the midst of a forest, and together with his wife, Françoise, provided her with food. Then there occurred an incident that showed the true character of Donadille's religious faith, and that of the other pastors in the Cevennes. It happened when Dr. Weill-Spire, a Jew in hiding in Collet-de-Dèze, swallowed poison rather than allow himself to be arrested by the French police, and was rushed to a hospital. Local residents stormed the police station and threatened that if the doctor died there would be trouble. Fearing unrest, Dutruch, the deputy prefect in Florac, asked Donadille to intervene and keep the situation from getting out of control. Furious at the deputy prefect, Donadille told him: "Do not forget that you are in the *camisard* [the Huguenot-Calvinist] countryside! Like their forefathers, the inhabitants here are ready to take up arms if the state commits acts opposed to their beliefs.

Don't ignore the fact that they have weapons. They turned in their bad weapons in the municipalities— but the good ones, they've kept them." With these words, Donadille left the deputy prefect's office. An hour later, the prefect called on Donadille. "I repeated what I had told the deputy prefect, insisting that the war of the Huguenots was not politically motivated, but a religious revolt, an upsurge of Christian conscience. And I concluded: the Protestants in the Cevennes, as well as the Catholics, with a few exceptions, are the spiritual children of the *camisards*. They do not agree with the iniquitous persecution of the Jews by the government, and they will oppose it with every means." Visibly moved, the prefect pleaded, "But what can I do? I receive compulsory orders from Pierre Laval that one must search for the Jews wherever they hide. . . . I am forced to obey the orders of my government." To which Donadille responded: "When you stand before God, he will not talk to you about Pierre Laval; he will ask what you yourself have done." Then Donadille counseled the prefect to tell his gendarmes to carry out the orders to look for Jews, but also to make them understand "that they are not obliged to find them." The prefect said, "I will see what I can do," and left Donadille's home. The result was that when the gendarmes came to Saint-Privat in search of Jews, they made it a point to stop over at Donadille's and stay there for quite a long time, thus allowing Donadille's family to alert the Jews to find another temporary refuge. Some people were then quickly moved to other locations, such as Jacques Rotenberg, who was taken by Pastor Wasserfallen to Viane (Tarn), and was fetched by other friendly pastors. Thanks to the help of the Protestant community, most of the Jews in the Cevennes survived.[67]

More Special Protestant Rescue Stories

In Lyon, we have the remarkable story of Pastor Roland De Pury. Born in Geneva, he studied theology in Paris, and in 1938 was appointed minister of the Protestant chapel on Rue Lanterne in Lyon. A man of abundant spiritual courage, on July 14, 1940, days after the fall of France and the installation of Marshal Pétain as France's new leader, to the adulation of the whole Catholic hierarchy, De Pury sent a defiant message from the pulpit. "Better a dead France than sold-out; defeated than thief. A dead France—one could weep for her, but a France that has betrayed the hope that the persecuted ones placed in her, a France that had sold her soul and renounced her mission, would reduce us to tears. She would no longer be France. . . . Already people no longer ask themselves whether this war was justified; they regret having done it because they lost it. As though defeat annulled the just cause of this struggle. As if truth was measured by its success." Soon thereafter, his home became a staging area for planning rescue activities of Jews. Traveling frequently to Switzerland, he coordinated activities with his colleagues there; in particular with Willem Vissert Hooft and Adolf Freudenberg, who urged the Swiss government to allow Jews access into Switzerland. In addition, he turned his house into a relay station for clandestine people, including *passeurs* on their way to the Swiss border, such as Mireille Philip, working out of the Le Chambon area, or those involved in helping prisoners in internment camps (Gurs, Rivesaltes, Noé, Récébédou). The Jewish activist and later historian Anny Latour was hidden in De Pury's home together with her husband, and Latour's friend, Rella Gottlieb, of the UGIF, referred to De Pury people in danger of arrest, especially children. The number of people received by him increased from day to day and at times he personally escorted people to the Swiss border. Soon after the Germans entered Lyon, on January 27, 1943, the Gestapo raided De Pury's home and caught him presiding over a meeting together with other clandestine and rescue activists, including Father Pierre Chaillet, Jean-Marie Soutou, and the Jewish Mrs. Bloch. All were taken to Gestapo headquarters for further interrogation. After hours of grueling questioning, Chaillet, who appeared under a different name, was freed (actually physically thrown out), without the Gestapo having succeeded in establishing his true identity; Soutou was eventually also released, and was able to flee to Switzerland; as for Rella Gottlieb, who also happened to be there, she was deported and perished. That evening De Pury held counsel in his home on what to do the following day when, as already prearranged, some Jews would be coming to fetch their false credentials. How could he alert them not to appear? It was decided that the Catholic lay worker Germaine Ribière, an associate of De Pury in the *Amitié Chrétienne,* would disguise herself as a cleaning woman washing the floors of the building, and thus able to warn visitors to immediately leave the premises. On Sunday, May 30, 1943, it was the turn of De Pury to be arrested and taken for questioning, on the charge of aiding the Resistance. Cardinal Gerlier and Pastor Boegner interceded on his behalf, but without success. Imprisoned for five months, he was released as a Swiss citizen on October 28, 1943, in exchange for German spies held in Switzerland, and he left for that country. After France's liberation, he returned to his Lyon post.[68]

The Calvinist pastor Pierre Toureille at first served as vice-chairman of an aid organization in Marseilles for refugees from Czechoslovakia, which also included Jews, and also as chaplain for Protestant foreigners in France. In November 1940, he was elected vice-president of the Nîmes Committee, a conglomeration of twenty-five Christian and Jewish organizations founded by Donald Lowrie of the American YMCA to help refugees in French internment camps. Later, from his base in Lunel (Hérault), near Montpellier, Toureille helped them with money, clothing, food, and books, as well as arranging their flight to Switzerland. He had a staff of nineteen people to assist him. He provided some of the Jews referred to him with documents stating that they belonged to the Protestant community and were thus under the church's protection. Anna Sperber, one of the Jewish beneficiaries of Toureille's aid, made contact with him through her husband's family in Switzerland, who turned to a Protestant organization, which in turn contacted Toureille. This was just in time, because the Sperber family, in Pézénas, near Beziers, was about to be deported (delayed thanks to a doctor's report of an illness in the family). In Anna Sperber's words: "On the fourth day [of our contrived illness], somebody called me to a drug store (three blocks away), where a long-distance call was waiting for me. Very scared, I heard a man's voice. It was Pastor Pierre Toureille, from a city a few hundred miles away from us. We had never heard from him before and I became suspicious, but it was a very kind voice that asked me how he could help us. At this very moment, I knew intuitively that now a little sunshine would come into our distress. From this moment, it was like a godmother's hands watching over us. . . . He helped us directly and indirectly. He gave us advice about how and where to flee. He sent us money wherever we were and also helped some friends we recommended to him." The Sperbers moved to several places and proceeded to Lyon, where they were assisted by the aforementioned Pastor de Pury—"a wonderful man"— who then forwarded them a few hundred miles away to Mens (Isere), a little town, with a letter of recommendation for the pastor there, named Pierre Gothié. Toureille also aided Robert Papet (Papst), who fled Germany to France, in 1934. In September 1942, Toureille had him brought from Metz, in the north of France, and looked after his and his non-Jewish wife's needs, "although," Papet adds, "I indicated on the form that I was of the Jewish race and of the Jewish religion." After the German occupation of the Vichy zone, in November 1942, Toureille provided Papet with a new identification under the name of Robert Parlier, and sent him to Pastor Charles Cabanis, in Bedarieux (Herault), where Papet/Parlier remained hidden during the whole month of December 1942. Toureille then referred the two to Pastor Luigi, in Camares (Gard), where Papet and his wife stayed for five more months. Then, in March 1943, Toureille invited Papet/Parlier to come to Lunel, and put him in charge of his office's administrative work. By then, Toureille was well aware that he was being watched by the French authorities. In fact, a Vichy internal security report, in October 1942, stated that Toureille "is very sympathetic to Jews and without doubt, helps them obtain the papers they need. . . . He is suspected of organizing the passage of foreigners to Spain." The report's conclusion: "I respectfully request that the Chief of the Regional Police order an active surveillance of the activities of Pastor Toureille." While the French were a little lax in following up this recommendation, when the Germans took over they raided Toureille's office and several times interrogated him. He was able to talk himself out, by explaining that his work was purely religious, nothing political.

With the war over, Toureille equivocated between agreeing to the Jewish children's return to their fold and a subtle attempt at evangelization. In a report by him on April 5, 1945, he urged maintaining the children within the Protestant fold, warning that "if we do not act, we will lose one after another of our children to Catholic or Jewish institutions." He strongly believed in a church that was aggressively evangelical; that the church's role was to "save men's souls," since "a church that does not evangelize is useless on earth." Like many other genuine Christians who hoped in their hearts for Jews to join the church, this did not conflict with his sincere feelings of helping Jews against their enemies. As stated by him, "Some of us would be ready again to run the same risks, and others, too, if necessary, in defense of the Jews." In a postwar letter, Pastor Toureille also underlined that "in my work, I never influenced Jews to convert; instead I gave them false documents, where they appeared as Christians." In 1988, Toureille's son, Marc Toureille, wrote to Yad Vashem, in appreciation of the planting of a tree in his father's name, that "because of the religious persecutions we had to endure and because of our religious education which was strongly based on Jewish history as told in the Bible, we French Huguenots always had a close sense of kinship to the Jews."[69]

In Nice, Pastor Edmond Evrard worked closely with Jewish rescue activists Joseph Bass and Moussa Abadi, and led groups of Jewish children to safety in Le Chambon. Actually, it was while on a visit to Le Chambon that he first became fired with the idea of lending a hand to help Jews. Returning to Nice, Evrard and his two grownup sons, in the guise of counselors in a Salvation Army summer camp, escorted fleeing Jews, dressed as Swiss Scouts, to the Swiss border. He also sheltered Jews for short periods of time and provided them with forged papers. Like many other Protestant pastors, he was sensitive to the religious needs of his Jewish wards. During the Purim festival, in March 1944, he put an annex in his chapel at the disposal of the Jews, so they could read the Scroll of Esther, as prescribed by the religion. While the reading went on, Evrard remained with the worshippers during the service while his sons stood on lookout in the street. The following festival was Passover, and here too Evrard exerted himself to make matzos (unleavened bread) available to his Jewish wards. On several occasions, he interceded with the Gestapo to effect the release of several Jews. In one case, he tried a risky tactic, by secretly promising a Gestapo agent who seemed more amenable than the others (but still was code-named "the killer") that if he were forthcoming, Evrard would after the war testify on the man's behalf. It was a risky step, but it succeeded. In another rescue operation in early 1944, involving a woman arrested in a maternity ward after she delivered a son, here, too, Evrard was able to acquire false identifications which showed the woman to be non-Jewish. With these papers, he went to see a Gestapo agent named Krauss, in February 1944. After the war, Evrard related what then transpired. "He behaved toward me in an unspeakable manner, and had me thrown against the door by a soldier, shaking me by holding on to my shoulders. . . . He threw me out because he had been ordered to do so, and if I returned he would then admit me. Which is what I did." To the surprise of Evrard, Krauss then told him that the woman in question would be freed, and so it happened. Writing about his rescue exploits after the war, Pastor Evrard stated: "What we did was altogether natural. We, other Christians, Protestants, and especially those of the Baptist Church, are nourished by the Bible. The history of the Jewish people is our history as well. Palestine is our second homeland. We love the Jews and we hold them in esteem. They are brave people."[70]

In nearby Cannes, Pastor Charles Monod provided fleeing Jews with false credentials and also arranged their flight to other locations. He remembered a telegram received by a collaborating pastor in Chatillon, in September 1943, with the following message: 'Send two Bibles marriageable format, deluxe edition; one more Bible for the road, hard binding; a Bible for Sunday School format." Monod was able to decipher the coded message as being a request to deliver two easy-going household Jewish couples for shelter; also, a young man of strong physique for farming purposes; and a child of Sunday School age.[71] In Belfort, Olga St. Blancat-Baumgarten, an officer in the Salvation Army, sheltered two young Jewish sisters (Giselle and Marianne Mohrer, born respectively, 1941 and 1939), starting July 1942, in her and mother's village home of Badevel. After the war, the Mohrer girls were sent to their maternal grandmother in England. In a 1988 letter to Yad Vashem, she wrote: "I thank Providence for having obeyed the commandment in Deuteronomy of love for fellow man— a precious heritage of Israel's election." At the Yad Vashem ceremony in her honor, she stated that when the phone rang and she was asked by a Red Cross representative whether she would take the children, "I knew that God was calling me, to test my faith. I could not but respond affirmatively."[72]

The story of Pastor Jean Severin Lemaire in Marseilles is one of the most edifying in the context of help to Jews, and we grant him the opening words. "After the French defeat, I lived in Marseilles, where I had been pastor since 1937 of an Evangelical community and a teacher of Bible. I was always opposed to the ideas and activities of what was known as the government of the State of France [Vichy], which I held, in principle and mostly on evidence, to be opposed to the ideas of a Christian and of the Gospels. I was especially struck by the mounting persecution of Jews in general, which began with the pursuit of foreign Jews. . . . I could not look on without actively aiding them—the hunted, whose numbers were on the increase. In the effort to try to help them, I contacted at the end of 1941 Joseph Bass [a Jewish activist who used the name Mr. André] . . . and learned of the organization he had founded to help those who were hunted, whether children, of military age, or elderly. This type of work I found to be just, and I decided to give it my full cooperation. We had many contacts with Christian and Jewish organizations. . . . We created in Marseilles, and throughout the southern Mediterranean region, an organization where Protestants, Catholics, and Jews of various shades of opinion worked fraternally—including Father de Parceval [a Dominican prior], who was later interned, Father Bremond, a Jesuit from Aix-en-Provence, Father Marie-Benoît, a Capuchin, Pastor Heuze (interned and deported), who was pastor of the Reformed Church in Marseilles, Joseph Lasalarie (attorney), Murzi (attorney), Israel Salzer (chief rabbi of Marseilles), Angelo Donati, Rabbi Hirschler, and many others. We helped many people avoid arrest and deportation, either by hiding them or arranging their passage into the Italian zone or abroad, or leading them to areas controlled by the Maquis [armed resistance], chiefly in the Chambon region." Then he was betrayed by a Belgian Jewish doctor posing as a fugitive but in reality forced to act as a Gestapo agent. How so? Lemaire had agreed to place at Bass's disposal the prayer hall he used for Sunday afternoon conferences. Denise Siekierski, a Jewish rescue activist, met people seeking aid at a different address, where she interviewed them to sort out those who were really in need of aid before directing them to Lemaire's conference hall. Dr. Siegfried Levy was seeking aid and claimed he had been tailed by the Gestapo. After interviewing him twice, and not suspecting anything, she referred him to Lemaire's address. He disclosed the information to the Gestapo, who came to arrest Lemaire on March 12, 1943, and mistakenly apprehended two men who happened to be waiting for a bar to open near the entrance to the pastor's chapel, and were suspected of being part of Lemaire's network. "That day I was not in Marseilles," Lemaire recounts, "but I had planned to give a lecture there the next day. Mr. André came to see me and asked that I leave Marseilles to join the Maquis and not show myself on Sunday. However, I felt it a matter of conscience to be there, and if necessary to be arrested, so that two innocent young men would be released. Two days later, Lemaire headed back to his Marseilles chapel and was promptly arrested. The two innocent arrested men were thereupon released. "I do not regret what took place, nor the decision I took. As a Christian and a pastor, I had to be a witness, irrespective of the consequences." Lemaire then underwent a long and arduous series of tortures at the hand of four Gestapo agents, to make him reveal his associates, but he stood firm. "Forty-eight hours later, I was led to a cell where Jews were kept. The Gestapo man declared: 'Because you love the Jews so much, we have placed you with them'." In that cell for two months, Lemaire had to contend with the very unhygienic conditions, more severe than in the non-Jewish cells, which he had to share with a group of elderly and young people, women and children and an eighteen-month-old baby, "for whom I asked for milk, instead of the watery soup which the Germans provided to the prisoners." Lemaire related the great suffering of that Jewish family. "I remember seeing the arrival of a Jewish family of thirteen people (the Vigderhaus family), father, mother, son, daughters-in-law, daughters, and a child. I must say that this child is alive because I managed to have him freed and the Red Cross came to fetch him due to my insistence. However, the mother, who was down with diabetes, begged the Gestapo to be allowed to go to Nîmes, and indicated the place in her closet where she had insulin for injections. She was told: 'It's unimportant, you will die sooner or later; you may as well die here.' And we helplessly witnessed the agony of this woman, who slowly and from day to day, for a period of eight days, lost her strength and suffered terribly. She expired, in extreme pain, in front of her children and her desperate husband. The children wanted at least to respectfully wash her body, but the guards simply dragged her out. I emphasize: they did not carry her but dragged her, and we don't know how the body was disposed of. Of this family of thirteen people, only the baby was saved. Another person, a daughter-in-law, survived the camps. All the others perished. . . . Then something extraordinary happened, which showed that there are no Jews, neither Greeks, nor pagans, nor Christians, but we were all people chained to the horror of our unspeakable sufferings. . . . Jews asking an evangelical pastor to give them God's blessings before leaving on their last journey. . . . Upon the request of the Jews, before leaving, I read to them a Psalm. . . . We then read together this Psalm, and together we prayed to the Almighty, the God of the Jews and of Jesus Christ, the God of the believers, to accompany them on their coming pilgrimage." In her testimony, Mrs. Francine Abravanel related seeing in the cell "a rabbi with a long beard, who prayed with us, observed the Sabbath, who always blessed us when people were taken away for deportation. It was he who raised our spirit, and it was this 'rabbi' who liberated the child." She then continued: "How astonished I was to recently learn that the man whom I took for a rabbi was the Protestant pastor Lemaire," who sported a long beard and was mistaken for a rabbi. After two months in this cell, Lemaire was moved to a non-Jewish cell, then in March 1944, he was deported, first to Mauthausen camp, then to Dachau, where he witnessed the horrors of these two camps, but fortunately survived. "Upon liberation, we returned, sick, tired, asking nothing from anyone and receiving nothing from anyone, wanting only to rest, calm and peace." As for the Holocaust, "one may forgive for himself; but society's justice cannot always forgive; political power cannot grant amnesty to every-thing; only God can forgive everything; but he has not given to people in their passions the right to invoke God's pardon, for they do not know his ways." Meeting Denise Siekierski in Marseilles, in 1984, who since the tragic event of March 1943, had been filled with pangs of guilt for having inadvertently caused Lemaire's arrest, he told her: "I know very well what you are going through, and I want to fully deliver you from this guilt complex with which you have lived these forty years. Things happened that way because God wanted it thus. It was a mission which I was forced to accomplish, and you should not feel guilty about it." Since then, Denise Siekierski, who lives in Jerusalem, when she has occasion to show groups of people from France the Yad Vashem memorial, makes it a point to show them the tree of Lemaire, and tell his story.[73]

Concluding Comments

From the preceding accounts, it is clear that the primary motivation of the clergy rescuers was the basic Christian obligation to extend help to people in need, following the example of the Good Samaritan story. As stated by Pastor André Trocmé of Le Chambon to a French police chief: "These people came to seek aid and refuge among the Protestants in this region. I am their pastor, in other words, their shepherd. It is not the role of a shepherd to turn over the sheep placed in his care." The history of suffering of the French Protestants at the hands of the Catholic majority undoubtedly also triggered a positive response to others in a similar situation, as bluntly stated by Pastor Marc Donadille to a high French official: "Do not forget that you are in the *Camisard* [Huguenot-Calvinist] countryside! Like their forefathers, the inhab-itants here are ready to take up arms if the state commits acts opposed to their beliefs." While most Protestant clerics make no claim of previous contacts with Jews, this was not always so with Catholic clergy. Father Roger Braun, a Jesuit, stated that he had gained much spiritually from contacts with Jews. "I acquired a greater respect for God, a greater love as well, and a much greater respect for the Law (Torah)." An additional factor for this cleric was the shame he felt as a young seminarian at the depiction on the façade of the cathedral in Strasbourg of the burning of the city's Jews in the fourteenth cen-tury, which led him to the conviction of forgiveness and reconciliation between the two faiths.

Did the hope of gaining additional souls for the Christian faith play an important role, especially in sheltering Jewish children in Christian institu-tions? Undoubtedly some may have been prompted by this consideration, especially in light of the importance attached in Christian thinking to the con-version of Jews, and there were probably cases of direct pressure. However, insofar as our record here reveals, while some may have harbored such thoughts, they did not manifest it openly; quite to the contrary. Our stories show that most clerics behaved quite differently. Monsignor Saliège, in Toulouse, reportedly instructed Sister Denise Bergon "You will have to lie; lie then whenever necessary; I give you all my absolution in advance." Father Raymond Vancourt, in Lille, turned down the request of the Jewish woman staying at his home to be converted, telling her, "Irene, I love you as a human being, and my respect for you as a Jew is deep and sincere; that's what you are. Don't ever ask me to do that. Even if you would ask me on bent knees, I would not do it and that's that." The same on the Protestant side. Pastor Pierre Toureille, in Lunel (Herault), who stated that "a church that does not evangelize is useless on earth" refrained from such attempts during the war years, and reiterated his conviction that "some of us would be ready again to run the same risks, and others, too, if necessary, in defense of the Jews." In Catholic convents, when conversions occurred, it was mostly either for the child's protection or to make him/her feel better integrated with the larger non-Jewish group. In the case of Jacqueline Eskinazi, baptized at her own request, the humanitarian factor of her rescuer nuns is proven by the strong ties between both sides after the war, and the acceptance of Jacqueline's return to Judaism, in her words, "with full understanding." Especially admirable are the accounts of how nuns helped their Jewish wards to practice their Judaism inside the walls of convents, as in the account of Mother Superior Marie-Gonzague Bredoux of the Abbaye Saint-Etienne convent, who fetched church candles for Mrs. Kraindel Dornfest to light on Friday eve to celebrate the Sabbath, and new utensils for use during the Passover festival. Similarly Sister Antoinette Masserey helped her young words to celebrate the Sabbath as religiously prescribed. A similar and even more pronounced attitude prevailed among Protestant clerics, with their greater attachment to the Hebrew Bible. Such as Pastor Edmond Evrard, in Nice, who at the approach of the Purim festival, in March 1944, placed an annex of his chapel at the disposal of the Jews, so they could recite the Scroll of Esther, while his sons stood out in the street as lookouts for possible approaching danger.

What is especially fascinating as a possible rescue motivation is the strong religious affinity that many clerics felt for Jews and Judaism despite the church's age-long "teaching of contempt." Such as Saliège's comment: "I cannot forget that Jesus' stem flourished in Israel, and produced its fruit. . . . How can you wish that I not feel tied to Israel like the bough the trunk has borne." Or Father Camille Folliet, in Annecy, who explained to French gendarmes why he was aiding Jews on Christmas eve, "The whole world is about to celebrate the holiday of hope and peace, promised to men of good will. Imagine what would have happened on the first Christmas if they had hunted Jews all the way to Bethlehem! The Savior would not have been born in a cave but in a prison, behind bars and barbed wire." This special relation toward Jews led some clerics to a feeling bordering on love for them. In Paris, the Russian Orthodox nun Maria Skobtsova, in the spring of 1942, wrote of the "election" of the Jews as a "great path." She ended her paean with the words: "Thou art persecuted again, O Israel. But what can human ill will mean to thee, thee who has heard the thunder from Sinai?" Father Albert Gau, of Carcassonne, during a Yad Vashem ceremony in his honor, spoke of the "grandeur" of the Jewish people, and ended with the words, "Do not fail us, for without you, we would lose direction. People of Jesus, I love you." Finally, the uniquely outstanding Marie-Benoît wrote in 1966 that the Jewish people cannot be exterminated because it lives by divine providence, for the fulfillment of religious aspirations, first "for its own good, then, for the good of all humanity. . . . Long live the State of Israel. May the God of Abraham, Isaac, and Jacob come to her help."[74]

Chapter 4
BELGIUM

Today we can almost certainly expect that this people, chosen by God, will produce many conversions, especially as they will no longer be precluded from [receiving] the overflowing gift of God's grace in view of the terrible suffering of this people. Thus, praying for the conversion of Israel seems to be needed, especially in these times. Bishop Louis-Joseph Kerkhofs, Liège, 1945.[1]

I never thought of trying to convert the Rosenberg children to the Catholic faith. I always respected their religious beliefs. . . . Because I foresaw that the children would, after the war, be returned to their family and to a Jewish environment. So I prefer a good Jew to a bad Christian.
Father Hubert Célis, Halmaal, 1965

Introduction

In the early Middle Ages, Jews settled in what later became Belgium. Over the following years, Jews underwent various tribulations, including massacres, in Brussels, Antwerp, and other locations, on false charges, such as being responsible for the Black Death plague. With the takeover of the country by the French Revolutionary armies in 1794, Jews were granted full freedom, and when Belgium became an independent country in 1831, Judaism was recognized as a legitimate religion. Most Jews resided either in Brussels and Antwerp; those in the latter city were mainly immigrants from Eastern Europe.[2] Days after the German invasion on May 10, 1940, the country's army capitulated and the government fled to England. In the absence of the ministers, the heads of the various ministries, known as secretary-generals, took over in a kind of mini-government. On the German side, a military administration was put in place, headed by General Alexander von Falkenhausen as military governor. The occupation lasted until September 1944, when Allied forces liberated Brussels and Antwerp, but the war continued on the fringes of the country, with the failed German winter offensive of

130

December 1944 in the Ardennes representing the last major German effort to turn the tide of the war. On the eve of the German invasion, the Jewish population numbered close to 66,000 (out of a total population of some 8 million), but fewer than 10 percent were Belgian citizens. The rest were recent immigrants from mostly East European countries. The Jewish population was concentrated in four cities: mostly in Brussels and Antwerp, and smaller numbers in Liège and Charleroi.[3]

The Germans lost no time in implementing severe anti-Jewish measures, which were to escalate to the deportation level. The military administrative office, headed by General Eggert Reeder, began enacting one restrictive measure after another. Ernst Ehlers, SS head in Belgium, was administratively subject to the military administration, but as an SS officer he was ultimately answerable to his SS chief, Himmler, and thus enjoyed much latitude and freedom of action.[4] The first anti-Jewish ordinance, on October 23, 1940, forbade the ritual killing of animals for food purposes. This was followed with a decree defining a Jew as a person with at least three Jewish grandparents, or even two Jewish grandparents if the person in question was a member of the Jewish community or was married to a Jewish spouse. As for people whose Jewish origin was doubtful, they "shall be treated as Jews, and shall be dismissed [from public service] until their origin be verified." Municipalities were ordered to keep a special register of all Jews (of at least fifteen years of age) in their communities. Then a decree ordered the registration of all Jewish-owned businesses. Jews were also prohibited from holding any public posts, from the practice of law or journalism, and from teaching in public schools, and their assets were to be liquidated. Jews were also forbidden to practice medicine and dentistry, and could no longer freely dispose of their goods. In September 1941, a curfew was imposed on Jews from 8:00 p.m. to 7:00 a.m., and they were furthermore forbidden to reside anywhere except Brussels, Antwerp, Liège, and Charleroi. Two months later, all Jews were ordered to register with the newly created Jewish (and Gestapo-controlled) umbrella organization, the *Association des Juifs Belges* (AJB). The organization's purpose, as spelled out in the decree, was to "carry out the emigration of Jews," a euphemism (although the Jewish leadership did not suspect this) for deportation to concentration camps. On May 27, 1942, the Germans imposed the wearing of the yellow star on the outer and visible parts of their garments. This went hand in hand with an edict obliging able-bodied Jews to perform physical labor in the form of building fortifications near the Atlantic coast cities in northern France. Some 2,200 Jews were affected, and most of them were eventually deported directly to Auschwitz. To tighten the trap on the Jews, a decree of June 1, 1942, warned the local population against sheltering Jews outside their residences (in the four permitted cities); that "any violation of this decree shall be punished with imprisonment and a fine . . . not only for the Jews but also for the Aryans who shelter them illegally"; and this could be followed with additional "security measures . . . by the police." By the time the deportation of Jews began in August 1942, in the words of historian Maxime Steinberg, the Jew had been "identified, registered, marked, confined to his home, regrouped in an obligatory organization, isolated from the rest of the population, despoiled of his goods and deprived of his professional economic activity. . . . He is now entirely at one's disposal for the Final Solution."[5]

By the summer of 1942, the Germans had finalized their plans for the start of the deportations. The first train left on August 4, picking up its human cargo at the Malines/Mechelen detention camp, where most Jews were interned. Additional convoys netted many of the non-naturalized Jews, who comprised over 90 percent of the Jewish population. The intervention of the Queen Mother Elisabeth spared for the time being the fewer than 10 percent of the country's Jews who claimed Belgian citizenship. However, in September 1943, the military governor reversed a previous decision and approved the deportation of these Jews as well. That month, the Gestapo head in Antwerp, Eric Holm, proudly proclaimed the city *Judenfrei* ("free of Jews"), although he knew very well that many Jews were hiding in the city and vicinity. An estimated 5,000 to 10,000 Jews managed to flee to France during the initial days of the German invasion, with many of them remaining there or continuing on to safer havens. All told, some 30,500 (including those initially taken to France for forced labor) were deported to camps in Poland (principally, Auschwitz) in twenty-eight convoys, and only 1,800 survived the rigors of the camp and death marches. Children below the age of fifteen constituted a large fraction of the deportees (16 to 20 percent). The remainder of slightly over 30,000 still on Belgian soil, in other words, about half of the original Jewish population, survived mostly in hiding (including approximately 5,600 children), thanks to the active and passive assistance of many Belgian citizens.[6]

As for the attitude of the population at large toward the ever-widening persecution of Jews, consideration must be given to the ethnic composition of the country, which is made up of two distinct ethnic groups, the Flemish and the Walloons, and is divided in half both linguistically and geographically. Flemish, a Dutch dialect, is spoken in the northern part, known as Flanders, bordering the Netherlands (including Antwerp), whereas French is spoken in Wallonia, the southern region that borders France (including Charleroi and Liège). The capital city of Brussels is an officially bilingual enclave. The dominant religion is Roman Catholicism, practiced by close to 80 percent of the population. On the whole, the population and the civil authorities (with the notable exception of Antwerp) were frankly repelled by the radicalization of the anti-Jewish measures. When, for instance, the yellow star decree was decreed, many people took occasion to show their sympathy with the plight of the Jews. "Salute them when passing; yield them a place in the tramway," urged one underground handout. Some clandestine papers explained that they supported antisemitic measures but only up to a certain limit. In the words of an underground journal: "Whether one is for or against antisemitism, there is one thing which one finds revolting: one does not thus place a whole group of people, a whole race, outside the pale of society." There were, of course, openly antisemitic groups that favored collaboration with the Germans and hailed the intensified persecution of Jews. For instance, an Antwerp lawyer, René Lambrichts, led an intense antisemitic campaign coupled with attacks on Jewish stores in his city. Then, there was the VNV (*Vlaams Nationaal Verbond*—National Flemish Movement), with 100,000 members in 1942, which lashed out at the Jews, deriding the "gentlemen of the Old Testament. The curtain has fallen. You may pack up, and vacate room for our own people." Similarly, the French-speaking Rexist movement, headed by Léon Degrelle, which also collaborated with the Nazis, took part in the hunt for hidden Jews. Belgium had a population of 8 million; after the war, 448,000 people were judicially tried or questioned with regard to collaboration with the enemy (most of them lived in the Flemish part of the country), and 3,000 were condemned to death.[7]

Belgian law made no distinction based on race or religion, but solely on non-citizenship. Thus in October 1940, when the German authorities asked the secretary-generals of the various ministries to introduce a registration system differentiating Jews from non-Jews, they refused to comply. Since the Germans refused to back off, the secretary-generals felt they had no choice but to obey. The lawyers association also refused to disclose the names of Jewish attorneys on its list, and asked for the opportunity to explain its opposition before the military governor. The request was turned down, but the Germans did not press the lawyers association on this point.[8] The Brussels Free University, in a letter addressed to the military government, refused to expel its Jewish academic staff. In November 1941, in the face of ongoing pressure to comply, the university elected to suspend its activities. A plan to create a semi-ministry to enforce the anti-Jewish measures (on the Vichy French model of a General Commissariat for Jewish Questions) was finally dropped, due to the outspoken lack of enthusiasm for the idea by the administrative heads of the various ministries. When the Germans tried to enforce the stamping in large red letters of the words *Juif-Jood* on identity cards held by Jews, they were again faced with opposition by the Belgian authorities (with the notable exception of the Antwerp municipality).

When the obligatory wearing of the star was announced, in May 1942, the metropolitan Brussels city mayors, headed by J. Coelst, and at the instigation of Jean Herinckx, the mayor of the Uccle section of the city, informed the Germans of their outspoken opposition to such a measure. "We have the duty to inform you," Coelst wrote to Dr. Gentzke, of the German military administration, "that you cannot force us to collaborate in its execution. A great number of Jews are Belgian [citizens], and we cannot agree to cooperate with a measure which deals such a direct blow to the dignity of every person, no matter who he is." The Germans, at least in the Brussels region, had to themselves distribute the stars.[9] In Antwerp, by contrast, the city fathers complied with the German request. This city has the dubious reputation of being the only Belgian community with a bad record for its treatment of the Jewish population during the war years. Even before the war antisemitic feelings and attacks were rampant, although the Socialist mayor, Camille Huysmans, tried to stem expression of the anti-Jewish sentiments by a series of local antisemitic organizations. On April 14, 1941, Antwerp experienced the only-reported pogrom in the country, when a mob of 200 people, spurred by antisemitic and pro-Nazi elements, invaded the Jewish quarter, vandalizing Jewish-owned stores and two synagogues, including the destruction of the Torah scrolls and religious artifacts, and ending with the torching of the synagogues. Similar incidents were repeated two days later. The German authorities, at first bemused by these attacks, finally intervened to put an end to this violence, since it interfered with the German designs not to alarm the Jewish population as to the ultimate designs on them. This did not stop the Flemish lawyers' association in Antwerp from expelling its Jewish members, and the municipality, in sharp contrast to Brussels, gladly accepted the task of stamping the identity cards of Jews with a large red-colored *Jood-Juif* sign, and placing its police at the service of the Germans when the roundup of Jews to the concentration camps began in August 1942.[10]

On the Jewish side, a clandestine rescue organization was created in September 1942, the CDJ (*Comité de Défense des Juifs*—Jewish Defense Committee), headed by Ghert Jospa and Chaim Perelman, for the purpose of aiding Jews to avoid arrest and deportation. Branch offices were opened in Antwerp, Charleroi, Namur, and Liège. The CDJ was financially supported by the American Jewish Joint Distribution Committee and several Belgian banks, and it worked closely with Yvonne Nèvejean, head of ONE (*Oeuvre National de l'Enfance*), the country's main and government-supported child aid agency, which opened its many doors to hundreds of Jewish children on the run. It also solicited the aid of the Catholic clergy, such as Archbishop Louis-Joseph Kerkhofs in Liège, Bruno Reynders of the Mont César abbey in Louvain, and Joseph André in Namur (whereof more will be told later). They are credited with having a hand in the saving of over a third of all Jews remaining on Belgian soil during the occupation, with the help of many non-

Jewish networks, religious and secular organizations, communities and individual people.[11]

Response by the Catholic Church

Like France, its southern neighbor, Belgium is a predominantly Catholic country, and the Catholic Church ran a vast network of primary and secondary schools, including the care and welfare of the sick and aged, institutions that were mostly in the hands of nuns and monks. The Germans, while suppressing political parties, left the church intact and undisturbed. As head, or primate, of the Catholic Church, Cardinal Joseph-Ernest Van Roey (also archbishop of Malines) took a firm stand against Nazi racist doctrines before the war. However, during the occupation, he felt that the situation required him to refrain from any openly critical statements. Insofar as the church's teaching on the Jews was concerned, the traditional negative theology was retained. In the 1880s, two Jesuits, Louis Delplace and Jo Heuvelmans, were believed to be the authors of a scurrilous attack on the Talmud, and the Jews were termed a "faithless nation of deicides." Heuvelmans accused the Jews of being behind a Masonic conspiracy to "reestablish the Israelite empire on the ruins of church and state." At the same time, there were few open anti-Jewish manifestations. After World War I, the idea of conversion of the Jews took hold among certain clergy over against the traditional denunciations and accusations, although the Catholic hierarchy remained aloof from such aims, with the notable exception of Monsignor Kerkhofs, in Liège, who favored a missionary approach.[12] During the 1930s, with the Nazi rise to power in neighboring Germany, one author in the *La Cité Chrétienne* considered the anti-Jewish measures justified from a theological point of view. This view was shared by the Dominican J. M. Oesterreicher, who wrote that since "Israel had abandoned God," the only remedy for the Jews was an "absolution of guilt" and conversion to Christianity. At the same time, these and other authors stood back from and even condemned the Nazi anti-Jewish excesses, especially the use of violence. One author in *La Cité Chrétienne*, shocked by the Nazi violence, wrote in 1938, "Never have we felt as strongly as now that, like all other people, the Jews are our brothers." A certain Abbé Du Moulin wrote that "the Germans are not qualified to punish the Jews for their crime against Christ,"[13] perhaps meaning that "punishment" was better left to God. After *Kristallnacht*, in November 1938, one Jesuit journal was even moved to call the faithful to respect "this glorious people," reminding its readers of the "ancient alliance" between Jews and Christians. A courageous cleric named Nagirnik in Louvain wrote, in 1935, of the hope of a fusion of Jews with Christians, adding: "One thing is certain . . . the church . . . has to start knowing the Jews as they are in reality," because this would dispel the false

Christian notion of the Jews as a "monster" people. The lay leader Camille Van Deyck, in Antwerp, founded in 1936 the Catholic Bureau for Israel in order to stem the antisemitic sentiments in that city, as well as to effect a dialogue between Jews and Christians, and it organized lectures attended by religious leaders of both faiths. However, in 1938, Cardinal Van Roey called for the bureau to be disbanded. The church justified this demand because "of the passions" the organization had aroused, which led to the "pouring of oil onto the flames of antisemitism," a statement which raises a lot of questions about the church's own attitude vis-à-vis that age-old animosity.[14]

At the same time, it is remarkable that many priests, monasteries, and Catholics in general extended help to Jews at considerable risks to themselves. Needless to say, the church's widespread infrastructure of convents, boarding schools, sanatoriums, vacation homes, and holiday camps facilitated their help to Jews on the run. Lieven Saerens, in his study of this facet, suggests the following positive factors which helped push aside prewar religious stereotypical convictions: traditional Christian charity, the view of Germany as the common enemy, and Paul's Epistle to the Romans, together with Augustine's similar conviction on the need to preserve the Jews, since they were needed for the final grand salvific event at the Parousia, the second coming of Christ.[15]

Returning to Cardinal Van Roey, he also intervened on behalf of certain Jews who were Belgian nationals and obtained their release, including Chief Rabbi Salomon Ullmann, who had been incarcerated in Breendonck camp, as well as baptized Jews, and Jews in mixed marriages who were in danger of deportation. In addition, he also let it be known that he was opposed to the baptism of Jewish children hidden in Catholic institutions, unless their parents had expressly authorized it before their deportation. He simultaneously alerted the Vatican, in a dispatch on August 4, 1942, which coincided with the departure of the first deportation train, about the "truly inhuman" anti-Jewish measures, which, he not unintentionally noted, affected even Catholics of Jewish origin. In December of that year, he again wrote to Rome on the subject of the Jews, informing the Vatican that the anti-Jewish measures were carried out with "a brutality . . . and a cruelty which have shocked the Belgian people." These communications were, of course, of a private nature. In public, Van Roey refrained from any protest against the persecution of Jews. Words pronounced from the pulpit were rather often more directed at "prayers for the conversion of the Jews." In the words of the historian Maxime Steinberg, "In this Catholic country where the word of the church counted . . . the hierarchy did nothing to express popular feeling about the Jewish Question." There was no protest by the church against the escalating antisemitic regulations of the Germans prior to the deportations themselves, for as reported by Van Roey's secretary, Canon Edmond Leclef, the cardinal felt that any such approaches would be useless.[16] Van Roey did not follow the example of his French colleagues, such as Archbishops Saliège and Théas, and even the pro-Pétainist, Cardinal Gerlier, who protested openly against the deportation of Jews, but limited himself to private and mild protestations, mostly not directly but through his secretary Leclef.

In Liège/Luiken, Monsignor Louis-Joseph Kerkhofs (of whom more will be said later) stood out among Belgian bishops in urging his diocesan clergy to take an active part in the rescue of Jews, and was himself instrumental in saving a number of Jews, including the local rabbi, Joseph Lepkifker, and his family. He also placed his diocesan children's holiday camps at the disposal of fleeing Jews, on top of taking a direct part in the creation of a large rescue network, which was headed by a Liège attorney, Albert Van den Berg. One of Van den Berg's rescue associates was a Dominican monk, Dom Bruno (Henri Reynders), of Mont César, near Louvain, who created his own rescue network, which saved close to 400 Jewish children. In addition, at the request of Queen Mother Elisabeth to the Egyptologist Jean Capart, his son, Father Pierre Capart, chaplain of the Catholic youth organization JOC (*Jeunesse Ouvrière Chrétienne*), agreed to place children in the four JOC homes under his supervision.

One should mention in this context that shortly before the start of the war, an increasing number of Jews had begun to seek conversion to Christianity in the mistaken belief that this would afford the church's protection in the event of war, and baptism was also in demand in 1939, when it was learned that the Brazilian embassy in Brussels would honor such documents when issuing immigration visas to Brazil. In May 1944, Van Roey repeated his reminder to the clergy that while children who had reached the age of seven could be considered adults for the purpose of baptism, but the bishop's authorization was still needed. Thus, Georges Meunier, of the St. John Nicholas parish in Brussels-Schaerbeek, testified that 175 Jews had been baptized in his parish church between 1939 and 1944, but with the permission of the cardinal's office. The requirement for the bishop's permission, however, could be circumvented if information on hand suggested that the child's parents would allow it to continue practicing the Catholic religion after the war. In this, Van Roey was merely repeating the traditional Catholic doctrine, as confirmed by the sixteenth-century Council of Trent, which upheld the age of seven as the age of reason, specifying that a child below that age could only be baptized with the parents' consent and if assurance could be given that the Catholic upbringing of the child would not be jeopardized. This left open the question of children whose parents had been deported to Nazi camps without consenting to their baptism. It was always possible that these parents would return to reclaim their children. Would the baptism of children under such conditions still hold up, in light of the fact that baptism, as a sacrament, could not be invalidated even when done illicitly? It was a complicated problem for the church in light of the eighteenth-century ruling by Pope Benedict XIV that the church was responsible for the continued Christian education even of children who were illicitly baptized without the consent of their parents. While no such doubts applied to children baptized at the age of seven and over, even here the bishop's approval was required, but here too exceptions to the rule were sometimes overlooked.[17]

Albert Van den Berg, in Liège/Luiken, who had been assigned by his bishop, Monsignor Kerkhofs, to organize a rescue network of Jewish children, sought the advice of Cardinal Van Roey on this point. Arriving in Malines/Mechelen, he was told by Monsignor Leonard Van Eynde, Van Roey's vicar-general, that Catholic institutions could admit Jewish children under the guise of abandoned children, but that the church had a more direct obligation to assist already-baptized children. In addition, to preserve the Catholic atmosphere in these places, Jewish pupils should be required to attend religious services, and their parents should, before the children were admitted, be made to understand that except for the Eucharist and other sacraments, their children would have to participate in the regular religious education taking place in these institutions. Kerkhofs is known to have favored a program of proselytizing among Jews, but he disapproved of doing it under wartime conditions (although the annual prayer for the conversion of the Jews was adhered to during the war years), and he always asked to be personally involved in cases involving the baptism of Jewish children whose parents were absent. In spite of this, it is known that children were baptized even without Kerkhofs' approval, especially in the *Notre Dame des Pauvres* Home in Banneux, as testified by its director, Abbé Louis Jamin, who proudly reported having baptized thirteen out of the thirty-three Jewish girls placed in his institution. Jamin wrote after the war the children were made to understand the difference between the two types of faith: one based on fear (Judaism), and the other, based on love (Christianity), which had replaced it. He also made a fantastic claim that some children had asked their rabbi about conversion and were told by him that "we believe that Christ is the Messiah, so there is no reason for you not to be baptized!" Jamin, of course, does not name the rabbi who counseled the children to deny their own religion.[18]

In Florence Matteazzi's study of the help to Jews by the Liège clergy, she related stories of Jewish children who came under pressure to convert. In her words, Abbé Marcel Stenne "could not resist trying to suggest baptism to the children in his home." David Herzslikovicz declined Stenne's offer, but four others gave in to the pressure and were baptized; two of them were sixteen and seventeen years old. Seventeen-year-old Léon Péguine explained his motivation at the time: "Okay, I will do it, to please him and in order not to have any problems." In Blegny-Trembleur, also in the Liège region, five girls were reportedly baptized in May 1944. One of them, Flore H., told of being lectured about the guilt of the Jews for the sin of deicide. She recalled another Jewish girl telling her mother, who had secretly visited her in the religious home, that she did not love the Jews because they had killed Jesus. Upon hearing this, her mother pushed her away, saying: "So, you don't love us any more!" Flore H. continued, "I believed, and if I sometimes asked why [the Jews killed Jesus], I was told that there was no 'why;' that this did not exist. . . . One must not ask why." Charles Erlbaum related that while in a religious institution in Bomal, a certain lady instructor, who attended to the hidden children's cate-chetical lessons, explained that "Jesus was killed by the Jews, and then it was altogether normal that God's anger was now striking the Jews, a people that one recognizes easily; they all have crooked noses, and they all have brown eyes, bent fingers, and curly hair, like the Negroes." Fearing for his safety, Charles took care to flatten his curly hair by continuously soaking it with black soap. Abbé Emile Boufflette is said to have subtly influenced his Jewish wards to convert. As told by Arnold Wolkowicz, who had just attained his thir-teenth birthday, Boufflette discussed with him questions of religion at length. He would say to Arnold: "Look here, the Jewish religion, that is very fine, but now we have a new faith. True enough, Jesus was Jewish, but he was also the Son of God." Arnold's response was: "Listen, you ask me a question to which I am not capable of responding. Let us leave it aside. I cannot answer, for you are more intelligent and more learned than me. . . . I will ask my father and he will give you an answer." At this, Boufflette stopped the conversation, and Arnold held on to his Jewish faith. Boufflette's religious enthusiasm did not diminish even after his arrest in 1944 and deportation to Gross-Rosen camp. It is reported that while in the camp he succeeded in having a Jewish prison-er baptized.[19]

What's more, the aura and decorum of the Catholic faith, and the natural desire of a child to be like everyone else and to be fully accepted, led some children to demand baptism. "We were all imbued with religion," the then eight-year-old Martin H. remembered of his stay in the St. Roch *Petit-Séminaire* in Hervé. "I prayed with all my heart, with all my soul; I had become a fervent Catholic." Equally for Nelly Rosen, hidden in Jamin's insti-tution in Banneux. "I am ever more desirous to follow God's light," she told the Sisters, "and I cannot refrain from asking you to afford me the happiness to become a child of the Good Lord, through baptism."

On the other hand, Tsivica-Cécile, the wife of Rabbi Joseph Lepkifker, of Liège, related that while she was hiding in a convent, the nuns brought her candles from the chapel for the Sabbath eve candle lighting. The rabbi's wife also related how Abbé Jamin tried to persuade her husband to convert. "He was a little strange, this Abbé Jamin," Cécile Lepkifker recalled. "I remember that one day, the monsignor was quite angry when he came to see me in the convent. He wanted to talk to me . . . 'You know, Madame, I suggest that Monsieur the rabbi should have himself converted, and become a priest. . . . But before speaking to him, I should like to have your opinion.' " The stunned rabbi's wife replied, "It is not nice to even come to tell me this. You want to break up our family and separate him from his children. No." When she later related the story to Bishop Kerkhofs, he told her: "Oh, don't pay attention to what Jamin says. He has all sorts of fantasies." Kerkhofs, however, was himself not beyond encouraging proselytizing among Jews, although not under wartime conditions. Before the war, he joined the *Archiconfraternitas Orationum pro Conversione Israel*, founded by Pope Pius X, whose stated purpose was the conversion of Jews. Also, after the war, in a September 1945 letter to the "fantasized" Jamin, Kerkhofs urged the creation of a permanent committee to encourage converted Jews to spend time in Banneux, where a shrine had been dedicated before the war in honor of the Virgin Mary. Such a committee, Kerkhofs added, would also "support the work of the conversion of the Jews." Similarly, in June 1945, in an address to his clergy, Kerkhofs asked them again to pray for the reprieve and conversion of Israel, adding that after they had undergone so much suffering, and having experienced Christian charity, one should earnestly implore divine mercy for the "redemption" of the Jewish people.[20]

The Benedictine monk Bruno Reynders was instrumental in almost single-handedly saving close to 400 children and had strongly discouraged the baptism of these children while under the impress of the war. Nevertheless, in line with traditional Catholic thinking, he took a strong stand against returning to the Jewish fold children who had undergone baptism while in hiding. The drama of these children unfolded immediately after the country's liberation in conflict between the Catholic establishment and newly reestablished Jewish community. In January 1945, Reynders composed a lengthy written opinion in which he contested the principle advanced by Jewish organizations that they automatically had legal rights over these children.[21] While admitting that some Christian rescuers might have acted overzealously by baptizing the children in their care without proper Catholic procedures, he added that these were only the exceptions. At any rate, he argued, in the interest of the children's safety, it was indispensable that they be taught to act like Christian children, and this had led some to become passionately attached to the Catholic religion. For such children, "it was impossible and cruel to refuse them for two years baptism and conversion," but this was done only upon the express consent of their parents, some of whom also had themselves baptized.

These children, Reynders argued, should therefore not be forced to return to their former faith. "However, an experience remains an experience," Reynders continued, "irrespective of the circumstances which provoked it, and it would be inadmissible to forbid the children to draw freely the consequences of this experience." Reynders also denied the Jewish claim to decide what constituted a Jew. If religion served as a criterion, Reynders countered, "there are so many Jews without religion! This is precisely the case for most members of the CDJ personnel and its children's homes." In CDJ homes, Reynders stated, children would be bereft of any religious instruction, even of the Jewish faith. If baptized children were to be released to such homes, it should only be done on condition that children who wished to continue practicing Christianity be allowed to do so, under the guidance of Christian tutors. Cardinal Van Roey supported Reynders' plea to the government to intervene and deny the CDJ's full tutelage over all Jewish orphans. [22]

Jewish leaders countered by rejecting the thesis of seven as an age of understanding, and argued that in the special circumstances of the Nazi period, such considerations were not applicable. Rather, one had to accept the age of reason as at least fifteen, since children below that age were not fully cognizant of what constituted happiness. At any rate, they argued, it was unthinkable to deny the Jewish community the right to reclaim its children, from which it had been separated due to the constraint of the Nazi occupation. In March 1945, Reynders and Abbé André met with Léon-Arieh Kubovitsky (Kubovy) of the World Jewish Congress (and later head of the Yad Vashem institute). The two prelates argued that children should in all fairness be turned over to those who had originally received them, namely their parents—but only to them, no one else. Kubovitsky countered that the Jewish community was the best judge of the wishes of the parents; and this community, which had been bled white by the loss of between five to six million of its members, aspired not to lose those of its children who had been saved from the Germans. No agreement was reached at the meeting. Finally, Reynders reduced his battle to seventeen of the children saved by him who wished to be baptized, and he vigorously opposed the return of five of them to the Jewish community, two of whom had already been baptized. It is not clear from the record how these differences were resolved, only that in the Liège region, the courts were more favorable to the Catholic claims. [23]

In contrast to Reynders, Father Joseph André, who saved dozens of children during the occupation in the Namur area, stated that he saw nothing incompatible between Jewish nationality and adherence to the Christian religion. During the intermediary period between the end of the occupation and handing over the children to Jewish hands, he took care to instruct dozens of Jewish children in a strictly Jewish-Zionist spirit, including lessons in

Hebrew. After the war, he reportedly hoisted a blue-white flag over the hostel building, and the rooms contained portraits of Zionist leaders (Weizmann and Herzl) and pictures of Zionist endeavors in Palestine. He also allowed a Jewish military chaplain to instruct the children in Jewish religion and history.[24] In fairness to Bruno Reynders, it should be pointed out that the Jewish children under his care testified to his neutrality in matters of conversion. Herman Krygier related how Reynders taught him the genuflections he was to practice so as not to stand out from the other boys. "In no instance, did he seek to convert me." Similarly, Bernard Rotmil stated that he and his brother Charles had once asked Reynders to have them baptized. "To my great surprise, he told us to wait until the end of the war, when we would be reunited with our parents." Nathan Zygrajch recalled that when Reynders was pressed by host families to have the children baptized, his response was: "We are responsible for the lives of these children, but their souls do not belong to us."[25] His effort was limited to children already baptized, whatever the circumstances attendant to this act. In summary, some, like Dan Dagan, wrote affectionately fifty years later of "the love, dedication, and care of those nuns toward a little Jewish child. To them, the significance of saving one soul, a soul created by God, was a total and uncompromising commitment."[26] Others, however, complained about the subtle efforts by their overzealous rescuers to obtain their conversion. It is at best a mixed bag.

Clergy Rescuers

Turning to clergy honored by Yad Vashem with the "Righteous" title, we begin with several accounts where the religious motivation for helping others in need apparently was dominant. In Brussels, Father Laurent Couppé, of the Redemptionist order, helped find sheltering places for the Goldberg family after some of them were arrested and deported. Places found included a convent close to Malines/Mechelen, for one family member, and another convent for another member. He kept in touch with them, including passing news from one to another. Couppé also found hiding places for four members of the Mydlarz family. On one occasion, when he tried to smuggle clothing to the father of the Goldberg family, who was being held in a Gestapo jail, he was apprehended and tortured in order to reveal the source of the parcel intended for Goldberg. He invented a story that someone had brought a package to him and asked him to deliver it to the prison. He was released; unfortunately, the elderly Goldberg was sent to Auschwitz and perished there. In a 1974 letter to Yad Vashem, Couppé wrote: "At the start of my religious life, I was taught the abnegation of one's self, love for fellow man—which is today known as considerateness and human solidarity. . . . During the events of the recent war, I did not at all think about the dangers facing me, nor of the gratitude I was eventually to receive. . . . I took the initiative and I helped where I could, and that was all. . . . Beyond people and their actions, there is a higher providence, of which Isaiah said, 'Your thoughts are not mine, and my ways are not yours. Thus says the Lord.' We found ourselves in the face of two immeasurable mysteries: the mystery of divine providence, which is love, justice, and holiness, and the equally unexplainable mystery of human freedom."[27]

Several Jesuit monks in the Brussels region were also active in help to Jews, in an operation spurred by Esther Grynpas and her Jewish-born but Catholic-baptized husband, Benedykt Grynpas (who in 1941 taught Greek and Latin at the St. Michel College in Brussels). She solicited the aid of Jean-Baptist Janssens, who during the occupation was the regional head of the Jesuit Order (after the war, he was elevated to father superior of the order, in Rome) and head of the Saint Jean Berchmans college, and he agreed to shelter large groups of Jews in his religious institution, many of them young people who were allowed to attend the class lectures. He also helped forge baptismal and other documents, thereby safeguarding many Jews from deportation. Another Jesuit father, Jean-Baptiste Decoster, helped find hiding places for Jews in flight. The Blinder family were among the fortunate people for whom Decoster arranged safe and separate sheltering places, some of whom Decoster provided with cassocks to disguise them as novices. He is reported to have said to a trusted colleague about the danger of disclosure and arrest: "If these persecuted people are taken, I would have the consolation to leave with them." Others of the Jesuit Order who helped the Grynpas couple included Emile Gessler, Alphonse Lambrette, and Ivan Lambrette. Father Henri Van Oostayen, who served as a chaplain with the Red Cross, and assisted the Grynpas network in the south of the country, was eventually arrested and deported to Bergen-Belsen camp, where he perished. "I repeat," Esther Grynpas wrote to Yad Vashem, "that thanks to the assistance and aid of the Jesuit fathers, I was able to save so many of our victims."[28] Already mentioned is Father Pierre Capart's role in the rescue of many Jewish children by placing them in the JOC (acrostic of Christian Working Youth) homes, located in Tourneppe, Schaltin, Leffe, and Banneux. Altogether some sixty Jewish children benefited from JOC's hospitality. In a Yad Vashem ceremony in his honor, in 1971, Father Capart stated: "I give thanks to the God of Abraham, Jacob, and David for allowing me to be his instrument. I thank our Lord Jesus Christ, who inspired in me paternal feelings towards these children torn from their parents. . . . Ladies and gentlemen, our century was one of the cruelest in history. It is dangerous for people not to uphold the meaning of God. For without God, one has no regard for fellow man. For isn't man a creature of God?"[29]

In Louvain/Leuven, 40 kilometers east of Brussels, Canon Armand Thiery, who seconded as a physics professor, assisted Mrs. Grunia Schicharewitch to find sheltering places. One such place was the garret of the prior of the Grand Beguinage, where she appeared under a different name, and which allowed her to continue her engineering work at the Louvain University for a while. When Thiery learned of the danger of German searches in that religious institution, he took Grunia to the Louvain suburb of Heverlee, where she was placed in a building reserved for visiting religious dignitaries. During Thierry's frequent visits there, he devised coded messages in Latin for use during emergencies. Thiery reportedly also aided other Jews in need. Grunia wrote of traveling with Thierry to Dinant, where "we visited many convents where he begged them to admit Jewish children." Learning of a German raid in a Louvain suburb, he asked Grunia to alert one of the rescuing families, the Mercier sisters, of the danger, thus enabling them to take preventive measures with regard to the Jews they were sheltering. Grunia rotated between several hiding places. Arrested in June 1944 (under her new name, and on suspicion of connection with the resistance), and taken to Malines, she was able to contact Thiery, who came to see her and was allowed to bring along food as well as to speak to her in the presence of two SS guards. However, they were dumbfounded by the prearranged Latin coded words with which Thiery advised Grunia on what to say to her prison interrogators, thanks to which she was able to be released. "He knew very well that I would not convert to Catholicism, for he was well aware of my spiritual belief," Grunia noted in her testimony, in which she asked that the "Righteous" title be awarded to her rescuer.[30]

We shall presently return to stories of rescues by clerics where the issue of conversion arose during the period of hiding, and the clerics' response to that challenge. As already mentioned, the bishop of Liège, Monsignor Louis-Joseph Kerkhofs, used his considerable authority to urge clerics in his diocese to save Jews from deportation. As told by Father Hubert Célis, the parson in Halmaal, near St. Truiden/St. Trond, northeast of Liège, in September 1942, he attended a meeting, convened by Kerkhfos, at the house of Father Mathieu Hendrikx, the dean of Hasselt, in order "to talk to them of the persecution of the Jewish people and ask for volunteers to help the Jews." As further related by Célis, "The bishop did not want to impose this on anyone, because of the risks involved, but he wanted his priests to know how proud he would be of those prepared to risk their lives to save others." It should also be underlined that Kerkhof's diocese was the only episcopate directly involved in help to Jews. In the words of historian Maxime Steinberg: "in the Liège diocese . . . it was the bishop who led the troops!" To streamline the rescue activities, Kerkhofs turned to attorney Albert van den Berg, who supervised the regional Catholic schools for undernourished children. In coordination with the CDJ, he placed many children in sheltering places. After his arrest in April 1943, his brother-in-law, Georges Fonsny, took over. The Van den Berg–Fonsny network covered the whole Liège region, and even beyond it—in Hainaut and into the Flemish-speaking region, and as many as twenty convents were involved. On a personal basis, Kerkhofs took charge of the local cantor, Joseph Lepkifker, who also seconded as rabbi, and his family. According to Rabbi Lepkifker, in July 1942, fearing deportation, he turned to Bishop Kerkhofs, "who was regarded by the entire population as the Prince of Charity. . . . Filled with a moving dedication, Monsignor Kerkhofs was able to shelter us from danger, and to escape from the furor of the enemy; myself at the episcopacy (clandestinely), as well as my wife, born Curt Tzivica, and my two sons, Mendel and Eli, respectively then aged five and three, as well as the greatest possible number of our coreligionists, and all this in the most disinterested manner, for over two years." Lepkifker testified that when he appealed to Kerkhofs for help, the latter told him: "You are now in a painful and dangerous situation. If the opposite had occurred, I would not have hesitated to turn to you to help me." According to one report, Kerkhofs personally accompanied the rabbi to a religious home in Fawes, having him dressed in a cassock, and introducing him as Abbé Botty (according to another sources, Rabbi Lepkifker arrived alone, but armed with a letter of introduction from Kerkhofs, under the name of Abbé Botty, and was then given a cassock by the home's chaplain). Lepkifker was hidden by the nuns in an attic, where he remained isolated from the Jewish children who were also hidden there. He was then moved to several places for his safety. As for the rabbi's wife, Tzivica-Cécile, she was taken with her younger son Elie, renamed Paul, to the Saint-Joseph home in Huy, which was headed by Sister Lutgarde, of the Soeurs de la Charité, who happened to be Kerkhofs' cousin. At a later period, Mrs. Lepkifker was moved to a little convent of six nuns named *Les Soeurs du Bon Secours,* where she remained until the liberation. According to one report, Kerkhofs personally brought her there in his car. Joseph Lepkifker's elderly parents were hidden for a time in the Buissonnets convent in Banneux. The Mother Superior, in a postwar letter, related how moved she was by the elderly Lepkifker, in whose eyes "one read all the sadness and nobility of his lengthy suffering. . . . Every evening, I went with a lantern in my hand, to secretly bring them moral support and food. I remember the majestic attitude of *M. le Grand Rabbin*, who welcomed me as if I were God's angel. He inspired within me such a deep and real respect that I, a Christian, did not hesitate to kneel before him to receive his solemn blessing"—an act quite unusual for a Catholic nun.[31] According to Georges Fonsny, the brother-in-law of Van den Berg, Kerkhofs asked that a file be opened for every child who asked to be baptized and whose parents were under arrest. Only after studying the file would he decide on the case. However, no such files were found, and it is not certain that this indeed was the case.

According to Leon Papeleux, who made a special study of the Kerkhofs–Van den Berg rescue network, it was credited with the saving of 229 Jews, eighty of them children. Other sources bring the number of children close to 200. The already mentioned Abbé Louis Jamin left a record of his role in this undertaking in a manuscript entitled *Chronique juive de Banneux*, including a list of thirty-three Jewish girls, thirteen of who were baptized. Apparently it dawned on Jamin that the presence of Jewish children under his supervision presented a unique opportunity to gain souls for his religion. In one reported case, he declined a girl's plea to be baptized. This happened on August 4, 1944, when a certain Paulette wrote Jamin a letter in which she asked to be baptized, explaining that "every morning I weep during Mass for I want to go to communion, but I cannot for I am not baptized. I ask that I be permitted. I will tell my mother that I want to become a Christian, even if because of this I could not see her again [her mother had told her she would not take her back if she converted]. Sir, I pray with all my little heart and I wait for your answer." On the letter, there is a note by Jamin: "We refused to baptize her—1944." Jamin himself stated: "Not once did we do this [baptism] with small children without the permission of the parents. Others who asked, we refused and waited for further events." Interestingly, the girls who were indeed baptized were of a mature age, such as eighteen and twenty. However, Jamin also baptized younger girls of whom we have no details. Jamin's dedication to the rescue of his Jewish wards is not open to question. Ruth (Helene) Karniel, writing from Kibbutz Ein Hanatsiv in Israel, recalled Jamin as an "extraordinary man. . . . He was a kind man. It was clear that he wanted to help Jews. . . . We lacked nothing except for the fact of not being able to see our family." She adds significantly, "They asked us to become Christians and to have us baptized. But they told us that it was forbidden to do so without the authorization of the parents."[32]

A number of children were hidden in *Le Petit Séminaire*, a Catholic college in Saint-Roch, near Liège. Jewish children were also placed in various Catholic retreat homes for children, in the Liège region, such as *La Colonie Episcopale des Enfants* in Stoumont (Ardennes region), headed by Abbé Marcel Stenne, where forty children were sheltered. Newly arrived children were told by Stenne to blend in with the other children and behave as they did. "Reveal to no one that you are Jewish and all will be well. If you have a problem, come to see me." David Herszlikovicz stated that he and the other Jewish boys were well integrated there, "and even served as acolytes and sang in the church choir. I was fortunate enough to have a good singing voice and soon became the soloist of the choir. As a soloist I traveled with the abbé and sang in the neighboring churches."[33]

Father Emile Boufflette's involvement in rescue and other clandestine operations ended in tragedy for himself. A vicar of the Saint-Christophe parish in Liège, he worked closely with Van den Berg as well as the CDJ. Together with his parents, he helped move children from one place to another and arrange false credentials for them, such as for the eight members of the Fremder family. He also helped people sought by the Germans to flee to France, and as far as Spain. Arrested in April 1944, he was deported to the Gross-Rosen concentration camp; then moved to Buchenwald, and Dora, where he was to die in March 1945, at the age of thirty-three.[34] Equally for Father Joseph Peeters, of Comblain-du-Pont, who helped many Jews with false credentials and sheltering homes with local farmers. Arrested in December 1942, he was sentenced to death. Kerkhofs intervened on his behalf via Cardinal Van Roey, but failed to prevent his execution, which was carried out in August 1943.[35] Several other clerics in the Liège region assisted the brothers Marcel and Albert Fremder . These included Louis De Gruyter and Joseph Lempereur, as well as Jacques Jacobs and Ivan Lambrette, of the Collège St. Hadelin, in Visé-Liège. The Fremder brothers point out that "neither the priests nor the Catholic families who participated in our plot to survive tried to convert us to Catholicism during this time. Their motives were purely humanitarian." On August 24, 1944, Father Jacobs was arrested and imprisoned in Liège. Two weeks later, the Americans liberated the city and Jacobs was spared deportation to a concentration camp in Germany.[36]

In Namur, the most celebrated rescue story is that of Abbé Joseph André of the St. Jean Baptiste parish. It all began in 1942, when he learned that Arthur Burak, a Jewish man he knew, faced deportation together with his family (wife and sons Norbert and Werner). André found a hiding place for Arthur and his family where they remained safe for two years, until the country's liberation. One week after the Buraks were safely sheltered, cousins of the Buraks also asked for André's solicitude, and he also arranged a sheltering place for them. This encounter with the Buraks led the unassuming abbé to embark on a grander rescue mission, benefiting not merely acquaintances but many other Jews as well. Making contact with the CDJ, André synchronized various rescue efforts with them, mostly of children on the run. As told by a Jewish activist, Mr. Vishnie: "I personally referred many people to Father André, and he always found hiding places for them and arranged their rescue. . . . It was not even necessary to knock on his door, for it was always open. No one ever passed through it without ultimately finding a suitable arrangement. Moreover, he kept tabs on all Jews whom he directed to secure shelters. . . . His role was especially significant in the rescue of children. I personally, and not only myself, passed over to his hands many children and kept them in his house until he found secure places for them. . . . There is no doubt in my mind that he is one of the most illustrious 'Righteous Among the Nations'—without equal in all Belgium." Traveling from place to place, he pleaded and cajoled at monasteries, convents, and private homes, for Jewish children to be taken in. In many instances, André did not wait to be approached but made the first move. As with Moshe Apter (born 1932), who related how André appeared in his family's Brussels home. "Mother opened the door. He was in a habit. He said: 'I know you are Jews. . . . I have come to save your son.' At first, mother did not want. . . . Father asked for a week's time to think. André promised that he would watch over me and return me at the end of the war." After leaving some money to help the Apters, he left, and later sent an emissary to pick up Moshe, and bring him to André's home in Namur. André then took the boy to a monastery in the Ardennes region. In 1943, Moshe and eighteen other children were returned to André, where they stayed for about a week. He then dispersed them in many places. "A week before the liberation, the man who originally took me brought me back to my home in Brussels. My parents were waiting for me. When I was in the monastery, André used to visit me, talk with me, and encourage me. When he visited Israel, he noticed me, called me Marcel, came over and embraced me. I don't think that he did that for the purpose of conversion."

Rabbi Harold Saperstein, a chaplain with the U.S. Army, who met André soon after the liberation, described him as "a gentle, frail fellow—humble in demeanor, with a gentle handshake and a bashful smile. Yet he proved himself to be of the stuff which spiritual heroes are made of." In that letter, written to colleagues in the United States, Lieutenant Saperstein also wrote about the necessity of reclaiming Jewish children kept in non-Jewish homes and religious institutions. "The job was a delicate one, requiring tact and diplomacy . . . one which demands the immediate attention of responsible Jewish organizations. The Jewish people can ill afford, after its overwhelming losses of recent years, the additional loss of any of the meager numbers of surviving Jewish children in Europe. In this particular case, even though no definite missionary activity was conducted among the children, and even though the *Vicaire* [André] personally evidenced at all times a broad and understanding spirit which can only be commended, it was obvious that unless action was taken these children might eventually be lost to the Jewish faith. The *Vicaire*'s work had been done and done well. For it, and for the similar work of other humble priests in many countries, the Jewish people must be eternally grateful." Saperstein wrote that he found Father André to be cooperative, and on October 1, 1945, all the remaining Jewish children in André's care left his home. The previous day, Rabbi Saperstein organized a farewell party to which the Catholic children of the parish were invited. Father André spoke on the universality of God and the brotherhood of man. Together with the rabbi, they were tossed in the air by the children, accompanied with shouts of praise for both. As the children boarded the van, André embraced each child and kissed it on the forehead. In Rabbi Saperstein's words, "He tried to smile and tears welled up in his eyes. Impulsively I put my arms around the little priest in his long black cloak on which he wore not a cross but a Magen [Star of] David and kissed him on both cheeks. . . . I rode in the truck with them. As we rounded the corner they let out a great cheer for the priest, who had really been a father to them." When Abbé André died, in 1973, his pallbearers included several of his former Jewish wards. He is credited with having saved several hundred Jewish lives.[37]

In a letter to the author in 1991, Rabbi Saperstein took issue with the late Rabbi Isaac Klein, who earlier had written of André's refusal to turn over the children in his care until the war's end (Belgium's liberation preceded the end of the war by eight months), when the children would possibly have been reunited with their parents returning from the camps. Saperstein, however, disagreed. "It is true that I found several young people who had chosen to embrace Christianity. However, their parents were alive and with them, and the conversion was apparently a pragmatic decision. I found the *Vicaire* to be more than cooperative in his eagerness to have the Jewish community, young and old, able to carry on their faith. He encouraged them to attend Sabbath and Holy Day services and to celebrate the festivals of Sukkot and Simchat Torah. He responded to my persuasion and turned over the children whose parents had not returned to me so that they could be brought back into the Jewish community." Rabbi Saperstein added that the last time he met *Le Vicaire* was when he visited New York. "I met him at the airport and brought him to my services that evening where he spoke and made a deep impression on the congregation. When we bade farewell to each other at the end of his visit, he said, 'I do not think we will see each other again in this world. But I know that in the World to Come we will meet each other face to face.' "[38]

We now return to Dom Bruno (Henri Reynders), already largely mentioned earlier in the discussion of his opposition to the return of converted Jewish children whose parents had disappeared in the Holocaust, and whose rescue record is quite fascinating. As the single largest rescuer of Jews (mostly children) in Belgium; his story therefore merits greater attention. Born in 1903, he was ordained a priest in 1928. Three years later, he earned a doctorate degree in theology from Louvain University. A visit to Nazi Gemany shocked him at the sight of a Nazi-led physical assault on Jews. As he later recalled, "My first contact with the problem of the Nazi persecution dated from July 1938. I was passing through Frankfurt and was taking a walk in a busy street. Everywhere in the street . . . defamatory signs: *Jude-Judas, Juden heraus, Hier sind Juden nicht erwünscht* [Jew-Judas, Jews Out, Jews Not Welcome Here]. This terribly shocked me." He was taken prisoner in the brief 1940 campaign and after his release returned to his base in Mont-César. Nothing much happened until 1942, when his superior asked him to leave for Hodbomont, near Theux, to serve as chaplain in a small home for the blind, sheltering some twenty people. Very soon, he learned that the home's "blind" director, Mr. Walter Bieser, and several other occupants were not blind at all, but Jews in hiding, and the other mostly blind people, including five or six children, were, indeed blind Jews who had been moved there from the Catholic Hospitalité children's home in Banneux, Monsignor Kerkhofs region. Toward the end of the year, when the Hodbomont home was no longer safe, Reynders went into action to find alternative hiding places with the help of the Van den Berg network. Beginning January 1943, he located ten sheltering homes in various parts of the country. Bruno made the rounds of these homes on his bicycle. In that dangerous endeavor, he is estimated to have pedaled forty or fifty times the equivalent of the *Tour de Belgique*, always busy improvising, and caring for the food, clothing, false credentials, change of names to non-Jewish-sounding ones, financial support to host families, some of which was covered by the Van den Berg network. Soon enough, the Gestapo got wind of Bruno's widespread activity, and he was forced to leave Mont-César to avoid arrest. Moving from Louvain to Brussels and other places, he changed his name several times, with constantly newly fabricated false identity cards, and listing as his profession teacher, Red Cross worker, and a married man with children. He placed Jewish children in many religious homes, such as Bellegem, Leffe, St. Marie in La Bouverie, the clinic in Jolimont, his sister's (Marie-Louise, known as Mother Thérèse) Benedictine convent in Liège, the Don Bosco convent in Tournai, and others, including the home of his parents and his brother, the dentist Jean Reynders, in Ixelles. An estimated 350 Jewish people (some say 390), including ninety adults, were helped by him, many of them referred to him by the CDJ.[39]

After the war, Reynders began to collect and organize the records of the children saved by him, listing the child's original name, borrowed name, and location of placement. He also listed some of the problems encountered, such as a convent, in Bellegem, where he was told by the Mother Superior to take back the children only recently placed there after she learned that they came from the French-speaking region of the country, and did no speak Flemish. In yet another incident, in the *Notre Dame des Anges* home in Néchin, near the French border, the Mother Superior took fright at the presence of Jewish children, and asked Dom Bruno to have them moved elsewhere. On the eve of the country's liberation, in August 1944, learning that five of his wards had been moved to an AJB childrens home Linkebeek, supervised by the Gestapo, Dom Bruno frantically tried to have them released before the Gestapo laid hands on them, and succeeded, using a plan secretly hatched with Jewish activists and Yvonne Nèvejean, head of the ONE.[40] The children he saved remembered him with great affection. Bernard Rotmil, writing to Dom Bruno in 1969, recalled his "friendly smile. . . . After twenty-eight years, you remain the most venerated and truest friend we have ever known." After the war, Bernard found the following passage in Bruno's journal: "I recall Bernard's appetite as a sixteen-year-old boy, and the difficulty I had in this regard because I had to pay for his upkeep at the place where he stayed in Louvain. One day, I dared tell him to try to control his appetite, and I recall his distraught face as he replied, 'But I am always hungry.' I was completely disarmed and could not cease reproaching myself. But nourishment was at that time a difficult and expensive thing." Bernard was finally taken to a farmhouse where the food was plentiful, and he remained there until the end of the war. Bernard saw his benefactor for the last time during the High Holiday services in a Brussels synagogue on the morrow of the liberation, in September 1944. When the rabbi announced the presence of Dom Bruno, the audience cheered him. "The children hung on his hands, and the parents tearfully thanked and blessed him. It took some time before calm was restored in the synagogue and the religious services could continue." Esther Krygier recalled him as "very kind and fatherly. He gave us a certain security. . . . He would lead us by the hand, and explain that where we were going one must not say that one was Jewish, not even trust another child. . . . He was the only one who had the gift to relieve all our fears." As earlier mentioned, when some sheltering families asked his permission to have the children converted, he replied, "We are responsible for the lives of these children, but their souls do not belong to us."[41]

Ghert Jospa's wife, Yvonne, was an activist in the CDJ—an organization to which Reynders was reluctant to turn over Jewish boys who had converted during their hiding period. In 1991 she described Reynders as a person for whom the human being was the main thing. Learning of his passing in 1981, Sacha Hirschovits wrote, "Father Bruno, for us you are not dead. Your lesson of dedication, of selflessness, of courage and love has not been in vain. We bear in our heart the path you have traced, and which will guide me till my last day." In 1991, friends and former wards gathered in Ottignies, Belgium, the place where he lived out the last years of his life, to dedicate a memorial, which reads: Father Bruno Reynders, Benedictine (1903–1981). Hero of the Resistance. Risking his life, he saved some 400 Jews from Nazi barbarism. Israel has proclaimed him a Righteous Among the Nations, and in his memory a tree was planted at Yad Vashem, Jerusalem.[42]

Returning to the Brussels region, we note the story of Father Jan Bruylandts, of the *Notre Dame de l'Immaculé Conception* Church in the Anderlecht section. He is credited with hiding a large number of Jewish children, including Jacques Caneau, who at the age of three was placed by Bruylandts in the home of his cousin, Marie Knops. While there, Jacques Caneau underwent baptism. As explained by his mother, Miriam Caneau, her son's baptism followed the discovery by his playmates that he was Jewish. Bruylandts suggested that he be baptized as proof of his Christianity. This was done with the complete agreement of his mother, as confirmed by her. Bruylandts also reportedly sheltered fifteen boys in a nearby house as well as in his own, and was assisted financially by Queen Mother Elisabeth through one her secretaries.[43]

Further southeast, in the wooded Ardennes region, in the village of Bougnimont, Abbé Georges Meurisse, in the summer of 1942, took into his home Ora Libeskind, aged nine, and her twelve-year-old brother. Meurisse took the children for daily walks and allowed them to attend church services with him. When Ora begged him to have her baptized, Meurisse consistently refused, saying that only when she was old enough to take responsibility for her acts would he allow her to consider conversion. In Ora's words: "He said to me then: 'Now you are a little girl, and I shall not allow you to change your faith. If, when you grow older, you still want to, I shall be happy to receive you into the bosom of the church. At the moment I need your father's consent, and honoring one's father is a sacred duty for children.' " At the end of the war, it was learned that the children's mother had perished in Auschwitz, and their father died in 1946. The children were then moved to a Jewish children's home.[44]

A similar and even more striking story, of allowing and even encouraging Jewish wards to remain faithful to their religion, is that of the Célis brothers. As related by Father Hubert Célis, after attending the earlier-mentioned priestly gathering convened by Monsignor Kerkhfos at the home of the dean of Hasselt in St. Trond/Truiden, Célis returned to his parish in the village of Halmaal. That same day, "for the first time in my life, a Jewish woman came to see me, accompanied by one of my parishioners. She was the mother of the Rotenberg children, and had arrived with her family in my parish after leaving Brussels, where life for Jews had become more and more unbearable. Mrs. Rotenberg wept profusely as she explained that she was about to be arrested at any moment, and wanted to be reunited with her children after the war— hoping she would survive. It was then that I gave her my word of honor, promising to save her children, and to give my life, if necessary, in that endeavor. Thank God, I remained faithful to my promise, and when I now see the children's happiness and their respective families, I give thanks to God for having given me the necessary strength. Following this promise, I placed the two girls, Régine (aged sixteen) and Sonia (two), with my father at St. Trond, and the two boys, Wolfgang (thirteen) and Sigmund (nine), with my other brother

[Father Louis Célis], a priest in Gotem, some 12 kilometers from Halmaal. On October 29, 1942, the children's parents, betrayed to the authorities by an unknown informer, were arrested: the father in my presbytery, and the mother in another parish home. . . . That same October 29, I was arrested for the first time, accused of helping the underground and Allied pilots, and for having hidden the Rotenberg children. . . . I was then asked to disclose the children's whereabouts. I refused. They began to insult me, and threatened to have me shot. This went on for about one and a half hours. I continued to respond calmly: 'I am in your hands; I know I will be shot but I will never speak. A priest is not a traitor.' The interrogator answered: 'I too am Catholic!' He had said enough, for at this point, I began to berate him as a Catholic for his behavior, saying: 'You are a Catholic, and have forgotten that the Virgin was a Jew, that Christ was Jewish, that He commanded us to love and help one another. . . . That He told us: "I have given you an example so that you do as I have done." . . . You are a Catholic, and you do not understand what a priest is! You do not understand that a priest does not betray!' The officer began to mumble, and excused himself by saying he had received orders to do the interrogation, and if he did not do it, he would himself be punished. I responded that I respected everyone who did his duty, so he must do his duty, but that it was useless to insist, for I would not talk! I was then freed, and hurried to disperse the Rosenberg children, who were taken to other places. On May 3, 1944, Régine was denounced by an informer and arrested in my father's home. This old man of about eighty years defended her like a lion, but was no match against the forces arrayed against him. The same day, I was arrested for the second time. By a fortuitous set of circumstances, I learned of the questions put to Régine and her answers, and this made it possible for me defend myself effectively. Régine was sent to the Auschwitz extermination camp, from where, thank God, she returned to us in 1945. I consider myself as having only done my duty. We are, after all, irrespective of our religious and political opinions, the children of the Good God; hence brothers who should help one another! This is precisely what Christ wanted to tell us when he asked us to help our fellow men. I never thought of trying to convert the Rosenberg children to the Catholic faith. I always respected their religious beliefs: (1) because I did not want to take advantage of their unhappy situation to influence their minds; (2) because Mrs. Rotenberg had placed her full trust in me, and I had given her my word of honor as a priest. I had no right to betray this trust, but had the duty to remain faithful to the word given, so as to be able to restore these children to their parents or their family in the same way they had confided them to me; (3) because I foresaw that the children would, after the war, be returned to their family and to a Jewish environment. So I prefer a good Jew to a bad Christian."

Wolfgang Rotenberg, in his testimony, wrote that while the boys were in hiding, Father Louis Célis took great care to make them pursue their religious practices. He was quite emphatic on this point, as the following example will illustrate. Noting that they were not donning the obligatory phylacteries on Saturdays, Célis inquired of his ecclesiastical superiors and was assured that this practice was not required on the Sabbath. The Rotenberg children eventually settled in the United States, but the ties between rescuer and rescued remained close in the ensuing years. In 1947, Father Hubert Célis led Regina to the canopy as she married Isaac Wolbrom. In 1965, he was present at their son's Bar Mitzvah celebration in a New York synagogue. On that occasion, Regina stated, "My children have no grandparents [they died in the Holocaust]. I think it is only fitting that Father Hubert should be on hand for my son's Bar Mitzvah because he was the last to see my parents." In a 1949 letter to an Israeli correspondent, Father Louis Célis belittled his deeds during the war: "And so, my very dear Mr. Rabinowitz, you insist on considering me a saint because I was unfortunately able to save only a few Jewish lives. But was this not an urgent and serious obligation of every person, Jew, Christian, or atheist, still worthy to be considered human? The only profound regret that I must always bear with me is for my not having been able to provide for the welfare of all the Jews in distress in Belgium and elsewhere, without any distinction whatsoever, and not having been able to hide them and thus fully remove them from this bloody persecution which, let's admit it, will forever remain an irremovable stain for the whole of Europe." In Regina's words: "He kept us alive. We can never do enough for him."[45]

Turning to nuns who helped Jews, we begin with the story of Sister Berthile Lerat, who served as Mother Superior of the Imelda Institute convent in Brussels, which included a childrens home where between forty and sixty Jews were hidden (not all of them at the same time). Some were brought there by the CDJ; others came accompanied by their parents. The adults did various chores, working in the kitchen, the gardens, and the laundry, while the children attended school classes. It is reported that Sister Berthile asked the parents' permission to baptize the girls. Most of the parents objected, but some consented. Her motive may have been simply to add a measure of security, since after the war no pressure was exerted on any of the girls to remain within the Catholic fold; none remained in the convent, and all returned to Judaism. Sister Berthile did not differentiate in the least between the girls who were baptized and those not, and all were treated equally. Myriam Goldfarb (then appearing as Maria Goffart) related the efforts of a certain Jesuit priest named Père Siméon to have her converted, which caused her parents to remove her to another location, but after the war, in gratitude for the rescue of their daughter, they made annual contributions to the Imelda Institute. Some of the girls spent as much as four years at this convent. Another nun, Sister Mechtilde, was especially dedicated to the welfare of the Jewish girls. The Jewish community honored both nuns in a public ceremony in 1980, at which many of the rescued girls participated.[46]

In nearby Anderghem, Sister Urbaine (Marie Joséphine Schoofs) was Mother Superior of the *Notre Dame du Bon Conseil* convent, which also claimed a boarding school. There, many Jewish girls with their parents were sheltered—the parents being assigned jobs in the kitchen and the garden. Teenager Helene Baumerder-Glowiczower first hid at the Imelda Institute, was transferred to Sister Urbaine's boarding school, where she found conditions and the atmosphere more to her liking (she had objected to the courses in sewing and knitting that she was required to attend at the Imelda Institute), and joined her cousin there. "I still recall today Mother Urbaine's office, when she welcomed me and my father—with a good welcoming smile; she immediately agreed to admit me in the modern humanities section; this seemed to me such a step forward that I felt as though reborn." Underground operatives brought ration cards for the Jews. After a nearby bombing raid, the institute was closed, and the girls were dispersed to other sheltering places. While there, Helene was required to participate in the Mass and recite the collective prayers, "but never, never did any of the nuns try to convert me to Catholicism."[47]

The following story exemplifies the circumstances under which some of the Jewish children were taken from their families and the traumatic experience of being taken to a Catholic religious institution. As told by Sarah Migdal, born in 1929, who was taken to the *Institut Notre Dame des Sept Douleurs* convent, outside Brussels: "I, coming from a very Orthodox Jewish family, I could not enter the convent. I refused, became hysterical, but somehow I was pushed and carried into the building, and the huge big double doors closed behind me. How I cried!! We were treated extremely well there. Good food and good nurses to take care of us. But emotionally I was drained. We were a total of maybe 100 children, all girls. We did everything the Catholic children did. We went to Mass every morning, and Salut every afternoon. But we were not the only eighteen children saved by the nuns. About the summer of 1943 [perhaps it was rather in 1944], in the afternoon, as we were having lunch, Mère Marie Eustelle opened the doors and took in about twenty Jewish children from another orphanage about a mile away, under the care and protection of the queen mother, Queen Elizabeth. The Gestapo had come to pick them up. The Mother Superior took them all to the basement. A few hours later, the underground picked those children up and placed them somewhere else. . . . All of us eighteen Jewish children remained at the convent until after the liberation. I was returned to my parents, who were fortunate to survive, but were shattered emotionally." Other former Jewish residents of this convent wrote similar testimonies on the good treatment by the nuns there. Rachel Dancygier (known as Céline Lagrange), born 1933, related that no one, including the Jewish girls, knew for sure who at the institute was Jewish or not, other than Mother Superior Agnes, as well as her principal assistant Sister Marie Eustelle, and Sister Marie Cécile, who was responsible for the medical well-being of her charges. As for Inge Schwartz, born 1937, she was four years of age when she arrived at this convent. When her parents came to visit, she asked their permission to accept baptism, "because I wished to be nicely dressed and well taken care, and receive gifts, and I wanted to do my private communion like the other small girls. They agreed, for I did not understand anything. I was only six years old. I was thus baptized as Agnes and did my private communion. I went to church, to communion, and to confession like the other children." After the war, her parents failing to return from the camps, Inge-Agnes was released to her aunt and left for Paris. It is not known how many others were converted, if any. What is certain is that everyone who wrote on their stay in this convent told of the affectionate treatment received at the hands of these three nuns. Andrée Geulen, a non-Jewish activist with the CDJ, which had referred most of the children admitted there, confirmed that forty-eight Jewish girls were sheltered there, and were well treated. She remembered the night in August 1944 when the Germans, before evacuating Belgium, decided to round up all the remaining Jewish children still in Jewish-operated orphanages, and the convent agreed to admit them before the Gestapo could lay their hands on them. "I personally moved some twenty small girls from the Jewish [Children's] Home in Wezembeek to the *Notre Dame des Sept Douleurs*, which was very near, who were admitted as an emergency measure."[48]

In Verviers, an Antwerp suburb, Sister Marie-Mathilde Leruth headed the La *Providence* orphanage, where many children were sheltered. Sylvain Brachfeld (known as Van Erp) who stayed there until April 1944, together with his sister Helene, related that there were several adult women along with the children: "Sister Marie always needed to keep an eye over the slightest conversation, for fear that a slip of the tongue would disclose [the identity of] her wards. The Jewish children did not attend communion or confession; but they participated at the services with the other children. One day, I overheard a conversation between several older boys . . . who were taking about the new arrivals and referred to them as Jewish. I immediately notified Sister Marie, who took the children aside and told them that there were no Jews among us." One day, to avoid a German raid, the children were taken on a pilgrimage to Banneux, which was not far from Verviers. In a 1968 ceremony in her honor at Yad Vashem, Sister Marie-Mathilde Leruth stated: "Be assured, Mr.

Chairman, that I do not ask any praise for saving Jewish children during the war; I only did my duty as a woman of charity, in welcoming them, and especially in loving them with all my heart. Their parents having being deported to Germany, it was only right that I give these little Jews the fraternal care and especially the warm affection which they lacked." Speaking of the martyred Jews, she continued: "Bowing my head before these ashes, commemorating your beloved who are no more, a feeling of profound sorrow engulfs my soul. I think of all your martyrs; I think particularly of the parents and relatives of my brave Jewish children whom I, like so many others, could hide during the war. There is nobody who can ever replace a father or a mother, but the memory lingers on."[49]

Farther north, in Louvain/Leuven, Sister Liguori (Martha Pauline Putzeys), Mother Superior of the *Mater Dei* Institute, admitted Jewish girls for shelter in the convent's two schools: boarding and day. A former student brought fifteen-year-old Rachel Rozenfeld and her younger sister Isabelle to the school but did not reveal their Jewish identity. When it became known to Mother Liguori, she reportedly wrote to the bishop for advice and was told to retain the girls. Between August 1942 and May 1944 the nuns at *Mater Dei* sheltered seventeen Jewish girls. Testimonies received by some of these wards confirm that Liguori never coerced the girls to convert. During the Easter holiday and summer vacation, the Jewish girls stayed inside the convent while all the other internees went home. In May 1944 the convent was evacuated because of the relentless air bombings and other hiding-places were found for all the girls. Rachel Rozenfeld related that the nuns showed extreme compassion for the plight of the Jewish girls. "Although they had vowed a life of silence, they felt it important to break their vows for us. Many nuns were astonished to see that we were not much different from other people. Many believed in our 'horns' and 'third eye'. Many had never seen or spoken to a Jew. If there were ulterior motives I can only think of one: Love thy neighbor."[50]

In Ruisselede, near Ghent, Sister Marie Chrysostome was the Mother Superior of a Carmelite convent that also served as a colony of needy children. Most of these children remained there for three months and were then replaced by others. The three Mendelovics (alias Fiers) sisters, Flora, Charlotte, and Betty, were admitted thereafter they could no longer stay in a preceding convent in Doel. Here, only a few nuns (Sr. Marie-Consulata, Sr. Marie-Amata, and Sr. Jeanne Marie) knew the girls' true identity, and later of a fourth girl brought there (Ruth Wallach, known as Marie Renée Leroy). Twice the Germans searched the convent. On one of these occasions, the girls were hidden in a cellar behind the sacks of potatoes, and another time in a cupboard. When the mother of the Mendelovics sisters wrote a coded letter to her daughters about the disappearance of a family relative, Chrysostome immediately invited her (in a return coded letter) to come to stay in the convent. Mrs. Mendelovics covered 90 kilometers on foot, walking along the railroad tracks by night and sleeping under bushes by day. She arrived in Ruisselede in May 1944, and remained in the convent until the liberation that September. Nobody in the convent knew or suspected that she was the girls' mother. After the war, it was learned that several other Jewish adults had been sheltered in the convent.[51] In Nivelles, southern Belgium, Mother Superior Marie Xavier, who headed the *Sacré Coeur* convent, in 1942 admitted the ten-year-old Noemi Perlmutter under the cover of a Catholic girl, named Micheline Pieraerts. She was afraid to lie to the Father Confessor about her real identity but was told by Xavier that in this case she had special dispensation, and should continue to lie, in the interest of all concerned, highly unusual and otherwise unacceptable advice from the mouth of a Catholic nun. During a German search, Xavier took Noemi into her own room, a place ordinarily restricted to members of the Order. Xavier never tried to convert the girl, who stayed in the convent until June 1945, when her mother was ready to take her back. It was only then that the other nuns learned her true identity.[52]

The need to keep the identity of hidden Jews a secret from many nuns in convents was also true in the story of the hidden Jews at the *Bon Pasteur de Bury-les-Roucourt* convent, near Bonsecout, in the Hainaut region, where Sister Marie de St. Augustin Nicolas served as Mother Superior. In October 1942, eight members of the Sapira family, three adults and six girls aged five to sixteen, after wandering aimlessly from place to place, in their despair knocked on the door of the convent, where Sister Nicolas took them in. She did not divulge the newcomers' true identity to the other Sisters and told the Sapiras to keep their presence discreet. The Sapiras had a room where they slept and spent the day, never stepping out. The Sapira girls, however, were allowed to attend classes together with the children of the orphanage. When five-year-old Rachel (alias Monique) came down with mastoiditis and needed an urgent operation, she was taken to the hospital by Sister Oalburge, a nun of German descent. Some other Jews also found shelter there. Sister Nicolas, who was old and sickly, would say: "I pray to God every day that he may grant me life to bring this task to a good end, for I would not like to force such responsibilities on whoever will come after me." An underground organization provided the refugees with ration cards. Upon liberation, when the Sapiras left the convent, Sister Oalburge accompanied them to the railway station. With tears in her eyes, she said: "You know that I am German. Although the other Sisters did not always trust me, I knew all the time who you were, but I would not have hurt you for anything in the world. I hope that you believe me, and that you will think of me."[53]

As for Sister Véronique Overkamp, she took in fifteen Jewish girls in a girls home in St. Georges sur Meuse. One of the girls, Edita Leeuwarden, born in 1930, and her sister, were first placed in a convent outside Brussels, where they stayed for close to two years. When the Mother Superior told Edita's mother that in light of the danger of German searches, her daughters could no longer remain, she was able to make contact with the earlier-mentioned Father Bruno Reynders, who took Edita and her sister to Sister Véronique's girls home. According to Edita, the especially affectionate treatment received from Sister Véronique aroused the anger of the Mother Superior there, who threatened to have the brave nun moved elsewhere if she continued to show special favor to the two sisters. In fact, as testified by the other Jewish wards, Sister Véronique gave special attention s not only to the Leeuwarden sisters but to the other Jewish girls in the home. In her postwar statement, Sister Véronique underlined that she had not differentiated between the girls but attended equally to everyone who needed her special attention. Danger lurked from sudden German visits. In the words of Sister Véronique: "One day, in 1943, I was visited by a German officer who asked for us to admit forty officers. I accepted his demand and kindly showed him around the interior of the home. He was fascinated. At this point, a group of children came down from the dormitories. . . . 'What are these children here for?' he asked me. 'They are tuberculosis children,' I answered him. 'What? Tuberculosis? Oh, none of my officers will be here,' and he couldn't leave the house fast enough. Luckily, I got away."[54]

We finish this section on rescuer nuns with one of the most dramatic stories, involving the Sisters of the *Très St. Sauveur* convent, in the Anderlecht section of Brussels. In the words of Mother Superior Marie-Aurélie (Eugénie Leloup), written in 1945, she began to admit Jewish girls on September 1, 1942 and eventually took in a total of fifteen. When the Germans staged a massive roundup of Jews in this section of the city, and the Gestapo visited the convent asking whether any Jews were to be found there, the answer, of course, was in the negative. Nine months passed in relative tranquility. "We lived in a perpetual state of unease; we were haunted by the fear of denunciation. The fatal day arrived." It was May 20, 1943, between nine and ten in the morning, when the Gestapo invaded the premises for the second time. Sister Marie-Amélie pleaded with them: "Sir, you are not going to take our small children, am I right?" The Gestapo responded: "It is not up to us, Sister; we act upon the call of a higher power." The twelve children present were told to dress quickly. One German, trying to mask the real purpose of the raid, told the nuns: "One must not frighten the children; on the contrary, one must encourage them. We are taking them, not to kill them, but to reunite them with their families." When the children had gathered in the office with their packages, one German screamed: "But some are missing!" In fact, three of the children, having been baptized at the request of their parents, were elsewhere, in class with the nuns. "I told them this. To which they said: 'It is not the religion that we seek, but the race.' " The Gestapo decided not to wait for the classes to end at noon, but instead they told Marie-Aurélie they would return the following morning, between 10:00 and 11:00 a.m., and to make sure that no one was missing. Marie-Aurélie was at her wits end: "What are we to do? One must act." She called the CDJ, and also alerted Abbé Jan Bruylandts, who left immediately for Malines and asked to see the cardinal. His response, according to Sister Marie-Aurélie, was disheartening: "It is better that I do not intervene; it would only aggravate the situation. But," he told Bruylandts, "do everything in your power to save them." Bruylandts then left to see Queen Elizabeth, and was told by her secretary that she would try to do something. "Myself," Sister Marie-Aurélie testified, "I did not know what to do. I prayed and to the last moment placed my trust in God. At one moment, before the door of the tabernacle [the receptacle containing the consecrated Eucharist], I said: 'Little Jesus, save us.' " A little before the curfew hour of 10:00 p.m. there was suddenly a heavy pounding on the door. Two young men forced their way in with revolvers in their hands. "Hands up!" they shouted. In the meantime, another group of people penetrated the office and ripped out the telephone line. There four men (three of them Jewish) and a woman—all members of the resistance, led by Paul Halter. One nun managed to slip Marie-Amélie a quick message: "I will lock you up in your room. Come quickly, since you are still ill. This will enable us to say tomorrow [probably meaning to the Gestapo] that you've seen nothing. This way you will not be taken away." The children were weeping. One girl comforted the others: "Don't weep, these are not the Germans; you know, you are being rescued." To reassure the children, some of the men spoke a few words in Yiddish. Within a quarter of an hour all the children were ready to leave. Some were happy; others, not knowing where they were being taken, wept. The invading party left, locking the nuns in the office. An hour passed before the nuns decided it was safe to alert the Belgian police about the "kidnapping." Upon arrival, the police freed the nuns, who with tears in their eyes acted out a pre-orchestrated story that the children had been snatched by Gestapo-looking people. The Belgian police dutifully filled out a report and left, alerting the Gestapo to what had happened, but knowing very well that by the time the Gestapo arrived, at 11:30, the following morning, the children would undoubtedly be safe and sound. When the Gestapo arrived, they angrily questioned the nuns. Gestapo: "Do you approve what these men did?" All the nuns in one voice: "Oh, no, Sir." Gestapo: "Who was awake then? Who opened the door to the intruders? How many of them were there? Were they masked? Did they have a Jewish appearance?" ("No, not at all.") Did they speak French or

Flemish? Were they all armed? ("Yes, all.") "Why didn't you scream? ("Scream? But we did not dare. They said that they would shoot if we called out.") Realizing that they had been duped, the Gestapo agents left very disappointed. The nuns feared further interrogations, but nothing of the sort took place. They then learned that the children were in good hands. Sister Marie-Aurélie added: "In recognition of heaven's protection of our little ones and ourselves, a cave in honor of the Virgin of Lourdes was dedicated in our courtyard."[55]

Turning to the Protestant side, in this overwhelmingly Catholic country, we have one noteworthy story, that of Alexandre Doulière and wife Elmire, in Docherie, Charleroi region. They belonged to the Evangelical Mission, a group of deeply devout Christians, mostly poor and hard-working people, who followed a fundamentalist interpretation of the Christian faith. The Doulière sons, Richard and Ivan, eventually became pastors in this church. As told by Gert Koppel, in June 1942, his family living in Brussels learned that a cousin of theirs, who had in the meantime fled to France, had received a letter from an evangelical church in Brussels, known as *La Mission Belge Evangelique,* inviting him to a ten-day overnight camp in August 1942, called Camp Limauges, near Ottignies. In the cousin's absence, Gert decided to take his place and went there. When he returned from the camp, his family received a summons to report to the Malines/Mechelen internment camp. The Koppel parents then turned to their son Gert to investigate whether the *Mission Belge* could help them. Gert was referred to a certain Pastor Odilon Vansteenberghe, who, after consulting his colleagues, decided to take the Koppel family under his protective wing. In the meantime, Gert was invited to return (this time with his sister Ilse) for another session in Camp Limagues, starting August 1942. There he befriended Richard Doulière. "I remember that I spoke with him, and told him about our predicament once the camp ended, namely, that we had ignored the German deportation orders and were therefore in danger and needed to find shelter. Richard Doulière—now a retired pastor of the *Mission Evangelique Belge*, living in France—was moved to action by my appeal." Richard turned to his parents, and after listening to their son's pleas, Alexandre and Elmire Doulière decided to shelter Gert in their La Docherie home. As for Gert's sister Ilse and father John, they were sheltered by two other families, belonging to a splinter evangelical group, known as The Brothers, or *Assemblée des Frères*. In total, Gert was moved to seventeen different families; all save one were evangelical Christians. Some sheltered him for a day or two; others, for weeks and months. "All the families that sheltered me were motivated by only two considerations: to save my life and to fulfill their religious convictions. They admired the Jewish people and wanted to save my life as a moral act dictated by God's law. They received no money for sheltering me; just the opposite. They were required to feed another mouth while food was scarce, and since I was in hiding, they were obviously not provided food ration coupons for me. This was a significant additional strain on the families' resources."

In a letter to Yad Vashem, in 1998, Richard Doulière (he was fourteen in 1942) wrote that his family's action during the war years was not based merely on humanitarian feelings, "but also, as Christians, we love the Jewish people, and we believe in the many promises made to it. I am a pastor, and during my sermons and conferences, I underline the soon-to-be fulfillment of all the promises made by God to Israel." In a 1991 article, Pastor Richard Doulière expanded on the Judeo-Christian symbiosis, underlining that "this persecuted and exterminated people was God's people, of our God." That both "true" Christianity and Judaism have in common the same root, namely "the Torah." He then referred to Paul's likening, in Romans 9–11, of Israel to an olive tree on which the church was grafted, and repeated Jesus' words to the Samaritan woman that salvation is of the Jews. Doulière followed this up by mentioning Isaiah's prophecy of the Jews being a light unto all the nations. "One must emphasize, before adding anything else, that Judaism is the only revealed religion," and "that the time will come when, according to the book of the prophet Isaiah, the nations will prostrate themselves before Israel, saying: 'God is to be found only among you, and there is no other God but Him.' " Doulière then asked, "So, where then does the true originality of Christianity reside?" Here Doulière fell back to the traditional Christian rendition of the significance of faith over works, and Israel's supposed failure to read the new message correctly. "It is in the gospels that one must look for traces of the shock that the teaching of Jesus provoked among his people." Without consulting the Jewish viewpoint on this or that point, Doulière reassured his readers that the day would come when the Jews would realize their mistake, that Jesus did not come to overcome the Law, but "to fulfill it"; that is to change "the interpretation that the Jews of that period had with respect to the Law." Similarly for Paul, who did not advocate the abolition of the Law, but objected to seeing in the observance of the Law a precondition for salvation, for the Law represented a "condemnation." In conclusion, "Christianity did not abolish Judaism, and had not substituted itself against it. The essential difference resided in discovering the attitude adopted toward the Law . . . as powerless in producing a justice acceptable to God, in considering its intrinsic weakness, in discovering the need for grace and the readiness to receive it from God outside any consideration of merit." Doulière restated the traditional Christian viewpoint of the preeminence of faith [in Jesus] and grace over the observance of Torah prescriptions, while at the same time hoping for a Jewish conversion which would heal the centuries-old rift between the two faiths, which to

Doulière were but one religion, essentially the one proclaimed by the church as the "true" spiritual Israel.[56] We have here encapsulated a subtle critique of Judaism , side by side with a true admiration for Jewish tenacity, coupled with the hope of Israel's conversion to the "true" religion—all this in the mouth of a rescuer of Jews.

Chapter 5
The Netherlands

They tried to massacre the Jews but they did not succeed.
God fulfills his promise and the Jewish people is still there,
dispersed all over the world. They who persecute the
children of this people will never flourish.
Rev. Pieter B. Müller, Nijverdal, 1952

The Jews were attacked as Jews by Hitler. We Dutch were not
strong enough to withstand this attack. . . . The only thing we can
do now is to make it up to the Jews and let them be what Hitler
did not permit them to be: Jews. . . . We must bring Jewish chil-
dren back to the homes which Hitler forced them to leave.
Pastor Jacob Kalma, Lekkum, Friesland, 1946

Introduction

The modern Jewish settlement in the Netherlands coincided with the country's independence from Spanish rule in the late sixteenth century. Portuguese Jews who had been forcibly converted to Christianity in their home country but who remained secret Jews (known as Marranos), and the descendants of such people living in Antwerp, Brussels, and Italy, began to settle in the Netherlands, where they were permitted to practice their Judaism openly. They were followed by Jews fleeing the Cossack pogroms in Poland in 1648–49, which had devastated many Jewish communities. In the Netherlands, Jews enjoyed tolerance and security of life and property, and in 1795, under pressure from the French Revolution, Jews were granted full civic rights. By and large, there was little hostility to Jews. Under a "gentlemen's agreement," Jews were debarred from certain professions, but in general they considered this but a slight nuisance. The country knew none of the violent and physical attacks on Jews (pogroms) prevalent in many East European countries. The principle of religious tolerance remained a cornerstone of Dutch political and social life. This went so far that, strange as it may sound, a few Jews were actually members of the Dutch Nazi Party before the war. On the eve of the German invasion, In May 1940, 140,000 Jews resided in the country (including 15,174 refugees, mostly from Nazi Germany), representing 1.6 percent of the total population of 8.9 million. Amsterdam alone counted 75,000 Jews, or over half of the total Jewish population.[1]

The German invasion of the Netherlands began without warning on May 10, 1940. After the massive bombing of Rotterdam a few days later, the Dutch army capitulated. It was the start of an occupation that was to last until the end of war in May 1945. In Nazi eyes, the Dutch were a lost Germanic tribe to be ruled with an iron fist. Hitler appointed a fellow Austrian Nazi, Dr. Arthur Seyss-Inquart as Reich commissioner, with five German commissioners-general serving under him, to supervise and control the Dutch administration. Hans Albin Rauter, for instance, the commissioner-general responsible for interior security (all branches of the German and Dutch police), was an SS general and largely dependent on his boss, SS-head Heinrich Himmler. The fact that, in contrast to France and Belgium, the German control of the Netherlands was both military and civilian is generally regarded as having helped facilitate the deportation of Jews.[2]

The first anti-Jewish laws affected some 2,000 Jewish civil servants who were summarily dismissed. When, as a result, Lodewijk Visser, president of the Dutch Supreme Court was forced to resign, no protest was heard from the still-functioning Dutch civil administration. This was followed by the compulsory registration of all Jewish-owned businesses and enterprises with a Jewish partner. These firms were then liquidated at ridiculous below-value prices or turned over to trustees. Jewish bank and financial assets were also frozen. When all Jews were ordered to register with local authorities, they promptly complied, since they were accustomed to obeying the law in a country known for its traditional deference to authority. In doing so they unwittingly signed their own death warrants, as became evident when deportations began a year later. In the words of one commissioner-general, "all Dutch Jews are now in the bag (*erfasst*)." All told, 157,000 registrations were filed, comprising 159,806 people; of these, "full Jews" amounted to 140,245, and "half-Jews" (*Mischlinge*) 19,561. The full Jews, by racial definition, included people who had been baptized into Christianity, of whom 1,245 were Protestants, and 700 were Catholics.

A further edict banned marriages between Jews and non-Jews, and subsequently having sexual relations was added, under penalty of imprisonment in a concentration camp. An initial group of such "offenders," wearing a large *R* (for "'race defiler") sewn on to their clothes, arrived in the Amersfoort camp, where they were given "special treatment." Then came travel restrictions, and many Jews were cleared from certain cities and forced to move into Jewish-designated areas in Amsterdam. Jews were also barred from public places, such as museums, cinemas, libraries, parks, zoos, restaurants, hotels, and public markets, as well as from fishing spots; telephones and radios were removed from Jewish homes, as well as privately owned vehicles. A curfew was instituted for Jews between 8:00 p.m. and 6:00 a.m., and shopping was permitted only for two hours. In April 1942, the Germans imposed the forcible wearing of the yellow star, required of everyone six and older.[3]

By the summer of 1942, the Germans were ready for the final step: the deportation of the Jews to the death camps in the East. In the Netherlands the Jews were destroyed with a singular thoroughness, unmatched in other West European occupied countries. The geographic position of the country, bounded by all sides by German-controlled countries, the flat terrain, with no woods to hide, and the concentration of Jews in a few large cities all contributed to place the Dutch Jews in a natural trap. SS chief Hans Rauter was in charge of this killing operation, and was assisted by three principal lieutenants: Willi Lages, Willi Zöpf of the Gestapo (Eichmann's man), and Ferdinand Aus der Fünten. When the latter suddenly informed the Nazi-appointed Jewish Council, on June 26, 1942, that henceforth people aged sixteen to forty would be sent for labor in Germany, the council head, David Cohen, protested that "this type of labor service runs directly counter to all the tenets of international law." Aus der Fünten replied, "It is we who decide what is international law. . . . After all, we are the victors."

Most Jews, unaware of the fate awaiting them, and frightened into submission, showed up with their families, in the mistaken belief that they stood a better chance of survival if all stuck together. The whole operation was swiftly and efficiently organized, so that by September 1943, during a fifteen-month period, over 100,000 of the original 140,000 Jewish population were deported to Auschwitz and Sobibor concentration camps, where most were straightaway dispatched to the gas chambers upon arrival. The killing process of the remaining Jews (those imprisoned by the Germans, and others discovered in hiding) continued right up to the liberation of the country in May 1945. In general, Jews were first diverted to a theater in central Amsterdam known as the *Hollandse Schouwburg* ("Dutch Theater"), which had been converted into a staging area for arrested Jews. After a short stay there, they were taken in groups to Westerbork camp in the northeastern part of the country. From there, trains left at regular intervals to the death camps in the East. A special German unit seized the household furniture left behind by the deported Jews, for distribution to ethnic Germans in other countries.[4]

People working for the Jewish Council were exempted in the initial stages of the deportation. Hans Calmeyer, a German working in the Office of Administration and Justice, was responsible for saving close to 3,000 Jews by certifying their non-Jewish or only semi-Jewish ancestry, mostly on the flimsiest of evidence. A small group was able to leave the country after acquiring passports from certain Latin American countries. Other groups, such as those employed in the diamond industry and in the Philips electrical firm, as well as by the German army, were initially spared, but were eventually also deported. To save themselves, the 4,000 Jews of Portuguese ancestry hired a race expert to prove that they were not racially Semites. The ploy failed, and with the exception of a few, the rest were deported and perished in the gas chambers.

In the case of Jews in mixed marriages, estimated at close to 20,000, the decision was not to deport them but to sterilize the Jewish males. About 600 men were actually sterilized; the others were given false sterilization certificates by sympathetic doctors (including a German physician named Dr. Eduard Meyer), but the operation was not carried out. Some were, nevertheless, eventually rounded up and deported. According to one estimate, in 1944, out of the original 20,000, only 8,610 of the intermarried Jews were still at large.

As for the half- and quarter-Jews, this problem touched a raw nerve with the Nazis, since it involved deciding whether to destroy people who carried as much as half of "pure" Aryan blood in their veins, and some were spared. The fate of the baptized Jews was the subject of many discussions and arguments. German policy in the Netherlands was to not recognize baptisms carried out after January 1, 1941, protests by the various churches notwithstanding. In fact, even people baptized before that date suffered the same fate as plain Jews. [5]

* * *

Statistics vary on the number of Dutch Jews who did not comply but went into hiding (known as *onderduikers,* "people who dived," in Dutch). Some place the figure at 25,000, of whom 15,000 or 16,220 who survived in this way; others number the lucky survivors at 10,000 out of 22,000 who went into hiding; still others, only 8,000. According to one estimate, some 4,000 Jewish children and 8,000 adults owed their survival to "diving." More recent studies suggest the number of 24,000–25,000 Jews in hiding or passing as non-Jews under false identity (including 4,000 children) of whom 16,000–17,000 made it safely through the war. Added to these were 2,000 who escaped to other countries; 1,000 who remained in Westerbork camp and were not deported; 5,000 who survived the camps in Poland; as well as some 7,000 *Mischlinge.* Whatever the figure, the Jewish fatality rate of 105,000 deaths, or 75 percent of the original 140,000 Jews, is the largest for any West European country. Not a few of the hiders were constantly on the move to avoid detection, with some rotating to as many as twenty places. One child broke the record. He was moved to thirty-seven different addresses—the highest number registered.

The northern provinces of Friesland, Groningen, and Drenthe (all Protestant strongholds, with strong Calvinist representation) were considered preferred destinations, due in part to the less dense populations there. Many also hid among the Catholics in the southern Limburg province, where local residents were relatively less blondish and more black haired than elsewhere, making it easier for fleeing Jews to blend in. Many people made individual arrangements when seeking hiding outlets. However, there were a number of networks that specialized in help to Jews, such as the legendary Joop Westerweel, in Rotterdam, who worked closely with a Jewish Zionist pioneering group, centered in Loosdrecht. On the home front, the LO (*Landelijke Organisatie voor Hulp aan Onderduikers*—National Organization for Assistance to Divers), the brainchild of the Calvinist minister F. Slomp, with as many as 14,000 members by 1944, assisted many thousands (Jews and non-Jews) with hiding places, ration cards, identity papers and money. The clergy played a pivotal role in organizing and expediting contacts between different areas even before the LO had come into existence. Students also set up their own rescue networks, such as the Utrecht Children's Committee and the Amsterdam Student Group, as well as individual people, such as Arnold Douwes, who created his own network, operating in Nieuwlande (Drenthe), the Calvinist minister Leendert Overduin in Enschede, the Ten Boom family in Haarlem, the Calvinist Bogaard family in Nieuw-Vennep, and the NV group that operated in Amsterdam and Heerlen (Limburg).[6]

For many of the rescuers, helping Jews was a direct experience in Christian mercy, compassion, and love. As related by a rescuer: "Difficult though it was to understand how the Lord could allow so much evil and injustice, we felt that it was all part of His plan, and that comforted us in those dark days." At the same time, Dutch feeling toward Jews remained ambivalent, with some rescuers making no secret of their dislike of Jews. "Granted they are not a pleasant kind of people. But after all, they are human beings" was one Amsterdamer's reaction." There were, of course, more friendly responses. One woman, who survived by passing as a non-Jew and working on a farm, struggled with herself whether to disclose at the end of the war that she was in truth Jewish. "I did not have the faintest idea how they felt about Jews, and for all I knew they might have been rabid antisemites." Finally overcoming her hesitation, she told them the truth, adding that perhaps they were sorry for having helped her. The hostess said: "I am sorry, but only because, had I known, I would have tried to help you even more."[7]

As for the Dutch civil authorities, the record is anything but praiseworthy. They assumed a compliant attitude vis-à-vis their German masters and bent to the Nazi demand for all civil servants to sign an Aryan Declaration form in the interest of preventing "general chaos in all areas." The Dutch railroads, as well, which took Jews to the German border, rolled without any hindrance; not a single train failed to run on schedule. The Dutch Nazi Party, better known as the NSB (*Nationaal-Socialistische Beweging*—National Socialist Movement), which before the war mustered only 4.22 percent of the parliamentary votes, by 1944 had installed NSB mayors in 55 percent of all Dutch cities. Significantly, immediately after the liberation, 120,000 to 150,000 people were imprisoned for collaboration with the enemy. Of these, 66,000 were sentenced by special courts and tribunals. Many of them were quickly released in response to pressure by the Dutch churches.[8]

On the other hand, many academicians and students showed greater moral stamina. In response to the German demand for the dismissal of Jews from the civil service, half of the university professors signed a letter of protest to Seyss-Inquart, and students at the universities of Leiden and Delft (two of the country's nine universities) went on strike in protest over the dismissal of Jewish professors. At the Leiden Technical University, Professor Cleveringa, the dean of the Legal Faculty, spoke up in November 1940 in defense of his Jewish colleague, the jurist Professor E.M. Meijers, "this noble son of our people, this man, this father to his students, this scholar, whom foreign usurpers have suspended from his duties." Cleveringa was later arrested and deported to Buchenwald. In addition to the academic protest, a significant public reaction, the first of its kind in Europe, took place in the early phase of the Nazi anti-Jewish measures. In February 1941, when local Nazis raided the Jewish quarter of Amsterdam, which led to Jewish resistance, the Germans retaliated by arresting 389 Jews and deported them to Mauthausen camp, where only one person survived. This spurred a Communist-led strike that paralyzed the entire transportation system, the largest factories, and the public services, and lasted for three days. Unfortunately, this public protest had no effect on the Nazi intent to rid the country of its Jews.[9]

As for the Dutch police, in general they obeyed German orders when it came to arresting Jews. There was a complete overhaul of the Dutch police organization, and its head was replaced by a man more sympathetic with Nazi designs, who went so far as requiring policemen to undergo ideological-retraining programs to bring them in line with Nazi thinking on the Jewish issue. Special Jewish departments were set up in various Dutch cities, staffed with detectives and police officers whose sole purpose was to track down Jews in hiding. These men were organized in "columns" (*Kolonne*) and paid a bounty for each Jew caught. The bonus was steadily raised by the Germans, from an original 7.5 guilders to 37.5 guilders per head, for greater motivation. They would roam the streets to check the passes of people who "looked Jewish," and also relied on denunciations. The most infamous of these groups was the Henneicke Kolonne, consisting of thirty-five men, who managed to arrest around 3,400 people during a six-month period. Not surprisingly, Gestapo chief Willi Lages, at his postwar trial, claimed that without the support of the Dutch police, "it would have been practically impossible to seize even 10 percent of Dutch Jewry." In addition, Dutch paramilitary collaborationist units, such as the NSB Home Guard (Nederlandse Landwacht), were also active in the hunt for Jews.[10] In a few isolated cases, Dutch policemen refused to carry out the order to arrest and pick up Jews for deportation. For instance, in Grootegast, Dirk Boonstra and ten other policemen stood firm in their refusal to arrest Jews. Boonstra was dispatched to Dachau, where he perished. The others were imprisoned for various periods.[11]

* * *

As for the churches, they were divided into three main groups: approximately 36 percent Catholic, 34 percent mainline Dutch Reformed (*Hervormde Kerk*), 8 percent Calvinist (*Gereformeerde Kerk*) and other fundamentalist groups. In October 1940, many clerics of the Dutch Reformed Church read from the pulpit a protest against the Aryan Attestation by civil servants. In March 1941, when the Germans ordered notices placed on public buildings denying access to Jews, the churches again protested. On February 17, 1942, Catholic and Protestant church representatives again protested to the Nazi governor, Seyss-Inquart, about the treatment of Jews. This was reportedly the first time in Dutch history that the two major denominations acted in unison; they co-signed a protest document against the anti-Jewish measures. In his reply, the Nazi governor underlined that "in our treatment of the Jews there can be no talk of mercy; only, at best, of justice. The Jewish problem will be solved by the Germans and no distinction will be made between Jews and Jews."

Despite the failure of this protest, with the start of the deportations in July 1942, all the major churches again joined in a signed memorandum stating their "sense of outrage at the deportations of Jews"; a step which ran counter to "divine commandments of justice and charity." Seizing on a loophole in the wording of the protest, which also mentioned the arrest of baptized Jews, the Germans decided upon a temporary concession; namely, Jews baptized before January 1, 1942 would be exempted from deportations; that is, of people not yet arrested (those already arrested remained imprisoned). A week following this German concession, the Protestant Reformed Church suggested that the church protest be read from the pulpit on Sunday, July 26. The Roman Catholic and Calvinist church leaderships agreed to do likewise. At this juncture the Germans, wishing to pull the rug from under the feet of the defiant churches, assured that if the protest were not read publicly, baptized Jews would not be harmed. At this, the main Protestant church backed off, but the Roman Catholic and Calvinist churches went ahead with their decision. Johannes de Jong, the Catholic archbishop of Utrecht, in his pastoral letter, denounced the anti-Jewish measures as contrary "to God's commands of justice and mercy." The German retaliation was swift and brutal, mainly against the Catholic Church. On the night of August 1–2, 1942, many of the 690 Catholic Jews were arrested and deported to the death camps, including the noted convert and philosopher Edith Stein, arrested with her sister Rosa in the Carmelite convent in Echt (Limburg province). The two were taken to Auschwitz and gassed upon arrival. In September 1942, SS chief Rauter proudly wrote to his boss, Himmler, that in contrast to Archbishop de Jong of Utrecht, who "did not abide by our original agreements," the mainline Protestant church fell into the trap, and the Nazis succeeded in breaking up the united Protestant/Catholic front. Rauter gloated: "Archbishop de Jong declared at a Conference of Bishops that he would never again form a united front with the Calvinists and other Protestants." Rauter was now satisfied that "the storm of protest raised by the churches when the evacuation [i.e., deportations] began has thus been greatly undermined and has now subsided." Himmler appended the words "*Sehr Gut* [excellent]" to the report. Two years later came the turn of the Protestant-baptized Jews. Despite the earlier assurance, in September 1944, 500 Protestant Jews were deported to Theresienstadt camp, of whom only 150 survived.

In the meantime, in May 1943, the churches again voiced a protest; this time against the forced sterilization of Jews married to non-Jewish spouses. Signed by nine Protestant and Roman Catholic churches, the statement warned Seyss-Inquart that "even your Excellency will have to give account one day" for the violation of the biblical command "be fruitful and multiply (Genesis 1:8)," for "sterilization is a physical and spiritual mutilation directly at variance with God's commandments . . . and undermines true Christian human life." The statement went on to lecture the Nazi governor that "the commandments of the God and Judge of all the earth apply to you as much as to anybody else and all the more in view of your high position. . . . It is your Excellency's duty to stop this shameful practice of sterilization. . . . The living God has the power to incline even the heart of your Excellency to repentance and obedience." Seyss-Inquart did not reply.[12]

Calvinists were in the forefront of those who aided Jews. Numbering only 8 percent of the population, it is estimated that they accounted for assisting 25 percent of the Jews who went underground. Calvinist pastors also played a major role in various rescue networks. Pastor Leendert Overduin, in Enschede, ran a network that helped hundreds of Jews in many ways, and in distant places in the country. Overduin was arrested on several occasions and incarcerated for nine months, but survived. The NV group (*Naamloze Vennootschap*), dedicated to helping children, was created when Constant Sikkel, a Calvinist pastor in Amsterdam, was asked to help two children and enlisted the help of two brothers, Jaap and Gerard Musch, to find hiding places for them—and subsequently for many more. Generally speaking, at the institutional level, the churches tended to tread carefully when dealing with the German occupiers, but on the grass-roots level, many individual pastors were ready to commit themselves to help Jews, in which members of the Calvinist Church took a leading role.

Especially among Calvinists, the obligation to help the Chosen People had a strong impetus. True enough, some clerics made an attempt to convert their Jewish wards. The earlier-mentioned Reverend F. Slomp, one of the founders of the LO underground network, stated that hiding Jews among Christians was a perfect opportunity to convert them, noting proudly that "in the last few years more Jews had been baptized than in decades before the war"—certainly an exaggerated statement. Historian De Jong observed that of the estimated 3,500 Jews in hiding in Calvinist households, a few years after the war only 125 had been converted. In one unpleasant case, a Jewish couple lodged with a farmer in the northern part of the country had to be moved after fourteen days because the farmer insisted that if they did not want to become Christians, they would have to live with his animals. Another survivor wrote in his diary, in a sympathetic tone, of his rescuer's attempts to convert him: "Today auntie asked me if I wanted to become a Calvinist. I won't do it, I won't let myself be baptized. . . . Auntie doesn't understand it. She is afraid that I won't go to heaven if I don't become a Calvinist."[13]

Hardly had the war ended when, in August 1945, a royal decree announced the creation of a commission for War Foster Children, known by its acronym OPK, to decide on the future guardianship of Jewish children who had been hidden with non-Jewish families. These amounted to 3,481 children, of whom 2,041 had been orphaned, and were now claimed by distant relatives or Jewish organizations. A bitter struggle was now waged over these war orphans. The Netherlands was the only Nazi-liberated country in Europe in which such a sorry situation prevailed. OPK's head, Dr. Gesina van der Molen, who belonged to the Calvinist Church, not only refused to sign the Aryan statement required of all teachers during the occupation, but was much involved in the rescue of Jewish children. Her concern for the children's welfare was sincere, but as a fundamentalist Christian she had difficulty accepting the legitimacy of Judaism, and she fought to prevent the return of these children, which led to an open conflict with Jewish organizations. In the heat of this debate, in July 1946, she declared that there was no such thing as a Jewish community in the Netherlands, since "Dutch Jews have such diverse beliefs that they can't be considered as being one. To call all theses varieties one 'Jewish community' is incorrect." It is well to remember that the dominant opinion in her church still maintained that Christianity had replaced Judaism and that the church had become God's Chosen People. Thus, while during the war years Gesina van der Molen had risked her life to save Jewish children, this paradoxically did not conflict with her viewing Judaism as a thing of the past. Perhaps this had to do with her strong Calvinist convictions, whose theology held that while the Jews remained God's original Chosen People and were consequently to be preserved, Christianity had replaced Judaism as the true carrier of the biblical message.[14]

The Jewish community reacted by maintaining that the issue of the Jewish war orphans was a Jewish one and therefore, in accordance with Dutch tradition, these children should be turned over to it. To this end the Jewish community established its own war orphans commission, appropriately named *Laezrath Hayeled,* "To the Child's Aid." In the weekly *De Vlam* ("The Flame"), which originally appeared as a resistance paper, one author contended that it would be no great loss if the professing Jewish community assimilated into a socialistic society and ceased to exist, adding: "Do we view Judaism as religion? As a race? Do we want, in the Year of Our Lord 1945, to accept racial theories? . . . Shall we take the Nazi way?" Especially galling to the Jewish community was the OPK's self-assumed prerogative to interpret the wishes of the children's deceased parents, More painful to Jewish sensitivities, a mostly Christian commission, headed by a devout Calvinist chairman, took it upon itself to determine the importance of membership in a Jewish congregation, including questions of circumcision and religiously consecrated marriages. If the parents had not had a kosher household and did not regularly attend synagogue, their Jewishness was put into question by the Christian majority members of the commission. Jews countered that there was little doubt but that most of the victimized parents would have wished their children to grow up as Jews after the war, as members of some sort of Jewish community, and that even completely non-Orthodox parents would have objected to their children being brought up in another religion. The head of Laezrath Hayeled pointed out that it would be equally unthinkable "that a commission comprised primarily of non-Catholics could speak out about the question of what the sacraments mean, baptism, confession, marriage (etc.)." In the end, an estimated 360 children remained with non-Jewish families. The others were returned to their parents, relatives, or other people and Jewish organizations.[15]

One dissenting voice in the chorus of anti-Jewish indignation was that of Pastor Jacob Kalma of the Dutch Reformed Church, in the village of Lekkum, Friesland province, who campaigned for the return of the Jewish children to their people. During the occupation he had saved Jews from the Nazis. After the war, he put his pen to use to justify the continued existence of the Jewish people as a religious community. In two pamphlets published during the OPK controversy (one of which was entitled *Redt de Joden*—"Save the Jews!"), Kalma stated: "The Jews were attacked as Jews by Hitler. We Dutch were not strong enough to withstand this attack. We are culpable as well. The only thing we can do now is to make it up to the Jews and let them be what Hitler did not permit them to be: Jews." He added: "No one denies his background, be it good or evil, fair or ugly, with impunity. . . .Anyone who 'converts' should know why he is rejecting the heritage to which he was born." Dissenting from the opinion of a child psychologist, advanced by OPK members, Kalma retorted: "We must bring Jewish children back to the homes which Hitler forced them to leave. By identifying completely with the child welfare position . . . one collaborates willy-nilly in the complete destruction (*Ausrottung*) of Judaism." The choice for the Dutch people was starkly clear. They had to choose between two alternatives "either preserving Judaism, including recognition of its spiritual value and meaning for the Netherlands as well," or "attempting, whether or not under the influence of antisemitism, through secularization or through conversion to liquidate that very same Judaism. Sharply put: either Christ or Hitler." Turning a patriotic page, Kalma thundered, "We are Dutchmen. . . . To prize freedom and tolerance has been a Dutch tradition. For a long time the Netherlands has offered the Jews a haven. Can this now be allowed to change?" Finally: "It is true: the Jews are divided, but with few exceptions they indeed wish to be Jews. It is both a Dutch and Christian obligation to make this possible. . . . Only thus can the dialogue between Judaism and Christianity commence, it being a matter of the utmost importance that this should take place." His, however, was a lone voice, and it is a pity that many of those who had acted so courageously in saving Jews from the Nazis could not rid themselves of a centuries-old prejudice which questioned the Jewish people's legitimacy as a religious community—in a country that prided itself on its rich tradition of religious tolerance.[16]

Rescue Accounts

While Catholics made up more than one-third of the population, there are only a few records of Jews hiding in convents and monasteries, unlike the situation in Belgium and France. Most rescue stories in the Netherlands took place in private homes, both of clerics and laypeople. The accounts of clerical help to Jews indicate that most of the helping clergy did not take advantage of the situation to try to steer their wards away from their religion—at least not during the war years. Consider, for instance, the story recounted by Lore Herrman, who together with her parents hid in the home of Pastor Evert L.

Smelik in Amsterdam. The pastor read aloud to his wards from the Hebrew Bible (Old Testament), but not from the New Testament, for in her words, "he said he did not want to take advantage of the situation, but simply wanted to strengthen the Jews in their own faith."[17] Similarly in the story of Elizabeth Santcroos, whose newborn son Peter was raised in the home of Protestant pastor Jelis-Jan Creutzberg and wife Francoise, in Nijmegen. It was quite by accident that Peter Santcroos arrived in the Creutzberg home, in Nijmegen. The story began on September 11, 1943, when Peter was born in a hospital in Naarden, North Holland. Nobody knew that his mother, Elizabeth, was Jewish, and thus nobody understood why she was so depressed after giving birth. Pieta Creutzberg, the nurse who attended Elizabeth, thought that the distraught mother might develop some confidence if she read to her from the Bible. Pieta instinctively chose to read from the Hebrew Bible, and Elizabeth could not help tell the nurse the truth about her identity. "Nurse Creutzberg did not lose any time," Peter's father wrote in his testimony to Yad Vashem. "She took the baby, left the hospital, and brought him to her parents in Nijmegen, Gelderland [region], who took care of him for sixteen months, under the most terrible circumstances." During this time, the Japanese shot the reverend's eldest son, in the Dutch East Indies, and Pieta's fiancé was killed by Germans. "I'd like to draw your attention," the child's mother Mrs. Santcroos wrote, "to the fact that Reverend Creutzberg never baptized the child, but considered it a great joy and satisfaction to himself and his wife to return a Jewish child unharmed to his parents and to Jewry."[18] A similar pro-Jewish attitude was that of Protestant Reverend Kleijs Kroon, in Noordwijk, who reportedly urged his congregants from the pulpit to assist Jews. In February 1941, he also voiced in writing his opposition to taking advantage of Jews wishing to convert in the false belief that they would avoid persecution. "It is wrong to abandon your religion under pressure," he wrote. "If, after the war, you still want to be a Christian, I will be happy to baptize you. At the moment, all you need is a forged baptismal certificate for your physical safety." He and his wife Henriette continuously sheltered Jews in their home, both in Noordwijk and in Amsterdam, to where Kroon was reassigned. Interestingly, after the war, one of the minister's daughters converted to Judaism and moved to Israel.[19]

In a slightly different setting, however, consider Reverend Jakob D. Koers, of the Dutch Reformed Church in Eibergen. He opened his home, where he lived with his wife and two young children, as a refuge for the Jacob Julius Zion family, but then made a subtle attempt to religiously influence his wards. In the words of Mrs. Zion, during her family's stay in the reverend's home, he gave her Christian religious books to read as well as the New Testament. When asked for her response to the contents of this literature, she answered that she was Jewish, and intended to stay such, was a Zionist and hoped after the war to go to Palestine. The pastor did not press the point, and continued to care for them during periods of danger and German searches.[20] Similarly, Pastor Gerardus Pontier in Heerlen, a Calvinist, assured Salomon Silber of his readiness to help him and his family, and showed them the place in his home where some of the Silber family could be sheltered. Upon parting from the youngish Salomon, "he gave me a little book—the New Testament, in Hebrew. I wondered why he gave it to me, but I saw that he was happy that I accepted and took it with me." Salomon Silber does not tell whether Pontier ever asked whether he had read the New Testament; evidently not. As we shall further see, the Calvinist pastor did not lack in courage in his dedication to his wards—the Silber family and numerous other Jews.[21]

Many Protestant clerics viewed the Jews as still being a divinely valid Chosen People, whose destiny was inextricably linked with unfolding of the final messianic drama, the second coming of Jesus. In a speech delivered in 1955 at a Jewish Reform chapel in Newport Beach, California, Hanna Kisjes-Goedhard, the daughter of Reverend Daniel Goedhart and wife Wilhelmina, from Hummelo, who had sheltered a Jewish family in their home during the war years, explained this belief. She told the worshippers that "there were three main reasons for my parents' decision to hide people—their profession, the location of their house, and their religion. . . . Now I am coming to the most important reason my parents had for giving shelter to Jewish fellow citizens, namely the religious one. . . . Since we were young we were told the stories from the Bible. My father was a very fascinating storyteller. Abraham, Isaac, and Jacob were living men for me. We learned about them and loved them—Moses, Joshua, Samuel (my first name is Hanna after Samuel's mother), Saul, David, the kings and prophets, the complete history of the people of Israel. . . . Of course in our case also we learned about the great Son of Israel, Jesus of Nazareth, who was a great source of inspiration for my parents. So how could they neglect the terrible fate of the Chosen People? They believed in biblical righteousness and Israel to be the holy tree with many branches, and the Christians as a wild shoot grafted into the religious tree. As a university graduate my father knew of the dreadful facts of history: the violence in Crusader times, the pogroms and many, many crimes committed by Christianity against the Chosen People. I think he was urged by conscience to put some good against that—be it ever so little." The Goedharts had sheltered for three long years the three members of the Itallie family: father Dr. Flip, wife Fan, and their eleven-year-old daughter Bertie.[22]

Reverend Bastiaan Ader, from Nieuw Beerta, Groningen province, was also fired with the religious obligation to save Jews. One of his wards recalled Ader once declining help to a non-Jew, saying, "I am sorry, I only deal with Jews," but he nevertheless also assisted non-Jews whenever possible. From the early stages of the occupation he frequently journeyed to and from Amsterdam, to the Joodsche Invalide hospital, formerly a Jewish old-age home, to offer hiding places to people who had no money or contacts. Ader's entire family—parents, sister, and in-laws—assisted him to hide as many Jews as possible. Ader was eventually caught and shot by the Germans. At the ceremony in his honor at Yad Vashem in November 1967, his wife Johanna reiterated her and her husband's religious bond with the Jewish people. "You should look at the future. Through all tribulations God is great and God is leading us to His holy future. Jews and Christians together will experience this holy future."[23]

Calvinist Minister Cornelis (Kees) Moulijn, in Blija, who together with his wife Annagnita (Anneke) helped many Jews, also gave voice to a special religious attachment to the welfare of the Jewish people. When told in 1975 of his elevation to the "Righteous" title by Yad Vashem, he responded: "Though we are grateful for the distinction, we very often feel ashamed that the we Dutch people did not do more to keep many more Jewish lives from the Final Solution. At any rate, we feel ourselves closely connected with your people and with the future of Israel, more, really, than with any other nation in the world."[24]

The religious belief in preserving the Jewish people also came out clearly in the postwar words of Reverend Pieter B. Müller, from Nijverdal. After the war he stated: "They tried to massacre the Jews but they did not succeed. God fulfills his promise and the Jewish people is still there, dispersed all over the world. They who persecute the children of this people will never flourish." During the war years, Reverend Müller and his wife Adriana took into their household (which included seven children) the young Abraham Meijers. To outsiders, Abraham, renamed Freddie, was presented as a nephew from the west of Holland who had moved east for health reasons.[25]

It goes without saying that, beyond a special attraction to the Jews as still the Chosen People, the Christian duty to aid the distressed and persecuted, as in the parable of the Good Samaritan, ran deep in the hearts and minds of clergy of all denominations. The Dutch Reformed vicar Pieter Miedema, in Drachstercompagnie, said in a sermon to his congregation: "If you refuse to open your house and heart to an innocent fugitive, then there is no place for you in the community of the righteous." True to his words, toward the end of 1942, the Miedemas (including wife Joekje) admitted the young Jewish Louis de Wied, after the pastor was unable to find another location for him. Louis's older brother David soon followed, and gradually more people were the recipients of the couple's charitable hospitality.[26] Calvinist minister Leendert Overduin, in Enschede, ran a rescue network that saved more Jews than any other cleric. Upon his arrest, he was asked by his German interrogators why he was risking his life to save Jews. He explained that his Christian belief obligated him to help anyone who suffered unjustly. In like manner, he continued, he would have to help his tormentors should they, in turn, be treated unjustly after the war. The answer left his interrogators speechless. After the war, indeed, when many sought revenge against members of the Dutch Nazi Party, Overduin appealed to the courts and pleaded that each former Nazi be afforded a fair trial. He even went so far as to camp on the steps of the home of the minister of justice in protest. Informed of the Yad Vashem decision to award him the "Righteous" title, he declined the honor, since he felt that no special reward was necessary for a person who simply acted on the dictates of his religious beliefs.[27] Similarly, the previously mentioned Calvinist pastor Gerardus Pontier, in Heerlen, when he learned from young Salomon Silber that his family had received a deportations summons, scheduled for August 25, 1942, he left the room to consult with his wife, then returned to announce that the two had decided to hide Salomon and his brother in their home. When Salomon blurted out that it was dangerous to harbor Jews, the pastor responded: "Don't worry, my child. We have decided to do so, and God will protect us. Son of Israel, we are happy to give you any help we can. It is the duty of every Christian to help people in danger." He then took the lad upstairs and showed him a room in the garret with two beds, saying that it would be waiting for the two brothers the following Monday night, and would be a comfortable and secure stay.[28]

Human nature being what it is, some clergy at first declined to help for fear of the authorities, but upon second thought and with some pressure from their colleagues, they changed their minds and, as demonstrated in the following, outdid themselves in aid to Jews. In autumn 1943, the Calvinist Leendert Overduin visited a colleague, Cornelis (Kees) Moulijn, who lived with his wife Annagnita (Anneke) in Blija, Friesland region, with their two young children, in order to enlist him in his rescue operation for Jewish fugitives. Moulijn at first demurred, but Overduin pressed on. Not making any headway, Overduin's parting words upon leaving were: "Ultimately, it is a matter of faith." This broke the ice. Moulijn ran after the departing Overduin, telling him that he and his wife had changed their minds. In 1974, recalling his initial hesitation, Moulijn wrote: "Even now, when I recall my first reaction, which was fear, I would never dare criticize any other Dutchmen for not having provided more help."

However, once he had changed his mind, a steady flow of Jewish fugitives came to hide in Blija, some of them personally escorted by Moulijn and his wife, all the way from Enschede, in Overijssel province. The first to come was a Jewish girl named Zus, followed by Reuben Kahane, an Orthodox Jew, who made his way on his own by train, and insisted on bringing along his phylacteries (*tefillin*) and a Torah scroll to the hideout. The pastor persuaded him that for his own safety it was better to leave these articles with him, since, as he stated, a vicar was expected to be conversant with the practices of other religions and these articles, if discovered with him they would not present an insurmountable problem. The man was then referred to a couple who lived nearby.

Josef Seligmann, another beneficiary of Moulijn's charity, stated that Moulijn distributed Jews among the farms in small villages. Of the pastor's 415 congregants, there was only one farmer who seemed to sympathize with the Germans, but he presented no threat after he was told that the Germans were also rounding up Jewish children, not merely adults. Shocked by this revelation, the man decided to take in a Jewish child. Together with the earlier-mentioned Pastor Jacob Kalma, Moulijn searched for safe addresses among his flock in Waaxens and Brantgum. Moulijn's wife, Anneke, was also involved in surreptitiously obtaining ration cards through her work with a leader of the resistance movement. Eventually, the Moulijns were themselves forced to go into hiding after the Germans learned of their links with the resistance. For a while, the Moulijns wandered from place to place, at times separated from each other.[29]

The previously mentioned Protestant pastor Evert L. Smelik, who hid many fugitive Jews among members of his parish (such as twenty-three-year-old Eric Zielenziger and Lore Herrman with her parents), declined the honors associated with the title when informed of his designation as one of the "Righteous" by Yad Vashem in 1978. His reasons given were a mixture of selfless modesty and religious piety. He wrote back: "It is a great privilege for a Dutchman to be honored by this sign of appreciation from the side of the Jews in Israel. . . . We remember with grief the victims we personally knew. With grief, but also *with shame* [Smelik's emphasis] that we did not do more to help and rescue them. I am afraid that I cannot accept the medal. My part in helping our friends was not very important, particularly in comparison with the share others had in saving threatened Jews. Perhaps some of the saved, with kind intentions, have exaggerated my slight interventions. I feel, rather, the shortcomings of our help. If we had really done our duty in the situation, we would have done a lot more and taken more risks. . . . Considering these arguments, I ask you not to expect me for the presentation of the medal. Far be it from me to offend you in any way, it is rather the contrary. My objections arise from personal feelings concerning my own behavior in the past. Dear sirs, please accept my feelings of gratitude for your intention and my continuous interest in the fate and difficulties of your esteemed nation. Yours."[30]

Some clerics helped only one or a few Jews; others went out of their way to help as many as possible, even beyond their capacity. After preaching in his church, in Drachstercompagnie, on the Christian obligation to help, Dutch Reformed vicar Pieter Miedema, together with his wife Joekje, decided to give a personal example, and toward the end of 1942 (a daughter was born to them in April 1942) they took in the Jewish boy Louis de Wied, who came to stay with them. Three months later, Louis's older brother David joined him. After moving the two to another location, the Miedemas arranged safe addresses for fourteen young patients who had fled from a Jewish tuberculosis sanatorium, while also taking in the Lezer family, and arranging a separate hiding place for the Lezers' two children, and supplying them with food and books. The Miedemas also hid a tailor named Josephon on the top floor of the vicarage, as well as sheltering a Jewish resistance man for a while. When he was arrested and executed, the Miedemas decided to move out of their home; Joekje and the children (a son had been added to the family) moved to her brother's home, while Pieter wandered from one place to another. It is estimated that throughout the occupation period Pieter and Joekje Miedema cared for at least twenty-three Jewish people.[31]

We return to Calvinist minister Leendert Overduin, in Enschede, Overijssel province—the man who probably stands out as the single largest clerical rescuer of Jews in the Netherlands. In September 1941, shocked and angered at the initial deportation of Jews from his city to Mauthausen camp, Overduin vowed to prevent any further deportations should they occur. For that purpose, he joined hands with Sieg Menko, chairman of the Jewish council in Enschede, in creating a rescue network. When the deportations resumed the following year on even a larger scale, Overduin and his sisters, Maartje and Corrie, set themselves to encourage the city's Jews to opt for hiding instead of responding to the deportation summons. As a result of the combined effort of the reverend, his sisters, and their Jewish associate, about 25 percent of the city's Jewish community was saved—700 to 800 in round numbers (also counting some Amsterdam Jews saved by Overduin), which represented the highest number of Jews saved by any other network in the country.

As told by Selien Brommet in her testimony: "We didn't even ask for help, but Reverend Overduin had seen our names on the list for transportation to the East. He came to my husband, whom he knew from the Jewish Council, and told him that we had to hide as soon as possible." Another survivor, Alice Israel, noted that as a Jew hiding in Overduin's home, "I could see for myself how he worked day and night to find addresses for Jews in need. He worked together with the police in Enschede and warned the Jews who were in danger." M. Seligman, another beneficiary of Overduin's generosity, wrote that "no wonder the Germans and their collaborators wanted to catch him. For months he did not sleep at home but wandered from place to place in and around Enschede, never ceasing to work for the benefit of Jews." When he visited his charges to distribute ration cards as well as to check on their treatment by their hosts, he sometimes came disguised as a baker, another time as a chimney sweep, or a plain blue-collar worker. Once, when Selien Brommet and her husband hadn't heard about their two-year-old son for a very long time, Overduin made a special trip to Bolsward, in distant Friesland province, to bring the Brommets a recent picture of the child. "I can't even explain what this meant to us," Selien adds. "I tell you this so that you can see how much understanding he had, and the risks he took to bring information about the nearest kin." For Jews who had been dispossessed of their funds and could not pay for their upkeep, the Overduin network raised money mainly from non-Jewish manufacturers. Overduin was arrested several times by the Germans, but released for lack of proof. Finally, after interrogating him unsuccessfully for several months, the Germans kept him locked in jail until the end of the war.[32]

In Grubbenvorst, Catholic Father Henricus Vullinghs saved the lives of at least forty-three Jewish refugees with the help of his co-workers in the resistance. It began in the summer of 1942, just after the start of the deportations in Amsterdam, when the first contingent of fleeing Jews began arriving in Grubbenvorst, with Vullinghs providing safe houses for all the Jews sent to him. Eventually, Vullinghs became one of the most active representatives of the LO clandestine network in Limburg, working alongside many others, including the curate Jean Slots. Vullinghs ensured that the Jews were able to find shelter with farmers in the area, although he did not always disclose to the hosts the Jewish identity of the fugitives. He also arranged addresses in nearby communities and often visited his wards to check on their well-being, and when necessary arranged their transfer to new addresses.

Avraham Perlmutter, one of the many Jews helped by Vullinghs, related his meeting with the tireless cleric. "It was a dark and cold winter night in December 1943, when I arrived at the railroad station of Venlo in the province of Limburg. Holding my small valise containing all my earthly possessions, I was anxiously surveying the near-empty station platform. I was told by my underground contact that a man was to meet me there and take me to my next hiding place. It was already more than a year and a half since I had gone into hiding, and I had stayed in close to a dozen different locations in various parts of Holland. During that time I had many close encounters with disaster, but also met unbelievably courageous people, who at the risk of their own lives were helping Jews to avoid deportation. . . . After several minutes a tall man came walking up to me and after asking my name, requested that I follow him. I was greatly reassured when I noticed his clothing was that of a priest. This was my first view of the brave and righteous Father Henricus Vullinghs of the parish church of *Maria ten Hemel Opneming* of Grubbenvorst. After leaving the train station Vullinghs asked me to sit on the back of his bicycle, and he quickly pedaled along the Venlose Weg toward Grubbenvorst, and then along Kloosterstraat to the house of Peter and Gertrude Beijers. After a brief discussion in the local dialect, which I only partially understood, Pastor Vullinghs left." Father Vulling's expansive involvement in sheltering people (including non-Jews) sought by the Germans eventually led to his arrest in May 1944. He was deported to Bergen-Belsen camp, where he tragically died.[33]

We continue with more stories of special interest. Reverend Peter Lambooy and his wife Anna Magdalena were on home leave from missionary work in Indonesia when the Germans invaded the Netherlands. Instead of returning, Lambooy took up the post of part-time minister in Hilversum. The Lambooys had nine children and were active members of the underground. When their Jewish neighbors, the Birnbaums, were ordered moved to Amsterdam, Anna Lambooy brought them food every week on her bicycle, imploring them to come and hide, but they refused out of fear of retaliation on family members. Later, the Lambooys hid the children of friends of the Birnbaums—thirteen-year-old Bernard and his sixteen-year-old sister Paula Gellert. At first, Bernard studied at home with Mrs. Lambooy, a teacher by profession. Later, her husband, the reverend, forged documents for Bernard so that he could attend school. Bernard kept faith with his Jewish origin, and when the Lambooy family said grace, Bernard blessed his food with his head covered with a skullcap that Mrs. Lambooy kept for him. One incident almost brought tragedy to the family. As related by one of the pastor's sons: "It was in 1942 that we kids stupidly talked too loud in our garden about the oppression of Jews, and our new neighbors, the Garons, heard our conversation. She turned out later to be a Nazi agent. She jumped to the conclusion that I was a most bad guy with intentions to help Jews. The same evening I was arrested by the Gestapo and brought to the Kleine Gartman Plantsoen prison, where I was beaten and thrown over a chair. My left kidney was badly injured then and never recovered. They found a *judenstern* [yellow star] in my pocket, made by a girlfriend of my sister to show at school, and wished to know where I got it from. They still haven't gotten an answer! Finally they assumed I had found it by accident, and because I was still a youth, they released me after a month; my father being fined 3,000 florins (about $1,500)."[34]

We return to the Calvinist pastor Gerardus Pontier, who lived with wife Dora and their four children in a large vicarage in Heerlen, Limburg province, a predominantly Catholic region in the southern part of the country. He is best known for his role in the clandestine rescues of the NV group, organized in Amsterdam for the purpose of saving Jewish children. Here we tell how he became involved in the rescue of a Heerlen Jewish family, the Silbers. It began on a summer day in July 1942, when Pontier stopped Salomon Silber, the eldest son of the Orthodox Silber family, on the street and told the surprised boy to come to him if he ever needed help. As related by Shlomo-Salomon Silber: "One day, I was walking in the street with my younger brother wearing the yellow star inscribed with the Hebrew letters *Jood* (Jew) in the center. . . .The man who saved our lives and those of five hundred Jewish children brought us this wonderful message of keeping faith in mankind. We met in the street. I saw how he looked at us when he was bicycling, and when he approached us, he got off his bicycle and greeted us kindly. He was a man of about fifty years old; blue eyes, short-cut gray hair, very tall and heavily built. He smiled and asked how we were faring these days during the bad times. I told him that we were in danger. The Nazis could pick us up any day and send us to a concentration camp; 'God knows what will happen to us.' Hearing this, he said: 'They are doing satanic work, and it is terrible to hear about it.' He closed his eyes for a minute as though he were praying and left us with words of hope: if we ever were in need of help, he would be ready to help us. His name was Reverend Pontier."

The Silber family consisted of the parents and four sons aged between ten and twenty. Soon thereafter, the family received the dreaded deportations summons and had to decide who would report for deportation and who would go into hiding. Abraham, the physically strongest of the sons, decided to report (he luckily survived the depredations of the camps), so it was left for the two other brothers to approach Pontier to solicit his promised help.

As told by Salomon: "I was ashamed to go, feeling somehow helpless and not seeing what he could do for us. . . I finally got the idea to go to him with some books that were very dear to me and ask him to keep them until the war was over. In the back of my mind I thought that perhaps these books would also interest a clergyman. When I finally mustered enough courage to go to him, I stood in front of the door . . . and rang the bell. Reverend Pontier opened the door himself and invited me to enter the house and follow him upstairs to his study. He told me to sit down and wondered why I was so pale and looked so sad. I told him about our present situation and the deportation order, and asked if he would kindly take care and save my books. He agreed and advised me to put my name in the books. 'Not your real name, one never knows.' I signed 'Sieg' instead of 'Solomon.' When I got up to leave, he asked if he could do anything else to help. He assured me that he was our friend and that I should tell him everything. This man emanated so much confidence and warmth, one felt immediately that he was a protector. To tell the truth, I was really waiting for him to offer to help us. I then told him that the policeman had brought the deportation order and that we had to leave our house on August 25, 1942 for an assembly place near the railway station for deportation to Germany. After listening to my story, he left the room for a few minutes and returned with his wife. Mrs. Pontier had such a kind and noble face. She was a brunette, her blue eyes were full of tenderness. She looked at me with pity, and her lips started trembling and tears filled her eyes. Her husband was also very sad and serious. He told me that he had spoken with his wife and they had decided to take two boys into their home until the war was over. Words failed me and I felt like choking. It was like a dream, but somehow I managed to blurt out: 'It is very dangerous for you to have Jews in your home.' 'Don't worry, my child. We have decided to do so, and God will protect us. Son of Israel, we are happy to give you any help we can. It is the duty of every Christian to help people in danger.' He then took me upstairs and showed me a room in the garret with two beds, saying that the room would be waiting for us when we come on Monday night, and that it would be comfortable and secure. . . . My steps carried me home quickly, where the whole family was waiting; their faces were pale and tense. I told them what had happened and especially what Reverend Pontier had said: 'I am your friend and I feel your pain. I can take two of you into the house.' Mother broke into tears and said that this man was a guardian angel, sent from heaven. . . . Which one of us would go into hiding and who would be deported? Shabbat evening, father said the Havdalah prayer: 'In you I trust, O God.' He had tears in his eyes; he felt that this was the last Sabbath we would be together."

Around the same time, in July 1942, Jaap Musch, of Amsterdam, one of the soon-to-be heads of the NV group, visited the pastor asking him for a list of reliable parishioners whom he could approach to shelter Jewish children. Both men went out to persuade local Calvinist families to get involved. The first children began arriving in Heerlen in October 1942. In order to speed up the process of locating safe addresses, Jaap Musch's brother, Gerard, and his colleague, Dick Groenewegen van Wijk, moved to Heerlen. Thus. in the second half of 1942, the Pontiers, Jaap, Gerard, and Dick established the basis of the NV's work. By late April 1943, approximately eighty children, mostly from the Amsterdam region, were already hidden in and around Heerlen. In the meantime, the deportation of the rest of the Silber family appeared imminent and it was decided that the Silber parents would be the ones to go into hiding in Pontier's home. The Pontiers' eldest daughter, Lies, vacated her room for the fugitives and moved in with neighbors. On November 6, 1943, the Gestapo raided the Pontier home. Finding the pastor sitting behind his desk, they arrested him but did not further search the premises and thus did not find the Silbers upstairs. Pontier was incarcerated for six months, part of which he spent in solitary confinement. In May 1944 he was released, thin and emaciated. After regaining some strength, he once more dedicated himself to the

NV's rescue activities.[35]

Let us return to the story of Reverend Bastiaan Ader. This Protestant pastor, who lived with his wife Johanna in Nieuw Beerta, Groningen province, made a special commitment to save Jews. Nettie Samuels, a friend of his wife, was the first person to be hidden in Ader's parsonage. A friend of Nettie's soon joined her at the hideout, and from that time on, it was decided that people should hide in pairs as much as possible, on the belief that two people provided support and comfort for each other during the long hours of the day when absolute silence had to be maintained. Known affectionately as Uncle Bas (and also as Gerard van Zaanen when working with the resistance), Ader was hardly ever at home because he traveled to many different places to find homes willing to take in Jews, whom he then fetched from the Joodsche Invalide hospital in Amsterdam. Mrs. Ganor, one of Ader's beneficiaries, worked at the Joodsche Invalide. She recalled her dramatic meeting with Ader. The date was October 9, 1943. "My friend Mep (who worked in the kitchen) was called to the office, where Ader was waiting and suggested she hide at his place. She asked whether I could join her; thus, I was called to the office where I met Reverend Ader. . . . At 6:00 p.m., that evening, we packed some light packages and went to the address indicated by Ader, a Christian living near the railroad station. We journeyed to Groningen, and he then took us to his parents' home, where we stayed for nine months, from September 1943 to May 1944. . . Later we learned that the reverend had been involved in dangerous acts, such as breaking into food depots and other resistance activities. In his home, he hid two women for a full year." At times, there were as many as nineteen people hiding in his home at the same time. Leonie Berger-Cahn, another of his beneficiaries, told how Ader was especially interested in women without ostensible Jewish features, since he felt he could easily place them as household governesses. "Reverend Ader came personally to bring me a new identity card and asked me if everything was in order [in her sheltering home]. Later, his niece Nel Appel brought ration cards each month."

In early 1944, as the danger of detection increased, Ader decided to move his wards to the southern province of Limburg. However, a relocation required a lot of thought. How could one move a large group of fugitives such a long distance without being noticed? Ader's solution was original. German soldiers returning from their furloughs in Germany traveled on a late afternoon train that crossed into the Netherlands around midnight. When the train pulled into the pitch-black station, the soldiers were fast asleep. As the train was filled with German soldiers, there was no identity document control, and so Ader managed to sneak the fugitives onto the train, where they could mingle with the few non-military Dutch passengers and thus travel across the country as far as Brunssum and Heerlen, with some dropping off in

Amsterdam.

The Germans were now desperately on the lookout for Ader because he had passed to raiding food ration stations and falsifying documents. They finally caught up with him, and in August 1944 arrested him in Haarlem after some-one he trusted betrayed him while he was on a mission to place a young girl in hiding. In November of that year, in retaliation for the murder of a German soldier by a Dutchman, the Germans executed five of their Dutch hostages, including the imprisoned Reverend Ader. His execution took place one month before his thirty-fifth birthday and sixteen days after his second son Eric was born. While in prison, Ader wrote some poems that he managed to smuggle out to his wife, who had them published. In one of them, he grappled with the existential problems of his impending death:

Not for myself do I want to push back these walls,
Panting for room and crying for justice!
I know I am trapped in a merciless tangle,
I am acquainted with the fate I have been assigned.
Not for myself: I have fought fiercely and unrelentingly,
Neither by day nor night have I asked for rest;
Sharing the suffering of those doomed ones,
And now am sailing to the distant, lit-up shore.
It's only that I still owe so many deep words
To her who always waits for me;
That I still have to put a small child to sleep
And softly kiss it good night![36]

In Rotterdam, a large port city infested with Germans in uniform, Gerrit Brillenburg-Wurth served as the Calvinist minister in the Breeplein section. In April 1943, when he learned that Hendrik de Zoete was in need of a hiding place, Brillenburg-Wurth immediately set himself to seek a place among his parishioners. After a stay at the home of the Groeneveld family, it was time to move on, and Brillenburg-Wurth again came to the rescue by suggesting that De Zoete and wife Sophia hide in the church in the attic between the ceiling and the roof. There the De Zoetes stayed until the end of the war. Brillenburg-Wurth confided in the sexton of the church, Hendrik De Mars, who was already hiding four Jewish people under the same church roof. An alternative hiding place was prepared at the opposite end of the church, above the organ pipes. A bed was placed on the joists, and a plank bridge about 60 by 150 cen-timeters served as the only possibility to stand or walk, because the other planks between the joists were too narrow to support a person. Over the next year Reverend Brillenburg-Wurth and his wife Gerda brought food to their wards, approaching the church from a little garden, and continuing via a hatch in the ceiling of a little storeroom. Brillenburg-Wurth also took upon himself the unpleasant task of daily emptying the pail filled with the people's bodily waste.

After a year, Reverend Brillenburg-Wurth was picked up by the Germans and held as a hostage, together with other prominent people known for their outspoken opposition to the occupation. Sexton De Mars and his wife Anna Hendrika took over the duties of caring for the hidden people in the church's garret. De Zoete wrote of the great vigilance exercised by the hidden people, especially during Sunday services, so as not to make the slightest noise and betray their presence. "From time to time we gathered in the home of the sexton in the evening, and on these occasions he taught us handicrafts, or we exchanged thoughts about Christianity and Judaism in the presence of Reverend Wurth. It was in the home of the sexton, too, that a baby was born to another Jewish family, with the help of an ophthalmic surgeon." A month before the end of the war, the Gestapo and the German police (the notorious *Grüne Polizei*) raided the church premises and the sexton's house and arrested Hendrik de Mars. His wife Anna took over caring for the Jewish wards. Fortunately for Hendrik, he was liberated at the end of the war, but his health suffered greatly and he died five years later after a prolonged illness.[37]

In Breda, southern Netherlands, a Catholic priest, Father Antonius J. Scheermakers, told one of the nurses in the maternity institution under his supervision (he was also in charge of a nearby monastery) to admit a Jewish woman for hiding, with the words: "We are in this world to help our fellow men." Thus, in early October 1943, Henriette Cahen-Elion, in her sixth month of pregnancy, was admitted to this institution, known as Moederheil, and generally reserved for unmarried mothers. Up to then, Mrs. Cahen had moved from one place to another, including a stay in a hospital under false pretenses, before entering Moederheil under the assumed name of Marietta Eliens (her husband had already been deported). In order to avoid annoying questions about Mrs. Cahen's non-Catholicism, she was listed as belonging to the Baptist Church. She gave birth on January 26, 1944, and her baby was official registered as Geertruida Helena Eliens, the child of an unknown father. During her stay, another Jewish woman, Gre van Bueren-de Vries, also expecting a baby, was also admitted in the institution. Normally, women stayed at Moederheil for a week after giving birth, but Mrs. Cahen and several other Jewish women were allowed to stay there until the liberation of Breda, on October 29, 1944.[38]

In Beneden-Leeuwen, Elisabeth Dasberg (born 1931) and her foster parents were hidden in the local Roman Catholic parish church of St. Alphonsus, headed by Father Petrus Zijlmans, for a period lasting from early February

1943 to the liberation. Only a few people knew the true identity of the Dasbergs. In his postwar memoirs, Father Zijlmans wrote that the Dasbergs came with the intention of staying for only two days before heading to Geffen. "They were in a state of exhaustion after walking from Kesteren, where they had previously hidden with a farmer. I agreed to admit them. What else could I do? Send them to their death? There was not the slightest chance for them to be admitted by one of my congregants. It was better for me to take the risk upon myself rather than a congregant with a family. . . . To hide them meant for us risking one's life. If they were discovered, our fate would be the concentration camp or execution. . . . The problem of food was eventually solved. But where were we to hide them? Many people visited the priest's home, and it was forbidden for anyone to feel their presence."

On Monday, the sacristan and his servant went to work in the attic. They built a small enclosure made from cartons and wooden boards. "An electric cord was taken from the presbytery to make it possible for them to light a stove during the cold weather and at certain times boil water for tea, etc. We darkened the windows, and made an old closet into a toilet, and the rest of the attic was ready for sleeping. . . . The walls were very thin, so it was permitted only to whisper and walk on one's toes. At night, we locked the church earlier, so they could come downstairs, and walk around a bit, pray and stretch their limbs. . . . The sacristan brought food to them at lunchtime, and at night slices of bread for the following morning."

On August 24, 1943, Father Zijlmans was informed of an impending Gestapo visit. "I inquired whether they would also search inside churches, and was told, only rarely. However, for better security, we prepared a place for three people to lie down in a storeroom in the garden where firewood was kept. . . . On Saturday, August 4, the Gestapo had still not arrived. . . . We decided to risk having the Jews return to the space above the church. After a few weeks stay there, we were faced with another problem due to the arrival of Germans for military exercises, with the possibility that they would use the church for this purpose (to practice shooting from the windows). On several occasions, they tried to enter the church, but I had the church locked and sent the sacristan with the keys into town and, thus, it could not be opened. So they did not break in. So we sought another hiding place. We found it above the holy altar. The sacristan improvised a small room with electric heating in front of the round window. . . . He placed a door in front of a hole in the wall used for entrance to the girls' section, on which he hung a long black curtain that was usually used during funerals, and added several chairs. We also took out the lamp in the girls' section. Now, everything seemed safe as far as possible, and there they stayed until the day of liberation."[39]

Finally, in Helden, near Venlo, Catholic Father Leonard Hendriks, also known as Brother Bernardinus, headed a project with a group of monks of the Huize Koningslust monastery to rehabilitate released prisoners within the walls of their abbey. In May 1943, Bernardinus admitted seventeen-year-old Yehuda Pimental, a fugitive from Amsterdam, and he remained hidden for a year and a half, until the liberation of the area in September 1944. Bernardinus met Yehuda at the train station, and as they bicycled to the abbey, he told the surprised youth what his cover story would be: he was to pretend to be a released convict and was to act a little disorderly, in order not to stand out! Brother Bernardinus would also teach him to pray for the same reason, and he would live in a small cell, just like the others. In Yehuda's words, "He asked me to act like a Catholic. However, he never exerted pressure on me to try to influence me to go over to the Catholic religion. On the contrary, I spoke to him of Eretz Israel, where I wished to live after the war, and he said he would come to visit. Indeed he came twice to see me, at my expense, and then came again to attend my daughter's wedding." The inmates had few restrictions; they were free to come and go as they liked, and there was plenty of food, despite the wartime conditions. Bernardinus took care of everything, for Yehuda in particular, but without drawing attention to it. Yehuda was not the only Jew among the ex-convicts. There were other Jews hidden in different places in the monastery. One hid in an attic above the church for two years, but because he looked so conspicuously Jewish, he was not allowed to walk around freely. Bernardinus personally brought him food several times a day and talked to him for hours at night, to keep the boy from sinking into despair in his secluded condition.[40]

Chapter 6
POLAND

A Jewish problem exists, and will continue to exist as long as the Jews remain Jews. . . . It is a fact that the Jewish influence upon morality is fatal. . . . But let us be just. Not all Jews are like that.
Cardinal Augustyn Hlond, 1936

These people are our brothers. They have souls just as we do. In the heavenly court, it is not they who will not be condemned, but those who murder them today.
Father Michal Kubacki, Warsaw, 1943.

Jews in Poland up to World War II

As we move from western to eastern Europe, we encounter a different brand of antisemitism—a grass-roots prejudice, unashamedly open, and often turning into violence against the Jewish population. The churches unfortunately carry much blame for creating this hostile climate. Interestingly, Jewish life in Poland began on a positive note. Starting from about the tenth century onward, Jews fled to Poland to escape the massacres and expulsions that took place in Germany and other central European regions because of the Crusades, the blood libels, and the Black Death, and also to escape their general feeling of insecurity in these lands. Rabbi Moses ben Israel Isserles, in the sixteenth century, even coined a pun in Hebrew for the name "Poland," explaining it as deriving from two Hebrew words, *poh lin* ("here we shall rest"). Polish kings and princes encouraged Jewish immigration as a way of fostering economic activity, especially King Casimir III (known as The Great), and Jewish communities sprouted in many cities of the Polish kingdom. By special charter they were under the king's protection and were granted the right to practice their religion and engage in commerce, although they were barred from the guilds.

From time to time, pogroms against Jews broke out, which in Kraków, in 1495, led to their expulsion from the city proper to nearby Kazimierz. The Roman Catholic Church in Poland, ever suspicious of Jews being granted too many rights, demanded that they be restricted to certain areas and be reduced to an inferior and humble social status. In 1267, a church synod in Wroclaw called upon believers not to be "misled by the superstitions and evil habits of the Jews who live among them." In the fifteenth century, Cardinal Zbigniew Olesnicki opposed the intent of King Casimir IV to grant certain rights to the Jews, or, as he termed them "the scourge of the Jews." He warned the king, "Do not imagine that in matters touching the Christian religion you are at liberty to pass any law you please. No one is great and strong enough to put down all opposition to himself when the interests of the faith are at stake. I therefore beseech and implore your royal majesty to revoke the aforementioned privileges and liberties. Prove that you are a Catholic sovereign, and remove all occasion for disgracing your name." As a result of this pressure, Jewish privileges were repealed, only to be later reinstated by the Polish kings.

In 1648 the Jewish population counted approximately 300,000 people, and Jewish life was organized around the Kehillah, and consolidated into a Council of the Four Lands (Great Poland, Lesser Poland, Ruthenia–Ukraine, and Lithuania), which enjoyed a semi-autonomous status. Many famous rabbis left a mark on Jewish religious life, among them Shalom Shakhna of Lublin and Moses Isserles of Krakow. In the eighteenth century, Israel b. Eliezer Ba'al Shem Tov founded the modern Hasidic movement in western Ukraine. However, in 1648, the Cossacks, led by Bogdan Chmielnitsky, rose up against their Polish overlords and also turned their wrath against Jews. The Chmielnitsky massacres of 1648–49, and the subsequent wars with the Tatars from Crimea and the Swedish incursions, brought widespread destruction of Jewish communities. Thousands were killed, and many were forced to convert. Poland itself lost much territory in the east. In spite of this tragedy, the Jewish population continued to grow, reaching 750,000 in 1764 (of whom 550,000 were in Poland and western Ukraine, 200,000 in Lithuania). Beginning in 1772, Poland underwent several partitions between Russia, Austria, and Prussia, and by the end of the eighteenth century, it had ceased to exist as an independent country.[1]

The new Poland arose in 1918 out of World War I with a population of about 30 million people, a third of whom were not Poles but Ukrainians, Jews, Belorussians, and Germans. In 1931, there were some 3,100,000 Jews in the country, which accounted to 9.8 percent of the total population, the second-largest ethnic minority (Ukrainians, 13.9 percent; Belorussians, 3.1 percent). The declaration of Polish independence in 1918 and the following two years were marked by pogroms (violent attacks on Jewish communities) in many places in more than 100 towns and villages during an initial three-month period. In the 1930s, the government encouraged an economic battle against the Jews, but stopped short of physical violence. Very few political groups resisted the antisemitic tide, with two, the Endecja and the Sanacja, favoring outspokenly antisemitic platforms. Some went further and resorted to violence, especially after Hitler's rise to power in neighboring Germany. Pogroms spread in many cities without any serious hindrance from the authorities. In the words of the Polish-Jewish historian Emmanuel Ringelblum, there prevailed in the country a situation of "constant turmoil" against Jews. In the universities, many lecture halls imposed separate seating for Jews and non-Jews, the so-called "ghetto benches." Restrictions against employment of Jews also prevailed in the civil service, government schools, state banks, and state-run monopolies.

Most of Poland's Jews stood out from the Polish norm because of their special traditional dress, food habits, mannerisms (typical gestures, facial expressions, bodily movements), different names and especially surnames, wide use of the Yiddish language (lack of Polish), and their attachment to Judaism in a country where being a Catholic was synonymous with being Polish. Most Poles did not regard the Jews as part of what Helen Fein called "the universe of obligation . . . that circle of people toward whom obligations are owed, to whom rules apply and whose injuries call for expiation by the community." Large portions of the Polish people still believed that Jews practiced ritual murder of defenseless Christian children to get blood for use in baking the matzah for the Passover festival. One year before the war, near the end of 1938, the government spokesman, General Skwarczynski, stated in parliament "that the solution of the Jewish Question has to be achieved most of all by the most conspicuous reduction in the number of Jews." The Germans were soon to show the general how this cold be done "most conspicuously." Emmanuel Ringelblum wrote, "Poland before the [Second World] war became the leading antisemitic country in Europe, second to Germany alone." In the meantime, the Jewish population slid into poverty and increased pauperism as the government pursued the economic strangulation of Polish Jewry. Even before the German conquest, the Jews of Poland already in some respects bore the earmarks of a conquered population.[2]

Regretfully, the Catholic Church in Poland did not try to contain the anti-Jewish trend. On the contrary, it added fuel to the fire. From the perspective of the church, the Jewish presence presented a serious threat to Polish self-realization. This message was repeated over and over in Polish journals, and by prelates high and low. The prolific Catholic cleric Józef Kruszyński in one of his writings lashed out at the Talmud, which he claimed instructed Jews in wickedness. Brother Paul Kuczka, in *Kultura*, accused Jews of advocating divorce, free-love, and birth control. "We stand before a life-and-death struggle with Judaism. The fate of the church and the nation hangs in the balance," and therefore "Christian ethics allows you to defend yourself against an aggressor, even if the aggressor should thereby lose his life." The Jesuit periodical *Przegląd Powszechny* wrote in 1936: "One should let the Jews be, but eliminate them from the life of Christian society. It is necessary to provide separate schools for Jews so that our children will not be infected with their lower morality." Another Catholic journal (*Przewodnik Katolicki*, "Catholic Guide") described antisemitism as a badge of honor. "It means you love your own nation more than strangers." The contrary meant "you wear a Jewish coat, and hundreds of Poles shiver from the cold for lack of work."

The primate of Poland, Cardinal Augustyn Hlond, in 1936, lent fuel to the antisemitic fire in a pastoral letter that was read from the pulpit in most churches: "A Jewish problem exists, and will continue to exist as long as the Jews remain Jews. . . . It is a fact that the Jews fight against the Catholic Church; they are free-thinkers, and constitute the vanguard of atheism, of the Bolshevik movement, and of revolutionary activity. It is a fact that the Jewish influence upon morality is fatal, and their publishers spread pornographic literature. It is true that the Jews are committing frauds, practicing usury, and dealing in white slavery. It is true that in schools, the influence of Jewish youth upon Catholic youth is generally evil from a religious and ethical point of view." At this point, the prince of the Catholic Church may have felt that he had gone a bit too far, so he made a slight retraction—very slight. "But let us be just. Not all Jews are like that. . . . I warn against the fundamental unconditional anti-Jewish principle, imported from abroad [Nazi Germany]. It is contrary to Catholic ethics. . . . It is not permissible to hate anyone. Not even Jews. One does well to prefer his own kind in commercial dealings and to avoid Jewish stores and Jewish stalls in the markets, but it is not permissible to demolish Jewish businesses, destroy their merchandise, break windows, bomb their houses. One ought to fence oneself off against the harmful moral influence of Jewry . . . . and especially should boycott the Jewish press and demoralizing Jewish publications. But it is not permissible to assault Jews, to hit, maim, or bruise them. . . . When divine mercy enlightens a Jew, and he accepts sincerely his and our Messiah, let us greet him with joy in the Christian midst." This from a prelate who was considered to represent the moderate wing of the church![3]

One of the most prominent clerical antisemites was Monsignor Stanislaw Trzeciak, author of an anti-Jewish book *The Program of Jewish World Politics: Conspiracy and Deconspiracy.* Basing himself on a New Testament passage, "You are of your father the devil, and your will is to do your father's desires" (John 8:44), Trzeciak accused Jews of "satanic" work in Russia, Mexico, and Spain, and of trying to demoralize and revolutionize Poland. He then added, again quoting the New Testament: "If your hand or your foot causes you to sin, cut it off and throw it from you" (Matthew 18:8). The Catholic Church produced a formidable religious press in Poland, including two daily newspapers, the *Maly Dzienniek* ("Little Daily"), published by the Franciscan friars at Niepokolanow, and the *Glos Narodu*, in Kraków, and both took turns at bashing the Jews. After *Kristallnacht* in Nazi Germany, in November 1938, *Maly Dziennik* ran an article under the heading: "What to do with the Jews? Nobody wants them." It also published letters from readers expressing such sentiments as: "Don't buy anything from Jews. . . . England, France, and Denmark don't want them; why should Poland be the haven for the world's Jews? . . . Let them find a place in Madagascar, Cameroon, Tanzania, or Guiana." As for *Glos Narodu*, under the control of the Kraków archdiocese and its archbishop, Cardinal Adam Sapieha, it stated with regard to the *Kristallnacht* pogrom: "The Third Reich is in the process of breaking the shackles the Jews have laid upon Germany's economic and cultural life. Nonetheless, we cannot approve the methods of their actions, even though we recognize their purpose. . . . Every nation—and certainly Germany—has the right to defend itself from subjection to so foreign a nationality as the Jews and their injurious influence on social life. . . . But always within the limits of ethics, i.e., the limits drawn by the universal Christian morality that views every human being as a neighbor. . . . Instead of protesting, Jews should realize that it is necessary for them to emigrate from Europe as quickly as possible. . . . We see clearly that Nazism has had and does have its reasons for coming out resolutely against Jews. We do not praise its barbarous methods, but we recognize the reason for its war [against the Jews] as valid." Then came the German invasion; from a nation that Polish antisemites naively looked to for guidance and praised for its radical antisemitism. Polish nationalists were now about to get a taste of a different kind of Nazi radicalism; the intent to destroy the Polish nation as an independent political and cultural entity.[4]

German Policy in Occupied Poland

Following the swift German victory in September 1939, the country was divided between Germany and the Soviet Union, with 22 million Poles falling under German occupation. Some of them lived in the territories annexed by Germany; what was left of Poland was renamed the *Generalgouvernement* and ruled from Kraków by a Nazi governor-general, Hans Frank. Two million Poles were counted as *Volksliste*—ethnic Germans who enjoyed special privileges denied to other Poles. The rest, some 4 to 5 million Poles, came under Soviet rule. In the annexed areas, the Polish administration, the local government, and all existing Polish organizations were banned. The Poles were ruled by a whole array of German military and security forces, including the SS, German police, and Wehrmacht units (some 500,00 troops, which rose to 1.1 million in 1944), who instituted a five and a half year reign of terror. Intent on wiping out the country's intellectual elite, the Germans shot to death some 900 clerics, and 1,345 more perished in concentration camps. Nearly 200 academics from the prestigious Jagiellonian University and the Mining Academy, in Kraków were arrested, and twenty were executed. By February 1940, more than 200,000 Poles and 100,000 Jews had been expelled from the annexed lands. The largest Nazi camp system was set up on Polish soil, including the extermination camps at Chelmno, Treblinka, Sobibor, Belzec and, of course, the infamous Auschwitz-Birkenau complex. During the 1944 Polish uprising in Warsaw, an estimated 150,000 civilians lost their lives. Polish loses, other than the nearly 3 million Jews, accounted for over 2 million lives; that is, 9.6 percent of the country's population. Most Polish journalists, 45 percent of Polish doctors, 40 percent of Polish professors, 45 percent of the lawyers, 30 percent of the technicians, and 20 percent of the priests are estimated to have not survived the occupation.[5]

According to Nazi plans, the whole of Polish territory was to be successively cleared of most of its population and simultaneously be gradually incorporated into the German Reich. The overwhelming majority of Poles, considered fierce nationalists, would be removed to distant Siberia (after the victory over Russia). A small fraction was to remain as helots, slaves needed to maintain a feudalistic type of society in the new 1,000-year Reich. No mercy was to be shown to this population, no temporary alliances formed with collaborationist elements, no rudimentary forms of autonomy of the minutest sort to be tolerated. Poland was simply to disappear from the map as a separate political entity. No attempt was made to draft Poles into auxiliary military units, as took place in Lithuania, Latvia, and Ukraine. As noted by Nazi governor Frank in his diary: sooner or later, "we will have to wipe Poland off the map. . . . It is clear as daylight that the Vistula country will be as German as the Rhineland." The whole of occupied Poland "was simply to be treated as a concentration camp. The only people who would be allowed any freedom of movement would be the guards." The prolongation of the war and the setbacks of the Russian campaign made it impossible to put this horrific plan into practice, but it manifested itself in the unusually cruel repressive measures against the local population. The Zamosc region in the Lublin district was chosen as the first area for the implementation of a full Germanization program. Of the 691 villages in the county, an estimated 297 were wholly or partly evacuated by July 1943. Some 110,00 Poles (including Jews) were removed from this area and replaced by 25,000 German colonists. The Germans reserved the right to impose the death penalty even for minor infractions, and no Pole felt completely safe. The cumulative effect of this unremitting German reign of terror accelerated the disintegrating forces in society and led to the drastic impoverishment of the population.[6]

As horrific as the measures applied to the Polish population appear, Jews fared even worse. They were to be totally eliminated. In September 1939, the *Generalgouvernement* totaled 2.1 million Jews, whereas 1.2 million Jews lived in the Soviet zone. Up to the German invasion of Russia in June 1941, a little less than 2 million Jews remained in the German zone (close to 200,000 fled to the Soviet zone). Moreover, from 1941, tens of thousands of Jews from other occupied countries were added to the Polish Jews already there, either in the ghettos, such as Warsaw and Lodz, or directly to concentration and death camps, such as Auschwitz and Sobibor. It is estimated that up to 4 million of the 6 million Jews victims of the Shoah (of which slightly over a million were especially brought there from distant lands) were slaughtered by the Germans on Polish soil.

In occupied Poland, Jews lost all traces of their civil and legal status, and were left without any umbrella organization, save the Gestapo-created and - controlled Jewish councils (*Judenrat*), through which Nazi demands were funneled. One restriction followed another in quick succession: Jews were prohibited from changing their places of residence, were barred from traveling by train, from theaters and cinemas, had to wear a white armband with a blue Star of David on the right sleeve on their outer garments, and were subject to forced labor. Non-Jewish firms were forbidden to employ Jewish workers and officials, and 112,000 Jewish-owned businesses and shops and 115,000 workshops were confiscated, as well as bank accounts. German soldiers sported with Jews; pious men had their beards shaved off with blunt instruments that tore their skin or had their beards burned off. Swastikas were branded on the scalps of some victims; others were subjected to "gymnastics," such as riding on the back of another victim, crawling on all fours, singing and dancing, or staging fights with one another. Synagogues were randomly vandalized or burned down, and it is estimated that several hundred synagogues were destroyed in the first two months of the occupation.

The Germans soon moved to the next step—concentrating all Jews in sealed-off ghettos. Lodz became the first sealed ghetto, followed by Warsaw, Lublin, and Kraków. The sites selected as ghettos were usually the most crowded and neglected sections of the cities. Attempts to leave the ghettos were punishable by death. The Warsaw and Lodz ghettos had over 600,00 Jews imprisoned in them, with the Warsaw ghetto becoming nothing less than a concentration camp for half a million Jews, without any link to the outside world. Workshops in the ghetto provided some economic subsistence, at ridiculously low wages. In the ghettos thousands of people died every month from malnutrition (by 1942 the Germans had allotted 2,613 calories per person for themselves, 669 for Poles, and 184 for Jews) and lack of medicine. In Warsaw the killer disease was typhus, and in Lodz it was tuberculosis. In these two large ghettos a total of 54,616 deaths were record in 1941—43,238 in Warsaw and 11,378 in Lodz—a mortality rate of 90 and 76 per 1,000 respectively. In August 1942, German governor Hans Frank declared, "We are starving 1,200,000 Jews to death; that is self-evident, and if the Jews do not die from hunger, anti-Jewish decrees will have to be speeded up, and let us hope that this is what will happen."

With the invasion of the Soviet Union in June 1941, special killings units, notoriously known as *Einsatzgruppen*, began a mass slaughter of Jews by shooting hundreds of thousands of Jews in front of open ditches where they were buried. Then came the death-camp stage. In December 1941, gas was first used to kill people at Chełmno camp, northwest of Łódz, where a total of 55,000 Jews were killed. Three more extermination camps were established as part of *Aktion Reinhard* in 1942: Bełzec, Sobibór, and Treblinka. Additional concentration camps established on Polish soil included Plaszów, Majdanek, Janówska (in Lwów), and Auschwitz-Birkenau—here more than 1 million Jewish lives were extinguished by gas, beatings, and exhaustion. In July 22, 1942, the Warsaw ghetto began to be emptied. This took until mid-September, and all told 300,000 Jews were deported to Treblinka, where most were gassed on arrival. That same summer, 30,000 Jews from the Lwow ghetto were deported to Belzec and murdered, with thousands of others killed in Majdanek camp near Lublin. At the high point of the killing spree, in 1944, as many as 20,000 people were gassed in one day in Auschwitz camp. In Majdanek camp, to solve the problem of overcrowding, the Nazis shot 18,000 people in one day on November 3, 1943. The Kraków ghetto underwent a similar liquidation, with many herded into the nearby Plaszów labor camp, made infamous by the brutal behavior of its commander, Amon Goeth. By early 1943, most Polish Jews had been exterminated, with only 250,000 still kept in various work camps. By end of 1943, only 60,000 Jews remained in the Lodz ghetto, and they too were murdered in August 1944. When the curtain came down on the German occupation in Poland, close to 3 million Polish Jews had been murdered—up to 90 percent of the prewar Jewish population.[7]

Trapped as they were inside the ghettos, many Jews nevertheless tried to survive by fleeing to the so-called Aryan side; some by contacting non-Jewish friends and acquaintances (in the Warsaw ghetto, telephones were still functioning). Once one was on the other side, there were two possibilities: to remain "above the surface," in Ringelblum's words, or go underground. "In the first case, the Jew turns into an Aryan: he provides himself with Aryan papers and lives legally." People tried to hide their melancholy and pensive look—their sad eyes, and women bleached their hair blond, to remove the dark and curly Jewish-looking hair. In the second case, a Jew, especially one with a Semitic appearance, sought a hiding place. Jewish women, under assumed names often hired themselves out as servants and housemaids. Others tried to save themselves by registering for forced labor in German firms, based on falsified documents, known as *Kennkarte*, with assumed non-Jewish names. Jewish children were secretly spirited out of the Warsaw ghetto in various ways; some, through the help of the social welfare department of the city, headed by Jan Dobraczynski, Wanda Wyrabowa, and Irena Sendler. The children were then dispersed either with private families or, more commonly, in children's homes, orphanages, and care centers for children, many of them connected with religious institutions. Then there was the issue of religion, in a country where religious observance mattered much. In the words of Nechama Tec, "There was so much a good Catholic had to know that a Jew could hardly avoid making some slip," especially with regard to Catholic rituals. Nechama Tec and her sister, both hiding under assumed names, memorized prayers and tested each other over and over again.[8]

German threats of punishment had to been taken seriously. On October 15, 1941, Hans Frank published an ordinance stating that Jews found outside their permitted residence areas were subject to punishment by death; and so were people who offered them shelter. The following month, the German governor of the Warsaw district reminded the population that "the same [death penalty] applies to those who knowingly give shelter to such Jews or help them in any way (such as taking them in for a night, giving them a lift in a vehicle of any sort, etc.)." This was followed by the stern admonishment: "Sentences will be imposed by special courts in Warsaw. I stringently call the attention of the entire population of the Warsaw district to this new decree, as henceforth it will be applied with the utmost severity." These stern admonishments were replicated in other cities. In no other occupied country was aid to Jews punished with such harsh measures as in Poland. Non-Jews caught helping Jews were sometimes shot and buried in Jewish cemeteries or in open fields, as a sign of disrespect and humiliation for the Catholic non-Jew.[9]

Attitude of Local Population Toward Jews

The antisemitic frenzy on both the governmental and grass-roots level led Ringelblum to state that prewar Poland was "the leading antisemitic country in Europe, second to Germany alone." The situation became even worse under the Nazi occupation, for in Ringelblum's words, "after the German invasion, there was a revival of antisemitism in the full sense of the term"; and among the population it remained "predominant in general." In February 1940, a seven-day pogrom took place in Warsaw under the watchful eyes of the Germans. Assailants armed with sticks, clubs, and crow-bars, shouting "Kill the Jews" and "Long live independent Poland without Jews," broke windows, pillaged shops, and beat Jews on the street into unconsciousness. The Polish police did not intervene, and Polish civic organizations kept their silence. Ringelblum was a witness to the incessant attacks on Jews on Warsaw streets by local Poles. "We . . . reproach the Polish community," he wrote from his hideout, "with not having tried to dissociate itself, either in words—sermons in the churches, etc.—or in writing, from the antisemitic beasts that cooperated with the Germans . . . or not having done anything whatsoever to weaken the impression that the whole Polish population of all classes approved of the performances of the Polish antisemites." Underground activist Jan Karski, in his report to the Polish government-in-exile in February 1940, wrote that the attitude of the Polish populace toward the Jews "is overwhelmingly severe, often without pity. . . . This bring them, to a certain extent, nearer to the Germans. . . . 'The solution of the Jewish Question' by the Germans—I must state this with a full sense of responsibility for what I am saying . . . is creating something akin to a narrow bridge upon which the Germans and a large part of Polish society find themselves in agreement."[10]

While Polish antisemites, even at their most vicious, never advocated extermination as the solution of the "Jewish problem," the lack of sympathetic interest in the fate of Jews on the part of the surrounding population facilitated the commission of the crime by the Germans. There were many, too many, whose animosity and antipathy toward Jews was not mitigated by the Jewish tragedy. In 1947, the Catholic writer Jerzy Andrzejewski observed that Poles "could look straight in the face of Polish men and women who were dying for freedom. They could not do so in the face of the Jews dying in the burning ghetto." In the words of historian Yehuda Bauer: "The majority of Poles evinced an indifference, often rather hostile, to the fate of the Jews, expressed in a lack of basic human interest in their fate. A fairly large minority was actively hostile to the Jews, and a smaller minority was friendly and helpful." Unfortunately, those who were friendly to Jews, and particularly those who were actively engaged in helping them, had to keep silent, while the antisemites, often coming from the lowest social strata, did not feel inhibited from voicing their opinions aloud even in public—in trams, trains, or workplaces." So much of the genocide took place on Polish soil that Poles could have no illusions as to the intentions of the Germans once the mass murder had begun. Ringelblum lamented the Poles' "satisfaction that Warsaw had in the end become *Judenrein;* that the wildest dreams of Polish antisemites about a Warsaw without Jews were coming true"; and satisfaction "that the Germans had done the dirty work of exterminating the Jews." Writing from his hideout on the Aryan side, he added that upon viewing the blazing ghetto, put to the torch by the Germans to quell the Jewish uprising there in April 1943, people expressed more regret about the buildings destroyed than the human lives lost. As one Pole stated: "Although we don't approve of the methods, one must

admit that Hitler did for us what we were incapable of doing so thoroughly."
He related the story of how a pious woman explained what was happening to
the Jews: "In Holy Week, the Jews tormented Christ. In Holy Week [April
1943], the Germans are tormenting the Jews." Adam Polewka, a person who
saved Jews, writing in 1946, recalled a saying among the Poles under the
occupation, "The Germans will throw stones at Hitler dead, because he
brought about the downfall of the German people, but the Poles will bring
flowers to his grave as a token of gratitude for his freeing Poland from the
Jews." A teacher in a village near Lublin, an educated man, wrote: "We
[Poles] must never forget that we also have something to thank the Germans
for. Though their methods of exterminating the Jews are inhuman and revolting—what is going on in Majdanek is horrible— . . . yet this is the only way
to solve the problem. The Jews should have been wiped out long ago. They
have done it instead of us, and it's a good thing that they have. The Germans
will leave, and Poland will remain for the Poles." A Jewish underground
activist in Bialystok ghetto, Mordecai Tenenbaum-Tamaroff, who was shot
during the short-lived uprising in the ghetto, lamented that "had it not been for
the Poles, for their aid— passive and active—in the 'solution' of the Jewish
problem in Poland, the Germans would never have dared to do what they did."
The evidence on this count is overwhelming.[11]

On the inbred antisemitism of many strata of the Polish people, consider
what Nechama Tec says about the Homars, who sheltered her and her family—of course, in return for pay. "They were so warm and friendly that I was
hurt when I discovered that they were antisemitic, and totally uninhibited
about being so. . . . The Homars never even tried to deny that they hated the
'real' Jews, and insisted that such a Jew was everything bad and evil. At the
same time they liked all four of us." Similarly, Nechama was aghast at the virulent antisemitism of the gentiles who made up her social circle. "Although
my friends were not interested in Jews as living and suffering beings, Jews
were a part of their everyday speech, constantly referred to as symbols of
greediness, dishonesty, and guile... It was hard for me to understand and
accept that those I thought of as kind, considerate, and helpful were often the
most vehement in their remarks about Jews. . . . I could not doubt that their
friendship would turn into denunciation if they knew who I really was." One
such friend was named Janka. "One evening, as we were resting on the grass
away from the others, she began telling me a story that had to do with Jews
catching Christian children, murdering them, and using their blood for matzah."
When Nechama protested, Janka responded surprisingly: "How strange, Krysia
[Nechama's Polish cover name], that you should ask such a thing. Everybody
knows Jews do that, but they're smart, they do it secretly! . . . You're still a baby,
young and dumb, that's what you are!" A Jewish child hidden among non-

Jews was told not to allow himself to be turned over to his Jewish family after the war, because the Jews "drank the blood of Catholics on their holidays." After he was returned to his mother, she related, "He hated everything Jewish. . . . 'All Jews are thieves and swindlers,' he would say, with firm conviction. 'They killed the Lord Jesus and now they kill Christian children to mix their blood in the matzos.' "[12]

Polish underground journals also entered the fray against the Jews. *Naród*, for instance, happily announced in August 1942: "Before long Warsaw will be saying farewell to the last Jew. . . . Will sorrow follow in the wake of the coffin, or weeping, or perhaps joy? . . . For hundreds of years an alien, malevolent entity has inhabited our northern suburb [i.e., Warsaw]—malevolent and alien from the point of view of our interests, as well as our psyche and our hearts. So let us not strike false attitudes of the sort adopted by professional mourners at funerals—let us be serious and honest. . . . We are not going to pretend to be grief-stricken about a vanishing nation which, after all, was never close to our hearts." There were many similar comments during and immediately after the war. The literary critic Kazimierz Wyka wrote that "the Germans have committed a crime murdering the Jews. It is on their conscience—but for us it is a sheer benefit, and in the future we shall reap more benefits, with a clear conscience, without blood on our hands." The example of Zofia Kossak-Szczucka, a devout Catholic and well-known writer, a member of the Polish underground and founder of Żegota, an organization dedicated to helping Jews, is a good illustration of how antisemitism could go hand in hand, in one mind, not only with pity for Jews but also with appeals to help them. In her celebrated August 1942 proclamation, entitled "Protest," she decried the Polish silence in the face of the massacre of Jews."We feel sorry for the Jews as individuals, as human beings, and whenever possible, if they are lost or in need of shelter, we should help them. We are bound to condemn those who inform on them. . . . But we cannot pretend to be sorry if a nation which, after all, has never been close to our hearts, disappears. . . . The dying are surrounded on all sides by Pilates washing their hands. This silence can be tolerated no longer. Whatever the motives for it, they are base and ignoble. He who is silent in the face of a murder becomes an accomplice of that murder. He who does not condemn assists. We therefore raise our voice, Polish Catholics. Our feelings toward the Jews have not undergone a change. We have not stopped regarding them as the political, economic, and ideological enemies of Poland. . . . Our awareness of these feelings does not free us from the *obligation to condemn the crime.* We do not wish to be Pilates. . . . We *protest* from the depths of our hearts, overcome with pity, indignation, and dread. This protest is demanded of us by God, God who does not permit murder. . . . He among us who does not support this protest is not a Catholic.

We also protest as Poles. . . . He who does not understand this, who dares to link the proud, free future Poland to base joy at the misfortune of his neighbor—he is indeed neither a Catholic nor a Pole." Alexander Artman was hidden for about six months in the home of Zofia Kossak, until her arrest by the Gestapo for complicity in the underground. This courageous woman could not refrain from including jarring anti-Jewish sentiments in this otherwise moving appeal. In the words of Polish publicist Antony Polonsky, "Certainly, the striking combination of a call for sympathy combined with distaste for the victims was not untypical in occupied Poland." This document reveals the tragic complexity of the relations between Poles and Jews. For if a founder of Żegota was antisemitic, what could one have expected of the average Pole, who doubtless would have lacked Kossak's extraordinary ethical sensibility?[13]

Insofar as the Polish clergy is concerned, Ringelblum charged that they behaved "almost with indifference" to the Jewish tragedy unfolding before their eyes. This was no surprise, he added (and as we have earlier seen from the prewar period), because the Polish church was distinguished "for its remarkably antisemitic attitude." The recently beatified Maksymilian Kolbe, of the Franciscan Order, before the war published the *City of the Immaculata*, with a circulation of almost a million, as well as the *Maly Dziennik*. Arrested in 1941, he was taken to Auschwitz, where he was killed when he took the place of another man selected to be killed as punishment for a prisoner who had escaped. Before the war he was notorious for his antisemitism. He denounced the "perverse Jewish-Masonic press, the liberal-socialist press, the Jewish press, [which] strikes at the foundation of the church." He accepted as authentic the forged *Protocols of the Elders of Zion*, which purports that the Jews have hatched a conspiracy to take over the world. He accused the Talmud of inciting Jews against Christians. "They teach, moreover, that it is allowed for a Jew to cheat or rob a Christian. . . . This work, which includes twelve big volumes and which breathes hatred against Christ and the Christians, is put in the heads of the rabbis, and they are obligated to instruct the people on the basis of it." Jewish leaders have allowed themselves to be "seduced by Satan, the enemy of humanity." He then adding apologetically, "That is not to say that among the Jews it is not possible to find honest people." Helena Szereszewska, a Jewish woman staying in a Catholic women's institution in Warsaw under an assumed name, often had to endure a priest's sermon justifying what was befalling the Jews. "Everything that is happening to the Jews," he said, "is only a atonement for their heavy sins, ordered in heaven above. The Germans are merely the avenging rod of the Lord. . . . It is forbidden to oppose this divine judgment." She sadly commented, "In our struggle for life, we [she and several other Jewish women passing as Christians] were forced to sit quietly and resign ourselves to these words."[14]

Dr. Zygmunt Klukowski, a chronicler connected with the Polish underground, in his entry of October 22, 1942, wrote of "our" gendarmes and the Blue Police at work. "They have been ordered to kill every Jew they catch on the spot. They are executing this order with great zeal. Since morning, they have been bringing the corpses of the Jews killed from different parts of the town [Szczebrzeszyn], mostly from the Jewish quarters, on horsedrawn carts to the Jewish cemetery, where they dig large pits and bury them. Throughout the day, Jews have been routed out from the most varied hideouts. They have been shot on the spot or brought to the Jewish cemetery and killed there." Also to be feared were ordinary civilians who participated in the hunt for Jews. S. Zeminski, a Polish teacher from Lukow, made the following entry in his diary on November 8, 1942: "On 5 November, I passed through the village of Siedliska. I went into the cooperative store. The peasants were buying scythes. The woman shopkeeper said. 'They'll be useful for you in the round-up today.' I asked, 'What round-up?' 'Of the Jews.' I asked, 'How much are they paying for every Jew caught? An embarrassed silence fell. So I went on, 'They paid thirty pieces of silver for Christ, so you should also ask for the same amount.' Nobody answered. What the answer was I heard a little later. Going through the forest, I heard volleys of machine-gun fire. It was the round-up of the Jews hiding there."[15]

Help by Non-Jews

In the face of such hostility and danger, Jews lost hope and certainly did not expect much help from the non-Jewish side. By and large, they were right, but there were nevertheless some people of great courage and humanitarian feeling who braved the risk. They had to face, at one and the same time, the danger of arrest and death from Germans and the hostility of their own people (insofar as Jews were concerned), yet they responded positively to appeals for help from destitute Jews. On the organizational level, Żegota, the Council for Aid to Jews, came into being in September 1942 and began fully operating in December of that year. It was dedicated to helping Jews who had escaped from the ghettos and were living clandestinely in the Aryan parts of Poland's cities. Its sphere of activity was mainly Warsaw, with smaller branches in Kraków, Lublin, Lwów, and other cities. The sole Polish organization to help Jews, Żegota was instrumental in saving thousands of Jewish lives. It was represented by a wide range of Polish political parties, as well as two Jewish activists, Leon Feiner and Adolf Berman. At its peak, Żegota assisted some 4,000 Jews, mostly in the Greater Warsaw area (where an estimated up to 20,000 Jews lived in hiding or were passing as non-Jews). In August 1943, Emmanuel Ringelblum, who as we noted, was very critical of the antisemitic sentiments among wide strata of the Polish people, was spirited out of the

Trawniki concentration camp by a Żegota courier, Teodor Pajewski, and a Jewish woman, Shoshana Kosower; and then was hidden with other Jews in Warsaw. As he noted in his cramped hideout, "I am writing this in the hideout on the Aryan side. I am indebted to the Poles for having saved my life twice during this war: once, in the winter of 1940, when the blessed arm of the Polish underground saved me from certain death, and the second time when it got me out of an SS labor camp, where I would have met my death either in an epidemic or from a Ukrainian or SS bullet." He then wrote of the bravery of his rescuer, Mieczyslaw Wolski, understandably mentioning him under an assumed name, one of the many Poles who braved the risks facing them in their effort to save Jews. "There are thousands of idealists like these in Warsaw and in the whole country," Ringelblum noted in his hideout; "whether of the educated class or the working class, who help Jews most devotedly at the risk of their lives." Tec makes an important observation on the rescuers' motivation. "Given the pervasive antisemitism, Poles who saved Jews were acting in opposition to the expectations of their countrymen, and were thereby inviting their censure. . . . Moreover, the pervasiveness of antisemitism made it hard even for the rescuers themselves to escape from anti-Jewish images and ideologies." When it came to helping Jews, rescuers "had to be moved by forces which were beyond the realm of reason. . . . Perhaps when the actions of people revolve around life and death more basic forces come into play and the less pressing conventional influences tend to recede into the background." Not to forget the danger the rescuers faced from the Germans, who imposed the death penalty for aiding Jews. Yad Vashem has honored thousands of these knights of the spirit with the "Righteous" title.[16] It is estimated that between 40,000 and 60,000 Jews survived in hiding, although Polish historians, trying to defend their country's honor, raise the figure to as much as double that number of Jews saved and even more. Naturally, not every Jew who sought rescue on the Aryan side survived the war. Perhaps only half managed to survive. The total number of Jews in hiding, at one time or another, could well have been above the 100,000 mark. In addition, many Jews hiding on Aryan papers survived exclusively owing to their own efforts, combined with such factors as looking Aryan and having an opportunity for employment.[17]

As for help by the clergy, which we shall deal with later at greater length, there were isolated cases of help to Jews. Ringelblum left us a record of a few brave clerics. In the village of Kampinos, the local parish priest delivered a number of sermons calling on his congregation to aid their fellow-men, the Jews, in a nearby camp. As a result of these sermons, the peasants "threw bread over the wire to feed them, etc. Some of the youngest Jewish children were taken into church orphanages and convents." Or a certain Mr. Z., a former Evangelical clergyman, "a Pole of exceptional moral worth." He hid four Jewish children in his home, two of them free of charge and the other two for 600 zloty a month. He also helped adults to the best of his ability. His wife opposed him, and he had to conceal his expenditures from her. Ignacy Kasprzykowski, a Methodist clergyman, who lived in a villa near Warsaw, sheltered adults and children in his house. Interestingly, of the three clerics mentioned by Ringelblum, only one was a Catholic—strange in a country predominantly Catholic. Also worth noting is the greater willingness of the Catholic Church to help baptized Jews, of whom there were several thousand. Masses were held for them in two churches in the Warsaw ghetto, the Church of all Saints and the Church of the Holy Virgin Mary, and the Catholic welfare association, Caritas, opened free kitchens for them. Ringelblum's sad conclusion: "To sum up what we have said about converts, it should be stressed that the help extended to them was fine work on the part of the Polish clergy, but it was not done to help Jews." One area, however, where the church did act was in the rescue of Jews in nunneries, where many Jewish children and adults were hidden; the exact figure is not known; certainly in the hundreds, and most likely even more.[18]

The Polish Underground and the Postwar Period

Sadly, in Poland, antisemitism was to a great extent compatible with patriotism. It flourished everywhere, even in the underground, of which the largest, most popular, and best organized organization was the Home Army (Armia Krajowa or AK). The Home Army did not as a rule accept Jewish units, and all efforts made by the numerous Jewish armed groups to contact the Home Army in this regard were unsuccessful. However, those willing to conceal their Jewishness from even their closest comrades were accepted in the smaller left-wing underground unit, the Armia Ludowa. Not a few members of the Home Army took part in the murder of Jews, especially Jewish partisans in the forests. Jewish partisans were often labeled "bandits" by the underground high command, an echo of the language used by the Nazis themselves. Not content with refusing to help Jewish underground units, the Polish underground even called upon its men—unbelievably!—to hunt them down. As spelled out in an order of the day on September 15, 1943, by General Bor-Komorowski, commander of the Home Army, "to take armed action" and "liquidate the leaders of the bands," who in his words were accused of raiding local farms in search for food. As stated by the Polish publicist Antony Polonsky, "Nothing in the order indicates any sympathy for fugitives from the Nazi genocide; no appeal is made to villagers to provide them with the food and shelter that otherwise they could only seize by force; and no understanding is shown of their predicament." AK armed units in the forests needed no further coaxing, and they soon passed over from a negative attitude or indifferent disposition to actively participating in pursuing and destroying Jewish armed groups. The evidence is too abundant to be denied. The situation worsened in 1944, as liberation from the Germans approached Poland's doorsteps. In March 1944, the NSZ (*Narodwe Siăy Zbrojne*, National Armed Forces), a violently antisemitic underground organization, was incorporated into the Home Army and began an extensive campaign of murdering Jewish partisans and Jews who had succeeded in escaping from the ghettos. The Home Army, while not approving this massive hunt for Jews, declined to condemn the NSZ's murderous forays, on the excuse that it was not "the right time."[19]

The attitude of the Polish political parties was not much different. A document drafted at the end of 1943 by the Home Army described the positions of the various underground organizations on the Jewish future in postwar Poland. Nine of the thirteen parties advocated either "emigration of all Jews" (some made an exception for Jews who had participated in the fight for independence), "liquidation of the Jews," or "removal of the Jews." Only three parties were in favor of "full and equal rights for all citizens." No wonder that in his report to the Polish government in London in September 1941, the then commander of the Home Army, General Stefan Grot-Rowecki, wrote bluntly: "Please take it as an established fact that an overwhelming majority of the population is antisemitic. Even the socialists are no exception. There are only tactical differences about what to do. Hardly anybody advocates imitating the Germans." Roman Knoll, a senior official in the Polish government's representation in occupied Poland (known as the *Delegatura*), in an August 1943 memorandum, stated a viewpoint shared by many. "The mass murder of Jews in Poland by the Germans will reduce the dimensions of the Jewish Question in our country; it will not liquidate it entirely. . . . In the Homeland as a whole . . . the position is such that the return of the Jews to their jobs and workshops is completely out of the question, even if the number of Jews were greatly reduced. . . . . .The government is doing the right thing in reassuring world opinion that there will be no antisemitism in Poland, but this can only happen if the Jews who survive the pogrom make no attempt to return en masse to Polish towns and cities." Knoll advocated that the future Polish government join in the effort to move the Jews to a self-established state anywhere else in the world.[20]

The killing of Jews by antisemitic Poles, including those in the underground, went on up to the end of the German occupation of Polish soil—and even afterwards. All over Poland, Jews who had survived the Holocaust were waylaid and killed, including women and children. The immediate postwar years were the worst in anti-Jewish violence in the history of Polish-Jewish relations. From 1944 to 1947, between 1,500 and 2,000 Jews were murdered, most of them specifically because they were Jews, and mostly when they returned to their former cities to find out the fate of their families or reclaim homes and businesses. Jews were pulled from trains to be beaten and murdered. In about a dozen cities and towns, Jews lost their lives in pogroms, the worst occurring in Kielce in July 1946, where forty-two Jews were killed and more than 100 wounded. In Lublin, two members of the Jewish community were received by the bishop, Stefan Wyszynski. He refused to make a public statement on the Kielce incident. Instead he told them that the contribution of Jews to Polish life was negative, and suggested that they should strive energetically to acquire a statehood of their own in Palestine and possibly also a colony in South America. Kazimierz Wyka, a professor of literature, wrote: "The only country in Europe where antisemitism is still alive, leading to political and moral crimes, is Poland; the country where Jews have been most thoroughly wiped out and where resistance against the occupation was the strongest. And yet it is there that Nazism has planted its bastard seed."[21] As for the saved, their rescuers pleaded with them not to tell anyone about it, for fear of retribution. In Nechma Tec's case, the Homars wanted her family to leave the city of Kielce without revealing their true identity. "They did not want anyone to know that they had helped a Jewish family to survive. We were stunned. They were not actually sorry or ashamed for having saved us, but they undoubtedly felt that their friends and neighbors would not approve of what they had done. After all, they had to continue living among these people." In another rescue story, this time in Lwów, "our host asked us not to come back to visit him, or for any other reason it would go hard for him if it were known that he had hidden Jews. Many of the Poles didn't like the idea that even a few Jews had been saved." This made the survivor Leon Wells comment, "How sad was the situation in Poland that when a man proved he possessed high, idealistic qualities, he should be ashamed and unpopular for doing such a fine deed!" In June 1945, only 55,000 surviving Jews had registered with local Jewish organizations. However, a much larger number had survived, nearly 380,000, which included the many who had managed to flee to the interior of the Soviet Union, and many of these returned to their former homes. They represented only 12 percent at the most of the original Jewish population in Poland; the other 88 percent, of an originally 3.2 million population, had perished. By 1951, the Jewish population had shrunk to 80,000, and the numbers continued to diminish in the following years, down to 30,000 in 1959. Most of the remaining Jews left during the government-sponsored antisemitic drive of 1968–69, which resulted in the virtual dissolution of the Jewish community as an identifiable group.[22]

It took almost a half a century for winds of change to appear. A pastoral letter on Christian-Jewish relations and antisemitism was read on January 20, 1991 during Masses in all Roman Catholic churches in Poland, signed by the primate, Cardinal Józef Glemp of Warsaw. It included the words, "We are especially disheartened by those among the Catholics who, in some way, were the cause of the death of Jews. They will forever gnaw at our conscience on the social plane. . . . We must ask forgiveness of our Jewish brothers and sisters. . . . We express our sincere regret for all the incidents of antisemitism which were committed at any time or by anyone on Polish soil. We do this with the deep conviction that all incidents of antisemitism are contrary to the spirit of the Gospel." Nine years later, in August 2000, Polish Catholic bishops apologized for the church's past toleration of antisemitism and hostility toward non-Christians, stating that "antisemitism like anti-Christianism, is a sin." The letter, read in Catholic churches, asked forgiveness "for those among us who show disdain for people of other denominations or tolerate antisemitism."

We conclude with the words of Polish author Jan Blonski, "To purify after Cain means, above all, to remember Abel. . . . The Christians of the past and the church itself were wrong. They had no reason to consider Jews a 'damned' nation, the nation responsible for the death of Jesus Christ, and therefore as a nation which should be excluded from the community of nations. If this did happen, it was because Christians were not Christian enough. . . . The church sustained hostility toward Jews. . . . We must say first of all: Yes, we are guilty. We did not take Jews into our home, but made them live in the cellar. When they wanted to come into the drawing-room, our response was, Yes, but only after you cease to be Jews, when you become 'civilized.' . . . One can share the responsibility for the crime without taking part in it. Our responsibility is for holding back, for insufficient effort to resist. . . . If only we had behaved more humanely in the past, had been wiser, more generous, then genocide would perhaps have been 'less imaginable,' would probably have been considerably more difficult to carry out, and almost certainly would have met with much greater resistance than it did. To put it differently, it would not have met with the indifference and moral turpitude of the society in whose full view it took place." Let the reader be comforted by the thought that some 6,000 Poles have been honored by the Jewish people through Yad Vashem for risking their life to save Jews. These brave men and women suffered more than their counterparts in West European countries. The dangers facing them were far greater than elsewhere: death at the hands of the Germans and ostracism, if not physical violence, by their own kinsmen. These rescuers are the true humanitarian heroes of the Holocaust—the best and bravest of them all.[23]

Clergy Rescuers

We begin with nuns because proportionally many more women religious than male clerics were involved in the rescue of Jews in Poland. Of the fifty-six Polish clerical rescuers honored with the "Righteous" title, thirty-eight were women; that is, close to 68 percent. At the same time, the figures are too small to draw any definite conclusion. We start with the story of Matylda Getter, the mother provincial of the Franciscan Sisters of the Mary Family. Founded in 1857, this order had more than 100 houses, spread over the country, with its provincial seat in Warsaw. Aside from its many orphanages, it had four homes for the crippled, two for the epileptic, three for retarded children, four for totally handicapped children, and two for unwed mothers. During the occupation, the Order's Sisters sheltered 250 Polish children and, according to one estimate, as many as 550 Jewish children from the Warsaw ghetto (perhaps an exaggerated figure). One of these was Marguerite Acher (born Frydman). On September 9, 1942, she and her sister were taken by a friend of their mother to the convent of the Family of Mary, where Matylda Getter admitted the two despite their pronounced Semitic looks. The following day, they were moved to the Order's house in Pludy (numbering 120–140 children, of whom at least forty girls were Jewish), accompanied by Sister Agnela Stawowiak, its Mother Superior. A small amount of money was paid for the upkeep of the two girls; first by friends, then by their mother, who fled from the ghetto in February 1943. The payments stopped when the mother was taken to Ravensbrück concentration camp in August 1944, but the two girls stayed on in the convent until May 1945, when their father came from Budapest and their mother returned from Germany. To outsiders, especially the Germans and the Polish police, the children were presented as of unknown parents. Hanna Faigenbaum (born Zaitman), another hidden child, first stayed for two months in a rest home managed by the nuns, where all the residents were Jewish, before being moved to Pludy. After the war, Hannah was almost killed as she accidentally happened to walk into a Polish anti-Jewish riot in Kraków. Wanda Rozenbaum, another resident of the Pludy home, who arrived there as a fourteen-year-old refugee from Warsaw, was assigned to knitting socks and shawls. She reported seeing many Jewish faces among the girls. Bianca Lerner (born Kranc, in 1929), also from the Warsaw ghetto, related being personally welcomed by Matylda Getter. Bianca added that some of the priests and nuns were openly antisemitic. "How do you know?" she was asked. "I could tell." In Pludy, her name was changed to Janina Marzec, and before she arrived there she was taught by her Polish benefactor not to speak a too refined Polish, but instead mostly colloquial. She then moved back to the Warsaw home, on Hoza Street. Bianca was by then well versed in the Catholic religion and attended prayers constantly. Her first crisis occurred a week after her arrival: what to do about confession and communion, and her benefactress, Matylda Getter was not present. "I was afraid as to who was antisemitic and who was not." She expressed her fears by praying a lot. Food was scarce because of war conditions, and the girls slept in a large, unheated room. "One morning I woke up with a rat on my bed. He was cold and hungry too." When Getter visited Hoza, she sent for Bianca to inquire whether she was all right. "She impressed me as a good person, a really good Christian." Bianca stayed there until August 1944, when she was given a revolver and trained to fight in the Polish uprising. In Bianca's words, Matylda Getter "never tried to push me to convert." According to the Polish author Wladyslaw Smolski, only a very few Jewish children were baptized, and all of them were older children; they were converted only at their own express request of the children involved and after a long period of catechetic preparation.

Sister Louisa recalled that Matylda Getter assigned several dozen Jewish girls to her charge. The Germans came many times, and it was simply a miracle that they did not find anything. In addition, people of goodwill helped a lot; the head of the village always warned the nuns of a coming police raid and told who was suspected of collaborating with the Germans. Such as a certain policeman, who helped the Germans in the hunt of Jews. He would suddenly appear and "threatened that he would shoot on sight any Jewish child in our precinct." The Sisters also had to contend with a certain Gestapo officer who was a frequent visitor. "He roared like mad, stamped his boots, and threatened us with death if he ever found a Jew in the institution. My Lord, if he had only known the actual facts, he would have had to have us shot fifty times. One Sister, who had been resettled from Poznan province and had a perfect command of German, always tried to distract him while we were hurriedly hiding those children whose appearance seemed most telling. We were frightened. Our Mother Superior [Matylda Getter] was very frightened because she was more responsible than anyone else. Being an elderly person, critically ill with cancer, she seemed near collapse." In early 1943 Getter brought a young woman with a ten-year-old daughter to Pludy. "Both looked all right, and when the mother peroxided her hair you could not tell she was Jewish. But she had one weakness: she took fright easily. She taught English to our girls. Well, we once had a very narrow escape with Rena (that was her first name) in the last month of the occupation when that rabid Gestapo man burst into the orphanage. He came just as we were sitting with the girls in the corridor. In all likelihood, he would not have done her any harm, because she did not look Jewish and had a right to be there as a teacher. But her nerves let her down. She fled to the girls' dormitory, where my bed stood behind a screen. All of a sudden I heard the officer roar. I jumped into the dorm and what did I see? The

Gestapo man had glanced behind the screen and saw Rena there. She was there all right, covered with my quilt, a bonnet on her head. He turned to me and—I know some German—asked if she was a nun. Naturally I answered yes. Then he pulled away the quilt and saw Rena's lay dress. That was a moment in my life! I thought both of us were done for. He called me a liar and dragged poor Rena by the hair into the yard, where he had already rounded up several people caught in Pludy and environs. When I ceased trembling, I felt enormous pity for Rena even though she had let us down in such a foolish manner. I did not know one thing, though: did he take her on the assumption that she was Jewish or because she seemed to him politically suspect? I prayed. A few minutes went by and . . . I could not believe my eyes. Rena, safe and sound, reappeared in the corridor. It was a miracle that she had escaped death. Immediately, I gave her a habit that from then on she never failed to put on whenever the rabid Gestapo man set foot in the orphanage."[24]

Maria Górska, who belonged to the Order of Ursuline Sisters (*Siostry Urszulanki Szare*) in Warsaw, saved the life of Janina ("Jasia") Kon (changed to Kaniewska) and her aunt Zofia Rozenblum-Szymanska, as well as countless other Jews. Born in 1933, Janina was smuggled out of the Warsaw ghetto in August 1942 by her aunt, and both were able to find refuge: the aunt in the convent of the Ursuline Sisters in Ozarow near Warsaw, and Janina in the convent of the Immaculate Sisters (*Siostry Niepokalanki*) in Warsaw. Sister Górska kept in touch with Janina's parents in the Warsaw ghetto until they were deported; as well as with an aunt who was hiding in a convent in Ozarow. In her statement, Maria Górska wrote that she and other Ursuline sisters had opened a home in Milanówek for debilitated children and children from broken homes that accommodated around 100 children between the ages of three and fifteen. During the war the home also sheltered many Jews. The Jewish children, who had false credentials, were referred there either by their families or by non-Jewish acquaintances of the families, as well as by Jewish organizations active in the rescue of children. "In most cases we knew very well that the children were Jewish. However, even in cases where we did not know for sure, and only suspected they were Jewish, it was never mentioned and never the subject of discussion, and we took the children as they were." The children remained in the home even when their sponsors could not keep up with payments. Luckily, none of the Jewish children was discovered. Some adult Jews were also sheltered, such as Dr. Zofia Szymanska, and two adult sisters of the Kurz family, hidden in the Ursuline home in Vislana. The Mother Superior (Pea Lesniewska) was quite helpful, in view of her excellent contacts with an organization that assisted Jews. Górska's main responsibility was care of the children's kitchen, on top of her teaching assignment in biology. She was also sent out to pick up stranded children near the ghetto walls and bring them to various convents. When danger threatened, Górska immediately organized the transfer of the Jewish children elsewhere for varying periods, whether a few hours or several days or weeks. Górska related the case of a Jewish girl whose head was bandaged to hide her obviously Jewish features when she was moved from Warsaw to Brwinow. "At a certain moment, in the train station, I sensed the suspicion of a Polish policeman, who was surprised to see a nun with a infant in her arms, especially a child with beautiful black hair and eyes (this child was later nicknamed 'the Spaniard'). The Polish policeman accepted my explanation, but I took advantage of the arrival of a train which was not going in the direction of Brwinow but the opposite way, in order to slip away and escape from the policeman, who could have discovered that the child was Jewish."

Sister Górska spoke candidly on the issue of conversion of these children. "We usually baptized the Jewish children in those cases where we were told that this was crucial for their survival, especially so as not to arouse suspicion that they were Jews. We wanted all the children to be present every day for confession and prayers. Some of the Jewish children became very attached to the Christian religious rites, but we made them understand that they would not be required to be committed [to accept Christianity when they grew up]. From my contact with tens of Jewish children, I noticed that they needed much empathy and expressions of love, since in the beginning they kept to themselves, which could have aroused suspicion. I decided to break down the wall between them and us and gain their confidence. . . . Today [1985] in our convent there are several nuns who have been with us after the Holocaust. No one ever came to ask for these Jewish girls, and when they grew up they asked to remain with us and be inseparable from us. . . . Most of the surviving children we returned upon the end of the war or several years afterwards to their families or to representatives of the Jewish community who were armed with appropriate documentation testifying a relationship to these children. . . . Not one of the Jewish children who were sheltered by us, and especially in the Milanówek house, did not return to his family in a much better condition." Sister Górska then went on to mention the names of some of the Jewish children: "Stenia Jankowska, daughter of a Lodz doctor . . . the Raniszewski sisters, who moved to Paris. . . . Some of them moved to Israel and after some years sent us letters of thanks and good wishes." She added, "This human experience helped me to better understand the human soul and heart, and especially the soul of a child who suffers through an experience as terrible as the Holocaust."[25]

Another story concerns Lilian Lampert (born 1931). After her father was lost in the Holocaust, friends provided her and her mother with false credentials, and through their contacts with the nuns of the Order of the Immaculate

Conception, they secured Lilian's acceptance (under the assumed name of Ludwika Baczewska) in the nuns' boarding school in Warsaw, headed by Sister Wanda Garczyńska. "The nuns knew of my identity and I retained my real name. They showed great courage by providing refuge for a Jewish child with red hair and Semitic features." She led a relatively peaceful life in the school. "I was treated exactly the same way as any other child at school. . . . I even continued my piano lessons. Only my outings outside the compounds were curtailed, understandably, for my own safety." Summers and holidays were spent at the order's affiliate in Szymanów, where the nuns conducted a boarding school for high school girls. Since Szymanów was more isolated, and hence seemed more secure, it was decided to transfer Lilian there permanently, and her mother, hiding in Warsaw, visited her occasionally. Lilian was not the only Jewish child there. "I remember, sometime in 1943–44 the arrival of another red-haired girl, and the nuns' efforts to bleach her hair, which attracted my curiosity. He name was Jasia. That's all I knew at that time. She too survived the war." At a later date, the convent in Szymanów was subjected to constant random inspections by the Germans, who requisitioned part of the convent's building to billet soldiers. "So, under one roof, there were Catholic nuns, their pupils, some of whom were Jewish, and German soldiers—none trusting the others." In the fall of 1944, Lilian was sent to rejoin her mother, who was hiding in the village of Zaręby Kościelne, near Grójec, where she remained until the area's liberation in February 1945. Lilian still affectionately remembers some of the nuns: Irenea, Brigida, Wanda, Teresa, Deodata, Blanka, Bernarda; also Father Skalski. According to the order's records made available to Yad Vashem, a total of twenty Jewish children were cared for.[26]

Mother Superior Bronisława Beata Hryniewicz and Sister Stanisława Jóźwikowska, of the *Dom Serca Jesusowego* convent, in Skórzec village, Siedlce region (60 kilometers east of Warsaw), took in two Jewish sisters: five-year old Barbara-Batya Faktor-Pichotka and eleven-year old Esther. In 1941, having previously escaped from the Warsaw ghetto, the two girls wandered through many villages, mostly in the Siedlce region. Arriving in Czerniejew, exhausted, hungry, and shivering from the cold, they were taken in by a compassionate woman, Władyslawa Cabaj, but were betrayed by neighbors. The Polish police took them for questioning in the nearby village of Skórzec. Refusing to part from them, Cabaj went along, arguing to the police chief that the two girls were really Christians and it would therefore be a sin to kill them. The police relented and Batya was placed with a local family. But after a while the family refused to keep her any longer, and the headmaster went to complain to the village head. By coincidence, Sister Stanisława Jóźwikowska happened to be present during this altercation, and she volunteered to ask her superior for permission to admit the girl to the convent. She returned the following morning with a carriage, and took Batya with her. It was January 1943. "The nuns welcomed me warmly, cleaned off the dirt which clung to me during the many months of wandering, tended my wounds, and fed me." She then fell ill for several months, and was tenderly cared for by Mother Superior Hryniewicz. After she recovered, she was taught the Christian catechism, and in September 1943 she was admitted into the local school's second grade. When the principal discovered that Batya did not have a baptismal certificate, he complained to the police and the village head. Batya's older sister Esther saved the situation, claiming her sister's baptism had taken place in a distant Warsaw suburb whose records were no longer available. The principal would not yield, so in desperation Esther confessed that she and Barbara-Batya were in truth Jews, hoping that at least Batya would be spared, since she was in the special care of Mother Superior Hryniewicz. To her surprise, the Mother Superior suggested that Esther also move into the convent even though she was well treated by the Polish Swiatek family with whom she was staying. The two nuns kept the identity of the two sisters a secret from the other nuns. Batya: "All this time, I did not know that my sister had revealed our true identity, and the nuns also kept this fact from me, in order to allow me a feeling of security, and prevent pain and fear." After the war, the two girls' elder sister Reginka searched for them and found them. The Jewish community offered the Mother Superior a monetary reward, but she declined, stating: "I did what was required of me as a Christian, and not for money."[27]

The Order of St. Joseph's Heart (*Sw. Jozefa Serca*), in Przemsyl, sheltered many Jewish children. The nuns in charge, after the sudden demise of the Mother Superior, and the illness of her replacement, included Eugenia Wąsowska (Sister Alfonsa), Anna Grenda (Sister Ligoria), Rozalia Sidełko (Sister Bernarda), and Leokadia Juśkiewicz (Sister Emilia). Sister Alfonsa was made responsible for the "Jewish section," and under her stewardship, a total of thirteen Jewish children (ten girls and three boys) were kept in the orphanage until the city's liberation in July 1944. Children were often received under dramatic circumstances. In July 1942, a mother smuggled her child out of the city ghetto and deposited it in front of the orphanage gate. The ensuing scene was exactly like the story of Moses, as told in Exodus 2:6: "And when she opened it she saw the child, and behold the child wept. And she had compassion on him and said, 'This is one of the Hebrew children.' " The baby girl's crying aroused the nuns and they took her in. In another episode, four-year-old Hedy Rosen and her mother, after wandering for a long time, arrived in front of the orphanage. Panting for breath and on the verge of collapse, Hedy's mother looked into her daughter's eyes and told her quietly: "You have no choice. From now on your name is Jadwiga Kozowska and you are a Christian Pole." After repeating several verses of a Catholic prayer with her, she placed Hedy near the convent's entrance and disappeared behind a tree. Hedy stood there alone and wept. Her cries alerted the nuns, who opened the gates and brought the child inside. Hedy's mother had in the meantime found work in a nearby village under a new identity, and on occasion brought food to the orphanage for her daughter's sake. "I was forbidden to show the slightest sign that I knew her," Hedy related, "for fear of the other children. I had to disregard her completely." Sister Alfonsa saw to it that the children did not lack food or clothing, and when the ration cards did not suffice, she went out to collect alms in order to increase her funds. Various tactics were used to avoid detection. One was to tell the Jewish boys, in Alfonsa's words, "that if a stranger comes to the convent and asks a boy what he wants to be when he grows up, he should say a priest.". Unable to repress the severe traumatic experiences that had prompted their placement in the orphanage, the Jewish children were prone to sudden bursts of hysterical weeping. "Sometimes at mealtime a child would cry and throw his food on the floor," Sister Alfonsa recalled. Miriam Klein remembered some of the children screaming at night and wetting their beds. "Sister Alfonsa always knew how to calm us. Sleeping with us in the small room she was alert to every noise and often got up at night to place an additional blanket on the frightened children." Immediately upon the city's liberation, Sister Alfonsa took the thirteen Jewish children to the newly constituted Jewish committee in Przemysl and promptly turned them over. "They were Jewish children and belonged with Jews," she emphasized. Recalling her stay at the orphanage, Miriam Klein remarked, "I was privileged to experience calm and mental relaxation, and there I discovered the best and most beautiful of women." The danger faced by these nuns were frighteningly real, in light of the public announcement by Dr. Heinisch, the German district head in Przemysl, in July 1942, that "Every Ukrainian or Pole who does anything to interfere with the campaign to expel Jews will be shot dead. . . . Every Ukrainian or Pole who tries to hide a Jew, or to assist him in hiding, will be shot dead."[28]

Still in Przemysl, we have the story of Aniela Kotowska (Sister Klara) and Irena Bielawska (Sister Honorata), who saved the Weitman family. In October 1942, the Weitmans fled from the Przemysl ghetto, aided by Bozenna Zlamal, who arranged for Avraham Weitman's daughter, Bilha, born in 1939, to be admitted to the Benedictine convent headed by Sister Klara (Aniela Kotowska), a Lithuanian-born nun ("a very prominent person; an outstanding woman," in Avraham's words), who also promised to find a separate hiding place for Avraham's wife. Zlamal also arranged for the Weitmans' son Jacob, born 1936, to be admitted to the religious orphanage section of the convent.

Sister Klara then accompanied Bilha's mother to a separate convent, of the Felician Order, and after a long discussion, the elderly Mother Superior agreed for Mrs. Weitman to stay there, on condition that she remain enclosed in a cell-like room. When Avraham visited his wife, he was told by Sister Honorata that he should first try to obtain false credentials and live outwardly as a non-Jew. He returned to inform her that he had failed to obtain the necessary documents, so she invited him to join his wife in her cell. "This was not a simple matter for them," Avraham recalled, "for husband and wife were not allowed to be together in one room in the convent, which was against their Christian custom." In the Weitman cell, there was also a Jewish girl, named Lila Blumenkrantz (born 1937), who was allowed to mix with the other non-Jewish girls. She would relate how she was told that the Jews had tortured Jesus. In her free time, she spent much time praying in front of the church's crucifix. "I remember I began to deny that I was Jewish. . . . There was a large picture in the convent, showing blood dripping from the hands and feet at the place of the nails. This picture always aroused compassion in me. If they, the Jews, did this, then I wanted no part of them." One day, she went up to Sister Honorata and said: "Sister Benedetta says that the Jews murdered Jesus. I swear that my grandfather was a good man, who could not even harm a chicken, so how could he have possibly murdered Jesus?" Avraham remembered that when this girl fell ill, she uttered the following prayer: "Jesus, since the Jews killed you, I have pains in my ears. Since you suffered, I too will suffer." Lila once asked to be baptized, fearing that that she might not live much longer and she wished to enter paradise, since as a Jew she had been told she would be sent to hell. She also told Sister Klara: "Don't bring my mother here, for she is a Yellow [Jewish], and looks like a Jew, and she would cause us all to fall." Sister Klara, indeed, had Lila baptized when, because the fighting front was drawing near, she began to fear that falling shrapnel might kill the child. Lila was then eight years old. Soon thereafter, Lila's parents having perished in the Holocaust, her grandmother appeared and took the child away. As for Bilha, the Weitmans' daughter, she was kept separate from her parents, but they were allowed to glance at their daughter from time to time through an perture in the wall. Avraham Weitman described Sister Klara as "an angel in human dress" because of her kindheartedness and compassion for the dozen Jews hidden in the convent. When Avraham no longer had enough money to pay for food and board, his fears were stilled by Sister Klara, "Don't you worry; we shall keep you until the war's end." Not all the nuns in the convent knew of the Weitmans' presence. In Avraham's words: "Some were anti-semites, and we had to watch out to make sure they did not find out." Upon the area's liberation, Sister Klara confessed to her bishop that she had sheltered Jews, and was told to bring the Weitmans to him for a serious talk.

Avraham went himself and was asked by the bishop "whether he knew that Jesus had aided us, and thanks to him our lives were saved. Therefore, it was time for us to become Catholics, since the Jewish faith, the Jewish religion, had not protected us, and we had been saved only thanks to Catholic people." Avraham answered: "Sir, bishop, I am not a believer, but I am a born Jew. How can one change a religion, when one does not see any importance in this?" But the bishop insisted: "We want the Jews to accept the Christian religion." Fearing a resurgence of antisemitism (in Przemysl itself, sixteen Jews were murdered by people active in the Polish underground), the Weitmans quickly left the country and headed westward to liberated Germany, from where they sent packages and money to Sister Klara. Avraham's lengthy testimony ends with the words: "I wish to underline that Sister Honorata was a terrible antisemite; she strongly hated the Jews. She told us that once, on her way to church during a visit to Tarnow, she had passed some Jews on their way to the synagogue wearing their tallith (prayer shawls), and that this sight had spoiled her day. She could not stand the sight of a Jew." Questioned by interviewer: "Then how come she saved you?" Avraham Weitman: "I asked her why she had saved us, and she answered that it was 'God's finger;' that God wanted it. On the other hand the Lithuanian nun [Sister Klara] was an outstanding person. . . . She saved many Jews. She was not a person, but an angel. . . . And she had great troubles, not necessarily from the Germans, but from her own Poles. Had they known that she was saving Jews, they would have murdered her."[29]

The horrific events of the Holocaust changed the lives of two nuns, as related in the following two stories. Sister Dolorosa (Genowefa Czubak) was a nun in the Order of St. Ignatius of Loyola, in Pruzana (now in Belarus). In January 1942, she suddenly took ill. Since there were no non-Jewish physicians in the area, the sisters took counsel and decided to approach Dr. Olga Goldfajn, who was confined to the ghetto with the town's other Jews. Dr. Goldfajn agreed to accompany Sister Marianne, who was dispatched to bring her by means of a dental surgeon's permit, and both hurried to the cloistered walls of the convent. "She made a good impression on all the Sisters and myself as well," Sister Dolorosa related, as she quickly recovered from her illness. In August 1942, as Nazi anti-Jewish measures increased in severity, with many evicted from the ghetto and shot over open graves. Olga Goldfajn managed to drop in on Sister Dolorosa for a quick visit, ostensibly to see how her patient was recovering. "Mrs. Goldfajn remarked that it might be the last time we would be seeing her," Sister Dolorosa recalled. "I tried to comfort her. She then asked me whether I would be prepared to shelter her if necessary. I did not answer in the negative in order not to sadden her, but, not having anticipated such a request, I did not think seriously about what I was saying." Dolorosa heard herself promising she would help one way or another. In November 1942, Olga Goldfajn secretly met Sister Dolorosa near the ghetto's barbed wire. "She looked terrible. Mrs. Goldfajn admitted to me that she had tried committing suicide but the injection had proved not potent enough. Seeing the hand of destiny in this, she begged me to hide her. Overcome with pity, I told her to come see me that same evening." Returning to the convent, she pleaded with the other Sisters not to mention her encounter with the Jewish woman doctor to anyone. "I was quite worried. Maybe I was wrong to consent to hide her," Dolorosa agonized silently. That evening, the distraught Dr. Goldfajn came, and she hid in the convent for five weeks, until matters had somehow quieted down again in the ghetto and she felt it safe to return. It was now December 1942. When this incident was reported to her superior in Bialystok, Sister Dolorosa was reprimanded for admitting a lay person to the convent, against the order's regulations. On January 28, 1943, when the Nazis launched another *Aktion* on the ghetto's remaining Jewish population, with posters appearing in public places threatening the death penalty for anyone caught helping Jews, "that evening, I could not eat anything," Sister Dolorosa remembered. After prayers, Dolorosa was informed by the convent's superior that she had better not repeat her previous "mistake." "Very depressed, I took sleeping pills, hoping to immediately fall asleep." At about two o'clock at night, Sister Dolorosa suddenly woke up. "My heart seemed to have turned to stone, so heavily did it weight on me." Several minutes later, the night-guard Sister ran up to Sister Dolorosa's room with the news that Dr. Goldfajn was at the convent's gate. She had escaped from a column of Jews about to board a train transporting them to their death. That evening, Dr. Goldfajn was given a nun's habit and provided with two legally issued work-permit cards, one in her name, the other in the name of a Sister from another city who had left her card while on a visit at the convent. The two women then left the convent. Dr. Goldfajn was to be known hereafter as Sister Helena. After spending the night in the home of a forester, the two women were henceforth committed to the life of wandering nuns, supporting themselves with alms from kind-hearted souls and passing through many towns and villages on foot, by horse-drawn carriage, or by train. Passing through Wielka Dąbrowa, they saw trains packed with Jews on their way to Treblinka camp. Sister Dolorosa remembered how "the condemned people broke holes in the sides of some of the cars, throwing out their children through the openings. At times, adults too jumped, so as to die on the spot and bring their sufferings to an end. Poles could not help them, for Nazi guards guarded the tracks. There were some who pillaged the dead, exploiting the tragedy of others. The preceding Sunday, the priest at Sokolow had cursed, in his sermon, this shameful behavior of some Catholics." The two women reached Sister Dolorosa's hometown of Olszyny, where they remained in the security of Sister Dolorosa's family for a full fifteen months. One Sunday Olga asked to be allowed to join Sister Dolorosa for Mass. "If people see us together, it will be safer," Olga reasoned. "I refused," Sister Dolorosa related. "For me, Holy Communion is God, for you it's bread. The fact that you belong to a different religion does not disturb God, but my behavior must conform to the regulations and teachings of the church." To others, "Sister Helena" was introduced as a former student nurse who due to a religious experience had taken a nun's vows. She freely treated the ill and sick, and her reputation as a healer began to spread, because all her prescriptions produced wonders. After the liberation, Sister Dolorosa was informed of her expulsion from the Order of St. Ignatius of Loyola. Accepting the verdict, she removed her nun's habit and resumed her maiden name of Genowefa Czubak. As for, Mrs. Goldfajn ("Sister Helena"), she left Poland for Israel, where she worked as a physician in a hospital. Before her death in 1964, she took care to leave a most treasured memorabilia of her wartime years with the Beit Lohamei Hagetaot Museum outside Haifa for permanent safekeeping—a photograph of herself and her benefactor, both in nuns' habits.[30]

For our second highly unusual story, we move westward to the Vilnius region, now in Lithuania, where we meet Anna Borkowska, also known as Sister Bertranda. The story unfolds in Kolonia Wilenska, located between Vilnius and Vileika, where Anna Borkowska served as Mother Superior of a Dominican convent. She was then about forty years of age. After the horrible massacres of Jews in the nearby Ponary forest in the summer months of 1941, Anna Borkowska consented to allow seventeen members of an illegal Jewish pioneering group to hide in the convent for brief spells of time. The nuns in the convent had until this moment been completely cut off from the outside world, obeying the strict rules of the Benedictine Order. Now the convent of nine nuns was bristling with activity, with the youthful Jewish men and women sheltered behind the secure walls of the Dominican convent plotting an eventual uprising in the Vilna ghetto. They worked side by side with the convent nuns performing laborious work in the fields. To conceal the Jewish group's activities from the eyes of suspicious neighborhood peasants ever watchful of the unusual comings and goings of the convent, the Jewish young people were given nun's habits to wear when they cultivated the nearby fields. "They called me imah [mother]," Anna Borkowska fondly remembered. "I felt as if I were indeed their mother. I was pleased by the arrival of each new member, and was sorry that I could not shelter more of them." Recalling those who passed through the convent walls, Anna mentioned Arieh Wilner: "I gave him the name Jurek," the code-name under which he was to be known for his exploits in Warsaw, where he was eventually to perish during the Warsaw Ghetto uprising of April 1943. As a member of the *Hashomer Hatzair* (Young

Guard) Zionist socialist movement, he held to Marxist opinions. "Two different worlds met," Anna stated. "Nevertheless we found points of contact, or rather bridges, since each of us wished to be able to look into the other's soul. We had respect for each other's convictions; we exchanged our mutual intellectual achievements, not without some sort of influence on each other. In our conversations we tried to escape from the monstrous reality into the world of ideas. . . . Those who survived and even more those who died will remain forever in my memory. In the whole ocean of small, gray events in life, the moments when one gambles for high stakes are the most beautiful and valuable. Such moments occur only once in a lifetime." Then there was Abba Kovner, the moving spirit of the Vilna underground. His brother Michas (Michal) had hidden for many weeks in a hole in an attic without light and air, and in Borkowska's words was as pale "as a holy wafer." Another Jew who hid there called the convent "the only spark of light that shined in the general darkness; the only place where one found brotherhood and human compassion. The Mother Superior had become elevated in the hearts of those who stood in her presence to the symbolic image of the ideal person." In the convent cells, Abba Kovner issued his famous clarion call of rebellion, the first of its kind in Nazi-occupied Europe, which opened with the ringing words: "Let us not be led like sheep to slaughter!" This manifesto, secretly printed in the convent and distributed inside the ghetto on January 1, 1942, served as inspiration for many ghetto and partisans fighters. When the time came for Abba Kovner and his comrades to return to the ghetto, they told Anna Borkowska, "If we are to die, let us die the death of free people, with arms in our hands." She rushed to join them. "I want to go with you to the ghetto," she pleaded with Abba; "to fight and fall alongside you. Your war is a holy war. Even though you are a Marxist and liberated from religion, you are noble, for there is religion in your heart. A great God—now you are closer to Him than I." Kovner told her she could be of greater help by smuggling in weapons. The noted Yiddish poet Abraham Sutzkever recalled that "the first four grenades . . . were the gift of the Mother Superior, who instructed Abba Kovner in their proper use. . . . She later supplied other weapons." As suspicions mounted, the Germans arrested Anna Borkowska in September 1943, closed the convent, and dispersed the Sisters. One nun was sent to a labor camp. As for Abba Kovner, he survived the Holocaust as a fighting partisan and, moving to Israel, became a man of letters, author, thinker, and poet. He sought the good nun but was wrongly informed that she had passed away. Then, suddenly, in 1984, he was told that Anna Borkowska, to whom he had dedicated a poem entitled "My Little Sister," was indeed alive and residing in Warsaw. Suffering from a terminal illness to which he would succumb only a few years later, Kovner rushed to her side, to present her with a Yad Vashem medal and certificate of honor. She wondered, "Why do I deserve this honor?" To which Abba Kovner replied: "You are Anna of the Angels." Addressing the audience, Kovner recalled, "[When] the angels hid their face from us, this woman was Anna of the Angels for us; not of the angels that we invent in our hearts, but of angels that create an eternal life for us."[31]

Turning to male clerics, we begin with the story of Michał Kubacki, in the Warsaw region. He helped Halina Engelhard, a teenaged girl who successfully jumped off a deportation train during the Warsaw ghetto uprising. Returning to Warsaw, she remembered her mother's instructions, moments before she jumped (her mother had stayed on the train): "Go to Father Kubacki at the Basilica Church. Take tramway number 5 and ride to the last stop. He will surely help you. Go and believe in your luck." When she reached the church, Kubacki arranged birth and baptismal certificates for Halina and concocted a story that she was a childhood acquaintance and now a refugee from Plock. Kubacki slowly taught Halina the Catholic prayers and customs. She and her work-mate Hela (who did not know Halina's true origin) were assigned to prepare meals for several hundred poor neighborhood people, as well as for the children in a school near the church. One day Halina met Father Stanek, a protégée of Kubacki, with a Jewish-looking girl of eight or nine years who was known as Zosia. She had large, black, sad eyes and long braids. Zosia was assigned to adorn the altar with flowers and other light household chores. Before long the church office began to receive complaints about keeping a Jewish girl, so Zosia was moved to a private home. This led Halina to begin discussing religious matters with Stanek. Stanek's position was that for God what counted was not whether one was a Christian but whether one acted kindly toward other people. As for Father Kubacki, according to Halina, he lectured on the need to help Jews. "These people are our brothers," he would state. "They have a soul just like us. In the heavenly court, it is not they who will be condemned, but those who murder them today. In God's eyes, it is man's behavior that counts, regardless of his religion. Be he a Buddhist, Jew or Muslim, if he believes in one God and keeps his commands, God loves him. A good Catholic is not one who keep the religious rites and regularly attends church to pray, but the one who obeys the commandment relating to fellow men, and extends a helping hand to others in need." These were rather unusual words coming out of the mouth of a Catholic priest in wartime Poland. As suspicions about Halina's Jewishness mounted, she decided to leave, and with the help of acquaintances she found lodging in a municipal homeless shelter where more than 100 women came to spend the night, mostly from the lower and poorer strata; many of them alcoholics and street walkers. After a short stint there, Halina was referred to Sister Bernarda at the Saint Magdalena convent, who in turn sent her to another convent, where Halina shared a room with two other women, and was assigned to set the tables and help feed the children there. A few days later, Sister Bernarda came to visit. "How are you, my daughter, do you feel well here? Are you hungry? And the work, is it too hard? . . . Remember, my girl, that you are Jewish. Be proud of it. The Jews gave the world great people; our Lord Jesus, he too was Jewish. When the war is over, go to Palestine, live and work there. Only there will you be really happy." Then she left. Later on Halina learned that the Gestapo was after Bernarda for helping Jews and she had to go underground. Halina soon found that there were other Jews hiding in the content. She later left the convent with two other Jewish women. They were subsequently were killed by Polish collaborators. Luckily for Halina, she survived.[32]

In the Bialystok region, northeast of Warsaw, fifteen-year-old Joseph Kutrzeba jumped from a deportation train in October 1942 and roamed the Polish countryside, hiding in forests, fields, and barns, while at the same time, posing as a Pole, he asked the farmers to give him work and shelter him. In Hodyszewo he ran into a priest, Józef Perkowski, to whom he disclosed his identity. The priest referred him to Father Stanisław Falkowski, a young vicar who was posted in the off-the-beaten-track village of Piękuty Nowe. "From the moment of my arrival (on foot, through the snow, at night) in Father Falkowski's house, the latter took me in, deloused me, treated the boils on my body, and sheltered me, first in his house, and later arranged for me to stay with several Polish farmers in the area (who were not aware of my true identity). This went on for about one year. Incidentally, his superior, the parish priest, was aware of my true identity all along and helped all along. His name was the Rev. Roch Modzelewski." In time, people began to suspect that the boy was Jewish. After consulting with Modzelewski, Falkowski arranged for him to obtain a new identity card that made it possible for Joseph to "volunteer" for work in Germany. Joseph recounted the following example of Falkowski's dedication to his survival. "One night, during my stay with a farmer on the outskirts of a village, the Polish partisans (AK) wandered in. I became enthused on meeting them and asked if I could join them. They agreed and suggested where I could meet them in few days thence, since I had indicated that I would have to seek Father Falkowski's permission or at least to take my farewell of him. When I subsequently told the priest of my plan, he declared himself vehemently against it, citing the following reasons: first, he said, I lacked the physical stamina to survive the rigors of the partisans' life; second, he warned that, however regrettably, the Polish partisans (AK) harbored antisemitic elements, and while they were dedicated to the struggle against the Germans, nevertheless, on discovering a Jew among them, they would put him away mercilessly. The priest did not want to expose me to those dangers, he said. The above episode illustrates the heroism of Father

Falkowski. It goes without saying that, by allowing me to join the Polish partisans, the priest could easily have 'gotten rid' of me. Even later, while I was in Prussia working in a factory, Father Falkowski kept in touch with me the whole time, writing letters to me and keeping up my spirits, and also sending me food packages. If, while in Prussia, I had been discovered and forced to reveal who had harbored me in Poland, Father Falkowski would have faced mortal danger." Joseph Kutrzeba added that on a recent visit to Poland, Father Falkowski told him he had harbored other Jews, adding, "I do recall him saying that a couple of Jews he had helped were caught by accident and executed."[33]

As for Adam Sztark, he was rector of a Jesuit church in Slonim and a priest in Zyrowice. In Slonim, he helped to save Jewish children by issuing predated Catholic birth certificates. He reportedly sneaked into the ghetto hoping to help the people inside. In June 1942, when the Slonim ghetto was being liquidated, Sztark stealthily crept outside the ghetto perimeter, hoping to pick up Jewish children to take to safe places, such to the gardener Jozef Mikuczyn, who hid a Jewish boy brought to him. He also saved adult Jews on the run. According to the testimony of Rafal Charlap, Sztark called upon his parishioners to extend help to Jews. Jesuit Father Vincent Lapomarda stated that in the summer of 1941, when the Germans exacted a "contribution" in gold from the Jews in the Slonim ghetto and they could not raise the required amount, Father Sztark organized the collection of golden crosses from his parishioners. When the Germans learned of Sztark's involvement on behalf of Jews, they arrested him in December 1942, in his home in Zyrowice. The following morning, he was taken to Górki Pantalowieckie. Ordered to undress, Sztark refused. The Germans allowed him to be shot in the black robe of the Jesuit order.[34]

In Lublin, southeast of Warsaw, Jozef Górajek helped seven-year-old Eugene Winnik and his mother. In 1942, the two had fled from the Warsaw ghetto and gone to live with a family in the village of Niezabitow, to whom they were referred by friends who did not inform the family that the arrivals were Jewish. Eugene's father stayed behind in the ghetto and died in the Holocaust. Eugene and his mother attended church services every Sunday in the church in nearby Wawolnica served by Father Górajek, who was well aware of their true identity. When it was time for Eugene to receive his first communion, Górajek attended to his needs. However, a group of villagers began to suspect that the two were Jews, "and they went to the priest and said that he must not under any circumstances give me a communion because I was a Jew. The priest was very angry with the villagers. He told them that I was a Catholic, that I would continue to receive communion, and that they were never again to say such a thing." Out of respect for the priest the villagers kept their peace throughout the war years. During this entire period, Jozef Górajek continued to protect mother and child. In 1987, Father Górajek wrote to Eugene Winnik, living in California: "We helped many people in those difficult times. How many documents we issued to prove the Catholic faith and Polish nationality, and how many Jewish children we baptized. I am not writing this to exalt my actions; I did it because I love my fellowmen and more so when his life is in great danger."[35]

In Dobczyce, near Kraków, Franciszek Orzechowski saved ten members of the Gletzer and Lipski families by moving them from one place to another, including assisting them to escape to Hungary. He had previously provided them with food and medicine while they were in the ghetto. Rena Gletzer Lipski, born 1924, told how she met Orzechowski in 1941 in Dobczyce, where her brother and wife lived, near the home of the priest's uncle, and this is how contact was made. Since it was forbidden for Jews to move about freely, Orzechowski took the initiative by making contact with members of the family, and transferred Rena's family from Dobczyce to another location when it was feared that they would be deported. He organized horses and carts for ten people and moved them at night. Later, they were compelled to flee this place and go to Kraków. To achieve this, Orzechowski again took it upon himself to move them; this time, in individual stages. On one occasion, Orzechowski helped smuggle a child of Rena's family out of the ghetto. In March 1943, during the final liquidation of the ghetto, Rena and her mother managed to flee through the sewers and then contacted the priest. He took the two women to some people for hiding and then rotated them from place to place. He managed to get Rena and her parents across the Polish-Slovakian border, and then they proceeded on their own to Hungary. Rena emphasized that Orzechowski's help was voluntary and without any compensation. After the war, Rena kept in touch with him from Belgium, and sent him packages of food and clothing.[36]

* * *

As we end this chapter on aid by Polish clergy, we mention again, as noted earlier, the prevalence among them of a religious antisemitism that had to be taken into consideration by their Jewish wards. Lila Blumenkrantz, for instance, was constantly reminded that the Jews had tortured Jesus. She defended herself to Sister Honorata by innocently swearing "that my grandfather was a good man, who could not even harm a chicken, so how could he have possibly murdered Jesus?" The same in the Benedictine convent in Przemysl, where Avraham Weitman and his family were sheltered by Irena Bielewska (Sister Honorata). He described her as "a terrible antisemite; she strongly hated Jews" but saved them because it was a religious obligation.

Also to be noted is Avraham's statement that Aniela Kotowska (Sister Klara), whom he described as "an angel," feared more from her own people than the Germans, for had the Poles "known that she saved Jews, they would have murdered her." This is probably an overstatement, but it nevertheless reflects the anti-Jewish climate in the country as a whole, which also affected many of the clergy. Similarly for Joseph Kutrzeba, who was discouraged by his protector, Father Stanisłlaw Falkowski, from joining the Polish Home Army (AK) underground because if they discovered he was Jewish, they "would put him away mercilessly." There were, of course, exceptions to this rule. Father Michał Kubacki, in Warsaw, sheltered Halina Engelhard and preached on the need to help Jews. "These people are our brothers," he would say. "They have a soul just like us. In the heavenly court, it is not they will be condemned, but those who murder them today." And Sister Bernarda told her: "Remember, my girl, that you are Jewish. Be proud of it. The Jews gave the world great people; our Lord Jesus, he too was Jewish."

On the issue of baptism, the sources in our study are too few to draw any conclusions. Interestingly, Maria Górska, of the Order of Ursuline Sisters, who saved many Jews, testified after the war that Jewish children were baptized because it was crucial for their survival in that they were then able to go to confession and prayers with the other children. At the same time, she explained, the children were made to understand that this would not obligate them to remain Christian once the war was over, and the children were later turned over to Jewish organizations. Her convent nevertheless won some Jewish souls. In closing, it should be emphasized that the overriding motivation of clergy rescuers of Jews was compassion for their sufferings coupled with a Christian duty to help others in need; motivations powerful enough to overcome the traditional Christian anti-Jewish prejudice; and for some, a conscious or subliminal hope that some of their wards would eventually adopt the Christian faith. In light of the great danger for those who saved Jews—danger both from the brutal German occupiers and from their own antisemitic kinsmen—Polish rescuers occupy an elevated position of selfless devotion and great courage, unmatched in any other country.

Chapter 7
Lithuania

The church cannot help you. Personally, I can only weep and pray.
Archbishop Vincentas Brizgys, to a Jewish delegation.

If you wish to respect my feelings, please marry according to the law of Moses and Israel, with my friend Rabbi Oshry.
Father Bronius Paukštys, to one of his Jewish wards, 1945

Founded in the thirteenth century, Lithuania became a major power especially after it entered a union with Poland in the sixteenth century. In Lithuania (which for a greater part of its history was joined with Poland in a single kingdom), Jews were granted the right to practice their religion and to trade and engage in various crafts. In 1795, Lithuania was annexed to Russia and remained so up to the end of World War I. Throughout the centuries, the Jews of Lithuania lived in relative peace, and developed world-renowned religious seminaries that attracted students from distant lands and produced great talmudic luminaries, such as Elijah ben Solomon Zalman, the Gaon of Vilna. After World War I, in independent Lithuania, the Jewish population in 1923 numbered 154,000 (7.5 percent of the total), mainly concentrated in the larger towns, with 25,000 in the capital city of Kaunas (Kovno). At first, Jews enjoyed full civil rights and were guaranteed religious and cultural autonomy. However, by the end of 1920s, this lenient policy dissolved, especially after the country's democratic institutions ceased operating in 1927 under the dictatorship of Antanas Smetona, which was accompanied by antisemitic demonstrations and pogroms. In October 1939, after the fall of Poland, the Russians ceded the formerly Polish province of Vilnius (Vilna) to Lithuania, adding some 100,000 Jews to the country's population, which now numbered over 250,000. But Lithuania's independence was short-lived, and in the summer of 1940, the Soviet army occupied the country and forced its annexation to the Soviet Union. There began a process of Sovietization, which especially affected the economic and cultural structure of the Jewish populace; the closing of commercial establishments and the renowned rabbinical academies. Some

Jews, naturally, profited from the new change of government, which was accompanied by the abolition of the former discriminatory measures against them. Then in mid-June 1941, a week before the German invasion, the Soviets staged a mass deportation of 40,000 "enemies of the people," involving many non-Jewish officials of the former government and anti-Soviet activists, but also including 7,000 Jews, who were exiled into the vast interior of the Soviet Union. Many Lithuanians blamed the Jews for both the loss of their country's independence and for the mass exile of many of the country's intellectuals, charging that many Jews occupied important positions in the Communist establishment and the secret police (NKVD), and overlooking the fact that these people considered themselves anything but Jewish. Many dyed-in-the wool nationalists swore revenge on the Jews on the day of reckoning when "we will yet slaughter the Jews"—not merely the small percentage of well-known Jewish Communist officials, but all Jews, most of whom were traditional and religiously observant people, far removed from any Communist inclinations. One poster warned that in the new Lithuania, liberated from the Communists, "there will be no civil rights and no possibility of existence for any Jew."[1]

On June 22, 1941, when Germany invaded the Soviet Union, most Lithuanians welcomed them as liberators, and many willingly and initially even enthusiastically collaborated with them. They were soon frustrated in their hopes of gaining independence under German suzerainty. Instead the country was placed under direct German control as part of the Ostland Commisariat (which included Latvia, Estonia, and Belorussia, now Belarus), and Adrian von Renteln was appointed commissioner general to govern the country. The local administration headed by Juozas Ambrazevicius, which had intended to restore an independent Lithuania, was quickly suppressed. This did not prevent the leading nationalist circles from continuing to urge collaboration with the Germans on the grounds that they were battling a common enemy: the Soviet Union. This situation prevailed for as long as the Germans were winning. Starting in 1943, with the German defeat at Stalingrad, Lithuanian nationalists began to sound a different tune, and sought a rapprochement with the Western Allies, to ward off another Soviet takeover of their country. Despite this many Lithuanians responded favorably to German appeals to enlist in German-sponsored military units.

From the first days of the occupation, so-called Lithuanian partisans, later organized in "battalions," who had trained in Germany in advance of the invasion, began to take things into their own hands, especially when it came to killing Jews. On June 22, 1941, the date of the German attack on the Soviet Union, Lithuanians began staging mass killing pogroms, murdering many Jews in the streets. When German troops entered Kaunas, locals staged a raid on the city's Jews, killing them in the most brutal ways with clubs and hatchets (which even shocked their German overlords). Many students and intellectuals took part in the mayhem. By the end of October 1941 (four months into the German invasion), 80,000 Jews had been done to death; by the end of December 1941, 85 percent of the country's original 235,000 Jews had been decimated, mostly by Lithuanians; that is, by Lithuanian militia or police (some led by German officers at the highest command levels), who willingly volunteered to perform this dastardly act; the remainder was done by German special killing units, the notorious *Einsatzgruppen*. In the Ponary forest outside Vilna, thousands of Jews were killed by Lithuanian guards commanded by only one German officer. Similarly for the Jews in Kaunas, who were taken to military bastions, such as Fort 7 (2,500 Jews killed on July 7, 1941) and Fort 9. The remainder were mostly herded into the three ghettos: Vilnius/Vilna (15,000–20,000), Kaunas/Kovno (15,000–17,500), and Siauliai/Shavli (4,500–5,000). Many communities were thus wiped out in sudden attacks, with no one left to tell the story of their martyrdom. In Lithuania, Jews were killed not in gas chambers but by mass shootings, on many occasions after having been forced to dig their own graves. Lithuania was the first country where most Jews were exterminated during the initial phase of the occupation, and mostly by the people of the country. As reported by SS General Stahlecker, who commanded *Einsatzgruppe A,* the large-scale liquidations perpetrated by Lithuanian auxiliaries took place "without a hitch" as a "spontaneous reaction to their oppression by the Jews for many years." To cite one example, a unit of 300 men commanded by the Lithuanian journalist Klimaitis perpetrated the mass murder of 1,500 Jews in Kaunas. After the initial killings subsided, the Germans went ahead and imposed severe restrictions on the surviving Jews. The Vilnius ghetto was liquidated in 1943 and most of its Jewish inhabitants exterminated. Some were sent to concentration camps elsewhere. A handful were kept alive in the city as vital laborers, but they too (some 2,000) were killed on the eve of the city's liberation in July 1944. In Kaunas and Siaulai, some of the few remaining Jews were able to survive until the liberation. In summary, of the 225,000–235,000 Jews in Lithuania under German occupation, only an estimated 3,000 were found alive when the Soviet army liberated the country (including those who fled into the forests to join or create partisan units). Several thousand more survived the concentration camps and forced marches.[2]

How did the country's mostly Catholic establishment react to the mass murder of Jews by their own people? On June 30, 1941, after reading Hitler's *Mein Kampf*, Archbishop Juozapas Skvireckas, head of the Catholic Church in Lithuania, wrote in his diary about the danger of the Jewish-Bolshevik poison and pointed out that Hitler's thoughts on the Jews "are truly interesting; in his words there is much truth, a sharp eye for seeing reality. . . . Hitler is not only the enemy of the Jews, but a man who thinks correctly." When the Jews of Kaunus urgently appealed to him to help stop the killings, Archbishop Vincentas Brizgys, who because Skvireckas's advanced age was the actual head of the church, declined on the excuse that an intervention on behalf of Jews might do harm to the status of the Catholic Church in Lithuania, and he dared not take such a responsibility upon himself. A Jewish request for him to issue a pastoral letter was similarly rebuffed, on the excuse that "the church cannot help you. Personally, I can only weep and pray." Both of these leading clerics congratulated Hitler for "freeing" their country, and called on their countrymen to enlist in German military units. An SS memorandum reported that Brizgys, in a letter to the faithful, forbade priests to extend aid to Jews. The memo stated that "all the Catholic clergy . . . fully support the steps taken by the Germans. . . . Insofar as the Jewish Question is concerned, the church's position is clear. . . . Priests were forbidden to intervene in any way on behalf of Jews." As for Jews seeking to convert to avoid persecution, the SS memo went on: "Up to now, we did face cases of conversion, and Catholic priests have opposed this type of conversion, for in their opinion the Jews would not have converted to Christianity for religious reasons, but only to benefit from it." Some clerics, however, did try to help, especially in light of the increasing German military setbacks in Russia in 1943 and the approaching front, together with misgivings at Lithuania's not being granted the freedom they had hoped would result from collaboration with the Germans. Among these priests was Jonas Žemaitis, of the Lauraj orphanage, in Sakiškes, near Vilnius, who reportedly sheltered many Jewish children who had escaped from the Vilnius ghetto.[3] Following are the stories of other clerical rescuers in greater detail.

* * *

We begin with a very unusual Catholic cleric, who showed an unbounded love for Jews and Judaism, in stark contrast to his coreligionists. A the height of the mass slaughter of Jews in October 1941, Father Polikarpas Macijauskas, rector of the church and monastery of Kalainiai, sheltered several Jewish people in his monastery, with the Jewish women dressed as nuns. He preached incessantly in church: "If a person, very much afraid of the sun's light, comes to you, feed him and give him shelter, for thus our Lord Jesus told us." He continued delivering this message in public even after it was learned that a priest had been shot at Fort 9 for preaching a similar message. In the area where Macijauskas lived, another priest, L. Jankauskas, headed a Lithuanian killing unit, while others served as chaplains in similar units. Jewish survivors report that Macijauskas never asked his Jewish wards to convert as a precondition for his help. Esther Kreingel related that "on several occasions, I heard from this priest that the Jewish religion was the first one based on the belief in one God, and it will remain the last." She added that he would remind the Jews under his care of the dates of the Passover, Rosh Hashanah, and Yom Kippur festivals, so that they could properly observe them, given the terrible conditions of those days. "On the bitter Yom Kippur, when the Jews in nearby Zagar were murdered, he lit a memorial candle in his church, and said the Kaddish in the original language." Eventually, fearing for his life, he fled and went into hiding.[4]

Also in the Vilnius region, we note the story of Father Juozas Stakauskas, the director of the Vilnius State Archives. When the Nazis decided to store looted books and documents in the archives, they asked Stakauskas to find a suitable storage place, and he chose a former Benedictine monastery. This was also the place he felt most suitable for hiding Jews—eventually twelve people. The hidden people kept quiet during working hours while Germans in an upstairs room sorted the looted materials. Stakauskas's resolve to help Jews may have dated from 1939, when he took lessons in English from one of his future Jewish woman wards, who spoke of him to her relatives, including Dr. Aleksander Libo, who supplied Stakauskas with medicine, not knowing that he was also a priest. In one of their meetings, Stakauskas told Libo: "If the situation in the ghetto becomes unbearable, come to me at the archives. Perhaps I will be able to hide all of you." This was in the spring of 1943. That October, Libo and others sneaked out of the ghetto and made their way to Stakauskas's office. When he appeared, he turned pale, because the workers would soon be coming, and he told them to move to the attic. The building, which had once served as a Benedictine convent, was now an archival center, with only Sister Maria Mikulska, a Polish nun, living on the premises. When Stakauskas asked her in Libo's presence whether she would help some Jews who were in his care, she responded: "If your honor is prepared to face hanging, so am I." Libo recalled that from his hiding place in the building's attic, "I could see from the window the Gestapo leading Jews (women and children, beaten, and weeping) from the wrecked ghetto. From time to time, one heard buildings exploding." Stakauskas would visit the group after working hours with news about what was happening on the outside. After about a month in the attic, Stakauskas's secretary Joasia took them to the nearby St. Catherine Church. "The church was packed. We kneeled at the entrance, and after a few minutes Sister Maria Mikulska appeared and signaled to us to follow her. We entered a dark corridor. She told us to take off our shoes, and via the corridor we came into a place already occupied by the attorney Grzegorz Jaszunski and his wife, and the engineer Jakub Jaffe with his wife." The hiding place was an empty space in the basement, blocked off by rows of files that almost touched the ceiling, and the people slept on opened books. The hiding place was divided in two; a dark storeroom for food and coal, and a lighted room with four beds, a closet with kitchen utensils, and behind it, bookcase. A stove in the room made it possible to warm food. The Nazi office was located on the floor above the hiding place. Food for the twelve people was arranged by Stakauskas's secretary Jadzia or by Sister Mikulska. Jaszunski described Stakauskas as "a strange person; not a practical person, very dedicated; I should say, an idealist. He considered it his duty to save people, particularly Jews." In all, he hid and care for over a dozen Jews. Stakauskas would visit the group every three or four days, and stayed with them for about an hour in conversation. He would say: "Either we will survive all of us or we will perish." One woman died in the hideout, and was buried there in a coffin made out of flooring planks and buried beneath the floor. The dozen others survived. This situation lasted until the city's liberation on July 15, 1944.[5]

Moving westward, to Kaunas, we begin with the story of Bronislovas Paukštys who saved many Jews, among them numerous children. A monk in the Salesian order, he is described as a modest and shy person, friendly and good-hearted. He had at his disposal an office in the monastery building and a bedroom nearby, rooms that during the Nazi period served as temporary sheltering places for many Jews. In contrast to Archbishop Brizgys, who turned down a request by a Jewish delegation for the church to become involved in rescuing Jews, Paukštys saw the Nazi conquest as a tragedy for his people and country, and the persecution of Jews as genocide, plain and simple, that one had to oppose. Avraham Tory, one of his wards, related, "Father Paukshtys revealed to me in my hideout, after I escaped from the ghetto, that he had been reprimanded by his superiors for jeopardizing the church and for raising doubts in the eyes of the occupation authorities about the credibility of the church." After the war, Paukštys wrote to a priest friend in the United States: "I did what I could at the expense of my family [i.e., the monastic order to which he belonged]. I sometimes had nothing in my pockets, not even a few cents to buy the most basic foods for my family. To help others I was forced to flee my home three times from the Gestapo. . . . So many worries! So many sleepless nights! So much exhausting wandering! So many fears were my portion!" Penina Tory, another witness, recounted her daughter's rescue by Paukštys. "Of all my terrible and hair-raising memories of the Holocaust, one ray of light shines forth—the image of a wonderful person—Father Bronius Paukštys. The very appearance of a man like Bronius Paukštys instilled in our hearts the hope that not all was lost, that not all men had turned into predator animals or cowards. That there were still people with morals and conscience, good-hearted and compassionate, and on top of that, gifted with a unique courage and urge to combat evil." The plan was to save her daughter by spiriting her out of the doomed ghetto to the monk's house; then take her to his brother, a professor of agriculture and owner of a farm. "When I went to meet him, I was afraid I would be scolded for not coming at the prearranged time. Instead, he greeted with a smile on his lips. It turned out that the original plan could not be carried out. I stayed for ten days with my seven-year-old girl in a room of his monastery. Thrice a day, he would bring us food. It was then decided to send my daughter to his brother, Professor Juozas Paukštys, who lived at the other end of the city. . . . Immediately after the liberation, when I went to see him in Kaunas, he welcomed us with as much joy as if he were seeing his brother and sister just returning from hell. Out of deep emotion, he even kissed me. He then opened a drawer and removed an envelope which I had given him the day Shulamit was sent to the village. It contained the only valuables I had left, so that he could use them for Shulamit's upkeep. The envelope also contained a ring. I begged him to accept it as a token and modest remembrance of us. He stubbornly refused. He would remember us even without a memorabilia."

Another of his wards, Rachel Levin-Rosenzweig, told of meeting Paukštys in 1943, when on several occasions she was sent by the Kaunas ghetto underground to obtain Aryan papers from him for several of her women friends. "He always received me with great friendliness, inquired about me and my family, and asked why I was not asking for Aryan papers for myself." In July 1944, she fled from the ghetto and went to see someone whose address had been given to her, but that person refused to take her in. "I did not know where to turn, and I decided to approach Father Paukštys. With a heavy heart I mounted the steps leading to his room and in my heart the sole prayer 'If only he will be there.' The moment I entered he recognized me; he did not ask where I had come from or why. My self-assurance gave way and I burst out in bitter weeping, for my whole family was still with the Germans. He then turned to me with great warmth and said: 'At least, it's good you're here, my daughter; I will protect you; be no longer afraid.' I was assigned a room adjoining the church, which I did not leave for two weeks. Food was brought to me, water to wash, and clean clothes. Father Paukštys visited me every day; he would bring me books and talk with me. He told me about his life and studies, his life as a monk in Italy, his family and his work. He discussed moral issues: love of fellow man, religious tolerance, and nonviolent resistance. He was concerned about the question of revenge. He was a very pious man, but not once did he raise the religion question, and he respected me for my outspokenness. I gave him to understand that I was not religious, but that Jewish values were sacrosanct to me. Outside, the Germans were distributing fliers stating that any house where Jews were found would be destroyed and its owners killed." Recalling him many years later, Rachel wrote: "In the despondent darkness of the Holocaust; at a time of the dimming of the world's lights, the image of the Lithuanian priest Paukštys rises as a shining star, and this noble Christian person is worthy that his memory not be forgotten." Dr. Masha Izinavod-Rabinowitz, who was also aided by Paukštys, was once asked by him whether she prayed. "When I answered in the negative, he remarked, 'Too bad. It's unimportant to which God one prays. But I am grateful that you have told me the truth.' " After the war, she went to thank him for his help and to ask his blessings for her upcoming marriage. He said: "If you wish to respect my feelings, please marry according to the law of Moses and Israel, with my friend Rabbi Oshri (who had then moved to the United States). We fulfilled his wish in the synagogue court on Maironus Street." Later, those he had helped tried to persuade him to join them in their flight from Lithuania, in light of the danger facing him from the Communists. He declared: "I cannot abandon my flock; here I belong, and I must fight the Bolsheviks as I fought the Nazis." In 1946, the Communist regime arrested him and sent him to Siberia, where he was assigned to crushing stones for ten years. He returned to Lithuania in 1956, but was forbidden to officiate at his former ministry. For a long time he traveled from village to village secretly holding Mass. From Israel, his former wards sent him packages of clothing and medicine. When he died in 1966 at the age of sixty-nine, many of his former Jewish beneficiaries attended the funeral.[6]

We now come upon a religious person of a different type. Although not officially a cleric, he was accepted by others as an itinerant monk of some sort. For many Jews, he was the savior of their lives. Born into a Lithuanian farming family near Taurage, Bronius Gotautas did not go to school and was not fully literate for the rest of his life. Reared in a devout Catholic atmosphere, he dreamed of becoming a monk, but his lack of education, especially reading and writing, prevented his acceptance by the monastery of his choice. Instead, he was allowed to live on the monastery's premises, serve the monks, and be at the disposal of the Father Superior. He was also given the task of peddling religious books and pamphlets in towns and villages as an additional source of income for the monastery. Thus he regularly moved from place to place, walking barefoot in the summer, visiting market fairs, with a knapsack full of religious literature. He wore a tattered brown cassock covered with innumerable patches, and a belt around his loins. Nicknamed Broliukas ("Little Brother"), he was a well-known figure, and many adored him as a saint. He lived an ascetic life; he wore clothes that were patched but clean. He did not have a permanent address. He would sleep where the night caught up with him. His wide contacts facilitated his mission of helping Jews. He prevailed upon other clerics to provide him with baptismal certificates that he distributed to Jews, besides finding sheltering places for them. Sarah Finkelbrand was one of the many Jewish people he helped. After losing her husband, killed in Fort 9, Sarah decided to save herself and her four-year-old son. One day, while outside the ghetto perimeter at her work site at Kaunas airport, she slipped away and headed for a nearby monastery, where she was accosted by a priest who rebuffed her call for help. A local pharmacist, to whom she went to ask for a dose of cyanide, instead referred her to Gotautas. She met him at a prearranged place and he pulled two identity cards from his knapsack, one for Sarah; another for her sister-in-law. Gotautas repeated with her the new name under which she was soon to be known. He also gave her the address of someone to see and told her how to get there. A week later, Sarah, her son, and her sister-in-law slipped through the ghetto barbed wire and headed for the designated home. The following morning, Gotautas arrived and took them to Panemune, where he arranged separate hiding places for both women under their new non-Jewish identities. Sarah Finkelbrand gave him her late husband's hardly worn sweater during the exceptionally harsh winter of 1941–42, certain he needed it because of his itinerant lifestyle. The next time she saw him he was not wearing the sweater. She asked about it. "I gave it to someone who needed it more than I," was the curt reply. His help was not limited to Jews; he also gave assistant to escaped Russian POWs. The Gestapo was on his trail and finally, with the help of an informer, he was finally apprehended and sent to the notorious Stutthof concentration camp. He survived the rigors of the camp, and after the war, fearing the Communist regime in his homeland, he moved to West Germany.[7]

Still in and around Kaunas, Father Vytas Baltutis assisted the Gail family after they fled from the Kaunas ghetto, arranging a shelter for them with a farming family. Baltutis, a young priest, knew Miriam Gail from high school. In 1943, the Gails learned that Baltutis was serving as a priest in a region close to the German border. Miriam wrote to him asking for help. On Christmas 1943, he came to Kaunas to meet Miriam. When he first suggested that she convert, Miriam responded that she would willingly go through the motions but only if it would save her family. He responded that with God's assistance he would help her family and there was no need to convert. Returning to his region, he located the Antanas Kupraitis farming family, who agreed to shelter Miriam, her brother Isser, and her sisters Masha and Esther. The Gails remained hidden with the Kupraitis in a bunker for six months. Baltutis also helped other Jews with hideout locations.[8] Another cleric who aided Jews was Vaclovas Martinkus, who took the child Mordehelis Michnikis, born in 1940, to the Jeronimas and Marija Bukontas farming family in the village of Dapsiai after having him baptized. The child's parents, originally from Židikai, near Kaunas, perished in the Holocaust. The child was adopted by the Bukontas, and only much later, as an adult, did he learn the truth of his origin.[9] Also meriting mention is Father Stanislovas Jokubauskis in Kaunas, who hid many Jewish children who had been smuggled out of the ghetto and brought to him.[10]

Moving to Siauliai, north of Kaunas, we note the moving story of Vincas Bila and Adolfas Kleiba. Dr. Paulina Tucker was an eye specialist whose patients included a priest named Bila, who preached that the murder of Jews was a sin. One night in December 1943, Paulina escaped from the Siauliai (Shavli) ghetto and approached Bila, and he readily admitted her into his home. After a short stay there, he moved her to Father Kleiba, who lived 15 kilometers from Siauliai and came to get her. On the way there, Father Kleiba told Paulina that he was already hiding two Jews, Dr. Shabtai Pasvalecki and Yehuda Livyatan. Pasvalecki, who did not look Jewish and spoke a good Lithuanian, worked as Kleiba's assistant. As for Livyathan, he was hidden in the priest's attic. Livyathan's wife, Penina, while in the Siauliai ghetto, had obtained a false identity card from a priest who was antisemitic but responded to her pleadings. She and her husband Yehuda had later fled from the ghetto and knocked on the priest's door. He was surprised to see them but admitted them for a night's stay. He then took Yehuda to another priest. The two clerics decided that Yehuda's Jewish looks and inability to speak Lithuanian made it necessary to hide him, so they brought him to Father Kleiba. As for Penina, armed with false credentials, she moved from place to place, and survived, while remaining in touch with her husband in Kleiba's home. Kleiba reportedly hid four Jews in all. On one occasion they decided to leave the priest's home in order not to endanger him further but he refused, stating that in case of arrest he was prepared to die with his charges. After the war, Kleiba urged the four not to remain in Lithuania but to head for Palestine, since, in his words, that was the country where Jews belonged, whereas in Lithuania they would have to contend with antisemitism. When Penina Livyatan was about to leave, he handed her some gold coins, but she refused to take them. He pressed the money on her, saying that he had accepted a gold watch from Yehuda as a gift when he was in hiding there. Kleiba did not want it to appear as if he had saved Yehuda in return for the watch gift and therefore forfeit paradise. Then he blessed Penina, placing his hands on her head. From Palestine, Penina corresponded with Kleiba, who was suffering from a kidney ailment. In his last letter, he wrote: "You flew away like birds from their nest, and left me alone in my pains." He died soon thereafter.[11]

Continuing with the story of Antanas Gobis, he saved the youngish Judith Zakstein in Panevezys. She had been separated from a group of Jewish children and had nowhere to go when she met Gobis. Seeing her in tears, he comforted her, "My child, do not be afraid, do not weep. I will be both father and mother to you." He took her to the home of a teacher and then to other locations. He paid for her upkeep and visited her regularly to make sure she was well taken care of. When a non-Jewish child died, Gobis secretly gave the child's name to Judith (Tereza Massite). The end of the war found Judith in Zarasey, near Dvinsk. Gobis told her that "as God had seen fit to save some of the Jews from the Holocaust, it was up to me to go back to my people and the surviving members of my family." When her cousin Zorah Sarveris, a soldier in the Red Army, traced her in Zarasey, Gobis arranged a farewell party, attended by local priests, which lasted late into the night. Her cousin stayed in the priest's house that evening. The following morning, the cousin, taking note of the cross around her neck, asked her what she wished to do. She responded, "I shall behave according to what Father tells me." Sarveris waited for Gobis to return from church and with a heavy heart asked: "Father, what do you say?" Gobis turned to Judith: "My daughter, I bless you, and order you to return to your brother [Sarveris had introduced himself as her brother]. When you grow up, marry only a Jew, and I also bless you to have many children, for your people have suffered much; a suffering unparalleled in human history." He then placed his hands on her head, blessed her, and said: "If you desire to go to Palestine, I shall pay for your trip. Return, Judith; return to your people and to your family! They need you! I, too, will not forget you. We'll remain good friends." Sarveris said that "the frank and straightforward words of this righteous man caused a trembling and excitement in my heart, and his open and trustworthy words also made an impression on Judith." She joined Sarveris and his wife in Vilnius, and from there went to Israel.[12]

In Varniai, Telshiai region, Father Juozas Gasiunas helped Chaya Sher (born 1927) by arranging a hiding place for her with local families. Before this she had been in the Telshiai ghetto. She survived a killing raid and after climbing out of the ditch where the bodies were thrown had hidden with the family of a local fisherman, who referred her to Gasiunas. He reportedly also hid a group of Jews in his home.[13] As for Kazys Kavaliauskas, he intervened to save Miriam Schneider, born 1924, in Zagary. He accomplished this by bringing a non-Jewish woman named One Navickiene to the local police station. She claimed that she was the real mother of Miriam, who had been born out of wedlock and given up for adoption by the Schneiders. From the record it is clear that Kavaliauskas came up with this ruse after Judith told him her true identity and he decided on the spot to save her. A colleague, Father Jonas Teišerskis cooperated by falsely testifying that he had baptized the girl at birth before turning her over to the Jewish Schneider family.[14] Also worth mentioning is Vladas Požela, the prison chaplain in Šiauliai, who reportedly furnished a false document to Fania Pentko, thus obtaining her release from jail and thereby saving her life.[15] We end with Vladas Taškunas, a young Catholic seminarian in Alsedziai, who helped find a hiding place for Sarah Feidelman, born 1922, with a local inhabitant, from January 1942 until the liberation in October 1944.[16] This is all we have of clerical help to Jews in Lithuania, during the Holocaust, in a country drenched with so much Jewish blood.

Chapter 8
Russia, Belarus, and Ukraine

*When I face an audience of Jews who are ready to listen to me, I
cannot help but see them as fellow men exposed to eternal
perdition. . . . And if there is a spark of religious sentiment in the
soul of any of them, it might be kindled under the influence of the
uttered words of the Holy Scripture . . . an opportunity to bring
them nearer to Christ's teaching.*
Metropolitan Andrei Sheptitzky (1902*)*

*My house is like the house of the patriarch Abraham. Whoever
comes in hungry leaves sated. You may bring me any Jew you
meet. Everyone is invited to visit here.*
Baptist preacher Nikolai Oshurko to a fleeing Jew, Ukraine, 1942

The first Jews in the vast expanse of the Russias apparently settled in the
Kiev region, fleeing from persecution in the Byzantine Empire. They were
joined by Jews from the former Khazar kingdom, whose monarchs and many
inhabitants had converted to Judaism in the first half of the eighth century.
Gradually Jewish communities expanded northward. In general, Jews fared
badly under the czars. In 1742 Czarina Elizabeth Petrovna ordered the expulsion of the Jews living in her kingdom, stating: "I do not want any benefit
from the enemies of Christ," but it is not known to what extent the order was
carried out. With the annexation of Polish lands at the end of the eighteenth
century, tens of thousands of more Jews were added to the Russian Empire.
Over the centuries, the Russian government was troubled by the large presence of Jews in its territory, and favored either their assimilation or expulsion.
In the meantime, the czars restricted Jewish habitation to an area in western
Russia known as the Pale of Settlement. Czar Nicholas I (1825–55) tried to
impose a forced indirect conversion by ordering the conscription of Jewish
youth into the army for long terms of service. In addition, special schools for
Jews were created with teachers who were either Christians and assimilated
Jews. The stated purpose was "to bring them nearer to the Christians and to

uproot their harmful beliefs which are influenced by the Talmud." Under Alexander II (1855–81), Jews experienced a relatively more tolerant approach. By the end of the nineteenth century, the Jewish population had mounted to five million. The assassination of Alexander II in 1881 led to an outbreak of pogroms against Jews, who were accused of being in alliance with revolutionary elements. The new czar, Alexander III (1881–94), issued anti-Jewish laws (known as the May laws of 1882) that restricted Jewish rights. Konstantin Pobedonostev, chief procurator of the Holy Synod (the governing body of the Russian Orthodox Church) and notorious leader of the Black Hundreds, who staged many of the pogroms against the Jews, formulated the church's policy vis-à-vis the Jews in the motto: "One-third of the Jews will convert, one-third will die, and one-third will flee the country." The antisemitic policy, continued under Nicholas II (1894–1917), led to pogroms in 1903, in Kishinev and other parts of the country in which many Jews lost their lives. Elements of Russia's antisemitic circles produced the forgery of a supposed Jewish plot to control the world, known as *The Protocols of the Elders of Zion*, which stoked the fires of anti-Jewish hatred, and still does in many places. In 1913, the government launched a blood libel trial in Kiev in which Mendel Beilis was accused of killing a Christian child, but he was eventually exonerated. These antisemitic measures caused a mass emigration of Jews from Russia, especially to the United States, and about two million Jews left between 1881 and 1914. The February 1917 revolution abolished all restrictions affecting the Jews. In the Civil War that followed the Bolshevik Revolution of October 1917, many Jews fell victim to the opponents of the revolution, known as Whites (as against the Communist Reds, whose Red Army was commanded by the Jewish Leon Trotsky). Many Jews were massacred, especially in Ukraine, by Whites under the leadership of Petlura. It is estimated that 530 Jewish communities were attacked under the slogan of "Strike at the Jews and save Russia," and there were more than 60,000 fatalities.[1]

Of the five million Jews in the Soviet Union, half were killed during the German occupation. In preparation of the invasion (codenamed *Barbarossa*), orders were issued to exterminate all the Jews as quickly as possible. These orders were carried out by special killing squads known as *Einsatzgruppen*. In Kiev, close to 34,000 Jewish men, women, and children were murdered within a two-day period (Sept. 29–30, 1941) in the Babi Yar valley. The *Einsatzgruppen* carried out one deadly *Aktion* after another, in which 40 percent of the Jews in many regions were murdered. By the end of 1941, a third of the entire Jewish population of eastern Belorussia had been exterminated. The Minsk ghetto, with its 100,000 Jews, remained in existence until October 1943, when it too underwent killing raids; approximately 10,000 Jews escaped into the forests, where many joined partisan units. In the Romanian-controlled area of Ukraine, known as Transnistria, Jews were herded into concentration camps where many died from hunger, cold, epidemic diseases, and occasional killings. In addition the Romanians conducted major killing raids in the Ukrainian city of Odessa, where 26,000 Jews were killed during the four-day period of October 23–26, 1941, and also in Iaşi (Jassy), which is actually in Romania.

The local population in Russia was by and large indifferent to these unprecedented mass killings. Some participated in the killing of Jews, seeing them as the authors or collaborators of the Stalinist repressions of earlier years. The Nazi-propagated notion of a vicious Judeo-Bolshevik adversary fell on willing ears; many (especially in Ukraine and Lithuania) welcomed the German army as liberators, and were led to believe that killing Jews, irrespective of age, sex, and political affiliation, was an appropriate way to participate in the struggle against communism. Local policemen and German-organized militia actively engaged in killing Jews; in fact, they outnumbered the relatively limited number of soldiers (3,000) serving in the *Einsatzgruppen,* who were spread over the vast distances of the conquered regions of the Soviet Union. It is doubtful whether the Germans could have accomplished the shooting of an estimated 1.25 million Jews within so relatively short a time without the collaboration of native law-enforcement and security organs. In a September 17, 1941 dispatch, a German official noted that in Khmelnik, Ukraine, after the murder of 229 Jews, "the reaction of the population at the liberation from Jews was so overwhelming that the result was a special thanksgiving prayer." In Belorussia and Russia proper, the reaction was less enthusiastic, but the population was, in general, not opposed to the drastic steps applied by the Germans toward the Jews, and some made sure not to miss out on the opportunity to loot Jewish property. There were, however, some people who, in spite of the personal danger, sheltered Jews and were apprehended and put to death. Mayor Senitsa of Kremenchuk, Ukraine, was shot for his complicity with a local priest named Romansky to register Jews as Christians and provide them with false credentials. In Lviv, eight of the fifty-three people sentenced to death by special German courts were shot for sheltering Jews (*Judenbeherbergung*).[2]

Before inquiring how the churches responded to the frenzied German onslaught on the Jews with the support of local law-enforcement forces, a few words need to be said about the structure of the churches in Russia and Ukraine. In both regions, the Russian Orthodox Church was the dominant denomination, followed by the Roman Catholic Church (in western Belorussia), the Uniate Church (a denomination that practiced an Orthodox rite but accepted the authority of the Catholic papacy), and various Baptist groups. The Russian Orthodox Church was headed by a patriarch whose seat was in Moscow and who was recognized by the Soviet regime. However, in Ukraine there was a separate Autocephalous Ukrainian Orthodox Church. This strongly nationalist church was headed during the war, with Nazi support, by Metropolitan Panteleimon, and his assistant Filofei. As for the Uniate Church, it was headed by the charismatic Metropolitan Andrei Sheptitzky, who was also an important figure in the Ukrainian nationalist movement, and maintained his church's allegiance to the Vatican and the pope. The extent of his collaboration with the invading Germans is still a subject of spirited debate. Like other Ukrainian nationalists, he greeted the Germans as liberators from Russian communism and urged his Ukrainian countrymen to help them win the war. However, by August 1942, Sheptitzky had become disenchanted with the Nazi overlords of his country, due to the terror tactics they employed against opponents of their policy and their lack of concessions with regard to Ukrainian national aspirations. In a letter to the pope, he mentioned the murder of over 200,000 Jews and for the first time condemned the Nazis as worse and "more devilish" than the Communists, likening German behavior to that of "a band of crazy people or wild wolves." Notwithstanding this, in Sheptitzky's mind, Hitler's Germany represented the lesser of two evils, by comparison with Stalin's Russia. This led him, in early 1943, to give his blessing to the creation of a Ukrainian SS Division to fight alongside the Germans, and he appointed clerics from his church as chaplains, headed by a certain Vasyl Laba. The division's oath-taking ceremony took place in Sheptitzky's cathedral, and the service was conducted by his assistant, bishop, Yosif Slipyi. At the same time, Sheptitzky was not indifferent to Jewish pleas for help, especially on behalf of children, and he allowed them sheltered in his church's institutions, such as Zvi Chameides (now Barnea), who was hidden in Studite church orphanages, first in Uhniv, then in Bzuchowitze, where he met other Jewish children in hiding. From there, Zvi and his brother Leon were was taken to a Studite monastery in Lviv, where they met Father Stek Marko, who escorted them to separate hiding places.[3]

Members of the Orthodox Autocephalous Church also harbored pro-German sentiments. Archbishop Polikarp, in Lutsk and Kovel, convened a church synod which called upon the Ukrainian people to help the Germans win a quick victory in the war. The church's head in Rovno, Bishop Platon, in a pastoral letter, praised Hitler, "who consistently leads an uncompromising struggle against the anti-religious Communist regime," adding that "we will assist the German army in every way to conclude this war in victory." Special church services were held in Kharkov to celebrate Hitler's birthday on April 20, 1942, during which mention was made of his "genial significance . . . in rescuing the Ukrainian people and all of Europe from godless communism."

Sadly, in 1942, clerics of the Autocephalous Orthodox church openly called on their flocks not to assist Jews. Such as the call of a priest in Kovel, in May 1942, not to provide Jews with bread, water, and shelter, and to inform the Germans about any Jews in hiding, for, he stated, the Jews were to be wiped off the face of the earth. On the eve of the liquidation of the city's Jews, a special thanksgiving prayer was held in church, conducted by Ivan Guba, in which God and Hitler were praised in one breath. After being sprinkled with holy water, Ukrainian policemen left the church to launch a killing spree on the city's Jews. There were only a few clerics in Ukraine who helped Jews—a few lone voices in a sea of hatred spawned from the pulpits of many churches.[4]

* * *

Turning to clerics who aided Jews, we begin with Aleksey Glagolev of the Russian Orthodox Church. His father, Alexander Glagolev, a priest in Podol (a Kiev suburb) and professor of theology, had acquired a good knowledge of biblical Hebrew and of Judaism and its rituals. During the pogroms in Kiev in October 1905, he confronted the rioters with a cross raised on high, at which sight they turned on their heels. Later, during the framed-up ritual murder trial of Mendel Beilis in 1913, Alexander Glagolev was asked by the court to give an opinion. He denied that the Jewish ritual prescribed the use of blood from Christian children, there being no intimation of this anywhere in Jewish religious literature. His son, Aleksey Glagolev, was the senior priest of a church in Kiev. During the Babi Yar massacres in September 1941, Aleksey and his wife Tatiana saved some of the Jews by hiding them either in the church or in his home and other safe places. Isabelle Minkin-Yegoruchev, for instance, hid temporarily with her non-Jewish husband's relatives, who referred her to Aleksey Glagolev. Glagolev's wife Tatiana volunteered to give her a passport (with the picture appropriately replaced) and a baptismal certificate, and referred her to some peasant acquaintances in the nearby village of Zlodievka (name changed after the war to Ukrainka), where she stayed for eight months. When the local authorities became suspicious and summoned her to answer questions about her identity, she managed to talk her way out but decided to leave the area. Late in the evening of November 29, 1941, she headed back to Glagolev's home, where she remained sheltered together with her daughter Ira, hiding in the bell tower of Glagolev's home. She related that Glagolev helped other Jews, among them Tatiana Shevelev and her mother Yevgenia. Glagolev found old blank baptismal forms, on which he entered slightly forged new names. Armed with this document, Tatiana and her mother were admitted into a house belonging to Glagolev's church.[5]

As for Miriam Druch, née Yakira in 1933, she lived in the Dubno region, where her father was able to get her a false certificate under the name Marusia.

Then, with the help of others, she was taken to the home of the Russian Orthodox priest Ignatiy Grogul, who lived with his wife Varvara in the village of Velike Zahore, located in a wooded area. There Miriam/Marusia stayed from fall of 1942 until the area's liberation. Part of the time, she was hidden; other times, she tended the cows and did household chores. On occasion, the Groguls journeyed to Dubno and brought back greetings from Miriam's parents; they did not survive. As danger mounted, Miriam had to remain in hiding all the time and was allowed to move around only indoors, with the curtains drawn. She had to hide (under the bed or elsewhere) whenever visitors showed up. After the liberation, Miriam joined a cousin in Dubno and left for Israel.[6] Tlusta, in eastern Galicia, was a town with about 5,000 residents, including 3,000 Jews. When the Russians retreated in June 1941 in anticipation of the German advance, local Ukrainians armed with all sorts of makeshift weapons decided to rob and kill the Jews. At this critical point, Father Antin Izvolski organized and led a group of people to protect the Jewish population. In this dramatic confrontation, Izvolski's group succeeded in repelling the rioters. Izvolski continued to help Jews during the years of the German occupation as far as possible, including sheltering some in his home, and preaching in church on the duty of Christians to protect the Jews. Luckily for him, he was not harmed although a priest in a nearby village who also spoke out in favor of the Jews was murdered.[7]

We continue with a few more stories pertaining to Ukraine. In Nepolokovtsy village, in the Chernovtsy region (Cernovici, under Romanian rule), Izakh and Adelya Gaber and their two children, Dora and Genrich, were assembled in the village square by Romanian and German soldiers together with the rest of the village's fewer than 100 Jews. They were about to be machine-gunned to death when Father Ivan Sherbanovich appeared on the scene to investigate the commotion. A Romanian officer, taking him for a Jew, pushed him into the crowd with the other Jews. Taking off his coat to reveal the large cross around his neck, he begged and pleaded with the Romanians not to shoot the Jews. After some haggling the soldiers acceded to his request and told the Jews they could leave.[8] Further to the east, in the village of Zabuzhye, Vinnitsa region, one night in December 1942, Semeion Borochovski escaped from the nearby camp at Pechora and went to the home of Father Fiodor Zavirukha. He was given food and told to spread word that anyone escaping from the camp would be welcome in the priest's home to rest and eat and would be given additional food. Even some escaping children were taken into Zavirukha's home for brief spells. Some adults also hid in his home for a while.[9] In Genivyan, on the Bug River, Dora Beigel, born 1924, and her family were sheltered by Vladimir Dlozhevski (and wife Maria), as well as other fleeing Jews. The Beigels remained in the priest's cellar for two months. After the police undertook a search of the house but failed to find them, the Beigels decided to leave. Father Dlozhevski helped them to cross the Bug River and reach the Vorochilovka ghetto in the Romanian sector, which seemed at the time to be a safer place. The priest continued to help them by sending money and food until the area's liberation in March 1944.[10]

Turning to Belarus, we have the story of the Russian Orthodox priest Konstantin Komar, whose wife Maria had befriended Dina Lesker before the war. While she was confined in the Pinsk ghetto, the Komars invited her to visit them and give chemistry lessons to their two daughters. In time they decided to shelter Dina rather than allow her to return to the ghetto. After converting, she received from Father Komar a new certificate in the name of Galina Shavel, with which she freely circulated in the city, and even joined the church choir. Fearing betrayal by people who knew her, she moved to the village of Dobroslavka, where she stayed with the priestly family of Peotr Tsikhotski until the area's liberation. She then returned to Pinsk to resume her teaching career.[11] Also worth noting is the story of Anton Ketchko who served as pastor (presbyter) of a Protestant evangelical church in Minsk, the capital of Belarus. During the occupation, the city council asked Ketchko to supervise two of the city's municipal orphanages, knowing very well that there were many Jewish children there. Anton Ketchko and wife Nina immediately agreed. Supported by a trustworthy staff, Nina brought food and other necessities from their parishes for the benefit of the children. During German searches, the Jewish children were locked up in the basement, with other children replacing them to make up the count of all the children. A friendly German official, who attended services in Ketchko's chapel, gave him advance warning of German checkup raids of the premises. The Ketchko daughter Lida once found a Jewish boy wandering aimlessly in the field after his parents had been shot, and she brought him home, where he was sheltered for a while before being moved to the orphanage under Ketchko's care. Of the 126 children in the two orphanages under Ketchko's care, 72 were Jewish. Some of them were gradually turned over for adoption. After the war, in November 1945, Ketchko was arrested for reasons not fully clear and sentenced to ten years at hard labor in a camp. He was released in 1953, after Stalin's death.[12]

We now return to the Studite Church, which was centered in western Ukraine (formerly eastern Polish Galicia), and to Kazimierz Sheptitzky, also known as Brother Klement, the superior general of the Studite monastic order and the brother of the church's head, Andrei Sheptitzky. As told by Adam Daniel Rotfeld, born 1938, his father Dr. Leon Rothfeld, an attorney, was the legal representative of the Studite monastery in the town of Univ. In late 1942, under instructions from Klement Sheptitzky, and with the agreement of Adam's parents, the Studite monk Varnava took Adam into the monastery orphanage of the Assumption of the Virgin Mary in Univ. This was last time that Adam, renamed Danylo Chervynsky, saw his parents. There were fifteen other children in the orphanage, including two Jewish boys, Leon Chameides and Odet Amarant. Kurt I. Lewin, born 1925, son of Rabbi Ezekiel Lewin of Lviv, was another recipient of Brother Klement's aid, referred to him by Metropolitan Andrei Sheptitzky. The Studite monks sheltered Kurt and his brother in their monasteries for two years. Kurt was renamed Roman Mytka and introduced as a novice, with Klement providing him with false identity and baptismal documents. Kurt had moved there from his previous hiding place in the monastery of St. John the Baptist in Lyczakiv (a suburb of Lviv). After a stay in the monastery in Univ, he was taken to the St. Andrew house in Luzky, in the Carpathian Mountains, and then to the St. Josaphat monastery in Leopolis. Father Mark Stek, the superior of the Studite monastery of St. John the Baptist in Lyczakiv, near Lviv, was responsible to Klement for the arrangements to shelter Jews in Studite monasteries and convents. These included Kurt's brother, the sons of Rabbi Chameides, Mrs. Abraham and her daughter, the Podoszyn family, the son of Amarant, and two families sheltered by Brothers Lazar and Teodosy (Tadeusz Cerbrynski) in a shoe factory they managed, and others. After the war, in November 1945, Kurt Lewin assisted Father Stek and a fellow cleric, Father Anton Ryzak, both disguised as Jews to escape with him from Communist-controlled Poland to Germany.[13] Brothers Lazar and Teodosy were also instrumental in saving Avraham and Feiga Fink, and their two daughters, Hanna and Gila, aged respectively twelve and six. The Finks were hidden in the factory's cellar, whereas the children were turned over to the care of Sister Helena Witer, also known as Ihumenia Jozefa. At night, Avraham Fink occupied himself with work in the shop, and remained hidden during the daylight hours, and the two monks took care of the Finks during the whole period of hiding. Ihumenia Jozefa was in charge of the convents of the Studite church, where she sheltered Jewish children referred to her by Metropolitan Sheptitzky. After personally admitting the children and examining their condition, she dispersed them in the church's convents in the Lviv region. Some of the children were baptized, but at the end of the war, they reportedly were all returned to Jewish hands. Rabbi David Kahana's wife was sheltered by Ihumenia Jozefa in a convent in Skalat after she fled from the Lviv ghetto, while her husband, Rabbi Kahana, found shelter in Sheptitzky's compound (the only Jew to be sheltered there). Metropolitan Sheptitzky also instructed Father Nikanor, head of the Studite Order in Lviv, to gather fleeing Jewish children and disperse them in the area's Studite monasteries and orphanages.[14]

Metropolitan Andrei Sheptitzky headed the Uniate Catholic Church in western Ukraine, centered in Lviv, known as Lwów under Polish rule. During the Nazi occupation, he was involved in the rescue of a number of Jews, especially children. Zvi Barnea (formerly Chameides) related how in September 1942, as a ten-year old boy, he was brought by his father, Rabbi Kalman Chameides, to Sheptitzky's official residence, located near his St. George's Cathedral. As Rabbi Chameides unfolded the bitter fate of the Jews, the venerable Metropolitan Sheptitzky comforted the rabbi with the words, "After the storm the sun always shines." Several days later, Zvi was admitted to a Uniate church orphanage; thence, to various monasteries, where the Uniate monks ensured his safety. He was later joined by his younger brother, Leon, and met other Jewish children in hiding, including Nathan Lewin, the brother of Kurt Lewin. Likewise for the 1931–born Ludwig Podoshin, sheltered by a Uniate priest, whereas his parents were hidden elsewhere in adjacent church buildings. Lili Pohlmann (born Stern), was also helped by Sheptitzky's church, together with her mother, Cecylia Stern, where they hid in several convents in the Lviv region. Her immediate benefactor was Sister Helena Witer (Ihumenia Jozefa), who headed the sisterhood of the Studite church.[15] Rabbi David Kahana, one of Lviv's eminent prewar rabbis, was one of those sheltered by Sheptitzky. The two had known each other before the war. When Kahana came to tell him about the August 1942 massacre of 7,000 Jews, "I could discern that the man was shocked. Many tears flowed from his eyes as he listened to my litany on the liquidation in the Lviv ghetto." In June 1943, fleeing from the Janowska camp, Kahana was temporarily sheltered in the metropolitan's private library before being placed in a Uniate monastery. Kahana survived in hiding until the city's liberation by the Russians in July 1944.[16]

The story of Sheptitzky's activities during the war years proved much more convoluted and complicated than at first sight. He was an important political figure in the Ukrainian national movement, which was known for its fierce antisemitism, and which clamored for independence from Russia, in partnership—for lack of a better choice—with Nazi Germany. Lviv, Sheptitzky's center of operations, counted some 160,000 Jews when the Germans swept into the city on June 30, 1941. Then one *Akzion* (the Nazi euphemism for violent deportation and killing raids) followed another without let-up, with the active participation of many Ukrainians in and out of uniform, until the Jewish community was totally decimated, and on November 23, 1943, the city was festively declared *Judenrein,* "clean of Jews." A large population of 160,000 Jews had been decimated within less than three years, with the active participation of many Ukrainians, and under the watchful eye, and literally under the window, of the most venerable religious and political figure in town, Andrei Sheptitzky. News of the ongoing reign of terror on the city's Jews reached Sheptitsky's ears in the Uniate Church compound on Mount Yur from many prelates, who told him of the extermination of the Jews in his city; especially because, in the words of Kurt Lewin, "the outrage perpetrated against the Jews was carried out with the assistance of a large segment of the Christian population." Sheptitzky's response to these unprecedented horrific events was and is still the subject of heated debate among students and survivors of the Holocaust. [17]

As the incontestably foremost religious-spiritual figure in Ukrainian society in Lviv and eastern Galicia, uppermost in Andrei Sheptitzky's mind were the national aspirations of his adopted Ukrainian people. As a political figure, he was president of the Ukrainian National Council, revered and respected by every faction in the movement even though they sometimes resorted to violence against each other. The Communists loomed in his mind as the personification of a double evil, against both God and the Ukrainian people, and he therefore looked forward to a German-Ukrainian alliance, which would ensure an independent Ukraine.[18] As a Christian clergyman, he was not free from the traditional Christian theological antisemitism, and his often-reported friendliness toward Jews was colored by ulterior considerations, as is given ample testimony by the following passage from a surprisingly frank prewar admission of his true motivations: "When I face an audience of Jews who are ready to listen to me, I cannot help but see them as fellow men exposed to eternal perdition. That is why I consider it my duty to take advantage of this opportunity to convey to them at least a word of the Lord's revelations. I accomplish this while talking to them. Indeed, I do it in their tongue and language. . . . This is the only way to bring the revealed truth closer to the listeners' souls. . . . And if there is a spark of religious sentiment in the soul of any of them, it might be kindled under the influence of the uttered words of the Holy Scripture . . . Every thread of Christian love for one's fellow man which links the faithful with nonbelievers may become, by the Grace of God, an opportunity for bringing them nearer to Christ's teaching."[19]

In 1942, in a communication to the Vatican in which he bewailed the Nazi killing of Jews, Sheptitzky added the consolable afterthought that perhaps this was part of a greater divine plan, for "among the massacred Jews there are many souls who have converted to God, because never in all the centuries were they placed in a situation like the present one, facing for months on end the possibility of a violent death."[20] The theological justification of the cruel fate of the Jews at the hands of the Nazis came out again in an intimate conversation with Rabbi Kahana, whom he was sheltering in his own residence. As related by Kahana, Sheptitzky asked him, late one evening: "Have you ever thought about it and asked yourself, What is the source of the hatred and savage persecution of the Jewish people from ancient times until the present? What is its origin?" He then quoted from Matthew 27:25, where the assembled Jews at the crucifixion site are said to have shouted that Jesus' blood be "on us and our children." "If you ponder this and take into consideration the relevant chapters in the New Testament," Sheptitzky told the rabbi, you will understand what is happening to the Jews. The next day, agonizing over the pain he had caused the frightened rabbi, Sheptitzky apologized. At a time "when the Jewish people bleed to death and sacrifice hundreds of thousands of innocent victims, I should have known better than to touch upon this subject. I knew that such a conversation aggrieved you greatly. I ask you to forgive me." He regretted having added to the rabbi's pain but not the religious justification for the persecution of the Jewish people, a theology from which he did not retract.[21]

Insofar as his collaboration with the Germans is concerned, Sheptitzky's support for the organization of a Ukrainian Legion to help the Germans dates back to January 1940, months before the invasion of the Soviet Union, when he met with Professor Hans Koch and Dr. Otto Waechter, respectively of the *Abwehr* (military intelligence) and of Nazi governor Hans Frank's office. Two Ukrainian battalions (*Nachtigall* and *Roland*) were formed, both commanded by German officers, and both under the religious care of a military chaplain appointed by Sheptitzky, and they marched into Lviv with the German army.[22] On July 2, 1941, several days after the German occupation of Lviv and the three-day pogrom of the city's Jews by local Ukrainians, Sheptitzky, in a printed pastoral letter to the Ukrainian people, blessed God for the "new period in the life of our motherland. The victorious German army . . .we welcome with joy and appreciation for our deliverance from the enemy." In the words of historian Shimon Redlich, Sheptitzky's response to the German invasion "was positive and even enthusiastic."[23] During the "Petliura Days" pogrom, starting on July 25, 1941, Sheptitzky, disregarding the renewed shedding of Jewish blood in his city, called on Ukrainians to assist the Germans and cooperate with them. Toward the end of August 1941, as the killings of Jews in Lviv intensified, Sheptitzky, in a dispatch to the Vatican, stated categorically that "we are indeed obliged to support the German army, which freed us from the Bolshevik regime, so that it can bring this war to a positive conclusion, which—God granting—will eliminate atheistic and militant Communism once and for all." Still favoring a alliance with Germany, in February 1942, as chairman of the National Council, Sheptitzky added his signature to those of other nationalist leaders in a letter addressed "To His Excellency, the Fuehrer Adolf Hitler," in which they protested the German reluctance to include more Ukrainians "in the armed struggle against their traditional enemy," and assuring Hitler that the "leading circles in Ukraine" were still willing to cooperate with Germany "in order to establish the New Order in Ukraine and throughout Europe." There is little doubt that Sheptitzky knew that in Hitler's mind the New Order meant a Europe without Jews. This letter, however, which was stopped by the German censor in Lviv and never reached Berlin, drew a sharp German reaction—the dissolution of the Ukrainian National Council, headed by Sheptitzky, and the postponement of any further discussions about an independent Ukraine.[24] Some reports state that in February 1942, he wrote to SS-head Himmler protesting, not the killing of Jews, but the use of Ukrainian militia in that sordid undertaking. There is, however, no record of the letter, nor of Himmler's reaction to this purported letter.[25] Sheptitzky was more outspoken in a later communication to the Vatican on August 29, 1942; after the dissipation of hopes of Ukrainian independence, and the ongoing enslavement of the local population to suit German military needs. In this letter he expressed his horror at the "regime of terror that is becoming more intolerable every day"; a regime that "is perhaps even more evil than the Bolshevik. . . . it is almost diabolical. . . . They treat the villagers like Negroes in the colonies. . . . It is very simply as if a pack of raving or rabid wolves had fallen upon a poor people." The Nazis, he continued, represented "a caricature of every idea of civilization and order . . . hatred of everything good and beautiful."[26] These protests, however, were voiced in private; the Ukrainian populace in western Ukraine, who equated Jews with the hated Communists, knew nothing of it, and they continued to commit the worst excesses against the Jews in their midst, with no dissenting voice from Sheptitzky. However, in November 1942, Sheptitzky did go public with a pastoral letter under the heading "Thou Shalt Not Kill," in which he decried the random killing of innocent people, leaving their wives and children helpless. At the time, most Ukrainian Jews had already been liquidated, so the reference to helpless women and children could not have meant them (all Jews irrespective of sex and age were killed), but pertained to the internecine warfare between Ukrainian factions, and between Ukrainian and Polish nationalists, which was beginning to assume alarming proportions. At any rate, the Jews were not mentioned by name, although he may also have had them in mind, as his supporters claim in his defense; but for the unsophisticated masses, many of who participated in the massacres of Jews, this had to be clearly spelled if it was to have any impact.[27]

Sheptitzky undoubtedly was caught between his sincere desire to stop the massacres of Jews and his lifelong passionate goal to gain independence for his beloved Ukrainian people, which, in the context of the Nazi-Soviet war, called for some form of collaboration with a Germany headed by Adolf Hitler.[28] Even more baffling to the student of this charismatic person is his giving his blessings to the creation of an Ukrainian division in the ranks of the SS in early 1943, in an effort to stem the Soviet army's advance. After giving his consent, he was unable to participate in the oath-taking ceremony for health reasons and referred this task to his coadjutor, Bishop Yosif Slipyi.

Sheptitzky, however, appointed five military chaplains, one of whom gave a sermon on the struggle against Bolshevism at a Mass celebrated for the soldiers by Bishop Slipyi. During the division's twelve-month existence, it was involved mainly in the pursuit of anti-German partisan elements in Slovakia and Slovenia, as well as Jews hiding in the forests.[29] Since the Ukrainian cause was apparently uppermost in his mind, Sheptitzky could not bring himself to discipline and rein in compatriots involved in an unbridled killing spree against the Jews, and thereby he failed the great moral challenge posed for him by the events of the day. While the killings continued, he met with the leaders implicated in these acts, both Germans and Ukrainians, continued to urge collaboration with the Germans even to the point of encouraging the creation of a Ukrainian SS division, and at the same time, in private, denounced the Nazis for their inhumane behavior and personally helped to rescue some Jews. In his relations to Jews during the Holocaust, Sheptitzky yielded "a complex picture of diverse and often contradictory reactions," according to the historian Shimon Redlich."[30] Another historian, Hansjakob Stehle, in a book dedicated to the memory of Sheptitzky, asked: "What was it that had moved the Metropolitan, despite his deep abhorrence of Nazi rule, once again to give his blessing to collaboration with the German regime, even under the SS emblem? . . . What motivated him, just one year before the total collapse, to support the formation of a Ukrainian SS division?" The man still remains a riddle.[31]

We conclude with some fascinating stories about Baptist ministers and laymen, sometimes referred to as Sabbatarians, who together with other Protestant fundamentalists stood out from their neighbors in their willingness to rescue Jews. Their communities were spread over the Volyn region in northern Ukraine and adjacent Belarus. One cannot speak here of a firm and hierarchical church structure, but, in the true sense of classical Protestantism, of a priesthood of all believers. They also held the notion of the Jews as the Chosen People, to be protected and preserved for all time. The following stories will exemplify this further.

Fanya Bass-Rosenfeld, born 1922, fled from Rafalivka, near Rovno, Volyn region, in August 1942, and headed in the direction of the Baptist habitations, where she begged for food. Finally arriving at the home of Filip and Teklya Konyukh, in Mulchitsy village, she slept over that night. The following morning, Filip Konyukh took her to the Baptists' weekly gathering at preacher Konon Kaluta's home in the nearby village of Mlynok. As the unofficial head of the local Baptist community, Kaluta preached on the obligation to save Jews. He would take Fanya to his community's assembly, where they gathered for prayers on Sundays, and Fanya participated in readings from the Bible. When the fiercely antisemitic Bulba partisans invaded the village, Kaluta moved Fanya to his sister in a nearby village, where she stayed for two months, and then was sent to hide with another family. Sender Apelbaum, born 1926, who was also aided by the local Baptist community, recalled the words of welcome from one of the faithful: "I consider it a privilege to be the lucky one to whom God has sent a Jew." Apelbaum added: "Wherever we met Baptists, they impressed me as great friends of the Jewish people, and believers in an obligation to save them."[32]

As for Alexander Schwartzblat-Sarid, the story also began in Rafalivka, when he fled from the Germans in September 1942, and together with two companions headed for the Baptist habitation in the Pinsk area (Polesia, today in Belarus), a region known for its marshlands. Reaching Yurkovo, they were met by a man who invited them in. It was Ivan Oshurko, who immediately began to prepare food for his guests. He explained that his father, a preacher in nearby Propobeidnik, would arrive the following morning. When Nikolai Oshurko appeared, holding a Bible under his arm, he greeted the new arrivals warmly. Then, in Alexander's words: "He opened the book and read from it: 'Blessed is the Lord who delivered the children of Israel from Egypt.' He then added: 'Blessed be the Lord who will gather the children of Israel from all corners of the world.' He proceeded to open a sack filled with rye, took a handful in his hand, shook it twice, and said movingly: 'See how the seeds gather in one place, so you too; after the war you will gather in the Holy Land.' He added: 'A remnant will be saved,' then closed his eyes." The three guests then sat at the table with the other members of the family, who numbered eight people. The household grandfather stood up and, with closed eyes, said: "Lord, save my family and the children of Israel." They then sat down for breakfast. Nikolai dispersed the three, whereas Alexander stayed with the Oshurkos for eight months. "He called me *Nibozh* (son of God), and I called him *Deydushka* (grandpa)." For two months Alexander remained hidden from strangers and only two families knew of his presence. "It was a great honor for them to save me." They gave him a book in Polish on bee tending, and Alexander in turn taught mathematics to their two small children. He usually stayed in the hayloft and joined them for meals. When winter settled in, he was allowed to sleep in the home. Grandpa Nikolai (same name as his son) once told Alexander: "My house is like the house of the patriarch Abraham. Whoever comes in hungry, leaves sated. You may bring me any Jew you meet. Everyone is invited to visit here." His son Nikolai had great influence over his community, which he led in prayers and sermons. Alexander would on occasion leave their home to visit other Jews in their hiding places and listen to their stories. In the spring of 1943, Alexander finally left the Oshurko family for good when he moved to a partisan-controlled area.[33]

Especially moving is the story of Savko and Okseniya Mironiuk and Ivan Yatsyuk, in the Lutsk region, Volyn province. They saved young David Prital, who had been obliged to move on after staying with a friendly Polish family over the winter of 1942–43, but where? He recalled the prewar business trips with his grandfather in the Ukrainian countryside. They had visited a farmer whom his grandfather had described as a saint, who belonged to one of the Baptist sects in the region. David remembered the strange prayers and cere-monies of these believers, held on the shores of the Styr River, where they had themselves baptized. The maidservant in his parents' home had also been a Baptist, and David fondly recalled her spirituality and her love for the Jewish people. He resolved to seek them out and, with their help, to reach the Ludmir ghetto or join up with friendly partisans. Proceeding in the direction of Dubno, and after a long walk in the night, he approached one of the Baptist homes. Out stepped a man in peasant's garb walking directly toward David. As they passed each other, the man stopped, looked David in the eye, hesitated for a moment, then, taking him by the hand, invited him in. "God has brought us an important guest," he joyfully remarked to his startled wife. "Come, let us thank the Lord for it." The man's name was Ivan Yatsyuk. He and his wife fell on their knees and murmured a silent prayer. David listened as they thanked God for the privilege of meeting a son of Israel and implored Him to help the saving remnant—the Jews hiding in forlorn fields and distant forests. Rising from prayer, they invited David to supper. Before partaking of the food, Ivan read from the Bible, and told David: "Try to understand; I too am a Jew." To David's astonishment, Ivan continued: "I am spiritually a Jew, and this encounter with you gives me much food for thought because it confirms the words of the prophets that a saving remnant will be spared." Deep in the night, Ivan took David to a neighbor's home, since his own place was not too secure because of its next-door to the home of a rabid Jew-hater. From then on, David rotated between several Baptist homes. One evening, Ivan told him: "We usu-ally place our trust in our fellow believers. But man is, in the final account, tested in adversity and in difficult situations. Tonight we shall take you to a farmer who does not know you. His attitude and response will test the sincer-ity of his faith. There is no danger to you. At the most, he will refuse you his hospitality and we shall take you elsewhere. But to us, his response will be a serious indication of the strength and depth of his faith." David knocked on the man's door and presented himself as a homeless person seeking shelter for a few nights. There ensued an argument between the man and his wife, who strenuously objected to taking in a stranger. When the man said he would not open the door to strangers, David despairingly replied: "What a world this is, when a Jew is refused shelter!" At that, the Baptist farmer turned to his wife: "But it's a Jew; how can we refuse him?" The door suddenly swung open and David was heartily welcomed. On another occasion, a Baptist farmer, notic-ing David's dejected mood, sat down near him and said: "I see you're sad and depressed. Allow me to sing you a song to strengthen your spirit." He began to hum Psalm 126, "When the Lord returned the captives from Zion," in the original Hebrew language! On yet another occasion, David found temporary lodging in the home of another Baptist couple, Savko and Oksenya Mironiuk. There he met Ignatz, a Jewish boy in hiding. Yaslenski, another Baptist with whom David stayed for a few nights, saved David's life during a violent confrontation with Ukrainian nationalists. Denounced by an informer, David was about to be shot in Yaslenski's barn, when his protector confronted the Ukrainians, "Do you realize what you're about to do? This Jew is wandering—estranged and homeless. What has he done to you? The blood of this Jew, if you kill him, will scream out for eternity and haunt you for the rest of your lives. Let him go!" Amazed and taken back at these words, the raiders relented and left. David's life had been saved in the nick of time.[34]

We move to the village of Zavalov in eastern Galicia, where a group of two dozen Jews fleeing from antisemitic Bandera partisans, in the fall of 1943, knocked on the door of Leon and Maria Bilecki and asked for help. This family of Baptist foresters helped the Jews to build a bunker in the nearby forest, while lifting their spirit by sitting up with them and reading verses from the Bible. In the words of Yitzhak Lev, one of the rescued people: "It was hard to believe that there were still people like these, especially Ukrainians, who not only acted in this way for Jews, but also risked their lives and those of their families. . . . They asked us to pray together with them. . . . They brought us a Bible in Polish and Ukrainian."[35] Similarly, Lukian Kondratiuk, a forester near the village of Ozhenino, Rovno region, together with his wife Fedora, sheltered the Kluchnik brothers, Motel and Idel, beginning in September 1942. Lukian's son Feodor (born 1925) explained that his family helped the two brothers and other Jews because "we acted thus in accordance with our evangelical belief, which obligates us to love the people of Israel."[36] Iosif Nechipor, a poor Baptist farmer, living with his sister Yulia near the village of Kontenivka, in the Polish Lublin region, sheltered four members of the Tsukerman family. When they came to his house and asked for aid, he said that God must have sent them and it was his obligation to save them.[37] These are but a few of a larger number of stories about Baptist families who considered it not only an obligation, but a great Christian privilege, to save Jews, whom they viewed as God's elect people, even though they lived amidst a population where many elements considered it a duty to be rid of the Jews in whatever way possible.

Chapter 9
Central and Southeastern Europe: Czech Lands, Slovakia, and Romania

> *The greatest tragedy of the Jewish nation lies in the fact of not having recognized the Redeemer and of having prepared a terrible and ignominious death for Him on the cross. . . . Also in our eyes has the influence of the Jews been pernicious. The church cannot be opposed, therefore, if the state with legal regulations hinders the dangerous influence of the Jews.*
> Catholic bishops, April 1942, Slovakia

> *I have only fulfilled toward my Jewish wards what I learned from their great teachers and prophets.*
> Pastor Přemysl Pitter, 1966, Czech Republic

Czech Protectorate

Up to the end of World War I, the western part of Czechoslovakia was administered by Austria and the eastern part of Slovakia by Hungary in what was then the Austro-Hungarian Empire. In the new state of Czechoslovakia, the Jewish population in 1930 was 357,000; of whom 117,000 lived in Bohemia and Moravia, 137,000 in Slovakia, and 102,000 in Carpatho-Russia.[1] The city of Prague, the capital of Czechoslovakia, claimed one of the oldest Jewish communities in Europe, going back as far as 970 C.E. Up to the modern period, the Jews of the city underwent intermittent persecutions. They were forced to move out of the protected castle city and across the river Moldau (Vltava) to what became the Jewish quarter of Josefov, where they built the Old Synagogue (*Altschul*), the oldest standing synagogue in Europe. As more Jews streamed into Prague, the authorities imposed one humiliating restriction after another: special dress, segregation in a crowded neighborhood, moneylending as the only permitted profession, higher taxes, even a decree that only eldest sons were allowed to marry and found new families, their brothers having to remain single or leave Bohemia. In 1541, King Ferdinand I bowed to local pressure and ordered all Jews to leave within two years, but they were allowed to return in 1545. In 1557, the king again expelled the Jews, and they were again allowed to return several years later. As elsewhere in Europe, the clergy fanned anti-Jewish feelings. Weathering these persecutions, Jewish life continued to prosper, and Prague became an important religious and talmudic study center. Things began to improve under Emperor Joseph II (1780–90), and in the following years the onerous restrictions were gradually removed, with full emancipation granted in 1852. Up to and after 1918, with the establishment of the Czechoslovak republic, Jews participated in the cultural life of the country, including famed authors like Franz Kafka, Max Brod, and Franz Werfel. In the Slovakian region, Andrej Hlinka's Slovak People's Party had an outspokenly antisemitic plank. With the rise of Nazism in Germany, the German minority in the Sudetenland came out in the open and also advocated antisemitic measures. On March 14, 1939, Slovakia declared its independence and became a vassal of Nazi Germany. The next day the remaining parts of Bohemia and Moravia were occupied by Germany and transformed into a "protectorate," while Hungary took over the Carpatho-Russia region at the eastern extreme of the dismembered country (after the war, this region was annexed to the Soviet Union and incorporated into the republic of Ukraine). On March 15, 1939, when the Nazis marched into Prague, the city counted about 56,000 Jews, and altogether there were 118,000 Jews in the whole of Bohemia and Moravia. By October 1941, 26,600 Jews had managed to escape, while 1,291 were deported to Poland, and 88,000 remained. Of these 73,600 were dispatched to Theresienstadt (Terezin) camp, of whom 60,400 were sent to Auschwitz and other death facilities in Poland, to be gassed; only 3,220 survived the depredations of the camps. About 5,200 died on Czech soil by execution and from other causes. On liberation day in Prague, May 5, 1945, there were only 2,800 Jews alive in Bohemia and Moravia who had not been deported (half of them in Prague); most of them were partners in mixed marriages. Theresienstadt was something of a "model" camp designed to fool visitors from the Red Cross about the true nature of concentration camp life. Prisoners there were encouraged to draw, paint, and engage in artistic and cultural activities; that is, until their deportation to the death facilities in nearby Poland.[2]

As for clergy rescuers of Jews, so far we know of only one person, Přemysl Pitter, an evangelical pastor (Bohemian Brothers) in Prague. He founded a home for abandoned and neglected children in the poorest section of Prague. During the Nazi period the authorities prevented the Jewish orphanage from getting milk, but he provided it to them on a regular basis. He was interrogated by the Gestapo, but resumed his milk deliveries as soon as he was released. He also raised money for Jews in need and sheltered in his orphanage some Jews who were married to gentiles and felt threatened. In addition, he visited

Jewish families to lift their spirits and moved some of the threatened Jewish children to a children's home in the town of Myto. In his sermons, he urged his congregants to assist Jews in need. In one sermon, he said: "Trees don't grow to the sky, and better days are ahead, and you will be rewarded from heaven for all you have done for the Jews." At the end of the war, he went to liberated Theresienstadt to collect the surviving Jewish children and take them to convalescent homes. Thirty-five of these children eventually left for Israel. When he received the "Righteous" award in 1966, in Switzerland (where he settled after he was forced to leave his home country, now under Communist control), Pitter stated: "There can be no question of receiving a reward. I have only fulfilled toward my Jewish wards what I learned from their great teachers and prophets. The appreciation toward me from the Jews is for me a great appreciation in my often thankless work."[3]

Slovakia

Slovakia was independent during the war years, but was allied to Nazi Germany. Thus this overwhelmingly Catholic country, ruled by a priest, Father Josef Tiso, faced the challenge of whether it would try to temper the antisemitic zeal of its German ally or rather, as was in fact the case, fan the flames and join in the open season against Jews. The Jewish population in 1939 amounted to approximately 89,000 souls, not counting the area Slovakia was forced to cede to Hungary. One of the first actions instituted by Tiso's government was an anti-Jewish law and the confiscation of Jewish-held enterprises and businesses, and able-bodied Jewish men were sent to labor camps. In 1941, in an effort to clear the capital city of Bratislava of its Jewish inhabitants, 10,000 of the 15,000 Jews were expelled. Some were sent to the labor camps and others to the towns of Trnava, Nitra, and other parts of the country. In February 1942, the Germans formally requested the Slovak government to furnish 20,000 "strong and able-bodied Jews," supposedly for labor assignments. However, the Slovaks suggested that instead of men only, the workers should be accompanied by their entire families, in "the spirit of Christianity." The Germans complied, and charged the Slovaks a fee of 500 German marks "as charges for vocational training" for every deported Jew. In return, the Germans promised that the Jews would never be returned to Slovakia, and no further claims would be made on their property. In other words, the Slovak regime could take possession of this stolen property while the owners were dispatched to the gas chambers. Between March 1942 and October 20, 1942, about 60,000 Jews were deported to Auschwitz and other parts of Poland, to be killed. Thousands of others fled to neighboring Hungary, still free of direct German rule. An additional 5,000 Jews sought protection through conversion to Christianity, of whom the Protestant and Greek Orthodox churches took the lion's share; the Catholics did not bestow baptism too lightly. A Protestant minister named Sedivy was accused by the authorities of having performed no fewer than 717 baptisms of Jews.[4] This caused the government to question the sincerity of the conversions. In the final account, conversion did not always help, and many were deported to the death camps in Poland. Some 25,000 remained in the country—many in hiding; others were exempted from deportation because they were considered "economically vital" by the regime (to the great displeasure of the Germans), and still others were married to Christians. In the fall of 1944, as a result of the Slovak uprising, the Germans entered in full force, and close to 14,000 Jews were deported to the concentration camps. On the eve of liberation (April 30, 1945) there remained only about 4,000–5,000 Jews in Slovakia, either in hiding or circulating with false credentials. The rest had perished in the Holocaust.[5]

Some time after the deportations began in 1942, the Vatican stepped in and asked for clarification of the destinations of these people. The Germans countered by claiming that the deported Jews were having a good time, and were accompanied by rabbis and doctors, and that the converted Jews even had priests to officiate to them. To fool those remaining behind, the Germans had the deportees, upon arrival at Auschwitz, write encouraging postcards to friends and acquaintances at home. Under pressure by the Slovak bishops, Prime Minister Adalbert Tuka asked the Germans to allow a mixed commission to inspect one of the camps to which the Jews had been sent. SS Colonel Adolf Eichmann responded, on June 2, 1942, with an evasive excuse as to why this was not necessary. The Slovak leaders kept insisting, and as a result the Germans agreed that the Jews who had not yet been deported would be concentrated in labor camps on Slovak soil, a situation which prevailed until the German takeover, at which time the deportations resumed.

The response of the churches to the wholesale destruction of the Jewish community is a pretty grim picture. The minority Lutheran Church did, however, take a stand. On May 20, 1942, a meeting of Lutheran bishops, under the chairmanship of Vladimir Cobrda and Samuel Stefan Osusky, issued a pastoral letter which excused the government for finding it "necessary to solve this problem [Jewish] in a just, humane, and Christian way," but stated that it was also necessary to take into consideration that "all men are endowed with the right to live, to earn an honorable livelihood, and the right to family life. It also protects the honor of the Jews as human beings." Thus the racial laws were "contrary to the Christian faith . . . contrary to human feelings, to justice, and to the law of God; they are in no way related to love... If members of the Evangelical Church participated in these deeds, they must be severely condemned." Since only about 13 percent of the Slovak population was Protestant, and the rest Catholic, the important question was what stand the

Catholic hierarchy would take on the mass deportation of the Jewish population. This question assumed special importance in light of the heavily clerically orientation of the Slovakian leadership; the country's president, Monsignor Josef Tiso, was a priest as well as a member of the Hlinka Slovak People's Party. Clergymen also served in the cabinet, and had committed themselves to making Slovakia a model Catholic state. The Nazi point of view was represented by the prime minister, Adalbert Tuka, and the interior minister, Alexander Mach. Moderates and extreme Catholics were united in their antisemitism and their willingness to remove the Jews from the country. The Vatican was represented by Monsignor Giuseppe Burzio, the Holy See's nuncio, who arrived in Slovakia in June 1940. Two months earlier, on April 18, 1939, the government's first Jewish legislation defined Jewishness based on religious factors. When the government ordered that Catholic children of Jewish origin were to leave Catholic schools and henceforth attend Jewish ones, the Vatican secretary of state, Cardinal Luigi Maglione, instructed Burzio to intervene to protect the right of these children to a Catholic education. The Vatican's intervention did not help, for a year later, on September 9, 1941, a new Jewish Code enacted a definition of Jewishness based on racial terms. Here too, Monsignor Burzio again tried to protect converted Jews, and he protested to Tiso that 3,000 Catholics would be obliged to wear the Star of David. He was reassured that this provision would be waived for those who had been baptized before September 10, 1941.[6]

In the Vatican, Cardinal Maglione told Slovak ambassador Sidor that "the Holy See cannot remain indifferent to the painful situation of so many of its children of Jewish origin. . . . They are in a state of great moral, social, and economic inferiority, so great as to practically oblige many of them to heroic actions to remain faithful subjects of the church and, perhaps, to lead some of them into extreme necessity." Not a word of protest about the improper treatment of Jews who were not Catholics. On October 27, 1941, Burzio reported to his superiors in the Vatican what he had learned from Slovak army chaplains on the Russian front about the killing sprees of the mobile *Einsatzgruppen*. This report may have been the first information to reach the Vatican about the massacres of Jews, at least from one of its own diplomats. The Vatican's reaction to Burzio's dispatch, written by Cardinal Tardini, came after a long wait, on December 20, and was couched in generalities voicing a humanitarian concern about innocent victims, but asking him to inquire whether it was Slovak units on the eastern front or Germans who were committing the atrocities. Burzio's reply, on March 11, 1942, reassured the Holy See that the Slovak units had clean hands; the massacres had been committed solely by Germans. "All the Jews in a given place were concentrated at a distance from any inhabited area and killed by machine-gun fire."[7]

Shortly before the deportation of Jews was scheduled to begin, Burzio, the papal nuncio, rejected Prime Minister Tuka's assurance that there was nothing inhuman or unchristian in such an action. He countered, in fact, that "the deportation of 80,000 [actually only 60,000 were deported at this stage] people to Poland at the mercy of the Germans is the equivalent of condemning a great part of them to death." The nuncio in Switzerland, Archbishop Felippo Bernardini, wrote to Rome from Berne on March 11, 1942, transmitting an appeal by Jewish leaders that the pope intervene to mitigate or cancel the deportation of Slovak Jews. Bernardini contacted Maglione again on March 19, relaying the request for papal intervention from Jewish leaders in preponderantly Catholic Slovakia. On March 13, Archbishop Angelo Rotta, the nuncio in Budapest, similarly passed on an appeal urging the pope to attempt to persuade Tiso to cancel the deportation orders, which included Catholic Jews. Attached to Rotta's letter was an appeal from the Jewish community of Bratislava to the pope. "Most Holy Father! The Jewry of all Slovakia, 90,000 souls, has recourse to Your Holiness for help and salvation. We are condemned to destruction. . . . Everything has already been taken away from us (money, linen, clothing, businesses, houses, funds, gold, bank accounts, and all household appliances), and now they want to banish us, as Slovak citizens, to Poland and to send each of us, without money or material goods, to certain destruction and starvation. No one can help us. We place all our hope and confidence in Your Holiness as the safest refuge of all who are persecuted. . . . . Would your Holiness kindly influence the president of Slovakia [Father Tiso], so that, in the name of mankind and neighborly love, he will receive us and not permit our banishment?" A week later Rotta sent a second appeal, this time from the chief rabbi of Budapest, asking the pope to intervene with the Slovak government. At the Vatican, Cardinal Maglione summoned the Slovak ambassador, Sidor, and told him that the Vatican "would like to hope that such information does not correspond to the truth, not being able to consider that in a country which intends to be inspired by Catholic principles, they had to adopt regulations which were so grave and of such painful consequences to so many families." What especially alarmed the Vatican were rumors that the Germans were planning to send several thousand Slovak Jewish girls to act as prostitutes for their front-line troops in Russia. The pope himself was so upset by this news that he instructed Maglione to protest again and appeal to Tiso's sentiments as a priest to prevent this outrage. As it turned, Jewish girls were indeed deported to Poland—not to serve as prostitutes, however, but to be murdered in concentration camps. The deportation of Slovak Jews went on as scheduled. In a long report on March 31, 1942, Burzio reported on the Slovak government's determination to deport all its Jews, even "in the most cruel manner." The government, he said, took full responsibility for the decision and denied that there had been pressure from

Germany. The Slovak parliament passed legislation on May 15, 1942 to retroactively legalize the deportations, depriving Jews of citizenship, and expropriating their property. Exempted were Jews baptized before March 13, 1939 or married to Christians before September 10, 1941, as well as those granted special privileges by Tiso. Burzio reported that the priests who were members of parliament had either voted in favor of the law or abstained, but none had voted against it. One such was Bishop Vojtassak of Scepusio, who claimed that it was best if the ecclesiastical authorities did not create obstacles for the government and for the president, since the Jews were Slovakia's worst enemies, and therefore things should be allowed to run their course.[8]

On April 26, 1942, as the deportations went into high gear, the Catholic bishops issued a pastoral letter to the faithful that began with a broadside against the Jewish people. The Jews, the bishops declared, were a cursed people because of their act of deicide. "The greatest tragedy of the Jewish nation lies in the fact of not having recognized the Redeemer and of having prepared a terrible and ignominious death for Him on the cross. . . . Moreover, the influence of the Jews has been pernicious. In a short time they have taken control of almost all the economic and financial life of the country to the detriment of our people. Not only economically, but also in the cultural and moral spheres, they have harmed our people. The church cannot be opposed, therefore, if the state with legal regulations hinders the dangerous influence of the Jews." The bishops tempered their ire by reaffirming the need to act humanely toward the Jews. They had the right to private property acquired by their own labor and also the right to have their own families. It was a reaffirmation of the classical church position that Jews were to be allowed to subsist, but in a lowly status, while simultaneously accused of crimes so heinous (deicide and social destructiveness) as to make such existence, and co-existence with the larger Christian community, hardly possible. Rabbi and author Irving Greenberg cited the response of the Slovak Archbishop Kametko to a plea for help from the Hasidic Nitra Rebbe in 1942: "It is not just a matter of deportation. You will not die there of hunger and disease. They will slaughter all of you there, old and young alike, women and children, at once—it is the punishment you deserve for the death of our Lord and Redeemer, Jesus Christ— you have only one solution. Come over to our religion and I will work to annul this decree." There were hardly any voices in the Catholic establishment opposing the deportation of Jews—perhaps only a very few. One was Bishop Pavol Jantausch, known to be unequivocally opposed to the deportation of the Jews. It is related that he saved the lives of a rabbi and his wife by driving them around in his car until the deportation train had left.[9]

In early 1943, reports of a possible renewal of the deportation began to circulate. On February 17, the Slovak bishops wrote to the government asking that converts not be deported, especially Catholic converts, because it would make a terrible impression if converted Catholics were abandoned by a Catholic state. That same month, Sister Margit Slachta, in Hungary, suggested that Slovak Jews be interned on Slovak soil, thereby preventing their deportation. On April 7, 1943, Cardinal Tardini, in the Vatican, commented: "In Slovakia the head of the state is a priest. Therefore the scandal is greater, and greater too is the danger that the responsibility can be shifted to the Catholic Church itself." He added that "it would be opportune for the Holy See to again issue a protest. . . . This will make known to the world that the Holy See fulfills its duty of charity rather than attracting the sympathy of the Jews in case they are among the victors, given the fact that the Jews, as much as can be foreseen, will never be too friendly to the Holy See and to the Catholic Church."[10]

On April 7, 1943, Monsignor Burzio took up the Jewish issue with Prime Minister Tuka. Tuka affirmed that it was his task to rid Slovakia of the Jews, whom he described as criminals, and bragged that he was doing this as a practicing Catholic. He claimed to have a clear conscience and the consent of his confessor for what he was doing. The deportation, he emphasized, was being carried out not under German pressure, but on the government's decision and initiative. Baptized Jews (estimated at close to 10,000), he assured the nuncio, would continue to be exempt. In his report to Maglione, on April 10, 1943, about his stormy meeting with the prime minister, Burzio indicated that Tuka was adamant. The prime minister had declared: "When it is a matter of Jews, it is useless to invoke principles of Christianity and humanity. I do not understand why they try to prevent me from carrying out my mission, which is to rid Slovakia of this plague, this band of malefactors and gangsters. . . . The Jews are an asocial and inassimilable race; they are a pernicious and deleterious element, whom it is necessary to eradicate and eliminate without regard." He then suddenly changed course and assured Burzio that "It is my plan to send a commission to ascertain the condition of the Jews deported from Slovakia. If the news of atrocities proves to be true, I will not permit one more Jew to cross the Slovak border." Tuka then defended his Catholic credentials: "I am a convinced and practicing Catholic; I attend holy Mass every day and receive Communion quite frequently; and I am at ease in my work; for me the supreme spiritual authority, more than the bishops, more than the church, is my conscience and my confessor." Burzio, in an attempt to mitigate the behavior of this very Catholic nation, asked diplomatically: "May I at least . . . communicate to the Holy See that the deportation of the Jews of Slovakia did not occur through the initiative of the Slovak government, but under external pressure?" Tuka's response proved disappointing. "I assure you on my honor as a Christian that it is our will and our initiative. This, yes, is true, that I was offered the possibility of realizing my plan, and I certainly did not refuse it. . . . As a functionary of the Vatican, you have done your duty and I will do mine; let us remain friends, but the Jews will depart." The bait thrown by the Vatican representative was left untouched.[11] In the words of John F. Morley, "The Vatican's options were more extensive in Slovakia than in other countries. It was a heavily Catholic country with a priest as president and a prime minister who prided himself on being a practicing Catholic. . . . Yet the Vatican did not act. It issued no threats of excommunication or interdict against the president, the prime minister, or the people. . . . Vatican diplomacy was content to limit itself to the narrow confines of strictly Catholic interests, and an opportunity for a great moral and humanitarian gesture was lost."[12]

Turning to the few Catholic clergy rescuers acknowledged and honored by Yad Vashem, we begin with Michal Maslej, a Greek Catholic priest in the off-the-beaten-track village of Olšavice, near Levoca, who reportedly never tired of preaching to his flock on the duty to help all people in distress. It is told that from the pulpit he reprimanded one villager for accepting payment from a refugee in return for bread. "Such a disgrace must never occur again," he thundered at the greedy man. Not content with preaching, he took an active part in rescue work, arranging sheltering places for Jews who fled to the area after the suppression of the Slovak uprising in September 1944. He personally took the Eugen Hartmann family into his home and helped find a safe place for the Ludovit Fuchs family. The village was liberated on January 25, 1945; during the preceding period none of the villagers betrayed the presence of the fifty Jews in Olsavice to the authorities. When the Communist government removed Maslej from his post in 1950, many of the Jews he had helped to survive now assisted him, and he was grateful for their help. Later on he was restored to his pulpit.[13] In another story, Peter Dudinsky, a Greek Catholic priest in the village of Hodermark, arranged for the Schaechter family, in nearby Podolinec, to hide with the farmer Michal Lesny. The Schaechters moved in with him on May 25, 1942. Later, in the fall of 1942, Dudinsky provided Malvina Schaechter with false credentials. Around the end of 1942, the priest helped Malvina's brother Emil to relocate to a safer hiding place with the forester Misutka. Dudinsky also helped other Jews with hiding places and false identities.[14] Similarly, Stefan Gallo, a priest in Ireg village (name later changed to Jarok), aided Robert Freund (born in 1930), whom he knew from before. Introducing the youngish Robert as a distant relative, he had him serve as an altar boy at Mass. When news spread that Gallo was sheltering a Jew, Robert left, was caught, and sent to Auschwitz, which he survived. Gallo also helped the Jewish Ressler family, who hid in nearby caves (previously used by vineyard workers,) by providing them with food and other things.[15] Finally, in Trencin, in 1942, Imberta Sinska, the Mother Superior of a Notre

Dame convent and orphanage, admitted Eva Poriezova (born 1935), at the request of a local priest. After the German takeover in late 1944, Eva was moved into the nuns' quarters and presented as a niece of one of the Sisters, while her parents were sheltered in the convent's school. It is also reported that nuns of the same Notre Dame order, in Klastor pod Znievom, especially Sisters Jana Novotna and Vilma Cermanova, sheltered the three children of the Kemenyova family: Eva, Maria, and Magda.[16]

Turning to Protestant rescuers, we begin with Vladimir Kuna, the Evangelical pastor in the city of Liptovský Svatý Mikuláš in northern Slovakia. He sheltered as many as twenty-six Jewish children in his church orphanage, and in the case of Laco Teschner, the mother as well, who served as a cook. He also took care to protect the true identities of hospitalized Jewish children. After the suppression of the Slovak uprising, Kuna was arrested in November 1944 and taken to the Gestapo in Bratislava, suspected of having assisted his brother, an underground member. Released from jail in January 1945, Kuna was placed under surveillance by the Gestapo. When an SS unit took over the orphanage, the children were removed to the nearby city of Ružomberok, where the local Evangelical community cared for them. Martha Nimrod, a former Jewish child survivor, wrote that in spite of pressure from the church, Kuna did not try to influence the Jewish children to convert. After the war, Pastor Kuna explained: "I considered it a matter of course that I should help those in need of help. . . . [I] was motivated solely by that love which is described by St. Paul in chapter 13 of his Epistle to the Corinthians."[17]

Julius Derer, a Lutheran Evangelical pastor in Modra, headed a girls boarding school and orphanage in that city, which included Jewish children (such as Gertruda Kaufmann, her sister Vera, and Jana Graf-Tanner). Although the parents had pretended the children were Christians when they left them in his care, Derer knew the truth. Derer generally knew about German raids in advance and hid the Jewish children elsewhere. Gertruda, for instance, was hidden in a wooded area behind the building, then returned to the orphanage after the Gestapo left. During one such raid, the Gestapo first questioned Derer in his home, but he was able to signal to his son to rush to the school and alert his daughter, who worked there as a teacher. She in turn took the Jewish children out into the garden, at a distance from the school building. According to Jana Tanner, née Graf, some of the Jewish children in the boarding school were arrested and taken away, but at least six others in the orphanage were not discovered and survived. Derer also arranged a hiding place for a Jewish doctor named Werner, who had served as Tiso's private physician but was threatened with deportation.[18] In Banska Bystrica, the parents of Oliver Spielberger (today Dov Sokol), born 1925, turned to a friend for help in the summer of 1942. He, in turn, referred them to Vojtech Schaffarovsky, an Evangelical pastor in the village of Kyjatice. Schaffarovsky utilized an empty space in his birth register to enter a notation that the six-member Spielberger family had been baptized on November 25, 1938. The date was important, because the Slovak government had decreed that it would only recognize conversions that had taken place before March 14, 1939, when Slovakia became independent. The Spielbergers then submitted the baptismal documents given them by Schaffarovsky to the local officials. This protected the family from deportation until the German occupation in late 1944, when the family went into hiding, while Dov joined the partisans.[19] We also note the tragic story of Jan Bakoss, an Evangelical pastor in Banska Bystrica, who was executed by the Germans in January 1945 for his participation in the Slovak uprising. He assisted many Jews (as many as 300 according to one report) by providing them with false documents, such as conversion certificates. According to one witness, he told a group of converted Jews that he was doing this in order to save them, and after the war, they could decide whether they wished to remain Christians or not. He also helped Jews with money from a special fund that he managed.[20] Finally, Pavel Teriansky was the pastor in the village of Nemecky Grob (today Velky Grob), near Trnava. When the Jewish dentist Dr. Ludovit Feldmann was ejected from his home in Zilina and ordered to move to Nemecky Grob, he and his family (wife Alzbeta and daughter Margita), were warmly welcomed by Teriansky, and Ludovit was allowed to practice dentistry in the village. In 1943, the Feldmanns were ordered to move to another village. Still later, in August 1944, during the Slovak uprising, when Teriansky learned that the Feldmanns were in distress, he had a church aide secretly bring them to his home, where together with his wife Margita, the three Feldmanns were sheltered. In March 1945, when German soldiers were billeted in his home, Teriansky arranged for the Feldmanns to be hidden in the barn of a friendly farmer. It is reported that Teriansky also gave shelter to several other Jews.[21]

Romania

Romania was known as Dacia in Roman times. Jews have lived there since the era of the Khazars, who converted to Judaism in the ninth century. Centuries later, local rulers granted special charters to attract Jews and encourage them to found commercial centers. Greek Orthodox prelates shaped the first codes of anti-Jewish laws, such as the one in 1640 that denounced Jews as heretics and encouraged Christians not to have any dealings with them. Romania (then consisting of Walachia and Moldavia) became independent at the Congress of Berlin in 1878, but its independence was made conditional on the granting of civil rights to Jews. Instead more antisemitic measures followed, and Jews were denied the right to practice law, teaching, and the other free professions. On the political front, both major political parties, the Liberals and the Conservatives, sponsored antisemitic platforms, and in 1910 the first specifically antisemitic party, the National Democratic Party, was founded under the leadership of university professors A.C. Cuza and Nicolae Iorga. The escalation of anti-Jewish measures led to a mass emigration of Jews, and by the beginning of World War I about 70,000 left. In 1924, there were 796,000 Jews in an enlarged Romania (5 percent of the total): 230,000 in Old Romania (known as Regat), 238,000 in Bessarabia, 128,000 in Bukovina, and 200,000 in Transylvania. In 1929, Corneliu Zelea Codreanu, a leader of the student movement, formed the Archangel Michael League, which later became the Iron Guard, a paramilitary organization with an extremist antisemitic platform. In 1937, a pro-Nazi regime was installed under Octavian Goga. This was, at the time, Europe's second officially antisemitic government after Nazi Germany. The Goga government lasted only forty days, and during this time it did its best to promulgate antisemitic measures. By January 1938, a quarter of a million Jews, about one-third of the total Jewish population, were deprived of their rights as citizens. On September 6, 1940, King Carol abdicated, and General Ion Antonescu became the country's leader, with Mihai Antonescu as prime minister. A government was formed with many Iron Guard ministers, who styled themselves as Legionnaires; thus the Nationalist-Legionary State. Radu Lecca was appointed general commissar for Jewish questions. In August 1940, a Statute of the Jews was passed that in effect canceled the citizenship of most Jews and prohibited mixed marriages. Romania adopted a definition of Jewishness that included baptized Jews as Jews, including baptized children of unbaptized Jewish parents, and the baptized wives of Christian husbands. That same year, Romania was forced to give up Bukovina and Bessarabia to the Soviet Union, northern Transylvania to Hungary, and southern Dobruja to Bulgaria, which reduced the country's Jewish population by close to 300,000—only 342,000 remained. In January 1941, the Iron Guard tried to seize full power; After three days of bloody street fighting in Bucharest, the putsch was crushed by the army, but before it was over, it had been widened into a pogrom—the Jewish quarter was invaded, synagogues and stores demolished, and private homes devastated. In many areas, Jews were lynched, with a total of 630 reported fatalities. To make up for lost territories, Romania was tempted to join Germany in the invasion of the Soviet Union, in June 1941, on the promise of gaining the land between the Dniester and Bug rivers (renamed Transnistria). It contributed nearly a million men, and suffered heavy losses in the battles of Odessa and Stalingrad.

Romania's entry into the war on the side of Nazi Germany was the event that precipitated the start of the Holocaust in Romanian-conquered lands. The government applied two separate policies, one for Jews in the annexed territories, and another for Jews in pre-World War I Romania and southern Transylvania. In the first area, mass murder by Romanian troops, assisted by SS killing squads, claimed 160,000 lives, with the surviving 185,000 expelled to Transnistria, and with tens of thousands dying en route. In Transnistria itself, 90,000 died under Romanian rule, while 25,000 Jews were massacred in Odessa. In Iaşi, part of Romania proper, rumors spread that Jews were helping the retreating Soviet army, and that some had even fired on Romanian troops. The Romanians reacted with a murderous massacre of the city's Jews that dwarfed the Bucharest outburst of the Iron Guard. At least 4,000 Jews died in the pogrom. Thousands of others were dispatched in cattle cars from the battle zone to the interior of the country, and many of them died in the padlocked cars from suffocation and starvation. During the first few months of the war, up to September 1, 1941, half of the 320,000 Jews in Bessarabia, Bukovina, and Dorohoi (part of Old Romania) were murdered, with the rest concentrated in ghettos and special camps, or moved to camps in Transnistria. Exemptions were given only to people essential to the economy, most notably 16,000 inmates of the ghetto of Cernauti (now Chernovtsy). In Bessarabia, the only chance of avoiding evacuation was a baptismal certificate, so baptism became a widespread practice. According to an unconfirmed and probably exaggerated German report, 40,000 Jews availed themselves of this saving opportunity.

In Transnistria, Jews were concentrated in camps under Romanian army command, where they lived in a state of semi-starvation; in some cases, reduced to eating grass or a diet of cattle feed that caused paralysis and other illnesses. In the Golta region, Colonel Modest Isopescu, who ran the camps at Bogdanovka, Dumanovka, and Akmecetka, ordered the mass shooting of inmates in Bogdanovka. These were carried out near a precipice overhanging the Bug River. Stripped of their belongings, standing naked in temperatures of 40 degrees below zero, the victims were shot and their bodies fell into the river. The shootings continued for several days, with the participation of Ukrainian police, until December 30. At the end of the operation, 48,000 Jews had been massacred. Isopescu extended his killing operations to the two others camps. At Dumanovka, 18,000 Jews were shot, and at Akmecetka, 5,000 were killed. In summary, in the Golta district alone, more than 70,000 Jews were massacred in mass shootings. By May 1942, about two-thirds of the Transnistria Jews were dead—as many as 90,000, or slightly more. After the Red Army's rapid advance toward the Bug River in 1943, the Romanian government began to explore the possibility of evacuating Jews from the region, with an eye on possible negotiations with the Allies. Antonescu ordered all killings to stop, and even toyed with the idea of allowing the surviving Jews to return to Bukovina and Romania proper.[22] In Romania proper (Moldavia and Wallachia and southern Transylvania), on July 22, 1942, Vice-Premier Mihai Antonescu consented to German demands for deportations to Poland to begin in September, but then backed off on the promise to deliver the 300,000 Jews. As the Russian advance proceeded, Romanian reluctance became gradually more pronounced. Finally, with the Russians on its doorstep, Romania stepped out of the Axis camp on August 24, 1944, and the following day declared war on Germany. The Holocaust there was over for good. While 350,000 Jews, or 57 percent of the Jewish population, survived, the fatality rate was 264,900 Jews murdered. Of this number, 166,000 perished during the first months of the war; the rest during the deportations to Transnistria or in the camps and ghettos of this region, where some were murdered, and others died from epidemics and famine.[23]

Most Romanians belong to the Greek Orthodox Church. Adherents to the Roman Catholic Church numbered just over 1 million, or 6.6 percent of the population, and another 1.3 million were Eastern Rite Catholics (especially the Uniate Church in Transylvania) in union with the Vatican. The papal envoy was Archbishop Andrea Cassulo. Like the nuncios in many other countries, he was mainly interested in the status of baptized Jews and in trying to attract Jews to the Catholic faith, although the mainline Orthodox Church made no attempt to convert Jews. In November 1941, thousands of Jews, fearing for their lives, turned to Catholic bishops for conversion. Earlier, in February 1939, Cassulo asked the Vatican to help the estimated 50,000 converted Jewish families (probably an exaggerated figure) emigrate to Spain, but nothing came of it. Romanian legislation passed in August 1940 stipulated that converted Jews would still be considered Jews. Cassulo pressed on, and asked that Jewish converts be allowed to give their children a Catholic education, a right formally guaranteed by the Concordat signed between the Vatican and Romania in 1939. The Vatican secretary of state, Cardinal Maglione, urged Cassulo to remind the authorities that forbidding the conversion of Jews to Christianity on racial grounds was a violation of the Concordat. When baptized Jews were included among the deportees to Transnistria in late 1941, Cassulo intervened again, and on December 4, 1941, he wrote to Prime Minister Mihai Antonescu: "To involve these Catholic families, without distinction, in the obligations, restrictions, and conditions of life of their former co-religionists would make it impossible for them to lead a religious life, or to give their children the religious education to which they are obliged and have the right. Neither special privilege nor protection is being sought, but only that conditions favorable to the moral and spiritual life of Christians be permitted." On the question of conversion the Vatican told Cassulo that if, during the six-month period of instruction and preparation for conversion, the conduct of the applicant was in accord with Catholic principles, the conversion could take place. If, however, doubts existed about the application's motives, the baptism was to be postponed.[24]

Difficulties continued in regard to baptized Jews. When the Ministry of Religion asked the Bucharest archdiocese to hand over its baptismal registers so that it could ascertain the details of the Jewish baptisms, the archbishop of Bucharest refused, and agreed to provide only a list of those already baptized. On September 30, 1942, the foreign minister announced that the government would not recognize baptisms of Jews in northern Bukovina and Bessarabia that had taken place during the short period of Soviet occupation (1940–41). Cassulo was instructed by the Vatican to intervene on behalf of these converted Jews, who reportedly numbered in the thousands. When Cardinal Maglione asked Cassulo to inquire about the fate of the 3,000 or 4,000 converted Jews already deported to Transnistria, Cassulo decided to check for himself, and he visited the area from April 27 to May 5, 1943. While his main concern remained with the baptized Jews, his visit was a morale-booster for the Jews in Romania, since they felt that Cassulo had brought both material comfort and moral encouragement to the deported Jews in Transnistria. Upon his return, Cassulo asked the prime minister to allow 8,000 orphans from Transnistria to be returned to Romania proper. In summary, according to historian John F. Morley, Cassulo was possibly the most active of the Vatican diplomats in matters concerning Jews, although his primary interest was the fate of Catholic Jews. He responded effectively and willingly to the appeals of Jewish leaders, particularly when the Jews of Old Romania were threatened, and he went beyond the strict lines of ecclesiastical interests and acted on behalf of people who were being oppressed—mostly, however, baptized Jews.[25]

The only story known to Yad Vashem of a Romanian clergyman helping Jews is that of Gheorghe Petre. An Orthodox priest who was later awarded the "Righteous" honor, Petre was tried by a military court in Sirova-Golta on February 16, 1944, on charges of complicity, in collusion with an army officer, in trafficking letters and money for the Jews of the Crivoe-Ozero and Treibude ghettos in Transnistria. Petre (also known as Pătru) had been sent to the war zone in November 1942 by the bishopric of Ramnicu, and was assigned to the parish of Sirovo, district of Golta (Pervomavnosk). There he agreed to help the Jews of the Crivoi Ozero and Trei Dube ghettos and alleviate their sufferings. Traveling back to his post in Transnistria, he obtained three pairs of winter socks, a woolen shirt, a pair of boots, and 1 kilo of candy for certain Jews in the Crivoi-Ozero ghetto. He had to travel 12 kilometers by coach to get there, and returned to his parish partly on foot because of partisan activity in the area. Questioned by the military police, he managed to burn the incriminating letters and photos in his possession (which some Jews had given him to forward to their loved ones). Charged by a military court in Tiraspol with having aided Jews, Petre responded: "I helped them in accordance with the precepts of Savior Christ." He submitted the parable of the Good Samaritan as his defense. Due to the lack of incriminating witnesses, no penalty was imposed on him.[26]

Chapter 10
HUNGARY

We do not dispute the fact that the Jewish Question must be resolved in a legal and just manner. Therefore we do not object, but actually hold it desirable, that in the economic system of the country the necessary measures be taken and the rightfully objectionable symptoms be remedied.
Cardinal Jusztinián Séredi (June 1944)

The simple fact that people are persecuted only because of their racial origin is a violation of the natural law. If the good Lord has given them life, no one has the right to take it away or deprive them of the means to exist.
Monsignor Angelo Rotta (May 1944)

Jews in Hungarian History

The Holocaust in Hungary, in mid-1944, which engulfed over 550,000 Jewish lives, tragically came at a time when level-headed Germans could no longer doubt that their country had lost the war. Despite its gloomy prospects, Nazi Germany was determined not to allow any letup in its extermination campaign, and the large Jewish community in Hungary loomed large in the minds of the Nazis as a job still undone. Jews first came to present-day Hungary (then known as Pannonia) in the wake of the Roman armies. Over the years, important communities developed in Buda and elsewhere. A church council in Buda in 1279 prohibited Jews from leasing land and compelled them to wear the Jewish badge. In practice, this and other decrees were not applied strictly because the king objected. Jews were expelled from the country in 1349, but their return was authorized in 1364. Occasionally, anti-Jewish riots broke out in Buda and other locations. Jews lived relatively undisturbed in central Hungary after it was incorporated into the Turkish Ottoman Empire in 1541. In the Hapsburg dominions of Hungary, however, Jews continued to fare badly. A blood libel in Bazin in 1529, for instance, ended with thirty Jews burned at the stake. In the modern period, most of the restrictions were abolished in 1859–60, and Jews were authorized to engage in all professions and settle in all localities. The number of Jews in all parts of the Hungarian kingdom (including present-day Slovakia and northern Transylvania) rose to 910,000 in 1910. In Hungary proper, as in Germany, the overwhelming majority of Jews (divided between the Orthodox and the Reform-Neologists) viewed themselves as members of the Hungarian nation, spoke the language, and contributed to its culture. In addition, the Jews were the backbone of the middle class, and of much of the professional and commercial activity. A short-lived Communist regime came to power in Hungary after its defeat in World War I, which included a considerable number of Jews in the upper ranks of the government, led by Bela Kun. It was quickly suppressed, accompanied by riots and acts of violence against Jews; the number of victim of this so-called White Terror has been estimated at 3,000 fatalities. The declared policy of the new government remained antisemitic, though of a moderate kind. A sharper anti-Jewish turn took place in the late 1930s as a result of the strengthening of rightist circles and growing German-Nazi influence. The number of Jews had by then been reduced as a result of territorial losses, and in 1930, they numbered 444,500 souls. The Jewish population rose again in early 1941, to 725,000, representing close to 5 percent of the total population of 14.7 million, as a result of the territorial acquisitions granted by Nazi Germany. An estimated 401,000 lived in the pre-1939 Hungary, 145,000 in areas acquired from dismembered Czechoslovakia, 150,000 in northern Transylvania (formerly Romania), and 14,000 in the Backa region (from dismembered Yugoslavia). Added to this figure were an estimated 60,000 baptized Jews divided among Catholics (43,000), Calvinists (12,000), Lutherans (3,000), and other denominations (3,000). Some figures place the number of converted Jews as high as 100,000.[1]

The Holocaust Period

Hungary's rapprochement with Nazi Germany in the 1930s was based on a hope for German help to regain territories lost at the end of World War I. Thus Hungary entered into a full alliance with Nazi Germany. This included sending troops to fight the Soviet Union in June 1941, which ultimately cost Hungary close to 200,000 casualties. However, when Hungary's leader, Miklós Horthy, met with Hitler in Klessheim Castle on April 7, 1943, the scales of war had by then turned to Germany's disadvantage, and Hungary was beginning to seek ways to disengage itself from the German stranglehold. Horthy defensively argued that he had done the utmost by restricting the economic base of Jewish existence, but he could not, after all, kill every one of them. Hitler interrupted, stating that wherever the Jews were left alone, they brought brute misery and depravity. They were complete parasites. They had to be treated like tubercular bacilli threatening a healthy body. Nations that did not defend themselves against the Jews, Hitler warned, had to perish. Upon his return, Horthy told his ministers that Hitler had accused him at "not having permitted the Jews to be massacred."[2] A year later, the situation for the Jews in Hungary was to undergo a dramatic change for the worse when, without warning, Germany invaded the country on March 19, 1944, and a new pro-German government was installed, headed by Döme Sztójay, who also served as foreign minister. Andor Jarosz, the new minister of the interior, was in charge of Jewish affairs.

In 1938, well before it gave in to the more extreme German demands, Hungary had enacted the Jewish Law which restricted the number of Jews in the liberal professions, the governmental administration, and commercial and industrial enterprises. The term "Jew" was defined to include not only members of the Jewish religion but also those who had converted after 1919 or who had been born of Jewish parents after that date. In 1939, the second Jewish Law ratified by parliament further extended the application of the term "Jew" on a racial basis, and so did the third Jewish Law in 1941. The Hungarian definition of Jewishness was far-reaching and included anyone who had two Jewish grandparents but had been raised Jewish or was married to a person with only one Jewish grandparent; plus those who had a Jewish mother and an unknown father; or a half-Jewish mother and an unknown father if not baptized as a child. Thus the total number of people officially registered as Jewish was more than 803,000, and as many as 850,000, including up to 100,000 converts to Christianity. In 1939, Hungary introduced a unique labor service system designed for Jewish men of military age, 80,000 of whom were drafted and organized into unarmed labor battalions assigned primarily to war-related work projects, such as building and repairing roads, clearing forests, digging trenches, and building tank traps, at home and along the fronts in Ukraine and Serbia. More than half of these men in these mobile forced-labor units did not survive the war. On top of this, in January 1942, the Hungarian army murdered more than 1,000 Jews in the Bácska region of Yugoslavia, while in the summer 1941 it seized 18,000 Jews near Kamenets-Podolski in occupied Poland and turned them over to SS troops, who proceeded to massacre them.

With the German occupation in March 1944, the final tragic step was put in motion: mass deportations to the gas chambers in Auschwitz. It should be borne in mind that the perpetrators, both Germans and Hungarian, knew that the war was lost when they started the deportations. The deportations were run principally by Hungarians, orchestrated by state secretaries László Endre and László Baky in the Ministry of Interior, with the aid of a relatively small German SS force commanded by Adolf Eichmann. At first, Jews were dismissed from all public services, their businesses were closed, and any assets worth more than 3,000 pengö (about $300) were confiscated, as were cars, bicycles, radios, telephones, bank accounts, and valuable art objects. Food rations for Jews were reduced, with restrictions on butter, eggs, rice, and meat. Special shopping hours were established in Budapest. Then came the obligatory wearing of the Jewish Star, followed by curfew hours and ghettoization in designated apartment buildings. Thus, the Jews found themselves fully isolated from the rest of the population and ready for the next stage—deportation to the death camps.

Deportations to Auschwitz began on May 15, with daily transports of 2,000–3,000 leaving from the provisional ghettos under the supervision of very brutal Hungarian gendarmes. From May 14 to July 8, a total of 437,000 people were deported from every part of the country except Budapest. The bulk of the transports reached Auschwitz by freight train, where most were gassed upon arrival. Each freight car was supposed to carry about forty-five people but in practice eighty to a hundred were usually crammed in, including the sick, elderly people, and babies, many of whom died during the three to five days of the journey from lack of water and ventilation. With the rest of the country cleared of Jews, it now was the turn of Budapest, where 220,000 Jews were crowded into apartment houses located near factories and railway stations, with all the apartments marked by a 12-inch Jewish star. A series of interventions by foreign governments, including Sweden, the Vatican, and the International Red Cross, brought a halt to the deportations on July 8. It looked as if the Jews of Budapest, the only remaining Jewish community in the country, were now safe. But a dramatic turn of events again made the situation change for the worst.[3]

On October 15, 1944 the pro-Nazi Arrow Cross Party of Ferenc Szálasi seized power with German help, unseated Horthy, and initiated an unprecedented reign of anti-Jewish terror in the capital city, with Arrow Cross extermination squads killing Jews at random and dumping their bodies into the frozen Danube River. Father András Kun, a Minorite monk, wearing a gun and an Arrow Cross armband, personally tortured and arrested Jews before their execution. Father Kun was also involved in the January 11, 1945, massacre of the patients and staff of the Jewish Hospital on Maros Street, where he reportedly ordered the Arrow Cross to fire in the "holy name of Christ." Most of the city's Jews were then moved to a central ghetto, although a smaller segment remained in buildings and neighborhoods protected by various neutral states (Switzerland, Sweden, Portugal, Spain, and the Vatican). On November 8, 1944, to overcome the physical impossibility of further transports to Auschwitz due to the Russian advance, a group of about 25,000 Budapest Jews were marched on foot to Hegyeshalom on the Austrian border. They were followed by other contingents of thousands more. Many perished along the road on this

Death March. The anti-Jewish terror in Budapest took place as Soviet troops closed in on the city, shelling it from several directions. On January 17, 1945, the Pest side of the city was liberated by Soviet troops, and they completed their occupation of the whole city with the capture of Buda on February 12, 1945. The number of losses sustained by Hungarian Jewry, within the eleven-month period of the German occupation were staggering. Of the 825,000 people considered Jews within the borders of Greater Hungary, about 565,000 perished, and about 260,000 survived the Holocaust. This included 69,000 Jews in Budapest's central ghetto, 25,000 in the international protected ghetto, and an estimated 25,000 in hiding in the city and environs; the rest were survivors from concentration and labor camps.[4] We shall now survey the response of the churches to the cataclysmic catastrophe of the Jewish community.

Response by the Churches

In 1941, Hungary counted 9.8 million Catholics, 2.8 million Reformed Protestants (Calvinists), and 729,000 Evangelicals (Lutherans), as well as 665,000 who belonged to no denomination or religion. Both before and during the Nazi era, these three major Christian denominations were strongly antisemitic, portraying the Jews as a people who had betrayed God and were forever cursed because of the crucifixion of Jesus. On the Catholic side, the Jesuit Béla Bangha (1880–1940) expressed the wish to see Hungary free of Jews; in 1919, Father Gyula Zakany claimed that it was the fault of the Jews that Hungary's territorial integrity had been violated. József Grősz, the archbishop of Kalocsa, argued that the pro-Nazi Arrow Cross was compatible with Christ's cross. Istvan Hasz, the bishop of the armed forces, concurred with Nazi ideas, arguing that "against the Jews, the destroyers of the country, any offense is permissible."[5] In summary, there was a consensus among church leaders that the country had a Jewish problem and that this imaginary problem required an urgent solution. One of the central figures of clerical antisemitism was Ottokár Prohászka, the bishop of Székesfehérvár (during his tenure 1906–1927), who accused the Jews of "eating us up, and we have to defend ourselves against this epidemic of bedbugs. It is absolutely true that there are good Jews, but Jewry is foreign, a foreign power that suppresses Christianity, conquers and exploits us . . . a cunning, faithless, and immoral race, a bedbug invasion, a rat campaign. There is only one question: How do we defend ourselves?" This cleric exerted a profound influence on public opinion for several decades. If church leaders objected to Nazi antisemitism, it was not so much for the anti-Jewish campaign, which they welcomed, but for the excessive methods used. Their interventions to moderate the carnage proved to be too little and too late. Church leaders found themselves unable to ride the tiger they had helped unleash.

The first sign of discontent between the churches and the government was when the star decree was imposed, because it meant that tens of thousands of Christians of Jewish parentage, even including members of the clergy, would soon have to appear in the streets wearing a Jewish symbol. This was too much for the church to swallow silently. Cardinal Jusztinián Serédi, the head of the Catholic Church (with the title of prince primate), immediately ordered his clergy not to wear the Jewish star. On April 4, 1944 the government appeared to relent, exempting members of the Christian clergy, as well as the wives, widows, and children of exempted veterans. But Prime Minister Sztójay turned down Serédi's request for Jewish converts not to wear the star. At the same time, Serédi and Sándor Raffay (representing the Evangelical churches) justified the adoption of the antisemitic laws by emphasizing the "threat" that Jewish cultural, political, and economic influence represented for the national interests of Christian Hungary. This preoccupation with the special interests of converts and Christians of Jewish origin was characteristic of most church leaders throughout the war. In the words of the historian Raoul Hilberg, "In waging the struggle for the baptized Jews in the first place, the church had implicitly declined to take up the struggle for Jewry as a whole. In insisting that the definition exclude Christians, the church in effect had stated the condition upon which it would accept a definition that set aside a group of people for destruction."[6]

Under pressure from some local clerical leaders, including Bishop Vilmos Apor of Györ, Cardinal Serédi met with Prime Minister Sztójay on April 13 and April 16 to submit a memorandum in the name of his fellow bishops. Quickly passing over the violation of human rights with regard to the recent anti-Jewish measures, Serédi came to the most pressing point on their minds: the rights of converts. He argued that they should be separated from the Jews because they had themselves already done so by virtue of their conversions, and therefore they should be exempted from the measures enacted against Jews, and be removed from the jurisdiction of the Jewish Council and from wearing the Star of David. In addition, Serédi asked permission for priests falling under the jurisdiction of the anti-Jewish laws to have non-Jewish servants. In his reply of May 3, the prime minister assured the primate that the government had already exempted priests of Jewish origin and would do everything possible to ensure the economic interests of Christians whose parents were affected by the anti-Jewish laws. As to the yellow star, Sztójay emphasized that it was not a symbol of the Jewish religion, but "a convenient means for the necessary identification from the administrative point of view of those of the Jewish race." He added that he would not object if converts wore a cross as well as a star. Not satisfied with Sztójay's letter, Serédi again insisted on separating baptized Jews from their former co-religionists: "I must again repeat my demand for a differentiation between converted Jews and Jews adhering to the Israelite faith. This applies especially to cases in which Christians of Jewish origin are to be housed with Israelites in the same flats, houses, ghettos, labor camps, etc. As Christians are separated from Jews in the labor battalions, so too they should be separated in the above cases. This at least we owe our Christian coreligionists." At this meeting, the prince primate did not deplore, let alone mention, the injustice and inhumanity of the escalating anti-Jewish measures. His silence may have been interpreted by Sztójay and his government as a sign that they could proceed with their more sinister designs against the Jews without objection by the church.[7]

The cardinal's apparent indifference to the plight of the Jews bewildered the papal nuncio, Angelo Rotta, and some other bishops. On May 27, Bishop Apor urged Serédi, to issue a pastoral letter on this issue, or to give the bishops a free hand to inform and guide their parishioners. The Vatican nuncio, on June 8, inquired of Serédi why he and the bishops of the Catholic Church were not taking a more resolute stand against the government's anti-Jewish measures. Serédi shot back a sardonic observation that the Vatican itself maintained diplomatic relations "with the very German government that is carrying out the atrocities."[8] On June 15, Bishop László Ravasz, of the Protestant Church, proposed to Serédi the issuance of a joint public declaration, and on June 27, Rotta, the nuncio, conveyed the pope's desire that the "Hungarian bishops take a public stand in defense of Christian principles and in support of those compatriots that were unjustly affected by the racial laws, and especially in behalf of the Christians." Yielding to the pressure, Serédi began working on a pastoral letter. The final text, adopted after consultation with Apor and Gyula Czapik, the bishop of Eger, and dated June 29, opened with a restatement of the general principle of the inviolability of human rights as understood by the church. It read in parts: "No one may be lawfully punished for the crimes of other human beings who belong to the same race, nationality, or religion, if he personally had no part in the commission of such crimes." Serédi then deplored the violation of this religious principle taking place in the country, adding "We need not list in detail the measures which are well known to you along with the manner of their execution, and which violate or even deny the inherent rights of some of our fellow citizens, even some who are together with us, members of our holy faith, only because of their origin." Before specifically mentioning the Jewish issue at hand, Serédi could not help avoid firing a broadside at the Jews that undid the whole purpose of the pastoral letter—the protection of the Jews. "We also have no doubt that a part of Jewry has had a guilty and subversive influence on Hungarian economic, social, and moral life. . . . We do not dispute the fact that the Jewish Question must be resolved in a legal and just manner. Therefore we do not object, but actually hold it desirable, that in the economic system of the country the necessary measures be taken and the rightfully objectionable symptoms be remedied." With this, Serédi turned to what really concerned him, the plight of baptized Jews. "However, we would neglect our moral and pastoral duty if we did not make very certain that the just shall not suffer, and our Hungarian fellow citizens and Catholic believers not be offended merely because of their race." Trying to correct the impression given by his earlier words that he was not concerned about the deportation of the Jews, Serédi stated: "We are nevertheless deeply grieved that during our negotiations we simply could not obtain what we would have liked best, that the unjust violations and deprivation of rights, mainly the deportations, should finally be terminated. . . . We restrained ourselves and waited. But now, when we see with great shock that our negotiations have been almost without success . . . we solemnly disavow our responsibility."

This as yet unpublicized pastoral letter was brought to the attention of István Antal, the minister of justice, who promptly stopped its distribution. The letter was reportedly read in some churches that received it before the government interdict was issued. On July 6, Antal visited Cardinal Serédi in his summer residence and warned about the possibility of a pro-Nazi Arrow Cross takeover of the government if the church moved against the present regime. Serédi said he would withdraw the pastoral letter if the prime minister acquiesced to the demands outlined in his earlier memoranda with regard to the exemption of baptized Jews from the anti-Jewish measures and to the return of such people if they had already been deported. Antal accepted these two conditions, whereupon Serédi instructed all parish priests by telegram to refrain from reading his pastoral letter. Two days after this meeting, coinciding with Horthy's order to stop the deportations of Jews (bowing to outside pressure), Sztójay brought along a letter to summarize the government's position concerning Jews and its concessions with regard to Jews of Christian faith—namely, the creation of a special organization made up of converts, which was to be independent of the Association of Jews. As for the Jews in Budapest (the only remaining Jewish community), Sztójay assured the cardinal that their deportation had been suspended until further notice; if it should resume, "the Christian Jews will remain in the country," although confined in segregated apartments, and would be allowed to practice their Christianity. Similarly, parents, brothers and sisters, and wives and children of pastors of the Protestant churches would also be excused from wearing the yellow star "and all associated consequences."

Sztójay's assurances must have reassured the cardinal, for he agreed to a compromise formula under which, on July 8 and 9, the state radio was to broadcast to all parishes Serédi's explanation that the pastoral letter was designed only for the information of the priests and church officials, and was not to be read from the pulpit. Instead, the following was to be announced: "Jusztinián Serédi . . . informs the Catholic faithful in his name . . . that he has repeatedly approached the royal Hungarian government in connection with the decrees relating to the Jews and especially the converts and is continuing his negotiations in this respect." Following up on its success in suppressing the pastoral letter, the government, on July 12, asked Serédi to have preachers abstain from adopting any political attitude or making any political criticism. To this Serédi replied, "I cannot stop sermons broadcast on the wireless from saying 'Thou shalt not kill! Thou shalt not steal!' Yet today many people might regard even that as politics."[9] Serédi now turned to the increased requests for conversions, and on July 24, 1944, he instructed his clergy that such petitioners were to be treated with extreme caution, and only be accepted if sincere in their adoption of the Christian faith. As for what the cardinal termed "paper Christians," probably having in mind Jews who wanted to adopt the Christian faith in the mistaken belief that this would provide them safety from persecution, their conversion was to be denied. This was the primate cardinal's final word on the Jewish issue, and he remained silent during the reign of terror of the Arrow Cross regime, when Budapest Jews were targeted for destruction.[10]

While Serédi was cowed into silence, several other leaders of the Catholic Church did have the courage to speak out. One was Baron Vilmos Apor, the bishop of Győr, who was so relentless in his protests that the government threatened to imprison him. In his Whitsunday sermon, he declared: "And he who denies the fundamental laws of Christianity about love and asserts that there are people and groups and races one is permitted to hate, and advocates that there are men whom one may torture, be they either Negroes or Jews, no matter how much he may boast of being Christian is in fact a pagan and clearly guilty. . . . And all who approve such tortures and participate in committing them commit a serious crime and will not receive absolution until they make amends for their sin."

Equally outspoken was the public stand of Áron Márton, whose diocese covered all of Transylvania, although his bishopric had its seat in Alba-Iula in the Romanian-held part of Transylvania. The sermon he delivered in St. Michael's Church in Koloszvár-Cluj on May 18 was mimeographed and distributed in other parts of the country. "The basis of the church's attitude and consistent position is the fundamental belief of Christianity that we are all God's children and are all brothers in Christ. . . . For us, however, my dear brothers, the fundamental premise of our belief, the command to love one's fellow man, still holds, and its open acceptance and practice is even more of a duty today than in former times. The name of Christian, which has been used so many times as a symbol with so many meanings, compels us to do so, my brothers! He who sins against his fellow man endangers one of the great achievements of the 2,000-year work of Christianity—the idea of the brotherhood of man. He proceeds not in a Christian but in a pagan spirit and willingly or unwillingly joins those drives that split nations into races, separate social classes, and selfish unions. . . . I have been informed that my parishioners, starting at the easternmost borders of the church district, have been greatly shocked by news of the restriction of freedom and uncertain fate of certain people, and have followed with great concern the measures lately carried out against the Jews. I was most pleased to hear of this moral conception, opinion, and judgment of my worshippers; I mention this with great pastoral pride because this is the conception, opinion, and judgment of the broad masses and at the same time the happy sign that the true Catholic spirit is deeply rooted and still alive in our people's souls as a living force."

In a later sermon to newly consecrated priests, Bishop Márton warned that they might face persecution by the authorities for upholding the divine command "you shall love your neighbor as thyself." If so, this would not be a mark of shame, but of great honor and distinction. He also addressed a confrontational letter to Prime Minister Sztójay in which he stated in no unclear terms that "with all due respect, but with full consciousness of my personal responsibility, I warn his excellency that for these terrible deeds, it will not be just one person, even the prime minister, and not solely the members of the government, but the entire people, who will have to bear the consequences. For you are placing the guilt for innocent blood on our heads." He then asked for the anti-Jewish decrees to be annulled. In an even more strongly worded letter, this time to Minister of Interior Jarosz, Márton stated: "We knew and honored you as a devoted and faithful Catholic. But now, in light of your anti-Jewish decrees, we are forced, sadly and angrily, to have doubts about your Christianity. . . . With all due respect . . . I ask you to annul your recent decrees. And if you are not able to do so, then resign from the post of interior minister which you hold today." It goes without saying that Bishop Márton's outspoken words were not well received by the Hungarian authorities. Rebuked by Jarosz, and fearing for his safety, he left for Alba-Iulia, the bishopric's seat on the Romanian side, at the end of May 1944 and, having become a persona non grata, did not reenter northern Transylvania until after the war.[11]

As for Bishop Apor, he had already spoken up earlier when Serédi refused to make public his pastoral letter. Apor wrote to him: "It fills me with great sorrow that Your Eminence has finally renounced his intention of publicly defending universal human rights, humanity, and the sacrament of baptism in a joint pastoral letter to all the Catholic faithful. . . . The present government regards this as a sign of weakness in us and as an encouragement to proceed further along the path it has taken. . . . Most of the faithful learn nothing of our fundamental attitude and our practical measures. How can they! We are thus responsible for the fact that many Hungarians are taking part, more or less in good faith, in the enforcement of merciless regulations and are applauding a doctrine that should be condemned. I know very well that by taking public action we may expose ourselves to certain vexations . . . But I am convinced that we must take this risk, and that in the final analysis the convictions of the faithful and the position of our church would emerge strengthened from the struggle. Should Your Eminence decide in no case to take any public action, [then perhaps he would allow] each individual bishop to be given a free hand to inform and guide the faithful of his own diocese. But first and foremost, I beg Your Eminence once again to issue a pastoral letter to all dioceses bringing home to our people clearly and unequivocally all the leading principles of morality and religion in the context of the present situation." On June 17, Apor wrote again to Serédi urging him to take a stand against the government, for "sin cannot be condoned even when it is committed by the state authorities. . . . We should step forward into the limelight." Serédi answered evasively that it was necessary to wait because negotiations were still in progress. On July 15, Apor wrote again to Serédi, suggesting that the cardinal address a personal appeal to Hitler simultaneously with a memorandum to the Hungarian government, "[to] make it clear how strongly the racial principle is to be condemned, and that by adopting and applying it the Hungarian government is abandoning the foundations of justice and Christian morality." To which Serédi responded that "to turn to Hitler was an unfruitful approach already tried by others, even by the pope himself [hardly true!]. It was all been in vain. Experimenting with a memorandum is also useless, because the government would either not understand it and act in accordance with it, or else would not dare to understand it or not wish to understand it."[12]

Endre Hamvas, bishop of Csanad, also spoke out against the radical anti-Jewish measures. On June 25, 1944, he preached a sermon to seminarians in Szeged whom he had just ordained, stating, "In the name of Christianity, hundreds of thousands of people are being robbed of their property and their dwellings and deported because of their race, which they cannot help, and all this in a manner which immerses them in a real sea of suffering, exposes their health and their lives to uncertainty, and degrades their human dignity. Among these hundreds of thousands there are innocent children, defenseless women, helpless old people, pitiable invalids. . . . Married people and family members are mercilessly parted from each other because one of them is a Jew. We must say it aloud, so that people do not ruin their consciences through error: none of this can be brought into harmony with Christianity! Some people seek to justify themselves by stigmatizing the whole race as guilty. Yet Christian morality says that the sinner shall be brought before the court and given the opportunity to defend himself. . . . God's commandments protect the rights of all—those of Negroes and those of Jews too—their rights to property, to freedom, to health, to existence. We do not say this because we are friends of the Jews, but because we are friends of justice. God has given every man certain fundamental rights without regard to differences in nationality, race, or social class. These rights are proper to every human being, and they may not be taken away from him by any power. . . . If we leave out of account the commandment of love and mercy in our dealings with the Jews, then we cannot count on these commandments being protected, nor can our little ones, our wives, or our old people." Hamvas succeeded in retaining 200 baptized Jews in Szeged, thus saving them from deportation.[13]

The reaction of the Protestant churches to the anti-Jewish measures was not fundamentally different from that of the Catholic Church. Although they agonized over the plight of the Jews, especially over the *manner* in which the "Jewish Question" was being solved, their primary concern was the welfare of converts. Like his Catholic counterpart, Bishop Dr. László Ravasz, on April 6, 1944, asked the government to exempt from wearing the yellow star all officials and employees of the Protestant churches who were of Jewish parentage, including teachers, cantors, deacons, and church wardens, and for the establishment of a separate Christian Jewish Council not linked to the government and the German-controlled Jewish organization. Sztójay's response was identical to the one given Serédi, emphasizing that the Jewish Question was being solved not on religious but on racial grounds. "The Jews are a race," Sztójay told Ravasz when they met on May 9, "and thus the regulation of the Jewish problem is not a question of religion but of race." The Protestant churches focused on the fate of the converts and demanded permission for ministers of the various denominations to serve the spiritual needs of their congregants in the ghettos. Ravasz met with Horthy on April 12, 1944, and was assured that "only a few hundred thousand Jews are scheduled to leave the country with the labor battalions. No harm will befall them, not a hair on their heads will be touched." When Ravasz learned of the true nature of the deportations, he approached Serédi to suggest a joint protest. As reported by Sándor Török (a baptized Jew), who was present, Serédi angrily threw his skullcap to the floor and declared: "If His Holiness the pope does nothing against Hitler, what can I do in my narrower jurisdiction? Damn it."[14]

In the meantime, in a June 1944 letter, Reverend József Éliász, the leader of the Good Shepherd committee (*Jó Pásztor Bizottság*), in a message to Protestant bishops, proposed that a delegation of Christian leaders go to Prime Minister Sztójay and threaten that unless the government halted the deportations, all the churches would be closed, church bells would toll while the deportations took place, and sacraments would be refused to those involved in the deportations and their families. The suggestion was rejected. At the same time, Ravasz pressed on, and on behalf of the Protestant churches (Dr. Bela Kapi, of the Lutheran Church, Jarros Vasarhelyi, of the Reformed Church, and other bishops) presented the government, on June 23, with a memorandum stating that "Jews have been crossing the frontier in sealed cars day after day and have disappeared from our sight bound for an unknown destination. Each of these cars contained about seventy or eighty people of different sexes, ages, and social standing and of both Israelite and Christian faith. . . . The journey leads to final destruction. The solution of the Jewish Question is a political task . . . But once the solution of the Jewish Question challenges the eternal laws of God, we are in duty bound to raise our voices, condemning but at the same time imploring the head of the responsible government. We cannot act otherwise. . . . [We] condemn every action which outrages human dignity, justice, or charity." Ravasz then turned to the matter that was closer to his heart, the fate of the baptized Jews. "As bishops of the two Protestant churches we protest against devout members of our congregations being punished only for being considered Jews from a racial point of view. They are being punished for a Jewish mentality from which they, and in many cases their ancestors, have solemnly disconnected themselves." Reverting to the issue at hand, the massive deportation of Jews, Ravasz stated that he was not protesting the government's decision to deal with the Jewish issue, only "against the very idea of a senseless and cruel destruction of the Jews." Sztójay's response restated the standard lie that Jews were simply being taken for labor purposes. As for the non-able people accompanying those capable of performing hard labor, the prime minister explained that "a strong family affinity is characteristic of the Jews, and the authorities, therefore, did not wish to separate families. They did not want the Jews working abroad to feel anxious about the families they had left behind, nor the families to worry about the fate of the deported Jewish men."

Finding the government's response unsatisfactory, Ravasz decided on a pastoral letter of his own, to be read in Protestant churches on July 2. The letter stated in part that it found "utterly regrettable the events which have accompanied the segregation and deportation of the Jews of Hungary, whether Jews or Christians by faith. Having stated that this mode of solving the Jewish Question violates God's eternal laws . . . we condemn all modes of action which violate human dignity, justice, and mercy," and ask the government "to put an end to the cruelties." Alerted by Ravasz's threat to go public, Stephen Antal, minister of religion and education, accompanied by Secretary of State Nicholas Mester, visited Ravasz on July 11 and told him that the deportations had ceased (but this was due to outside pressure and not the Hungarian churches). They gave similar assurances to Cardinal Serédi, with regard to the special treatment of converts. Like his Catholic counterpart, Ravasz backed off and canceled the reading of the pastoral letter. Instead, on July 12, ministers of the Protestant churches were instructed to read a text at services the following Sunday stating "that in connection with the Jewish Question, and particularly the baptized Jews, [the churches] have repeatedly taken steps with the appropriate government officials and will continue to do so."[15]

Vatican Nuncio Angelo Rotta

Angelo Rotta was the cleric who stood out most forthrightly in directly confronting the issue of the Jewish tragedy in Hungary. He was not a member of the Hungarian clergy but the Vatican ambassador, or nuncio, in the country, and the dean of the diplomatic corps. Between March 23, when the Sztójay government was installed, and May 15, when the mass deportations began, Rotta frequently contacted the prime minister, pleading for moderation and the redressing of injustices. These contacts were made either in person or through Gennaro Verolino, the secretary of the nunciature. During the first phase of the Final Solution program, however, the nuncio, like the Hungarian church leaders, was especially concerned about the fate of converted Jews. In contrast to the others, however, he did not stop at that, but gradually took up the cause of the Jewish community as a whole. On May 15, 1944, Rotta wrote to the Hungarian government to protest the deportations. He stated: "The Hungarian government is prepared to deport 100,000 people. . . . The whole world knows what deportation means in practice. The apostolic nunciature considers it to be its duty to protest against such measures . . .; it once again appeals to the Hungarian government not to continue this war against the Jews beyond the limits prescribed by the law of nature and the commandments of God, and to avoid any proceedings against which the Holy See and the conscience of the whole Christian world would be compelled to protest. . . . The mere fact that human beings are being persecuted simply because of the race to which they belong is in itself a violation of natural law. If God gave them life, no one is entitled to take it from them if they have committed no crime, or to rob them of the means they need to live. To take antisemitic measures without any regard for the fact many Jews have become Christians though baptism is a serious offense against the church." At the time, Rotta limited himself to asking that converts be exempted from the antisemitic measures, and that fundamental human rights be observed in the implementation of whatever measures were enacted. On May 25, 1944, dismayed by the start of the deportations, Rotta cabled the Vatican secretary of state, Cardinal Luigi Maglione, urging him to persuade Cardinal Serédi to play a more active role, since "to the surprise of all, the Hungarian episcopate has not taken any steps. Perhaps a direct action by the Holy See will be beneficial." In a further communication to Maglione, on June 18, 1944, Rotta reported that unfortunately the number of deportees had passed the 300,000 mark, and complained about the lack of a forceful response by Serédi. Rotta also asked for a direct intervention by the Holy See to stop the deportations.[16]

On June 6, meeting with Sztójay, Rotta strongly condemned the way the Jewish problem was being solved. "Now you can see what the application of race theory leads to in practice. People who were born Christians, or who have been Christians these thirty to forty years, are treated in the same unjust way as the other Jews." Sztójay responded that the deportation of the Jews was not a question of race destruction but of aiding an ally in need of manpower. In choosing between racial Magyars and Jews, "it is therefore only natural that we prefer to place the racial Jews living here at the disposal of our ally, the more so as the racial Jews are generally representatives of destruction. As for the Christian Jews, a council of baptized Jews had been established." Rotta asked about the logic of deporting people under sixteen and over sixty years of age, as well as of those unable to work. Sztójay's reply: "The Germans say that the Jews work harder if their families are with them." Rotta countered that when seventy-year-old, even eighty-year-old men, and also women, children, and invalids were being dragged off, one is bound to ask what kind of work such helpless creatures as these could carry out? The answer was that the Jews were simply being given the opportunity to take their relatives with them. Rotta: "And what about cases where the old and the sick are deported or where they are not the parents of persons? . . . When one remembers that the Hungarian workers who go off to Germany to work are not allowed to take their families with them, it seems amazing that this great favor is accorded only to Jews." At loss for an answer, Sztójay launched an attack on the Jews, accusing them of being "defeatists" and of siding "with the other side even though the victory of Bolshevism would engulf Hungary." Rotta admitted that "there was a certain Jewish danger, the elimination of which was necessary," but he emphasized that it should be done with due respect for Christian morality and the rights of the church. He also asked that baptized Jews be allowed to leave their dwellings earlier on Sundays and church holidays, and not be required to wear the yellow star. He included parents of priests, and holders of papal and church decorations, in the request. Sztójay agreed to this. In a further note to Rotta on June 30 the government reassured him of its special concern for baptized Jews as shown by the creation of a separate organization headed by the apostate Sándor Tőrők, the League of Christian Jews (the organization existed only on paper), and confirmed that relatives of Christian clergymen would be exempted from wearing the yellow star."[17]

Soon after the Arrow Cross takeover, Rotta visited the new foreign minister, Baron Gábor Kemény, to implore him to use moderation with regard to

Jews. On October 21, Rotta had a long exchange of views with Szálasi, who promised not to resume the deportations. When the new government did not honor its promise, the nuncio invited his diplomatic colleagues to a meeting. On November 17 a new memorandum was sent to Szálasi by Rotta and the Swedish ambassador, Ivar Danielsson (countersigned by Harald Feller for Switzerland, Jorge Perlasca for Spain, and Count Pongrácz for Portugal), protesting the renewed persecution of Jews, and stating that everyone by now knew what lay in store for the deportees—not work, but a "cruel reality." As even small children, old men, and invalids were being deported, it was quite clear that work was not the purpose. "On the contrary, the brutality with which the removal is being carried out makes it possible to foresee what the end of this tragic journey will be." The memorandum included a threat that the countries at war with Hungary might seek retaliation, including the possibility that "all Hungarians abroad would be exposed if the deportation and annihilation of the Jews is continued; not to mention the fact that in the event of an occupation of Hungary the occupying forces could apply the same methods to the Hungarian people."

Rotta followed this up by issuing letters of protection to thousands of Jews on the pretext that they had applied for conversion to the Catholic faith and therefore were under the protection of the nunciature, and should not be harmed until their conversion process was completed. The letter of protection was a device also used by several other diplomats, notably Raoul Wallenberg of Sweden and Carl Lutz of Switzerland. To Nina Langlet, who, together with her husband Valdemar, represented the Swedish Red Cross, Rotta disclosed that he had received permission from the authorities to issue no more than 2,500 Vatican letters of protection, but in fact had turned out over 19,000 such documents (some sources place the number at 15,000). Jozsef Lowi, for one, testified that in the summer of 1944 there were rumors among men in his labor company unit (number 101/343) that people who converted would not be deported. Twenty-two men of the company announced their willingness to convert in order to save themselves. Thereupon the non-Jewish company commander informed the nunciature that he would allow a priest to visit his men only if letters of protection were issued to all 250 men in the company. Soon thereafter, a priest came and gave the commander Vatican letters of protection for all of the men. As for the twenty-four who wished to become Catholics, the priest "converted" them after less than two hours of instruction. The nunciature also issued certificates of protection to everyone who submitted a baptismal document, without checking whether it was genuine—this at a time when many forged baptismal documents were being produced and sold. The nunciature also took under its protective wings around twenty-five religious institutions and houses, flying the Vatican flag and therefore considered extraterritorial, where several thousand Jews were sheltered. The Arrow Cross militia often raided such buildings and murdered many of their inhabitants, but nonetheless the houses were safer than being on one's own in the open.[18]

During the infamous Death March of thousands to the Austrian border, in November 1944, with many succumbing or being shot by Hungarian gendarmes for not keeping up with the rest, Rotta authorized the issuance of pre-signed blank safe-conduct certificates to rescue Jews from the horrendous march. When he learned that Sándor György Ujváry, of the International Red Cross, was distributing false baptismal certificates, Rotta reportedly reassured him by stating: "What you are doing, my son, is pleasing to God and to Jesus, because you are saving innocent people. I give you absolution in advance. Continue your work to the honor of God." Rotta gave Ujváry a personal authorization which stated that on November 19, 1944, the apostolic nuncio in Budapest had entrusted him with the task of inquiring after all people of Jewish origin under the protection of the apostolic nunciature who had been removed from Budapest contrary to agreements legally concluded between the apostolic nunciature and the Hungarian government, and to bring them back home, and asking the military and civil authorities to give Ujváry the fullest support in carrying out this duty.[19] Rotta also persuaded a twenty-one-year-old Catholic seminarian, Tibor Baransky (at the time known as Báránszky), to distribute letters of protection. Baransky related that Monsignor Rotta summoned him several days after he had obtained letters of protection for the Jewish Szekeres family, in late October 1944. Impressed by the young seminarian's audacity, he asked: "Can you fool the Nazis like you fooled me?" Rotta had learned that nearly fifty baptized Jews were being held for deportation and he needed someone to rescue them. Baranszky: "The papal nuncio asked me if I would go the factory the next morning and get them out. I said no." Rotta did not give up. "The nuncio then offered me the keys to a small Opel." It was the nuncio's private limousine, with which Baranszky was to impress the Arrow Cross guards at the factory. Arriving there late at night with a list of fifty people, he managed to free forty. His success pleased Rotta, who appointed him secretary responsible for the department dealing with "protected" people. In that capacity, Baranszky distributed hundreds of letters of protection and took care of the 3,000 Jews in the Vatican protective houses. During the November Death March to the Austrian border, Baransky overtook the marchers and succeeded in bringing back a large number to Budapest, where he had them placed in exterritorial houses. For this purpose, he received from Rotta on the nunciature letterhead a letter similar in content to the one given Ujváry, and signed Angelo Rotta, Apostolic Nuncio, November 20, 1944. Orit Mozes testified in 1976 that Baranszky saved her and thirty other Jews in November 1944, when she was arrested for stepping out during curfew, and was taken to the cement factory for deportation, Baransky suddenly appeared, in priestly garb, and announced: "Whoever has a Vatican letter of protection, should approach him. I and another thirty people approached him. He took us out and set us free." Asked after the war how the Holocaust could be explained, Baransky said: "I say God gave you a free will. A free will is a knife. You can make beautiful carvings. Or you can kill."[20]

As the Soviet army closed its ring around Budapest and began bombarding it, the government asked all accredited diplomats to leave the city, Rotta announced that he would stay behind to protect the Jews in the embattled city. On December 25, Rotta assembled the remaining diplomats of the neutral powers for the last time, and issued a note to the Szálasi regime on behalf of the Jewish children, who at this point were being forced to move into the ghetto. "We hear it asserted that the Jews are Hungary's enemies, but even in wartime, justice and conscience condemn all hostile action directed against children. Why, then, compel these innocent creatures to live in a place which in many ways is like a prison; where the poor little ones will see nothing but the misery, suffering, and despair of old men and of women who are being persecuted simply because of their racial origin? All civilized peoples show consideration for children, and the whole world would be painfully surprised if traditionally Christian and chivalrous Hungary was to take action against these little ones. . . . Allow all children (together with their mothers when the children are not yet weaned) to remain outside the ghetto in the refuge homes organized by diplomatic missions or in the various Red Cross institutions." Rotta stayed behind during the dreadful siege of Budapest, which lasted until the city's total capture by the Russians on February 12, 1945. In summary, while at first Angelo Rotta showed greater concern about the plight of the baptized Jews, he gradually abandoned this distinction and pleaded on behalf of all Jews in danger of deportation and death. Monsignor's Rotta's behavior is to be contrasted with the lackluster and passive attitude of Cardinal Jusztinián Serédi, the head of the Catholic Church in Hungary, who declined to lend his great authority to an effort to stem the avalanche of anti-Jewish measures by a government that claimed fidelity to the Catholic faith.

Clergy Rescuers

Turning to stories of rescues by members of the clergy, as recorded at Yad Vashem, we begin with Catholic clerics. Most of the rescue operations took place in the Budapest area, the only remaining Jewish community, when the pro-Nazi Arrow Cross seized power and instituted a reign of terror against the Jewish populace. Our account starts with Father Janos Antál. He was the provincial (highest-ranking official) in the Salesian Order of St. John Bosco and of its three locations in the Budapest area, Esztergom, Óbuda, and

Rákospalota (or Ujpest), when Istvan Anhalt met him. Anhalt was in a labor battalion of the Hungarian Army that happened to be marching from Sátoraljaujhely in eastern Hungary toward the Austrian border. It was November 29, 1944, and as Istvan watched the long column of Budapest Jews (women, children and old men) equally on the forced march, he resolved to make his escape. That night he managed to slip away from his unit and enter a nearby Catholic institution. It turned out to be the Esztergom center of the Salesian Order. Asked what he wished, he responded that he wanted to see the man responsible for music at services. After being tested at the piano, and telling of his studies in the Academy of Music in Budapest, Istvan came to the point. "I told him that my life was in danger; I want to avoid having to go to Austria and asked if he could help me get to Budapest." His interlocutor was visibly shaken, and the Salesian fathers agreed to help him reach Budapest. Istvan was given a handwritten note which stated that he was a member of a paramilitary organization. A monk then accompanied Istvan to the nearby rail-way station, where he boarded a train for Budapest. Arriving there, he looked up the home of Professor Jenő de Kerpely, one of the country's best-known cellists. After spending a night with his host, Istvan decided to look up the nearby Salesian address. A priest told Istvan that he regrettably could not offer him shelter there, as the place was already overcrowded with Jewish refugees. Instead, Istvan was escorted to the Salesian Order's main house, in Rákospalota, dressed in a cassock. Arriving there, he was led into the office of the provincial, the head of the entire Salesian Order: Father Janos Antál. "He smiled at me, and his voice was calm, bespeaking kindness and understanding. I immediately felt that I would not have to 'explain' or plead much with this man." After briefly telling his story, Istvan was told to try a certain cassock. Antál laughingly told the surprised Istvan: "I took it from a visitor who just left. You see, I am too short, and my cassock would not do for you. Tomorrow we shall adjust its length to fit you." Istvan was then shown a place to spend the night. The next morning, Antál gave him a set of identity documents issued in the name of a Salesian seminarian who happened to be absent, since the Russians had already occupied his place of residence. Dressed in the monk's cassock, Istvan could now circulate freely in the city, visit friends and relatives, and return to the Salesian monastery to pass the nights. Three weeks later, on the night of December 15, 1944, the Arrow Cross staged a raid on the Salesian house and discovered about forty Jews hidden in the basement, as well as an illegal printing press. Father Antál was taken away together with the Jews. Istvan luckily escaped arrest after showing his papers, which proved to be in good order. He was now asked by Father Adám Lászlo, the administrative head of the house, who had become the priest in charge in Antál's absence, to deliver an urgent letter to the Vatican nunciature in the Buda section of the city, where Istvan was heading (to return to the De Kerpely home), and alert them to the arrest of Antál. Istvan carried out this mission, and, as he learned later, the nunciature's intervention led to the freeing of Antál as well as Father Lászlo, who, as the administrative head of the place, was charged with personal responsibility for sheltering the large group of Jews. The unfortunate Jews were taken away and shot by the Arrow Cross men. After the war, Istvan Anhalt maintained contact with Father Antál until the latter's death. In 1975, safely established in Canada, and having resumed his musical career, Anhalt dedicated an opera entitled *La Tourangelle* to Antál's memory.[21]

Also in Budapest, Albert Pfleger, a French-born monk of the Marist Order, obtained authorization from his superior, Brother Louis Pruczer, to admit fleeing Jews to the Champagnat monastery. In this endeavor, he was aided by Valdémar and Nina Langlet of the Swedish Red Cross, who provided letters of protection and food. He discounted Nina Langlet's warnings that Arrow Cross militiamen were active in the neighborhood of the Marist cloister with the words: "If the Nazis attack us, we shall go to jail with our protégés. If not, our task will only be half done." Margit Schneller was one of the people sheltered there, starting November 8, 1944. She and her family were given Pfleger's own room, while he slept on a nearby stairway. One of the Jewish wards, Olga Vértes, related how she once saw Brother Alexander Hegedűs, known as Frère Joseph, carry an old Jew into the cloister on his back after finding him unconscious in the street. With so many people sheltered in the monastery (according to one estimate as many as seventy), it was sometimes necessary for fifteen people to huddle in one room. In this huge rescue undertaking, Brother Pfleger was aided by the other monks of the order, who exerted themselves to locate new hiding places in other religious or private houses for people who could no longer be admitted to the Marist compound because of the overcrowded conditions. Word soon got on, and on December 9, 1944, the Gestapo raided the place and arrested the monks and the Jews still there. Though tortured, starved, and deprived of medical care, the monks refused to reveal the whereabouts of the other Jews or the names of those who had helped in the rescue operation. Several weeks later, thanks to the intercession of the Swedish Red Cross and the papal nuncio, they were released. After the war, recalling his rescue by the Marist monks, one of the beneficiaries said: "They considered it the most natural thing to help us. . . . If not for their humane deeds, I would not be here today able to testify on their behalf. We survivors express our deepest gratitude to them from the depths of our hearts." In addition to Albert Pfleger, the courageous monks included François Angyal, Jean-Baptiste Bonetbeltz, Bernard Clerc, Ferdinand Fischer, Alexandre Hegedűs (Br. Joseph), Ladislas Pingiczer (Br. Etienne), and Louis Pruczer.[22]

Father Jacob Raile headed a Jesuit college that sheltered 150 refugees, many of them Jewish with Raile providing them with false baptismal certificates. To fend molestations by Arrow Cross militiamen, he had some of his wards (who included many army deserters) dress in police uniforms and stand in front of the building. One of his associates was the Jesuit Joseph Zrinyi. During the siege of Budapest, he stayed in the Buda section with his family and in response to an appeal from Raile sheltered Jewish children. A member of Raoul Wallenberg's staff brought Zrinyi fourteen Jewish children for hiding, most of them baptized Protestants. Raile also sent him a baptized Catholic woman. Food was provided with the help of the Swedish Red Cross. After the liberation of the city, the children were turned over to their friends and relatives; all survived. One of Raile's Jewish wards, Andrew (Andras) Gyarfas, born 1922, reported that in October 1944 he was taken in by Raile in the Jesuit monastery on Horanszky Street, where he was reunited with his father. His brother John joined them there a few days later. Raile arranged for several relatives of the Gyarfas family to be hidden in adjoining institutions headed by nuns. In Gyarfas's words: "As for the question of his motivation, I would presume it was basically to give protection to Jews who had converted to the Catholic faith, but this protection was also extended on humanitarian grounds to many others, such as the well- known Orthodox cantor Linetzky and his family." The people sheltered by Raile, in addition to the three Gyarfases, included Cantor Linetszky, Dr. Kornhauser, Hugo Kemeny, Lesley Huszar, Dr. Ladanyi and son George, Robert Halmos and sons Robert and Paul, and Lesley Reeves. A story related by Monsignor Béla Varga has Father Raile joining Raoul Wallenberg and a third person to visit Gestapo headquarters after learning from a Gestapo agent that some prominent Jews were about to be deported, They succeeded in extricating some of these people, including Samu Stern, president of the Hungarian Jewish Council. Stern was sent elsewhere, but all the others were taken to Raile's hiding place.[23]

We briefly mention several other Catholic clerics who aided Jews. Ferenc Köhler belonged to the Lazarist Order, and like Baransky, he worked closely with Angelo Rotta, who gave him protective passes, which he distributed in Hegyeshalom, during the November 1944 Death March. It is reported that he slipped into the line of marchers and wrote down names, which he then filled in on his empty forms. Quarreling with the guards, who abusively termed him a Jew and a "servant of the Jewish pope," and even threatened to kill him, he managed to have many Jews freed. On one occasion, when some guards were about to physically assault him, Köhler held up his pectoral cross and said: "I am not afraid. Shoot me if you have the courage." They relented and withdrew.[24] Father Pal Klinda, in April 1944, opened a workshop that manufactured trousers and coats for the Hungarian army. A good many girls were employed there, and in time it became a sheltering place for as many as between forty or sixty Jewish women. In November 1944, the Arrow Cross raided the place and took away many of the girls, but it later released them in fear of intervention by a foreign agency. Father Klinda also spirited twenty women into Swedish protective houses. In April 1945, sixty former residents of the garment workshop added their signatures to a statement in favor of Klinda and his rescue efforts. Klinda died that same year; also caused as the result of physical abuse by the Arrow Cross during one of their searches of the workshop.[25] Father Pawel Boharczyk was a Slovak priest stationed in Vác, where he participated in a conspiracy to hide the Jewish identity of a group of eighty children and youths who were posing as Catholics and were sheltered in a children's home belonging to a Jew, but under the protection of a Polish refugee organization. To protect their cover, the children were made to attend church, and Boharczyk was invited to come and teach them prayers and behavior appropriate to Catholic children. With the German invasion in March 1944, the children were quickly dispersed elsewhere in Budapest.[26] We also mention Father Gilbert Nagymanyoki, who first sheltered some Jews in a children's home under his supervision, then arranged a hiding place for the Jewish Koves family.[27] Kelemen Krizosztom, who headed the Pannonhalma monastery in western Hungary, sheltered thirty-five Jews there, including Gyorgy Grosz-Gereb.[28] Finally, Ferenc Kálló, an army chaplain who admitted Egri Istvan and other Jews to a Budapest military hospital by falsely claiming that they needed medical treatment, was brutally murdered by Arrow Cross militiamen.[29]

Turning to nuns who aided Jews, Sister Margit Slachta's is the most impressive story. In 1923 she founded the Sisters, or Society, of Social Service (also known as the Gray Nuns because of their simple gray habit), a Benedictine order. In 1943, Sister Margit aroused some resentment when, in a Catholic monthly, she urged people to pray not only for their sons who were fighting on the Russian front, but also for the unarmed Jewish labor units whose job was to clear mine fields. The deportations of Slovakian Jews, which began in the spring of 1942, prompted her to see Cardinal Spellman of New York when he visited the Vatican in the spring of 1943, and he arranged for her to meet with Pope Pius XII. She pleaded with the pope to intercede on behalf of the 20,000 Slovakian deportees already suffering in German camps, and asked for his help in providing them with food and shelter. She recalled later: "He [Pius XII] listened to me all the way through. He expressed his shock. I can say the following: he listened to me but said very little." After the German takeover of Hungary on March 19, 1944, Sister Slachta called the Sisters for a conference in the society's training center in Oradea, Transylvania. She implored them to help the local Jews. "Is it the conviction of every Sister of Social Service that a moral organization can be safe for the future only when it lives up to its moral convictions? Are we willing, in the name of fraternal love, to take the risk of being interned, or carried away, if the community is being dissolved, or even of losing our own lives? If so, even if all these things were to happen, yet if in the soul of every Sister of Social Service the ideal of Christianity still lives, the community will be found worthy to have a future and will deserve life even if only one Sister of Social Service is left alive. What does it help us if our work, our property, our lives are left to us, but when we come to give account we have to hide our faces shamefully before the eyes of God." According to one estimate, the Society of Social Services harbored between 900 and 1,000 mostly Jewish men, women, and children in its houses in Budapest before placing them with reliable private people.[30]

Dr. Gábor Markus was one of Slachta's beneficiaries. He was a third-year medical student in 1944 when, after the Arrow Cross takeover on October 15, 1944, he was admitted to one of the society's homes in Máriaremete, a small community just outside Budapest. "I was immediately accepted with a warmth and kindness that made me believe they had been waiting for me. I soon found out that in the two houses that made up the convent there were approximately ninety men and women hidden. . . . Every care was taken to keep our presence invisible. I was overjoyed to find there an aunt and uncle of mine and two cousins, both young girls. . . . They did not try to convert those of us who were not Christians [some of the sheltered people were baptized Jews] . . . but they offered us consolation, hope, and guidance, and the door of the chapel was always open to anyone who wished to pray, or just to meditate." Dr. Miriam (Magdalena) Gross-Shlomi was another of the fortunate people. She had lost her husband in a Hungarian labor battalion. Moving to Kosice (then part of Hungary), in 1943, with her four-year-old son Menachem, she was admitted to one of the society's houses through the intercession of Sister Sara Salkahazi, who had known her husband as a fellow employee when she worked for a local journal before she joined the society. In the summer of 1944, when the Gestapo searched all of the society's facilities in the city, Sister Salkahazi moved Miriam and her son to Budapest; then to a society home in Jankovits Telep, near Lake Balaton, where Miriam was provided with a false identity. Dressed as a nun, she was assigned work in a rest home for women workers, and attended services with the other nuns. In one of the society's other houses, she met other Jews in hiding. She remembered a police raid that took place while Slachta happened to be visiting. Slachta approached one of the men who was questioning the children about their origin. She said to him: "Sir, why are you asking such unimportant questions? Are we raising bulls here, where one needs to know a lot about its lineage? We are merely saving souls." The man angrily retorted: "You have all sold out to the Jews," but he ended the interrogation and left. When the situation there proved too dangerous, Salkahazi brought Miriam back to Kosice, where she was hidden in one of the society's buildings. Miriam related that Sister Slachta once talked to her about converting to Christianity. When Miriam declined, Slachta apologized and expressed her admiration for Miriam's stalwart position, and never brought up the subject again. The society, together with the Holy Cross Society (founded in the 1930s to protect the interests of Catholic converts), baptized many Jews in order to protect them from the Hungarian authorities, knowing very well that the act was not motivated by belief in Christian faith but as a way to avoid persecution.

Sister Sara Salkahazi tragically died a martyr's death at the hands of Arrow Cross militiamen. When they raided one of the houses where Jews were sheltered, she was taken away together with the hidden women. Together with a great many Jews rounded up elsewhere, they were all marched that same night to the banks of the Danube, where they were shot to death, and their bodies dumped into the river. Salkahazi's body, riddled with bullets, was found lying on the riverbank. Earlier, she had composed a prayer that included the following words: "If the persecution of the church or the sisters takes place, and my death should not be in the plans of Thy Divine Wisdom and Providence, yet deign to accept it, with all its suffering, as a ransom for my Sisters, especially in place of the life of the aged, the sick, and the weak." Following this tragic event, Sister Slachta sought refuge in a Carmelite convent, and remained hidden until the city's liberation.[31] Sister Vilma Bernovits, who worked in the same home with Sara Salkhazi, suffered the same martyrdom as her colleague, shot by Arrow Cross militiamen for harboring Jews.[32] Roza-Katalin Peitl was another of the society's nuns who helped find hiding places for Jews on the run in Budapest and other locations. Among those she helped were Dr. Szcucs Albertné, Szekely Zoltan, Sperak Jozsefné, Sandor Palné, Szekely Otto, Lukin Laszloné, and Hetenyi Varga Karoly.[33]

Zsuzsanna Ván was the Mother Superior of the Society of the Holy Virgin (*Szüz Mária Társasága*) in Budapest, located near the Arrow Cross headquarters. She sheltered many fleeing Jews, children as well as adults, such as Valentine Füzéki and Edith Körmeni, as well as János Berger. Mrs. Füzéki, born 1937, and her brother were sent by her father to Sister Ván's convent in late 1944, where they stayed for a while in a separate room, then in the convent's shelter, because of the shelling by the Russian army. Eventually their mother joined them. In Valentine's words: "We were afraid; we were cold; we were in darkness because of the lack of electricity; we did not have water so we had to melt snow; we were dirty, scabby, and lousy, but still alive. We had almost nothing to eat but beans and peas and garlic as vitamin. But still alive." As to what led Sister Ván to admit adults in addition to the children already sheltered, in her words: "A lady came to the nunnery in December 1944. She had no place to go. She wanted to stay. I rejected her. 'I'll be killed,' said the lady but I still rejected her, because we had danger and worry enough with the children. I said goodbye and started upstairs. I took two or three steps, then could go no father. I was unable to take the next step. I called the lady back. She was the first adult." To which Valentine Füzéki adds: "It was so simple, wasn't it? Susanna Ván could not go any farther."[34] Also meriting mention is Hildegard Gutzwiller, the Mother Superior of the *Sacre Coeur* order, who sheltered a large group of Jews (forty children, eighty women, and ten men), such as Agnes Klein-Van Gorp.[35] As for Sister Margit Juhász, she hid Avraham Farkasz, his wife and three children for a while, then arranged another hiding place for them, introducing the woman as her sister, whose husband was a front-line soldier.[36]

Turning to Protestant pastors, help to Jews came from clerics and religious organizations that before the antisemitic persecutions in Hungary had dedicated themselves to missionize Jews and help baptized Jews avoid arrest. Later on, especially after the rise to power of the Arrow Cross party, the same clerics extended their help to all Jews in need. Gábor Jenö Sztehló was foremost among them. An Evangelical minister in Budapest, he represented the Protestant Good Shepherd (*Jo Pásztor*) Committee, originally established as an association of Jewish converts to Protestantism. Before the war, Calvinist Pastor Jószef Éliász (himself of Jewish extraction) headed the committee, which was focused on aiding converts, such as Dr. Edit Beregi, a Protestant Jewish woman, and her family. Similarly with Dr. M. Kűlloi-Rhörer (Mária Székely), who worked as a secretary and translator in Éliász's office; she was born a Lutheran but was of Jewish extraction. Margit Weisz, another convert, was forced to wear the star, and Éliász agreed to shelter her and her child. In October 1944, Éliász went underground, and his work was continued by Gábor Sztehló. The work of the committee was especially crucial during the Arrow Cross period, when it kept hundreds of children in thirty-two homes. Although some of the homes were raided by the Arrow Cross and the police, remarkably little harm befell the children entrusted to Sztehló's care. One of the beneficiaries was the seventeen-year-old Tibor Berger (later, Samuel Ben Dov), who escaped from a labor battalion and returned to Budapest carrying a forged document stating that he was a Hungarian Christian refugee. "I went to the Evangelical institution and presented my papers to the director, a minister named Gábor Sztehló. He looked at it and at once said: 'This document is forged, and you are Jewish, but don't worry. I shall place you in one of our institutions in the city.' " Tibor soon became aware of the many Jewish children among the Christian refugees in the institution; some of the nurses and nannies were also Jewish. Soon Arrow Cross men forced their way into the building and hauled all the Jewish children to the ghetto. Tibor fled again and made his way to Sztehló's office in the Buda section of the city, on the other side of the Danube River. Making his way safely over the guarded bridges, he was warmly received by Sztehló, who gave him a document stating that he was a messenger for the Red Cross. During the Soviet siege of Budapest, Sztehló transferred thirty-three children with forged documents to the cellar of his private home, where he was hiding with his family and cared for them until the city's liberation. It is estimated that 500 Jewish children were saved this way.

Pal Foti, another recipient of Sztehló's aid, related that around the end of October 1944, he escaped from a forced labor unit and made his way to Pastor Sztehló's office in Buda. Arriving there, he introduced himself as Emil Pasztor. " 'I am an Aryan . . . and this is my only document,' I said. 'All right my son . . . you don't have to convince me,' Sztehló responded and continued, 'I will send you to one of our Swiss Red Cross children's homes, and you shall work as a messenger.' " After alternating between several places, on New Year's 1945, Pal secretly made his way to Sztehló's home, where he met forty other hidden people. "Mrs. Sztehló served us hot soup. Days passed, as we stayed in the cellar, which was an air raid shelter. They had one son, four years old and a daughter of two. . . . Pastor Sztehló never wanted to convert any of us. It was he who made me go to the synagogue on Yom Kippur 1945 [after the liberation]. Thinking back to this time of man's inhumanity to man, the person of Pastor Gábor Sztehló, with his great courage and humanity, gave me back my faith in my fellow men." Another of Sztehló's Jewish wards recalled the Bible reading and prayer every evening. At the same time, "Pastor Sztehló made no attempt to convert us, but he knew that faith in God was absolutely essential to help us overcome our sense of abandonment and terror. Quite naturally, he shared with us the religion he professed, Christianity. Although I never converted, I have retained a deep gratitude for the spiritual comfort I received, which was critical to my survival and that of my friends during those horrible times." No precise estimates exist, but by all accounts the number of Jewish children saved by Sztehló's institution runs to several hundred.[37]

Reverend László Michnai, an Adventist minister, also saved many Jews. As reported by Yehudit Carmeli, she and her parents Jenö and Lina Vámosi, and sister Agnes received forged identity papers from him. After the Arrow Cross takeover, he took them to Vác, a small town north of Budapest, and there housed them with friends. He also sheltered many Jews in his house (according to one report as many as thirty). Michnai was known as a philosemite, and he constantly endangered himself by moving his wards from place to place. Michnai gave Lina Vamosi, her husband, and two daughters the Christian documents he had with him, in the name of his wife and his two daughters. Then, on October 18, 1944, he moved them out of Budapest to a safe place outside the city; and thence to a village near Vác, with an Adventist farmer's family.[38] A somewhat unusual case is that of Pastor András Keken, who sheltered Jews (both baptized and not) in his church. In 1944, he was accused by the Arrow Cross of baptizing Jews too quickly, waiving the regular study and indoctrination needed for such an important rite. He defended himself by claiming that he had in fact rejected many Jewish candidates for conversion because they did not meet the requirements and had actually only baptized about forty people from the hundreds who had applied to him. This disclaimer served him ill after the war, for in 1948 he was charged with refusing to convert Jews who had approached him and thus with having condemned them to the hands of the antisemitic authorities. It was also charged that in 1944 he had accused several other clerics of being too lax in conversion procedures. A good many witnesses at the hearing (some of them baptized Jews) testified that he had sheltered them either in his Budapest church or in his home; the witnesses included Miklós Szász, Magda Völgyesi-Tauszig, Jolán Fejér, Edith Szász-Dobó, Jenö Falvay, Erzsébet Frankl, Ágnes Féher-Varga, Margit Varga-Czinner, and Márta Gloetzer-Broschko.[39]

We also have the extraordinary story of Jane Haining, a native of Scotland, and member of the Reformed Presbyterian Church, who in 1932 was sent to Budapest to head the girls' home of the Scots Jewish Mission. The Scots Mission was established in Budapest in 1841, with the purpose of converting Jews, and a school was opened in 1907 to instruct Jews interested in Christianity. During the Holocaust years, many of the 400 boarder girls were Jewish; according to one report, of the 315 pupils and 48 boarders, 224 and 31, respectively, were Jewish. In Haining's words: "We try to surround these girls with a Christian home atmosphere and, without trying to thrust religion down their throats, to instill into them, consciously or subconsciously, by practice as well as precept what Christianity means. . . . We have, for each day, a Bible lesson when the Jewish children must learn the New Testament. . . . Our girls all leave us at about fourteen to fifteen years of age; and again, according to the law of Hungary, no child may change its religion officially until it is eighteen years of age." One woman wrote thankfully after the war that through Haining's influence, her mother became a convert to Christianity. In 1942, conversion courses were suspended, to facilitate a quick conversion process so as to save those asking it. In the words of one Scottish minister: "Those people were not making the conversion out of their free will and choice, circumstances forced them to do it. . . . It would not [have been] humane to burden them further with another act of force, and therefore I suspended the six-week introductory course. I had to do this without being able to consult with the church in Edinburgh." When the Nazis ordered all the Jewish girls to wear a star on their clothes, Jane Haining wept as she sewed on the identifying Stars of David. When she was arrested by two Gestapo agents on April 25, 1944, appeals went out to Bishop Ravasz, to Prime Minister Dome Sztójay, and to the head of state, Miklos Horthy—all to no avail. She was charged with working among Jews, weeping when seeing the girls attend class wearing the yellow star, dismissing her non-Jewish house-keeper, listening to the BBC, hosting many British visitors and visiting escaping British POW's, and sending them food parcels. Deported to Auschwitz on May 15, she died there on July 17, 1944.[40]

We end with several brief accounts. Pastor Imre Szabo founded the Julianna religious boarding school for Protestant-baptized Jewish children. During the Arrow Cross period, he also sheltered several fleeing Jewish children.[41] Emil Koren worked with Gábor Sztehló, who sent him Jewish children for shelter. After the war, Koren became a Lutheran deputy bishop.[42] Albert Bereczky, a Calvinist pastor in Budapest, was initially concerned with helping baptized Jews avoid arrest and harm, as with Maria Vida and her parents, who had converted to Protestantism in 1919, and had joined Bereczky's church. During the German occupation, he provided false credentials for her and family, and also arranged hiding places for them. With the intensification of the persecution, Bereczky moved on to helping Jews as well. Mrs. Levendel Laszlone, one of the unconverted Jews he helped, received false credentials from Bereczky for herself and her daughter, as well as temporary asylum in the Calvinist church. She stayed there for only a week, because she was worried about her mother in the ghetto and visited her. On returning to the church, she learned that everyone hidden had been killed by a gang of Arrow Cross militia led by the Catholic monk András Kun (executed after the war). After the war, Bereczky was nominated bishop of the Calvinist Church.[43] Also meriting mention is the Greek Orthodox priest Jozsef Csedrik, in Duszina, near Munkacevo, who sheltered Ervin Selmeczi-Schwarcz and Otto Mozes, who had escaped from a labor battalion in October 1944.[44] Victor Janos sheltered a group of Jews in his Budapest home, including thirteen-year-old Erzsébet Herman and her mother.[45] Finally, Andor Jarosi, in Kolozsvar/Cluj, sheltered the young Anna Kadar in his home during the tragic roundup of the city's Jews and their deportation to Auschwitz.[46] This concludes the list of Hungarian clerics awarded the Righteous title by Yad Vashem for help to Jews.

Chapter 11
The Balkans:
Croatia, Serbia, Bulgaria, and Greece

Christian non-Aryans, especially Catholics, [should] be separat-
ed from other non-Aryans of the Jewish religion; . . .
district officials [should] be ordered not to place Catholic
non-Aryans in the same category with other non-Aryans
when taking administrative measures.
Archbishop Alojzije Stepinac, to Croatian pro-Nazi government
(May 1941)

We cannot be callous to the pain of the Jews as if they were
strangers or spectators. . . . The Holy Church . . . should speak
up for the oppressed and persecuted Jews, regardless of whether
they are converted or not.
Metropolitan Stefan (Bulgaria, 1942/43)

We are all the children of the same Father, for God created us in
his own image, and we are obligated to extend our help to our
fellow men, and not allow Satan to rule over us. . . .
I have made my cross, have spoken with God, and have
decided to save as many Jewish souls as I can.
Metropolitan Damaskinos (Greece, 1943)

Croatia and Serbia

Jews have lived in what was until recently the federated republic of
Yugoslavia since Roman times, when the area was known as Pannonia. Until
the modern period, much of what is now Serbia (converted to Greek
Orthodoxy) was under the rule of the Ottoman Turkish Empire, while Croatia
(converted to Catholicism), to the north, was ruled by the Austrian Empire.
Jewish settlements existed in Belgrade, Zagreb, and other cities, and they

experienced intermittent good and bad times until late in the eighteenth century, when Jews finally gained full civil liberties. Croatia became an independent state for the first time in its history when Germany invaded Yugoslavia on April 10, 1941, and dismembered it into separate entities. The rest of the country was gobbled up by Germany and its allies: Serbia and Slovenia were controlled directly by Germany, while Italy, Hungary, and Bulgaria divided the remainder of the spoil. Only half of Croatia's population of 6.3 million, were Roman Catholics; the others included Greek Orthodox Serbs (1.9 million), Muslims (700,000), ethnic Germans (170,000), Hungarians, Gypsies, and some 40,000 Jews. An radical pro-Nazi regime, based on the Ustaša fascist party, came into being, headed by Ante Pavelić Pavelić, who was both head of state and prime minister, and termed himself *Poglavnik* ("Leader") in good Nazi style. Croatia has one of the worst records of atrocities committed against Jews and other minorities during World War II. The new government closed ranks with Hitler's Germany in launching a vicious persecution campaign against the country's Jews, most of whom were either executed on Croatian soil or delivered to the Germans for deportation to the death camps. In addition, the Croat Ustaša, which depicted itself as a Catholic bulwark in the southern Balkans, undertook a campaign of ethnic cleansing against the large Serb minority and the small Gypsy population, but leaving the Muslims (in Bosnia-Herzegovina, also annexed to Croatia) in relative peace.[1] In the course of the war, a half a million Serbs were killed, a quarter of a million were expelled o Serbia, and 200,000 converted to Catholicism.

As one of its first acts, the Croat government issued several decrees modeled on the German Nuremberg laws, defining Jewishness, requiring the wearing of a yellow star with the letter *Z* (for *Zidov,* "Jew") on it, confiscating Jewish property, and conscripting male Jews for forced labor in the salt mines and elsewhere. Some 5,000 Jews fled to the Italian zone of occupation, where the Italian authorities refused to molest them, declaring that doing so would be "incompatible with the honor of the Italian army." Thousands of Jews were sent to concentration camps on Croat soil, the most notorious being Jasenovic, south of Zagreb, the country's capital, where 20,000–25,000 Jews were slaughtered, along with 600,000 Serbs and Gypsies. It was one of the most brutal and notorious camps to have dotted the European landscape. There were no gas chambers; inmates were killed in the most cruel and primitive fashion by shooting, hanging, knifing, and hacking to death. One of the camp's commanders was a former priest, Miroslav Filipović-Majstorović, who reportedly killed scores of prisoners with his own hands. By the end of the year, two-thirds of Croat Jewry were incarcerated in one of the eight concentration camps on Croat soil, where most were killed soon after their arrival. In the summer of 1942, the Croat government asked the Germans to remove the remainder of the Jews to German-operated concentration camps, and said it was willing to pay 50 German marks for each Jew removed from Croatia, in gratitude for the "final solution of the Jewish problem" in Croatia. Total Jewish losses amounted to 30,000, or 80 percent of the prewar Jewish population. In Serbia, to the south, under direct German occupation, the destruction process of the 8,000 Jews moved even more swiftly, and the killing was taken over by the German military. Around 15,000 Jewish women and children were asphyxiated in special gas vans installed in motor vehicles. In June 1942, the Germans proudly announced that the Jewish problem had been solved in Serbia; they had all been killed—except, of course, for the few in hiding.[2]

The Catholic Church enthusiastically welcomed the establishment of the Croatian state and was happy about the goal of its leaders to purify the state by eliminating the non-Catholic elements (with the exception of the Muslims). Many Catholic priests, mainly of the lower clergy, took an active part in the murder operations. Ivan Saric, the bishop of Sarajevo, reportedly justified the persecution of Jews, stating that the Jews, as the descendants of those who hated Jesus, and persecuted him to death, were responsible for the present moral and economic disaster in Europe. "Their appetite grows till only domination of the whole world will satisfy it. . . . Satan helped them to invent socialism and communism."[3] The dominant religious figure in this Catholic country was Archbishop Alojzije Stepinac. As head of the Catholic Church, he gave his blessings, at least publicly, to many of the government's actions. Privately, and in messages to government ministers, Stepinac voiced misgivings and even protests at some of the extreme measures against political opponents and ethnic minorities, but in public he was a loyal supporter of the Ustaša government and its "Leader," Pavelić, on whom he bestowed the church's blessings at the many political ceremonies which he, as the leading church dignitary, dutifully attended. Far from condoning the brutal excesses of the regime, Stepinac felt it was wiser to try restrain the regime's inhumane militancy through private appeals to Pavelić and his ministers, rather than by uttering public denunciations from the pulpit. At the same time, Stepinac and the Catholic clergy were not, in principle, averse to repression short of mass expulsion and murder. Stepinac also held sway over the military chaplains, but he did little to restrain their vociferous enthusiasm for the regime's brutal policies. In July 1941, in a letter to Pavelić, Stepinac appealed for a more humane application of the measures against the state's enemies: allowing people to settle their personal affairs before being deported, not to use overcrowded sealed trains for deportations, provide the sick with medicine, allow Catholic priests to conduct Christmas services for camp inmates and to administer the last rites to those on the verge of death, since, in the words of Stepinac, "the dying begged for a priest to prepare them for death." By and large the regime ignored such requests by Stepinac.[4]

Stepinac also applied himself with some vigor in defending the rights of baptized Jews and those religiously married with Catholic spouses. In May 1941, he told Interior Minister Andrija Artukovic that while one could view with favor the government's "wish to eliminate every bad influence which would destroy unity," he asked for special treatment of baptized Jews—so that "Christian non-Aryans, especially Catholics, be separated from other non-Aryans of the Jewish religion. . . when taking administrative measures," such as exempting them from wearing the distinguishing yellow star badge. Similarly, the Bishops' Synod convened by Stepinac in November 1941, appealed to the government to carry out measures against the Jews in a humane manner "as far as possible," and especially so the baptized Jews. "We therefore turn to you . . . to let personal and civil liberty and their property be returned to those Jews and their descendants, who after having been converted should not be regarded anymore as Jews," the bishops wrote. Stepinac similarly protested against the state's planned annulment of marriages between Jews and Catholics in marriages sanctioned by the church. "For this reason," Stepinac wrote to Artukovic, "I call on you . . . to differentiate, in that order, between Catholic non-Aryans and non-Aryans [i.e., plain Jews]." In his official communications to the government, Stepinac also pleaded that the Jewish Question not be solved "in a most brutal manner," without regard to Christian teachings. Punishment should be proportionate to "the injustice done by the Jews," but should not include innocent Jews. The government, of course, saw this as a green light to continue its anti-Jewish measures, and dismissed Stepinac's appeal for the measures to be applied more humanely.

In private, behind the scenes, Stepinac was willing to assist Jews who appealed for his help. Thus, in December 1942, in response to an appeal by the remnants of the Jewish community in Zagreb, he offered one of his estates as a refuge for the sixty remaining residents of a Jewish old age home. In addition, he tried to save the life of Dr. Miroslav (Shalom) Freiberger, the chief rabbi of Zagreb, but without success. The rabbi was deported to a German concentration camp, where he perished. At the same time, while visiting the Vatican in May 1943, at a time when the killings of Serbs, Jews, and Gypsies was at a high pitch, Stepinac had only words of praise for the Ustaša leadership. He praised it for abolishing abortion, "which had been initiated primarily by Jewish and [Greek] Orthodox doctors," and also for eliminating pornographic literature; here, too, the culprits were "Jews and Serbs." Earlier, in February 1942, Stepinac lauded Pavelić for his "renovation" of the country based "on the eternal foundations of Christ's principles contained in the

Bible." After the war, the communist-installed Yugoslav regime put Stepinac on trial for collaboration with the Ustaša regime, and sentenced him to a long-term imprisonment. He died while in confinement.[5]

The Vatican did not formally recognize the new regime and therefore was represented by an apostolic "visitor," the Benedictine abbot Giuseppe Ramiro Marcone, rather than a nuncio. The Croat regime, however, treated Marcone as a *de facto* nuncio, and he attended all functions of an official nature. In August 1941, Marcone reported to the Vatican on the opportunity presented by the persecution of Jews to gain souls for the Catholic Church. "Supernatural motives and the silent action of divine grace cannot be *a priori* excluded from this. Our clergy facilitates their conversion, thinking that at least their children will be educated in Catholic schools and therefore will be more sincerely Christian." In the summer of 1942, Marcone reported a conversation with Eugen Kvaternik, chief of the Croat police, who told him that two million Jews had already been killed. In Kvaternik's words "the same fate awaits the Croat Jews particularly if old and incapable of work." At about the same time, on August 4, 1942, Rabbi Freiberger appealed to Pius XII for help. "Now, at the moment when the last remnants of our community find themselves in a most critical situation—at a moment when decisions are being made about their lives—our eyes are fixed upon Your Holiness. We beseech Your Holiness in the name of several thousand women and abandoned children, whose supports are in concentration camps, in the name of widows and orphans, in the name of the elderly and the feeble, to help them so that they may remain in their homes and spend their days there, even, if necessary, in the most humble circumstances." The response, received via Marcone, was the standard Vatican formula that it had always desired to bring help and relief to the suffering, and would continue to do so.

The Vatican's real concern was and remained the baptized Jews. In March 1943, Marcone reassured Cardinal Maglione that "I have insisted to Pavelić that above all, families resulting from mixed marriages and, in general, all the baptized Jews, should not be molested. Pavelić has always promised to respect the Jews who had become Catholics or were married to Catholics." It is estimated that several thousand people fell under this category, and most were spared, but some were deported in spite of the Croatian government's promise to the contrary. As for the non-baptized Jews, evidently their fate was of little concern to Marcone and his superiors in Rome. Not once did the Catholic Church in Croatia or the Vatican issue a protest or condemnation of the actions taken by the Croat authorities against the Jews. In the words of Morley: "The record of Croatia on the Jews is particularly shameful, not because of the number of Jews killed, but because it was a state that proudly proclaimed its Catholic tradition and whose leaders depicted themselves as loyal to the church and the pope." The church failed to use its prestige in this self-pro-claimed Catholic country to try thwart the murderous actions of the regime against the Jews and other non-Catholic minorities.[6]

There is very little information in the Yad Vashem archives about Catholic clerics in Croatia sheltering Jews. The known few include Dragutin Jesih, who saved Milivoj Radicevic (today Dan Baram), born 1931, by hiding him and his mother Erna in the cellar of his church, near Ščitarjevo, from 1942 until 1944. Jesih made no secret of his opposition to the Pavelić regime. One night in late 1944, armed Ustaša men invaded Jesih's home, took him out, knifed him to death, and threw his body into the Sava River. Dan Baram and his mother were able to escape.[7] Also to be noted are the two nuns Jozica Jurin (Sr. Cecilija), the Mother Superior of a Catholic convent in Split, and Sister Karitas, who admitted fleeing refugees, including Jews, for shelter. Jurin had been in touch with the Jewish community in Split, who sent refugees to her from time to time. Toward the end of 1941, four-year-old Avraham Albahari from Sarajevo was brought there and given a new name—Bata. At that time, there were seven other Jewish children under the care of Sister Karitas, who knew of their origin (including Erna Papo, Iso Poljoka, and Avraham Albahari). The area where the convent was located was initially under Italian control. With the coming of the Germans, in September 1943, the convent underwent searches by the new masters. At such times, the Jewish children had to be quickly hidden in various other locations.[8] These represent the only clergy in Croatia honored with the "Righteous" title. As for clerical rescuers in nearby Serbia, we have the case of Svetozar Milenkovic, the local Greek Orthodox priest, in Raska. In February 1942, he sheltered Hermina Fenje and her two daughters, Magda and Ica, in his house for several days, which he shared with his wife Vida. The Milenkovices then arranged for the Fenje fam-ily to leave the village for another region, in the mountains, where it was felt they would be safer.[9]

Bulgaria

A Jewish settlement is known to have existed in Macedonia in Roman times, as well as later, when the area was part of the Byzantine Empire. More Jews trekked down to present-day Bulgaria from Hungary and Germany, or arrived via ship from Spain. In 1878, Bulgaria gained partial independence under Turkish suzerainty, and in 1908, full independence, at which time Jews were granted equal rights. In 1940, most of the country's 6.2 million inhabi-tants belonged to the Orthodox Church (87.5 percent). The Jewish population in 1943 (including the annexed territories) was 63,400, or about 1 percent of the population, of whom 51,500 lived within the pre-1940 borders, half of them residing in the capital city of Sofia. In 1933 a Nazi-oriented movement came into being, the Union of Bulgarian National Legions, known as the Legionnaires' Association. This was followed by the founding of a youth organization, Branik, modeled on the Nazi Hitler Youth, and a fascist organization, known as the Ratnitsi ("Warrior"), led by Petur Gabrovski, who served as minister of the interior during the war years. On February 15, 1940, King Boris III, who earlier had obtained dictatorial powers, appointed the pro-German Bogdan Filov as prime minister, and on March 1, 1941, Bulgaria formally joined the Axis. On that day, Hitler forced Romania to cede southern Dobruja to Bulgaria. A month later, following the conquest of Yugoslavia and Greece, Bulgaria obtained a further long-dreamed bonus, Macedonia and Thrace, and thus the fulfillment of a Greater Bulgaria.

Following in the footsteps of its Nazi ally, in August 1940, the government introduced the Law for the Protection of the Nation, which curbed the rights of Jews. The law specified, "The Jews are an evil and foreign element among the Bulgarian people that acts against the state." Jews, therefore, could not be elected to public office, and Jewish civil servants had to resign immediately; mixed marriages between Jews and Bulgarians were prohibited; Jews were restricted to their current places of residence; and Jewish economic activities were severely restricted. All Jews were required to register and to submit to the Ministry of Finance a statement of their total wealth within seven days of the law's publication, and a special tax was imposed on the Jewish community. Exceptions were provided for Jews who had converted to Christianity, were married to non-Jews, or served in the military. Furthermore, all Jewish males between the ages of twenty and forty were liable to conscription into special labor battalions, for work in the mountains and forests. Finally, all Jews aged ten and over had to wear a yellow badge on their clothing. The law defined as Jewish, anyone with three or more Jewish grandparents. Such a person would not be considered Jewish if he had been married in a Christian rite to a non-Jew before September 1, 1940. The law was supported by the fascist organizations, the students union, the merchants' association, and trade and business groups. Opposition was voiced by the writers, lawyers, and doctors union. Twenty-one leading writers sent a protest letter to the prime minister, stating: "On behalf of civilization and on behalf of Bulgaria's good name, we beseech you not to accept the law, the repercussions of which would put a dark stain on our legislation and leave an intolerable mark upon our national memory." But it was to no avail.[10]

The Holy Synod of the Bulgarian Orthodox Church, headed by Metropolitan Stefan of Sofia, also voiced its opposition. At first, the primary concern of the Bulgarian Church was for baptized Jews. However, it also voiced grave reservations about the law's application to the whole Jewish population—that is, all Jews. On November 15, 1940, the Holy Synod petitioned the government to treat Bulgarian citizens of Jewish origin who had converted, or were willing to do so, in the same manner as Christian Bulgarians. The petition added that Jews should not be singled out for counter-measures, because the Bulgarian Orthodox Church believed that we are all children of one fatherly God, and therefore certain provisions with regard to Jews should be annulled, because of their basic injustice. "Let no account be taken of laws against the Jews as a national minority," the statement continued," but let purposeful steps be taken against the real dangers to the spiritual, cultural, economic, public, and political life of the Bulgarian people, from whatever direction these dangers come." The petition was signed by all the metropolitan bishops: Stefan of Sofia, Mihail of Dorostol and Cherven, Paisi of Vratza, Sofroni of Tarnovo, Yosif of Varna and Preslav, Kiril of Plovdiv, Filaret of Lovech, and Evlogi of Sliven. Kiril had already in 1938 written a pamphlet condemning antisemitism, and he presently issued his own personal condemnations of the government leaders. In early 1941, Metropolitan Stefan convened a plenary session of the Holy Synod, which passed a resolution agreeing to send a letter of protest to the prime minister. "The principle of racism which is the basic idea on which the above-mentioned law is founded . . . in this case the Jewish race, has no justification, and therefore . . . one cannot turn the Law for the Protection of the Nation into a means of oppression and persecution of the Jewish minority in the land." These protests came to nothing, and on January 21, 1941, the discriminatory law was passed by parliament; it was ratified by the king's signature two days later.[11]

On August 26, 1942, the government established a Commissariat for Jewish Questions, at the insistence of Interior Minister Petur Gabrovski, the architect of the anti-Jewish legislation. Aleksandur Belev was appointed commissar. Jewish community boards were stripped of their powers and placed under the authority of the commissariat, whose expenses were to be financed by the blocked bank accounts of the Jews. In other words, the Jews themselves would have to pay the enormous cost of their persecution. Everything conceivably Jewish had to be marked: apartments, stores, business correspondence, bills, and even merchandise. Everything of monetary value in the possession of Jews was confiscated, including motor vehicles and bicycles, and Jews were forbidden to be on the street except for four or five hours a day to shop.

In a report to the Holy Synod on September 14, 1942, Metropolitan Stefan (born Stoyan Popgueorguiev) stated his concern about the converted Jews who were affected by the new decree. "Already wearing the life-giving cross, they are also forced to wear the Jewish Star of David. . . .They can live neither with Christians nor with Jews who have not converted. . . . There have never been any borderline Christians in the history of our holy church! . . .

Those who belong to the holy church are fiercely and relentlessly persecuted without being guilty or having committed any sin, just because of their origin." Stefan also deplored the escalated persecution of Jews as "uncharacteristic of and averse to the Bulgarian people. . . . This phenomenon throws the dark shadow of barbarity and brutality over the good reputation of the Bulgarian people as a tolerant and benevolent nation." Linking the fate of the converts with that of all Jews, Stefan went on: "We cannot be callous to the pain of the Jews as if they were strangers or spectators." On September 9, 1942, Stefan preached a sermon in which he restated the traditional Christian view of Jewish guilt: "God punished the Jews for the crucifixion of Jesus in that He expelled them from their country and had not given them a country of their own. And thus, God has determined the destiny of the Jews." He mellowed these harsh words with a reminder: "However, men have no right to exercise cruelty toward the Jews and to persecute them. Christians especially ought to see their brother in Jews who have accepted the Christian religion and to support them in every way. . . . It is in God's hands to punish twice and three times, but it is forbidden for Christians to do such a thing."[12]

Bowing to German pressure, on February 2, 1943, Interior Minister Gabrovski assented to a demand by SS officer Theodor Dannecker that all Jews living in Greek and Yugoslav Macedonia and in Thrace, administered by Bulgaria, would be surrendered to the Germans for deportations. On February 22 1943, a formal agreement to this effect was signed by Belev and Dannecker, and on March 3, the government approved the surrender of 20,000 Jews into German hands. The plan called for the deportation of 8,000 Jews from Macedonia and Pirot, 6,000 from Thrace, and 6,000 from Bulgaria proper, for a total of 20,000. Starting March 4, 1943, some 12,000 Jews were deported from the Bulgarian-occupied countries by Bulgarian soldiers and police, who turned them over to the Germans. With a few exceptions, all of them died in Treblinka. Belev was still short of the 20,000 Jews stipulated in the agreement with Dannecker, so he decided to fill the quota with Jews from Bulgaria proper, beginning with the Jews of Kustendil. When Dimitur Peshev, the vice president of the Subranie (parliament), learned of the planned deportation of Jews from his city of Kustendil, he organized a parliamentary protest and presented the prime minister with a petition protesting the deportations signed by forty-two deputies. Stunned by this organized protest (backed up by protests from prominent public figures), the government relented, and the deportations were temporarily halted. Peshev was made to pay the price for his insubordination by a parliamentary reprimand and removal from the vice-presidency.[13] Momentarily stunted, the government soon renewed its anti-Jewish drive, and by end of May 1943 it ordered the eviction of the 25,000 Jews of Sofia to the countryside, whence—away from the glaring public eye—it would be easier to deport them should such a decision later be made. As a result, about 19,000 Jews were driven from their homes in Sofia and forced to live in twenty provincial towns, with many as eight to ten people to a room. Their property was put up for auction, and their homes were given to the poor. In addition, several hundred prominent Jewish families were sent to a camp in Somovit, which came close to being a Bulgarian concentration camp.

In anticipation of the deportation of Jews from Bulgaria proper, Abraham Alfasi, head of the Jewish community in Sofia, went to see Metropolitan Stefan to ask him to intervene. Stefan immediately went to the palace and asked King Boris to cancel the order to deliver the Jews to the Germans. The Metropolitan threatened that if the government attempted to carry out the deportation, he would order the gates of the churches and monasteries opened to shelter the Jews. On April 2, 1943, Stefan called for a plenary session of the Holy Synod. It unanimously decided to send a letter of protest to Prime Minister Filov and Interior Minister Gabrovski, stating that the church deplored the Law for the Protection of the Nation, which had become an instrument for "restricting and persecuting the Jewish minority in our country. . . . These citizens of our country are deprived of the most elementary rights, and the Department for Jewish Affairs is free to do with them as it wishes; sending them to camps and deporting them from the country. Our people . . . cannot tolerate injustice, cruelty, and violence against anybody. It cannot accept what is being done now to the Jewish minority. . . . The Holy Synod of the Bulgarian Church cannot ignore its divine command and its holy duty. It must, in accordance with the teaching of the Gospel concerning love of one's neighbor, raise a compassionate and defending voice in aid of the suffering and wronged people; it must beg, guide, and convince, so that the measures against the Jews may cease or at least be eased. God's law, which transcends all human laws, definitely obliges us not to be indifferent in the face of the sufferings of innocent people of whatever race."[14]

During that session, Metropolitan Kiril of Plovdiv described events in his city. "On March 10, some 1,500 to 1,600 people from Plovdiv were arrested and detained in a school, before being deported to Poland. In the morning I was told what had happened. I sent a note to His Majesty the King, in which I pleaded with him in God's name to show mercy toward these miserable people. After that I asked to speak to the police commissioner, who was in Plovdiv that day, but couldn't get in touch with him. I looked for the district police chief, but was told he was also absent. Then I called out his deputy and asked him in a rather civil manner to tell the government that so far I had always been loyal to it, but now will act at my own discretion as my conscience as a bishop dictates to me. Then some converted Jews came to see me.

I comforted them and told them they could find shelter at my home. They can arrest them in my home! Later on, an order was received at about noon, much to the delight of those arrested, to let them free." Metropolitan Stefan added that "the Jews now seek shelter with the church. We cannot turn them away. Their suffering is inhumane. I could understand if the government told them they were not wanted in the country and gave them six months to leave with all their possessions, but when a boy comes to your house and tells you to pack your things in two hours and be ready to leave for some unknown place—this is unheard of and never before seen in our country. Some horrible things happened to the Jews from Aegean Thrace. The persecuted Jewish community is calling for our help, and we cannot deny them sincere Christian care and attitude. The Holy Synod cannot turn a deaf ear to the pleas of these wretched people." Metropolitan Kliment of Stara Zagora added that "we cannot remain indifferent to the fate of the persecuted Jewish minority because we would be condemned by God and we would find ourselves in the same position as the Levite and the priest from the parable of the Good Samaritan, who went past the wounded man without looking at him. It is cruel and unjust to drive someone out of their home. There are other purely Christian reasons for which we have to stand up for the Jewish minority and voice our protest against the government's actions." Similar opinions were voiced by the other metropolitans present.

Metropolitan Kiril (born Konstantin Markov) especially stood out for his favorable and warm attitude toward Jews, which was not diluted by theological considerations, as in the case of Metropolitan Stefan and others, who mixed their words with the doctrine that the Jews were eternally punished for refusing to acknowledge the Christian Messiah. According to Suzanna Behar, the daughter of Shmuel Behar, the rabbi of Plovdiv—her father and Kiril often met in the rabbi's house or in Kiril's—"He never failed to send good wishes to us on our great Jewish holidays." On March 10, 1943, when Kiril learned of the arrest of the city's Jews, he immediately took steps to have them released. "When we came back home, there was a knock on the door, and there stood Patriarch Kiril, dressed in his ceremonial vestment, a smile on his face. He and my father hugged each other. They spoke for about twenty minutes." Another witness, Sarina Molho, remembered that on March 10, 1943, as a ten-year-old child, she witnessed Bishop Kiril making his way to a place where Jews were gathered and assuring them that "I will not allow any of you to leave Plovdiv"; and that same afternoon they were released. Another report has Kirl informing the king that he will start a campaign of civil disobedience, including personally lying down on the railroad tracks in front of the deportation trains, if the planned operation was carried out.[15]

When Sofia's Jews faced expulsion, Rabbis Daniel Tsion and Asher Hananel, together with two other leaders of the Jewish community, Adolf Chaymov and Menachem Moshonov, sought out Stefan, on the morning of May 24, 1943, for his intervention against the decree. As related by Moshonov, Stefan "after he had listened to us, he calmed us and promised to continue to do everything in his power to prevent the deportation of the Jews from the country." He added that he would see the king that same day during the ceremony in honor of Saints Kyril and Methodius, and would speak to him about this matter. He seemed to be very moved and full of hope." According to Stefan's account, as reported to the Holy Synod on May 27, 1943, Rabbi Hanannel said to him, "If we did not fear deportation to Poland, we would not be ill at ease. We have no other homeland than Bulgaria. . . . Let them draft all of us fit for work, because many are already in work groups, and send them to internment camps, but we need confirmation that we will not be deported from Bulgaria." Taking his leave from them, Stefan left for the cathedral, for the festivities of Kiril and Methodius Day, and "as I was entering the cathedral a group of mothers approached me and asked me to take their children—some of them converted, others not—and dedicate them to God and homeland, but not allow their deportation from the country. This tormented my soul on the morning of this great festive service. I was terrified of God, and inconsolable grief and fear for Bulgaria and its children gripped my heart. My soul was torn in dark foreboding, and my heart was wept for lost national values and imminent hardships and misfortunes because we enrage God and harm ourselves when we persecute the defenseless." Returning home, he drafted a letter to the king. It read in part: "My heart is broken! I have a presentiment that we will be punished severely for what we have done to the Jews because our acts are disrespectful of God and harmful to the nation. The blood of the innocent thirsts for revenge. . . . Jesus Christ says we should not persecute lest we be persecuted because 'measure for measure.' I apologize for this clumsy letter but I did not have much time." A day later, another Jewish dignitary visited Stefan. Solomon Mashiach related what took place during his visits to Stefan on May 25 and 26. "After I locked the door, and told him of our travails, he listened to me, then said. 'This I cannot permit as long as I am alive. . . . I shall speak with the king immediately. I wish you to hear our conversation.' " Stefan then placed a call and was connected to the king. He said: "Boris, my son, I am not at all satisfied with you. One hears lately of many things done to our Israelite brethren. This is unworthy of you and of the Bulgarian people." The king asked what Stefan had in mind. Stefan: "Things have come to my knowledge which I would rather not believe. They are a disgrace and a shame to you and to the Bulgarian people. I cannot explain them to you by telephone. If you wish, come to me, or I shall come to you at once." The king began to stammer, and said he could not receive Stefan that day, but only on the following one. Stefan replied: "Boris, let it not be too late. Pull yourself together, my son." Then Stefan said to Mashiach: "Come tomorrow morning, between nine and ten. He is trying to give me the slip but I shall not permit him to bring such a disgrace, even if I should lose my head." The next morning, Mashiach returned to Stefan, who picked up the phone and told the king: "Boris, you forget yourself. You are avoiding me and hiding. You know that for me there are no secrets under the sun." Stefan then sent a telegram to the king, paraphrasing a moral lesson from the Sermon on the Mount (Matthew 7:2): " 'Do not persecute, lest you be persecuted. With what measure ye mete, it shall be measured to you again.' I know, Boris, that from heaven God will keep watch over your actions." It was unheard for a church prelate to address the king in such harsh terms. The government, however, remained adamant, and the expulsion of Jews from Sofia was carried out.[16]

On May 28, 1943, the police raided the offices of the Sofia bishopric and, impounded, among other things, 386 applications for conversion by adults of Jewish origin and 104 for children. Another raid followed on June 1, and more written material, including certificates of baptism, was confiscated. Stefan reported to his colleagues on June 23, 1943, about the threats to him by the pro-fascist Father Paisi Union. "I have committed the sin of being unconditionally devoted to the church and to my country, having refused to be pragmatic and accommodate to the winds of change. I have chosen to be the antithesis of the silent resignation of the middle way and selfish conformity. . . . People should be told the truth and shown the lie. People should know that the state cannot be good to some and brutal to others." After the war, in his memoirs, Metropolitan Stefan recalled his long confrontation with the government on the Jewish issue, which he termed "another black page in the history of our country. . . . The majority of our people were bitterly asking the question: Why this slavish subordination and blind imitation of Hitler's wild march against the Jews? . . . We appealed to the people, the government, and our head of state to stop the persecution and prevent the deportation of Jews to Poland, and to bring home those already in camps."[17] Fortunately for Stefan, events inside and outside Bulgaria soon made it politically unfeasible for the government to continue the anti-Jewish drive. On August 28, 1943, King Boris II died under mysterious circumstances after returning from a visit with Hitler. This, coinciding with the German reverses on the Russian front, led to the replacement of Gabrovski, and the reshuffling of the government in September 1943. At the end of May 1944, a new government was formed, which in August abolished the Commissariat for Jewish Affairs and abrogated all anti-Jewish legislation. Finally, with the Soviet Army on its doorstep, on

September 9, 1944, Bulgaria reneged on its Axis alliance and declared war on Germany. The Bulgarian Jews had been saved.

In the words of the historian Frederick B. Chary: "No other institution with comparable influence so consistently opposed the government's antisemitic policy as did the Holy Synod of the Bulgarian Orthodox Church. No other man with comparable influence so opposed the government's antisemitic policy as did Metropolitan Stefan."[18]

Greece

Jewish settlement in Greece dates back to Roman times and even earlier. The first-century Jewish historian Philo listed Jewish communities in most parts of the Peloponnesus. In fact, many of the debates engaged in by Paul of Tarsus took place in synagogues in Jewish settlements in Greece (such as his Letters to the Thessalonians). In the Byzantine period, Jews underwent various forms of persecution. During the Middle Ages and down to the modern times, Greece was subject to many conquests and divisions, changing hands between the Byzantine emperors, the Normans of Sicily, the Saracens, the Crusaders, the Venetians, the Genoese, the Seljuk Turks, the Bulgars, and finally the Ottoman Turks. In general, Jews fared badly under Christian rule and better under Turkish Muslim rule. In the sixteenth and seventeenth centuries, the Jewish population increased with the influx of Jews expelled from Spain. Under Turkish rule, Salonika emerged as the largest Jewish community in Greece, where Spanish Jews retained until the modern period a strain of medieval Spanish known as Ladino. After its absorption into the Greek state in 1912, Salonika, renamed Thessaloniki, remained one of the leading centers of European Jewry and was known proudly as "Mother of Israel" by its Jewish inhabitants. On the eve of World War I, the Jewish population in the country counted close to 100,000 souls.

The German attack in World War II, beginning on April 6, 1941, led to the division of Greece into three zones. The Italians were given Epirus, the Ionian islands, central and southern Greece, and Athens (with its 13,000 Jews); the Germans held central Macedonia, the city of Thessaloniki (with its close to 60,000 Jews), and a strip of land at the eastern edge of Greek Thrace, and the Bulgarians occupied Thrace. A satellite regime was headed by Constantine Logothetopoulous and Ioannis Rallis as prime ministers.[19] In Thessaloniki, the Germans moved quickly to impose anti-Jewish measures, including the looting of synagogues, community offices, and libraries, with some leveled to the ground. The first public display of violence came on July 12, 1942, when the Wehrmacht commander ordered the male Jews of the town to assemble in Eleftheria (Freedom) Square to register. They were deliberately humiliated, while crowds gathered to watch the spectacle, with 10,000 men kept standing in the sun for hours, and some eventually collapsed in the heat. At the end of the day some of the men were released, but 6,000 to 7,000 men (some say 9,000) between the ages of eighteen and forty-eight were registered for forced labor and sent to malaria-infested swamps, where many of them died from sickness and starvation. A year later, the uprooting and deportation process in Thessaloniki was accomplished with unprecedented rapidity, in the space of a few months. The victims were fooled into silence and compliance by being told that they would take up life anew in the Polish city of Kraków, where the local Jewish community would welcome them with open arms. Polish paper money was distributed. The deportation of Thessaloniki's Jews began on March 15, 1943 and continued for several months. The majority were sent to Auschwitz, where 37,400 were immediately gassed. Few of the remainder, who were consigned to forced labor, returned home. An estimated 3,000 escaped from Thessaloniki to Athens, where Jews were safe because it was then under Italian occupation. The renowned Thessaloniki community, the great center of Sephardic Jewry, had come to a swift end.[20]

As in neighboring Bulgaria, the head of the Greek Orthodox Church, Metropolitan Theophilos Damaskinos, took a strong stand against the deportations. On March 23, 1943, when he learned of the deportations in Thessaloniki, Damaskinos, supported by a group of scientific, professional and intellectual leaders, addressed a strongly worded protest to the prime minister, Constantine Logotheropoulos, which read in part: "The Greek people have recently learned, with great surprise and grief, that the German military occupation forces in Thessaloniki have begun the gradual expulsion of Jews living in Greece, and that the first groups of displaced Jews are already en route to Poland. The grief of the Greek people is even deeper because . . . Greek Jews not only have been valuable contributors to the final progress of the country, they generally have been loyal and have shown full understanding of their duties as Greek citizens. . . . Our holy religion repudiates any racial or religious distinctions, supremacy or inferiority, stating that 'there is neither Jew nor Greek' (Galatians 3:28), and condemns every tendency to create distinctions on grounds of racial or religious differences." Then, retreating somewhat from these praiseworthy words, Damaskinos continued that he did not intend "to defend or criticize international Jewry and its activities in the sphere of the political and financial problems of the world," but was only interested in the lives of the Greek Jews. He demanded that "if, however, the Germans insist, against every hope, on their policy of expulsion, we think that the government, as the holder of the remaining political power in our country, should take a firm stand against these actions. It should be made clear that full responsibility for this injustice will rest with the foreigners. Let no one forget that all acts committed during this difficult period, even those committed against our will and beyond our power, will one day be examined in our nation; it will ascertain the responsibility of everyone. On that day of national judgment, the moral responsibility of those in authority, who have failed to express by some courageous gesture the unanimous anguish and protest of the nation against all actions which are derogatory to our unity and pride, such as the expulsion of the Jews, will weigh heavily." The memorandum was countersigned by twenty-nine prominent figures, including the president of the Greek Academy; the rectors of the university and the Polytechnic Institute; the chairman of the Association of Writers, Painters, and Artists; lawyers, surgeons, industrialists, and the chamber of commerce. On March 24, 1943, Damaskinos penned an equally forceful letter to Guenther von Altenburg, the German diplomatic representative in the Italian-administered city of Athens, in which he pointed out that "since the era of Alexander the Great and his descendants and through all the centuries of Greek Orthodoxy down to the present time, our relations with the Jewish people have always been harmonious. We believe that, in your high office as ruler of our country during the present war, you will not hesitate to accept our present request and decide, even if provisionally to suspend the expulsion of Greek Jews from Greece until the Jewish Question can be examined in the light of a special and detailed investigation." Needless to say, these appeals proved fruitless.

After Italy surrendered to the Allies on September 8, 1943, the Germans swept into Athens and environs, and began planning the destruction of the Jews in that region. SS officer Dieter Wisliceny summoned Elias Barzilai, the grand rabbi of Athens, and gave him three days to provide addresses and other information about the Jewish community. Exactly what happened next remains something of a mystery. One version has it that a delegation led by the rabbi went to see Damaskinos, who declared that, to his deep regret, he did not see how he could do anything further on behalf of the Jews, despite his willingness to help them. The only alternative was to go into hiding or disappear. When the rabbi requested permission for the Jews to hide in the churches, the archbishop replied: "Willingly, but it is a mistake to think that you will be safe there. They will not hesitate to seize you. However, I could, with the help of the English, arrange a transfer to the Middle East for those Jews who are prepared to go." Another version has it that Damaskinos issued a circular to all priests, parishes, and convents, exhorting them to lend succor and safety to the victims of Nazi barbarism, although no copy of this circular has been found, and the directive may have been delivered by word of mouth through Damaskinos's secretary, Jean Georgakis. What is certain is that over the weekend of September 23–25, 1943, Rabbi Barzilai, hidden in a mail truck, was spirited out of Athens by the Greek underground (EAM/ELAS) and moved into the hills of central Greece, where he, with his wife and daughter, survived the war with underground support. As for Damaskinos, he reportedly met with Panos Haldezos, who headed the Athens municipality, and told him: "I have made my cross, have spoken with God, and decided to save as many Jewish souls as I can. Even if I were to endanger myself, I will baptize Jews, and you will issue municipal documents, so that they obtain identity cards, as Christian Greeks." He then asked Angelos Evert, head of the Athens police, to issue false identity cards to protect all those in hiding and help others to escape.[21] Other Jewish communities also suffered depredations. In Jannina, on March 25, 1944, 1,700 Jews, representing 95 percent of the Jewish population, were deported to Auschwitz. Similarly for the 2,800 Jews on the island of Corfu, whereof 1,800 were deported and destroyed, and the 1,700 Jews on the distant isle of Rhodes, close to the shores of Turkey, who were sent by boat to Piraeus, then by train to Auschwitz, to be gassed. In the final accounting, the statistics of Jewish losses were staggering. Of the some 80,000 Jews in Greece at the start of the war, fewer than 10,000 survived.[22]

As to clerics who extended help to Jews and were awarded the "Righteous" title by Yad Vashem, we begin with Metropolitan Joachim Alexopoulos, the bishop of Volos, who was on good terms with the chief rabbi of the city, Moshe (Moisis) Pessach. On September 30, 1943, the Jewish New Year, the rabbi was ordered to report immediately to the German military governor, Kurt Rikert, and to submit, within twenty-four hours, a list of the names of the Jewish community in Volos, which at the time numbered 872 souls. Rabbi Pesach immediately contacted bishop Alexopoulos and asked him to find out what the Germans intended. The bishop, who was on good terms with the German consul, Helmut Sheffel, was told that it was better for the Jews to leave the city at once, before the stated deadline. Alexopoulos informed the rabbi and handed him a letter of introduction to the priests in the villages surrounding Volos, urging them to help the Jews in every way. The letter read in part: "I heartily recommend the teacher, bearer of this letter, and I ask every brother who is going to meet him, to listen to him carefully and in good will, and to give him any kind of assistance for anything he may be in need of for his life as well as for his flock, so that they do not become victims of this difficult situation." With the help of the underground, the whole Jewish community was able to slip away into hiding, with the exception of some 130 people who stayed behind, and were arrested by the SS, who then proceeded to blow up the synagogue, and pillage the houses and the shops of the Jews. The rest, 74 percent of the Jewish community, had left in time and survived. When the Jews returned to Volos in November 1944, after the departure of the Germans, Alexopoulos issued a statement urging the local inhabitants to return to them any valuables they had left in their hands for safekeeping. Many years later, he confided to a distant relative, "I feel particularly happy because I helped to save the Jews of Volos, and I thank God because my instructions to priests and Christians to protect our fellow-citizens were heeded."[23]

On the island of Zakynthos (Zante), Metropolitan Demetriou Chrysostomos, together with the local mayor, Lukas Karrer, succeeded in preventing the deportation of the island's Jews. In September 1943, the German commander asked Mayor Karrer to turn over a list of the Jews on the island. There are several versions of what then happened. According to one account, the mayor and Metropolitan Chrysostomos, the local bishop, bribed the German commander with an expensive gold ring inset with a beautiful diamond. After this incident, much later, a new officer, named Alfred Lit, appeared on the island who issued a twenty-four-hour ultimatum to the mayor to deliver the Jews or face death. The mayor alerted his men to take the Jews to the hills or hide them with Christian friends in the countryside. That same evening the mayor escaped on a fishing boat to another island. The Jews remained hidden until the German departure on September 12, 1944. Another version has it that Metropolitan Chrysostomos, who had studied philosophy in Munich and was fluent in German, told Lit: "The Jews of Zakynthos are Greeks, peace loving and industrious. They are pureblooded Zakynthans and totally harmless. I beg you to rescind the criminal order." When the commander remained adamant, the bishop pulled out a sheet and said: "Here, take the list of the Jews on Zakynthos." He had scribbled his own name on the paper. He added: "I am at your mercy, you can arrest me, not them. If this does not satisfy you, then know that I will march together with the Jews straight into the gas chamber." The German commander, taken aback by the bishop's words, relented. In yet another version, this incident took place with another German commander, who had replaced Lit, and it happened in the last weeks of the German stay on the island, which was rampant with resistance activities. At any rate, Zakynthos, counting 275 souls, was the only Jewish community in Greece where no deportation took place, and much of the credit goes to two principal heroes, the mayor and Bishop Chrysostomos.[24] In another rescue story, in Thessaloniki, Metropolitan Georgios Alexiadis Guenadios reportedly helped raise funds to support Jews who went into hiding. When he learned about the planned action to deport the city's Jews, Guenadios tried unsuccessfully to get the Germans to stop the deportation. He then cooperated with Damaskinos in Athens, and with Greek Red Cross and Jewish representatives to save Jews from deportation.[25]

Turning to Catholic clerics who helped, we note first Father Irénée Typaldos, from Patras, of the Greek Catholic Church, who was attached to the Spanish embassy in Athens. Joseph Nehama, a leader of the Jewish community in Greece, related: "When the Germans assembled the Jews of Thessaloniki prior to their deportation, Typaldos hastened there on July 30,

1943, in order to save from deportation at least those Jews with Spanish citizenship. It is told that when the Germans refused to release a group of 367 Jews claiming Spanish nationality, Typaldos asked to accompany them to the concentration camp. However, the Germans only agreed that those Jews would be deported in more comfortable cars than their Greek coreligionists and that their jewelry and valuables, which had been confiscated from them in the transit camp, would be turned over to Typaldos for safekeeping in the Spanish embassy for subsequent return to them. In addition, Typaldos hid a number of Spanish and Greek Jews and looked after them until the liberation. As the administrative head of the Greek Catholic orphanage in Athens, he was able to arrange hiding places for Jewish children; at times even giving temporary refuge in his home, as with the Saltiel children (Salomon-Nico, fourteen, and Serge-Theodore, five), as well as the Ben-Sasson family.[26]

In Athens, we also have the stories of two nuns. Sister Elisabeth (Hélène) Capart was of Belgian origin and the sibling of Father Pierre Capart. She served as headmistress of an important Catholic school for girls, and contacted the International Red Cross, the Greek police, and various humanitarian organizations, in an effort to help persecuted Jews. On February 1, 1944, she was arrested by the Gestapo, but was released on March 24 after vigorous efforts on her behalf by influential Greek friends. She continued to help Jews.[27] Returning to the Thessaloniki region, for our final story, Sister Joseph was a nurse in the hospital of the *Soeurs de la Charité de St. Vincent de Paul*, in Calamari, where she was responsible for the nursery. One day a baby girl was brought in and left with the nuns. It was Rena Sciaky (today Molcho), born in April 1942. Her father, Albert Sciaky, had escaped to the partisans; her mother, Eda, joined her parents on her revalidated Spanish citizenship, and thus they were saved. The baby was left with a relative who had Italian citizenship, and who subsequently placed the infant, in April 1943, on the doorsteps of the Calamari church. Sister Joseph was especially fond of Rena, and left her work in the hospital in order to dedicate herself to the baby girl. To ward off suspicion, she approached the Citterichs, an Italian couple who lived in Thessaloniki with their young son, and asked Mrs. Lina Citterich if she would agree to claim motherhood of the baby in order to forestall any problems with the Germans. Lina responded favorably. The baby was then baptized and registered as Lina's daughter. Rena was now called Gilberte, and spent time intermittently with the nuns and in the Citterich home. Since the convent was located near the sea, whenever the Germans approached the area, Sister Joseph would take the baby in a small boat and row away until the Germans had left. Rena's parents survived the war, and in May 1946, Sister Rochette, the head of the convent, took the baby by plane to Paris so she could be reunited with her mother.[28]

Chapter 12
Italy and the Vatican

> *The Jews have not recognized our Lord, and so we cannot*
> *recognize the Jewish people. The Jewish faith was the foundation*
> *of our own, but it has been superseded by the teachings of Christ,*
> *and we cannot admit that it still enjoys any validity. . . .*
> *If the Jews persist in settling in Palestine, we will be*
> *ready with churches and priests to baptize you all.*
> Pope Pius X to Theodor Herzl, 1904

> *We are slaves of egotism, and are only free when we abandon*
> *our selfness. I therefore thank my Jewish brothers and sisters,*
> *who liberated me from the slavery of egotism. I wish to state that*
> *it is a privilege to be part of the chosen people in a time of*
> *humanity's downward slide. . . . The thinking of the philosopher*
> *Levinas will help everyone to understand how much we are in*
> *debt to Judaism, and how close we are to it.*
> Father Arturo Paoli, 1999

History

Jews have lived in Italy without interruption from the time of the
Maccabees (second century B.C.E.) until the present day. In past times, they
often enjoyed good relations with the rulers; Julius Caesar, for instance, was
favorably disposed toward Jews, and granted them certain exemptions to
enable them to fulfill their religious duties. Paul's Letter to the Romans, with
its significance for future Jewish-Christian relations (chaps. 9–11), attests to
the presence of a sizable Jewish community deserving of his attention. At the
same time, the growing friction between Jews and Christians led Claudius to
expel both in the years 49–50, but the decree was short-lived. With the suppression of the revolt in Judea in the year 70, a large number of Jewish prisoners were brought to Rome. One estimate places the number of Jews in Italy
in the first century at 50,000, of whom over half lived in or around the city

of Rome, where they were served by twelve synagogues. Jewish communities were also reported in other Italian cities, including Sicily.

For Jews, the official acceptance of Christianity by a weakened Roman Empire in the fourth century spelled the transition from an era of relative tolerance to one of subjugation. As earlier mentioned, Christianity oppressed Jews and Judaism but did not seek to eliminate them because of its need for their physical preservation as a witness people of ancient truths. From the fourth century onward, the church fathers increased their efforts to restrain Jewish religious activities, limit their political rights, and curb them both socially and economically. Laws were promulgated prohibiting conversion to Judaism, marriages between Jews and Christians, and barring Jews from owning Christian slaves. Clerics mounted attacks on Jews and incited the populace to destroy their places of worship. In 388, for instance, Philaster, bishop of Brescia, encouraged the populace of Rome to set fire to a synagogue. Ambrose, bishop of Milan, praised the population of Aquileia for doing the same, expressing sorrow that the synagogue in Milan had not been similarly treated. The legal codes of the emperors Theodosius and Justinian (529–34) established a new status for the Jews as inferior citizens. During the Middle Ages, Dominican friars forced Jews to attend conversionist sermons in Lombardy and elsewhere. In Rome, Popes Julius II, Leo X, Clement VII, and Paul II were well disposed to the Jews under their jurisdiction. Through all this, Jewish cultural and spiritual life did not suffer despite the vicissitudes. Besides the religious academies (yeshivot), Jews counted among them philosophers, grammarians, physicians, lexicographers, geographers, poets, and dramatists.[1]

As Italy opened up into the Renaissance, it simultaneously began to close Jews into ghettoes, with Venice leading the way in 1516, and then copied in many other parts in Italy and elsewhere in Europe. The Age of the Ghetto lasted well into the nineteenth century. All the ghettos except for the one in Leghorn (Livorno) were locked at night. Jews who stepped outside the ghetto were obliged to wear a distinguishing badge on their garments to identify them. Jews were barred from most professions except medicine, but under restricted conditions. When the French revolutionary armies entered Italy in 1796–98, the walls of the ghetto were demolished and the Jews received equal rights, but with the fall of Napoleon in 1815, the old conditions were restored. Leo XII, in 1823, in one of his first pontifical acts, ordered the Jews back into the ghetto "to overcome the evil consequences of the freedom they have enjoyed." When emancipation finally dawned for Italian Jewry with the dismemberment of the Papal States and their integration into a unified Italy in 1870, Jews flocked into political, military, academic, professional, administrative, and commercial fields, and many attained high positions, including government ministers. But the Jews were a small and insignificant minority, numbering in 1931 only 47,485.[2]

Fascism originated in Italy with Mussolini's ascension to power in 1922. Surprisingly or not, until late 1937 the Fascist government did not formally interfere with the social and legal rights enjoyed by Jews, although even in its early phase, Mussolini criticized the "alien character" of the Jews, with their international, cosmopolitan contacts. In his earlier days, Mussolini publicly condemned racism and antisemitism, and had cordial talks with Zionist leaders. He assured the chief rabbi of Rome, Angelo Sacerdoti, that Fascism was entirely free from antisemitic tendencies. However, this changed as Italy aligned itself closer with Nazi Germany, and in September 1938, the first two laws against Jews were passed, one forbidding them to study or teach in any school or institution of higher learning; the other ordering the deportation of all Jewish aliens who had found refuge in Italy after 1919. It also prohibited marriages between Jews and non-Jews, and forbade the employment of Jews in the army, government, municipal service, and public institutions, as well as the hiring of non-Jewish servants by Jews. In addition, Jews were not permitted to own radios, visit holiday resorts, enter public libraries, publish newspapers, or be partners in business firms with "Aryan" Italians. Jews were defined as people with two parents "of the Jewish race" regardless of religion. Thus, the Catholic offspring of two Jewish parents who had both converted to Catholicism were considered Jewish, and this created serious dilemmas for the church. Despite these severe restrictions, some Jews still mistakenly thought that converting to Christianity was the road to safety. In 1938–39, the Jewish community recorded 3,910 cases of apostasy, as against 101 in the previous two years. Over 5,000 others preferred to emigrate, and in consequence the Jewish population dropped to 35,156 in 1939, or 0.8 percent of the total population.

With Italy's entry into World War II, several thousand Jews of foreign nationality as well as about 200 Italian Jews were incarcerated in Ferramonti and other internment camps. By contrast with German camps, conditions were on the whole bearable. Families lived together, and there were schools for the children as well as a broad program of social welfare and cultural activities. The work imposed on the inmates only involved services required for the camp itself. This is as far as Italian Fascism went in declassifying Jews as full citizens. Late in the summer of 1942, Italian Jews were called up for labor, and the Jews of Rome were forced to wash the retaining wall of the Tiber River. Women were usually not called, and the work itself rarely lasted more than a few weeks. As the war progressed, Italian treatment of Jewish refugees softened, and enforced residence became more common than internment. Until the German occupation in September 1943, Mussolini's government did not release a single Jew to the Nazis for deportation. What is more important, Italian officials at the highest levels, including army generals, refused to turn over Jews to the Germans and their collaborating allies for deportation. They resorted to every imaginable scheme and subterfuge, including bureaucratic excuses and lies, to resist repeated German demands for the deportation of Jews, going so far as to ignore Mussolini's own directive, at times with his tacit consent. The Italians could not bring themselves to follow the Nazi logic and allow human lives to be destroyed simply because the intended victims had been born Jewish. Delasem, a government-approved Jewish association, founded in 1939, helped about 2,000 Jewish refugees emigrate abroad. It also provided food, clothing, medicine, and living allowances to about 9,000 other refugees. [3]

On July 25, 1943, with defeat staring Italy in the eyes, Mussolini was arrested and replaced by Marshal Pietro Badoglio, who a little over a month later, on September 8, 1943, surrendered to the Allies, who already occupied the country's southern third. That same day, the Germans occupied the rest of Italy, from Rome northwards. The Holocaust of Italian Jewry had begun. Tragically, almost all of Italy's approximately 34,000 Jews lived in the German-controlled part of the country, with 8,000 to 10,000 in Rome, which experienced the most terrifying event of the Holocaust in Italy. The new pro-Nazi Italian government (known as the Salò Republic) ordered all Jews without exception to be interned in special concentration camps. In Rome, in a single day in October, the Germans arrested over 1,000 people, who were dispatched directly to Auschwitz, where most were gassed on arrival. At least 835 more Roman Jews were arrested before Rome was liberated on June 4, 1944. From Rome the operation shifted to the northern areas, Trieste, Genoa, Florence, Milan, Venice, and Ferrara. The two most important concentration camps on Italian soil were Fossoli and Bolzano in northern Italy—way stations on the road to death camps in Germany and Poland. Many Jews managed to flee to Switzerland. Others found their way through the front line to southern Italy or joined the anti-Fascist partisans in the mountains. The statistics for the losses by the Jewish community are not staggering when compared with other countries under German rule. Of the 38,000 Jews in September 1943, when the Germans took over, 7,000 crossed into Switzerland (or reached the Allied lines in the south), of whom 1,000 were forcibly returned, which leaves 6,000 who reached a safe haven. Of the 32,000 left on Italian soil, some 10,000 were arrested, of whom 8,360 were deported, and 7,750 of these people died. People in hiding therefore accounted for 22,000 souls. In summary, four-fifths (or over 80 percent) of the Jews of Italy survived the German occupation, thanks to the help of Italians in all walks of life, and especially of many of the clergy—probably more so than any other country, and this makes Italy the Catholic country that saved the highest percentage of Jews.[4]

The Vatican and the Jews

Before recounting stories of clergy rescuers on Italian soil, something more needs to be said about the Vatican's past relations toward Jews and its behavior during the German occupation of Italy. Over the centuries, the Vatican's treatment of the Jews varied considerably. Some popes expressed hostility and promulgated anti-Jewish measures; others tried to restrain antisemitic violence by the faithful and reconfirmed the right of Jews to a separate existence and the practice of their religion. Gregory I (590–604) is especially significant for Jewish history. Although he, like others, condemned the Jews for their refusal to acknowledge Christianity, he afforded the Jews protection in Rome and elsewhere against vexations at the hands of local bishops, insisting that although he desired the conversion of the Jews, he was opposed to attaining this by violence. Several papal bulls (official statements by the head of the Roman Catholic Church) protected Jews from assaults against their persons, property, or religious practice, from conversionist pressure, and various accusations, such as poisoning the wells during the Black Death plague. On the other hand, there were popes who fulminated against the Jews. Innocent III, in *Etsi non displiceat*, in 1205, addressed to the king of France, accused the Jews of usury, blasphemy, even murder. The Fourth Lateran Council (1215), convened by Innocent III, sought to place the Jews in a position of perpetual serfdom and introduced the regulation compelling them to wear a distinguishing sign on their garments. *Etsi doctoribus gentium*, by Benedict XIII, in 1415, was one of the most complete collections of anti-Jewish laws. In 1542, Paul III authorized the establishment in Rome of a Spanish-type Inquisition, and appointed as its head the fearsomely ascetic Pietro Caraffa, who, in 1553, sentenced a Franciscan monk who had converted to Judaism to burn at the stake, and presided at the burnings of dozens of Marrano Jews (Jews forced to convert to Christianity). Pope Julius III ordered all copies of the Talmud seized and burned, and this directive was carried out on Rosh Hashanah, the Jewish Near Year, on a huge pyre built in the middle of Rome's Campo dei Fiori. Vast numbers of Talmud volumes and other Hebrew-language books seized from the homes in Rome's ghetto were tossed into the conflagration; a bonfire was lit; the burning of the Talmud had come to Rome. The year was 1553, the beginning of the Renaissance. The attacks became more violent under Paul IV (1555–59), who was none other than the earlier-mentioned grand inquisitor Caraffa. He prohibited Jews from possessing any religious book except the Bible, and placed the Talmud on the Index of Forbidden Books. In July 1555, he issued the bull *Cum nimis absurdum,* which used very uncomplimentary language and stated that Christians were not permitted to address Jews as "Sir." Jews were to live on a single street, or in a distinctive quarter cut off from other sections of the town or city, which was to have only one entrance. That year, all of Rome's Jews were rounded up and brought to the district beside the Tiber that would thenceforth serve as the ghetto, and which was to exist until late in the nineteenth century (1870). In the words of John Carroll: "For three hundred years [until 1870], the keeper of the keys of the Jews' first and, until modern times, last and most squalid concentration camp was the keeper of the keys of Peter."[5]

Particularly galling to Jewish religious sensibilities was the requirement to listen to sermons calling for abjuring of Judaism and conversion to Christianity. In 1278, Pope Nicholas II, in *Vineam soreth*, ordered the selection of trained men to preach Christianity to the Jews. *Sancta mater ecclesia*, by Gregory XIII in 1584, ordered the Jews of Rome to send 100 men and 50 women every Saturday afternoon to listen to conversionist sermons which were delivered in a church near the ghetto. Replying to a plea for relaxation of the anti-Jewish measures from the Austrian statesman Metternich, Pope Gregory XVI, in 1843, wrote: "The prohibitions on the Jews, forbidding them from employing Christian servants or wet-nurses, from owning real estate . . . from living—where there is a ghetto— outside its walls, mixed in and confused with Christians, are prohibitions founded in the sacred canons. These, in order to guarantee Christian religion and morality, command the separation of Christians and Jews. Aside from the fact that the Jews are forbidden such ownership by the sacred canons as a nation of deicides and blasphemers of Christ, and sworn enemies of the Christian name, there is also the danger that the Jews will seduce and pervert those who rent from them or peasants who depend on them." In 1848, Pope Pius IX finally ordered the demolition of the gates and walls of the ghettos in Rome and other towns of the Papal States. Jews were still subjected to conversionist pressure, and in many cases women and boys were pulled out of their homes and into the House of the Catechumens by the police, after witnesses reported that they had idly expressed an interest in Christianity. This went on well into the nineteenth century. The notorious kidnapping of the child Edgardo Mortara in Bologna occurred in 1858, and of Giuseppe Coen in Rome as late as 1864. In the Mortara affair, the police broke in and snatched the six-year-old child from its parents on the claim that the nurse had him secretly baptized. Pope Pius IX turned down appeals by the child's parents and the French ambassador, to return the Mortara child to his parents. He told the French ambassador that the six-year-old boy "pleaded that he be allowed to remain Christian and that he not be made to leave the church." Under such circumstances, the pope concluded, "it is impossible for the head of this church, for the Representative of

Jesus Christ on earth, to refuse this child, for he begged me with an almost supernatural faith to let him share in the benefit of the blood that Our Lord shed for his Redemption. It is impossible to eject from Christianity this soul, even though it entered the Catholic faith through irregular means. . . . My decision is irrevocable."[6] The child was lost to the Jewish people.

The Vatican's anti-Jewish stance did not change much in the following years. In 1904, Pius X met with Theodor Herzl, founder of the Zionist movement, and told him: "The Jews have not recognized our Lord, and so we cannot recognize the Jewish people. The Jewish faith was the foundation of our own, but it has been superseded by the teachings of Christ, and we cannot admit that it still enjoys any validity." The pope assured Herzl that he prayed for the Jews in the hope that they would see the light. "If the Jews persist in settling in Palestine, we will be ready with churches and priests to baptize you all." In 1939, Archbishop Dalla Costa of Florence stated: "As for the Jews, no one can forget the ruinous work they have often undertaken not only against the spirit of the church, but also to the detriment of civil coexistence. . . . Above all, however, the church has in every epoch judged living together with the Jews to be dangerous to the faith and to the tranquility of Christian people. Hence the laws promulgated by the church for centuries aimed at isolated the Jews." Paradoxically, these harsh words by Florence's highest cleric did not stop many clergy of that city from extending aid to Jews during the German occupation. Pius XII, as well, in his encyclical *Mystici Corporis Christi*, in June 1943, seemed to imply that Judaism was nothing but a living corpse; for "on the gibbet of his death Jesus made void the Law with its decrees, [and] fastened the handwriting of the Old Testament to the cross, establishing the New Testament in His blood. . . . On the Cross, then, the Old Law died, soon to be buried and to be a bearer of death."[7]

The Lateran Treaty of 1929 with the Italian government established the sovereignty of the Vatican State over 108.7 acres in Rome, as well as an additional 160 acres of extraterritorial buildings and institutions. Archbishop Francesco Borgongini Duca was appointed the first Vatican ambassador, or nuncio, to the Kingdom of Italy, a post he retained until 1953. Soon thereafter, the Italian racial laws of 1938 created tension between the Vatican and the Italian government, not because of the discriminatory aspects against the Jewish population, but solely with regard to baptized Jews still regarded as Jews by the new laws. While priests continued to perform marriages between Catholics and converts whom the law regarded as Jewish, these religious unions had no legal validity in Italy. As an additional obstacle to church-state relations, the law held that the offspring of Jewish parents was considered Jewish regardless of whether the child or either of his parents had been baptized. Father Pietro Tacchi-Venturi, a Jesuit priest who served as intermediary

Vatican and the Italian government, protested that the converted evoted sons of the church even if of Jewish blood, and asked that of mixed marriages, baptized in infancy, be recognized as Aryan even if one parent was non-Italian. In August 1939, Tacchi-Venturi also asked the government to permit baptized children to attend Catholic schools, and to allow baptized Jews to marry Italians with full civil recognition of their marriages. Nothing came of these demands. Needless to say, neither the pope nor any other church authority opposed the Fascist government's efforts to strip unconverted Jews of their rights. In late 1938, the Italian government declared Jews undesirables, threw Jewish children out of school, and fired large numbers of Jewish adults from their jobs. Neither the pope nor the Vatican hierarchy uttered a single word of protest. As Mussolini sarcastically stated on August 16, 1938, in a private note to the Vatican: "The Jews, in a word, can be sure that they will not be subjected to worse treatment than that applied to them for centuries by the popes who hosted them in the Eternal City."[8]

In September 1938, Pope Pius XI exclaimed to a group of Belgian pilgrims: "Listen carefully: Abraham is defined as our patriarch, our ancestor. . . . Antisemitism is a hateful movement, with which we Christians must have nothing to do. . . . Through Christ and in Christ we are the spiritual descendants of Abraham. . . . Antisemitism is unacceptable. Spiritually, we are all Semites." Sadly, the pope's words were never printed in Italy. The article in *L'Osservatore Romano* reported the audience with the Belgians but omitted any mention of the pope's reference to the Jews. Equally unfortunate, Pius XI did not raise his voice against the Italian anti-Jewish laws in 1938, which tried to toe the Nazi Nuremberg laws. Not a word against them.[9] That same year, Pius XI decided that some kind of public statement on antisemitism was needed, and invited an American Jesuit priest, Father John LaFarge, to draft an encyclical on the unity of humankind that would condemn both racism and antisemitism. LaFarge enlisted the head of the Jesuit order, the Polish Father Wladimir Ledóchowski, who in turn added two others: a German, Gustav Gundlach, and a Frenchman, Gustave Desbuquois. In their draft statements, the three Jesuits, while condemning racism, fully reflected the church's centuries-old anti-Jewish attitude. The Jews, they stated, "blinded by a vision of material domination and gain," had failed to recognize the Savior, and their leaders "had called down upon their own heads a Divine malediction" which doomed the Jews "to perpetually wander over the face of the earth." The church's hopes for the Jews' ultimate conversion "do not blind her to the spiritual dangers to which contact with Jews can expose souls, or make her unaware of the need to safeguard her children against spiritual contagion." The church asked only that states exercise "justice and charity" in any steps they took to protect Christian society from the Jews. Statements hardly complimentary in a year which saw the torching of all the synagogues in Germany by baptized, if unbelieving, Christians. Weak as it was, the encyclical condemning racist antisemitism was never issued. A Dutch Jesuit scholar sighed in relief: "God be praised that this draft remained only a draft." [10] Pius XI, however, did make a pronouncement on racism. *Mit brennender Sorge* ("With Deep Anxiety"), issued the previous year on March 14, 1937, was read from the pulpit in all German Catholic churches on Palm Sunday, March 21. *Mit brennender Sorge* began with a protest against the Nazi regime's violations of the Concordat treaty of 1933, followed with a condemnation of racism. Jews are not mentioned by name in the encyclical, but it refers to them in a disparaging way, as "the story of the chosen people, bearers of the Revelation and the Promise, repeatedly straying from God and turning to the world." No word on the four years of the escalating Nazi reign of terror against the Jews. [11]

The debate is still open as to how much the Vatican knew about the Nazi atrocities against the Jews and its responses to them. Other than Pope Pius XII, the chief policy-makers in the Vatican were the secretary of state, Cardinal Luigi Maglione, and his two chief deputies, Monsignors Giovanni Battista Montini (the future Pope Paul VI) and Domenico Tardini. In addition, the Holy See had papal nuncios in Berlin, Rome, Vichy, Budapest, Bucharest, Berne, Madrid, and Lisbon, as well as apostolic delegates in Istanbul, Athens, London, and Washington, and other representatives elsewhere, most notably Zagreb and Bratislava. Papal diplomats received information from prelates and priests, who in turn collected information from the faithful, including soldiers, guards, and civilians who witnessed atrocities and were sometimes disturbed by them. Vatican envoys were able to send communications by diplomatic pouch or telegraph, or could entrust messages to the many priests permitted to travel to Rome. The evidence on hand clearly demonstrates that the Vatican was well informed, before other governments, about the large-scale massacres of the Jewish people by the Germans, as will be illustrated below. The Vatican response to the terrible information flowing in was a combination of minimizing the news coupled with an apologetic claim that the Holy See was powerless to do anything about it.

On August 21, 1941, Cardinal Maglione received an appeal to intervene with the Croatian government to restrain its anti-Jewish measures, Maglione instructed the Vatican's representative in Zagreb, Giuseppe Marcone, to urge "moderation" on the Croatian leaders, but to do it "confidentially and always in such a way that an official character cannot be attributed to your steps." One wonders what Maglione was afraid of. On March 19, 1942, Felipo Bernardini, the nuncio at Berne, forwarded to the Vatican a report received from Jewish sources (Richard Lichtheim of the Jewish Agency and Gerhart Riegner of the World Jewish Congress), which stated that most of the Jews in Bucovina,

Romania, numbering 170,000, had been forced to leave their homes and were transported at the beginning of winter in open freight cars to Russia. "By the time they reached the Russian frontier, a quarter of them were already dead," Bernardini added. Furthermore, "in Bessarabia thousands of Jews were executed by firing squads, including children, the aged, the sick, and even hospital patients." Ten days earlier, on March 9, 1942, Giuseppe Burzio, the Vatican representative in Slovakia, informed Maglione that "the deportation of 80,000 people to Poland at the mercy of the Germans is the equivalent of condemning a great part of them to certain death." The following day papal nuncio Bernardini in Berne sent Maglione the same information, begging the pope to intervene, "to save, if possible, so many people from atrocious sufferings." Nuncio Angelo Rotta, in Budapest, forwarded two similar requests for intervention on behalf of the Slovakian Jews.

Information about what was happening to the Jews also flowed from other reliable sources. Such as from Italian chaplains, who frequently traveled through central Poland with Italian troop trains on their way to the eastern front; they moved about freely and had unrestricted access to Vatican City. In May 1942, a hospital train chaplain, Pirro Scavizzi, wrote directly to the pope about the mass killings in Poland. On October 7, 1942, he sent another account: "The elimination of the Jews by mass killings is almost total, without regard even to nursing babies. . . . It is said that over two million Jews have been killed. . . . Poles are allowed to take refuge in the houses of the ghetto, which daily is being depopulated by the systematic killings of Jews." At the end of August 1942, Metropolitan Sheptitzky, in Lviv, Ukraine, wrote to Pius XII that "the number of Jews killed in this small region has certainly passed 200,000. As the army moves east, the number of victims increases." A month later, on September 26, 1942, Myron C. Taylor, President Roosevelt's diplomatic representative, personally delivered an urgent communication to the Vatican about the "systematic massacres of the Jews," which "have reached proportions and forms which are horribly frightful. Incredible killings take place every day"; moreover, he said, the Warsaw ghetto was reportedly being liquidated and Jews were being killed in special camps, one of which was Belzec; Jews were being deported from Germany, Belgium, Holland, France, and Slovakia, and "sent to be butchered." Taylor asked Maglione if the Vatican had any information to confirm these reports, and any ideas about what should be done. In spite of these horrific reports emanating from the Vatican's own sources, according to Cardinal Montini, Pius XII was skeptical of the Taylor report, and stated, "I don't believe that we have information that confirms . . . this very grave news."[12]

More terrible news continued to land on the Vatican's desks. On September 18, 1942, after meeting with Count Malvezzi, who had just returned from

Poland, Monsignor Giovanni Montini wrote that "the massacres of the Jews have reached fearful and execrable forms and proportions. Incredible slaughter takes place every day; it seems that by the middle of October they want to empty entire ghettos of hundreds of thousands of languishing unfortunates to make room for the Poles." On May 5, 1943 an official at the Vatican Secretariat of State prepared a memo summarizing the situation of the Jews in Poland: "In Poland, there were, before the war, about 4,500,000 Jews [actually 3,250,000]; it is calculated now that there remain . . . only 100,000. . . . There is no doubt that the majority have been killed." In light of all this reliable information, the pope could not remain totally silent, but he still refrained from any direct mention of what was happening to the Jews. Thus in his Christmas 1942 message, Pius XII mentioned "the hundreds of thousands who, without personal guilt, are doomed to death or to a progressive deterioration of their condition, sometimes for no other reason than their nationality or descent." Again, on June 2, 1943, addressing the Sacred College of Cardinals, he spoke of the people who suffer "for reasons of their nationality or descent." The pope never used the words "Jew," nor did he mention or name the perpetrators.[13] The fact that Pope Pius XII did not publicly condemn the Holocaust does not mean that he did nothing to help the Jews. The thousands of Jews hidden in religious institutions throughout Italy were there with his knowledge and consent, and perhaps in some cases at his own instigation. According to Susan Zuccotti, the best that can be said of him is that he allowed others to take great risks and that he fulfilled his institutional mandate at the expense of moral leadership. Rome was liberated on June 4, 1944, and after that date the pope had no reason to fear that the Vatican City would be invaded and that fugitives hidden in Vatican properties in Rome would be seized if he displeased the Nazis and Fascists. He still elected not to speak out after June 1944, when it was safe to do so. To the U.S. diplomatic representative, Harold H. Tittman, the pope said, "If I should denounce the Nazis by name as you desire and Germany should lose the war, Germans everywhere would feel that I had contributed to the defeat, not only of the Nazis, but of Germany herself. . . . I cannot afford to risk alienating so many of the faithful." To which Tittman added: "It was difficult for us to argue these points effectively with the pope, and in the end we were obliged to resign ourselves to the failure of our attempts." One cannot help but agree with Susan Zuccotti's conclusion that "the pope and his diplomatic officials knew enough about the Jewish genocide to believe and understand that it was a disaster of immense, unprecedented proportions. Given what they knew, they should have acted vigorously." John Morley concurs. In his words: "The sad conclusion is that the tragic events in Poland were not able to move the pope or his secretary of state to face the reality of a situation whose cruelty was unparalleled in human history. A more sobering conclusion might be that diplomatic relations with Germany were considered such a premium that no word or deed could be permitted that would endanger them."[14]

On October 16, 1943 (Black Saturday), the Germans conducted a large-scale raid in Rome, literally under the windows of the pope, which netted 1,259 Jews, of whom 1,007 were dispatched to Auschwitz. The Vatican's failure to make an effective response is indicative (far more than any other example) of its hands-off policy with regard to the Holocaust. Not a single word of public protest. The Vatican secretary of state, Cardinal Luigi Maglione, summarized what took place in a meeting with the German ambassador, Ernst von Weizsaecker. Maglione told him: "See if you can save so many innocent people. It is sad for the Holy See, sad beyond telling, that right in Rome, under the eyes of the Common Father, so many people have been made to suffer only because they belong to a particular race." Maglione: "The ambassador, after several moments of reflection, asked me, 'What will the Holy See do if events continue?' I replied: The Holy See would not want to be put into the necessity of uttering a word of disapproval. . . . I wanted to remind him that the Holy See, as he himself has perceived, has been so very prudent so as not to give the German people the impression that it has done or wished to do the least thing against Germany during this terrible war. . . . Your Excellency has told me that you will attempt to do something for the unfortunate Jews. I thank you for that. As for the rest, I leave it to your judgment. If you think it more opportune not to mention our conversation, so be it." Relieved by Maglione's conciliatory words, Weizsaecker reported to Berlin on October 17 on his meeting with Maglione: "The Curia is dumbfounded, particularly as the action took place under the very windows of the pope, as it were. . . . It is being said that in French cities, where similar things happened, the bishops took up a clear position. The pope, as supreme head of the church and bishop of Rome, could not lag behind them... The pope, although harassed from various quarters, has not allowed himself to be stampeded into making any demonstrative pronouncement against the removal of the Jews form Rome. . . . He has done everything he could, even in this delicate matter, not to injure the relationship between the Vatican and the German government or the German authorities in Rome. . . . No objection can be raised to this public statement [i.e., a communiqué in the *Osservatore Romano* on the pontiff's "benevolent activity"], the less so as its text . . . will be understood by only very few people as having special reference to the Jewish Question. The whole affair could therefore be looked upon as liquidated."[15]

Clergy Rescuers

The large fraction of Jews saved in Italy were the beneficiaries of a charitable response by Italian clerics, almost all of them Catholics; more so than in any other country under German domination. In Rome itself, an estimated 4,000 Jews found shelter in churches, monasteries, and convents; with some 450 Jews hiding in Vatican-held buildings. Priests suspected of aiding Jews and opponents of the Fascist regime were treated with great brutality, and at least 170 priests were murdered in reprisal killings. In Rome, the raid of October 16, 1943 on the city's Jews caused a stampede of people seeking shelter in religious and secular institutions. Between forty and 100 women were hidden in the girls boarding school of the Sisters of Our Lady of Sion, on Janiculum Hill, and sixty-seven Jews disguised as patients were hidden in the San Giovanni Calibita Hospital. In 1961, an Italian historian, Renzo De Felice, published an impressive list of 100 female convents and fifty-five male-operated monasteries, schools, hospitals, and parish churches in the Rome region and Vatican-owned properties that sheltered Jews. He concluded that the women's institutions protected 2,775 Jews, for a total of 4,447 Jews sheltered everywhere. This figure has to be measured against the hundreds of parish churches, the 1,120 religious institutions for women, and 152 for men then existing in Rome. Only a few of them can be mentioned here, such as the Monastery of the Carissimi, Convent of Santa Rufina, the *Santa Maria della Divina Provvidenz*, and the *Instituto Pio XI*, a boarding school for boys run by the Salesian Order, which hid around seventy Jewish boys and adults. Some paid fees of about 40 lire a month, and some disguised themselves as non-Jews. It should not be overlooked that many of the Jews sheltered in Catholic institutions were in fact converts, relatives of converts, or spouses and children of mixed marriages. Also to be kept in mind is that after the October 16 *razzia*, many individuals who had escaped the roundup were refused admission to convents and monasteries, and according to some reports, others were admitted only upon the assurance that they would agree to convert. Settimio Sorani, of Delasem, recalled that after the liberation of Rome, "I went from convent to convent to bring out the Jewish children sheltered there, and more than once I was told that they had no 'Jewish children.' They had evidently been baptized, without much difficulty. All those whom it was possible to recover (about 300) were returned to family members or were sheltered in three children's homes."[16]

At times there was pressure from the Vatican to remove outside guests from Vatican City, but many of the prelates there strenuously resisted the expulsion order. "The matter," Cardinal Tardini recorded, "caused an uproar," and the guests apparently were allowed to remain.[17] Michael Tagliacozzo, who was twenty-two years old at the time, was admitted by Father Vincenzo Fagiolo to the prestigious Vatican-owned *Pontificio Seminario Romano Maggiore* after fleeing from his home during the great roundup on October 16, 1943. Michael remained hidden there until February 1944. Among the total of about 200 guests, there were an unknown number of Jews (perhaps as many as fifty-five, many of whom had converted to Catholicism years earlier). On February 4, Italian Fascists invaded the premises and arrested many of the hidden Jews, but Michael managed to escape. After aimlessly wandering for a few days, he ran into an Adventist minister, Pastor Danielo Cupertino, who hid him in his flat for two months, introducing to his family as a relative. On April 10, Michael returned to Fagiolo, and his aide, Father Pietro Palazzini, hid him in the basilica of St. Giovanni in the Vatican until Rome's liberation on June 4, 1944. After the war, Palazzini rose to the rank of cardinal, and played a role in the reforms of the Second Vatican Council (1962–65). Tagliacozzo recalled that "there was absolutely no pressure for conversion to Christianity. . . . Don Palazzini turned to me, knowing that among the refugees I was the closest to the Jewish tradition. He begged me to instruct him in the Jewish dietary laws, so that the sentiments of the refugees would not be offended. He gave me a Bible in Hebrew that inspired me with faith and hope in the future."[18] On June 2, 1944, on the eve of Rome's liberation, an official at the Vatican Secretariat of State calculated that about forty Jews were among the 160 fugitives in Vatican City. At least fifteen of the forty had been baptized, some during their stay in the Vatican City.

Vatican-held properties in the city were not always immune from raids by Fascist paramilitary agents and SS soldiers. The *Seminario Lombardo*, a Vatican property but without extraterritorial privileges, was raided on the night of December 21–22, 1943. After dragging the rector, Monsignor Francesco Bertoglio, out of the chapel, the invaders began a ruthless search of the premises. Many of the Jewish men whose rooms were on the fourth floor were able to escape to an adjoining building through a passage at that level. The invaders apprehended twelve or fifteen prisoners, including Jews. A similar raid that evening on the *Pontifico Instituto Orientale* netted some Jews. The *Basilica di San Paolo fuori le Mura* ("St. Paul outside the Walls"), traditionally the site of the martyrdom and burial of Paul, enjoyed extraterritorial status together with its large Benedictine monastery. On the night of February 3–4, 1944, the Germans raided the place and arrested sixty-four prisoners, including five Jews; about thirty others managed to escape. The Jews were deported to Auschwitz and perished.

The earlier-mentioned French Capuchin Benoît, now in Rome, was able to mask his identity by using the Italian-sounding name Padre Benedetto. From his headquarters in the Capuchin college at 9 Sicilia Street, Benoît launched an even larger rescue operation, in cooperation with Delasem (*Delegazione per l'Assistenza dei Emigranti Ebrei*, "Jewish Emigrants' Aid Society"), which aided thousands of Jews in the capital city. Benoît was appointed to the executive board of Delasem. Together with other Delasem officials he helped billet Jews with families throughout the city, and provided them with forged certificates, for which a printing press found in the basement of the Capuchin college had been put to use. When Delasem's head, Settimio Sorani, was arrested, Benoît was elected president of the Jewish welfare organization, and he presided over its secret meetings from inside the Capuchin compound. Under Benoît's guidance, several thousand Jews were helped to find hiding places. Three Jews sat on Benoît's committee, Giuseppe Levi (Sorani's secretary), Stefan Schwamm, and Aron Kasterszein; the last two had fled from France to Italy. Many Jews came to Benoît's base on Via Sicilia, looking for "the Father of the Jews," and this understandably risked compromising Benoît's rescue operation. Consequently, he decided to move his food and clothing distribution center to several other locations. Funds were funneled from various outside organs, including the American-based Joint Distribution Committee, or were raised locally, such as from Cardinal Pietro Boetto of Genoa. In 1961, Benoît wrote that in April 1944, accompanied by Sorani and two other people, he requested a Vatican loan, and was told: "The Vatican does not make loans; if it has it, it gives it." The supplicants left with nothing. Evidently irked by Benoît's large-scale assistance to Jews, on November 19, 1943, Monsignor Angelo Dell'Acqua, of the Vatican Secretariat of State, wrote: "I have repeatedly (and the last time very clearly) told Father Benoit, Capuchin, to use the maximum prudence in dealing with the Jews. . . . It can be seen, unfortunately, that he has not wished to heed the humble advice given him. . . . I have always believed . . . in using the maximum prudence in speaking with the Jews, to whom it would be better to speak less."[19] Needless to say, Benoît disregarded this counsel.

A problem arose when the Italian Fascist officials announced that refugees who had arrived after December 6, 1943, could no longer stay in the city. Benoît solicited the aid of the Swiss consul, Chauvet, who also represented the interests of France, and was willing to issue Swiss "letters of protection" to refugees from France who could produce documentation showing that they had arrived before the break-off date. Benoît had no problem fabricating false documents with his secret printing press, affixed with counterfeit stamps and seals, and based on fake hotel registers, which certified that the people in the endangered status had actually been in the city before December 6. As many as 200 Jews were saved in this way from being sent back to France and into the hands of the waiting Gestapo. When the Rome police asked the Swiss consul to hand over the list of French nationals provided with letters of protection, the consul alerted Benoît, who, together with his Jewish co-partner Stefan Schwamm, devised a plan whereby fictitious Hungarian names and passports, supplied by the Hungarian consul, were turned over to the Swiss consul for delivery to the police. Officials in the Rome police, of course, knew of

Benoît's clandestine activities but closed their eyes and preferred not to see. In addition, the police gave Benoît 1,300 ration cards as a goodwill gesture. Benoît, Stefan Schwamm (who used the name of Bernard Lioré) and Aron Kasterszein [20] visited the remaining embassies in Rome, asking their assistance on behalf of Jews on the run. Also solicited was a certain Protestant Pastor Ammenti of the Methodist Church, who in the words of Benoît "helped us much," and members of various clandestine political organizations (democrats, monarchists, and communists).

Benoît-Benedetto escaped several attempts to arrest him. Once, two Yiddish-speaking Gestapo agents pretended to be Jewish refugees and asked for help. Benoît, who had been tipped off, sent a monk to answer the door with a cover story and climbed out his office window. In April 1944, Benoît and Schwamm went to Milan to help a group of Jewish refugees make contact with smugglers who would take them across the Swiss border. While they were in Milan, Schwamm was arrested, but Benoît escaped to Genoa, where he was welcomed by Cardinal Pietro Boetto and his secretary, Monsignor Francesco Repetto. Secretly making his way back to Rome, Benoît went into hiding for a month until the liberation of the city on June 4, 1944.[21]

Immediately after the liberation, Benoît was honored by the Jewish community in a Rome synagogue, where he was invited to speak. "I ended my speech by recalling the great command of Moses, of the love of God and of one's neighbor, and then cried out: 'I love the Jews with all my heart.' " In December 1994, at another ceremony by the Jewish community to honor him and his colleagues, including Father Callixte, who had helped Jews imprisoned in the Ferramonti camp, he was given a Bible with the signatures of everyone present. A speaker then addressed the audience: "Who among us will ever forget this noble man? . . . We are sure and convinced that a place is reserved for them in the world to come. . . . My friends, let us stand up! Let us turn our eyes toward Father Marie-Benoît and all his brothers! They are the personification of goodness, of love, and of humanity. Let us salute them." The Jewish Labor Committee in New York asked Benoît then to be their representative in Rome for the distribution of funds and goods to Jewish refugees in need, to which Benoît consented. In 1966, Marie-Benoît was honored by Yad Vashem as a "Righteous Among the Nations." In 1978, informed that a tree had been planted in his name, Benoît wrote back: "What I did for the Jewish people, what I did to merit being called 'Father of the Jews' is but an infinitesimal contribution of what should have been done to prevent this most heinous and satanic slaughter of some six million Jews, which will undoubtedly remain mankind's foulest disgrace—a shame affecting all who participated or allowed it to happen. They wanted to exterminate the Jewish people. But the Jewish people is not to be exterminated. It is by divine providence that the Jewish people wishes to live and fulfill its divine goals—first, for its own good, then, for the good of all humanity. I hope that the tree planted in my name will be a sign of my attachment to Israel, of my fervent wish that its peaceful survival and its final and assured liberation will become a living reality, recognized by all, in harmony and peace. Long live the State of Israel. May the God of Abraham, Isaac, and Jacob come to her help."[22]

Father Antonio Dressino was head of the San Giacchino Church, in the Prato quarter of Rome, where he hid some twenty people. Before agreeing to do so, he reportedly asked his parish priests for their views. Several of them vetoed the proposal and even threatened to inform the police, but he fought vigorously and succeeded in winning a vote in his favor. Leopoldo Moscato, born 1928, and his father, Alberto, were hidden in the church attic, starting in October 1943, together with other people (Leopoldo's mother, Virginia, and found a refuge in the nearby convent of San Vincenzo, with the collaboration of a French-born nun, Marguerite Bernes). With the help of Pietro Lestini, a lay Catholic associate, a wall was built to close the entrance to the attic. Food was supplied only at night, through a window. Professor Arrigo Finzi, a psychiatrist, spent three months in the church attic, from February to April 1944, when he had to leave, because of rumors of an impending German search. Earlier, he and his brother Gilberto had hidden in the Catholic seminary of *Collegio Lombardo*, which they also had to leave from fear of a German inspection of the premises.[23] We also have the story of Fathers Francesco Antoniolo and Armando Alessandrini, who both served in the Salesian institute Pius XI College, a boarding and vocational school for about 100 pupils, in a Roman suburb, where at least twenty Jewish boys (and perhaps as many as seventy) were sheltered. Antoniolo was the director, and Alessandrini, the administrator. Most of these boys arrived there after the Black Sabbath, October 16, 1943. Some of them were foreign refugees in Rome, and the rest, local Italian Jews; some remained for a few days, others for several months. Some of the Jewish boys were registered as outside students and went home for the night. All had to attend the daily prayers, as well as the religious ceremonies, but there was no mention of any attempt at conversion. Only a small sum of money was paid for accommodations and tuition, but payment was never a condition for acceptance there. Included among those sheltered were Aldo Di Castro with his brother (their surname changed to Barbieri), Giuseppe Fua (surnamed Giuseppe Valente), and Tagliacozzo. Also Marizio Shlomo Rossi with his three younger brothers, Guglielmo, Gualtiero, and Franco, and his uncle Aulo Camerini, from December 5, 1943 until April 17, 1944, when they moved to the Franciscan *Penitenzeria Lateranense*, with thirty other Jews and non-Jews, partisans, former government officials, and waited out the German occupation.[24] We equally note the story of Alfredo Melani and

Alessandro Daeli, of the Church of *Santa Eurosia* of the Order of *San Filippo Neri*, in the Garbaella quarter of Rome. The two hid many Jews in their church after the October 16, 1943 raid on Roman Jews. These included the three members of the Ascoli family (Benedetto and sons Franco and Mario). During one raid, Fascist militia used machine-guns to smash in the gates. More than twenty Jews were reportedly hidden in the church, as well as deserters from the Italian army. Other Jews hidden included Adolfo Perugia, Flaminina Anticoli, Giuseppe Astrologo, Franco di Porto and Anna Perugia—all Roman Jews.[25]

Turning to nuns in the Rome region, we note the story of Virginie Badetti (Sr. Agnesa) and Emilia Benedetti (Sr. Augustine), of the convent of the Sisters of Our Lady of Zion (*Nostra Signora di Sion*). Badetti, a French national, was Mother Superior, and Benedetti was in charge of outside contacts. The two sheltered Jews on the run, such as Roberto Modigliani, his mother and grandmother, an aunt, and a brother. There they met many other co-religionists, including Dr. Ferruccio Sonnino, who related that some 100 people were hiding there, Jews and non-Jews alike; and, understandably, conditions were crowded. Included among the those hiding there were also Ruth Einberg, originally from Zagreb, with her uncle Sasha Konforty, who had escaped from an internment camp in Modena in September 1943, and on arriving in Rome had wandered the streets, until someone referred them to this convent. As an emergency measure, if anyone rang the gate bell, the two nuns would pull a special bell as a warning for everyone to hide and be silent. "The *suora* gave us their beds and we also slept everywhere on the floors," Ruth Einberg recalled. She mentioned a certain Sister Giuseppe "who especially loved me. I was then a nice young girl, always hungry, and she very often used to put her piece of bread under my pillow." They stayed there until the city's liberation.[26] Also meriting mention are Anna Bolledi (Sr. Emerenzia) and Maria Corsetti (Sr. Ferdinanda), of the *San Giuseppe al Casaletto* convent, which operated a girls' school, where they hid around thirty Jewish girls, plus several boys who attended the boys' class. Sister Emerenzia was the Mother Superior, and Sister Ferdinanda, the school's headmistress. The Jewish women who found refuge there were dressed in nun's habits and with false identity cards stating that they were Catholics from southern Italy who were unable to return home because of the Allied occupation there. While outwardly they were instructed to act in the Catholic fashion, no one interfered with their engaging in Jewish practices, such as celebrating Purim and Passover. The nuns at the convent were privy to the girls' true origin but kept silent. The girls remained there until Rome's liberation in June 1944. Among those sheltered may be counted Lia Levi and her two sisters (aged twelve, ten, and six), Roberto Calderoni with his brothers and sisters and parents, Emma Torre

Pugliese and her two daughters, Giuliana and Paola (aged nineteen and thirteen), six-year-old Marta Ravenna and her cousin, as well as her parents and grandmother.[27]

Sister Marguerite Bernes, a French-born nun of the Daughters of Charity, served as an assistant to the Mother Superior of the San Giaccomo (Joaquin) convent, but was, in truth, in charge, given the Mother Superior's advanced age. Sister Bernes hid Jews in the convent and in the attic of a nearby church, among them Anita Finzi and her children, Arrigo, Nora, and Alberto, as well as Rosetta Sermoneta. When the Gestapo raided the convent, many of the Jews escaped, including the Finzi children, and Bernes found them hiding places in other religious institutions. After the war, Bernes moved to Jerusalem and headed the *Saint Vincent de Paul* Hospice in Ein Karem, a home for mentally retarded children, and was honored by the city of Jerusalem as a Distinguished Citizen. Responding to a letter in 1988, inviting her to a ceremony, she wrote: "I am a Daughter of Charity, a person who, instead of marrying and building a proper family, decided to give every day of her life to God, praying and serving the poor, the children, and other people in need of help. Here in Israel I have worked since 1952 for the poor handicapped children. According to our religious rules, there is no place during the day or the night for pleasant meetings or other things like that. We pray, we work, we rest . . . and again the same. . . . Please excuse me. Think about our eighty Jewish children, little ones who cannot know the pleasure of living with their parents. Every moment we can be with them and give them all possible love is very precious."[28]

Moving outside Rome to the north, we stop first in Florence, where Cardinal Elia Dalla Costa appointed his secretary, Monsignor Giacomo Meneghello, as his liaison with the Jewish Delasem organization. Dalla Costa also asked for help from Father Cipriano Ricotti, a Dominican priest at the *Convento di San Marco*, as well as Father Leto Casini, a parish priest from nearby Varlungo. Dalla Costa provided Casini and Ricotti with letters of introduction to use in their search for lodgings for Jewish fugitives. Ricotti coordinated his activities with Rabbi Natan Cassuto, and Casini distributed false documents and monthly subsidies provided by Delasem. As recalled by Casini, Dalla Costa "summoned me to his palazzo with a telephone call one evening in October . . . and after describing the tragic situation of the foreign Jews to me . . . asked if I would put myself at the disposition of a committee to search for lodgings, obtain food supplies, provide identity cards—naturally false; in sum, do everything possible to save those persecuted people." Father Casini agreed. On one occasion, much to his surprise, he was refused assistance by a hostile prelate. This occurred in January 1944, when Casini had to change trains in Perugia while on his way to deliver Delasem funds to the bishop of Foligno. The connecting train to Foligno was delayed, and, the weather being bitterly cold, Casini went to see the archbishop of Perugia, hoping that he could leave the money with him, to be relayed to Foligno by someone else. But, as Casini wrote later, "I had barely mentioned the 'Jewish problem' . . . he didn't let me finish the sentence, and showing me the door, asked me to leave." Casini had to sleep in the open that night, behind a gate. Father Casini was eventually arrested in Florence together with Rabbi Cassuto. Casini was freed and ordered to leave town, but Cassuto was deported to Auschwitz. As for Father Ricotti, Rachel Matilde Cassin recalled meeting him at the San Marco monastery, where they discussed ways to help Jewish refugees who had fled to Florence. At times he put up Jews in his private room in the monastery, an act strictly forbidden by the monastic rule. Fleeing arrest by the Fascist authorities (of the pro-Nazi Salo regime), Ricotti escaped to a Dominican monastery in Prato but returned to Florence to resume his rescue works despite the risks this involved. Ricotti was aided by several other clerics, including Giovanni Simeoni, Angelo Della Torre, and Giuseppe De Zotti.[29]

Ruth Mayer and Mina Goldmann were members of a group of thirteen women and children who crossed into Italy from France and were referred by Casini to Father Giovanni Simeoni at the *Santo Spirito* convent in Florence, where they were hidden in the cellar, with the nuns bringing them food at night. Simeoni visited them every day with news of the outside world and words of encouragement. After the Mother Superior, fearing for her nuns' safety, would no longer keep the women, Simeoni took it upon himself to transfer the people, in separate parties, to Treviso, which was near his hometown. This entailed a risky train journey with people who had no papers. The trips went through without a hitch, and in Treviso he confided his wards to three clerical colleagues, Leto Casini, Angelo Della Torre, and Giuseppe De Zotti, who took over. The women and children were again separated and hidden with families or in convents. De Zotti took Ruth Mayer and her mother to his parents' home, in Mestre, near Venice, where they remained for one and half years. Sabine Selzer-Adler also recalled the trip to Treviso with Simeoni, who for that purpose was dressed in civilian clothes on the train journeys. When Simeoni learned that a certain Mrs. Tarnower was pregnant and close to delivery, according to Sonja Rosenstrauch, he placed her in a clinic. They threw her out when they learned that she was Jewish, but Simeoni took her and her six-year-old son to his parents' home, where she delivered a boy. He also moved Lina Glatt and her seventeen-year-old daughter Ruth to the parents of Father De Zotti, and others he dispersed with village families or in regional convents. In addition, Della Torre arranged a hiding place in the *Concretto del Montello* retirement home for Sabine Selzer-Adler, Stella

Schwarzwald, and another family with two daughters. After a German raid, Della Torre moved the women to a Franciscan monastery in Treviso, and provided them with false identities and proper clothing.

Returning to Father Ricotti, he aided the Pacifici family; Wanda Pacifici was referred to Casini, who gave her the addresses of several religious institutions in Florence to try. With her two sons, she trudged from place to place all day on Saturday, November 19, 1943, knocking on doors, but was turned away. Toward evening, and at her wits' end, she was finally admitted by Sister Sandra-Ester Busnelli, who as Mother Superior headed the Missionary Franciscan Sisters of Maria (*Suore Francescane Missionarie di Maria*) in Florence, but the two brothers, Emanuele and Raffaele, were allowed to stay for only one night. The following day, they were moved to the Santa Marta Institute, in Settignano, near Florence, a boys' educational home, headed by Sr. Folcia Marta and assisted by Sr. Benedetta Vespignani, where they stayed for eleven months, from November 1943 until the liberation in June 1944, under the forged name of Pallini. A week after their arrival there, on November 27, 1943, the Gestapo and local Fascists raided the Busnelli convent and arrested all forty Jewish women, most of them foreign nationals, including Wanda Pacifici, and deported them to Auschwitz. Busnelli was also arrested, but was released thanks to the intervention of Cardinal Della Costa. Wanda's husband, Rabbi Riccardo Pacifici, had been arrested earlier in Genoa, in November 1943, when he was lured early in the morning from his hiding place to his synagogue, where he was apprehended and deported to Auschwitz. Both parents perished. Emanuele Pacifici related that every night, before going to bed, they had to wish good-night to and kiss the crucifix worn by one of the nuns, but when she faced the Jewish boys, she used to cover the crucifix with both hands.[30]

Father Giulio Facibeni headed the *Madonnina del Grappa* orphanage, in the Rifredi quarter of Florence. In cooperation with the earlier-mentioned Giovanni Simeoni and Leto Casini, he saved five Jewish boys and one adult. Willy Hartmeyer, Louis Goldman, and brother Harry were hidden in the orphanage compound. The boys, originally from Germany, had fled on foot from France to Italy in September 1943 with their families, and moved through several Catholic institutions. They escaped a Nazi raid on November 5, 1943, while Goldman's father was deported. The next morning, Fathers Giovanni Simeoni and Leto Casini, who were hiding the Goldman mother and other Jewish women in a convent, contacted Facibeni's orphanage (holding some 200 boys), and Facibeni instantly consented to hide the boys, and they remained there until the liberation of the Rifredi quarter on August 11, 1944. Facibeni invented a cover story for them, claiming that their father was a prisoner of war on the Russian front and their mother was stranded in the liberated southern zone of Italy. The boys were also given new names: Harry became Francesco Capaldi, and Louis, Nicola Capaldi. Facibeni provided them with separate accommodations in a small building to reduce the risk of being unmasked by the other boys. Four other Jews were hidden in the orphanage. During the German retreat, in July 1944, the orphanage was raided on suspicion of aid to the partisans. Louis and some other boys were hauled in for questioning. Louis managed to talk himself free and on his way back he ran into Facibeni, who had learned about Louis's arrest, and was frantically on his way to the German headquarters to offer himself in exchange for the boys. Facibeni was at the time suffering from Parkinson's disease. In the words of Louis Goldman: "As his Parkinson's disease worsened, he often asked me to accompany him on his orphanage rounds, shuffling in little steps and leaning on my arm for support. He was no longer able to shave, so I did it for him every second day. Here is an unusual tableau: a young Jewish boy in hiding shaving an elderly, highly esteemed church dignitary." Louis related how Facibeni was viewed as a saint, with people dropping to their knees and vying to kiss his hands as they met him in the streets. He never tried to convert anyone. On the contrary, in Louis Goldman's words, he "always admonished us to never lose our faith."[31]

Still in the Florence region, sixty-year-old Giulio Gradassi served as parish priest in Castiglioni, a Florence suburb, where he lived with his elderly parents. He saved the lives of the Pick family—mother Henia, son Dr. Rubin Pick, and daughter Sonia—who had arrived in Trieste in 1935 from Poland. After the German invasion, they decided to head for Rome, but when they arrived in Florence, local clerics suggested that they stay there. Dr. Pick was first sheltered by Father Luigi Gragani of the *Santa Felicita* Church in Florence; his mother and sister in the La Calza convent. Three weeks later, feeling threatened, Gragani turned Pick over to Gradassi, who sheltered him in his home. Sometime later, in December 1943, Henia and Sonia were warned by the Mother Superior of the threat of arrest; they escaped and headed for Gradassi's home. It was a rainy night, and Gradassi, who suffered from tuberculosis, rode on his bicycle to look for an alternative hiding place for the two women. He returned, feverish with a severe cough, but happy to have found a new safe place for them. A month later, when they had to leave again, Gradassi decided to move the two women into his home, and Rubin to another parish. At the approach of Passover, he offered to bake matzos for them, knowing they were observant Jews and ate only ritually permitted food.[32]

Also of note is the Protestant minister Tullio Vinay in Florence, who helped Jews find safe places, and aided in their flight either to the south to the liberated area of Italy, or north toward the Swiss border, as in the case of Saul and Hulda Campagniano and their two young children, Sara and Reuven. In

November 1943, Hulda was left alone with her two children and the four children of her brother Natan Cassuto, rabbi of Florence, after her husband, her brother, and her brother's wife were arrested and deported, and after she fled from a convent because of a German raid. Vinay at first thought of spiriting the group either north or south, but this plan was dropped in light of the many young children. Instead, he arranged separate hiding places for Hulda Campagniano and her group.[33] In summary, it is estimated that in Florence and environs, at least twenty-one monasteries and convents, along with parish churches and trusted parishioners, participated in sheltering over 300 fleeing Jews.

Moving farther to the center of Italy, we come upon the town of Assisi, with its many religious shrines, and the story of how the local bishop, Giuseppe Placido Nicolini, decided to turn the town into a haven for fleeing Jews. Assisi is located in the foothills of the Apennines, and in 1943 it had a population of about 5,000, not one of them Jewish. Christians came to pray at the shrines of St. Francis, founder of the Franciscan Order, and St. Clare, of the Poor Clares Order. During the German occupation of Italy, several hundred Jews, as well as others fleeing the Germans—anti-Nazi Italians and downed Allied pilots— found shelter there. To synchronize the rescue operations, Bishop Nicolini set up a committee, staffed mostly by priests, to help newcomers find shelter and accommodation. Nicolini appointed Father Aldo Brunacci, a canon at the San Rufino Cathedral, to head the committee, and the latter promptly recruited several priests to help him.[34] The committee's main purpose at this point was to help newcomers put their papers in order, obtain ration cards, and find lodgings at reasonable prices—all ostensibly quite legal acts. The committee collected information about available apartments or rooms in farmhouses, hotels, and inns, and passed it along to the refugees. Bishop Nicolini also authorized the transformation of monasteries and convents into sheltering places. Jewish religious objects were hidden in a walled-up enclosure in the basement of the bishop's residence. In Brunacci's words, "The work was not done by workers, but by the bishop himself, who used a trowel to build the walls while I held a lantern. When a wall had to be broken into, I would wield the pick while the bishop held the light for me. These operations were performed whenever we had to restore the objects to individuals who were leaving Assisi even before the end of the war." According to Brunacci, most of the Jews in Assisi came from Trieste, and he arranged their sheltering in monasteries and convents, even those that were *clausura*—closed to outsiders. Men were dressed as monks, and women were taught to act like pious Christians. Yom Kippur was observed inside the monasteries and convents, with the nuns, on one occasion, preparing a break-the-fast dinner at the end of the day. In Brunacci's words: "When the guests sat down at table to take their first meal after the fast and looked around, they no longer felt like strangers, and they understood that in the bond of love they had been welcomed as brothers and sisters. I recall what a day of intense emotion that was!" Some quipped that Assisi boasted the only convent in the world with a kosher kitchen. A Jewish woman refugee who died while in hiding was buried in the local cemetery without the usual Catholic rites. On the way to the cemetery, Brunacci and his entourage passed a German patrol, "whose members immediately stood at attention, never knowing that the coffin they saluted contained a Jewish lady." After the war, an inscription was placed on the tombstone, headed by a Star of David: "Kerfa Feld Clara, widow Weiss, born in Vienna on September 15, 1887 and peacefully died in Assisi, on November 9, 1943, where she found loving hospitality during the Nazi persecution."

The churches, convents, and monasteries in Assisi that sheltered Jews included the Basilica of St. Francis, Saint Quirico, the Church of St. Francis; the *Laboratorio Saint Francesco*, the Convent of the German Sisters, and the Cathedral and Diocesan Seminary. As for the clerics associated in this rescue conspiracy, Brunacci mentioned the following: Fathers Michel Todde, Rufino Nicacci (of the St. Damiano monastery), Federico Vincenti, and Monsignor Minestrini. Included among those helped were Professor Emilio Viterbi (a chemistry professor, renamed Ernesto Varelli), his wife Margherita (renamed Vitelli), both from Padua, and their daughters Grazia and Mirjam; also, the sisters Rachel (Hella) Lev and Mira Barsiah (both née Baruch), together with their parents, who found refuge in the convent of the Stigmatic nuns, where they remained from the end of 1943 until the town's liberation on June 1944. They told of meeting other Jews in hiding there, and said that Nicacci often came to visit, bringing food and false papers. They, as well as many others, lived openly in Assisi, but under assumed names, and even attended local school. The locals, who suspected the truth, kept their silence. Nicacci reportedly referred many Jews to the Clarisses Sisters (the Poor Clares), a mendicant order of nuns who ran a guest house at the monastery of San Quirico. He also recruited a local printer to fabricate documents in his shop at night, and accompanied Jewish fugitives by train to Florence, where they were met and taken to Genoa and ultimately to safety. Niccaci was eventually arrested and imprisoned in Perugia. Somehow he survived. The rescue operation continued until Assisi's liberation on June 17, 1944. Before that, Brunacci was also arrested and tried in a Perugia court, but he held his own and did not disclose anything. He was eventually released through the intervention of papal officials, on condition that he would leave Assisi and remain in the Vatican. After the war, he stated that "in all, about 200 Jews were entrusted to us by Divine Providence; with God's help, and through the intercession of St. Francis, not one of them fell into the hands of their persecutors." Ending his recollections of that period, Brunacci stated: "Jews and Christians venerate the same book, the Bible, whose opening chapter reminds us that we are created in God's image and likeness. God is our Father, and we are all brothers and sisters."[35]

In Nonantola village, a group about 120 Jewish children, most of whom had arrived there from the Italian zone of occupation in Dalmatia (Yugoslavia), found temporary shelter in the Villa Emma building—that is, until the arrival of the Germans on September 8, 1943. The children then sought refuge in the local Catholic seminary. Yosef Itai, who was in charge of the children, reported that the seminary rector told him that "for a thousand years, no woman has entered this place. May the Lord be blessed." Itai further reported that in one of the seminary's rooms, he sat up with Father Aldo Beccari, one of the teachers, talking about Marxism and religion, "about man and evil, about despair and hope. He viewed us as equals, without any conversion attempts. He had dedicated his life to fighting evil, and he saw us as victims of evil." Beccari took it upon himself to look after the needs of the children, and arranged for the older children to be put up with nearby farmers. This was a temporary measure, and ways had to be found to save the children. At first it was planned to transfer them to the south, already freed by the Allies, with Itai dressed as a priest (Beccari had him photographed in priestly garb). This plan proved too risky, so it was dropped in favor of an alternative plan—escape to Switzerland via a northerly route. Beccari was able to recruit trustworthy people to take the children to the Swiss border. The group successfully crossed the border on Yom Kippur 1943, traveling there by train with forged papers provided by Nonantola's doctor, Giuseppe Moreali. Soon thereafter, Beccari was arrested and interrogated in a Bologna jail, but he kept silent about the missing Jewish children, and he remained imprisoned until the liberation. Years later, he wrote to Itai, who had settled in an Israeli kibbutz: "It would be difficult for me to erase the memory of the terror and sufferings of those days or of my joy at doing the small good which was my duty and which had to be done."[36]

The next story takes us to Father Beniamino Schivo, the rector of a seminary in Citta di Castello, Perugia province, where in 1941 he met the Korn family (Paul and Johanna and their daughter Ursula, born 1925). The Korns had fled from Germany. At the start of the war, they were interned in Citta di Castello, where a friendly priest referred them to Father Schivo. In Ursula's words: "From that moment on, Father Schivo became our protector, our one and only best friend. He put me in a convent so that I could go on with my schooling, otherwise not permitted under penalty of law, and gave us food to supplement what was given us to eat. He helped us in every way to stay alive, risking his own life, and would do it again and again, as he is the kindest man I have ever met in my life." Things moved rather smoothly, considering the wartime conditions. Upon the arrival of the Germans on September 8, 1943, when the hunt for Jews began in earnest. At this point, Father Schivo and another young priest took the Korns by night through German patrols up into the hills to a summer villa of the Salesian nuns. It took them eight hours in freezing temperature to get them in an abandoned large shed outside the convent. The temperatures were freezing t. On Christmas 1943, he came to bring something to eat. "He had walked for nine hours in the hills through German patrols, without his priestly robe on, so that he could bring us some comfort, and he stayed with us until dawn." As the Allies advanced northward, the situation became too dangerous for the Korns to stay on. So a priest took Paul Korn high up in the mountains, while his wife Johanna and daughter Ursula hid with partisans in a wooded area, always under the watchful eyes of Schivo. "Finally, we could no longer run, so in the middle of the night he took us back to Citta di Castello and hid us in the convent of the Sacred Heart, where we were dressed as nuns and locked in a room, and only the Mother Superior knew about us." When the Germans broke into the convent looking for partisans, Father Schivo took his wards to his seminary and locked them in a room, visiting them every night to bring comfort and food. This continued until the area's liberation by the British on July 14, 1944.[37]

Benedetto Richeldi was a priest in Massa Finale, and during the war years he saved ten Austrian and Yugoslav Jews. This happened after the German invasion, when the wife of Dr. Maurice Levi approached Richeldi on the street to tell him that she and the others had been arrested. Richeldi succeeded in having them released and placed in a boarding school in Montablanc. In December 1943, Richeldi transferred them for a week's stay in surrounding farmhouses, while he planned their escape to Switzerland, equipped with false documents. That same month, Richeldi and the Jews went to Modena, where he turned them over to a guide with instructions to proceed by train to Milan, then to Como and Lanzo d'Intelvi, and finally across the Italo-Swiss border. Responding to Yad Vashem on learning he had been elevated to the "Righteous" title, Richeldi wrote in 1974: "As we had hoped, it seems that everything turns out for the better. Israel has its land, with Jerusalem, the Holy City. What you have accomplished arouses the admiration of the whole world. The nations will no longer kick the Holy City around. I always prayed that God would not abandon His people, and God has now stabilized His people's condition. The desert blooms. Long live Israel and its leaders."[38]

Next we meet Father Gaetano Tantalo in Tagliacozzo Alto, who saved the dozen members of the Orvieto and Pacifici families (Rabbi Riccardo Pacifici's sister Judita Orvieto, her family, and her parents, Mario and Gilda). Tantalo harbored the two families in his own home for nine months. He introduced them to outsiders as relatives who had been forced to evacuate their homes. Sensitive to their religious needs, he supplied them with Bibles, greeted them with "Shabbat Shalom" every Friday evening, helped find out when Passover began according to the Jewish calendar, and supplied new dishes and helped organize the necessary ingredients for the baking of the matzos (unleavened bread). "For him, it was a holiday, and he thanked God for the privilege of doing such a great deed," Emanuele Pacifici stated. After Tantalo's death, a small piece of matzah, evidently from the 1944 Passover Seder, was hidden among his belongings. In July 1944, the two families were able to leave Tantalo's home and headed for Rome.[39]

We now turn to an unusually heartwarming story, involving a religiously devout Jew, Herman Gerstel, born 1921, and a Catholic priest, Arturo Paoli. As recounted in Gerstel's testimony, during the war, he fled from Belgium to France, where he obtained a false identity under the name Joseph Gruber, supposedly born in Hagennau, Alsace. With Italy's surrender in September 1943, he and his wife fled to Turin, Italy, by train. Arriving in Livorno, exhausted, the two slept over in a stranger's home, but were told to leave the following morning. They somehow managed to move along, and when they reached Lucca, Mrs. Gerstel was on the point of delivering a child. It was just before the Jewish holiday of Passover 1944. Clerics in Lucca had arranged for her care, especially Father Arturo Paoli, who sent his sister to look after her needs. Mrs. Gerstel gave birth to a girl, aided by Paoli's sister. As for Herman, he decided to ask for shelter in Paoli's religious seminary and he was readily admitted. Paoli used to sit up late into the night discussing religious matters with Gerstel. "Our discussions continued until I declared to him that I would never change my faith, and asked him whether he was willing to change his faith. We remained close friends." Paoli used to come regularly to pick up Gerstel's laundry at his hiding place. One day, the Germans raided the seminary building. At the time Gerstel was in the library, with the door locked. He heard the Germans ask who was inside, and the reply that it was just an office, and no one was there. The Germans responded by screaming that they did not understand Italian. They began pounding the heavy door, but failed to unlock it and left in frustration. After this incident, Paoli spirited Gerstel out of the building and that night took him to the home of an elderly priest, who welcomed Gerstel with the words: "You are my child, and I will save you with my blood" (*Tu sei figlio mio io te salve con mia sangne*). On September 6, 1944, the Americans liberated Lucca. The war over, Gerstel eventually settled in Strasbourg, France, and closed the page on his life during the Holocaust. Over fifty years after his rescue at the hands of Paoli, Gerstel experienced a change of heart and decided to look him up. Finally locating him in Brazil in 1988, he penned a letter to his former rescuer, which said in part: "Dear friend, you will be shocked. Do you know who is it that is writing to you? It is the young Jewish talmudist (1944), with whom you debated the Gospels from midnight to two o'clock on certain days, during the sad days of 1944, in the Lucca seminary." Responding to Yad Vashem's announcement that he had been elevated to the "Righteous" honor, Paoli wrote back: "I deserve no honor, for I am conscious of having done what I had to do. I shake your hand for your noble and necessary work, at this time when humanity has a tendency to mix goodness and evil." At the ceremony in his honor in Brasilia in November 1999, Paoli spoke of the theological significance of the Holocaust. "There are no words capable of describing the Holocaust. For some of us, it was a time to discover that the direction of life is in a state of total imbalance between egotism and total abandonment of one's self. All of life is to be found in this asymmetry. No one living in this age can say that he never harmed anyone else, or did not cause injury to the rights of others. We are slaves of egotism, and are only free when we abandon our selfness. I therefore thank my Jewish brothers and sisters, who liberated me from the slavery of egotism. I wish to state that it is a privilege to be part of the chosen people at the time of humanity's downward slide. During this period, Jewish intellectuals became the guides of the modern period. Such as Martin Buber, Hans Jonas, Emmanuel Levinas, and others. . . . I wish to end my speech, which was meant to be words of thanks, with the words of our teacher: 'The purpose of man is to save man.' It is hard for one who is not involved in Christian life to grasp the true meaning of these words, but it must be emphasized that the thinking of the philosopher Levinas will help everyone to understand how much we are in debt to Judaism, and how close we are to it. This closeness will no doubt help us during the time of peace to which we all look forward so much, after all the violence and injustice we went through."[40]

Moving to northern Italy, we begin with Cardinal Pietro Boetto, the archbishop of Genoa, and his secretary, twenty-eight-year-old Father Francesco Repetto. A few weeks after the German occupation, Valobra, a Delasem representative, came to ask him if Cardinal Boetto would agree to continue the assistance to Jews in the region that up to then had been the responsibility of Delasem. In Repetto's words: "I took this [request] to the cardinal. . . . Standing in front of the cardinal's desk . . . The cardinal paused for a moment, but he did not think about it for long; he said: 'They are innocent, they are in grave danger; we must help them regardless of all our other problems.' " Valobra delivered to Boetto all the Delasem records of contributions received and of individuals helped. Boetto in turn asked Repetto to coordinate activities with the Delasem staff, and he kept scrupulous records of the distribution of money, and recruited bishops and archbishops throughout northern Italy to help in this endeavor, thus creating rescue networks that saved hundreds, if not thousands, of Jews. One of his first recruits was the bishop of Chiavari, whose diocese was a resort town on the coast near Genoa. Many Jewish names appear on a list provided by Repetto after the war, including Rabbi Riccardo

Pacifici, who was later captured and deported. The help included shelter in religious institutions, false documents, hospitalization under false names, and escape to Switzerland. According to another witness, the attorney Giuseppe Sala, Repetto asked Cardinal Ildefonso Schuster in Milan to coordinate rescue efforts. Schuster, who before the German occupation had been friendly to the Mussolini regime, experienced a change of heart and agreed to cooperate with Repetto. On Schuster's request, Sala enlisted a growing group of helpers, and Milan became the center of a network that escorted hundreds of Jews across into Switzerland, as well as many others fleeing the Germans (British prisoners of war, political dissidents, and draft dodgers). In Turin, Cardinal Maurilio Fossati agreed to distribute Delasem funds to foreign Jews in the area, via his secretary, Monsignor Vincenzo Barale, who worked closely with both Repetto and Delasem. Barale distributed funds from Delasem to needy Jews, and allocated money to individual priests throughout his archdiocese and beyond, for distribution to indigent Jews in their parishes, estimated as many as 475. Barale was arrested in August 1944. Cardinal Schuster intervened on his behalf, and he was moved to a religious institution outside Milan, where he lived under strict government surveillance. In July 1944, it was the turn of Repetto to go underground to avoid arrest. Father Carlo Salvi took over from him and continued the rescue operation. In 1955, the Jewish community in Italy honored both clerics with gold medals for their rescue of many Jews.[41]

In Turin, the thirty-nine-year old Dominican Giuseppe Girotti hid many Jews in his monastery, apparently without even informing his superiors. Before that, he taught theology in Turin. He had also written commentaries on Isaiah and Ecclesiastes, and had begun writing one on Jeremiah as well. Among those he aided were Emma Weil and her mother, who were sheltered in a convent for several months, and he provided her father with a false identity card. Denounced and caught while moving a wounded Jewish partisan to the house of his father, Girotti was arrested on August 29, 1944, and deported to Dachau, where he was murdered by lethal injection on April 1, 1945, on the eve of liberation. It is reported that while in Dachau, he continued to write his commentary on the Book of Jeremiah.[42]

Father Dante Sala was another cleric who smuggled Jews across into Switzerland—by his own reckoning, as many as 106 people, among them the Modena, Almoslino, Corinaldi, Capagnano, and Lampronti families. He worked closely with several rescue networks in this widespread undertaking. Twice a week, he would guide groups of five, seven, ten, or at most twelve people to the Swiss border. He also arranged fake ration cards and identities, as well as warm clothing for the people on the road. Some groups converged at the Milan train station and then proceeded to Como, and from there to the border town of Cernobbio, where Sala met them. After negotiating with border smugglers on the price per person, he would turn the fleeing Jews over to them. On December 4, 1943, while engaged in one such mission, he was arrested arrested in Como and brutally interrogated. After two months in prison his superiors were able to get his trial moved from a military to a civil court, and he was ultimately released for lack of sufficient proof. After his release, Sala continued his rescue operation.[43]

Sister Maria Angelica Ferrari was the Mother Superior of a Dominican convent in Fossano. The story begins in France, from where Dvorah Schneider fled to Italy in 1943. On reaching Fossano she jumped off the train with her two children, Louis and Regina, after a rumor spread that the refugees were about to be deported, and was severely injured. Taken to a local hospital, she was visited by the local bishop, Monsignor Dionisa Borra, who arranged for her children to be sheltered: Louis, in a Dominican school; Regina, in the convent headed by Sister Ferrari, the only one there who knew she was Jewish. When Regina took sick that winter, Ferrari moved the girl to her private quarters, which was against convent rules, and the child remained there until fully recovered. Recalling Sister Ferrari's help, Regina stated: "To me, she looked like the Madonna. Her soft eyes seemed sad, yet warm and deep. And she became my mother—*mia Madre*—watching over me and treating me like her own special child. In her presence, I always felt safe and secure." At bedtime each night one of the nuns would come to her room to make sure that Regina made the sign of the cross by folding her arms on her chest. Then Regina would say her prayers, for God, the bishop, the Mother Superior, her mother, her father [who was in a concentration camp], and her brother Louis. "I was thoroughly dedicated to religion, and wore my cross and medals with pride. Mixed with my Catholicism, however, was my attachment to something else I did not really understand. I knew words I had heard my mother speak before I entered the convent that had important meaning to me. At desperate moments, she had prayed to God—as I had learned to do in the convent—although she did it in a different language. In my own moments of despair and loneliness, I would sound those same words with the same depth of emotion as she had done. As I pushed my rosary beads, Latin would turn Yiddish, and Hebrew, and back again; from Catholic to Jewish to Catholic, from *mia Madre* to *mominu* and back again. . . . The nuns watched me closely because I was their little angel child. They had a great sense of pride in their little protégée. I tried so hard to be good and obedient. Whenever a nun lost her place at prayer, she knew she could be reoriented by Reginetta [as Regina was then known]. The better I was, the more the nuns loved me and cared for me. Therefore, I felt safe and protected. . . . Much of my energy in church was generated toward prayer for the end of the war. I pushed and pushed my rosary beds, saying *Guttenu, Guttenu* [God, God]. They were magical words to me—

the words He would answer to bring us peace—and I still remember exactly where I was sitting in the chapel on the day that my prayer for peace actually ended with the news that the war was over." Visiting her mother on occasion, she once noted her mother covering her head and walking to the sink, above which was a light bulb. "Cupping her hands, she began moving her arms in circular motions around the bulb and praying to God in Hebrew. It seemed foreign and familiar, frightening, yet comforting. This was her Sabbath ritual which she felt safe to share with me."

When the mother came to fetch her daughter (and her son), one of the nuns angrily shouted at her, *puta, puta,* for according to Regina, the nuns were disappointed to learn that Reginetta was really Jewish and would no longer be staying with them. As for the Mother Superior, she "was driven by a fundamental faith which left her no alternative but to care for me. We knelt together and prayed each day in front of a statue of the Madonna and child, and she simply followed her faith in watching over me. Hers was a pure love, perhaps compounded by this unique opportunity to raise the child that she had forsworn ever having herself when she entered the Dominican order. . . . Between us, she did not in any way attempt to deny my Jewish and family heritage [a secret closely kept from the other nuns], for every day she prayed with me for the return of my father [who survived the depredation of the camps] and kept the flame of family reunion lit in my heart. Simply put, Maria Angelica Ferrarri saved my life; she was human in a time of gross inhumanity, loving and faithful in an age of pathological hatred."[44]

Also deserving mention is Sister Maria Giuseppina (Barbara Lavizzari), the responsible nun in the Benedictine convent at Ronco di Ghiffa, Novara district. When news spread of the massacre of the Jews in Meina, on the shores of Lake Maggiore, in September 1943, the Torres fled with their two daughters, Adriana and Renata, together with an old grandmother from the Milan region, where they lived. After much wandering and searching, they contacted Sister Maria Giuseppina, who immediately agreed to shelter the three people. Jewish women were already present inside the convent—perhaps baptized Jews, or from mixed marriages. The three Torres were given a separate room, where relatives were permitted to visit them on weekends. They state that there was no pressure on them with regard to religion throughout their stay there. In December 1943, an aunt joined them in their sheltered room. When someone betrayed the Jews' presence there, Sister Giuseppina moved two women of the Torres family to the *clausura* section of the convent and had them dress in nun's habits, while the youngish Renata and Adriana left to join their parents in their new hiding place.[45]

In Venice, Cardinal Adeodato Piazza reportedly viewed Jews as Christ killers, doomed by God to perpetual chastisement, and held that they presented a constant danger to the Christian community and church. At the same time, when it came to converted Jews, Cardinal Piazza felt pain over their travails and asked the Holy See to save them. That is, the baptized Jews only.[46] By contrast, Piazza's colleague in nearby Trieste, Bishop Antonio Santin, did not conceal his concern for unbaptized Jews. It is reported that he delivered an astounding speech in the presence of Nazis and their Fascist collaborators. "I am asking for this law of humanity in the name of Christ, also for the sons and daughters of that people from whose womb He came as a man and in whose midst He lived and died." No harm befell Santin, but his pleas did not produce the desired results. Close to 1,200 Jews from Trieste were deported to Auschwitz, of whom only a hundred survived.[47] In closing we mention the tragic end of twenty-two-year-old Father Aldo Mei, who was shot beneath the old walls of Lucca on August 4, 1944, for hiding just one Jew and some partisans.[48]

Chapter 13
Switzerland and Scandinavia

> *The Lord spoke to Cain: "Where is your brother Abel?" He*
> *answered: "I do not know. Am I my brother's keeper? " . . .*
> *Today, God's scrutinizing and inquiring eyes are focused upon us*
> *Christians . . . and He demands of us, "Where, where, where!*
> *Where is your brother, the homeless Jew?"*
>
> Rev. Paul Vogt, Basel, 1944

Switzerland

There were 18,000 Jews in Switzerland on the eve of the war. In the early years of the Nazi regime, several thousand German Jews passed through Switzerland on their way to other destinations. To regulate and stop the entry of Jews into the country, the Swiss police chief, Heinrich Rothmund, suggested to the Germans on September 29, 1938, that all passports held by Jews be marked with a large red *J*. Thus it was as a result of a Swiss initiative that the Nazis introduced this discriminatory practice. On August 13, 1942, the border police was instructed to send back civilian refugees from France who had entered Switzerland illegally, with the exception of political refugees. Most of the people affected were Jews, but even so, thousands made it into the country illegally between August 1, 1942 and the end of the year. This development led to a new decree, on December 29, 1942, ordering that foreigners arrested while crossing the border or in the region of the border (within 10 kilometers) must be turned back immediately. The only exceptions were parents with children less than six years old. In the first seven months of 1943, 1,821 refugees were sent back and 4,733 admitted. Those admitted were sent to special camps, some of which were labor camps. Jews made up the vast majority of the refugees. After the Italian armistice in September 1943, several thousand more Jews entered Switzerland. In summary, a total of 300,000 foreigners passed through Switzerland during the Nazi period, which included 115,000 people fleeing the military draft in their countries. An estimated 30,000 of those admitted were Jews.[1]

As to the response of the Swiss churches (overwhelmingly Protestant), on November 17, 1941, one hundred pastors signed a resolution condemning antisemitism, declaring it incompatible with membership in the church, and calling upon members to prayer for the suffering Jewish people and to do everything they could to alleviate this suffering, since, quoting the words of John 4:22: "salvation comes of the Jews." In June 1942, a similar declaration issued by the Council of Pastors in Geneva also included words of praise for Jewish converts to Christianity, adding that "the race from which came the prophets and the apostles, and to which Jesus Christ belonged, deserves our respect. We owe Jews a debt of gratitude, and if Christians pray to God for the conversion of the chosen people, they must also implore divine mercy for persecuted Israel." Finally, in October 1943, the churches addressed the matter of the refugees pounding on the doors of the country. The Church Council of Zurich called for the government to freely admit the refugees in the spirit of the Good Samaritan. This was followed, in November 1943, with a similar call by the Swiss Union of Reformed Pastors: "In the name of Jesus we demand that our authorities put a stop to the driving back of refugees to their death, until final measures are taken, and to grant them a safe, Christian asylum."[2] On June 22, 1943, the Swiss Protestant Relief Society, in a letter to the Swiss Jewish Union of Congregations, declared its solidarity with Jewish suffering and its deep regret at Christian antisemitism: "We regret every word of contempt we Christians have ever uttered against Jews. . . . We regret that we Christians were not more loyal to our Master and thus failed courageously to struggle, in time, against every expression of antisemitism. On this day of your mourning we implore the almighty for his mercy. . . . 'God be merciful to us sinners.' " In July 1944, in light of the tragic events in Hungary, the Council of the Synod of Berne condemned the deportations of Hungarian Jews as "a monstrosity unparalleled in history, as well as a grievous sin and guilt before God."[3]

Reverend Paul Vogt stands out as the Swiss cleric who deplored in strong terms the church's silence in the face of the Nazi extermination of the Jews. Consider, for instance, his sermon on June 27, 1944, in the *Leonhardkirche* in Basel: "The Lord spoke to Cain: 'Where is your brother Abel?' He answered: 'I do not know. Am I my brother's keeper?' The Lord answered: 'What have you done? Behold, thy brother's blood cries out to me from the earth' (Gen. 4:8–10). Today, God's scrutinizing and inquiring eyes are focused upon us Christians . . . and He demands of us, 'Where, where, where! Where is your brother, the homeless Jew? . . . Thou protective and nursing Christian mother who loves your children, where are the homeless Jewish children today? . . . Where are the widows, the orphaned, the hungry, the thirsty and the strangers?' . . . God's inquiry always concerns the brother. . . . Today and here the question focuses very clearly on the brothers of the people of Abraham. Where are they all? You Christians, tell me, where? Cain gave the classic response of those shirking their responsibility: 'I don't know!' From his response, one can glean a thinly veiled allusion of rebellion: 'O God, of what concern is it to You where my brother is? And what does where my brother is have to do with me?' . . . Today, Christians respond in the same classic fashion of irresponsibility: 'I do not know where the Jew is! Nor does it concern me in the least.' O Holy God, it is with profound shame and deep fear that we come before Thee today. Thou hast inquired of us regarding our brothers the Jews. . . . We are not worthy of standing before Thee, because we Christians loved so little and had so little faith. . . . In the midst of our Christendom, godlessness seeks to exterminate the entire Jewish people, and we can no longer prevent it. . . . O Father, have mercy, have mercy, forgive us our enormous sin . . . O help, so that Your earthly church truly repents in sackcloth and ashes for ignoring Your words and will, and for its contempt of Your promise. . . . Tear us out of our indifference, all our Cain-like thoughts and perspectives. . . . Help Your earthly flock truly become the protector of the disenfranchised, the worthless, homeless, and helpless. Have mercy upon the persecuted Jews. Have mercy upon the sorrow-laden Jews!" Vogt followed this up, on July 14, 1944, with a direct appeal to the Swiss government: "I beg of you—in the name of the Jewish people who knock on my door, in the name of our master Jesus, who through the humblest of his brethren knocks mightily on the doors of our Swiss houses, which fortunately have been spared, and who knocks on the doors of our hearts—to do everything that will transform the will of the Swiss people to active assistance. Why were we Swiss, in our dear homeland, spared through God's wonder? Surely not to live each day without a thought [of the matter]. Certainly not for the purpose of celebrating endless parties and smugly praising our own virtues. And most assuredly not to self-righteously criticize and judge other nations. . . . If this is the purpose of our being spared, then we will appear before history and future generations as petty, ugly, and mean."[4]

Dr. Vissert Hooft, the secretary general of the World Council of Churches, and Dr. Adolf Freudenberg, director of the Refugee Department, also acted to relieve the plight of Jews, especially those who had managed to reach Switzerland either on their own or with the help of Protestant organizations in France. Pastor Hans Schaffert visited the internees in the Gurs internment camp in France and helped some ("too few unfortunately," in his words) to escape to Spain and Switzerland. As in August 1942, when, during the deportations from the Gurs camp, he supplied some fleeing Jews with small amounts of money and helped them reach the Spanish border. In a 1966 letter to Yad Vashem, he wrote, "To this day, I redden with shame and anger at the murder and injustice done by us, the baptized, of whom I too am one, in our country and outside it. More than ever I know that whoever sins against Israel sins against God's property and God himself. This is not a question of sentimentality but of the deepest theological conviction."[5]

Scandinavia

The German occupation in Denmark was unique in many ways. The king and the Danish government remained in place, and the Germans even had a diplomatic representative. Germany granted Denmark a degree of autonomy unusual for an occupied country, and did not press the government on the Jewish issue. This lasted until August 29, 1943, when the government resigned after the Germans declared martial law and disbanded the small Danish army. SS general Dr. Werner Best, the German envoy, received full powers as Reich plenipotentiary. At the time there were 7,700 Jews in the country. The Germans planned a deportation action against them in one fell swoop, to take place on the night of October 1–2. When news of this leaked out, it was met with disbelief. The bishop of Copenhagen, Dr. Fuglsang-Damgaard, on September 28, assured the leaders of the Jewish congregation that the rumors were baseless. However, when he learned that the roundup was, in fact, in the offing, he drafted a letter on behalf of the country's bishops, under the heading "Protest," to be read in all churches. It went as follows: "Wherever persecutions are undertaken for racial or religious reasons against the Jews, it is the duty of the Christian Church to raise a protest against it for the following reasons: (1) Because we shall never be able to forget that the Lord of the Church, Jesus Christ, was born in Bethlehem, of the Virgin Mary, into Israel, the people of His possession, in accordance with God's promise. The history of the Jewish people up to the birth of Christ includes the preparation for the salvation which God had prepared in Christ for all men. This is also expressed in the fact that the Old Testament is a part of our Bible. (2) Because a persecution of the Jews is irreconcilable with the humanitarian concept of love of neighbor which follows from the message which the Church of Jesus Christ is commissioned to proclaim. . . . Therefore, we desire to declare unambiguously our allegiance to the word that we must obey God rather than man." No bishop or pastor, to the best of our knowledge, was arrested because of the public protest.[6]

The Germans, of course, were not inhibited by the bishop's message, and went ahead with the roundup of Jews. On the night of October 1–2, 202 Jews were captured in Copenhagen, and 82 elsewhere. About 200 others were arrested later. The great majority, however, were saved thanks to a massive rescue operation undertaken by the Danish underground, which ferried most of the country's Jews across the Sound waterway to Sweden. A total of 7,220 people, including 5,919 full Jews, 1,301 part-Jews, and 686 non-Jews who were married to Jews, was ferried across. Tragedy struck on October 6, 1943, in the fishing town of Gilleleje, where forty or fifty Jews had been hidden up in the loft by the church warden. The group had come directly from Copenhagen; the children were deep in sleep after being injected by local doctors. More people were added, for a total of eighty. Just the day before, seven fishing vessels had managed to get 102 men, 76 women, and 28 children to safety in Hoganas, Sweden. It was bitterly cold outside, there was no light and no heat, and Pastor Kjeldgaard Jensen comforted the people and allayed their fears. However, news of the Jews hiding in the church garret was betrayed to the Gestapo in Elsinore, and it decided to investigate, with reinforcements from the Danish police. At around midnight, German police set up machine guns and searchlights around the church, and proceeded to arrest the eighty Jews holed up in the church. Only one person escaped, by hiding in the clock tower between the bells. Thirty-eight were later released because they were "half-Jewish." The rest were sent to the Theresienstadt (Terezin) concentration camp. Reverend Jensen had a nervous breakdown the next morning when he learned of the arrests; he felt personally responsible for them. On November 29, 1943, the bishops jointly wrote to Dr. Best: "It with deep sorrow and disappointment that we perceive, through developing circumstances, that our appeal to the German authorities about the Jewish Question has not born fruit. . . . [Our] deep sympathy with our deported countrymen is undiminished... We wish to suggest to the Danish church communities that they should send help to the interned Jews, in the form of gift parcels, through the Red Cross." The Germans allowed the gift parcels to be delivered to the Danish Jews incarcerated in Theresienstadt. Of the 475 Jews who were sent there, all saw it through the war with the exception of fifty-three who died. Denmark was the only occupied country to actively resist the Nazi regime's efforts to deport its Jewish citizens, with the participation of its churches.[7]

The Germans conquered Norway in April 1940, and a pro-Nazi party headed by Vidkun Quisling was appointed to head a puppet government. There were 1,700 Jews at the time of the invasion, mostly in Oslo and Trondheim. In October 1942, arrests of Jews began; at first only men aged sixteen and over, but later all men and the women as well. Those picked up were sent by boat to Germany; thence to Auschwitz. In a letter to Quisling on November 10, 1942, the Norwegian bishops stated that Jews had the legal right to reside and earn a livelihood in Norway for ninety-one years, but now they were being deprived of their property without warning. Furthermore, they were being punished like the worst criminals, wholly and solely because they were Jews. "When we now appeal to you, Mr. Minister-President, it is not to defend whatever wrongs the Jews may have committed. If they have committed crimes, they shall be tried, judged, and punished according to Norwegian law just like all other citizens. But those who have committed no crime shall enjoy the protection of our country's justice. . . . The church has God's call and full authority to proclaim God's law and God's gospel. Therefore, it cannot remain silent when God's commandments are being trampled underfoot. And now it is one of Christianity's basic values which is being violated; the command of God which is fundamental to all society. . . . Stop the persecution of Jews and stop the race hatred which, through the press, is being spread in our land. . . . By the right of our calling, we therefore warn our people to desist from injustice, violence, and hatred. He who lives in hatred and encourages evil invokes God's judgment upon himself." This was followed on two consecutive Sundays with prayers from the pulpit for the Jews—November 15 and 22, 1942. The only exception to this unified stand was Bishop Jacob Mangers, head of the Catholic Church, who declined to join the Protestant church leaders in denouncing the persecution of Jews. His interest was restricted to Jewish converts to Catholicism. A total of 763 Norwegian Jews were deported, of whom 739 perished. About 900 escaped to Sweden with the help of the underground. It is still not known how many clergymen, if any, were involved in the rescue effort.[8]

Before the war, the borders of nearby Sweden were sealed to Jewish refugees who did not have visas. In 1938, Sweden even returned to Germany refugees who had entered illegally. By late 1942, and especially during 1943, with Germany beginning to lose the war, Sweden's policy changed, and it agreed to accept any Jewish refugees who entered its territory, as in the case of those from Norway and Denmark. In May 1944, the Swedish legation in Budapest began to provide transit visas and protective passes for Hungarian Jews who had contacts with Sweden. Raoul Wallenberg was dispatched to the Swedish legation in Budapest in early July to work exclusively to aid Jews. As a result of Bernadotte's efforts to obtain the release of Scandinavian prisoners in Ravensbrueck and other German concentration camps, Himmler consented to allow non-Scandinavians from Ravensbrueck to join the Scandinavian group. As a result, several thousand Jewish women inmates from the camp left for Sweden in the latter part of April 1945. It is estimated that a total of 12,000 Jewish refugees were admitted in Sweden during the war years.

As for the response of the churches, more than 95 percent of Sweden's citizens were members of the Swedish Lutheran Church, which was headed by bishop Erling Eidem. Although opposed to Nazi Germany, he had to consider the views of the many clerics in the Swedish church who sided with Germany, especially those in the diocese of Göteborg, the second-largest city. The diocesan journal, the *Göteborgs Stifts-Tidning*, argued that Hitler was a good Christian, criticized democracy, and equated godless Bolshevism with

Judaism. As Eidem bewailed in 1941, "Unfortunately it seems to be the case that a pro-Nazi attitude (including antisemitism and worshiping Mars) is not unusual among the clergy." Eidem attempted to limit the clergy's antisemitism.[9] There were, of course, others, such as Olle Nystedt, chief pastor of the Stockholm congregation, who spoke out against the deportation of Jews in nearby Norway, in a sermon entitled "If We Remain Silent, the Stones Will Cry Out." Bishop Eidem, on November 30, 1942, asked Foreign Minister Günther to help the Jews in Norway who had not yet been deported. "My sincere and earnest wish is that the Swedish government must take whatever step is possible to help those unhappy people by providing visas for transit to Sweden or by some other method." At the same time, playing it safe, in late 1942, Eidem declined to publicly appeal for an end to the persecution of the Jews. Explaining his silence, he stated that for Sweden "it is much wiser that their voices be spared for the future, for the time when the world war has come to an end. . . . My opinion is not determined by cowardice but by an honest desire to be an instrument for reconciliation and goodwill." He felt that if one had to make a choice, German rule was preferable to that of Soviet Bolshevism. In July 1944, Eidem again declined an appeal by Rabbi Isaac Herzog to protest the German persecution of Jews, a position which he maintained until the end of the war. As already noted, the Swedish church in Berlin, under pastors Erik Perwe and Erik Myrgren, was active in sheltering Jews, baptized as well as full Jews.[10]

Chapter 14
Conclusions

From our study of clergy rescuers of Jews, one may be tempted to conclude that Christian clerics were able to overcome the deep anti-Jewish bias of church teachings when they committed themselves to aid Jews in distress during the Nazi period. This would be a far-reaching conclusion, not supported by evidence. Rather, it is most probable that while many of the rescuers held, to various degrees, to the traditional teaching on Jews, they did not feel that this conflicted with the religious obligation to aid Jews who would otherwise be destroyed by a regime whose philosophy and behavior conflicted with those of Christianity. At the same time, many of the rescuers admired the Jews for their tenacity through ages of sufferings. This went hand in hand with a belief that the Jews, as still a Chosen People, had an important role to play in the unfolding of the final divine drama for the salvation of mankind; in fact, that it could not happen without Jewish participation. Hence, the necessity to preserve them. Finally, and this remained a strong motivation—the basic and fundamental Christian obligation to extend assistance to those in desperate need, of whatever faith and people. It must also be pointed out that members of the lower clergy, less addicted to hair-splitting theological teachings, found it easier to disregard or minimize whatever anti-Jewish input they may have been exposed to during their training for the priesthood. At the other end of the spectrum, and with a few notable exceptions, higher ecclesiastical clerics were too much blinded by the *Adversos Judaeos* tradition to be able to act courageously in face of the moral challenge presented by the murderous Nazi antisemitism.

No major differences are detectable between Catholic and Protestant clergy rescuers, except that in countries where Protestants were a minority and had undergone suffering at the hands of a Catholic majority, as in France, they were more prone to identify with the plight of the Jews and come to their aid. This also had to do with the greater Protestant reliance on the Hebrew Bible, and with a tendency to see the Jews as very much still God's Chosen People despite their refusal to accept the Christian Savior. Thus a relatively greater proportion of Calvinist pastors, especially in the Netherlands, participated in rescuing Jews. At the same time, a word of caution: in overwhelmingly Protestant Germany, Protestants showed no greater sympathy for Jews than was displayed by their Catholic counterparts.

Finally, the issue of conversion of Jews under Christian care. It is hard to draw any definite conclusions. At the same time, the unique opportunity presented by the placing of children of a tender and impressionable age in the care of Christian clergy was too tempting for people trained in the exclusivity of their faith not to attempt, mostly in subtle ways, to influence the minds of these tender children. Insofar as this study is concerned, most clerics held back from overt pressure, and kept faith with the human and religious decency to allow those under their care to decide for themselves on the merits of the Christian faith—but out of a free choice arrived at, preferably after the war years. We shall now examine how the events of the Holocaust led the churches to a reexamination of their stance vis-à-vis Jews and Judaism.

Chapter 15
Post-Holocaust

You are our favored brothers and, in a certain sense, one can say
our elder brothers. . . . The Jews are beloved of God, who has
called them with an irrevocable calling.
Pope John Paul II (1986)

It did not happen immediately, but the Holocaust—a mass murder unprecedented in history, perpetrated by baptized Christians with the blessings of not a few clergy— sent shock waves through Christianity, and led to a slow, laborious, and unmistakable rethinking of the religion's basic tenets with regard to Jews and Judaism, and this process is still ongoing. We shall presently discuss some of the issues involved in this self-reexamination.

Problem: Anti-Judaism Heritage
In a 2001 lecture at Yad Vashem, Franklin H. Littell stated that "nothing is more traumatic for a professing Christian than to have to come to terms with the fact that in the heartland of European Christendom, millions of Jews were systematically murdered by baptized Christians—never rebuked, let alone excommunicated, by the churches' leaderships." A minister of the Methodist Church as well as a professor of religious history, Littell is a well-known Holocaust interpreter who for many years was concerned by what the legacy of the Holocaust, which he terms an "alpine" and "watershed" event in history, posed for Christianity.[1] Marcel J. Dubois, another well-known Christian theologian, concurs: "While I consider it a distortion of fact to say that Holocaust was the work of Christians—even though many of its perpetrators were *de facto* Christians—I admit that there is ample evidence that the centuries-old Christian anti-Judaism prepared the soil for modern antisemitism and the Holocaust. The Holocaust could not have happened if the Christians of Germany, Europe, the world, had taken an unequivocal stand against the Nazi program of persecution and extermination of the Jews. The reason why no such stand was taken, why so few prophetic voices were raised, is the

strong antisemitism of the West, one of the roots of which has been Christian teaching."[2] It goes without saying that, in the words of Jon D. Levenson, it strains the historical imagination to claim that nearly two millennia of Christian demonization of Judaism and the Jews played no role in laying the ground work for the Final Solution.[3]

The anti-Jewish polemic gained strength as the nascent church claimed that it had superseded Judaism and was henceforth the true Israel. In 1975 Littell wrote that Christian superseding, or displacement theology, ominously "already rings with a genocidal note."[4] As Carroll observed, since the church claimed that the Jews had forfeited their right to continue in existence, did this not imply a justification of their removal?[5] Not surprisingly, Hitler cynically reminded Bishop Berning and Vicar General Prelate Steinmann, in April 1933, that his *Judenpolitik* was only carrying out what the church had actually done for centuries, but in recent times, due to its ever increasing enfeeblement, had failed to achieve.[6] For theological reasons the church forbade the killing of "corporeal Israel," preferring to keep the Jews in their degradation and oppression as living evidence of the truth of Christian faith, while the theology of substitution left no room for the recognition of Judaism as of any religious significance, for as depicted at the entrance of the Strasbourg cathedral, a veil covers the face of the synagogue. Anti-Judaism thus became an expression of Christian self-affirmation. The "sins" of the Jews were stressed more and more, and the Jew became, in the eyes of Christians, the embodiment of treachery and evil. The anti-Judaic arguments were repeated, over and over again, in Christian sermons, biblical commentaries, and theological tracts. Christians found it difficult to preach or teach anything without touching on the Jews in some way.[7] James Carroll recalled that when he was studying for the ministry, "we young students of the New Testament . . . knew that, from what we thought of as its origins, the church had defined itself as the replacement of Judaism, and that because Judaism had refused to yield to that claim, the church had further defined itself as the enemy of Judaism."[8]

Marcel Dubois posed the agonizing question: "Anyone studying Christian anti-Judaism will eventually have to confront what for many of us is the most difficult question of all: is anti-Judaism part and parcel of Christian dogma? . . . Is anti-Judaism endemic to Christian theology?"[9] Paradoxically, Pope Pius XII and many Christian prelates failed to see that they, too, would eventually be threatened in the event of a Nazi victory in the war. As noted by Otto Dov Kulka and Paul Mendes-Flohr, "Since Judaism was the root of Christianity, the 'Final Solution' of the Jewish Question was not only an intrinsic objective of the Nazi apocalyptic vision, but also a necessary precondition for its successful struggle against the church. Hence, the 'Final Solution' of the Church Question, albeit postponed by Hitler for tactical reasons . . . would inevitably follow the 'Final Solution' of the Jewish Question." Klaus Scholder, a church historian, concurs with this estimation. "The Jewish and Christian questions in the Third Reich were much more closely linked than the Christian churches were willing to acknowledge. Only Hitler's defeat in the war spared the Christians the violent realization of this fact." If, in the words of Alice Eckhardt, Auschwitz was "the decisive event that will forever divide time into a 'before' and an 'after,' " then the church was called to reappraise its age-old teaching of contempt against the Jewish people. How has the church faced up to this challenge?[10]

Postwar Vatican Declarations

The Catholic Church, as the largest, most powerful, and most influential Christian church, waited two decades after the end of the war, but then, in the *Nostra Aetate* document, which followed the 1965 Vatican II Ecumenical Council, it dealt with the Jewish "mystery" from a different and, for the first time, positive approach. The church could not forget, the document stated, that "she received the revelation of the Old Testament through the people with whom God in His inexpressible mercy deigned to establish the Ancient Covenant. Nor can she forget that she draws sustenance from the root of that good olive tree into which have been grafted the wild olive branches of the Gentiles." The church also acknowledged that from the Jewish people sprang the apostles, as well as most of the early disciples who proclaimed Christ to the world. While the Jews were mistaken in not accepting Jesus as Christ, "nevertheless . . . the Jews still remain most dear to God because of their fathers". As for Jesus's crucifixion, "what happened in His passion cannot be blamed upon all the Jews then living, without distinction, nor upon the Jews of today." While, indeed, the church supplanted the Jews as the new chosen people, and the church is the new people of God, the Jews should not be presented as repudiated or cursed by God." Finally, "mindful of her common patrimony with the Jews, [the church] deplores the hatred, persecutions, and displays of anti-semitism directed against the Jews at any time and from any source."[11] Much of what was said here was a repetition of the standard traditional Christian viewpoint with regard to the Jews, but voiced in less hostile and somewhat conciliatory terms. For the first time, the Catholic Church no longer claimed that it aimed at the disappearance of the Jewish community, but instead sought a living link with it, while at the same time clinging to the traditional message that the Jews had forfeited the right to be considered God's chosen people. Cardinal Bea, the moving spirit behind *Nostra Aetate,* stated that the Jewish people "is no longer the people of God in the sense of an institution for the salvation of mankind. . . . Its function in preparing the Kingdom of God finished with the advent of Christ and the founding of the church."[12]

The Guidelines which were issued after *Nostra Aetate*, starting in 1974 and up to 1985, were further positive steps in discarding the old devaluation of Judaism. They called for Christians to acquire a better knowledge of the religious tradition of Judaism, so that "from now on, real dialogue must be established. . . . Dialogue demands respect for the other as he is; . . . respect for his faith and his religious convictions. [The church will] strive to understand the difficulties which occur for the Jewish soul—rightly imbued with an extremely high, pure notion of the divine transcendence—when faced with the mystery of the incarnate Word. . . . The Old Testament and the Jewish tradition founded upon it must not be set against the New Testament in such a way that the former seems to constitute a religion of only justice, fear, and legalism, with no appeal to the love of God and neighbor. Jesus was born of the Jewish people, as were his apostles and a large number of his first disciples. Jesus used teaching methods similar to those employed by the rabbis of his time. The history of Judaism did not end with the destruction of Jerusalem, but rather went on to develop a religious tradition."

Furthermore, "The people of the Old and the New Testament are tending toward a like end in the future: the coming or returning of the Messiah— even if they start from two different points of view. It is more clearly understood that the person of the Messiah is not only a point of division but also a point of convergence. . . . Jesus was and always remained a Jew, his ministry was deliberately limited 'to the lost sheep of the house of Israel.' . . . There is no doubt that he wished to submit himself to the Law . . . that he was circumcised and presented in the Temple like any Jew of his time . . . that he was trained in the law's observance. He extolled respect for it. . . . His relations with the Pharisees were not always or wholly polemical. . . . It is Pharisees who warn Jesus of the risks he is running (Luke 13:31); Jesus shares, with the majority of Palestinian Jews of that time, some pharisaic doctrines: the resurrection of the body; forms of piety, like alms giving, prayer, fasting . . . and the liturgical practice of addressing God as Father; the priority of the commandment to love God and our neighbor. . . . It is noteworthy too that the Pharisees are not mentioned in accounts of the Passion. Gamaliel . . . defends the apostles at a meeting of the Sanhedrin. An exclusively negative picture of the Pharisees is likely to be inaccurate and unjust. . . . Criticisms of various types of Pharisees are moreover not lacking in rabbinical sources. . . . It may also be stressed that, if Jesus shows himself severe toward the Pharisees, it is because he is closer to them than to other contemporary Jewish groups. . . . The permanence of Israel (while so many ancient peoples have disappeared without trace) is a historic fact and a sign to be interpreted within God's design. We must, in any case, rid ourselves of the traditional idea of a people punished, preserved as a living argument for Christian apologetic. It remains a chosen people, 'the pure olive in which were grafted the branches of the wild olive which are the gentiles' (John Paul II)."

These are words never uttered before by any church since the dawn of Christianity. They testify to a radical change in the relationship of Catholic Church to Jews and Judaism.[13]

Polish-born Pope John Paul II, a witness to the Holocaust on his native soil, and head of the Roman Catholic Church from 1978 to 2005, took a giant step in drastically changing the traditional church theology of Jews in a most direct way. He displayed an unashamed fondness, if not more, for the Jewish people, and left a mark on the Catholic Church which his successors will find hard to disregard. In 1979, he visited Auschwitz, which he described as "the Golgotha of the contemporary world," and prayed there, first for victims who were Jewish and then for the other victims. In 1986, he visited the central synagogue on the banks of the Tiber in Rome, where he prayed together with Roman Jews. Significantly, he was the first bishop to visit a synagogue since the foundation of Christianity. His visit contrasted sharply with Bishop Ambrose's fulmination against the synagogues of his day. Recalling his visit to Auschwitz on this occasion, the pope stated: "This people that received from God the commandment 'Thou shalt not murder,' itself experienced a singular ordeal in killing." Reversing the teaching of substitution, the pope went on: "The Jewish religion is not 'extrinsic' to us, but in a certain manner, it is 'intrinsic' to our religion. We have therefore a relationship with it which we do not have with any other religion. You are our favored brothers and, in a certain sense, one can say our elder brothers. . . . The Jews are beloved of God, who has called them with an irrevocable calling." This led him to state further in 1997: "This people has been called and led by God, Creator of heaven and earth. Their existence, then, is not a mere natural or cultural happening. . . . It is a supernatural one. This people continues in spite of everything to be the people of the covenant, and, despite human infidelity, the Lord is faithful to his covenant." Words never spoken before by any pope! Finally, "the Christian must know that by belonging to Christ he has become 'Abraham's offspring,' . . . and has been grafted onto a cultivated olive tree. . . . If he has this firm conviction, he can no longer allow for Jews as such to be despised, or worse, ill-treated."[14]

In 1983, marking the fortieth anniversary of the Warsaw Ghetto Uprising, Pope John Paul II spoke with warmth of his affinity with Jewish neighbors in prewar Poland. "I remember, first of all, the elementary school in Wadowice, where at least one-fourth of my classmates were Jewish boys. . . . My eyes still behold, like a living picture, the Jews walking on the Sabbath to the synagogue near our high school. The two religious blocs, Catholic and Jews, were linked, so I assume, by the knowledge that they worshiped the same God." In 1993, the Vatican agreed to established diplomatic relations with the State of Israel, a sign that the old teaching that the Jews had been exiled from their ancestral homeland no longer applied. In a letter to Cardinal Edward Idris Cassidy, on March 12, 1998, John Paul II wrote that "the crime which has become known as the Shoah remains an indelible stain on the history of the century that is coming to a close. . . . [The church] encourages her sons and daughters to purify their hearts through repentance for past errors and infidelities. She calls them to place themselves humbly before the Lord and examine themselves on the responsibility which they too have for the evils of our time. It is my fervent hope that the document *We Remember: A Reflection on the Shoah* . . . will indeed help to heal the wounds of past misunderstandings and injustices. . . . May the Lord of History guide the efforts of Catholics and Jews and all men and women of goodwill as they work together for a world of true respect for the life and dignity of every human being, for we all have been created in the image and likeness of God."[15]

In March 2000, during a visit to Yad Vashem, Pope John Paul II commiserated with the tragedy of the Holocaust. "I have come to Yad Vashem to pay homage to the millions of Jewish people who, stripped of everything, especially of their human dignity, were murdered in the Holocaust. More than half a century has passed, but the memories remain. . . . Men, women, and children cry out to us from the depths of the horror that they knew. How can we fail to heed their cry? No one can forget or ignore what happened. No one can diminish its scale. We wish to remember. But we wish to remember for a purpose, namely, to ensure that never again will evil prevail. . . . The Catholic Church . . . is deeply saddened by the hatred, acts of persecution, and displays of anti-semitism directed against Jews by Christians at any time and in any place. . . . As bishop of Rome and successor of the Apostle Peter, I assure the Jewish people that the Catholic Church, motivated by the Gospel law of truth and love and by no political considerations, is deeply saddened by the hatred, acts of persecution, and displays of antisemitism directed against the Jews by Christians at any time and in any place. . . . I fervently pray that our sorrow for the tragedy which the Jewish people suffered in the twentieth century will lead to a new relationship between Christians and Jews. Let us build a new future in which there will be no more anti-Jewish feeling among Christians or anti-Christian feeling among Jews, but rather the mutual respect required of those who adore the one Creator and Lord, and look to Abraham as our common father in faith."[16] Then, standing bowed at the Western Wall, on March 26, 2000, the pope inserted the following message: "God of our fathers, you chose Abraham and his descendants to bring your name to the nations. We are deeply saddened by the behavior of those who in the course of history have caused these children of yours to suffer, and, asking your forgiveness, we wish to commit ourselves to genuine brotherhood with the people of the Covenant."

We Remember: A Reflection on the Shoah, a significantly titled work published in March 1998, is the most recent and authoritative Vatican document addressing the Holocaust and antisemitism. It states that facing the Shoah, "before this horrible genocide . . . no one can remain indifferent, least of all the church, by reason of her very close bonds of spiritual kinship with the Jewish people and her remembrance of the injustices of the past. . . . The fact that the Shoah took place in Europe, that is, in countries of long-standing Christian civilization, raises the question of the relation between the Nazi persecution and the attitudes down the centuries of Christians toward the Jews." Sure enough, the history of relations between Jews and Christians "is a tormented one," and has been quite negative. "In the Christian world (not the church directly) erroneous and unjust interpretations of the New Testament regarding the Jewish people and their alleged culpability have circulated too long, engendering feelings of hostility toward this people." This despite the Christian preaching of love for all, even for one's enemies. "Sentiments of anti-Judaism in some Christian quarters, and the gap which existed between the church and the Jewish people, led to a generalized discrimination, which ended at times in expulsions or attempts at forced conversions." The document goes on to distance the church's traditional but misguided *Adversos Judaeos* teaching from the antisemitism manifested in the Nazi movement. "The Shoah was the work of a thoroughly modern neopagan regime. Its antisemitism had its roots outside of Christianity and in pursuing its aims, it did not hesitate to oppose the church and persecute her members also." This statement, only partly true, disregards the eighteen centuries of anti-Jewish teaching and preaching by many church leaders. As is underscored by the Catholic priest and Holocaust interpreter Father John T. Pawlikowski: "*We Remember* leaves the distinct impression that there is no inherent connection between the Nazi ideology and classical antisemitism. This is basically inaccurate."[17] At the same time, the document admits that the anti-Jewish prejudices "imbedded in some Christian minds and hearts" but not in Christian teachings (a disclaimer not borne out by history) may have helped the Nazis in their fiendish acts, and also made some Christians less sensitive vis-à-vis the persecution of the Jews. Referring to anti-Judaism, "of which, unfortunately, Christians also have been guilty," it asks, "Did anti-Jewish sentiment among Christians make them less sensitive or even indifferent to the persecutions launched against the Jews by National Socialism when it reached power?" It implies that the answer is in the affirmative. It also asks rhetorically whether Christians gave every possible assistance to persecuted Jews. "Many did [actually, relatively only a few], but others did not," for which "we deeply regret the errors and failures of those sons and daughters of the church. . . . At the end of this millennium the Catholic Church desires to express her deep sorrow for the failures of her sons and daughters in every age. This is an act of repentance (*teshuvah*). . . . We pray that our sorrow for the tragedy which the Jewish people has suffered in our century will lead to a new relationship with the Jewish people. . . . The spoiled seeds of anti-Judaism and antisemitism must never again be allowed to take root in any human heart. . . . We deeply regret the errors and failures of those sons and daughters of the church." *We Remember* ignores the religious antisemitism that flourished even at, or especially at, the highest levels of the Vatican hierarchy, or the fact that Jews continued to suffer discrimination in papal Rome until that city was forcibly acquired by Italy in 1870; all such matters are silently passed over. Nowhere in *We Remember*, moreover, is there the faintest criticism of the wartime leadership of the church in the face of the Holocaust then taking place in Christian lands. At the same time, it speaks warmly of the church's relationship to the Jewish people, which is "unlike the one she shares with any other religion," and it calls upon all Catholics "to renew the awareness of the Hebrew roots of their faith" and to remember that "the Jews are our dearly beloved brothers." It also calls upon "our Jewish friends, whose terrible fate has become a symbol of the aberrations of which man is capable when he turns against God, to hear us with open hearts . . . while bearing their unique witness to the Holy One of Israel and to the Torah."[18]

Although *We Remember* is clearly one of the most important landmarks in Catholic-Jewish relations, it is in certain ways an apologia for the Catholic Church, an attempt by its leaders in the Vatican to absolve the church of any responsibility for the Holocaust and for the role the church played in the persecution of the Jews during its long history. The Vatican document makes a sharp distinction between anti-Judaism and antisemitism. The document overlooks the fact that the Nazi onslaught against the Jews took place in a climate of opinion conditioned by centuries of Christian hostility to the Jews. At the same time, the Vatican document is a very positive orientation toward the future. The faithfulness of the Jews to the "Holy One of Israel" and to the Torah is described as a "unique witness." No more mention of the Jews as a "witness people" to the truth of the Christian faith. In *We Remember* the teachings of contempt and supersession are finally discarded from the Catholic agenda. In the words of Cardinal Edward Idris Cassidy, who presided over the wording of the document, "It is in that direction that our relationship is now moving, toward a partnership based on what we have in common and directed to be a blessing to the world in which we live. We are very conscious of our diversity and respect it. Still, we are convinced that strengthening the bonds that unite us is the most effective way to ensure that never again will antisemitism prevail."[19]

Changes in the Catholic Church

The evolution of a positive Christian-Jewish relationship by the Vatican has been matched by similar steps in other Catholic communities. Already in 1975, the National Conference of Catholic Bishops in the United States stated its regret that early in Christian history "a de-Judaizing process dulled our awareness of our Jewish beginnings. The Jewishness of Jesus, of his mother, his disciples, of the primitive church, was lost from view. That Jesus was called Rabbi; that he was born, lived, and died under the Law; that he and Peter and Paul worshipped in the Temple—these facts were blurred by the controversy that alienated Christians from the Synagogue." This was followed by the conference's Committee on the Liturgy, which in 1988 pointed out that the arrest of Jesus took place outside the city because of his popularity among his fellow Jews; his interrogation before a high priest was not necessarily a Sanhedrin trial; his formal condemnation was by the Roman governor, Pontius Pilate; and the crucifixion was carried out by Roman soldiers, who mockingly affixed the title "King of the Jews" to the cross. The bishops called for a greater knowledge of the diversity of first-century Judaism, the emotions of the factions competing for leadership among the Sadducees, Zealots, apocalyptists, Pharisees (especially of the two major schools of Hillel and Shammai), Herodians, Hellenists, scribes, sages, and miracle workers of all sorts—with the rhetoric often running high. Hence, that Jesus and his teachings can only be understood within this fluctuating mixture of Jewish trends and movements of his age.[20]

In France, in a 1997 statement, Archbishop Olivier de Berranger, of Saint-Denis, admitted the church's guilt in remaining silent when the Vichy government launched its anti-Jewish measures even before the start of the deportations. "Today we confess that silence was a mistake. We beg for the pardon of God, and we ask the Jewish people to hear this word of repentance. We beg God's forgiveness and ask the Jewish people to hear our words of repentance." He also called for a reexamination of the traditional teaching of hostility toward Jews within the church which caused "a venomous hatred of Jews to flourish," the signs of which are still evident.[21] The Hungarian Catholic Bishops Conference, in 1994, termed the Holocaust "the greatest shame of the twentieth century. . . . Those who considered themselves members of our churches . . . failed to raise their voices against the mass humiliation, deportation, and murder of their Jewish fellowmen whether out of fear, cowardice, or opportunism. . . . We ask forgiveness before God." And in Poland, a bishop's Pastoral Letter in 1991 deplored the behavior of those Christians "who in some way had contributed to the death of Jews," a statement which fell short of the church's special role in creating a vicious anti-Jewish climate in that country.[22]

Changes in the Protestant Churches

Similar rectifying changes were also apparent, and even earlier, in some of the Protestant churches. In 1948, the First Assembly of the Council of Churches, meeting in Amsterdam, declared: "We must acknowledge in all humility that too often we have failed to manifest Christian love toward our Jewish neighbors, or even a resolute will for common social justice. We have failed to fight with all our strength the age-old disorder of man which anti-semitism represents. The churches in the past have helped to foster an image of the Jews as the sole enemies of Christ, which has contributed to anti-semitism in the secular world. . . . We call upon all the churches we represent to denounce antisemitism, no matter what its origin, as absolutely irreconcil-able with the profession and practice of the Christian faith. Antisemitism is sin against God and man." At a subsequent meeting in New Delhi, India, the Council of Churches noted that "Jews were the first to accept Jesus, and Jews are not the only ones who do not yet recognize him."[23] The National Brethren Council of the Evangelical Church in Germany, meeting at Darmstadt in April 1948, admitted its guilt in forgetting "what Israel really is, and no longer lov-ing the Jews. Christian circles washed their hands of all responsibility, justi-fying themselves by saying that there was a curse on the Jewish people. . . . In this way we Christians helped to bring about all the injustice and suffering inflicted upon the Jews in our country." The Tenth German Evangelical *Kirchentag*, in 1961, affirmed that "every hostility toward Jews is godlessness and leads to self-destruction. . . . [We are] against the wrong doctrine preached for centuries that God has cast away the Jewish people."[24]

The old idea of restorationism has gained ground since the Holocaust, espe-cially in certain Protestant churches. Restorationism is the belief that Jews will be restored to their homeland in biblical Israel as a sign of God's impending millennial reign, usually just before, after, or during a mass conversion of Jews to Christianity. Adherents of this belief feel a need to guard and protect the State of Israel, a creation that, viewed mythically, has major significance for them. In a certain sense, this is a replay of the old "witness people" idea, but viewed in positive terms; the suffering, exile, preservation, restoration, and ultimate salvation of the Jews are part of God's revelation for humanity as a whole. Thus the Jews' rejection of Jesus, it is claimed, did not end Israel's pivotal role in salvation history. Jewish unbelief has only caused the prophet-ic clock to stop, as it were, until the exiled people Israel could be reborn as a nation. Jewish restoration in the new State of Israel is, consequently, the infallible sign that God has begun dealing with Israel again.[25]

Into the Future

While many positive steps have been taken by various churches in the aftermath of the Holocaust, the challenges ahead are numerous. Public opinion on sacrosanct-held matters does not change easily. Richard S. Ellis related a telling reminder of this. In 2001, while visiting Rome, he joined a tour of the Vatican. The guide, in a booming voice, informed the group that the Jews had murdered Christ, and that Pontius Pilate acted merely to placate them. Ellis objected: "I am Jewish, and I strongly object to your version of the story of the death of Jesus." The guide: "I only speak the truth." Ellis: "You are blaming the Jews for killing Christ. Don't you realize that the crucifixion of Jesus has been used to justify two millennia of antisemitism sponsored by the church? Where's your sensitivity?" The guide: "Sorry, mister. It's all in the Gospels, and I take everything in the Gospels as the literal truth."[26] A Catholic cleric who rescued Jews during the Holocaust recently stated in a private communication to a Yad Vashem associate that the Jews, "for two thousand years, without respite, [have been] anti-Christian. I and my Jewish friends are bitter about this." He characterized the Jews as "a people whose forefathers murdered their Messiah, and coupled with their criminal act the whole people cried out 'May his blood be on us and on our children.'" William Shakespeare's *The Merchant of Venice* continues to convey a haunting image of the Jew as something alien amidst Christendom. Add to this that the anti-Jewish passages of the New Testament, a book considered sacred, will continue to be believed word for word, especially by those who cling to an uncritical and literal reading of the text.[27] The question then is, as Rosemary Ruether puts it, is it possible to eliminate anti-Judaism from Christianity and still affirm Jesus as the Christ? Or, as she phrases it more bluntly, "Is it possible to say 'Jesus is the Messiah' without, implicitly or explicitly, saying at the same time 'and the Jews be damned' "?[28]

The negation of Jewish existence is lodged so deeply in Christian doctrine, and so far below the level of awareness, that Christian teachers and theologians sometimes unwittingly endorse and repeat it. In the words of Gregory Baum, some Christian theologians get "cold feet" when faced with a radical reinterpretation of some of the church's age-old doctrines, including the theology of the Jews and Judaism. For nothing touches so near to the roots of Christian identity than its relation to Judaism. Some fear that as long as the Jewish religious tradition continues to reject the church's interpretation of the significance of Jesus, the validity of the Christian view is in question. This leads to the unsatisfied need of the church to prove that it has the true content of the Jewish Scriptures. From a Christian point of view, Jews dissent just by continuing to exist. Whatever the ultimate cause of this resentment, in Ruether's words, Christianity may have to settle for the sort of ecumenical goodwill that lives with theoretical inconsistency and opts for a *modus operandi* that assures practical cooperation between Christianity and Judaism.[29]

As Henry Siegman observed, there is a certain inevitability to the disappointment Christians will experience in their expectations of a dialogue with the Jews. Christianity chose to validate itself within Judaism, and expected Judaism to join its ranks or disappear. The living reality of Judaism poses for the Christian the question of ultimate truth. The existence of a thriving Christianity does not, however, pose a similar question of truth for the Jews. It is different with the Christian. He encounters Israel as part of his encounter with himself as a Christian—that is the enduring price Christianity has paid for its rejection of Marcion—and he cannot encounter the reality of the Jews, Judaism, and Jewish history without having to struggle at the same time with himself as a member of the *novus et verus Israel*. His relationship to Judaism cannot be of the same order as that to, say, Shinto or Hinduism. As stated by Karl Barth, in 1966: "We must not forget that in the last resort there is only one really big [and decisive] ecumenical question: our relationship to Judaism."[30]

From the Jewish perspective, there is room for dialogue and coexistence. In this context, the ideas of the Jewish philosopher Franz Rosenzweig come to mind. He stated that the manner in which Christians understand their revelation and await redemption turns their individual and collective lives into a journey. The Christian is always en route, the eternal pilgrim, making his way from pagan birth to baptism, overcoming temptation, spreading the gospel; and likewise the church, which considers all men brothers and therefore feels obliged to convert them or, if necessary, conquer them. Whereas Christianity prepares the redemption of the world through activity in time, according to Rosenzweig, Judaism answers a different call. Long before the revelation of Christianity and the opening of its history, the Jews, as the sole people of revelation, lived in a timeless, face-to-face relationship with God. They needed no mediator because they already had a direct rapport with the Father; they were given no historical task because they were already what they were destined to be. The Jewish people had already reached the goal toward which the other nations are still moving. Only an eternal people, not encompassed by world history, can at every moment bind creation as a whole to redemption while redemption is still to come. There are, then, two peoples awaiting their final redemption. Individual Christians focus on spiritual rebirth, every moment finding themselves at the crossroads of decision; individual Jews, on the other hand, live as links in a chain of generations running backward and forward; their rebirth happens communally as they procreate, as they guard memory of the past, and as they internalize their spiritual existence. Christianity needs Judaism if it is to perform this function: while it is busy converting the pagans without, the example of Judaism helps Christians to keep at bay the pagan within. If the Christian did not have the Jews at his back, he would lose his way. Christians are aware of this, too, and hence resent the Jews, calling them proud and stiff-necked. The very existence of Judaism and its claim to have experienced eternity shames the pilgrim Christian, who becomes antisemitic out of self-hate, out of disgust with his own pagan imperfections.[31] Marcel Dubois perhaps sums it up best: "Judaism and Christianity are both religions of redemption. That is to say, the central faith experience of each of them is founded on a saving act of the living God: for the Jews, the Exodus and Sinai; for the Christians, the death and resurrection of Jesus Christ. But the ultimate redemption, and man's reconciliation with God, remains for both faiths in the future.[32]

In this context, the stories of the "Righteous" clergy outlined in this study can serve as role models for a more constructive dialogue between Judaism and Christianity. These men and women of the church risked their lives and safety to save Jews out of fidelity to the biblical command "Thou shalt love your neighbor as thyself," and a conviction that it was to be applied to everyone—even those who hold to a different perception of man's true relationship to the transcendent divine being.

Clergy: Righteous Among the Nations

(Includes Names not Mentioned in Previous Chapters)
alphabetical by country of origin
Legend: C = Catholic; P = Protestant; O = Orthodox

Belgium (106)

Aan de Stegge, John	C	Delcuigne, Germaine (Aline)	C
Agnes Marie	C	Delepaut, Claire (Louise-Marie)	C
André, Joseph	C	Doulière, Alexandre and Elmire	P
Andrée-Frere	C	Doyen, Auguste	C
Baggen, Hélène	C	Eulalie, (Judith)	C
Beirens, Marie	C	Eustelle Marie	C
Berthile	C	Euthalie	C
Bertiaux, Zephirin	P	Feraille	C
Boufflette, Emile	C	Gessler, Emile	C
Bribosia, Germaine	C	Herbeck, Madeleine	C
Bruylandts, Jan	C	Hillegonda	C
Capart, Helénè	C	Hospel, Madeleine	C
Capart, Pierre	C	Houyet, Jean	C
Castecker, Jacques	C	Jacobs, Jacques	C
Cécile Marie	C	Jamin, Louis	C
Celis, Hubert	C	Janssens, Jean-Baptist	C
Celis, Louis	C	Juvent, Octave	C
Charensol, Ernest	P	Kerkhofs, Louis-Joseph	C
Chrysostome Marie	C	Künch, Theodore	C
Coenraets, Paul	C	Lambrette, Alphonse	C
Cottiaux, Jean	C	Lambrette, Ivan	C
Couppé, Laurent	C	Leboutte, Olivier	C
Coussemaeker, Agnes		Lefebvre, Jean	C
(Marie-Gérard)	C	Leloup, Eugènie (Marie-Amelié)	C
Coutuer, Léonce	C	Lempereur, Joseph	C
Darblay, Pierre	C	Lerat, Mechtilde	C
De Beukelaar, Petrus	C	Leruth, Marie	C
De Caunes, Anne-Marie (Didier)	C	Lombaerts, Edouard	C
De Caunes, Antoinette (Claire)	C	Lux, Theo	C
De Coster, Jean-Baptiste	C	Marie-Alphonse	C
De Gruyter, Louis	C	Marie-Louise (1)	C
De Pauw, Maria (Germaine)	C	Marie-Louise (2)	C
De Petter, J. D.	C	Massion, Jean	C
De Vogel, Ghislaine	C	Masurelle, Octave	C
Decort, Jean-Marie	C	May, Pierre	C
		Mechtilde	C

Meunier, André	C
Meurisse, Georges	C
Moguet, Madeleine	C
Naveau de Marteau, Berthe	C
Nicolas, Marie de St. Augustin	C
Odonia	C
Otto, Anna (Marie Dora)	C
Overkamp, (Véronique)	C
Paternotte, Marcel	C
Peeters, Joseph	C
Piedboeuf, Georges	C
Placide (Marie)	C
Putzeys, Martha (Liguori)	C
Rausch, Lucien	C
Reynders, Henri (Dom Bruno)	C
Richard, Julien	C
Richart, Jeanne (Marie Ignace)	C
Rixhon, Ernest	C
Robert, Edouard	C
Roberta	C
Royer, Madeleine (Ines)	C
Schoofs, Marie-Joséphine (Urbaine)	C
Sibille, Marthe	C
Smeets, Oscar	C
Steiger, Alberic	C
Stenne, Marcel	C
Stingers, (Cécile)	C
Thierry, (Marie-Thérèse)	C
Thiery, Armand	C
Van Acker, Véronique	C
Van Causbroeck, Georges	C
Van Oostayen, Henri	C
Van Schoonbeeck, Léontine (Marie)	C
Vandermolen, Marie-Alphonse	C
Xavier, Marie	C
Yvens, Cathérine (Emilie)	C

Belarus (4)

Imshenik, Vladimir	O
Ivanov, Vasili	P*
Ketcho, Anton	P
Komar, Konstantin	O
*Baptist	

Bulgaria (2)

Kiril (Markov Konstantin)	O (Bulgarian)
Stefan (Popgueorguiev Stoyan)	O (Bulgarian)

Croatia (3)

Jesih, Dragutin	C
Jurin, Cecilija	C
Jurin, Karitas	C

Czech Republic (1)

Pitter, Přemysl	P

England (2)

Walsh, Clare (Agnes)	C
Haining, Jane [Scotland]	P

France (19)

Adrien, Jean	C
Aguadich-Paulin, Denise	C
Albert-Marie	C
Allenait, Francine (St. Lucie)	C
Arribat, Joseph-Auguste	C
Bagny, André (Br. Louis)	C
Banc, Marie (Marie des Anges)	C
Baragades, Jeanne (Marie-Paule)	C
Barin, Anselme	C
Barot, Madeleine	P
Bengel, Robert	C
Benoît, Pierre-Marie	C
Berchmans (Jeanne) (Meienhofer Marie)	C
Berger, Marie-Thérèse	C
Bergon, Denise	C
Bernes, Marguerite	C
Beyls, Marguerite (Henrica)	C
Blain, Michel	C
Boccard, Raymond	C
Boegner, Marc	P
Bourdon, Joseph	P
Bovet, Jean-Charles	C
Brasche, Maurice	C
Braun, Roger	C
Bredoux, (Marie-Gonzague)	C
Brée, Elie	P
Brunel, Paul	P
Bunel, Lucien (Jacques)	C
Cabanis, Charles	P
Carbonnet, Raymond	C
Castillon, Marie	C
Chaillet, Pierre	C
Chalve, Marius	C

Chapal, Paul	P	Glasberg, Alexandre	C
Chazel, François	P	Gosselin, Louis	C
Chevalier, Alice (Marie-Angélique)	C	Granier	C
Chopin, Joséphine	C	Gret Henriette (Anne-Marie)	C
Coeuret, Francis	C	Guigues, Andréa (Marie-Gabrielle)	C
Coffy, Maurice	C	Guillaume, Irène (Marthe)	C
Cook, Robert	P	Guillon, Charles	P
Dallière, Emile	P	Haag, Daniela	C
Dallière, Louis	P	Haering, Paul	P
De Courrèges d'Ustou, Louis	C	Hammel, André	P
De Naurois, René	C	Hertel, Jeanne	C
De Pury, Roland	P	Hyacinthe	C
Delechenault, Marie-Louise		Imberdis, François	C
(Marie de Jesus)	C	Jacquet, Abel	C
Delesalle, Marthe (Annette)	C	Jolivet, Marius	C
Delizy, Charles	P	Joseph, Robert	P
Delord, Albert	P	Joussellin, Jean	P
Depo, Victoria (Marie-Gilberte)	C	Kamper, Emilie (Placide)	C
Dessaigne, Jeanne (Marie-Angèle)	C	Kolmer, Victor	C
Devaux, Théomir	C	Lafont, Marie-Julie	C
Donadille, Marc	P	Laurent, Yvonne (Louis de Gonzague)	C
Dreyer, Hélène (Marie de Jésus)	C	Le Caherec (Anne-Marie)	C
Dubois, Roland	P	Ledain, Roger	C
Ducasse, Raymond	P	Leenhardt, Roland	P
Dumas, André	P	Lemaire, Jean-Severin	P
Dumas, Antoine	C	Lhermet, Raoul	P
Dumoulin, Philemon	C	Llobet, Anne-Marie	C
Elias, Paul	C	Longeray, Claudius	C
Emmanuelle	C	Malolepszy, Madeleine	C
Espitallier, Jean	C	Manen, Henri	P
Evrard, Edmond	P	Marquet, Eugène	C
Exbrayat, Idebert	P	Marquet, Pierrette (Perpetue)	C
Favre, Louis	C	Martin, Gaston	P
Fleury, Jean	C	Masserey, Antoinette	C
Folliet, Camille	C	Matter, Annette	P
Folliet, Marie-Amedée	C	Mayrand, Auguste	C
Fouchier, Pierre	P	Menardais, Henri	C
Fournier, Claudius	C	Monod, Charles	P
Françoise-Elisabeth	C	Mopty, Pierre	C
Gagné, Félix	C	Morel, André	P
Gall, André	P	Murat, Marie-Angélique	C
Gallay, Simon	C	Nick, Henri	P
Gallon,Celestin (Aimé-Edmond)	C	Olivès, Laurent	P
Gau, Albert	C	Olivier, Marguerite	C
Genestier, Marcel	C	Panneley, Marie-Louise	C
Gerlier, Pierre-Marie	C	Parent, Jean	C
Girard, Pierre	C	Pasche, Marcel	P
Girardin, Antoine	C	Pasquine, Marguerite	C

Payot, André	C	Trocmé, André	P
Pean-Pages, Evangelina	P	Trocmé, Daniel	P
Pernoud,Gilbert	C	Tzaut, Paul	P
Perret, Léon	C	Uthurriage, Marie (St. Jean)	C
Pezeril, Daniel	C	Vancourt, Raymond	C
Piguet, Gabriel	C	Vandevoorde, Lucien-Henri	C
Pinet, Jeanne Dominique	C	Vergara, Paul	P
Planckaert, Emile	C	Veyrine, Germaine	C
Pollex, Roland	P	Vidal, Marie-Alice	C
Puech, Pierre-Marie	C	Villepelet, Georges	C
Ramade, Jeanne-Françoise	C	Viollet, Marie-Jean	C
Régéreau, Clotilde	C	Waffelaert, Marguerite	
Relave, Joseph	C	(Théophilus)	C
Rémond, Paul	C	Westphal, Charles	P
Révol, Henri	C	Zech, Magda	C
Ricard, Louis	C	Zufferey, Jeanne-Françoise	C
Ricard, Marie-Antoinette		*Salvation Army	
(Elizabeth)	C		
Richard, Joseph	C	Germany (24)	
Riebert, Roger	C	Arkenau, Aurelius	C
Rivet, Elizabeth	C	Barwitzky, Cläre	C
Robaeys, Germaine (Céline	C	Boettcher, Johannes	P
Robert, André de	P	Brandt, Guenther	P
Robert, Franck	P	Dilger, Alfred	P
Rocas, Georges (Julien)	C	Disselnkoetter, Walther	P
Rodien, Jeanne	C	Goelz, Richard	P
Rolland, Philomène (Marie-Etienne)	C	Goes, Elisabeth	P
Roques, Marguerite	C	Grüber, Heinrich	P
Rosay, Jean-Joseph	C	Held, Heinrich	P
Rose	C	Hoeffner, Josef	C
Roser, Henri	P	Lichtenberg, Bernhard	C
Roullet, Viviane	P	Maas, Hermann	P
Rousseau,Oscar	C	Mensching, Wilhelm	P
Roux, Marie-Thérèse	C	Middendorf, Heinrich	C
Saliège, Jules-Géraud	C	Mörike, Otto	P
Simeoni,Vincent	C	Poelchau, Harald	P
Simond, Albert	C	Ruf, August	C
St. Blancat-Baumgarten, Olga	P	Seebass, Julius	P
Stahl, Robert	C	Stoeffler, Eugen	P
Tafani, Josette (Marie-Pascale)	C	Sylten, Werner	P
Tartier	P	Symanowski, Horst	P
Terruwe, Jean	C	Weiler, Eugen	C
Théas, Jean-Marie	C	Wendland, Ruth	P
Thèbe, Louise	C		
Theis, Edouard	P	Greece (6)	
Thérèse-Lucie	C	Alexopoulos, Joachim	O
Tinel, Paul	P*	Chrysostomos, Demetriou	O
Toureille, Pierre	P	Damaskinos, Theophilos	O

Guenadios (Georgios Alexiadis) O
Joseph C
Typaldos, Irenee C*
*(Greek Catholic)

Hungary (34)
Adam, Laszlo C
Angyal, François C
Antál, Janos C
Baranszky, Tibor C
Bereczky, Albert P
Bernovits, Vilma C
Bonetbeltz, Jean-Baptiste C
Clerc, Bernard C
Csedrik, Jozef O
Fischer, Ferdinand C
Gutzwiller, Hildegard C
Hegedüs, Alexandre (Joseph) C
Jarosi, Andor P
Juhasz, Margit C
Kálló, Ferenc C
Keken, András P
Klinda, Pal C
Köhler, Ferenc C
Koren, Emil P
Krizosztom, Kelemen C
Marton, Aron C
Michnai, László P
Nagymanyoki, Gilbert C
Peitl, Róza-Katalin C
Pfleger, Albert C
Pingiczer, Ladislas (Etienne) C
Pruczer, Louis C
Raile, Jacob C
Salkahazi, Sara C
Slachta, Margit C
Szabo, Imre P
Sztehló, Gábor P
Ván, Zsuzsanna C
Victor, Janos P

Italy (54)
Alessandrini, Armando C
Amerio, Pasquale C
Antoniazzi, Maria C
Antonioli, Francesco C
Badetti, Virginie (M. Agnesa) C
Bassi, Angelo C

Beccari, Arrigo C
Benedetti, Emilia (Augustine) C
Bolledi, Anna (Emerenzia) C
Bortolameotti, Guido C
Braccagni, Alfredo C
Brondello, Francesco C
Brunacci, Aldo C
Busnelli, Sandra C
Bussa, Eugenio C
Carlotto, Michele C
Casini, Leto C
Cei, Maria Maddalena C
Corsetti, Maria (Ferdinanda) C
Cupertino, Daniele P
Daeli, Alessandro C
De Zotti, Giuseppe C
Della Torre, Angelo C
Dressino, Antonio C
Facibeni, Giulio C
Fagiolo, Vincenzo C
Ferrari, Maria-Angelica C
Folcia, Marta C
Girotti, Giuseppe C
Gradassi, Giulio C
Lavizzari, Barbara (Marie Giuseppina) C
Marteau
    (Marie de St. François Xavier) C
Meccaci, Vivaldo C
Melani, Alfredo C
Minardi, Luisa C
Niccaci, Rufino C
Nicolini, Giuseppe Placido C
Ollari, Ernesto C
Palazzini, Pietro C
Paoli, Arturo C
Raspino, Francesco C
Repetto, Francesco C
Richeldi, Benedetto C
Ricotti, Cipriano C
Rosadini, Luigi C
Rotta, Angelo C
Sala, Dante C
Salvi, Carlo C
Schivo, Beniamino C
Simeoni, Giovanni C
Tantalo, Gaetano C
Vespignani, Benedetta C
Vinay, Tullio P

Vincenti, Federico	C	Groenenberg, Isaac	P
		Hafmans, Jan-Willem	C
Lithuania (15)		Hamming, R.	P
Baltutis, Vytas	C	Heidinga, Jetze	P
Byla, Vincas	C	Hendriks, Leonard (Bernardinus)	C
Gasiūnas, Juozas	C	Hijmans, Abraham	P
Gobis, Antanas	C	Hoek, Henk	P
Gotautas, Bronius	C	Hoek, Laura van der	P**
Jokubauskis, Stanislovas	C	Hoogkamp, Rikkert	P
Kavaliauskas, Kazys	C	Houben, Maria (Eunomia)	C
Kleiba, Adolfas	C	Hugenholtz, Johannes	P
Macijauskas, Polikarpas	C	Kalma, Jacob	P
Martinkus, Vaclovas	C	Koers, Jakob	P
Paukštys, Bronius	C	Kok, Elisa	P
Požela, Vladas	C	Kroon, Kleijs	P
Stakauskas, Juozas	C	Lambooy, Peter	P
Taskūnas, Vladas	C	Leignes-Bakhoven, Helena-Cornelia	P*
Teišerskis, Jonas	C	Meima, Klaas	P
		Mesdag, Willem	P
Moldova (1)		Miedema, Pieter	P
Benya, George	O	Moulijn, Cornelis	P
		Müller, Pieter	P
Netherlands (68)		Nieuwenhuyzen, Johannes van	P
Ader, Bastiaan	P	Nijkamp, Frederik	P
Alberts, Gerrit-Willem	P	Oostenbrug, Teunis	P
Alderse-Baars, Johannes	P	Overduin, Leendert	P
Assendorp, Jan	P	Pliester, Matthias	P
Barends, Pieter	P	Pontier, Gerardus	P
Biemans, Martin (Lambertus)	C	Post, Hendrikus	P
Bijlsma, Johannes	P	Reinders, Willem	P
Boon, Dirk	P	Roorda, Binne	P
Bos, Jan van den	P	Schakel, Dirk	P
Bosshardt, Alida	P*	Scheermakers, Antonius	C
Brillenburg-Würth, Gerrit	P	Smeenk, Bernard-Daniel	P
Broekema, Eben-Haeser	P	Smelik, E. L.	P
Brouwer, Cornelis	P	Sweepe, Hendrik	P
Bruining, Nicolette	P	Tangelder, Theodorus	P
Buenk, Louis	P	Touwen, Lourens	P
Burger, Abraham	P	Ubbink, Gerhard	P
Cals, Paulina (Emerentia)	C	Val, Wandrinus	P
Cannegieter, Lambertus	P	Voet, Marcus van der	P
Creutzberg, Jelis-Jan	P	Vullinghs, Henricus	C
Drooge, San and Eddy van	P	Wesseldyk, Leendert	P
Faber, Adriaan	P	Zijlmans, Petrus	C
Frederikse, Theodoor	P	*Salvation Army	
Goedhart, Daniel	P	**Quaker	
Gommans, Engelbert	P	***Mennonite	

Poland (56)

Adamek, Małgorzata	C
Bartkowiak, Euzebia	C
Bednarska, Stefania	C
Bielawska, Irena (Honorata)	C
Boguszewski, Bruno	C
Borkowska, Anna (Bertranda)	C
Bykowska, Krystyna	C
Czubak, Genowefa	C
Drzewecka, Aleksandra	C
Falkowski, Stanisław	C
Frąckiewicz, Diana (Helena)	C
Galus, Bronisława Roza	C
Garczyńska, Wanda	C
Getter, Matylda	C
Gloeh, Feliks	P
Głowacki, Władysław	C
Górajek, Józef	C
Górska, Maria	C
Grenda, Anna (Ligoria)	C
Hryniewicz, Bronisława (Beata)	C
Jaroszyńska, Klara	C
Jóźwikowska, Stanisława	C
Juśkiewicz, Leokadia (Emilia)	C
Kołodziej, Władysław	P
Kotowska, Aniela (Klara)	C
Kubacki, Michał	C
Makowska, Bogumiła	C
Małkiewicz, Ludwika	C
Małysiak, Albin	C
Manaszczuk, Antonina (Irena)	C
Mazak, Stanisław	C
Michorowska, Julia (Bernardetta)	C
Mikulska, Maria	C
Mistera, Joanna	C
Neugebauer, Imelda	C
Orzechowski, Franciszek	C
Osiecki, Aleksander	C
Osikiewicz	C
Ostreyko, Jordana	C
Patrzyk, Jan	C
Pawlicki, Jan	C
Poddębniak, Jan	C
Polechajłło, Aniela (Stanisława)	C
Reiter, Johanna (Zygmunta)	C
Reszko, Marina	C
Romansewicz, Józefa (Hermana)	C
Roszak, Celina	C

Sidełko, Rozalia (Bernarda)	C
Siwek, Maria	C
Sosnowska, Julia	C
Sztark, Adam	C
Szymczukiewicz, Witold	C
Urbańczyk, Jadwiga	C
Wąsowska, Eugenia (Alfonsa)	C
Wilemska, Bronisława	C
Życzyński, Ignacy	C

Romania (1)

Petre, Gheorghe	C

Russia (2)

Klepinin, Dimitri	O (Russian)
Skobtsova, Yelizaveta (Maria)	O (Russian)

Serbia (1)

Milenkovic, Svetozar	O

Slovakia (9)

Boharczyk, Pawel	C
Derer, Julius	P
Dudinsky, Peter	C*
Gallo, Stefan	C
Inska, Imberta	C
Kuna, Vladimir	P
Maslej, Michal	C*
Schaffarovsky, Vojtech	P
Teriansky, Pavel	P

*Greek Catholic

Sweden (1)

Myrgren, Erik	P

Switzerland (4)

Bettex, André	P
Curtet, Daniel	P
Gross, Albert	C
Schaffert, Hans	P

Ukraine (14)

Dlozhevski, Vladimir	O
Glagolev, Aleksey	O
Grogul, Ignatiy	O
Izvolsky, Antin	P*
Kaluta, Konon	P*

Lazar	C**	Teodosy (Tadeusz Cebrynski)	C**
Nikanor	C**	Witer, Helena	C**
Oshurko, Nikolai	P*	Zavirukha, Fiodor	O
Sheptitzky, Klement	C**	*Baptist	
Sherbanovich,Ivan	C**	**Uniate	
Stek, Marko	C**		

NOTES AND SOURCES

Sources are listed simply by the author's name, with full details given in the Bibliography section. Where more than one book or article by the same author is cited, an abbreviated title of the relevant study is indicated. Full details of author, title, and publication are given for the occasional work cited only once. File number listings are for individual stories in the Yad Vashem archives, catalogued under: M-31, plus file number.

Introduction

[1] See, for instance, Tec, *When Light*; Oliner and Oliner; Fogelman.

Chapter 1   Antecedents

[1] David Flusser, the noted Jewish historian of Jesus, who identified with what he calls Jesus' "Jewish *Weltanschauung*" (life philosophy), wrote of "the unease experienced by many Christian thinkers and scholars . . . [who] have felt obliged to deal with the fact that the founder of their religion was a Jew, faithful to the Law [i.e., the Torah]." Flusser 15, 58; Carroll, 101.

[2] The appellation Yeshua already appears in the Hebrew Bible, and was widespread among Jews, such as the author of Wisdom of Sirach, or Ecclesiasticus. Four Yeshuas are counted by Nehemiah (e.g., 12:7) among the Jewish priests at the Jerusalem Temple. Josephus Flavius mentions twenty men with the name Yeshua; Flusser, 24.

[3] Luke 2:21, 39–52.

[4] According to Flusser, Jesus had four brothers and seven sisters. Flusser, 28.

[5] As at the moment of his death, when he cried out in Aramaic the words from Psalms: "*Eli, Eli, lama sabachthani*? That is, "My God, my God, why hast thou forsaken me?" Matthew 27:46. Cf. Mark 15:34. Other Aramaic expressions found in the New Testament: "*Talitha cumi*" ("little girl, arise"); "*Ephphatha*" ("Be opened"); "*Abba*" ("father")—Mark 5:41, 14:35, 15:34.

[6] Romans 15:8.

[7] John 3:2.

[8] Mark 14:12–14; Luke 4:15, 22:7–9; Matthew 26:17; John 7:14.

[9] Mark 14:12; Luke 22:15.

[10] Mark 3:1, 6:2, 11:11, 27; 12:35, 41, 14:49; Matthew 4:23; John 7:14, 28; 8:2, 20; 10:22–3; 18:20. The same in the case of Paul, who visited and preached in many syn-

agogues on his journeys outside Judea. Interestingly, in the Gospels Jesus is described as launching his career as a healer and wonder worker, rather than strictly a preacher, healing an abundance of people who came to him from all over. Mark 3:7–19, 6:56; Matthew 11:3–6. Likewise for his twelve disciples, whom Jesus sent out to "have authority to cast out demons." He may have interpreted his supernatural feats of healing as an unmistakable sign that the era of salvation had already dawned. Disease is of the devil, and the kingdom of God comes when Satan is conquered and rendered powerless; Flusser, 49.

[11] Ernest Renan, *Vie de Jesus*, 4th ed. (Paris: Michel-Levy, 1863), pp. 215, 221, 223, 236, in Isaac, *Jesus,* 49.

[12] Matthew 5:17–20.

[13] Mark 1:44. The word Torah is only very imperfectly translated by "Law." To the Jew it has a far-richer meaning and does not in the least imply a slavish following of a written document, even if the document has final authority; Isaac, *Jesus,* 65 f.; Rayner, 26.

[14] Mark 6:41, 11:29–31, 12:28–29; Matthew 14:19, 22:36–40; Luke 9:16; John 6:11. Leviticus 19:18.

[15] Matthew 6:9–10, 19:16–19; Luke 11:2.

[16] The Kaddish, in the Hebrew prayer book.

[17] Mark 2:27; Mekhilta on Exodus 31:14, in Flusser, 62. Flusser notes that Jesus' dictum "Not what goes into the mouth defiles a man, but what comes out of the mouth, this defiles a man" (Matthew 15:11) is completely compatible with the Jewish legal position. A person's body does not become ritually impure even when one had eaten animals forbidden by the Law of Moses; Flusser, 60.

[18] Mark 10:1–2; Matthew 18:7.

[19] Matthew 5:25, 6:41–2, 7:12; Luke 6:35, 37; Shabbat 31a, Avot 2:3. The Talmud similarly teaches that "transgressions between a man and his neighbor are not expiated by the Day of Atonement unless the man first makes peace with his neighbor." Also, "everyone who publicly shames his neighbor sheds his blood." (Babylonian Bava Mesia 58b); Flusser, 84, 91; Townsend, 235. It has been pointed out that if Jesus had really been a revolutionary against the Law and presented himself as a "destroyer" of Judaism, as Renan claims, how is one to explain that his most intimate disciples, the eleven, and along with them, following them, hundreds and thousands of converted Jews who were the first Christians, were totally unaware of it, and seemed to know absolutely nothing about it. The Acts of the Apostles record their respect and love for the Law, and even more their devoted attendance at the Temple, the most zealous being James, "the brother of the Lord" and the recognized leader of the Christian (Acts 2:46). As for new converts, the Jerusalem council decided that "it was necessary to circumcise them, and to charge them to keep the law of Moses" (Acts 15:5). Isaac, *Jesus,* 70–71.

[20] Leviticus 19:18. Several generations before Jesus, a namesake of his, Jeshua (Jesus!) ben Sirach, taught: "Forgive your neighbor's injustice, then, when you pray, your own sins will be forgiven. . . . Hate not your neighbor;" Flusser, 85. In the Testament of Benjamin, the following instruction appears: "The good man... shows

mercy to all men, sinners though they may be, and though they may plot his ruin. . . . If, then, your minds are predisposed to what is good, children, wicked men will live at peace with you" (4:2–3, 5:1); Flusser, 87, 99.

[21] This beautiful parable reads as follows: Jesus: "A man was going down from Jerusalem to Jericho, and he fell among robbers, who stripped him and beat him, and departed, leaving him half dead. Now by chance a priest was going down that road; and when he saw him he passed by on the other side. So likewise a Levite, when he came to the place and saw him passed by on the other side. But a Samaritan, as he journeyed, came to where he was; and when he saw him, he had compassion, and went to him and bound up his wounds, pouring on oil and wine; then he set him on his own beast and brought him to an inn, and took care of him. And the next day he took out two denarii and gave them to the innkeeper, saying 'Take care of him; and whatever more you spend, I will repay you when I come back.' Which of these three, do you think, proved neighbor to the man who fell among the robbers? He said: 'the one who showed mercy on him. And Jesus said to him, 'Go and do likewise.' " Luke 10:30–38.

[22] Luke 9:27.

[23] Isaiah 61:1–2, 58:6; Luke 4:18.

[24] Mark 15:26.

[25] Matthew 2:2; John 4:25–6; Luke 19:40; Acts 1:6.

[26] Luke 20:20–26; Flusser, 105; Rayner, 38.

[27] Luke 23:3, 37–38. In the Johannine version, Jesus' response to Pilate's question was: "My kingship is not of this world." John 18:33–37.

[28] John 5:18, 7:1, 8:44, 19–20. It is well to remember that the Gospel of John was written around the year 100 C.E., when the split between Christianity and Judaism and the hostility between them was an accomplished thing. See also Carroll, 92.

[29] John 2:23, 4:22, 6:59; 7:40, 8:30; Mark 1:32, 39, 2:2; Matthew 4:23, 9:35, 13:54; Luke 4:16, 44, 13:10, 22.

[30] Luke 4:22–30; Mark 1:22, 2:2; Matthew 4:24–5, 8:1, 15–30.

[31] Matthew 21:8–11, 46; Luke 19:47–8, 20:19, 21:38; Mark 12:12, 35. Also, Isaac, *Jesus,* 129. Cf. Midrash on Psalm 118: The people of Jerusalem used to say: "Save us, O Lord (Hosanna), and the pilgrims replied: "So be it, Lord." The people of Jerusalem used to say: "Blessed is he who comes in his name" and the pilgrims replied: We bless you from the house of the Lord"; Flusser, 134–135.

[32] Luke 23:27, 48. Mark 15:23. Flusser, 148, 170. Flusser also notes that in Luke, there is no single Jew who is not affected by the death of Jesus, whereas in Mark all the "non-Christian" Jews are enemies of Jesus. In Luke, the Jewish crowd mourns the crucified Jesus; in Mark they are against him. Flusser, 230, 235.

[33] Sandmel, 87; Flusser, 74; Carroll, 110. It is only with the elimination of the Temple and its priesthood that the Pharisees emerge as rivals—not of Jesus, but of his movement a full generation removed. That is why they are cast as enemies in the Gospels.

[34] "If there is a group of people and Gentiles said to them, 'Deliver one of yourselves to us and we shall slay him; if you do not, we shall slay all of you,' let all be slain and do not deliver to them a single soul in Israel; but if they single him out . . . let them

deliver him to them that all of them be not slain." Tos. Terumot 7:20 and Jerusalem Terumot VIII 46b; in Flusser, 205–206.

[35] Mark 13:2; Matthew 24:2. Isaac 275–276; Flusser, 135, 141, 200. It should be noted that the prophets Isaiah and Jeremiah likewise prophesied the downfall of the Temple, but in their case, not for refusing to accept their position as prophets, but for violating the moral precepts of the Mosaic code. Josephus, *Antiquities* 20:97–99. Paul was later mistakenly held by the Romans to actually be a similar messianic troublemaker; Acts 21:38.

[36] Mark 14:50. Parkes, 45; Flusser, 43, 144; Sandmel, 137.

[37] Luke 20:19; Matthew 26:5; John 11:45–48, 53.

[38] Mark 14:50; Matthew 26:56.

[39] Jules Isaac compares the trial of Jesus with that of Joan of Arc, sentenced by a tribunal of chief priests and scribes in 1431. "We have the complete and authentic text of her trial but not of the trial of Jesus, which was hurried through. Joan's trial for heresy and sorcery was conducted in accordance with all the rules of canon procedure and law, before church judges—the lord bishop of Beauvais; the abbots of the most important Norman abbeys and the canons of Rouen, people of distinction; doctors from the illustrious University of Paris, then the highest authority recognized in Latin Christendom; arbiters of kings and popes. This court was assembled to judge the peasant girl of Domrémy, a child, less than twenty years old. Lord Bishop Pierre Cauchon was Caiaphas. They condemned her. The irony is that they condemned her in the name of Jesus. They declared her "a blasphemer against God, a blasphemer against the saints, contemptuous of God even in His sacraments; a violator of divine law, sacred doctrine, and ecclesiastical sanctions; seditious, cruel, apostate, schismatic, engaged in a thousand fallacies about our faith"; and on all these counts rashly "guilty toward God and Holy Church." And when Joan, after the public abjuration, fell into their trap and was proclaimed "relapsed," the clerics delivered her to the secular arm, that is, the English occupation troops, to be burned alive in the Place du Vieux-Marché in Rouen. And it was a great spectacle, and among the spectators some laughed, other cried. Joan was rehabilitated, but not one voice in the church rose against the evil of her condemnation. Her judges were heaped with honors and rewards. Not the king of France (for whom Joan had sacrificed everything), nor the ecclesiastical authorities, intervened to save the young maiden." *Jesus,* 285–6.

[40] Isaac, 283. Josephus castigated Annas' affiliation with the Sadducees, that they "are indeed more heartless than any other Jews when they sit in judgment." *Antiquities* 20:199; in Flusser, 198.

The Babylonian Talmud and the Tosefta list the woes caused by high priestly families. Pesahim 57a: "Woe is me because of the house of Boethus; woe is me because of their staves [rods]. Woe is me because of the house of Hanin [Annas], woe is me because of their whisperings. Woe is me because of the house of Kathros [Kantheras], woe is me because of their pens. Woe is me because of the house of Ishmael the son of Phabi, woe is me because of their fists. For they are high priests and their sons are [Temple] treasurers and their sons-in-law are trustees and their servants beat the people with staves." The terms "whisperings" and "pens" would be allusions to secret denunciations, oral and written. These priestly families are also accused of defiling the Temple, desecrating the sacred sacrifices, displaying a disgusting gluttony, and so forth. Isaac, *Jesus,* 275. The Pharisees succeeded in having the high priest Annas the Younger deposed as a result of the illegal execution of James. Flusser, 198–99, 203.

[41] Matthew 27:25; Isaac, *Jesus,* 99, 132, 357, 389. The philosopher Philo, who lived in Alexandria, and died some twenty-five years later than Jesus (in the year 54), and whose works are extensive, does not even mention him, although he drew a severe picture of Pontius Pilate. Nowhere in his work is there the smallest allusion to Jesus. Flavius Josephus devoted only a few lines to him, and historians speculate whether some or all of them might not be pious interpolations. Some hold such passage to be inauthentic. Isaac, *Jesus,* 94–95.

[42] Josephus, *Jewish War,* 2:171–177. Philo, *Leg. Ad Gaium,* 38;302; in Flusser, 155–6.

[43] Flusser, 164–166, 209–210; Isaac, *Jesus,* 335.

[44] Mark 15:16–20; Luke 23:27, 34; Flusser, 224.

[45] Sandmel remarks sarcastically on the accusation that "the Jews" (not individual monarchs) killed their own prophets, with an imaginary accusation that "the Americans" killed Lincoln, McKinley, and Kennedy, not individual people; Sandmel, 136.

[46] Acts 3:1, 5:21, 34 ff.; 15:5; 21:24.

[47] Acts 8:1–3, 9:1–4, 26:9–11.

[48] Sin's grip on man is woefully described in heartrending passages in the Letter to the Romans. "I do not understand my own actions. For I do not do what I want, but I do the very thing I hate. . . . For I know that nothing good dwells within men, that is, in my flesh. I can will what is right, but I cannot do it. For I do not do the good I want, but the evil I do not want is what I do." Romans 7:15–23. Also, Ruether, *Faith,* 69; Sandmel, 9–10.

[49] Romans 4:15, 5:13, 7:7, 12–13; 1 Corinthians 15:56.; Acts 23:6.

[50] Romans 3:21, 4:9; Galatians 3:6, 23–24, 29; II Corinthians 3:11, 15; Sandmel, 10–11; Parkes 53–54; Gaston, 63; Ruether, *Antisemitism,* 242.

[51] Romans 9:6, 25, 27, 31–2; 10:2, 19; 11:11. Ruether, *Faith,* 105.

[52] Romans 11:15–24. Ruether, *Faith,* 106; Parkes, 54–55; Sandmel, 13–14.

[53] Ruether, *Faith,* 241; Parkes, 57; Sandmel, 8, 141; Maccoby, 9.

[54] Matthew 5; Luke 10:30–38; 1 Corinthians 13:4–7.

[55] Baum, *Antisemitism,* 137; Carroll, 90, Rayner, 30–31, 50.

[56] Sandmel 149, 160; Davis, *Anti-Semitism,* 61.

[57] Efroymson, 111–112, Carroll, 177.

[58] Efroymson, 100–101, 104, 108; Cohen, 484.

[59] The church anathematized those holding to the view that the Son is somehow inferior to the Father, and another one which saw in Christ two natures mechanically joined together rather than an essential and personal union. The accepted doctrine was of two natures "unconfused and unchanged, indivisible and inseparable" united in the person of Christ, the property of each nature being preserved; Parkes, 301.

[60] Isaac, *Jesus,* 239–40.

[61] Ruether, *Faith,* 226.

[62] Ruether, *Faith,* 63, 185; Ruether, *Antisemitism,* 234. Ruether adds: "The church looks at the synagogue with a jealous anger; the belief that the church itself cannot be whole until the synagogue repents and accepts the One whom they rejected. The church must pursue the synagogue down through the corridors of history and even to the end of time with this jealous demand. Paul lays the foundations for the idea developed in Augustine that not until the Jews are converted will Christ return and the salvation of the world, of church and synagogue, be complete"; Ruether, *Antisemitism,* 240. Carroll disagrees with this assessment, and claims that the Jew-hatred that stamped the beginning of Christianity is not essential to it as a religion; Carroll, 91.

[63] Ruether, *Faith,* 118, 121, 127, 128, 134, 136–137, 144; Parkes, 84, 154; Carroll, 201, Lazar, 47. At the same time, as stated by Justin Martyr: One must pray for them, such as the prayer on Good Friday, "Let us also pray for the perfidious Jews." In 1949, Pius XII authorized the change from "perfidious" to "unbelieving" or "without faith." Pope Paul VI removed the prayer altogether in 1965.

[64] Ruether, *Faith,* 125, 137, 151, 155, 161; Parkes, 83–84, 97, 100, 106.

[65] Ruether, *Faith,* 130, 175–179; Parkes, 158, 163–164.

[66] Ruether, *Faith,* 185–186, 189–190, 196; Parkes, 185.

[67] Parkes, 167, 187, 333, 363.

[68] Parkes, 184, 211–212, 214, 219; Ruether, *Faith,* 200; Carroll, 248.

[69] Ruether, *Faith,* 186; Haynes, 27–28, 30–32; Carroll, 218, 233.

[70] Haynes, 41, 89; Isaac, *Jesus,* 250, 329; Carroll, 359 (who reports the Edith Stein statement).

[71] 1 John 2:18–19, 22. In the legend of Theophilus, an unhappy and despairing cleric sells his soul to the Devil, through the mediation of a Jewish magician; Lazar, 46–47, 56; Carroll, 270–271, 624; Haynes, 40.

[72] Carroll, 372, 542; Lazar, 47; Isaac, *Jesus,* 250, 261–3; Davis, *Anti-Semitism,* 70.

[73] 366–368 Carroll; Isaac, *Jesus,* 249; Haynes, 47.

[74] These "Judaizers," were known as Marranos. They belonged to a large group of people who had been forced to convert to Christianity and were suspected of secretly continuing to practice Jewish rituals. Ruether, *Faith,* 202, 205–206, 210; Carroll, 333.

[75] Carroll, 275–276, 376, 379–380, 449; Ruether, *Faith,* 205.

[76] Haynes, 6, 64; Parkes, 57; Ruether, *Antisemitism,* 233; Katz, 29; Cohen, 487; Carroll, 59.

[77] Hayes, 67–75, 78–79, 81; Davies, *Antisemitism,* 118–119.

[78] Isaac, *Has Anti–Semitism,* 40, 56, 61; Davies, *Antisemitism,* 125; Ruether, *Antisemitism,* 183, 224–225; Carroll, 22.

Chapter 2 Germany

[1] Kulka and Hildesheimer, 557–559.

[2] Massing 6–8, 84; Tal, *The Catastrophe,* 94. I prefer the form "antisemitism" because, unlike the hyphenated "anti-Semitism," it does not imply being opposed to Semitic peoples (which would include Arabs), but is a code-word and euphemism for plain hatred of Jews.

3 Massing, 6–8, 55, 84; Mosse, *Toward,* 100–1; Tal, *The Catastrophe,* 94, 107, 109.

4 Racist ideas were wedded to another element of nineteenth-century popular thought, Social Darwinism, which propounded that the life and existence of peoples were conditioned by an eternal struggle among them for the survival of the fittest, and that the victors in this ongoing contest were superior and more valuable than the losing peoples. These ideas were solidified into a hard-core concept of the inexorable laws of "nature," an idea which Hitler referred to constantly. Maltitz, 27, 30, 222–223; Mosse, 30–32, 51–55, 100–101, 105–107; Cummings, 58–59; Massing, 82–83; Tal, *The Catastrophe,* 110; Schlette, 72–73; Hitler, *Mein Kampf,* 284 ff.

5Broszat 50; Hitler, *Mein Kampf,* 249, quoted by Ryan, 154; H. R. Trevor-Roper (ed.), *Hitler's Secret Conversations, 1941–44* (New York: Octagon Books, 1976), 116; Maltitz, 14–15, 36–37, 62, 268–269; Blackburn 35, 68–69, 73, 79; Hitler, *Table Talk,* 155, 158, 442, quoted in Maltitz, 37, 497; Hitler, *Mein Kampf,* 339, quoted in Kurth, 15.

6 Friedlander, 97, 103; Hofer, 280–281, quoted in Maltitz, 62; Bullock, 17; Vernon 301; Maltitz, 352, 378; Hitler, *Mein Kampf,* 59–63, 70, 129, quoted in Ryan, 156; Blackburn, 23; Broszat, 51; Tal, *Political Faith,* 29; *On Structures,* 4–5, 36; *Judaism and Christianity,* 92.

7Buchheim, 27, 33, 35, 39; Broszat, 32; Maltitz, 21, 232, 269, 272–273; Tal, *Political Faith,* 21, 30; *Judaism and Christianity,* 64, 76–77, 94; Ryan, 15, 158, 160; Blackburn, 13, 75, 76–77, 177–178; Conway, 19, 68, 177, quoted in Lyons, 1370.

8 Raynes, 395–396; Blackburn, 77, 79; Hitler, *Mein Kampf,* 6; Maltitz, 369, 373–376; Domarus, 264, 606; quoted in Maltitz, 372, 379; Speer, *Erinnerungen,* 367, 570; quoted in Maltitz, 379.

9 Hitler, *Mein Kampf,* 206 (where he writes that his decision to enter politics was prompted by his decision to combat the Jews. "There is no making pacts with Jews; there can only be the hard either-or. I, for my part, decided to go into politics"); Vernon, 4–5; Hitler, *Mein Kampf,* 70; quoted in Maltitz, 378; Friedlander, 102; Maltitz, 377, 389; Tal, *Political Faith,* 28, 47; Weiss, 312;. Müller, 65, 38; Blackburn, 154, 159–60; Ryan, 163. SS head Heinrich Himmler voiced similar anti-Christian thoughts: "Which of us, wandering through the lovely German countryside and coming unawares upon a Crucifix, does not feel deep in his heart . . . a strange but enduring sense of shame? . . . How different is the pale figure on the Cross, whose passivity and emphasized mien of suffering express only humility and self-abnegation, qualities which we, conscious of our heroic blood, utterly deny. . . . The corruption of our blood caused by the intrusion of this alien philosophy must be ended"; Blackburn, 67, 155; Lewy, 26, 51, 155; Conzemius, 91.

10 Hitler, *Table Talk,* 154, 178, 185, 266–267; quoted in Maltitz, 370, 372; Tal, *Political Faith,* 31.

11 Maltitz, 73, 130; Weiss, 286, 389; Bauer, *Remembering,* 1970–1971; Friedlaender, 102; Kuhn, 310; Tal, *Political Faith,* 29; *Yad Vashem,* 42; Gilbert, *The Holocaust,* 285.

12 Pulzer, 12–13; Weiss, 249, 251, 343–344; Hilberg, 5–6; Gerlach, 175; Rosenkranz, 131; Kulka and Hildesheimer, 574. In 1935, a Dutch motorcyclist on his way to Berlin took photographs of antisemitic signs in the towns he passed, such as: "Jews not

wanted here"; "The residents of this place want nothing to do with Jews"; "Jews enter this place at their own risk"; "The Jew is our misfortune. Let him keep away"; "Hyenas are scum, and so are Jews"; "Jews get out!"; Kulka and Hildesheimer, 563. The only known demonstration against the arrest and deportation of Jews was associated with what came to be known as the Rosenstrasse incident. When the Jewish husbands of non-Jewish spouses were arrested in a massive sweep in February 1943, their non-Jewish wives, numbering in the thousands, crowded around the portals of the building in the Rosenstrasse where most of the men were being held, calling and shouting for the release of their husbands. This incident was extremely disagreeable to the Nazi leadership, who could not bring themselves to open fire upon the women, who in consequence succeeded in having their husbands released. There was no other demonstration like this in the whole of the Hitler period, and there were certainly no demonstrations protesting the deportation of Jews; Gutteridge, 257.

[13] Bankier, 103, 105, 112, 131–132, 144, 155; Kershaw, 363–365, 370–372; Weiss, 348–349.

[14] Haynes, 88; Kershaw, 247, 254–255; Snoek, 36; Lyons, 1374; Gerlach, 231; Gutteridge, 269; Leuner, 108.

[15] Gerlach, 183, 194; Gutteridge, 52, 71; Heschel, 86–87.

[16] Gutteridge, 52, 94, 121, 232, 286; Gerlach, 147, 183, 231–232; Snoek, 37; Heschel, 82; Leuner, 100.

[17] Gerlach, 48–49, 80–81, 194, 231; Gutteridge, 53–54, 64, 71, 117, 190–191, 218, 231; Heschel, 80, 83, 86–87.

[18] Gerlach, 5, 31, 45, 48, 58, 123; Gutteridge, 97, 101, 132; Friedman, *Roads*, 426, 433; Leuner, 110; Lewy, 283. During the spirited debates on whether baptized Jews could be allowed to sit next to Aryan worshippers at church services, the following amusing as well ludicrously funny story was repeated by church people. Scene: A church service. The pastor stands at the altar. His opening words are, "Non-Aryans are requested to leave the church." No one makes a move. "Non-Aryans are requested to leave the church," he repeats. Again there is no movement. "Non-Aryans are required to leave the church at once." At this Christ comes down from the cross on the altar and quits the church; Gutteridge, 100; Gerlach, 69.

[19] Gerlach, 54; Gutteridge, 94, 99.

[20] Gerlach, 54, 105, 112; Scholder, 274–275; Weiss 352; Conzemius, 99.

[21] Gerlach, 77, 83; Gutteridge, 106, 331; Leuner, 100, 111. In a postwar declaration, the Evangelical Church admitted that while it had been opposed to the separation inside the church between Christians and baptized Jews, "the official church in general approved openly or secretly the Jewish policy and accepted the measures of the National Socialist regime both in and without the church"; Weiss, 352.

[22] Gutteridge, 137, 141, 196; Gerlach, 70, 104–105.

[23] Gutteridge, 42, 78, 111–113, 272–242; Gerlach, 14–16, 40, 111; Ericksen, *Remembering*, 68, 75, 93, 95.

[24] Scholder 275–277; Burton-Nelson, *Remembering;* Friedman, *Roads*, 443; Haynes, 82–84; Kelley, 85–86, 89; Robertson, 128; Davies, *Anti-Semitism*, 183; Eva Fleischner, *Judaism in German Christian Theology since 1945* (New Jersey, 1975);

24–25; Cohen, 483; Gutteridge, 297. It should be recalled that in the very year in which Bonhoeffer, according to Eberhard Bethge, his pupil and biographer, acknowledged, in Karl Barth's words, "the Jewish problem as the first and the decisive question," Bonhoeffer was able to write "The church of Christ has never lost sight of the thought that the 'chosen people' who nailed the redeemer of the world to the cross, must bear the curse of its action through the long history of suffering"; Bonhoeffer, 226–227; Bethge, 167.

[25] Niemoeller, 195–197; Friedman, *Roads,* 423, 434–435; Gerlach, 47–48; Gutteridge 102–103, 312; Weiss 226.

[26] Gutteridge, 186–187, 242–246, 353–354; Gerlach, 149, 198–200, 204; Snoek, 113; Leuner, 107.

[27] Gutteridge, 184–185; Gerlach, 107, 144–145, 147–148; Leuner, 114. After Kristallnacht, Berlin pastor Wilhelm Jannasch wanted the Confessing Church to issue a statement condemning the persecution of the Jews. It was not approved; Gerlach, 151.

[28] Gutteridge, 350–351; Gerlach, 215–217; Snoek, 108–110; Leuner, 107.

[29] Also meriting mention is a flyer distributed by Walter Hoechstaedter, a hospital chaplain serving in occupied France, printed in summer 1944 and distributed to German soldiers, condemning the persecution of Jews, and likening it to the witch hunts of the Middle Ages. Gutteridge, 248–252; Gerlach, 217–218; Leuner, 128–129.

[30] Gerlach, 169–172; Leuner, 101.

[31] Lewy, 11–3, 17–18, 20–21, 27, 107–108; Kershaw, 190–191, 247–248; Friedman, *Roads*, 428–429; Morley, *Vatican Diplomacy*, 105. One priest, with avowed Nazi sympathies until 1938, stated: "I must admit that I was glad to see the Nazis come into power, because at that time I felt that Hitler as a Catholic was a God-fearing individual who would battle Communism for the church. . . . It was not until after 1938 that I saw that Hitler and the Nazis hated Catholicism as much as they did Communism"; Friedman, *Roads*, 429.

[32] Hitler's response to the two religious dignitaries, in the original German: "*Man hat mich wegen Behandlung der Judenfrage angegriffen. Die katholische Kirche hat 1500 Jahre lang die Juden als die Schaedlinge angesehen, sie ins Getto gewiesen usw., da hat man erkannt, was die Juden sind. In der Zeit des Liberalismus hat man diese Gefahr nicht mehr gesehen. Ich gehe zurueck auf die Zeit, was man 1500 Jahre lang getan hat. Ich stelle nicht die Rasse ueber die Religion, sondern ich sehe die Schaedlinge in den Vertretern dieser Rasse fuer Staat und Kirche, und vielleicht erweise ich dem Christentum des groessten Dienst; deswegen ihre Zurueckdraengung von Studium und den staatlichen Berufen.*" In Hans Mueller, *Katholische Kirche und Nationalsozialismus* (Munich: Deutscher Taschenbuch Verlag, 1965), 129. Griech, *Pure Conscience,* 142; Lewy, 51, 270–271.

[33] Lewy, 276–277; Scholder, 271; Spicer, *Between*, 93, 96; Weiss, 315; Leuner, 104.

[34] Lewy, 107–112, 141, 164, 279; Kershaw, 219; Spicer, *Choosing*, 433, 435, 438; Carroll, 518. The Concordat notwithstanding, the Nazi regime did not hesitate to bear down strongly on the Catholic Church in various devious ways, including the closing of Catholic publications, false accusations, and concocted lurid descriptions of sexu-

al abuses in church institutions and religious orders. This forced Pope Pius XI to issue an encyclical letter to be read from the pulpit on Palm Sunday, March 21, 1937, entitled "With Burning Anxiety" (*Mit brennender Sorge*), in which he expressed dismay at the tribulations of the Catholic Church in Germany, in violation of the 1933 Concordat. Not a word on the ongoing and accelerated persecution of the Jews in Germany. He limited his statement to specific concerns pertaining to Catholic interests in Germany. Lewy, 140, 156–157, 174; Spicer, *Choosing,* 221–223.

[35] Lewy, 280–282, 287, 290; Spicer, *Choosing,* 110–111.

[36] Lewy, 265–267; Conway, 283; Kershaw, 340 (n. 26); Griech, *Pure Conscience,* 29, 47, 71, 79, 93, 110, 114, 125, 133–135, 140, 157, 187; *God's Name,* 111. An English translation of Von Galen's sermon may be found in Hugh Gregory Gallagher, *By Trust Betrayed: Patients, Physicians, and the License to Kill in the Third Reich* (New York: Henry Holt, 1990), 294–297. In truth, the euthanasia program was not completely cancelled but continued to operate at a reduced level.

[37] Griech, *Pure Conscience,* 219.

[38] Spicer, *Choosing,* 391–393; Leuner, 109–112.

[39] File 10292. See also, Spicer, *Choosing,* 406, 415–416, 420, 423–451, 453–460; Lewy, 284; Mann, 112.

[40] File 75; Gerlarch, 169; Gutteridge, 21, 207, 209; Leuner, 114–118; State of Israel, Ministry of Justice, *The Trial of Adolf Eichmann: Record of Proceedings in the District Court of Jerusalem,* vol II, Jerusalem, 1992; 736–751, 16 May 1961.

[4i] File 1614; Gutteridge, 211.

[42] File 74; Friedman, *Roads,* 439, 450–451; Leuner, 127.

[43] Krakauer et al.; Gutteridge, 217; Leuner, 129–133.

[44] File 412.

[45] File 4882.

[46] File 7924; Krakauer, 57–61.

[47] File 5039. See also the story of Elisabeth Goes, the wife of a Protestant pastor who was away in the army. She was one of the people who answered the call of the *Sozietaet* des Christlichen Naechstenliebe, and sheltered the Krakauers for five weeks; file 5074.

[48] See Beate Steckan's lengthy report in the Von Rabenau story, file 625.

[49] File 9.

[50] File 965.

[51] File 1867.

[52] File 3546. Data also collected from article by Erik Myrgren, "In the Valley of the Shadow of Death," 1984 (translated from Swedish by Rev. Dr. Göran Larsson, director of the Swedish Theological Institute in Jerusalem). Also from, Leonard Gross, *The Last Jews in Berlin* (New York: Simon & Schuster, 1982); especially chaps. 23, 36, 39, 40.

[53] File 7129.

[54] File 9242.

[55] File 10280.

[56] File 8084.

[57] File 5837.

[58] File 10066.

[59] File 10424.

Chapter 3 France

[1] Blumenkranz, 7–22; and Schwarzfuchs, *Encyclopedia, France,* 22–31.

[2] On October 7, 1940, a Vichy law deprived the Jews of Algeria (a French colony), counting some 115,000 souls, of the citizenship they had been granted in 1870. In Morocco and Tunisia, similarly under French rule, discriminatory laws were passed diminishing the rights of altogether 280,000 Jews, and in Morocco plans were under way to establish ghettos and internment camps for the Jewish population there; Zuccotti, *The Holocaust,* 56–57, Hilberg, 401; Lowrie, 58–9.

[3] Duquesne 264; Marrus and Paxton, 206. *Témoignage Chrétien,* in its issue of April-May 1942: "*les Juifs sont, à l'heure actuelle, dans l'impossibilité presque absolue d'exercer aucune profession remunératrice*"; Bedarida, 130–131. René Gillouin, a French Protestant, close to Petain, wrote to him in August 1941 that the new anti-Jewish laws were more severe than the 1685 revocation of the Nantes edict, which disenfranchised French Protestants. Joutard, 17, who cites Marrus and Paxton, 192; Pierrard, 302, Beradia, 127. At the same time, it should be pointed out that Vallat wished to go no further than these anti-Jewish measures. He felt contempt toward the Germans for their too inhuman approach to the Jewish Question. A follower of the royalist and conservative Charles Maurras, he was violently anti-German. His anti-semitism was according to him simply to restore the ancient "equilibrium" between real French and outsiders, but not further than this. His refusal to implement to wearing of the Star in the Vichy zone as well as to deliver Jews to the Germans, caused his removal and his replacement by the more virulent antisemite and the obsequiously pro-German Darquier de Pellepoix.

[4] Zuccotti, *The Holocaust,* 67–68; Marrus and Paxton, 363.

[5] Marrus and Paxton, 201, 400; Pierrard, 296 ; Hilberg, 400. Morley speculates that the high sources in the Vatican mentioned by Bérard may have included Monsignors Tardini and Montini (the future Pope Paul VI). Morley, *Vatican Diplomacy,* 51–53, 68, 311, 313. For a full account of Bérard's report, in the original French, see: *Le Monde Juif,* no 2. (October 1946).

[6] Marrus and Paxton, 197; Cohen, 328; Marrus, *Judaism and Christianity,* 309; Duquesne, 44–47. During his visit to the Vatican in January 1943, Suhard was received coldly by the sole French bishop there, Monsignor Tisserand, who felt that the French Catholic hierarchy had gone too far in its support of the Vichy regime; Duquesne, 51, 53, 59, 276. A religious pæan for Pétain was modeled on the Lord's prayer : "*Notre Père, qui êtes à notre tête, Que votre nom soit glorifié. Que votre volonté soit faite sur la terre pour qu'on vive. Demeurez, sans retour, notre pain de chaque jour. Redonnez l'éxistence à la France. Ne nous laissez pas retomber dans le*

vain songe et le mensonge. Et delivrez-nous du mal – O Maréchal!". A parochial bulletin in Pau praised Petain for "burying the Republic…, suppressing the Masons,… restoring God in school. . . . Long live the Marshal." Duquesne, 59, 61.

[7] The Catholic lay activist Germaine Ribière, who participated in the rescue of Jews, writes about the anti-Jewish climate among Catholic circles with whom she mixed, and *"cette aberration de la foi qui faussait le regard porté sur les Juifs, sur ce dont ils étaient victimes, et justifiait un certain silence et parfois plus."* Ribière, 9; Marrus and Paxton, 199, 200, 311; Pierrard, 296. Father Garail, who at the time filled an important position in the diocese office in Toulouse, questions Vallat's assertion on the church's approbation of anti-Jewish measures, since it conflicted with Saliège's known stand of opposition to the Vichy regime. Pierrard, 295, 297; Marrus and Paxton, 198.

[8] Marrus and Paxton, 189; Zuccotti, *The Holocaust,* 58–59, 61; Cohen, 336.

[9] Marrus, *Judaism and Christianity*, 316. On July 31, 1941, Rabbi Jacob Kaplan, who at the time was a deputy to chief rabbi Weill, wrote to Xavier Vallat, in which he pointed out that since the Jewish religion was the mother of the Christian religion, including the fact that Jesus and the apostles were Jews, he asked Vallat whether he did not realize that in attacking the Jews, the anti-Jewish laws were also attacking the founders of Christianity? Kaplan received an evasive response from Vallat ("let me simply point out that in the government's attitude there is no anti-Semitism, simply the application of reasons of state"); Hilberg, 398–9.

[10] Zuccotti, *The Holocaust,* 139–142; Duquesne, 150–159; Pierrard, 309–310, 312. Bedarida, 119–120, 128, 146, 177–178.

[11] Joutard, 218, 220–221, 236–238; Société, 15 (based on *Rencontre Chrétiens et Juifs, 1968*; 294); Marrus-Paxton, 203–204; Marrus, *Judaism and Christianity*, 315–316. Among some conservative Protestant pastors, such as Pastor Noël Noguet, it was felt that Boegner was going too far in his criticism of Vichy's Jewish policy, since theologically they argued the Jews would benefit from their current sufferings; Marrus, *Judaism and Christianity*, 316.

[12] Morley, *The Vatican,* 58; Marrus and Paxton 209, 236, 239; Zuccotti, *The Holocaust,* 94.

[13] Hilberg, 389; Zuccotti, *The Holocaust,* 81, 105, 107, 118, 189–190, 192–193, 206–208; Marrus and Paxton, 250, 252.

[14] Duquesne, 161, 260; *La Semaine Catholique de Toulouse*, April 16, 1933; 311–312.

[15] Duquesne, 258; Introduction in *Livre d'Or des Congregations Francaises 1939–1945,* 1948; also file 197. Marie-Rose Gineste, a Catholic lay worker, at the request of Théas, had typed up the bishop's pastoral letter of August 1942. To sidestep mail censorship by Vichy authorities, and simultaneously make sure that the bishop's letter be read from the pulpit on the following Sunday, Gineste volunteered to carry the bishop's message on her bicycle, for a long ride, lasting several days – throughout the parishes of the Tarn-and-Garonne department. "Thus, all the parishes of the Montauban diocese were in possession of the letter of protest by Monsignor Théas, which was read on Sunday, August 30, 1942." The only dissenting voice to the bishop's letter was the parish priest of Ardus, who was known for his pro-Vichy sympa-

thies, and Gineste avoided him. Returning from her long Paul Revere-type bicycle ride, Théas charged her to help hide fleeing Jews in the region's religious institutions, and provide them with the necessary false credentials. Gineste's bicycle is now on display at the Yad Vashem Holocaust memorial, in Jerusalem; file 3256.

[16] Zuccotti, *The Holocaust,* 146–147; Duquesne, 261; Marrus and Paxton, 272–273. Also, files 197 (Saliège), 197a (Théas), and 1769 (Gerlier).

[17] Marrus and Paxton, 277–8. *Catholiques du Tarn,* 26; Zuccotti, *The Holocaust,* 177.

[18] Zuccotti, *The Holocaust,* 214–215, 221–222, 240.

[19] Perthuis, 17–18, 21, 91; Duquesne, 268; Zuccotti, *The Holocaust,* 141–142.

[20] Zasloff,166; Nodot, 32–33; Joutard, 132, 252–253.

[21] In the words of Pastor Elie Brée: "in the face of a family, of a person, of a human being needing help, suddenly one is faced with the choice of either closing one's eyes, or to be someone *(d'être)* and to act"; Joutard, 240.

[22] Marrus, *Judaism and Christianity,* 327; Zuccotti, *The Holocaust,* 68–69, 75, 351; Joutard, 229, 240; Lowrie, 135. Other relief agencies also participated in helping to relieve conditions of people in these camps. They numbered some 25 agencies, comprising all denominations, including Jewish; such as the American-based YMCA, the Protestant CIMADE, the Jewish Joint and OSE organizations, and the Swiss Aid for Children. All these agencies coordinated their activities under what became known as the Nîmes Committee, with headquarters in Marseilles. Lowrie, 84; Latour, 38; Nodot, *Résistance,* 11. See also files 2142 (Holbek Helga), and 2142a (Resch-Synnestvedt Alice).

[23] *Le Plateau et l'Acceuil,* 27–29. Bollon, 2; Zuccotti, *The Holocaust,* 229.

[24] Gilbert, 233–236; Latour, 138; Zuccotti, 229; Bollon, 4–10; 13–21; Lowrie, 195, 199–200; Rittner, 102; *Le Plateau et l'Acceuil,* 7,8, 11, 21, 25, 36. Jacques Trocmé, son of Pastor Trocmé, relates an argument between his father and Boegner, in 1943, which if we are to believe the then 10–year old Jacques, is a bit unnerving. It, went on as following: Boegner to Trocmé: *"What I want to say is this; you must stop helping refugees."* Trocmé: *"Do you realize what you are asking? These people, especially the Jews are in very great danger. If we do not shelter them or take them across the mountains to Switzerland, they may well die."* Boegner: *"What you are doing is endangering the very existence not only of this village but of the Protestant church of France! You must stop helping them."* Trocmé: *"If we stop, many of them will starve to death... We cannot stop."* Boegner: *"You must stop. The Maréchal will take care of them. He will see to it that they are not hurt."* Trocmé: *"No";* Zasloff, 172. No wonder the two did not get along, and Boeger qualified Trocmé as "that impossible man." It is well to keep in mind that Boegner was not in principle opposed to aiding Jews; on the contrary, and as long as it was done silently and with circumspection. He may have feared that the large-scale and unrestricted rescue operation of Trocmé would jeopardize the tenuous position of the Protestant churches in a country overwhelmingly Catholic.

[25] Joutard, 199.

[26] Joutard, 202–3; Duquesne, 269.

[27] Gilbert, 250; Zuccotti, *The Holocaust,* 241.

[28] Zuccotti, *The Holocaust,* 241, 243 (based on Saul Friendlander, *When Memory Returns.*).

[29] Perthuis, 21, 60–65, 73–75, 78–85; Zuccotti 131–132; Lazare, 188–191; Lowrie, 229–235; Latour, 60–62; Nodot, 39–40. There are discrepancies in some of the accounts, as to what actually took place in Vénissieux camp, and the exact interchange of words between Gerlier and Angeli, as well as between Gerlier and Glasberg and Chaillet.

[30] Marrus and Paxton, 241, 335; Zuccotti, *The Holocaust,* 178. The Italian attitude prompted German Foreign Minister Joachim von Ribbentrop to openly protest to Mussolini, during his visit to Rome in February 1943. Mussolini promised to do something about it and appointed a special commissioner for Jewish affairs, Guido Lospinoso, to synchronize with the Germans anti-Jewish activities in the Italian zone in France. However, upon arrival on the scene, he acted rather differently, according to one report even promising one Jewish delegation: "I believe God has sent me here to help you: I am one of you, from way back (intimating he was a descendant of the Marranos); Latour, 148; Zuccotti, *The Holocaust,* 168. The comparable figure for the Netherlands with its original Jewish population of 140,000, is 105,000 casualties; in Belgium, some 25,000 Jews died of an original population of 57,000 at the start of the deportations in 1942; in Italy, Jewish losses were a mere 15 percent of the approximately 45,100 Jews in the country in September 1943, when the Germans overran most of the country. Hilberg, 392; Marrus and Paxton, 247–248, 267, 308; Zuccotti, *The Holocaust,* 161, 164–165, 237, 245, 256, 282–286, 365.

[31] File 7245; Friedman, *Their Brothers',* 53; Pierrard, 322–3.

[32] File 3099; Braunschweig et al.; Zuccotti, *The Holocaust,* 245.

[33] File 4730.

[34] File 762; Pierrard, 328; *Recontre,* 126–139.

[35] While in Gap, Werner Epstein on the point of arrest fled to a hospital. Father Joseph Richard helped him escape from the hospital, and both men eluded Gestapo agents posted on every path and street corner. The two crossed forests, and after a 20–kilometer trek, Father Richard turned over the Jewish fugitive to the Resistance. Files 870 and 1033.

[36] File 5532.

[37] Some of his philosophical writings include: *Les Derniers Commentateurs Alexandrins d'Aristote,* 1941; *Qu'est-ce que le Communisme?,* 1947; *Marxisme et Pensée Chrétienne,* 1948; *La Phénoménologie et la Foi,* 1953; *La Pensée Réligieuse de Hegel,* 1965; *Kant, sa Vie, son Oeuvre, avec un Exposé de sa Philosophie,* 1967.

[38] File 909.

[39] File 3734.

[40] File 4872; also Vulliez 90–92.

[41] I take this occasion to thank again Dr. Eva Fleischner, who met Father Gallay during her study tour in France, and solved the riddle of "Mr. Lebain."

[42] Files 4363 and 4245.

[43] Files 193, 3601 and 3558. See also, Perrot, 7, 43–60.

[44] File 6720.

[45] File 5161.

[46] File 5380.

[47] Files 1532 and 5638.

[48] File 9625.

[49] File 1807.

[50] File 4845.

[51] File 4768.

[52] File 3078; Friedman, *Their Brothers'*, 30–1; Stratton-Smith, 114, 127, 130, 162, 170, 196, 204; Hackel, 120–122.

[53] File 57.

[54] File 3444; Latour 77.

[55] File 5061. Also, Gilbert, 246–247; Landau, 21–42; Latour, 71. This account of Abadi's unorthodox approach to the bishop of Nice has a parallel in Joseph Bass's account of how he enlisted a Dominican monk, in Marseilles, in his rescue network. "I went to the Convent of the Dominicans, and asked to see the Father. He came – it was Father de Parceval. I had never met him before, and I said: 'I am a Jew with illegal status – but that isn't the issue. I'm not asking for help for myself, in terms of money or ID papers; I only want to know whether you are just going to make a lot of speeches and sermons, or whether – in thinking back to your patron Saint Dominique, who did so much to harm the Jews – you are prepared to *do* something to make amends... What will you do for us?' He was flabbergasted, but finally asked: 'But what is it you want of me?' I said: 'Whatever you wish to give – nothing or everything.' Whereupon he asked me to return the next day. I did, and he said: 'All right. I am at your disposal.'" Bass spent many nights in Latour's monastery, and held many clandestine meetings there. Latour, 115–116.

[56] Leboucher, 30.

[57] In French: *"On n'aurait pas cru cela de la part de la France."*

[58] File 201; Leboucher, 114. On July 8, 1945, Benoît spoke before a Jewish audience, on behalf of the International Council of Christians and Jews, on the theme of Judeo-Christian solidarity. "The Jews are the people chosen by God to preserve the true primitive religion of Adam and Eve in the midst of the idolatry of the other nations, and to prepare the coming of the Messiah... The Jews are, by the will of God, the legitimate inhabitants of Palestine, which they conquered and in which they remained for more than twenty centuries until the destruction of Jerusalem, after which they dispersed throughout the world in which they live, always faithful to the holy covenant of God, putting at the disposal of every nation their intelligence and their activity, though subject to untold suffering and persecution. The importance of the Jewish people is not in their numbers but in their sublimely divine vocation... The Jews, by the will of God, hold first place among the races of the earth, so that from this point of view humanity is divided into Jews and non-Jews, the Jews chosen by God to preserve and to give back to the world the true religion, and the non-Jews or Gentiles,...fallen to worship false gods and awaiting the liberation through Israel.... According to the Christians, Jesus Christ is the Messiah promised to the Jews. He did not intend to abolish the Mosaic Laws but to bring them to their fulfillment, insisting chiefly on the

two great precepts – the love of god and the love of one's neighbor…. Antisemitism is a movement of antipathy, a movement in which we Christians can have no part. For Christ and we in Christ are the spiritual descendants of Abraham… After more than thirty centuries, the Decalogue remains the indispensable basis of human progress and of lasting peace, and your synagogues, sanctuaries of the Holy Covenant of God, subsist and prove perpetually this fact to the entire world… For this reason Christians feel united with the Jewish people in a bond of special affection, and they love them, not only because they must love all men without distinction, but also because of a special predilection, through the obligation of a particular spiritual relationship, like older brothers, in the faith of the God of Abraham, of Isaac and of Jacob… This Jewish Christian friendship must be acknowledged. It cannot aspire to the fusion of two non reconcilable religions, for the contrast remains essential. Why do Jews continue to await the Messiah whereas Christians affirm that He has come and acknowledge Him in the person of Jesus Christ, the Savior of the world, the Revealer, Redeemer, and Sanctifier of all men? It is a mystery of Divine Providence which allows for particular ends we cannot understand; the differences of mind and human will. But as a mystery and like all mysteries it is the object of our admiration, and understood in this sense, can never give rise to hate and aversion but on the contrary, to the respect of conscience of the highest degree…" See also: James Rorty, "Father Benoit, Ambassador to the Jews," *Commentary* 2, Dec. 1946; also, Duquesne, 266; Friedman, *Their Brothers'*, 55–57; Latour, 152–153; Morley, *Vatican Diplomacy,* 64–67.

[59] File 3134.

[60] Philip Hallie, *Lest Innocent Blood be Shed,* New York: Harper and Row, 1979; 21, 233.

[61] Georges Menut, "André Trocmé, Un Violent Vaincu par Dieu." In, *Le Plateau Vivarais-Lignon : Accueil et Résistance 1939–1944.* Colloque du 1, 13, 14 octobre 1990. Chambon-sur-Lignon, France, 1990; 8.

[62] A film maker, in Los Angeles, California, Pierre Sauvage was born in Le Chambon in 1944, the child of Jewish refugees who sought shelter there. He has since consecrated much of his activity to the remembrance of Le Chambon and the teaching of its humanitarian message.

[63] Latour, 140–141.

[64] File 612; Zasloff, 30.

[65] Files 2698, 3979, 4072.

[66] *"Enfin, il y avait un adversaire clair. Le fameux choix: ou est le bien, ou est le mal, on était devant un mur, il fallait réagir, et donc il y avait deux réactions: je m'écrase et j'attends que cela passe et puis à un moment non on ne peut pas. Maintenant il faut devenir acteur. A ce moment là, il faut chercher à agir. C'est le moment ou j'ai dit a mon épouse 'tu sais, on ne peux plus rester comme ça.'"* See also file 2698.

[67] File 3370. Also, Joutard, 13–15, 26–33, 140–149, 188, 194–201, 232–235, 254–257, 282, 293.

[68] Files 1066.

[69] File 813. Also, Zasloff, 104, 188, 197, 237.

[70] File 6358.

[71] File 6958.

[72] File 3848.

[73] File 1039.

[74] Reverend Cyrille Argenti, in response to his elevation to the Righteous title, wrote that it was up to God to judge who is to be considered as Righteous. However, "I should hope that this decision by His people will prefigure His own." In the original French: *"Vous ne pouvez vous imaginer l'émotion que j'ai ressenti: être considéré 'Juste' par les représentants du peuple élu de Dieu. C'est bien plus qu'une décoration. Certes, Dieu seul jugera qui est Juste. Mais puis-je espérer que cette décision de son peuple préfigure la Sienne."* File 4592.

Chapter 4 Belgium

[1] Saerens, "The Attitude," 157.

[2] Schwarzfuchs, *Encyclopaedia, Belgium*, 416–418.

[3] Michman, Dan, *Encyclopedia,* 161–161; Lazare, *Belgium,* 446–447; Saerens, "Antwerp," 160–161. Also, Steinberg, *L'Etoile,* 76–77, 92.

[4] Steinberg, *Dossier,* 16–17. Michman is of the opinion that the military tried to moderate and restrain the anti-Jewish measures which it found itself constrained to enforce, vis-à-vis the SS; Michman, Dan, *Encyclopedia,* 162. Steinberg is of another opinion; that the military was more sensitive to public opinion in the country and its efforts were directed to implement these measures in a more astute and pragmatic way, so as not to arouse local opposition to the German occupation. One method was to pass the buck by requiring the Belgian administration to enforce many of the administrative anti-Jewish steps, while at the same time jealously guarding its own preeminent position as the final arbiter in the country. For more on the ongoing friction between the military and the SS with regard to the preeminent and ultimate authority and responsibility of these two branches in the implementation of the anti-Jewish measures, see Steinberg, *Dossier*, 32 ff.; and by same author in, *L'Etoile,* 25, 27; *Judenpolitik,* 211.

[5] To add to the AJB's legal appearance and the approval of Belgium's civilian administration to its creation, the organization's statutes were published in *Le Moniteur Belge* (Belgium's official gazette); Steinberg, *Judenpolitik,* 216. The Germans term *beherbergung* is translated in English as either "accommodation," "give lodging," "harbor," or "shelter." Garfinkels, 14–18, 38–42, 78–79; Steinberg, *L'Etoile,* 18, 57; *Patterns,* 353–355, 358, 362; *Judenpolitik,* 201.

[6] A small number of Jews, married to non-Jewish spouses, were exempted from deportation, but were interned. Several hundred Jews who were conscripted for work in the German armaments industry were also spared deportation. Michman, *Encyclopedia,* 162; Garfinkels, 8, 45, 54, 56–57, 62, 99; Steinberg, *Patterns,* 369–371; *Extermination,* 62; *Dossier,* 24, 39, 52, 139–162, 219; *Belgium,* 349; *Judenpolitik,* 203–206, 215, 218–219. Also, Riesel, 483.

[7] Steinberg, *L'Etoile,* 133–143, 171, 178; Michman, *Encyclopedia,* 164.

[8] By contrast, in neighboring Antwerp, there was greater support among attorneys for

the removal of Jews from its membership list, but there too in the final account, the opposition to such a step prevailed. Steinberg, *L'Etoile,* 115–116.

[9] Steinberg, *L'Etoile,* 65–6; Garfinkels, 43.

[10] Steinberg, *L'Etoile,* 64, 106–117, 122–129, 157–161, 176–179; *Dossier,* 55, 157; Garfinkels, 18–25, 29–33, 43, 48–53; Saerens, "Antwerp," 166–191; Brachfeld, *Collaboration,* 6–11.

[11] In his study of the CDJ, Steinberg lists 126 communities in the Charleroi region that helped with false credentials and registrations and with food ration cards; Steinberg Lucien, 186–187, and the book in general, starting page 71. Steinberg, Maxime, *Extermination,* 25–27, 38–43; Gotovitch, 280–281; Garfinkels, 88–90; Michman, Dan, *Encyclopedia,* 167; Matteazzi, 77–88. Andrée Geulen, Claire Murdoch, Paule Renard, and Brigitte Moens were among the non-Jewish operatives, who specialized in finding safe locations for Jewish children. Also worth mentioning is the attack carried out, with CDJ inspiration, on a deportation train on April 19, 1943, which was stopped by armed men as it neared Tirlemont, as a result of which 108 of those who jumped from the train were able to flee to safety. An additional 75 were recaptured, and 21 were shot by the Germans while trying to escape. Garfinkels, 10, 58–59, 77–82, 94–95; Steinberg, Lucien, 91, 98, 102–7, 130–7; Papeleux, 137, 165; Michman, Dan, *Encyclopedia,* 165.

[12] Van den Wijngaert, 226–267; Saerens, *Belgium, Attitude,* 117–119, 121, 126, 134.

[13] Gotovitch, 275 (based on *La Belgique Indépendante,* 44)

[14] Saerens, *Attitude,* 134, 138–139, 142–145, 150–151. Saerens suspects that the real motive of the Bureau's dissolution may have been the Bureau's too favorable presentation of Judaism, and that Van Roey had preferred for this organ to limit itself to a more missionary activity among Jews; 147.

[15] Saerens, *Belgium, Attitude,* 155. Some Catholic clerics hoped that the church's help to Jews during the war would elicit a greater conversion of Jews after the war, since in the words of the Liège diocesan journal "they will no longer be precluded from [receiving] the overflowing gift of God's grace in view of the terrible suffering of this people. Thus, praying for the conversion of [the people of] Israel seems to be needed, especially in these times"; Saerens, *Belgium, Attitude,* 157, n. 118. Van den Wijngaert, 231–233. See also Dom Bruno Reynders's list of several dozen various Catholic institutions where he placed hundreds of Jewish children; Blum, 32–34.

[16] Steinberg, *Remembering,* 466, 469 (based on Leclef, "Le Cardinal Van Roey et l'occupation allemande en Belgique," Brussels 1945; 286). Garfinkels, 58–61. A similar disclaimer was related to Liège attorney Van den Berg, who was told that "it had been shown by previous protests that the occupying authorities pay no heed to them, so that a protest would have every chance of failing like the previous ones which related to other matters" (*ibid.,* 470). After the war, a group of former resistance fighters addressed a letter to Van Roey in which they condemned his silence at the deportation of Jews and pointed out that the only protest evinced by him was when the German tried to silence church bells"; Matteazzi, 58, 60, n. 95. At the same time, the cardinal took a strong stand against the pro-Nazi Rexist movement, going so far, in 1941, as to forbid communion to Rexist members in uniform; Matteazzi, 61.

[17] Dequeker, 235, 238, 258–259; Papeleux, 154; Steinberg, 102. The Trent council also reaffirmed the irrevocable right of the parents to determine the religious education of their children (the principle of the freedom of man), but at the same time allowed baptism of children without and even against their parents' consent when the children's lives were in immediate danger, or in situations, such as in missionary regions, when the children are abandoned or sold by their parents; then the parents are considered to have given up their rights over the children; Dequeker, 241, 244–246, 263–264.

[18] See the case of David Natan Rapaport, who signed a statement in which he "accepts without any reserve for my above-named child, the program of the *Colonie Catholique*. . . . He would follow all the classes and lessons; with the only exception of the Sacraments since he is not baptized"; Papeleux, 141; also 152–154; Dequeker, 241–243. Jamin is reported to have baptized thirteen Jewish girls, of a total of thirty-three in his Banneux institution.

[19] Matteazzi, 215.

[20] Lepkifker's story appears in Matteazzi, 216, 223, 224–225, 244.

[21] Papeleux, 188.

[22] Papeleux, 186–195, 197.

[23] Papeleux, 200–201, 203.

[24] Dequeker, 249–251.

[25] Blum, 79, 89, 236, 249. Matteazzi, in her study of the sheltering of Jews by the clergy in the Liège region, found that of the twenty-one conversions researched by her, only three maintained links with their new faith, but after a while stopped practicing it, and only rarely attended church services. "In general, we may consider the result of the conversions to be negative, as the baptized people, for the most part, turned away from Catholicism"; Matteazzi, 228.

[26] Private communication by Dan Dagan to the author.

[27] File 866.

[28] File 530.

[29] File 697.

[30] File 1863. See also, later, the Sister Marie Xavier story, in the rescue of Genia's daughter. Father Pierre May, also in Leuven, was of help to Eduard Shalom Oppenheim; file 175.

[31] Garfinkels, 70. Steinberg, *Remembering*, 478. Celis Louis, file 1777; also Matteazzi, 100. Arrested in April 1943, Van den Berg was sentenced to five months imprisonment by a German court, for his involvement in the fabrication of false papers for Jews. Close to the end of his term in prison, he was picked up by the Gestapo and transferred first to Vught camp, in the Netherlands, then to Neueungamme concentration camp, in Germany, where he died toward the end of the war, in April 1945. Banneux became a famous pilgrimage site after Kerkhofs sanctified a shrine a site there when a local resident named Mariette Becco claimed that the Virgin Mary had made eight appearances to her in 1933.

[32] File 6678.

[33] File 3708a; Matteazzi, 166. Abbé Alberic Steiger headed the Val-Dieu monastery

in Liège. When Stenne was interrogated by the Gestapo on the charge of sheltering Jewish children, Steiger testified on his behalf, and managed to have Stenne set free; file 3708b.

[34] File 1361; Matteazzi, 202 ff.

[35] File 1362a; Matteazzi, 208–209.

[36] Files 1364, 1365. Also, *Mémorial, Collège St-Hadelin, Visé, 1881–1956* (Wagelmans: Visé, 1956).

[37] File 486.

[38] File 486 (André), and file 8546b (Lefèbvre).

[39] Blum, 5–15; Gilbert, 266–269.

[40] Blum, 27–28, 46–49.

[41] Blum, 16, 75, 80, 95.

[42] File 84, 103–104.

[43] Steinberg, *Remembering*, 474; Garfinkels (chap. 4).

[44] File 262.

[45] File 1777.

[46] File 5175.

[47] File 6551. While Yad Vashem awarded the Righteous title only to Mother Urbaine, the person who was ultimately responsible for the convent and the sheltered children, the other nuns who shared in the rescue effort received letters of thanks and appreciation. They included: Bertha Braekmans (Sr. Amalienne), Lucie Quevauvillers (Sr. Archangele), Hubertina Verstappen (Sr. Marie-Reine), Bridget Fitzgerald (Sr. Bridget), Marie-Josée Giet (Sr. Bernadette), and Franziska Catharina Weber (Sr. Rodriguez).

[48] File 6219.

[49] File 132.

[50] File 4666.

[51] File 6109.

[52] File 1862.

[53] File 5629.

[54] File 7605.

[55] File 9552. The three Jews in the group of five were Paul Halter, Toby Cymberknopf and Bernard Feneberg. The two others were Floris de Smet, and Andrée Ermel.

[56] File 8432.

Chapter 5 The Netherlands

[1] De Jong, *The Destruction,* 2; Presser, 325; Warmbrunn, 165; Michman, D., *Studies,* 262. Boas, 360; Moore, 162; Michman, J. 1046.

[2] Michman, D., 1046; Moore, 191, Hirschfeld, 18–20, 46–47. As for the German police, by contrast, for instance, with France, where the total German police force amounted to 3,000 men, in the much smaller Netherlands they constituted a much large force of around 5,000; Moore, 193. Himmler to Seyss-Inquart in 1941 wished him success in "the historically vital task of reclaiming 9 million lower-Germans for

the German people who for centuries have been estranged from Germandom, and leading them back to the Germanic community with a firm but very gentle hand." Hitler urged Mussert to have the Netherlands join the Reich and sacrifice selfhood just as Austria did. Hirschfeld, 27, 34, 46, 55–56; Warmbrunn, 23–26, 47, 262.

[3] Moore, 58, 64–65, 265; Hirschfeld, 143–145, Presser, 19, 26–27, 33–5, 115–117, 120, 221 (in which the figure for *Mischlinge* including "quarter-Jews" is given as 20,985; Hilberg, 368–369, 374; Michman, D., 1047, 1049–1051; Warmbrunn, 166.

[4] Hilberg, 365; Moore, 153, 192; Presser, 136–137, 156; Michman, D., 1045, 1054. Of the 34,313 people deported to Sobibor, only nineteen survived; Michman, D., 1055. In response to an appeal by a Jew for exemption due to the fact that he had lost one of his legs in battle during the German invasion, General Friedrich Christiansen, the commander-in-chief of German troops in the Netherlands, wrote back "A Jew is a Jew with or without legs," and the request was denied; Presser, 351.

[5] Moore, 116, 118–123, 127, 143–144; De Jong, *Netherlands and the Holocaust*, 16; Presser, 165, 305–310; Michman, D., 1054; Hilberg, 377. Presser claims that many more of the 1,146 men were sterilized; Presser, 202.

[6] On the various fatalities estimates, see Hilberg, 278; Warmbrunn, 68; De Jong, *Netherlands and anti-Nazi*, 10; Michman, D., 1055; Moore, 260; Fishman, *Journal*, 462. In addition, an estimated 300,000 non-Jewish people went underground, mostly to avoid forced labor in Germany. Moore, 146, 155, 168, 170–172, 174, 179–184; Presser, 282–283; Warmbrunn, 77, 187–189; De Jong, *Netherlands and anti-Nazi Resistance*, 8; Hirschfeld, 37.

[7] Presser, 396, 403; Warmbrunn, 265.

[8] This is to be contrasted with the Belgian civil service, which did not have German masters appointed over their heads, and could consequently act with greater freedom; in France, the existence of an independent administration in Vichy gave the French more leverage against German demands; Moore, 195, 198–199. Insofar as Belgium is concerned, with the exception of the Antwerp, the police refused to participate in raids on Jews. In the Netherlands, the room for maneuver enjoyed by individual policemen was much more restricted, owing to the constant and close control by the German leadership of the Dutch police. In addition, the 22,000 to 25,000 Dutch volunteers in SS units constituted the largest such figure in absolute numbers in comparison with other conquered nations. After the war, Mussert was tried and executed by the Dutch authorities. Moore, 204–206; Hirschfeld, 154, 256–257, 261–262, 275, 283, 287–295, 299; 302–318; Presser, 147, 293, 333–335; Warmbrunn, 85, 91, 122; Fishman, *Journal*, 462.

[9] Hirschfeld, 140–146; De Jong and Stoppelman, 216; De Jong, *Netherlands and the Holocaust*, 5; *The Netherlands and anti-Nazi*, 6; Presser, 27; Warmbrunn, 149, 151; Michman, D., 1048; Hilberg, 372–373.

[10] Moore, 199–203, 206–209; Hirschfeld, 174, 176–177, 179; Presser, 355, 392, who reports that one of the *Kolonne* men gave his occupation on a tax form as "Jew Catcher."

[11] Presser, 350–352; Moore, 200. Boonstra and his fellow "refuseniks" were honored with the "Righteous" title by Yad Vashem; file 3995.

[12] Warmbrunn, 157; Snoek, 126–127, 131–132; Moore, 127–129; Presser, 147–148, 313; Carroll, 541; Snoek, 129.

[13] Moore, 166.

[14] File 8228.

[15] Brasz 85; Fishman, *Wiener,* 32–33; *Journal,* 463; Presser, 543; Michman, D., 1056.

[16] Brasz, 87, 89; Fishman, *Journal,* 471, 473–475.

[17] File 1204.

[18] File 967.

[19] File 1860b.

[20] File 741.

[21] File 422.

[22] File 7406.

[23] File 423.

[24] File 900.

[25] File 6412. The special role of the Jewish people in Christian thinking also affected the behavior of lay Christians, mostly in the Protestant community, as in the following two examples. In Vlaardingen, near Rotterdam, Gerrit and Wilhelmina Don, who sheltered two Jewish boys in their house, stated in 1975: "We feel happy that our God gave us the opportunity to be active to save as many Jews as possible, people of the Old Nation, of whom our Savior Jesus Christ was one. . . . I personally trust in the Word of God, when He promised that his people will not be fully destroyed. So trust in the God of Abraham, Isaac, and Jacob, and He will do well." The other story took place in the city of Haarlem, North Holland province, and involves the already mentioned Ten Boom Calvinist family: Casper ten Boom, known as Grandpa, and his two daughters, Cornelia, known as Corrie or Aunt Kees, and Elisabeth, nicknamed Betsie or Aunt Bep, all of whom became legendary for their commitment to hide Jews in their home, as well as other fugitives from the Nazis. Arrested by the Germans, the eighty-four-year-old Casper held out for ten days before succumbing, dying while in jail. Writing after the war, Corrie ten Boom related that her father Casper, before his arrest, had even joined the Jews in hiding during their prayer sessions. Corrie, who was also arrested, survived the horrors of the Ravensbrück concentration camp. After the liberation, she stated that she wished "to start a Christian home in Israel, that would also serve as a center for tourists. From this center I would like to travel the world not only to evangelize but also in order to promote interest in and prayer for Israel." Files 980 (Don), and 330 (Ten Boom).

[26] File 5809.

[27] File 805.

[28] File 422.

[29] File 900.

[30] File 1204.

[31] File 5809.

[32] File 805.

[33] File 6339a.

[34] File 5854.

[35] File 422.
[36] File 423.
[37] File 48.
[38] File 831.
[39] File 9364.
[40] File 2607.

Chapter 6   Poland

[1] Ben Sasson, 712, 714, 716, 726; Guttman, *Encyclopedia, The Jews,* 1151–1152.

[2] Heller, 3, 50, 71–72, 100, 136–137; Ringelblum, 10–13, 15–16; E. Mendelsohn, *Encyclopaedia Judaica,* 740. Polonsky, states that in the interwar period in Poland, "the largest Jewish community in Europe was clearly in peril"; Polonsky, *The Fate,* 198; Michnik, b7, b9.

[3] Hlond's pastoral letter of Feb. 29, 1936, quoted from *Listy Pasterskie* (Poznań, 1936), 192–193; Modras, 184, 186–189, 190–191; Carroll, 271–289.

[4] Heller, 110–111, 113. See also Dariusz Libionka, "Alien, Hostile, Dangerous: The Image of the Jews and the 'Jewish Question' in the Polish-Catholic Press in the 1930s," *Yad Vashem Studies* 32 (Jerusalem, 2004); 227–267.

[5] Madajczyk, *Encyclopedia,* 1145–1148; Polonsky, *The Fate,* 199, 202.

[6] Madajczyk, *Polish,* 4, 6, 10; Datner, 7, 8; Gumkowski and Leszczynski, 12–15, 17, 20, 28, 31, 49, 73, 162 f., 215–216; Jan T. Gross, 72, 75, 83, 99, 166; Kamenetsky, 6, 43, 84–85, 65, 135, 139, 142 f.; Piotrowski, 39, 45–46, 73, 87, 95–96, 134; Koehl,121, 145, 184, 199; Muszkat, 5, 74; Szerer 16–17, 21, 43, 56; Korbonski, 7. Ringelblum, 6, fn. 13.

[7] Gutman, *Encyclopedia,* 1158, 1162, 1166; Ringelblum, 4–5, 58–59, 81(fn. 20), 82, 88m 165–6 (fn. 8); Trunk, 752.

[8] Turkow, 256 ff., 264–265; Tec, *Dry,* 36, 71; Tec, *East European,* 117; Meed, 255.

[9] Bartoszewski and Lewin, 632, 639–640, 642–643; Iranek-Osmecki, 265–266; Berenstein and Rutkowski, 30–1.

[10] Bartoszewski and Lewin, lxxxiv. Polonsky, *The Fate,* 195, 205, 207; Korbonski, 138; Ringelblum, 10, 35–38, 45, 49–53.

[11] Ringelblum, 7, 133–134, 183–185, 247; Kermish and Krakowski, in Ringelblum, 307–308, n. 1, p. 142; Kermish, in Ringelblum, xxvii, xxxii; Adam Polewka, "To boli," in *W trzecią rocznicę zagłady getta w Krakowie* (Kraków, 1946), 159–160, quoted by Kermish in Ringelbum, xxviii; Irwin-Zarecka, 146–147; Polonsky, 194–196; Prekerowa, *The Fate,* 75–76; Smolar, 43; Adam Shternberg, a Jewish fugitive in the Lwów region, and his wife, passing as Christians, were hiding in the house of the sister of Cardinal Wyszynski (who was also in hiding). She said to them, "There's, however, one important thing that Adolf Hitler is doing; he is attacking the Jewish lice, and we should erect a monument 150 feet tall from pure crystal." Shternberg continues, "My wife and I, who were passing as good Catholics 'agreed' to every word. We only asked, why of crystal? It is so expensive? She, a teacher and educator by profession, answered: 'So that every day, when the sun shines, all Polish

children will see and know the great deed done by Adolf Hitler, who burned the Jews"; Shternberg, 47.

[12] Tec, *Dry* 121–122, 143–144; Donat, 351, 355, 358–359.

[13] Kossak file, 577; Tonini, 81. In 1936, Kossak wrote, "Let's be absolutely honest. We're indifferent to what the Jews believe. It's a dismal and grotesque faith, but we are completely indifferent to it. . . . It's not a question of religion, but of race. We don't like the Jews because they are completely foreign to us, they belong to another race. . . . What needs to be said is this: I'm fighting the Jews for my right to exist on my own land, either I fight or I succumb, not because I'm a Catholic. . . . The Jews represent a real and terrible danger for us, and it's getting worse by the day. . . . Jews are people redeemed by the Holy Blood of Christ. They are my fellow creatures. . . . Polish youth must fight the Jewish invasion *in spite* and not *because* of religious belief"; Tonini, 84; Joseph Kermish, in Ringelblum, 292–293 (on Zofia Kossak's help to Jews); Krakowski, 141; *Zycie na niby* (Warsaw: Ksiazka i Wiedza, 1959), 199, in Smolar, 44. Some of the known antisemites who helped include Jan Mosdorf, Father Marcel Godlewski, and Jan Dobraczynski; in Smolar, 36; Polonsky, *The Fate,* 213; Steinlauf, 40.

[14] Ringelblum, 206–207; Kolbe file 2548; Szereszewska 158, 218, 222. On the rescue of baptized Jews inside the Warsaw ghetto, see Ben-Sasson, 153–173.

[15] Ringelblum, 42–43, 120, 122–124, 126, 128, 133–134; Kermish, in Ringelblum, xxv-vi; Kermish and Krakowski, Ns. 6, 7, in Ringelblum, 33–42; Meed, 114; Gutman, *Encyclopedia,* 1172. Tec writes that in her sample of 308 who survived thanks to help received from 565 Poles, 88 percent reported that at one time or another they experienced threats of and/or actual denunciations. 12 percent reported that they were blackmailed by friends or acquaintances; Tec, *East European,* 117.

[16] Tec, *East European,* 115, 117, 119, 121; Iranek-Osmecki, 271–273; *Yediot Yad Vashem* 12 (Hebrew), January 1957, p. 15. Ringelblum, 1, 245, 288 ff.; Kermish, in Ringelblum, 293–294, 297, 301; Kermish and Krakowski, n. 1, in Ringelblum, 1. Also Prekerowa, *Acta Poloniae,* 153–170, for a discussion of the extent of help to Jews, from a former associate of Zegota. For a discussion of the sheltering of children in convents, see Bogner, *Yad Vashem,* 235–285.

[17] Ringelblum, 247; Prekerowa, *My Brother's,* 73; Meed, 239.

[18] Ringelblum, 209, 211, 240, 242; Polonsky, *The Fate,* 220.

[19] Smolar, 41; Trunk, 776; Polonsky, *The Fate,* 219; Iranek-Osmecki, 250; Meed, 300, 302–303, 326–328; Goldstein 105; Ringelblum, 188; Kermish, in Ringelblum, 310, 314; Kermish and Krakowski 253–256; n. 38 in Ringelblum, 221; n. 35, in Ringelblum, 219; n. 32, in Ringelblum, 217; n. 9, in Ringelblum, 111–112; n. 27, in Ringelblum, 186–187.

[20] Polonsky, *The Fate,* 203–205, 208–209, 211; Trunk 776, 778; Smolar, 37, 40; Krakowski, 142; Kermish and Krakowski, in Ringelblum, xxvii–xxviii, 256–258; n. 41 in Ringelblum, 224–245.

[21] Steinlauf, 52, 61; Smolar, 46, 53, 55; Kermish, in Ringelblum, 315.

[22] Tec, Dry 214; Smolar, 46–47, 53, 55; Wells, 239; Steinlauf 55, 61; Gutman, *Encyclopedia,* 1174, 1176; Trunk, 771; Sfard, 780.

[23] Blonski, 35, 44, 46; Smolar, 67; *New York Sunday Times*, Jan. 20, 1991.

[24] File 3097. Also Bartoszewski and Lewin, 347–351.

[25] File 7668.

[26] File 2396b.

[27] File 6166.

[28] File 1929.

[29] File 2680.

[30] File 1851.

[31] The other nuns, also honored by Yad Vashem, include: Jordana Ostreyko, Celina Roszak, Imelda Neugebauer, Stefania Bednarska, Malgorzata Adamek, Julia Michorowska (Bernadetta), and Diana Frackiewicz (Helena). File 2862. Also Bartoszewski and Lewin, 513–525; Reizl Korchak, *Flames in Ashes* [Hebrew] (Merhavia, Moreshet, 1965), 16.

[32] File 7482.

[33] File 1175.

[34] File 9178. Also, Israel Gutman and Shmuel Krakowki, *Unequal Victims: Poles and Jews During World War II* (New York: Holocaust Library, 1986), 236–237. Bogumila Nojszewska, better known as Sister Maria Ewa of Providence, from the Order of the Sisters of the Immaculate Conception of the Blessed Virgin Mary, the director of the municipal hospital; she sheltered the young son of her Jewish colleague Dr. Kagan in her convent, as well as other Jewish children. The Germans were notified and shot her and the other nuns together with the children in front of an open pit. Part of this story appeared in a deposition by N. Kaplinski in the Yad Vashem Archives (03–2361).

[35] File 4298.

[36] File 3390.

Chapter 7 Lithuania

[1] Garfunkel, 48–50; Neshamit, *Rescue Attempts,* 289–293; Levin, 895–897; *Kivunim* (Hebrew), 30–32, 34, 36–38; Gar, *Encyclopedia*, 368, 374, 378, 382, 385. Helena Kutorgiene, honored as a "Righteous" for saving Jews, stated that "with the exception of a few individuals, all the Lithuanians . . . hate the Jews," and that "her kinsmen acted with such beastly cruelty that . . . I cannot believe my eyes and ears." Neshamit, *Rescue Attempts,* 294.

[2] Gar, *Encyclopedia,* 386–388, 390; Levin, *Kivunim,* 38–39; Garfunkel (Hebrew), 50–53, 55–56; Levin, *Encyclopedia,* 896–899; Arad, *Lithuanian,* 39–47; Gar, *Lithuanian, Details,* 21–23, 25–26; Gar, *Lithuanian, Ostland,* 27–29; Neshamit, *Dapim, Betweeen,* 152–161, 164–175; Neshamit, *Rescue Attempts*, 298. Ona Simaite, a non-Jewish Lithuanian librarian, expressed her shock at the participation of many of her kinsfolk in the murder of Jews, and stated that when she visited Jews in the ghetto (on the pretext of fetching loaned library books), "I told my Jewish acquaintances and friends that if I were in their place, I would hate all the Aryans [non-Jews] without exception. They calmed me by responding that they distinguished between their

friends and enemies"; Garfunkel, 56. No Latvian clerics are listed at Yad Vashem as "Righteous Among the Nations." In Latvia. There were some 70,000 Jews, of whom only an estimated 3,000 survived; a few by hiding with non-Jews; the rest in the forests or in concentration camps. The rest were killed in several large-scale actions in 1941–42, of whom 25,000 were shot in the Rumbula Forest, and 2,800 in Liepaja, on the shores of the Baltic Sea. See Ezergailis Andrew, "The Fate of Latvian Jewry," and Hagar Esther, "Liepaja"; in *Encyclopedia of the Holocaust,* vol. 6; 851–852; 874–876.

[3] Yellin, 420–422; Neshamit, *Dapim, Righteous,* 322–323; Neshamit, *Dapim, Between,* 161–164; Nishemit, *Rescue Attempts,* 312–316, 329–330; Levin, *Kivunim,* 39; Garfunkel 54, 59; Levinsonas and Guzenberg, 44–45, 92–93, 114–117.

[4] File 10500.

[5] File 917.

[6] File 2246.

[7] File 780.

[8] File 1873. After the war, Baltutis left the priesthood, married, and moved to Canada.

[9] File 6897a.

[10] File 8422.

[11] File 7326. See also Binkiene, file 274–276.

[12] File 1741.

[13] File 7616.

[14] File 9071.

[15] File 1856.

[16] File 6327.

Chapter 8 Russia, Belarus, and Ukraine

[1] The discussion on Russia applies to Belorussia as well, today independent Belarus, which became part of the Russian empire in the end of the eighteenth century. Following World War I, the area was split between Poland the Soviet Union; then fully reintegrated in the Soviet Union in September 1939. The 1897 census found Jews concentrated in the major cities, and in the following cities they constituted a majority: Minsk, Mogilev, Vitebsk, Gomel, and Bobruisk. Dinur, 1514–1518; Cholas, 169–170, 172–173; Slutsky, 434–473. Interestingly, the same Pobedonostev, in a conversation with Yelizabeta Pilenko, the future Maria Skobtsova, mentioned in the chapter on France, responded as follows to her question "What is truth?": "The truth is in love. Many think the truth is in love for those who are far away. But love for distant ones isn't love at all. If everyone loved the person next to him, the one who is by his side, then it would not be necessary to simulate a love for those in the crowd, those one does not see. So it is with action. Great acts in the faraway are no acts at all. The real act is the one near to us, small, inconspicuous. It does not consist in a pose, but in self-sacrifice, humility." See Stratton Smith, 34. Pobedonostev evidently saw no contradiction between his highly spiritual notion of love for the stranger and his outspoken radical antisemitism.

[2] Arad, *History,* 763–778, 793.

[3] Gilbert, 32–35.

[4] Arad, *History,* 797–808.

[5] File 4998.

[6] File 5567.

[7] File 5990. See also *Tlusta Memorial book,* Yad Vashem library, 100–101.

[8] File 9109a.

[9] File 6062.

[10] File 9863

[11] File 9485.

[12] File 7761.

[13] File 6304.

[14] Files 421a, c, e. Kurt Lewin has vividly described his war-time experiences, in hiding in several monasteries, in *A Journey Through Illusions* (Santa Barbara, Calif.: Fithian, 1994); especially chap. 2.

[15] Ivan Hirnyj, a former chauffeur for the Uniate Church, testified to his moving Jews (mostly children) from one Uniate home to another, on orders of Abbot Klement, Andrei Sheptizky's brother, who was responsible for the church's monks, and Father Kotiv. This included placing eight Jews in a shoe-factory in Lviv operated by Uniate monks. Michael Kuzyk, known as Brother Laurentiy, confirmed meeting Jews in the shoe factory, where he too was employed.

[16] Kahane, 139.

[17] Following is a summary of these killing raids: "Jail Action" of June 30–July 3, 1941: 7,000 victims; "Petlura Days," July 25–28, 1941: 2,000 victims; Action Against Soviet Sympathizers, July 1941: 2,000; Hostage Action, August 1941: 1,000; Bridge Actions, November 15 to mid-December 1941: 10,000; Expulsion Action, March 1942: 15,000; Blitz Action, June 1942: 6,000–8,000; Major Action, August 1942: 60,000; Special Action, November/December 1942: 15,000; Random Action, January 5–7, 1943: 10,000; Reprisal Action, March 17, 1943: 1,000; isolated actions during March 1943: 3,000; Liquidation Action, April to June 16, 1943: 20,000. Also Yones, chap. 6, 169 ff. Much of the information on the condition of Jews in Lviv under the Nazis is taken from this masterly study. Also, Redlich, *Bitter,* 61–76.

[18] Redlich, *Bitter,* 65.

[19] Redlich, *Bitter,* 64–65; also, Redlich, *Morality,* 150.

[20] Redlich, *Bitter,* 72.

[21] Kahane, 141–142. In a conversation with a French collaborator with Germany, Dr. Frederic, he reports that Sheptitzky agreed that Judaism represented a mortal danger to Christianity, but insisted that the extermination of the Jews was not permissible. Stehle, 125–144; Redlich, *Bitter,* 66, 72.

[22] Stehle, 126.

[23] Redlich, *Bitter,* 67.

[24] Stehle, 128–131; Redlich, *Bitter,* 67. Earlier, on July 22, 1941, Sheptitzky, in a telegram to Berlin, referred to the "New Order" which would be jeopardized by the

cancellation of plans for an independent Ukraine. Stehle, 127–128. Also, Kurt Lewin, *Aliti Mi-Spezia*. Sheptitzky Andrei file, 421

[25] No copy of this letter exists, but Rabbi Kahana claims that Sheptitzky showed it to him during a visit to Sheptitzky's study. It is thought that he handed the letter to Johannes Peters, a German ordained by Sheptitzky in 1937, who became his private secretary, and often traveled to Berlin, where he claimed to have posted the letter. Stehle, 131–132.

[26] Stehlel, 134; and Redlich, *Bitter,* 69.

[27] Stehle, 136.

[28] Following the suppression of the Ukrainian declaration of independence, Bandera urged action against the Germans. Sheptitzky, however, counseled moderation, in the hope of a change of heart by the Germans.

[29] Stehle, 138, and Franz W. Seidler, *Die Kollaboration 1939–1945* (Munich: Herbig, 1995), 484–487.

[30] Redlich, *Bitter,* 72–73. The man's immense popularity (and perhaps "untouchability" from harm) may be gauged by the fact that at his funeral, in November 1944, even a top Communist leader like Nikita Khrushchev (representing a movement and philosophy which Sheptitzky deeply abhorred and feared) was among the hundreds of priests and religious figures who attended.

[31] Stehle, 138; also, file 421.

[32] File 6498b.

[33] File 3930.

[34] Files 2555, 2556.

[35] File 4474.

[36] File 7487.

[37] File 9396.

Chapter 9 Central and Southeastern Europe:
Czech Lands, Slovakia, and Romania

[1] Yahil, 1188.

[2] Yahil, 1193–1194; Herman and Yahil, 964–975; Kulka, 1198–1199; Rothkirchen, 227–230.

[3] File 93. Also, Gilbert, 199–200.

[4] Charles Sidor, the Slovak ambassador to the Vatican, revealed on May 23, 1942, the abuses of Protestant clerics in connection with the conversion of Jews. He reported that in Zilina, a Calvinist pastor, Stefan Puskas, baptized 180 Jews in one day, 110 the next day, and 40 the day after that, for a total of 330 Jews baptized in three days. Similarly, 86 Jews were baptized in the parish of Vrutky, and 160 in Zvolen. In Nitra, another Protestant pastor reportedly baptized 80 Jews, and in Bratislava, a Protestant pastor baptized 276 Jews in one day. Likewise in other locations. The many Jews who flocked to the baptismal font mistakenly hoped that this would save them from deportation to the concentration camps. Morley, *Vatican,* 234.

[5] Kulka Erich, 1195–1197.

[6] Morley, *Vatican,* 72–101, 234; Snoek, 173–174.

[7] Morley, *Vatican,* 77–78.

[8] Morley, *Vatican,* 227.

[9] Haynes, 61; Morley, *Vatican,* 77–81, 85. Also, Eva Fleischner, *Auschwitz: Beginning of a New Era?* (Hoboken, N.J.: Ktav, 1974), 11–12.

[10] Morley, *Vatican,* 92–93.

[11] Morley, *Vatican,* 241–242.

[12] Morley, *Vatican,* 71–101.

[13] File 6625.

[14] File 4993.

[15] File 10018.

[16] File 8700.

[17] File 721.

[18] File 7103.

[19] File 9819.

[20] File 7404. Due to the lack of testimonies by direct witnesses, and the availability only of secondary hearsay accounts, Jan Bakoss's name has so far not been included in the "Righteous" list.

[21] File 10388.

[22] Hilberg, 485–509; Ancel, *Encyclopedia, Transnistria,* 1473–1476; Popisteanu, 1289–1291; Ancel, *Encyclopedia, Romania,* 1295.

[23] Lavi, 386–404; Ancel, *Romania,* 1289–1298.

[24] Morley, *Vatican,* 27–30.

[25] Morley, *Vatican,* 23–47.

[26] File 10060.

Chapter 10   Hungary

[1] Katzburg, 1088–1096.

[2] Hilberg, 524.

[3] Hilberg, 509–554. The pope's message to Horthy on June 25, 1944, read: "Supplications have been addressed to Us from different sources that We should extend all Our influence to shorten and mitigate the sufferings that have, for so long, been peacefully endured on account of their national or racial origin by a great number of unfortunate people belong to this noble and chivalrous nation. . . . Our fatherly heart could not remain insensible to these urgent demands. For this reason we apply to Your Serene Highness, appealing to your noble feelings, in the full trust that Your Serene Highness will do everything in your power to save many unfortunate people from further pain and sorrow." Although the word "Jew" was not mentioned in the message, as Pius XII habitually refrained from mentioning it throughout the war years, Horthy understood him to have meant the Jews. Levai, *Hungarian Jewry,* 26.

[4] Estimates vary slightly between historians. See Braham Randolph, *Encyclopedia of the Holocaust,* vol. 2, 698–703; Vago, 1088–1105.

[5] Braham, *Politics,* 1172.

[6] Hilberg, 514.

[7] Braham, *Politics,* 1176 ff.

[8] Braham, *Politics,* 1178.

[9] Levai, *Hungarian Jewry,* 79.

[10] Levai, *Black Book,* 117–122, 148–152, 197–226, 292–293, 360–361.

[11] Marton file 9471. Also, Braham, *Politics,* 1046–1047.

[12] Levai, *Hungarian Jewry,* 64, 85.

[13] Levai, *Hungarian Jewry,* 98–99.

[14] Braham, *Politics,* 1187.

[15] According to Rabbi Fabian Hershkovits (former chief rabbi of Budapest), Ravasz and his friends intended, by supporting the anti-Jewish law in 1938, to protect Hungary's national interests. "He did not understand that Europe, after Hitler had come to power, had become a powder–magazine; one should not light a match in a powder-magazine; that was Bishop Ravasz's historical mistake." Snoek, 65

[16] According to Father Pirro Scavizzi (1964), Pius XII stated: "Perhaps my solemn protest would have gained me the praise of the civilized world, but I would have brought on to the poor Jews a still more implacable persecution than the one they now suffer. I love the Jews." It is not clear what sort of "implacable persecution" the pope had in mind for people sent to the gas chambers. Levai, *Hungarian Jewry,* 111.

[17] Levai, *Black Book,* 197–201, 223–226; *Hungarian Jewry,* 21–24, 32–34, 36–38.

[18] Rotta file, 7690; Verolino file, 9632.

[19] Ujváry file, 3110.

[20] File 1548.

[21] File 5463.

[22] File 2008.

[23] File 4371.

[24] File 9963.

[25] File 6664.

[26] File 1113.

[27] File 10439a.

[28] File 8116.

[29] File 9957.

[30] Sheetz–Nguyen, 232. File 9962.

[31] File 495. Also, Sheetz–Nguyen, 229, 231. Martin Gilbert reports that Margit Slachta secured protective documents for Aaron Rokeach, the famed Belzer Rebbe, who had fled from Poland, where he lost his family to the Germans. She intervened on his behalf with the head of the Hungarian Secret Service, General Istvan Ujszaszy, and obtained for him both the identity card of a Polish non-Jewish refugee and an army uniform. Using these, he was able to leave Budapest for Romania, and then make his way to Palestine, together with his brother, Rabbi Mordecai, the Bilgoraj Rebbe; Gilbert, 337–338.

[32] File 9962.

[33] File 10107.

[34] File 4879.

[35] File 6611.

[36] File 3180. According to J. Levai, the following Christian institutions sheltered many hundreds of Jewish adults and children at the height of the Arrow Cross terror, most of whom survived, although some were discovered and killed: the Lazarist Fathers, Mother House of the Sisters of Mercy, Sophianum, League of Catholic Housewives, Convent of Our Lady of Sion, Convent of Franciscan Missionary Sisters, Hospital of the Convent of Saint Elizabeth, Society of the Daughters of the Heart of Jesus, Collegium Marianum, Collegum Theresianum, Champagnat Institute of the Marist Brothers, Mother House of the Daughters of the Heavenly Redeemer, Convent of the English Ladies, Central Seminary, House of Mercy in Obuda, Good Shepherd Community, House of the Society of Jesus, House of the Daughters of Divine Love, Institute of St. Teresa, Society of Catholic Craftsmen and Working Youth, Hám János Home of the Szatmar Sisters of Mercy, Convent of the Sacred Heart, Little Boarding House at the Caritas Headquarters, Collegium Josephinum (Society of the Virgin Mary), Union Eucharistica Sisters, St. Aloysius House of the Salesian Fathers, Cistercians Teachers' Training College, Carmelite Sisters. Levai, *Black Book,* 372.

[37] File 722. Also Gilbert, 342–348. As for Jószef Éliász, see file 3912.

[38] File 18.

[39] File 4037.

[40] File 6905.

[41] File 9860.

[42] File 3574.

[43] File 6998.

[44] File 8464.

[45] File 6063.

[46] File 8465.

Chapter 11 The Balkans: Croatia and Serbia, Bulgaria, Greece

[1] Marcus, 868–874; Milan Bulajić, *The Role of the Vatican in the Break–Up of the Yugoslav State* (Belgrad: Strucna Knjiga, 1994), 131, 137.

[2] Shelah, *Encyclopedia, Croatia,* 323–329, and *Jasenovac,* 739–740. Hilberg, 433–442, 453–458.

[3] Menachem Shelah, "The Catholic Church in Croatia, the Vatican and the Murder of the Croatian Jews," in *Holocaust and Genocide Studies* 4, no. 3 (1989), 327.

[4] Stepinac file, 617.

[5] German diplomats in Zagreb, however, considered Stepinac not fully trustworthy, as he definitely opposed Nazi racial ideas, and his political support of Germany was at best lukewarm. In 1944 a stone was thrown through his window. This was interpreted as a warning to Stepinac to mute his criticism of the regime. Stepinac Alojzije, file 617.

[6] Morley, *Vatican,* 147–154, 159–161, 165.

[7] File 5418.

[8] File 4209.

[9] File 9818.

[10] Ben Yaakov, 263–272.

[11] Chary, 188.

[12] Snoek, 182–183; Chary, 74, 189.

[13] Chary, 93–101; Hilberg, 473–484.

[14] Snoek, 186.

[15] Chary, 90, based on Haim Keshales, *Tova se sluchi v onezi dni*, unpublished manuscript at Yad Vashem; Chary, 192.

[16] Arditi, 374; Snoek, 181–193; Chary, 149, 151, 189.

[17] Abraham Alfassi, *Yad Vashem Archives* 03/963, 40–43; Arditi, 374. Also Stefan file, 9375.

[18] Chary, 188.

[19] Gafni and Marcus, 868–878.

[20] Gafni and Marcus, 878–879.

[21] Moissis, 54; Snoek, 28, 162. See also Damaskinos file, 547.

[22] Based on: Snoek, 28, 154–162; Hilberg, 442–453; Mazower, 235–261; Bowman and Kerem, 610–616.

[23] File 7795.

[24] File 1257a.

[25] File 546.

[26] File 549.

[27] File 548.

[28] File 3579a.

Chapter 12   Italy and the Vatican

[1] Milano, 1115–1125.

[2] Milano, 1126–1132; Kertzer, 63.

[3] Zuccotti, *The Italians,* chaps. 3–5; 28 ff.; *Under,* 42–44, Hilberg, 421.

[4] Zuccotti, *The Italians,* 272.

[5] Carroll, 449.

[6] Kertzer, 63, 82–83, 122.

[7] Kertzer, 29, 285; Elon Amos, *Herzl* (New York: Schocken, 1986), 395–396; Carrol, 603; Solomon Grayzel, "Bulls," in *Encyclopaedia Judaica,* vol. 4 (1971),1494–1497.

[8] Morley, *Vatican,* 189; Zuccotti, *Under,* 38, 139.

[9] Zuccotti, *Under,* 45.

[10] Zuccotti, *Under,* 33; Kertzer, 281. See also Georges Passelecq and Bernard Suchecky, *The Hidden Encyclical of Pius XI* (New York: Harcourt, Brace, 1997).

[11] Zuccotti, *Under,* 22–23.

[12] Zuccotti, *Under,* 104–6; Morley, *Vatican,* 138.

[13] Zuccotti, *Under,* 95, 99–100, 105, 109–112, 114; Morley, *Vatican,* 135–143, 146.

[14] Morley, *Vatican,* 146, Zuccotti, *Under,* 112. One report has it that when Dr. Edoardo Senatro, the correspondent of *Osservatore Romano* in Berlin, asked Pius XII whether

he would protest the extermination of the Jews, the pope reportedly answered, "Dear friend, do not forget that millions of Catholics serve in the German armies. Shall I bring them into conflicts of conscience?" Lewy, 304.

[15] Zuccotti, *Under,* 159–165; Morley, *Vatican,* 180–182; Lewy, 302.

[16] Zuccotti, *Under,* 198.

[17] Zuccotti, *Under,* 230.

[18] Zuccotti, *Under,* 205, 229. See also file 2578.

[19] Zuccotti, *Under,* 181, 184–185.

[20] Stefan Schwamm and Aron Kasterszein, before the Italian capitulation, led a group of Jews from Grenoble across the frontier into Italy and brought them to Rome, where they were cared for by Delasem. In Rome, Benoît recognized some of these refugees as people aided by him while in Nice. Schwamm and Kastersztein now collaborated closely with Benoît in aiding Jews in Rome and other cities still under German rule.

[21] Schwamm was deported to a concentration camp, which he luckily survived. Aron Kastersztein was also arrested and deported to Auschwitz, Stutthof, and Buchenwald. He too survived.

[22] Benoit file, 201.

[23] File 6747a.

[24] File 7320.

[25] File 8638.

[26] File 7768.

[27] File 7689.

[28] File 898.

[29] Files 174, 788. Zuccoti, *Under,* 252, 258.

[30] File 6176.

[31] File 7289.

[32] File 929.

[33] File 1989.

[34] Brunacci's introduction to Francesco Santucci's *The Strategy That Saved Assisi* (Assisi: Editrice Minerva, 1999); also, Zuccotti, *Under,* 263.

[35] Files 876 (Niccaci), 1235 (Nicolini), and 1236 (Brunacci). Also, 73–74, in Brunacci's introduction to Santucci's booklet.

[36] File 35.

[37] File 3362.

[38] File 790.

[39] File 1337.

[40] File 8417. Father Paoli had in mind the Jewish religious philosopher Emmanuel Levinas.

[41] Zuccotti, *Under,* 235. Another account mentions Massino Teglio as the Delasem man in Genoa, who worked closely with Repetto. See files 1055 (Repetto) and 1056 (Salvi).

[42] File 6025. Zuccotti also mentions Father Paolo Liggeri, in Milan, who provided the Vittorio Luzzati family with food and shelter. Liggeri was eventually arrested when eleven Jews were found hiding in his Instituto La Casa, and was deported to

Mauthausen, then Dachau; he luckily survived. His Jewish wards were deported to Auschwitz. As for the Capuchin Father Giannantonio Agosti in Milan, he reportedly assisted mostly baptized Jews, whom he hid in his monastery and helped to escape to Switzerland. Arrested, Agosti was deported to Flosenburg and Dachau. He, too, survived. Zuccotti, *Under*, 247–249.

[43] File 284.

[44] File 5533.

[45] File 9955.

[46] Zuccotti, *Under*, 268–269.

[47] Zuccotti, *Under*, 280–284.

[48] Zuccotti, *The Italians,* 213–214; *Under,* 243, 258.

Chapter 13 Switzerland and Scandinavia

[1] Yahil, 1441–1444. In 1944, the Swiss government allowed a trainload of 1,684 Hungarian Jews from Bergen-Belsen ("Kasztner train") to enter the country, and another trainload of 1,200 Jews from Theresienstadt was allowed in as a result of negotiations between former Swiss Federation president Jean-Marie Musy and SS chief Heinrich Himmler. See Musy file, 3841.

[2] Snoek, 209, 211, 219–220.

[3] Snoek, 225–226, 230. For Karl Barth's condemnation of antisemitism, coupled with his negative theology of Judaism, see above, chap. 2, "Germany."

[4] Krantzler, 110, 112.

[5] Visser 't Hooft file 462; Schaffert file 328.

[6] Snoek, 168.

[7] Snoek, 170.

[8] Snoek, 116–119

[9] Koblik, 85–87.

[10] Koblik, 80, 86, 88.

Chapter 15 Post-Holocaust

[1] Franklin H. Littell, "The Holocaust: Tragedy for the Jewish People, Credibility Crisis for Christendom," June 18, 2001, 6.

[2] Kulka and Mendes-Flohr, 502.

[3] Jon D. Levenson, "How Not to Conduct Jewish-Christian Dialogue," *Commentary* 112, no. 5 (December 2001), 32.

[4] Haynes, 17.

[5] Carroll, 59.

[6] Kulka and Mendes-Flohr, in *Judaism and Christianity*, 19.

[7] Baum, *Antisesmitism,* 144, 146; Carroll, 391; Ruether, *Antisemitism,* 228, 230. Ettinger, 41.

[8] Carroll, 552.

[9] Dubois, 502–503.

[10] Dubois, 500. Also, Kulka and Mendes-Flohr, 12, on the connection between eliminating Christianity together with the Jews, as well as the Klaus Scholder statement.

[11] Braham, *Vatican,* 111–112.

[12] Siegman, 258–259.

[13] Braham, *Vatican,* 116–119, 129–131, 135.

[14] Fay, 31, 38. 41–42; Braham, *Vatican,* 99.

[15] *Visit of Pope John Paul II to Yad Vashem,* 30.

[16] *Visit of Pope John Paul II to Yad Vashem,* 14–16.

[17] Rudin, 94

[18] Rudin, 93; Zuccotti, *Under,* 325–326.

[19] *Visit of Pope John Paul II to Yad Vashem* 10; Braham, *Vatican,* 17–18; Braham, *Yad Vashem,* 241–280; Rudin, 91; Morley, *Vatican,* 57.

[20] Fay, 63–70, 75–77, 79.

[21] Patrick, 1104, 1099; Braham, *Vatican,* 37.

[22] Braham, *Vatican,* 36–37.

[23] Visser't Hooft, ed., *First Assembly,* 161; *Third Assembly* (1962); Also, Snoek, 299.

[24] Snoek, 291–292, 294.

[25] Haynes, 51, 127, 133, 139, 153, 184.

[26] Ellis, *Midstream* 47, no. 4, 14; *Midstream* 47, no. 5, 7.

[27] Spiro, 35.

[28] Davies, *Antisemitism,* xvi; Ruether, *Faith,* 246; Siegman, 259–260.

[29] Ruether, *Antisemitism,* 231–233, 240; Baum, *Antisemitism,* 137–138, 145–146; Carroll 30.

[30] Siegman, 245; Werblowsky, 531–536.

[31] Lilla, 63–64. This calls to mind Sigmund Freud's observation that Christians "have not overcome their resentment of the new religion that was forced upon them, but they have shifted this resentment to the source from which Christianity came to them . . . Their hatred of the Jews is basically hatred of Christianity." Freud Sigmund, *Moses and Monotheism* (New York: Vintage, 1967), 11

[32] Dubois, 504.

BIBLIOGRAPHY

Abrahamsen, Samuel. *Norway's Response to the Holocaust*. New York: Holocaust Library, 1991; chap. 11.

Altshuler, Mordechai. "Soviet Union." In *Encyclopedia of the Holocaust* (1971), vol. 4; 1383–1390.

Ancel, Jean. "Romania." In *Encyclopedia of the Holocaust* (1990), vol. 3; 1292–1300.

———. "Transnistria." In *Encyclopedia of the Holocaust* (1990), vol. 4; 1289–1298.

Arad, Yitzhak. *History of the Holocaust: Soviet Union and Annexed Territories* (Hebrew). 2 vols. Jerusalem: Yad Vashem, 2004.

———. "Policies and Execution of the Final Solution in Lithuania" (Hebrew). In *Lithuanian Jewry: The Holocaust*, vol. 4; Tel Aviv, 1984; 39–47.

Arditi, B. J. *The Jews of Bulgaria Under the Nazi Regime, 1940–1944* (Hebrew). Tel Aviv: Israel Press, 1962.

Bankier, David. *The Germans and the Final Solution: Public Opinion Under Nazism*. Oxford: Blackwell, 1992.

Bar Efrat, Pinchas. *Hunters of Jews in the Netherlands During World War II* (Hebrew). Yad Vashem Archives, 103–107F.

Barlas, Chaim. "Operation Aliya from Lithuania." In Z. Shner and S. Derech (eds.), *Dapim*, second series, vol. 1. Beth Lochamei Hagetaoth: Hakibutz Hameuchad, 1970; 246–255.

Bartoszewski, Władyslaw, and Lewin, Zofia. *Righteous Among Nations: How Poles Helped the Jews, 1939–1945*. London: Earls Court, 1969.

Bauer, Yehuda. "Is the Holocaust Explicable?" In *Remembering for the Future*. New York: Pergamon Press, 1988, vol. 2; 1967–1975.

———. *The Holocaust in Historical Perspective*. Seattle: University of Washington Press, 1978.

Baum, Gregory. *Is the New Testament Anti-Semitic? A Re-examination of the New Testament*. Glen Rock, N.J.: Deus Books, 1965.

———. "Catholic Dogma After Auschwitz." In Alan Davies (ed.), *Antisemitism and the Foundations of Christianity*. New York, 1979; 137–150.

Baynes, Norman H. *The Speeches of Adolf Hitler*, vol. 1. New York: Howard Fertig, 1969.

Bédarida, Renée. *Témoignage Chrétien, 1941–1944*. Paris: Librairie des Éditions Ouvrières, 1980.

Bein, Alex. "The Jewish Question in Modern Anti-Semitic Literature: Prelude to the Final Solution." In Yisrael Gutman and Livia Rothkirchen (eds.), *The Catastrophe of European Jewry: Antecedents, History, Reflections.* Jerusalem: Yad Vashem, 1976; 40–89.

Ben-Sasson, Haim H. "Poland." In *Encyclopaedia Judaica* (1971), vol. 13; 710–732.

Ben-Sasson, Havi. "Christians in the Ghetto: All Saints' Church, Birth of the Holy Virgin Mary Church, and the Jews of the Warsaw Ghetto." In *Yad Vashem Studies* 31. Jerusalem, 2003; 153–173.

Ben Yaakov, Avraham. "Bulgaria." In *Encyclopedia of the Holocaust,* vol. 1 (1990), 263–272.

Berenstein, Tatiana, and Rutkowski, Adam. *Assistance to the Jews in Poland, 1939–1945.* Warsaw: Polonia, 1963.

Berman, Adolf-Avraham. "Hayehudim betsad ha-Ari." In *Encyclopedia of the Jewish Diaspora: Poland Series,* Warsaw vol. (Hebrew); 1953; 685–732.

———. *Mimei Hamachtereth* (Hebrew). Tel Aviv: Hamenorah, 1971.

Bethge, Eberhard. "Troubled Self-Interpretation and Uncertain Reception in the Church Struggle." In Franklin Littell and Hubert Locke, *The German Church Struggle and the Holocaust.* San Francisco: Mellen Research University Press, 1990; 167–184.

Binkiene, Sofia (ed.). *Ir be ginklo Kariai.* Vilnius: Mintis, 1967.

Blackburn, Gilmer W. *Education in the Third Reich: A Study of Race and History in Nazi Textbooks.* Albany: State University of New York Press, 1985.

Blonski, Jan. "The Poor Poles Look at the Ghetto." In Antony Polonsky, *"My Brother's Keeper"?* Oxford: Routledge, 1990; 34–52.

Bloom, Solomon F. "The Peasant Caesar." *Commentary* 23 (1957); 406–418.

Blum, Johannes. *Père Bruno Reynders: Héro de la Résistance, Juste des Nations.* Brussels: Les Carrefours de la Cité, 1991.

Blumenkranz, Bernhard. "France." In *Encyclopaedia Judaica* (1971), vol. 7; 7–22.

Boas, Henrietta. "The Persecution and Destruction of Dutch Jewry, 1940–1945." *Yad Vashem Studies* 6 (1967), 359–374.

Bogner, Nahum. "The Convent Children: The Rescue of Jewish Children in Polish Convents During the Holocaust." In *Yad Vashem Studies* 27 (1999); 235–285.

———. *At the Mercy of Strangers* (Hebrew). Jerusalem: Yad Vashem, 2000.

Bollon, Gérard. *Contribution à l'histoire du Chambon-sur-Lignon: Le Foyer Universitaire des Roches et la Rafle de 1943.* Cahiers de la Haute-Loire, 1996.

Bonhoeffer, Dietrich. *No Rusty Swords,* vol. 1 (ed. Edwin H. Robinson). London: Collins, 1965.

Bowman, Steve, and Kerem, Yitzchak. "Greece." In *Encyclopedia of the Holocaust* (1990), vol. 2; 610–616.

Brachfeld, Sylvain. *La Collaboration de la Police Anversoise aux Arrestations des Juifs de la Ville, Pendant l'Occupation Allemande de la Belgique* (1942). Herzlia, Israel: 2002.

———. "Jewish Orphanages in Belgium under the German Occupation." In Dan Michman (ed.), *Belgium and the Holocaust.* Jerusalem: Yad Vashem, 1988; 419–431.

Braham, Randolph L. *The Politics of Genocide: The Holocaust in Hungary,* vol. 2. New York: Columbia University Press, 1981.

————. "The Vatican: Remembering and Forgetting; the Catholic Church and the Jews During the Nazi Era." In Randolph L. Braham (ed.), *The Vatican and the Holocaust*; 13–47.

————. "Christian Churches." In *Yad Vashem Studies* 29, 2001; 241–280.

————. *The Origins of the Holocaust: Christian Anti-Semitism.* New York: Columbia University Press, 1986.

————. *The Vatican and the Holocaust: The Catholic Church and the Jews During the Nazi Era.* New York: Columbia University Press, 2000.

Brasz, Chaya. *Removing the Yellow Badge: The Struggle of a Jewish Community in Postwar Netherlands, 1944–1945.* Jerusalem: Hebrew University Press, 1995.

Braunschweig, Maryvonne, and Gidel, Bernard. *Les Déportés d'Avon: Enquête autour du Film de Louis Malle, « Au Revoir les Enfants ».* Malesherbes: Maury-Imprimeur, 1988.

Broszat, Martin. *German National Socialism, 1919–1945* (trans. Kurt Rosenbaum and Inge Boehm). Santa Barbara, Calif.: Clio, 1966.

Buchheim, Hans. *Glaubenskrise im Dritten Reich: Drei Kapitel nationalsozialistischer Religionspolitik.* Stuttgart: Deutsche Verlags-Anstalt, 1953.

Bullock, Alan. *Hitler: A Study in Tyranny.* New York: Bantam, 1961.

Burton-Nelson, F. "1934: Pivotal Year of the Church Struggle." In *Remembering for the Future.* Oxford: Pergamon Press, 1988. Supplementary volume.

Büttner, Ursula. "The Persecution of Jewish-Christian Families in the Third Reich." *Leo Baeck Year Book* 34 (1989); 267–289.

Carroll, James. *Constantine's Sword: The Church and the Jews.* Boston: Houghton Mifflin, 2001.

Chary, Frederick B. *The Bulgarian Jews and the Final Solution, 1940–1944.* Pittsburgh: University of Pittsburgh Press, 1972.

Cholawski, Shalom. "Belorussia." In *Encyclopedia of the Holocaust.* vol. 1; 169–174.

Cohen, Richard I. "Jews and Christians in France During World War II: A Methodological Essay." In Otto D. Kulka and Paul R. Mendes-Flohr (eds.), *Judaism and Christianity Under the Impact of National Socialism.*

Conway J. S. *The Nazi Persecution of the Churches, 1933–45.* London: Weidenfeld & Nicolson, 1968.

Conzemius, V. "The Church and the Third Reich." In Marcel Baudetteet et al., *The Historical Encyclopedia of World War II* (New York: Facts on File, 1980); 91–100.

Cook, Michael J. "Jesus and the Pharisees— the Problem as It Stands Today." *Journal of Ecumenical Studies* 15 (1978);441–460.

Cummings, Philip W. "Racism." In *Encyclopedia of Philosophy* 7 (1967); 58–61.

Datner, Szymon; Gumkowski, Janusz; and Leszczynski, Kazimierz. *Genocide, 1939–45.* Warsaw: Wydawnictwo Zachodnie, 1962.

Davies, Alan T. "Myths and their Secular Translation." In Alan Davies (ed.), *Antisemitism and the Foundations of Christianity.* New York: Paulist Press, 1979; 188–207.

————. *Anti-Semitism and the Christian Mind: The Crisis of Conscience After Auschwitz.* New York: Herder & Herder, 1969.

Delmaire, Danielle, and Hilaire, Yves-Marie. "Chrétiens et Juifs dans le Nord-Pas-de-Calais Pendant la Seconde Guerre Mondiale." *Revue du Nord*, April–June 1978; 451– 456.

Dequeker, Luc. "Baptism and Conversion of Jews in Belgium, 1939–1945." In Dan Michman (ed.), *Belgium and the Holocaust.* Jerusalem: Yad Vashem, 1988; 235–271.

Dinur, Benzion. "Ukraine." In *Encyclopaedia Judaica.* vol. 15; 1513–1519.

Donat, Alexander. *The Holocaust Kingdom: A Memoir.* London: Secker & Warburg, 1965.

Dubois, Marcel J. "The Challenge of the Holocaust and the History of Salvation." In Otto D. Kulka and Paul R. Mendes-Flohr (eds.), *Judaism and Christianity under the Impact of National Socialism;* 499–512.

Duquesne, Jacques. *Les Catholiques Français sous l'Occupation.* Paris: Bernard Grasset, 1966.

Efroymson, David P. "The Patristic Connection." In Alan Davies (ed.), *Antisemitism and the Foundations of Christianity.* New York, 1979; 98–117.

Ellis, Richard S. "A Jew in Rome: Christian Antisemitism and the Holocaust," Part 1, *Midstream* 47, no. 4 (May–June 2001); 14–24. Part 2, *Midstream* 47, no. 5 (July–August 2001); 6–35.

Ericksen, Robert P. "Christians and the Holocaust: The Wartime Writings of Gerhard Kittel." In *Remembering for the Future; International Scholars' Conference.* Oxford and New York: Pergamon Press, 1988. Supplementary vol.; 90–104.

————. "Genocide, Religion, and Gerhard Kittel." In Omer Bartov and Phyllis Mack, *In God's Name: Genocide and Religion in the Twentieth Century.* New York and Oxford: Berghahn Books, 2001; 62–77.

Ettinger, Shmuel. "Secular Roots of Modern Antisemitism." In Otto D. Kulka, and Paul R. Mendes-Flohr, (eds.), *Judaism and Christianity Under the Impact of National Socialism;* 37–62.

Ezergailis, Andrew. "Latvia." In *Encyclopedia of the Holocaust,* vol. 3 (1990); 849–853.

Fabre, Emile C. *Les Clandestins de Dieu: Cimade, 1939–1945.* Paris: Fayard, 1968.

Fay, William (ed.). *The Bible, the Jews, and the Death of Jesus: A Collection of Catholic Documents.* Washington D.C.: U.S. Conference of Catholic Bishops, 2004.

Fishman, Joel S. "Jewish War Orphans in the Netherlands: The Guardianship Issue, 1945–1950." *Wiener Library Bulletin* 27 (1973–74); 31–36.

————. "The Ecumenical Challenge of Jewish Survival: Pastor Kalma and Postwar Dutch Society, 1946." *Journal of Ecumenical Studies* 15 (1978); 461–476.

Flusser, David. *Jesus.* Jerusalem: Hebrew University Magnes Press, 2001.

Fogelman, Eva. *Conscience and Courage: Rescuers of Jews During the Holocaust.* New York: Doubleday, 1994.

Friedländer, Saul. *Nazi Germany and the Jews.* vol. 1: *The Years of Persecution, 1933– 1939.* New York: Harper Collins, 1997.

Friedman, Philip. *Their Brothers' Keepers.* New York: Holocaust Library, 1978.

———. "Was There an 'Other Germany' During the Nazi Period?" In Philip Friedman, *Roads to Extinction: Essays on the Holocaust.* Philadelphia, Jewish Publication Society, 1980; 422–464.

Gafni, Isaiah, and Marcus, Simon. "Greece." In *Encyclopaedia Judaica,* vol. 7 (1971); 867–882.

Gar, Joseph. "Lithuania." In *Encyclopaedia Judaica* (1971), vol. 11; 374–390.

———. "Details of the Destruction in Lithuania in the Einsatzgruppen Reports" (Hebrew). In *Lithuanian Jewry: The Holocaust,* vol. 4; Tel Aviv, 1984; 21–26.

———. "Ostland and Generalbezirk Lithuania" (Hebrew). In *Lithuanian Jewry: The Holocaust,* vol. 4; Tel Aviv, 1984; 27–29.

Garfinkels, Betty. *Les Belges face à la Persécution Raciale, 1940–1944.* Brussels: Université Libre de Bruxelles, 1965.

Garfunkel, L. "Our Account with the Lithuanians" (Hebrew). In *Lithuanian Jewry: The Holocaust,* vol. 4; Tel Aviv, 1984; 48–60.

Gaston, Lloyd. "Paul and Torah." In Alan Davies (ed.), *Antisemitism and the Foundations of Christianity.* New York, 1979; 48–71.

Gerlach, Wolfgang. *And the Witnesses Were Silent: The Confessing Church and the Persecution of the Jews.* Lincoln: University of Nebraska Press, 2000.

Gilbert, Martin. *The Righteous: The Unsung Heroes of the Holocaust.* London: Doubleday, 2002.

———. *The Holocaust: The Jewish Tragedy.* London: Fontana, 1987.

Gilman, Sander L., and Katz, Steven T. *Anti-Semitism in Times of Crisis.* New York: New York University Press, 1991.

Glenthoj, Jorgen. "On a Much More Central Point: Karl Barth's Attitude to the Aryan Paragraph 1933." In *Remembering for the Future.* Oxford: Pergamon Press, 1988. Supplementary vol.; 139–149.

Goldstein, Bernard. *Five Years in the Warsaw Ghetto.* Garden City, N.Y.: Doubleday, 1961.

———. *The Stars Bear Witness.* London: Gollancz, 1950.

Goldstein, Laurie. "To-be Pope criticized Nazis Early." *International Herald-Tribune;* Sept. 1, 2003.

Gotovitch, José. "Resistance Movements and the Jewish Question." In Dan Michman (ed.), *Belgium and the Holocaust.* Jerusalem: Yad Vashem, 1988; 273–285.

Grayzel, Solomon, "Bulls, Papal." In *Encyclopaedia Judaica,* vol. 4; 1494–97.

Griech-Polelle, Beth. *A Pure Conscience Is Good Enough: Bishop von Galen, the Nazis, and the Question of Resistance.* New Brunswick, N.J.: Rutgers University Press, 1999. Also in Omer Bartov and Phyllis Mack, *In God's Name: Genocide and Religion in the Twentieth Century.* New York: Berghahn Books, 2001; 106–122.

Gross, Natan. *Who Are You, Mr. Grimek?* (Hebrew). Tel Aviv: Moreshet, 1986.

Gross, Jan Tomasz. *Polish Society under German Occupation: The General-gouvernement, 1939–1944.* Princeton, N.J.: Princeton University Press, 1979.

Gumkowski, Janusz, and Leszczynski, Kazimierz, *Poland under Nazi Occupation.* Warsaw: Polonia Publishing House, 1961.

Gurevich, Nikolay. *A Religion Spurned: The Biblical Origins of Anti-Semitism.* Toronto: Anik, 2001.

Gutman, Israel. "The Jews in Poland." In *Encyclopedia of the Holocaust*, vol. 3; 1151–1176.

———. (ed.), *Encyclopedia of the Holocaust.* 4 vols. New York: Macmillan, 1990.

Gutteridge, Richard. *Open Thy Mouth for the Dumb! The German Evangelical Church and the Jews, 1879–1950.* Oxford: Basil Blackwell, 1976.

Hackel, Sergei. *Pearl of Great Price: The Life of Mother Maria Skobtsova, 1891–1945.* London: Darton, Longman & Todd, 1981.

Hagemann, Friedrich. *Prozess Bernhard Lichtenberg: Ein Leben in Dokumenten.* Berlin: Morus, 1977.

Hallie, Philip. *Lest Innocent Blood Be Shed.* New York: Harper & Row, 1979.

Hare, Douglas R. "The Rejection of the Jews." In Alan Davies (ed.), *Antisemitism and the Foundations of Christianity.* New York, 1979; 27–47.

Haynes, Stephen R. *Jews and the Christian Imagination: Reluctant Witnesses.* New York: Macmillan, 1995.

Heller, Celia S. *On the Edge of Destruction: Jews of Poland Between the Two World Wars.* New York: Columbia University Press, 1977.

Henry, Patrick. *Daniel's Choice: Daniel Trocmé (1912–1944),* 2003

Herman, Jan, and Yahil, Chaim. "Prague." In *Encyclopaedia Judaica* vol. 13; 964–975.

Heschel, Susannah. "When Jesus Was an Aryan; The Protestant Church and Antisemitic Propaganda." In Omer Bartov and Phyllis Mack, *In God's Name: Genocide and Religion in the Twentieth Century.* New York: Berghahn Books, 2001; 79–105.

Hilberg, Raul. *The Destruction of the European Jews.* New York: Harper & Row, 1979.

Hirschfeld, Gerhard. *Nazi Rule and Dutch Collaboration: The Netherlands under German Occupation, 1940–1945.* Trans. by L. Wilmot. Oxford: Berg, 1988.

Hoelzel, Alfred. "Thomas Mann and the Holocaust." In *Remembering for the Future; International Scholars' Conference, 10–13 July 1988, Oxford.* Oxford: Pergamon Press, 1988. vol. 2; 1496–1503.

Inkeles, Alex. "The Totalitarian Mystique: Some Impressions of the Dynamics of Totalitarian Society." In Carl J. Friedrich (ed.), *Totalitarianism.* New York: Grosset & Dunlap, 1964; 87–108

Iranek-Osmecki, Kazimierz. *He Who Saves One Life.* New York: Crown, 1971.

Irwin-Zarecka, Iwona. "Poland, After the Holocaust." In *Remembering for the Future.* Oxford: Pergamon Press, 1988. vol. 1; 143–155.

Isaac, Jules. *Jesus and Israel* (trans. By Sally Gran). New York: Holt, Rinehart & Winston, 1971.

———. *Has Anti-Semitism Roots in Christianity?* New York: National Conference of Christians and Jews, 1962.

Jansen, Hans. "Anti-Semitism in the Amiable Guise of Theological Philo-Semitism in Karl Barth's Israel Theology Before and After Auschwitz." In *Remembering for the Future*. Oxford: Pergamon Press, 1988. vol. 1; 72–79.

Jong de, Louis. "The Netherlands and Auschwitz." *Yad Vashem Studies* 7 (1968); 39–65; also in Yisrael Gutman and Livia Rothkirchen (eds.). *The Catastrophe of European Jewry*. Jerusalem: Yad Vashem, 1976; 299–318.

———. "The Destruction of Dutch Jewry." Address given at the Fourth World Congress of Jewish Studies, Jerusalem, July 26, 1965.

———. "The Netherlands and Anti-Nazi Resistance." Article sent to author.

———. "The Netherlands and the Holocaust." Article sent to author.

———. and Stoppelman, W. F. *The Lion Rampant: The Story of Holland's Resistance to the Nazis*. New York: Querido, 1943.

Joutard, Philippe; Poujol, Jacques; and Cabanel, Patrick, *Cévennes: Têrre de Refuge 1940–1944*. Presses du Languedoc/Club Cévenol, 1987.

Kahane, David. *Lvov Ghetto Diary*. Amherst: University of Massachusetts Press, 1990.

Kamenetsky, Ihor. *Secret Nazi Plans for Eastern Europe*. New York: Bookman Associates, 1961.

Katz, Jacob. "Christian-Jewish Antagonism on the Eve of the Modern Era." In Otto D. Kulka and Paul R. Mendes-Flohr (eds.), *Judaism and Christianity under the Impact of National Socialism;* 27–36.

Katzburg, Nathaniel, "Hungary," *Encyclopaedia Judaica*, vol. 8 (1971); 1088–1096.

Kelley, James P. "The Best of the German Gentiles: Dietrich Bonhoeffer and the Rights of Jews in Hitler's Germany." In *Remembering for the Future*. Oxford: Pergamon Press, 1988. vol. 1; 80–92.

Kermish, Joseph. "Yachasom shel Polanim el Hayehudim Bimei Shoah Umered" (Hebrew), in *Dapim Lecheker Hashoah ve-Hamered* 2b, 1973 (Beit Lohamei Hagetaot); 248– 258.

Kershaw, Ian. *Popular Opinion and Political Dissent in the Third Reich: Bavaria, 1933–1945*. Oxford: Clarendon, 1983.

Kertzer, David I. *The Popes Against the Jews: The Vatican's Role in the Rise of Modern Anti-Semitism*. New York: Alfred A. Knopf, 2001.

Koblik, Steven. *The Stones Cry Out: Sweden's Response to the Persecution of the Jews, 1933–1945*. New York: Holocaust Library, 1988.

Koehl, Robert L. *RKFDV: German Resettlement and Population Policy, 1939–1945*. Cambridge, Mass.: Harvard University Press, 1957.

Korbonski, Stefan. *The Polish Underground State, 1939–1945*. New York: Columbia University Press, 1978.

Krakauer, Max. *Lichter im Dunkel*. Stuttgart: Quell, 1980.

Krakowski, Samuel. "The Polish Underground and the Extermination of the Jews." In Antony Polonsky et al. *Poles, Jews, Socialists: The Failure of an Ideal*. London: Littman Library of Jewish Civilization, vol. 9, 1996; 138–147.

Kranzler, David. *The Man Who Stopped the Trains to Auschwitz*. Syracuse, N.Y.: Syracuse University Press, 2000.

Kuhn, Helmut. "German Philosophy and National Socialism." In *Encyclopedia of Philosophy* 3 (1967); 309–316.

Kulka, Erich. "Protectorate of Bohemia-Moravia." In *Encyclopaedia Judaica,* vol. 5 (1971); 1198–99.

Kulka, Otto D., and Hildesheimer, Esriel. "Germany." In Yisrael Gutman (ed.), *Encyclopedia of the Holocaust.* New York: Macmillan, 1990. vol. 2; 557–575.

Kulka, Otto D., and Mendes-Flohr, Paul R. (eds.) *Judaism and Christianity under the Impact of National Socialism.* Jerusalem: Historical Society of Israel and Zalman Shazar Center for Jewish History, 1987.

Kurth, Gertrud M. "The Jew and Adolf Hitler." *Psychoanalytic Quarterly* 16 (1947), vol. 1; 11–32.

Landau, Maria, and Sigaar, Jacqueline. *Le Réseau Marcel: Histoire d'un Réseau Juif Clandestin.* Paris, 2002.

Latour, Anny, *The Jewish Resistance in France (1940–1944).* New York: Holocaust Library, 1970.

Laureys, Véronique. "The Attitude of the Belgian Government-in-Exile in London Toward the Jews and the Jewish Question During World War II." In Dan Michman (ed.), *Belgium and the Holocaust.* Jerusalem: Yad Vashem, 1988; 287–306.

Lavi, Theodor. "Rumania." In *Encyclopaedia Judaica,* vol. 14 (1971); 386–404.

Lazar, Moshe. "The Lamb and the Scapegoat: The Dehumanization of the Jews in Medieval Propaganda Imagery." In Sander L. Gilman and Steven T. Katz, *Anti-Semitism in Times of Crisis.* New York: New York University Press, 1991; 38–80.

Lazare, Lucien. *Le Livre des Justes.* Paris: Jean-Claude Lattès, 1993.

———. *Rescue as Resistance: How Jewish Organizations Fought the Holocaust in France.* New York: Columbia University Press, 1996.

———. "Belgian Jews in France, 1940–1944." In Dan Michman (ed.), *Belgium and the Holocaust.* Jerusalem: Yad Vashem, 1988; 445–455.

Leboucher Fernande, *Incredible Mission.* Trans. by J. F. Bernard. Garden City, N. Y.: Doubleday, 1969.

Le Plateau et l'Acceuil des Juifs Réfugiés 1940–1945. Chambon-sur-Lignon: Société d'Histoire de la Montagne, 1990.

Le Plateau Vivarais-Lignon, Acceuil et Résistance 1939–1944: Colloque du 12, 13, 14 Octobre 1990. Chambon-sur-Lignon, 1990.

Leuner, H. D. *When Compassion Was a Crime: Germany's Silent Heroes, 1933–45.* London: Oswald Wolff, 1966.

Levai, Jenö. *Black Book on the Martyrdom of Hungarian Jewry.* Zurich: Central European Times, 1948.

———. *Hungarian Jewry and the Papacy.* Dublin: Clonmore & Reynolds, 1968.

Levin, Dov, "Lithuania." In *Encyclopedia of the Holocaust,* vol. 3 (1990); 895–899.

"On Relations Between Lithuanians and Jews During World War II" (Hebrew), *Kivunim* 2 (1979); 29–43.

Levinsonas, Josifas, and Guzenberg, Irina, *Hands Bringing Life and Bread,* vol. 2. Vilnius: Vilna Gaon State Jewish Museum, 1999.

Lévy, Paul, *Elie Bloch: Être juif sous l'Occupation.* La Creche: Geste, 1999.

Lewy, Guenther, *The Catholic Church and Nazi Germany.* New York: McGraw-Hill, 1964.

Libionka, Dariusz., "Alien, Hostile, Dangerous: The Image of the Jews and the 'Jewish Question' in the Polish-Catholic Press in the 1930s." *Yad Vashem Studies* 32 (2004); 227–267.

Lilla, Mark, "A Battle for Religion." *New York Review of Books.* vol. 49, no. 19 (December 5, 2002); 63–64.

Lindsay, Mark R. *Covenanted Solidarity: The Theological Basis of Karl Barth's Opposition to Nazi Antisemitism and the Holocaust.* New York: Peter Lang, 2001.

Littell, Franklin H. "Christian Antisemitism and the Holocaust." In Otto D. Kulka and Paul R. Mendes-Flohr (eds.), *Judaism and Christianity under the Impact of National Socialism;* 513–530.

———. and Locke, Hubert G. *The German Church Struggle and the Holocaust.* San Francisco: Mellen Research University Press, 1990.

Loeblowitz-Lennard, Henry. "The Jew as Symbol." *Psychoanalytic Quarterly* 16 (1947); 1:33–38.

Lowrie, Donald A. *The Hunted Children.* New York: Norton, 1963

Lyons, James R. "Idolatry: The Impact of National Socialism on the Churches of Nazi Europe." In *Remembering for the Future.* Oxford: Pergamon Press, 1988. vol. 2; 1368–1378.

Maccoby, Hyam. "Origins of Anti-Semitism." In Braham Randolph (ed.), *The Vatican and the Holocaust: The Catholic Church and the Jews During the Nazi Era.* New York: Columbia University Press, 2000; 1–11.

Madajczyk, Czeslaw. "Generalplan Ost." *Polish Western Affairs* 3, no. 2 (1962), Posznan.

———. "Poland." In *Encyclopedia of the Holocaust,* vol. 3; 1143–1151.

Maltitz, Horst von. *The Evolution of Hitler's Germany: The Ideology, the Personality, the Moment.* New York: McGraw-Hill, 1973.

Marchione, Margherita. *Yours Is a Precious Witness: Memoirs of Jews and Catholics in Wartime Italy.* New York: Paulist Press, 1997.

Marcus, Simon. "Yugoslavia." In *Encyclopedia of the Holocaust,* vol. 16; 868–874.

———. "Greece." In *Encyclopedia of the Holocaust* (1990), vol. 7; 868–880.

Mann, H.G. *Prozess Bernhard Lichtenberg: Ein Leben in Dokumenten.* Berlin: Morus, 1977.

Marrus, Michael R. "French Churches and the Persecution of Jews in France, 1940–1944." In Otto D. Kulka and Paul R. Mendes-Flohr (eds.), *Judaism and Christianity under the Impact of National Socialism;* 305–325.

———. and Paxon, Robert O. *Vichy France and the Jews.* New York: Basic Books, 1981

Massing, Paul W. *Rehearsal for Destruction: a Study of Political Anti-Semitism in Imperial Germany.* New York: Howard Fertig, 1967.

Matteazzi, Florence. *L'Attitude du Clergé face à la Shoa dans le diocèse de Liège (1940–1945).* Catholic University of Louvain, 1995–96.

May, Herbert G., and Metzger, Bruce M. *The New Oxford Annotated Bible with Apocrypha: Revised Standard Version.* New York: Oxford University Press, 1977.

Mazower, Mark. *Inside Hitler's Greece,* New Haven, Conn.: Yale University Press, 1993; chap. 19, 235–261.

Meagher, John C. "As the Twig was Bent." In Alan Davies (ed.), *Antisemitism and the Foundations of Christianity.* New York, 1979; 1–26.

Meed, Vladka. *On Both Sides of the Wall: Memoirs from the Warsaw Ghetto.* Beit Lohamei Hagettaot, 1972.

Meiri, Adam. "Hakenesiyah bepolin—ladin." *Maariv,* September 1, 1987; 10.

Menut, Georges. "André Trocmé, Un Violent Vaincu par Dieu." In *Le Plateau Vivarais-Lignon: Acceuil et Résistance 1939–1944; Colloque du 12, 13, 14 octobre 1990.* Chambon-sur-Lignon, 1990.

Michaelis, Meir, and Carpi, Daniel. "Italy." In *Encyclopedia of the Holocaust,* vol. 3; 721–730.

Michman, Dan. "Belgium." In Yisrael Gutman (ed.) *Encyclopedia of the Holocaust,* vol. 1. New York: Macmillan, 1990; 160–168.

———. *Belgium and the Holocaust: Jews, Belgians, Germans.* Jerusalem: Yad Vashem, 1998.

———. "Changes in the Dutch Attitude Towards the Jews on the Eve of the Holocaust" (Hebrew). *Studies in Dutch Jewish History* 3 (1981); 247–262.

Michman, Jozeph. "The Netherlands." In Yisrael Gutman (ed.), *Encyclopedia of the Holocaust,* vol. 3. New York, Macmillan, 1990; 1045–1057.

Michnik, Adam. "Poles and the Jews: How Deep the Guilt?" *New York Times,* March 17, 2001, B7–9.

Milano, Attilio. "Italy." In *Encyclopaedia Judaica,* vol. 9; 1116–32.

Modras, Ronald. "The Catholic Church in Poland and Antisemitism, 1933–1939: Responses to Violence at the Universities and in the Streets." In *Remembering for the Future.* Oxford: Pergamon Press, 1988. vol. 1; 183–195.

Moissis, Asscher. "La situation des Communautés juives en Grèce." In *Les Juifs en Europe.* Paris: Editions du Centre, 1949; 47–54.

Moore, Bob. *Victims and Survivors: The Nazi Persecution of the Jews in the Netherlands, 1940–1945.* London: Arnold, 1997.

Morley, John F. *Vatican Diplomacy and the Jews During the Holocaust 1939–1945.* New York: Ktav, 1980.

———. "Reaction of a Catholic Theologian to the Vatican's 'We Remember' Document." In Randolph L. Braham (ed.), *The Vatican and the Holocaust;* 47–69.

Mosse, George L. *Germans and Jews: The Right, the Left and the Search for a Third Force in Pre-Nazi Germany.* New York: Howard Fertig, 1970.

———. *Toward the Final Solution: A History of European Racism.* New York: Howard Fertig, 1978.

———. *Nazism: A Historical and Comparative Analysis of National Socialism.* New Brunswick, N.J.: Transaction Books, 1978.

Müller, Ingo. *Hitler's Justice: The Courts in the Third Reich.* Cambridge, Mass.: Harvard University Press, 1991.

Muszkat, Marian. *Polish Charges Against German War Crimes.* Warsaw: Glowna Komisja Badania Niemieckich Zbrodni Wojennych w Polsce (Polish Main National Office for the Investigation of German War Crimes in Poland), 1948.

Niemöller, Martin. *Here Stand I.* Trans. by Jane Lymburn. Chicago: Willett, Clark, 1937.

Neshamit, Sara. "The Righteous Among the Nations in Occupied Lithuania" (Hebrew). In *Dapim,* second series, vol. 1. Beth Lochamei Hagetaoth: Hakibutz Hameuchad, 1970; 317–324.

———. "Between Collaboration and Resistance in Occupied Lithuania" (Hebrew). In *Dapim,* Second Series, vol. 1. Beth Lochamei Hagetaoth: Hakibutz Hameuchad, 1970; 152–177.

———. "Rescue in Lithuania During the Nazi Occupation." In Yisrael Gutman and E. Zuroff, *Rescue Attempts During the Holocaust.* Jerusalem: Yad Vashem, 1977; 289–331.

Noakes, Jeremy. "The Development of Nazi Policy Towards the German-Jewish 'Mischlinge', 1933–1945." *Leo Baeck Year Book* 34 (1989); 291–354.

Nodot, René. *Les Enfants ne Partirons Pas! Témoignages sur la déportation des Juifs, Lyon et Région 1942–1943.* Lyon: Nouvelle Lyonnaise, 1970

———. *Résistance Non-Violente, 1940–1944.* Lyon, 1978.

Ogiermann, Otto. *Bis zum Letzten Atemzug: das Leben und Aufbegehren des Priesters Bernhard Lichtenberg.* Leipzig: St. Benno, 1983.

Oliner, Samuel, and Oliner, Pearl. *The Altruistic Personality: Rescuers of Jews in Nazi Europe.* New York: Free Press, 1988.

Paldiel, Mordecai. *The Path of the Righteous: Gentile Rescuers of Jews During the Holocaust.* Hoboken, N.J.: 1993.

———. *Saving the Jews: Amazing Stories of Men and Women Who Defied the Final Solution.* Rockville, Md.: Schreiber Publishing, 2000.

———. *Sheltering the Jews: Stories of Holocaust Rescuers.* Minneapolis: Fortress, 1996

———. "Sparks of Light." In Richard Libowitz (ed.), *Faith and Freedom.* New York: Pergamon Press, 1987; 45–69.

Papeleux, Léon. "Le Réseau Van den Berg qui Sauva des Centaines des Juifs." *La Vie Wallonne* 58 (1981); 129–208.

Parkes, James. *The Conflict of the Church and the Synagogue: A Study in the Origins of Antisemitism.* New York: Sepher Hermon, 1974.

Patrick, Henry. "The French Catholic Church's Apology." *French Review* 72, no. 6 (May 1999); 1099–1105.

Perrot, Alain; Nodot, René; and Pierrier, Jean-François. *Ma Vie pour la Tienne: Epopée Oecuménique de la Résistance chrétienne au Secours des Juifs Pourchassés et au Service de la Libération de la France.* Geneva: Le Courrier, 1987.

Perthuis, Valérie. *Le Sauvetage des Enfants Juifs de Vénissieux: le 26 août 1942.* Lyon: Éditions Lyonnaises d'Art et d'Histoire, 1997.

Phayer, Michael, and Fleischner, Eva. *Cries in the Night: Women Who Challenged the Holocaust*. Kansas City: Sheed & Ward, 1997.

Pierrard, Pierre. *Juifs et Catholiques Français: de Drumont à Jules Isaac (1886–1945)*. Paris: Fayard, 1970.

Piotrowski, Stanislaw. *Hans Frank's Diary*. Warsaw: Panstwowe Wydawnictwo Naukowe, 1961.

Polonsky, Antony. "Beyond Condemnation, Apologetics and Apologies: On the Complexity of Polish Behavior Toward the Jews During the Second World War." In Jonathan Frankel (ed.), *The Fate of the European Jews, 1939–1945: Continuity or Contingency?* New York: Oxford University Press, 1997; 190–224.

———. *"My Brother's Keeper"? Recent Polish Debates on the Holocaust*. Oxford: Routledge, 1990.

Popisteanu, Cristian. "Romania." In *Encyclopedia of the Holocaust*, vol. 3; 1289–1291.

Porter, Clifford F. "The Interpretations of Nazi Totalitarianism by Hannah Arendt, Leo Strauss, and Eric Voegelin." Doctoral diss., Claremont University Press, 2000.

Prekerowa, Teresa. "The 'Just' and the 'Passive'," in Antony Polonsky (ed.), *"My Brother's Keeper?" Recent Polish Debates on the Holocaust*. Oxford: Routledge, 1990; 72–80.

———. "Who Helped Jews During the Holocaust in Poland?" *Acta Poloniae Historica* 76 (1997); 153–170.

Presser, Jacob. *The Destruction of the Dutch Jews*. Trans. by A. Pomerans. New York: Dutton, 1969.

Pulzer, Peter G. *The Rise of Political Anti-Semitism in Germany and Austria*. New York: John Wiley, 1964.

Rayner, John D. *Towards Mutual Understanding Between Jews and Christians*. London: James Clarke, 1960.

Redlich, Shimon. "Metropolitan Andrii Sheptyts'kyi and the Complexities of Ukrainian Jewish Relations." In Zvi Gitelman (ed.), *Bitter Legacy: Confronting the Holocaust in the USSR*. Bloomington: Indiana University Press, 1977; 61–76.

———. "Sheptyts'kyi and the Jews During World War II." in Paul R. Magocsi (ed.), *Morality and Reality: The Life and Times of Andrei Sheptyts'kyi*. Edmonton: University of Alberta, 1989; 145–162.

Remembering for the Future: Jews and Christians During and After the Holocaust, 10–13 July, 1988. Oxford and New York: Pergamon Press, 1988.

Rencontre: Chrétiens et Juifs. vol. 71, 3ème Trimestre, 1981.

Résistance Non-Violente: La Filière de Douvaine. Douvaine, 1987.

Ribière, Germaine. *L'Affaire Finaly «Ce que j'ai vécu»*. Paris: Centre de Documentation Juive Contemporarine, 1998.

Riesel, Arye. "Re-education of War-Orphaned Jewish Children and Adolescents in Children's and Youth Homes in Belgium, 1945–1949." In Dan Michman (ed.), *Belgium and the Holocaust*. Jerusalem: Yad Vashem, 1988; 483–497.

Ringelblum, Emmanuel. *Polish-Jewish Relations During the Second World War*. Jerusalem: Yad Vashem, 1974.

Rittner, Carol, and Myers, Sondra. *The Courage to Care: Rescuers of Jews During the Holocaust.* New York: New York University Press, 1986.

Robertson, Edwin. "A Study of Dietrich Bonhoeffer and the Jews, January–April 1933." In *Remembering for the Future.* Oxford: Pergamon Press, 1988. vol. 1; 121–129.

Rosenkranz, Herbert. "Austria." In Yisrael Gutman (ed.), *Encyclopedia of the Holocaust,* vol. 1. New York: Macmillan, 1990; 126–132.

Rothkirchen, Livia. "The Protectorate Government and the 'Jewish Question,' 1939–1941," *Yad Vashem Studies* 27 (1999); 331–362.

———. "Bohemia and Moravia." In *Encyclopedia of the Holocaust,* vol. 1 (1990); 227–230.

Rudin, James. "Reaction of a Jewish Theologian to the Vatican's 'We Remember' Document," in Randolph L. Braham (ed.), *The Vatican and the Holocaust,* 241–280.

Ruether, Rosemary R. *Faith and Fratricide: The Theological Roots of Anti-Semitism.* London: Search, 1975.

———. "The 'Faith and Fratricide' Discussion: Old Problems and New Dimensions." In Alan Davies (ed.), *Antisemitism and the Foundations of Christianity.* New York, 1979; 230–257.

———. "Anti-Semitism and Christian Theology." In Eva Fleischner (ed.), *Auschwitz: Beginning of a New Era?* New York: Cathedral of St. John the Divine, 1977; 79–92.

Ryan, Michael D. "Hitler's Challenge to the Churches: A Theological Political Analysis of *Mein Kampf,*" in Franklin H. Littell and Hubert G. Locke (eds.), *The German Church Struggle and the Holocaust.* Detroit: Wayne State University Press, 1974; 148–164.

Saerens, Lieven. "The Attitude of the Belgian Roman Catholic Clergy Toward the Jews Prior to the Occupation." In Dan Michman (ed.), *Belgium and the Holocaust.* Jerusalem: Yad Vashem, 1988; 117–157.

———. "Antwerp's Attitude Toward the Jews from 1918 to 1940 and Its Implications for the Period of the Occupation." In Dan Michman (ed.), *Belgium and the Holocaust.* Jerusalem: Yad Vashem, 1988; 159–194.

Sandmel, Samuel. *Anti-Semitism in the New Testament?* Philadelphia: Fortress Press, 1978.

Schlette, Antonia R. "Chamberlain, Houston Stewart." In *Encyclopedia of Philosophy,* vol. 2 (1967); 72–73.

Schleunes, Karl A. (ed.). *Legislating the Holocaust: The Bernhard Loesener Memoirs and Supporting Documents.* Boulder. Col.: Westview Press, 2001.

Scholder, Klaus. *The Churches and the Third Reich.* vol. 1. London: SCM Press, 1987.

Schwarzfuchs, Simon R. "France: The Modern Period." In *Encyclopaedia Judaica* 7: 22–31.

———. *"Belgium,"* In *Encyclopaedia Judaica* 4: 416–418.

Sfard, David. "Poland." In *Encyclopaedia Judaica* 13: 778–785.

Sheetz-Nguyen, Jessica A. "Transcending Boundaries: Hungarian Catholic Religious Women and the 'Persecuted Ones' " In Omer Bartov and Phyllis Mack, *In God's Name: Genocide and Religion in the Twentieth Century.* New York: Berghahn Book, 2001; 222–242.

Stehle, Hansjakob. "Sheptyts'kyi and the German Regime." In Paul Magocsi (ed.). *Morality* and Reality: The Life and Times of Andrei Sheptyts'kyi. Edmonton: University of Alberta, 1989.

Shelah, Menachem. "Croatia." In *Encyclopedia of the Holocaust,* vol. 1 (1990); 323–329. "Jasenovac." In *Encyclopedia of the Holocaust,* vol. 2 (1990); 739–740.

Siegman, Henry. "A Decade of Catholic-Jewish Relations: A Reassessment." *Journal of Ecumenical Studies* 15 (1978), 243–260.

Slutsky, Yehuda. "Russia." In *Encyclopaedia Judaica,* vol. 14; 434–493.

Smolar, Aleksander. "Jews as a Polish Problem." *Daedalus* 116 (Spring 1987), 31–73.

Snoek, Johan M. *The Grey Book.* Assen, Netherlands: Van Gorcum, 1969.

Spicer, Kevin P. "Choosing Between God and Satan: The German Catholic Clergy of Berlin and the Third Reich." Doctoral diss., Boston College, 2000.

———. "To Serve God or Hitler." In John K. Roth and Elisabeth Maxwell (eds.), *Remembering for the Future,* vol. 2. New York: Palgrave, 2001; 493–508.

Spiro, Jack D. "The *Merchant of Venice* and Shylock's 'Christian Problem'." *Midstream* 47, no. 4 (July–August 2001); 33–35.

Steinberg, Lucien. *Le Comité de Défense des Juifs en Belgique 1942–1944.* Université de Bruxelles: Brussels, 1973.

Steinberg, Maxime. "The Judenpolitik in Belgium Within the West European Context." In Dan Michman (ed.), *Belgium and the Holocaust.* Jerusalem: Yad Vashem, 1988; 199–221.

———. "The Jews in the Years 1940–1944: Three Strategies for Coping with a Tragedy." In Dan Michman (ed.), *Belgium and the Holocaust.* Jerusalem: Yad Vashem, 1988; 347–372.

———. *L'Etoile et le Fusil: La Question Juive 1940–1942.* Brussels: Vie Ouvriere, 1983.

———. *Le Dossier Bruxelles Auschwitz: La Police SS et l'Extermination des Juifs de Belgique.* Brussels, 1980.

———. *Extermination, Sauvetage et Résistance des Juifs de Belgique.* Brussels, 1970.

———. "Faced with the Final Solution in Occupied Belgium: The Church's Silence and Christian Action." In *Remembering for the Future,* Supplementary vol. Oxford: Permagon, 1988.

———. "The Trap of Legality: The Association of the Jews in Belgium." In Yisrael Gutman and Cynthia Haft (eds.), *Patterns of Jewish Leadership in Nazi Europe, 1933–1945.* Jerusalem: Yad Vashem, 1979; 353–376.

Steinlauf, Michael. *Bondage to the Dead: Poland and the Memory of the Holocaust.* Syracuse, N.Y.: Syracuse University Press, 1997.

Sternberg, Itzhak. *Bezehut Acheret (Under Assumed Identity).* Beth Lohamei Hagetaot, 1984.

Stratton-Smith, T. *The Rebel Nun.* London: Pan Books, 1967.

"Symposium: A New Christian Document on Christian-Jewish Relations." *Midstream,* January 2003.

Szerer, Mieczyslaw. *Republic of Poland: German Crimes Against Poland.* London, 1945.

Szereszewska, Helena. *The Last Chapter* (Hebrew). Beit Lochamei Hagetaot, 1980.

Tal, Uriel. *"Political Faith" of Nazism Prior to the Holocaust.* Tel Aviv: Tel Aviv University Press, 1978.

———. *Jews and Christians in the Second Reich (1870–1914): A Study in the Rise of German Totalitarianism* (Hebrew). Jerusalem: Hebrew University Press, 1969.

———. "Forms of Pseudo-Religion in the German *Kulturbereich* Prior to the Holocaust." *Immanuel* (Jerusalem: Ecumenical Research Fraternity), no. 3, 1974; 68–73.

———. "On the Study of the Holocaust and Genocide." *Yad Vashem Studies* 13 (1979); 7–52.

———. "Aspects of Consecration of Politics in the Nazi Era." In Otto D. Kulka, and Paul R. Mendes-Flohr (eds.), *Judaism and Christianity under the Impact of National Socialism;* 63–95.

———. *On Structures of "Political Theology and Myth" in Germany Prior to the Holocaust.* New York: Holocaust Conference, 1975.

———. "Anti-Christian Anti-Semitism." In Yisrael Gutman and Livia Rothkirchen (eds.), *The Catastrophe of European Jewry: Antecedents, History, Reflections.* Jerusalem, Yad Vashem, 1976; 90–126.

———. *Christians and Jews in the Second Reich (1870–1914): A Study in The Use of German Totalitarianism.* Jerusalem: Hebrew University Press, 1969.

Tec, Nechama. *In the Lion's Den: The Life of Oswald Rufeisen.* New York: Oxford University Press, 1990.

———. *Dry Tears: The Story of a Lost Childhood.* Westport, Conn.: Wildcat, 1982.

———. "Sex Distinctions and Passing as Christians." *East European Quarterly* 18. no. 1 (March 1984); 113–123.

———. *When Light Pierced the Darkness: Christian Rescuers of Jews in Nazi-Occupied Poland.* New York: Oxford University Press, 1986,

Tittmann, Harold H. Jr. *Inside the Vatican of Pius XII: The Memoir of an American Diplomat During World War II.* New York: Doubleday, 2004.

Tonini, Carla. "Zofia Kossak: The Anti-Semite Who Rescued Polish Jews." In Bibo Arslan et al., *There Is Always an Option to Say "Yes" or "No": The Righteous Against the Genocides of Armenians and Jews.* Padua, Cleup, 2001; 79–88.

Townsend, John T. "The Gospel of John and and the Jews: The Story of a Religious Divorce." In Alan Davies (ed.), *Antisemitism and the Foundations of Christianity.* New York, 1979; 72–97.

Trunk, Isaiah. "Poland: Holocaust Period." In *Encyclopaedia Judaica* (1971), vol. 13; 752–774.

Turkow, Jonas. "On the Rescue of Children from the Warsaw Ghetto" (Hebrew). In *Dapim Lecheker Hashoah ve-Hamered,* Part B1; Beit Lohamei Hagetaot, 1970; 256–265.

Turowicz, Jerzy. "Polish Reasons and Jewish Reasons." In Antony Polonsky (ed.), *"My Brother's Keeper?" Recent Polish Debates on the Holocaust.* Oxford: Routledge, 1990; 134–143.

Vago, Bela. "Hungary: Holocaust Period." In *Encyclopaedia Judaica* (1971), vol. 8; 1096–1105.

Vernon, W.H.D. "Hitler, the Man: Notes for a Case History." *Journal of Abnormal and Social Psychology* 37 (1942); 295–308.

The Visit of Pope John Paul II to Yad Vashem. Jerusalem, March 23, 2000. Jerusalem: Yad Vashem, 2000.

Visser't, Hooft (ed.). *The First Assembly of the World Council of Churches,* London, 1949; 161.

———. *The Third Assembly of the World Council of Churches,* London, 1962.

Voegelin, Eric. *The New Science of Politics.* Chicago: University of Chicago Press, 1952.

———. *Die Politische Religionen.* Stockholm: Bermann-Fischer, 1939.

Vullizez, Hyacinthe. *Camille Folliet: prêtre et résistant.* Annecy: L'Atelier, 2001.

Warmbrunn, Werner. *The Dutch under German Occupation, 1940–1945.* Stanford, Calif.: Stanford University Press, 1963.

Weiss, John. *Ideology of Death: Why the Holocaust Happened in Germany.* Chicago, Ivan R. Dee, 1996.

Wells, Leon. *The Janowska Road.* New York: Macmillan, 1963.

Werblowsky, R. J. Zwi. "Jewish-Christian Relations: New Territories, New Maps, New Realities." In Otto D. Kulka and Paul R. Mendes-Flohr, *Judaism and Christianity under the Impact of National Socialism;* 531–536.

Wijngaert Van den, Mark. "The Belgian Catholics and the Jews During the German Occupation, 1940–1944." In Dan Michman (ed.), *Belgium and the Holocaust.* Jerusalem: Yad Vashem, 1988; 225–233.

Wijsenbeek, M. D. "Is There a Hiding Syndrome?." In *Israel-Netherlands Symposium on the Impact of Persecution.* Jerusalem, 1977; 68–73.

Wistrich, Robert S. "Helping Hitler." *Commentary* 102, no. 1 (July 1996); 27–31.

Yahil. Leni. "Denmark." In *Encyclopedia of the Holocaust,* (1990), vol. 1; 362–365.

———. "Sweden." In *Encyclopedia of the Holocaust,* (1990), vol. 4; 1436–1440.

———. "Switzerland." In *Encyclopedia of the Holocaust,* (1990), vol. 4; 1441–1444.

Yahil, Chaim. "Czechoslovakia." In *Encyclopaedia Judaica* (1971), vol. 5: 1188–1194.

Yelin, Meir. "The Few Who Helped a Lot" (Hebrew). In *Lithuanian Jewry: The Holocaust,* vol. 4; Tel Aviv, 1984; 418–426.

Yerushalmi, Yosef H. "Response to Rosemary Ruether." In Fleischner Eva (ed.), *Auschwitz: Beginning of a New Era?* New York: Cathedral of St. John the Divine, 1977; 97–107.

Yones, Eliahu. *Smoke in the Sand: The Jews of Lwow During the War 1939–1945* (Hebrew). Jerusalem: Yad Vashem, 2001.

Zasloff, Zela. *A Rescuer's Story: Pastor Pierer-Charles Toureille in Vichy France.* Madison: University of Wisconsin Press, 2003.

Zuccotti, Susan. *The Holocaust, the French, and the Jews.* New York: Basic Books, 1993.

———. *The Italians and the Holocaust: Persecution, Rescue and Survival.* New York: Basic Books, 1997.

———. *Under His Windows: The Vatican and the Holocaust in Italy.* New Haven: Yale University Press, 2000.

INDEX